DESTINY OF THE SOLDIERS

Fianna Fáil, Irish Republicanism and the IRA, 1926–73

DESTINY OF THE SOLDIERS

Fianna Fáil, Irish Republicanism and the
IRA, 1926–73

DONNACHA Ó BEACHÁIN ∽

Gill & Macmillan

*This book is dedicated to the memory of my
grandmother, Kathleen O'Brien, my aunt Meḋḃ
Ní Bhriain, and my father, Breandán Ó Beacháin.
Without their encouragement, love and support
I would have achieved little in life.*

Gill & Macmillan Ltd
Hume Avenue, Park West, Dublin 12
with associated companies throughout the world
www.gillmacmillan.ie

© Donnacha Ó Beacháin 2010
978 07171 4763 2

Index compiled by Cover to Cover
Typography design by Make Communication
Print origination by Carole Lynch
Printed and bound in the UK by MPG Books Ltd,
Cornwall

This book is typeset in Linotype Minion and
Neue Helvetica.

The paper used in this book comes from the wood pulp
of managed forests. For every tree felled, at least one tree
is planted, thereby renewing natural resources.

A CIP catalogue record for this book is available
from the British Library.

5 4 3 2 1

CONTENTS

ACKNOWLEDGEMENTS

I would like to acknowledge the courtesy and assistance I received from the staffs of the following libraries and archives: the National Archives of Ireland, Dublin, the British National Archives, Kew Gardens, the National Library of Ireland, National Photographic Archive, Dublin, University College Dublin Archives and the Fianna Fáil archives when they resided at Upper Mount Street, Dublin.

Much of the material presented in this book was gathered and composed as part of research conducted for a PhD thesis, awarded by University College Dublin. I appreciate the help rendered by my supervisor, Professor Tom Garvin and the departmental secretary, Jean Brennan during this process. Gratitude too is due to my colleagues at the School of Law and Government, Dublin City University and in particular the Head of School, Dr John Doyle.

A Marie Curie fellowship from the European Commission afforded me the time to complete the manuscript and prepare it for publication. It also brought me back to Ireland after almost a decade skirting the former Soviet empire.

My thanks to Fergal Tobin who proved an understanding editor and the many staff members of Gill & Macmillan who shepherded the manuscript through the publication process.

During the many years when the research for this book was conducted I profited from conversations with a number of people on Irish history and politics. In particular I would like to acknowledge the insights and argumentative skills of Paul McGuill, Renata Matuszkiewicz, Martin Naughton, John Kelly, Rossa Ó Muireartaigh, David Kuijper and Stuart Graham. I am also indebted to my mother, Deirdre and my sister, Caoilfhionn for their support.

Chapter 1 ⌒

LEGION OF THE REARGUARD

The revolutionary origins of Fianna Fáil, 1920–23

PARTITION

On 23 December 1920 an international boundary was constructed in Ireland by the arbitrary movement of the British imperial pen. The partition of Ireland received the British monarch's 'royal assent' on that date, having been approved by Parliament the previous March.

Not only was the concept of partition inherently undemocratic, considering that 80 per cent of the Irish population favoured independence from Britain, but its execution compounded the iniquity. As Joseph Lee has noted, 'the geographical boundaries did not attempt to follow the mental boundaries.'[1] The nationalist majorities in Cos. Fermanagh and Tyrone were greater than the unionist majorities in Cos. Derry and Armagh; and the new state included towns such as Derry and Newry, which had large nationalist majorities.

To satisfy the demands of a small regional majority, and to preserve British hegemony, a new state was established, ostensibly to protect a 20 per cent minority while simultaneously creating a new minority that made up 34 per cent of the population. In not one of the six counties was the unionist majority greater than the nationalist majority in Ireland as a whole. Taking cognisance of these facts, Lee states that the objective of partition was 'to ensure Protestant supremacy over Catholics even in predominantly Catholic areas,' and that it did not separate two warring peoples but actually brought them closer together.[2] During the principal debate on the Government of Ireland Act, David Lloyd George declared, with breathtaking honesty, that the measure conflicted with the aspirations of the great majority of the Irish people.

> If you asked the people of Ireland what plan they would accept, by an emphatic majority, they would say 'We want independence and an Irish Republic.' There is absolutely no doubt about that. The elected representatives of Ireland, now by a clear majority, have declared in favour of independence.[3]

The leader of the House of Commons, Andrew Bonar Law, outlined the alternatives to the bill, one of which was 'to give self-determination to the representatives of the Irish people: that is to create an Irish Republic'; but this option was rejected.

The undemocratic nature of the partition is clear when it is compared with the way in which the British subsequently handled the question in India.[4] There the Muslim minority, like the Irish unionists, had sought a partitioned state for an area far larger than they were entitled to on the grounds of their numbers and demo-graphic distribution. They were, however, confronted with a choice. Control over the desired area was dependent on the establishment of a federal relationship with the majority Hindu population. If they preferred complete separation they would be entitled only to rule those areas where they comprised an impregnable majority. However, the dissident unionist minority in Ireland were indulged to the extent that more than half the area under their control was nationalist in sentiment. But while unionists had a large appetite, they had poor digestion, and the forcible incorporation of so many nationalists in the new state merely sowed the seeds of future strife.

THE WAR OF INDEPENDENCE

Ireland was partitioned while Irish nationalists were engaged in an armed struggle against British rule. The insurrectionary spark had been struck in April 1916, when a body of men and women launched an insurrection in Dublin during which an Irish republic was proclaimed. Seven men—Patrick Pearse, Joseph Plunkett, Éamonn Ceannt, Tom Clarke, Seán Mac Diarmada, Thomas MacDonagh and James Connolly—signed the proclamation, knowing as they did so that they were also sign-ing their death warrants, as the rebellion was doomed from the start. The bulk of insurgent arms, imported from Germany, with which Britain was locked in a ferocious world war, were seized the day before the Rising, and it was actually called off by the nominal head of the Irish Volunteers, Eoin MacNeill.[5] A minority persisted with the rebellion, and for a week, hopelessly outnumbered, outgunned, and holding out in strategic buildings around the city, they fought the British forces. Much of Dublin city centre was destroyed, 450 people were killed and at least 2,600 wounded.[6]

After the surrender the British rounded up the insurgents and sentenced ninety of them to death. Most of these sentences were commuted to life imprisonment, including that of a 33-year-old mathematics teacher, Éamon de Valera, whose American birth proved decisive in saving him from the firing squad. But fifteen of the leaders were shot in Kilmainham Jail, Dublin, between 3 and 12 May.[7] As any seasoned observer of Irish politics could have forecast, and certainly as the leaders had hoped, the executions turned a military debacle into a stunning political victory. The Rising, like some before it, had been spearheaded by small armed groups—in this case a minority of the Irish Volunteers (under the control of the IRB) and the Irish Citizen Army—though it repre-sented a much larger body of opinion. Within two years the spirit of 1916 was institutionalised in a resurrected Sinn Féin, which eclipsed the moderate nationalist Irish Party that had garnered the majority of votes in Ireland for almost half a century.[8] In so doing, the 1916 Rising reinforced the belief among republicans that the sacrifice of honest patriots, however outnumbered militarily or electorally, would be vindicated.

In modern republican and Irish politics (and for much of the time these have been synonymous) 1916 is Year 1. Before 1916 the agitation of the Irish Party in the House of Commons in London, where it regularly held the balance of power, had promised a parliament for Dublin. Two failed legislative attempts, in 1886 and 1893, to introduce a domestic legislature (albeit with limited powers) had put politics to one side for a generation, and a spectacularly vibrant cultural revival filled the void in nationalist activity.[9] In 1910 the Irish Party once again held the balance of power, and it exacted its price for supporting the British Liberal Party: a reduction in the power of the House of Lords, and a third Government of Ireland Bill (commonly called the Home Rule Bill) to be introduced in Parliament.

By 1914 it seemed that the Irish Party had finally achieved a parliament for Dublin; but the outbreak of war meant that no such parliament would be established until the conflict had subsided. Eager to curry favour with the British elite (the better to secure generous terms for a Dublin parliament) and to compete with the Ulster unionists in demonstrating loyalty to the Crown, the leader of the Irish Party, John Redmond, urged Irishmen to join the British forces to fight in Europe. As the war dragged on and the British political elite seemed disinclined to resist unionist demands for separate treatment, the moment seemed ripe to some revolutionaries in the IRB for staging a rebellion.

The Irish Republican Brotherhood represented a different tradition of political agitation. Declaring itself the heir of the United Irishmen[10] and the Young Irelanders,[11] the IRB was a secret revolutionary organisation founded in 1858 by Irish exiles in New York.[12] Active throughout the latter part of the nineteenth century, it had co-existed, competed and co-operated with the Irish Party when it was led by the formidable Charles Stewart Parnell, and some prominent home-rule MPs were also members of the IRB. (Joseph Beggar, for example, was a member of the Supreme Council.)

With Parnell's demise the paths of the IRB and the Irish Party increasingly diverged.[13] Each organised and waited patiently, the Irish Party for British parliamentary arithmetic and wisdom to recognise the necessity of Irish home rule, the IRB for British vulnerability and Irish revolutionary consciousness to be exploited for achieving an independent republic. Home-rulers had confidently expected to be the leaders of a new legislature in Ireland—just reward for two generations of patient endeavour. But while thousands of Irishmen died in the First World War, 1916 was not to be the year remembered mainly for the slaughter of the Somme: it was to be for the defence of the General Post Office in Dublin by a few hundred republicans. Quite simply, what happened between 1916 and 1921 was a revolution.

In the two years following the 1916 Rising, Sinn Féin won a string of by-elections. In North Roscommon on 3 February 1917 George Plunkett became the first Sinn Féin member of the British Parliament, though, like all other Sinn Féin MPs who were to follow him, he refused to take his seat.[14] The election of Plunkett, the father of one of the seven signatories of the 1916 proclamation, represented a clear electoral endorsement of the actions and ideals of the 1916 rebels. Equally symbolic was the victory of the only surviving 1916 commandant, Éamon de Valera, who was elected MP for East Clare in July 1917.[15]

The election had been called to fill the vacancy occasioned by the death of Willie Redmond (brother of John Redmond), who had died fighting in the British army with the vain hope that his exertions might further the cause of home rule. De Valera's annihilation of Redmond's nominated successor, Patrick Lynch, indicated that the hegemonic grip of the Irish Party on the nationalist electorate was coming to an end.

As the British army was killing off the last of the 1916 rebels sentenced to death, John Dillon, the last leader of the Irish Party, had made an impassioned plea to the House of Commons for the executions to stop, saying, 'You are washing out our whole life's work in a sea of blood.'[16] The tidal wave that the Irish Party expected engulfed it during the 1918 general election. It was the first election held since 1911, and the Representation of the People Act (1918) enfranchised all men over twenty-one and all women over thirty, thus tripling the Irish electorate.

The Irish Party did not bother to contest twenty-six constituencies, but the scale of Sinn Féin's victory still came as a shock to the British government and conservative elements in Ireland. Of the 105 Irish seats the republican party took 73, the unionist party 26 (including those in the rotten-borough university seats), and the once-mighty Irish Party was reduced to a mere 6 seats, 4 of which were obtained through a pre-election pact that had divided eight Ulster seats with Sinn Féin. Britain refused to acknowledge that Sinn Féin's sweeping victory, fought on the platform of securing an independent Irish republic, necessitated discussing a new constitutional framework with republicans.

Sinn Féin resolved to act as if it had already secured a republic. A parliament, to be called Dáil Éireann, was established in January 1919. Membership was open to all Irish MPs elected in 1918, but as the unionists and home-rulers continued to attend the House of Commons in London, and as a majority of the Sinn Féin deputies were in prison, most members did not attend. Still, the new parliament opened in the Mansion House in Dublin amid great ceremony and pomp. The Proclamation of the Irish Republic (1916) was reaffirmed, and British forces were ordered to leave the country. The assembly adopted a Declaration of Independence and an Address to the Free Nations of the World, calling for support for the new republic. Alternative structures of government were established to compete with existing British institutions. A judicial system, commonly called Dáil courts, was established throughout the country. These achieved considerable support, not least because many parts of the country were not under British control, as the Royal Irish Constabulary was forced to withdraw from four hundred rural police stations during the war.[17] Moreover, having won control of twenty-eight out of Ireland's thirty-two county councils in the 1920 local elections, Sinn Féin was now entitled to receive and spend revenues throughout the country.

The exact nature of Sinn Féin's and Dáil Éireann's relationship with the IRA was a vexed question during the struggle for independence. The IRA's shooting of two members of the RIC at Solloghodbeg, Co. Tipperary, which marked the beginning of the War of Independence, was not sanctioned by the Dáil. Subsequent events, together with the fact that the Dáil assembled for the first time on the same day as the attack, helped to obscure the nature of the conflict.[18] Arthur Griffith,[19] for one, was outraged and described the action as the work of outlaws that would only encourage Britain to use its superior force.[20] Throughout the War of Independence, Griffith and many of the moderate wing of the movement only learnt of IRA activities from the newspapers. In particular, they condemned the actions of Michael Collins's elite assassination squad.[21] There was no regular channel of communication between the IRA brigades and the Dáil or, for that matter, IRA headquarters. This was not surprising, considering that both the IRA and the Dáil were declared illegal by the British and forced underground. Consequently, the IRA's fight to defend the Republic was carried out largely unhindered by any influence from the politicians, which encouraged a strong sense of autonomy among guerrilla leaders.

The first major attempt to clarify the relationship was made after de Valera, now President of the Irish Republic, returned from America in March 1921, when he publicly acknowledged that the IRA was the official army of the Irish Republic and secured Dáil approval for his stance. During this Dáil session Richard Mulcahy[22] suggestively commented that such recognition was timely, as the Volunteers had demonstrated that they would fight, and, with their effectiveness apparent, the Dáil was on safe ground acknowledging them.[23] It was not until November 1921 that the IRA was formally subordinated to the government of the Irish Republic and that the procedures for the granting of new commissions by that government were formalised.

The British government had responded to the independence struggle with military reprisals, martial law—selectively applied to individual counties and not applied throughout the country, in an attempt to deny the IRA belligerent status—and a plethora of security initiatives. David Lloyd George had repeatedly stated that, as Prime Minister, he would never negotiate with the IRA 'terror gangs' and boasted that he had 'murder by the throat.'[24] But, faced with what seemed to be a ubiquitous but elusive guerrilla foe that enjoyed a large measure of support, the British empire—the world's most powerful—found itself drawn into a costly, humiliating and deeply embarrassing war. A truce negotiated between IRA and British army leaders took effect from midnight on 11 July 1921. Though de Valera had met Lloyd George shortly afterwards, he controversially chose to stay in Dublin while his hand-picked plenipotentiaries—Arthur Griffith, Michael Collins, Robert Barton, Éamonn Duggan and George Gavan Duffy—negotiated the future of Anglo-Irish relations with Lloyd George and his colleagues between October and December.

While many knew that participation in the London talks would ensure that painful concessions would have to be made, the signed document brought back from the negotiations fell far short of republican expectations. The Republic, for which so many lives had been lost, was to be formally abandoned and replaced with an Irish Free State that would have extensive powers in twenty-six of the thirty-two counties. Partition was not reversed; instead, a Boundary Commission would review the competing territorial claims. Ireland was to become a dominion within the British Commonwealth; the King of England would be in law the monarch of Ireland; and Irish parliamentarians would have to swear an oath of fidelity to the King and his heirs before being able to carry out their parliamentary duties in the new Dublin assembly that would replace the 32-county Dáil Éireann. Britain would retain three naval bases in the Irish Free State (in addition to those in Northern Ireland), denying Irish autonomy in determining foreign and defence policies. And while the Free State would have substantial fiscal powers—a fact prized by Arthur Griffith—it would remain heavily dependent on Britain as well as being deprived of its industrial base in the north-east. Moreover, the Free State would have to pay millions of pounds annually as a contribution to the imperial debt, paying British military and police pensioners in Ireland and recouping the land annuities from Irish farmers.[25]

De Valera immediately rejected the Articles of Agreement for a Treaty Between Great Britain and Ireland (commonly called the Anglo-Irish Treaty), which had been signed without his consent, though the plenipotentiaries were under clear instructions to refer any draft agreement to Dublin for approval. In a letter to the Irish people de Valera claimed that the terms of the agreement were in 'violent conflict' with the wishes of the majority of the Irish nation as expressed in successive elections and stated that he felt it his duty to declare immediately that 'I cannot recommend acceptance of this Treaty, either to Dáil Éireann or to the country.'[26]

The conflicting sentiments about the Treaty found expression during the Dáil debate, which took place between 14 December 1921 and 7 January 1922. Pádraic Ó Máille summed up the feelings of some who voted for the Treaty by declaring unquestioning loyalty to his army leader, saying that 'what is good enough for Michael Collins is good enough me.'[27] Others, such as Richard Mulcahy and Collins himself, emphasised the relative military weakness of the IRA and the fact that they had not approached the negotiations 'in the position of conquerors dictating terms of peace to a vanquished foe.'[28] Both Barton and Gavan Duffy defended their decision to sign the Treaty by referring to Lloyd George's ultimatum, according to which a refusal to sign would lead to 'terrible and immediate war.'[29] Gavan Duffy declared that he was

> going to recommend this Treaty to you very reluctantly, but very sincerely, because I see no alternative . . . It inflicts a grievous wound upon the dignity of this nation by thrusting the King of England upon us . . . The complaint is . . . that the alternative to our signing that particular Treaty was immediate war; that we who were sent to London as the apostles of peace . . . were suddenly transformed into the unqualified arbiters of war; that we had to make this choice within three hours . . . and that monstrous iniquity was perpetrated by the man who had invited us under his roof in order, *mar dhea*, to make a friendly settlement.[30]

Not all those who supported the Treaty did so in a defensive, semi-apologetic manner or by conjuring up images of apocalyptic doom should an alternative route be considered. Some, like Griffith, concentrated on the positive attributes of the agreement and the powers that had been wrested from the British government. 'We have brought back the flag,' he told the Dáil.

> We have brought back the evacuation of Ireland after 700 years by British troops and the formation of an Irish Army. We have brought back to Ireland her full rights and powers of fiscal control. We have brought back to Ireland equality with England, equality with all the nations which form that Commonwealth, and an equal voice in the direction of foreign affairs in peace and war.[31]

Austin Stack, the son of a Fenian leader, an exponent of traditional separatist sentiment and now Minister for Home Affairs, demonstrated the extent of the ideological chasm during the Treaty debate when he rejected dominion status. Griffith had stressed that Ireland had now the same degree of independence as Canada, Australia and New Zealand; but these countries, Stack pointed out, had 'sprung from England,' and their ruling populations were 'children of England,' who regarded England as their motherland.

> This country, on the other hand, had not been a child of England's nor never was. England came here as an invader, and for 750 years we have been resisting that conquest. Are we now after those 750 years to bend the knee and acknowledge that we received from England as a concession full, or half, or three-quarter Dominion status? I say no.[32]

A difference between 'true believers' and 'pragmatists' could be detected. The pragmatist view stressed the gains that had been made: Britain had made Ireland an equal member of the British Commonwealth, with the same legislative and executive powers as Canada. The 'true believers' stressed what had been lost. Liam Mellows claimed that the Dáil

> had no power to agree to anything inconsistent with the existence of the Republic. Now either the Republic exists or it does not. If the Republic exists, why are we talking about stepping towards the Republic by means of this Treaty? I for one believed, and do believe, that the Republic exists, because it exists upon the only sure foundation upon which any government or republic can exist, that is, because the people gave a mandate for that Republic to be declared. We are hearing a great deal here about the will of the people, and the newspapers—that never even recognised the Republic when it was the will of the people—use that as a text for telling Republicans in Ireland what the will of the people is . . . The people are being stampeded; in the people's minds there is only one alternative to the Treaty and that is terrible, immediate war . . . That is not the will of the people, that is the *fear* of the people. The will of the people was when the people declared a Republic.[33]

De Valera introduced a proposal that he hoped might form the basis of a compromise between the two sides. Quickly dubbed 'Document No. 2', it was a subtle attempt to achieve more effectively the promise of the Treaty: a stepping-stone to the ultimate freedom and unity of the country. The central theme was that all power must be derived from the Irish people alone. To this end, a constitution would be enacted that explicitly declared that the people, not the British Crown, were the source of all governmental authority. In deference to British sensitivities, this independent Ireland would be 'externally associated' with the other states of the British Commonwealth in certain matters and would enjoy equal status with Britain and other Commonwealth members.

Another important distinction was made with the Treaty's provision that made Irish membership of the British Commonwealth a non-negotiable principle, violation of which would occasion an immediate resumption of armed conflict. Under the Treaty the Free State was an involuntary member of the Commonwealth, and its subordinate status to Britain was explicitly stated. De Valera's alternative would make Ireland's association with the Commonwealth a voluntary contract entered into by independent states in no way subordinate to another. A logical extension of this premise was the right of the Irish people to leave the Commonwealth if they so wished. If such a relationship were established the Irish government would recognise the King as head of the association. Moreover, if the British insisted that such a contractual relationship be sealed by the taking of an oath, then it would be an oath to *obey* the Irish constitution, to *abide* by the Treaty, and to *recognise* the king as head of that association. It is important to demonstrate how this differed from the provisions contained in the Treaty. If the Free State constitution was to be compatible with the Treaty it would have to contain an oath declaring fidelity to the King as King of Ireland. De Valera's alternative merely required that representatives obey the constitution, which stated that all power came from the people of Ireland. Everything else stemmed from this concept, and the oath was compatible with this democratic principle.

Document No. 2 represented a constructive attempt by de Valera to bridge the gulf that was emerging between those who accepted the Treaty and those who opposed it. However, the pro-Treaty deputies were convinced that 'neither renewed war—which they were offered—nor continued negotiations—which they were not offered— would bring them one iota nearer the realisation of their full demands.'[34] With the summary rejection of his alternative, de Valera became increasingly recalcitrant and resistant to compromise. Document No. 2 had been his attempt to reunite the Dáil, and its non-acceptance, he felt, absolved him from the compromises offered, which were becoming the subject of embarrassment and confusion in republican circles.[35]

De Valera's performance at this time has been criticised, largely because it is felt that he anticipated, as much as any of the plenipotentiaries—if not more so—the limitations the British would impose on negotiations. He had, after all, entered into talks with Lloyd George in July. His keen grasp of constitutional minutiae and semantics would have resulted in a different negotiating style, though it might not have produced a substantially different offer.[36]

While indulgence in counterfactual speculation throws up some tantalising possibilities, it can never alter the historical record. The republican movement was, as Cathal Brugha forecast, split 'from top to bottom.' When the result was announced, 64 votes had been cast for the Treaty, 57 against.[37]

A last-ditch effort to reject the Treaty by other means was attempted with a motion to re-elect de Valera as President of the Irish Republic. To murmurs of approval from pro-Treaty deputies, Arthur Griffith declared that it was 'most unfair to this Assembly that the personality of Mr. de Valera should be used as it is being used,' as 'everyone knows how difficult it is for a man personally to vote against President de Valera.'[38] This vote was also narrowly lost—60 votes to 58—with several abstentions, including de Valera.[39] Griffith was elected in his stead; but, in the light of the concessions made in London, de Valera pointedly asked whether he was going to be elected as President of the Irish Republic—the position he had held—or something else. Griffith equivocated. The Treaty stipulated that before the Irish Free State could be established a Provisional Government must take over the functions of the state and that this body was to be created by assembling the 'Parliament of Southern Ireland' that had been created by the same Government of Ireland Act (1920) that had produced a parliament in Belfast. What would happen to the large amount of funds that had been collected from republicans in Ireland and America for the functioning of the Republican government? Were these going to be used by the Provisional Government? And, as Dáil Éireann was a 32-county body and the Parliament of Southern Ireland was a 26-county body, what would happen to the Dáil representatives from the excluded six counties?

Many of the ambiguities were buried beneath a landslide of rhetorical commitments to putting a new constitution before the electorate, who would be asked to endorse the changes. Republican opponents of the Treaty insisted that it was the duty of Dáil representatives to keep the Republican legislature intact and functioning; the people had established the Republic, de Valera claimed, and only they could discard it. Griffith and the other Treaty signatories knew, however, that the British would not permit any elections until a Provisional Government was created in line with the Treaty.

Meanwhile, the anti-Treaty IRA, which had withdrawn its allegiance to the Dáil and was not controlled by any political party, established its headquarters in the Four Courts, Dublin.

THE PRO-TREATY EMBRYO

As a self-professed national movement, Sinn Féin was a broad coalition transcending sectional interests.[40] While the divisions within this coalition only became public during the Treaty debate, evidence of its fragility can be found at its source.

Despite being the founder of Sinn Féin, Arthur Griffith was 'no Sinn Féiner.'[41] The Sinn Féin constitution adopted in 1908 was 'far from revolutionary' and in fact proposed a central place for the King of England in any Irish constitution.[42] Griffith's monarchical policies and pacifist views did not endear him to many nationalists of a more radical hue,[43] so that by 1916 Sinn Féin as an organisation was moribund. The erroneous connection made by the British establishment between Sinn Féin and the Rising (which it called the 'Sinn Féin Rebellion') saved Griffith's organisation from political obscurity, occasioning the popular saying that 'it wasn't Sinn Féin made the Rising, but the Rising made Sinn Féin.'[44] Recruits flocked into the party, and the vast increase in membership ensured that the new Sinn Féin differed markedly from its predecessor.

Not all these new members were content to tolerate Griffith's titular leadership, but they were satisfied that the militants were in the ascendancy. 'The original Sinn Féiners were not in sympathy with the men of Easter week,' wrote a correspondent to the new Sinn Féin figurehead, George Plunkett, 'but the present Sinn Féiners, in the country at least, are heart and soul with them.'[45] The Rising also saved Arthur Griffith, who had opposed the insurrection but, 'fortunately for his future reputation,' was arrested in its wake and interned.[46] His 'dual monarchy' ideas survived the Rising, however, and the more militant republican elements thrown up after 1916 noted his 'undeviating attachment to a political settlement with a monarchical character.'[47] In this context his fervent support for the Treaty is not difficult to comprehend, for it achieved everything—and more—that his original Sinn Féin movement had set out to attain in 1905.

Griffith's unreserved enthusiasm for the Treaty contrasted with the reluctant support of others and indicated an important divergence of outlook. A fervent nationalist, Griffith was also a classic example of the 'native intellectual'[48] unable to fully reject the power that had moulded him. His economic policy and political objectives were shaped by a peculiar love-hate relationship with the British Empire. Griffith was not an anti-imperialist: rather he resented Ireland's subordinate position within the British Empire. Commending Australian Orangemen in 1913 for referring to the 'Empire of Great Britain and Ireland', Griffith confessed that he 'thought the expression was a good one and I often wondered why it was not more extensively used.'[49] This ambiguity in Griffith's position surfaced again and again throughout his writings. Indeed his series of articles called *Pitt's Policy* is virtually a lamentation for the lost possibility of Anglo-Irish imperialism and contains a strong suggestion that England cheated Ireland out of its equitable and fitting role as joint ruler of Britain's vast exploitative empire.

> One day in July 1800, the Peers of Ireland entered their Parliament House rulers of a nation—co-rulers of an Empire—and came out less than the equals of the most illiterate Hodge in an English constituency. Mr. Pitt had destroyed the partnership of Ireland in the rule of the Empire—he had made England not the predominant partner, but the owner of the firm.[50]

Griffith's political ideology was far removed from the revolutionary and radical voices of such individuals as James Connolly, Jim Larkin and Liam Mellows.[51] Ireland's subordinate position within the British Empire wounded Irish pride and prestige, but rarely did Griffith interrogate the imperial system itself. Indeed at times his writings lapse into a tone of longing and regret for the Irish superpower that might have been.

> An Anglo-Hibernian dual monarchy would be master of the world today . . . An Empire equally governed from Dublin and London was possible beyond all that the Empire had been . . .[52]

Griffith's vision for Ireland saw Britain not as a mother-country but as a twin sister—a dual monarchy. His analysis of foreign political situations did little to cultivate a reputation of anti-imperialism. While his sympathies were always instinctively with those who opposed England, no deeper examination of objectives, social structures or consequences was considered necessary. Like many of his contemporaries, Griffith viewed the Anglo-Boer War as a European conflict and unconditionally accepted the Boers as the true nation of South Africa. The interests and aspirations of Africa's native population were dismissed, which is all the more curious considering Griffith's two-year sojourn in the Transvaal. Indeed he declared himself 'in hearty sympathy with the civilisation of Africa.'[53]

Griffith's fixation with the work of the German economist Georg Friedrich List is also something of an oddity. An ardent imperialist, List had little time for the rights of small nations, advocating the incorporation of the Netherlands and Belgium in a

German superstate and arguing that Britain's rule in Ireland was a legitimate con-
quest that remedied the latter's deficiency in national resources and capabilities.[54]
Furthermore, List believed that only through an alliance with a more powerful state
was it possible for a small nation to retain its independence, and that even with such
an alliance the small nation would have to sacrifice some of the advantages of
nationality.[55]

Griffith's assimilation of many of the racist tropes of empire and his dubious ideological affiliations in international affairs were never more clear than in his lifelong
promotion of an Austro-Hungarian solution for Ireland. Griffith's elevation of
Hungarian nationalism revealed a conservative and imperialist streak, at variance
with ideals of egalitarianism and liberty. The coercive, oppressive rule of the Magyar
minority over the Slavic peoples—widely documented during Griffith's time—did
not seem to offer the 'parallel for Ireland' that he claimed. Aristocratic and land-
owning, their struggle for power was more analogous to that of the Anglo-Irish
propertied class than to any other comparable group in Ireland. Griffith's advocacy of
the Magyar cause is, however, consistent with his oft-derided nostalgia for 'Grattan's
Parliament' of the late eighteenth century.[56]

The confusion that Griffith's monarchical ideals aroused in republican circles was
recalled by Bulmer Hobson, who claimed that Griffith's talk of 'the King, Lord and
Commons of Ireland' had disillusioned the separatist youth that he had helped to
radicalise and 'lowered the national claim of independence.'[57] For several years these
fundamental differences were represented in numerous separate organisations, but in
the post-Rising euphoria the two main strands came together at the 1917 Sinn Féin
ard-fheis to provide a united front.

Writing some years later as president of Sinn Féin, Father Michael O'Flanagan
drew attention to the inherent duality of the Sinn Féin movement and noted that 'the
split was there from the very beginning.'

> The two vice-presidents elected [Griffith and O'Flanagan] were the two men of
> opposite views who formed the nucleus of the provisional committee. The two
> secretaries were Austin Stack and Darrell Figgis. The two treasurers were Laurence
> Ginnell and William Cosgrave. The highest votes for membership of the Standing
> Committee were given to John [Eoin] MacNeill and Cathal Brugha. When the so-
> called Treaty came, one of the original vice-presidents of the organisation
> [Griffith] became its foremost champion. The other [O'Flanagan] remained on
> the side of the Republic. One of the secretaries [Figgis] became an eloquent
> spokesman of the Free State cause, the other fought against it to his last breath.
> One of the treasurers [Cosgrave] became for many years the leader of the Free
> State majority party. The other died in harness in the ranks of the Republic. Of the
> two who came first in the list for the Standing Committee, the name of one
> [Brugha] will go down in history as that of the outstanding hero martyr of the
> Republican cause; that of the other as the leading intellectual champion of the
> policy of compromise. We had only one president. The President found it
> impossible to divide himself into two.[58]

This does much to explain the subsequent Treaty split. Reflecting these divisions is the fact that during the October 1917 ard-fheis two lists of preferred candidates were apparently circulated, representing the two major wings of the joint executive.[59] Such a manufactured coalition of opposites was to be mirrored five years later when Collins and de Valera negotiated the famous pact aimed at retaining some semblance of unity within republican ranks. In 1922, as in 1917, the personnel of the opposing sides remained much the same. The papering over of the considerable fissure in this formal baptism of the 'second' Sinn Féin did not prevent some from questioning the revolutionary credentials of those present and from airing doubts about their suitability to hold prominent positions within the movement.

The elections to the National Executive provoked a vociferous attack against Eoin MacNeill by Kathleen Clarke (widow of Tom Clarke, one of the executed 1916 leaders) and Constance Markievicz, who castigated him for his attempt to call off the Rising. De Valera stepped in and took MacNeill and his acolytes under his wing. Indeed he made a point of including MacNeill during the East Clare by-election hustings.[60] On his release de Valera had been a *deus ex machina* and succeeded in uniting Sinn Féin, but the conservative influx that followed 'widened the Sinn Féin front, but at the same time softened the character of the movement.'[61] And while de Valera proved adept at splitting ideological hairs, he could not, as O'Flanagan pointed out, divide himself in two when it came to a vote. This problem, so painfully obvious during the Treaty debates, would also be a feature of his tenure as leader of Sinn Féin and 'President of the Republic' in the years leading up to the establishment of Fianna Fáil.

The 1916 Rising thus facilitated a merger of the monarchist and pacifist members of the old Sinn Féin, the militant separatists that formed the bedrock of the new Sinn Féin, and a host of other individuals of various motivations and outlooks. But this unity was always precarious and dependent for its cohesion on British coercion.[62] The separatist movement was 'composed of an uneasy mixture of bureaucrats and guerrillas,' and in such circumstances revolutionary *élan* was continually threatened by bureaucratic rationalism.[63] The relationship between local units of the IRA and headquarters often strained, with the former believing that GHQ was out of touch with realities on the ground.[64] Moreover, contact with Dáil Éireann was tenuous at best. The politicos within Sinn Féin relied on press reports for their information on how the armed struggle was progressing; they had no effective say in how the war was conducted.[65]

It was only during the truce that many of the guerrilla fighters and administrative leaders came into contact with one another, and some were surprised to discover that they had a mutual antipathy. An occupational cleavage existed at some level within the movement, later evident in the Treaty split. Erhard Rumpf and A. C. Hepburn have commented that 'there seems to have been a predominance of professional people and possibly white collar workers on the pro-treaty side.' They are cautious, however, in placing too much emphasis on this, as occupational distinctions, they claim, are not sufficiently clear-cut to permit any general conclusions.[66] Tom Garvin has gone further and has claimed that a statistical analysis of the Dáil vote 'strongly suggests that the division was indeed one between administrators, who were pro-Treaty, and local guerrilla leaders, who were against.'[67] In addition, he notes that of the twenty-six TDs who held significant administrative positions in the Dáil government or the movement two-thirds voted in favour of the Treaty.[68] A similar cleavage can be detected within the IRA. Nine of the thirteen members of the GHQ staff agreed to support the Treaty, while eight of the nineteen divisional headquarters reported a majority in favour of acceptance. At the brigade level, however, opposition to the Treaty was between 70 and 80 per cent. These statistics suggest a vertical division within the IRA, with the highest echelons less opposed to the Treaty than those at the regional and local level.[69]

Personal loyalties also played a large part in determining the attitude of individual republicans to the Treaty. Some, like de Valera, found themselves opposing it despite relatively moderate inclinations, while 'there were those who followed Collins who would have been equally happy on the hillsides.'[70] Indeed, as Ronan Fanning has argued, Collins was temperamentally 'closer to the fighting men in the Four Courts than to some of his government colleagues in City Hall.'[71] These divisions, however, were largely internal to the Sinn Féin movement; others outside this ideological framework would also be making judgements.

Even before the Treaty was formally signed, many republicans had detected a softening of the Sinn Féin position and a revival of groups 'who did nothing to gain the victory, but will reap the gains of others.'[72] The Treaty brought out the job-seekers and the peace brigade and was the signal for the re-emergence of a plethora of interests implacably opposed to revolution. Joseph Sweeney, who was to become one of Collins's trusted generals in the new Free State army, remembers attempting to approach a depressed Collins shortly after the Treaty to seek clarification of the IRB position on the agreement only to find Collins besieged by 'a lot of fellows who were looking for jobs, the sort of self-seekers that follow in the wake of an agreement like this.'[73] Another pro-Treaty observer admitted that material rewards were offered and that there was 'an unseemly rush of friends and relatives for a share in the plums of office.'[74] Garvin notes that careerism was exploited to secure the allegiance of waverers and that Free State leaders 'offered jobs and promotions to key leaders to attract them away from "irregularism".'[75]

Collins himself was alert to the dangers of allowing ambitious sectional interests to exploit both the impasse facing the independence struggle and the lapse in fighting.[76] On 3 April 1922 he wrote to a friend, Patrick Daly:

> I am in sympathy with a majority of the IRA; I would wish them to continue now and finish the fight. I want to help them to do so. To postpone the struggle for 15 or 20 years would be a forlorn consolation. The 'big' businessmen and the politicians will come forward when peace is established and perhaps after some years gain control. Their interests will never demand a renewal of war.

WINSTON CHURCHILL AND THE CAMPAIGN FOR A CIVIL WAR

The signing of the Treaty caused a large section of the IRA to withdraw their allegiance from the Dublin parliament, contending that they had fought for and pledged allegiance to the established government of the Republic and would not countenance the disestablishment of that government. Shortly after the Treaty vote was announced,

Michael Collins, who emerged as head of the pro-Treaty Provisional Government (not to be confused with Dáil Éireann, over which Arthur Griffith presided), came under intense and sustained pressure from the British government to confront his anti-Treaty opponents militarily. Winston Churchill, Secretary of State for the Colonies and chairman of the Cabinet Committee on Ireland, made these demands particularly forcefully.

Collins's instinct was to patch up a deal with his erstwhile republican comrades rather than submit to Churchill's ever more belligerent demands. On 1 May 1922 the two wings of the IRA produced an agreed 'Army Document'—signed by eight officers, including Collins, Mulcahy and Dan Breen—in an effort to close ranks and preserve unity.[77] These efforts were mirrored by political developments, with Collins and de Valera entering into negotiations that yielded a pact for the forthcoming election. There would be an agreed Sinn Féin panel, and both pro and anti-Treaty sides would be represented according to their existing strength. Assuming that Sinn Féin secured a majority, the government would consist of an elected President, a Minister of Defence, who would represent the army, and nine other ministers proportionate to the Dáil division: five pro-Treaty and four anti-Treaty. The personnel would be selected by the respective sides, while the allocation of portfolios would rest with the President.

The joint manifesto referred to 'the coalition of forces represented in the Sinn Féin organisation,' which had been 'Ireland's strength' during the preceding years. Sinn Féin would continue to stand 'not for party, but for the nation,' and the coalition government would be composed of the men and women who had been 'tested through the time of trial' and who would 'best be able to meet the immediate national need.'[78] Griffith, whose opinion had been neither given nor sought, was appalled at the *rapprochement*: 'You have given them everything,'[79] he exclaimed to Collins; but he was forced to acquiesce. Griffith and Collins were to die within days of each other, and during their remaining weeks their former cordiality was never re-established.[80]

For Collins and de Valera, and for the majority of their supporters, unity had been preserved and a national catastrophe averted. But the unity of the republican movement, as far as Collins was concerned, was a means to an end. At the Sinn Féin ard-fheis on 23 May he told delegates that the pact would enable him to concentrate on the north-east.[81] Immediately after signing the pact he had written a terse note to himself: 'Above all, Ulster.'[82]

Churchill was outraged at the proposed agreement, which in his estimation would facilitate a united republican movement. He wrote to Austen Chamberlain, Leader of the House of Commons, on 13 May: 'It seems to me absolutely necessary to tell Griffith on Monday that we will have nothing to do with such a farce, nor will we pass any Act of Parliament creating the Free State or according a permanent status to the Irish Govt. on such a basis.'[83]

That an electoral pact between two groups that were—if only in theory—still members of the same party should have so infuriated the British government is curious, considering that it was itself a coalition of Conservatives and Liberals who had fought a pact election in 1918. Electoral pacts or coalition governments formed to meet particular political circumstances were not alien to British governments. For them, such governments were natural *ad hoc* arrangements designed to guide the country through difficult periods. Yet the Irish leaders agreeing to such a proposal, to meet a far more life-threatening crisis, was considered by Churchill to be a negation of democracy, despite the fact that all parties would be contesting. The real objection was a united republican party. The prospect of a political marriage between Collins and de Valera 'shattered Churchill's hopes that Republicanism would be eclipsed,' and Tom Jones (Deputy Secretary of the Cabinet) noted that he now wished 'to pull the whole [Treaty] plant out of the ground.'[84]

Churchill's disillusionment with the process was evident when the Cabinet met on 16 May. He stated his belief that if British forces were withdrawn from Dublin 'a Republic would be declared there.' Under such circumstances it might be necessary, he argued, to hold Dublin by armed strength as the 'English capital' and to convert the surrounding area once again into an English pale, an area of settlement under permanent military protection 'prior to reconquest.'[85] For Churchill the line between pro and anti-Treaty was becoming increasingly blurred, and he now saw the Irish leaders as 'men of violence and conspiracy [who] had hardly emerged from that atmosphere.'[86] He concluded balefully that 'there is really none too much difference between the Free State and the Republican parties . . . and there is a general reluctance to kill one another.'[87]

In the coming days and weeks Churchill would do his utmost to rectify this perceived chink in the Irish character. When Collins and de Valera formally signed their electoral pact on 20 May, Churchill summoned Griffith and Duggan to London. Collins hesitated, but Churchill rebuked him on 22 May, warning him 'not to allow anything to stand in the way' of the meeting.

On the following day the Cabinet approved a massive shipment of arms to the Unionist government in Belfast. The Unionist Prime Minister, Sir James Craig, had requested the weapons to protect the border from republicans and to 'restore order' in Belfast—a euphemism for suppressing Catholics. When Churchill telegraphed news of the approved arms, Craig expressed 'many thanks' and was 'greatly relieved.'[88] Churchill's official biographer notes that, even before the Cabinet decision, Craig 'was confident that Britain would now support Ulster in all she did'; and thus, on 23 May, he announced that his government would never accept any change in the border, irrespective of any recommendation of the Boundary Commission.[89]

On 26 May, Churchill spent three hours discussing the republican election pact with Griffith. Despite the fact that Collins had not yet reached London, Griffith made it clear that he was totally opposed to the pact. When the head of the Provisional Government arrived the following day, therefore, he was confronted with a British delegation well aware of divisions within the Irish government on the merits of the electoral pact.

The chance for the British to exploit these divisions and to scupper the pact arrived when Collins submitted his proposed constitution for the Free State. Lloyd George informed his Cabinet colleagues that the proposed constitution was totally unacceptable, as it complied with the Treaty neither in substance nor in form but was 'purely republican in character and but thinly veiled.' The position of the Crown representative was 'reduced to that of a sort of Commissioner.'[90] The Irish side claimed the right to make their own treaties, while the Irish Supreme Court was to be the final court of appeal and not the Judicial Committee of the Privy Council.[91]

Moreover, according to the Constitution the King was not part of the Irish legislature; he would not appoint ministers, nor would he summon and dissolve the parliament. 'The distance between their Constitution and the Treaty is almost as great as when the Prime Minister began his negotiations with Mr. de Valera,' Churchill complained. Lloyd George identified the republican constitution as the linchpin that held the pact together. As Calton Younger points out, Lloyd George knew that so long as Collins and Griffith were prepared to stand by the Constitution 'the Pact would hold together, the Irish would be united once more and the Dáil itself would have become, after all, a unanimous body of opposition to the Treaty.'[92] In the end, 'the stronger side got the Constitution it wanted.'[93]

The Irish leaders went to London in June with one constitution, only to arrive home with an entirely different one. It was a replay of the Treaty negotiations: those engaged were almost identical to those of the previous encounter, similar tactics were employed, and the result was much the same, with victory going to the physically superior side. The *Sunday Times* delivered a verdict summarising British government and, indeed, republican opinion: 'Instead of weakening the Treaty, as was generally expected in Ireland, it underwrites the Treaty, and underscores the Treaty in an emphatic manner. The English victory is plain.'[94] The pact was inoperative, although, as Younger comments, 'it is doubtful that Griffith shed many tears over that.'[95]

Faced with the unavoidable imperialisation of the constitution, Collins had to accept that there was no prospect of a coalition government and that the pact had been rendered ineffective in its objective of preserving unity. On 14 June, two days before the election, he made a speech to an audience in Cork that was widely interpreted as marking the end of the pact.[96]

As the text of the Constitution was published only on election day, it is doubtful that many had the opportunity to read it before casting their vote. As expected, the result was interpreted as a solid victory for the Treaty: 58 pro-Treaty deputies were returned, as opposed to 36 anti-Treatyites. 17 members of the Labour Party were also elected, as were 7 farmers and 6 independents; 4 Unionists were returned for the rotten borough of Trinity College.[97] The latter groups were all willing, if required, to take the oath of fidelity to the British monarch so as to enter the Dublin legislature, and their constituents were therefore considered to be in favour of the Treaty.[98]

Events now moved quickly as the country slid towards civil war. Churchill had been trying to orchestrate a military confrontation for months. On 5 April he had told the Cabinet that 'a point might come when it would be necessary to tell Mr. Collins that if he was unable to deal with the situation the British Government would have to do so.'[99] The moment had now arrived when this case would be put to the Provisional Government with renewed vigour. Churchill had interpreted the election result as giving a mandate for attacking the republican forces, and for a time it appeared that war between the Irish and English forces was inevitable. General Nevil Macready, commander in chief of British forces in Ireland, was instructed to draw up plans immediately for an attack on the republican forces in the Four Courts, but he astutely delayed, and the Cabinet calmed down.[100] A British assault would have united the pro and anti-Treaty sides, something to be avoided if at all possible.

One last effort would be made by the British to get Collins to draw the sword for them. In a strongly worded declaration, Churchill asserted that if the republican occupation of the Four Courts was not brought to 'a very speedy end' it would be his duty to inform the Provisional Government that the British regarded the Treaty as having been violated, that no steps would be taken to legalise its further stages, 'and that we resume full liberty of action.'[101] The situation had returned to that outlined at the Treaty table six months earlier: submit to the dictates of the British government or war would be resumed; and Collins's instinctive response was one of angry dismissiveness. 'Let Churchill come over here and do his own dirty work,' he snapped.[102] But it was obvious that Churchill would do just that, and Collins was forced to reconsider. At two o'clock on the morning of 28 June 1922 the Four Courts was surrounded; and at 3:40 a.m a note demanding the vacation of the building within twenty minutes was sent inside. When this was rejected, the artillery that had been supplied by British military headquarters in Dublin began firing. The Civil War had begun.

Churchill could not contain his delight. In a letter to Collins marked 'Private and personal' he described the events since the attack as having in them 'the possibilities of very great hope for the peace and ultimate unity of Ireland, objects both of which are very dear to your British co-signatories.' The artillery and other arms that had been long withheld, for fear of their use against British soldiers in the North, were now made available in unlimited supplies. In a telegram to Collins, Churchill warned that the shells supplied by the British

> will be of little use without heavier guns and good gunners. Do not fail to take both. Both are available.[103]

He also cabled that

> aeroplanes manned by own pilots will carry out any action necessary. They could be quickly painted Free State colours to show that they were an essential part of your forces.[104]

Six weeks after the attack on the Four Courts, Griffith died of a brain haemorrhage, and ten days later Collins was killed during an ambush at Béal na mBláth, near Crookstown, in his native west Cork. With Collins dead and de Valera on the run, Churchill was eager to banish the republicans from public life for ever. In a telegram to Andy Cope[105] he emphasised the dangers from the British point of view and outlined his plan to solidify the divisions of the Civil War.

> The danger to be avoided is a sloppy accommodation with a quasi-repentant De Valera. It may well be that he will take advantage of the present situation to try and get back from the position of a hunted rebel to that of a political negotiator. You should do everything in your power to frustrate this . . .[106]

To this end Churchill needed to enlist the support of the Provisional Government. With Griffith dead he feared that his successor as President might be 'some extremely doubtful person,' less responsive to British demands.[107] The appointment of William Cosgrave soothed these apprehensions.[108] A 'supporter of Griffith's monarchist Sinn Féin from its inception,'[109] Cosgrave was not, by his own admission, 'a leader of men' but was known as a moderate and effective Minister for Local Government during the War for Independence.[110]

Lest the new President entertain ideas of reconciliation with his erstwhile comrades, Churchill instructed Cope to 'make it clear to the Free State leaders that their fight against the Republicans must go on.' Even if 'the surrender of the rebels or rebel leaders' was forthcoming, they must not be allowed to reappear 'as Members of the Assembly . . . and ought to be rigorously shut out.' As an inducement to perpetuating the divisions within the Free State, Churchill, paradoxically, held out the prize of Irish unity.

> Never fail to point out in your communications with Cosgrave, Mulcahy and others that the only hope of a friendly settlement with the North and of ultimate Irish unity lies in a clear line being drawn between the Treaty party and the Republicans . . . Use your utmost endeavours to keep this position before their eyes, making it clear that you have my authority for speaking in this sense.[111]

Churchill expressed deep satisfaction that the Provisional Government had at last locked itself into an internecine civil war. Cosgrave had become, in Churchill's eyes, 'a chief of higher quality than any who had yet appeared,'[112] and his conduct during the Civil War assuaged British fears. 'And today they are dispersing the pickets of the Post Office servants who are on strike,' Churchill enthused. '*Responsibility* is a wonderful agent when thrust upon competent heads.'[113]

The summary executions of republican prisoners constituted a bloody baptism for the Free State, which formally came into existence on 6 December 1922. But by then British attention had turned to its other imperial problems. Ireland was quickly forgotten, receding into the dim recesses but for a short period during the deliberations of the Boundary Commission, when it appeared as though the 'dreary steeples of Fermanagh and Tyrone' might re-emerge. The effects of the Civil War would have a much greater and more enduring impact on the Irish people.

DE VALERA AND THE CIVIL WAR

There has been an erroneous tendency to equate de Valera's opposition to the Treaty with the IRA campaign to dislodge the putative Free State before it became firmly entrenched. This tendency has also encouraged the assumption that the anti-Treaty party led by de Valera was an integral and organic part of the republican forces, a view bolstered by the fact that de Valera 'deliberately fostered the idea that he both influenced the Volunteers and sympathised with their demands.'[114] In fact there was a clear division between the politicians and the Volunteers, the party and the army being two separate bodies. This was made clear shortly after the Treaty division when Rory O'Connor, representing the most strident anti-Treaty IRA opinion, told the press that 'some of us are not more prepared to stand for de Valera than the Treaty.'[115] Three months later O'Connor claimed he had not read Document No. 2, and denied suggestions that the army would obey de Valera. The IRA did not belong to any political party, he maintained, nor had de Valera anything to do with it.[116]

De Valera played a complex and ambiguous role during the Civil War. The military shake-up occasioned by the Treaty—with the rump of the IRB (controlled by Collins) and the GHQ staff supporting it but with the divisional commanders and the majority of the rank and file opposed—saw de Valera become increasingly impotent within the anti-Treaty movement. As civil war approached, power slipped perceptibly from de Valera's grasp, and he found himself more a spectator than the author of events. T. Ryle Dwyer has noted that,

> having stoked radical Republicans, he was no longer able to control them. He was pretending to lead while he was, in fact, being dragged along by his supposed followers. He made approving statements which concealed the differences with them, and he soon found himself compelled to serve the folly he had approved ... In the process he became a model of infuriating inconsistency.[117]

Examples of such inconsistencies are numerous. After the Treaty vote in January 1922 de Valera expressed the hope that 'nobody will talk of fratricidal strife,'[118] while two months later he told an IRA contingent at Thurles that they would have 'to wade through Irish blood, through the blood of the soldiers of the Irish government, and through, perhaps, the blood of some members of the government' to secure Irish freedom.[119] He then condemned the press as warmongers for reporting the speech. 'You cannot be unaware,' he wrote to the *Irish Independent*, 'that your representing me as inciting civil war has on your readers precisely the same effects as if the inciting words were really mine.'[120]

In March an IRA general army convention, composed of delegates from all units, withdrew its allegiance to the Dáil on the grounds that it had betrayed the Republic. Despite privately describing the IRA's repudiation of the Dáil as 'the greatest barrier we now have,' de Valera trenchantly defended the decision in public.[121]

His impotence was underlined by the fact that he was not informed, let alone consulted, on the momentous decision of republican forces to seize the Four Courts.[122] However, in an attempt to retain some semblance of control over events he strongly endorsed the seizure while privately entertaining doubts. On the same day as the capture of the Four Courts, addressing the 'young men and women of Ireland,' he declared that 'the goal is now in sight. Steady; all together; forward. Ireland is yours for the taking. Take it.'[123] It is not difficult to understand why, despite his private hesitancy, de Valera was the man most associated in the public mind with the republican occupation.

At the height of the Civil War, on 25 October 1922, de Valera announced the establishment of a Republican government in opposition to the Free State's Provisional Government. The path taken to this decision reveals something of de Valera's ideological flexibility and his desire not to create a political straitjacket from which he could not extricate himself. When the question emerged of attending the new Free State parliament, which was to assemble on 9 September, de Valera outlined the republican position in a private letter. In principle, abstention seemed appropriate, as the second Dáil had not been dissolved, and the question of the oath was unresolved. He continued:

> So far principle. Now expediency. Our presence at the meeting [of the Dáil] would only help to solidify all other groups against us. We would be the butt of every attack. We could not explain—we would be accused of obstructing the business and of 'talking' when we should 'get on with the work' . . . Finally, whatever chance there is of union in our own group, it lies more in the direction of abstention than attendance.[124]

It is clear from this that de Valera was able to distinguish between the tactical and the ideological factors that would influence any decision to enter the Dublin parliament.[125] It was also clear that circumstances would determine future action and decide whether tactical or ideological considerations would dominate. That de Valera wished to keep his options open is illustrated by his reluctance to make an unequivocal public statement on the issue, on the grounds that 'if we issue a statement it will tie our hands, and if at a future time a course other than non-attendance should seem wise we might find ourselves precluded from taking it.'[126] When presented with a formal request in August,[127] signed by Oscar Traynor, Peadar O'Donnell and other prominent republicans, to establish a Republican government, de Valera replied that 'this is no use . . . we can't maintain one, I fear.'[128]

Despite these reservations, de Valera hinted that he might agree if the proposed government enjoyed the allegiance of the IRA.[129] In this way he adroitly linked his support for a Republican government to the question of his position as head of such a government *vis-à-vis* the IRA Executive. When he proposed a meeting with the IRA leadership to clarify his position within the movement he had received a curt reply from Liam Lynch that brusquely turned down the request.[130] Eoin Neeson has commented that the letter

> underlined that the Army Executive not only was unlikely to give allegiance to a new authority, but considered itself the only proper anti-Treaty administration. It clearly shows how the political and military arms of the anti-Treatyites were drifting apart. The tone of Lynch's letter is that of a supreme commander, which he was, to a somewhat tiresome civilian representative, which de Valera certainly was not.[131]

Lynch's attitude infuriated de Valera, who declared that 'the position of the political party must be straightened out.' If it was official policy to leave all matters to the IRA, he argued, the obvious response of party members should be to resign their positions as public representatives. He bemoaned the fact that '*we* have all the public responsibility, and no voice and no authority.' If the position was not clarified, he threatened to resign publicly.[132]

In a private letter to Cathal Ó Murchadha of 13 September 1922 de Valera proposed that there were three options available to the republican movement.[133] The first was that the republican party should take control, acting as the legitimate Dáil. The second was that the IRA Executive should take control and assume responsibility. The third option suggested that a joint committee could be formed to decide policy for the party and the army. This was firmly ruled out as impracticable, as 'the task of riding two such horses as the Party and the Army will be too much for any Executive.' De Valera claimed that he preferred the second option, but the tone of his letter suggests that this was merely a bargaining tactic. His only argument in favour of this course of action was that it was 'most in accord with fact.' If the option was accepted, the IRA Executive would have to publicly accept responsibility, and 'this pretence from the pro-Treaty Party that we are inciting the Army must be ended by a declaration from the Army itself that that is not so.'

De Valera maintained that the natural corollary of this move would be that the party would cease to operate and that he would resign, an action 'I have long been tempted to take myself.' Therefore, if the IRA were to accept de Valera's 'preferred' option it would lose the assistance of Sinn Féin and the invaluable propaganda services it provided. Opponents would undoubtedly represent this as a division within the republican movement, and morale would be weakened as a result. Most importantly, they would lose de Valera, who, though often an irksome ally, was a crucial figurehead and provided much-needed political credibility for the anti-Treaty struggle.

It is not difficult to understand why the IRA did not choose this option, despite its disdain for civilian representatives. By presenting it in such an unattractive fashion it seems that de Valera was informing the Executive of the ramifications of a break with the party, which he claimed was necessary so as to clarify matters in the public mind. In contrast, the first option, that the republican party should assume control, which de Valera claimed to oppose, was expounded in a more cogent and appealing manner. He stated that this option

> would constitutionally be the correct one, and most consistent with our whole position. Of all times since the signing of the 'Treaty' the present is the most suitable time. I am against it, however.

The main justification de Valera presented for his opposition was that any Republican government would need the 'unconditional allegiance' of the IRA, and this was plainly not possible; and without such allegiance the proposed government would be 'a farce.' Once again de Valera was putting it up to the IRA to support a Republican government—or suffer the consequences. The manner in which de Valera presented his argument reveals much of his political style. Not for the first time, he portrayed himself as the reluctant politician, ready to serve but equally prepared to return to a quiet life outside politics. By presenting a number of choices he allowed the IRA to believe that it was deciding what course of action to take. In this way de Valera could claim later that his preference had been to retire publicly from the republican party and leave matters to the army but that, at the IRA's behest, he had reluctantly agreed to assume the supreme position within the anti-Treaty movement. He had not sought the army's subordination, de Valera could argue, but the IRA had suggested such a solution itself, against his advice.

Despite appearing reluctant at taking up a position of supremacy within the movement, it was clear that de Valera felt that the issue of a Republican government would be one in which he could gain control of events by subordinating the IRA to his authority. In the end he secured the desired allegiance of the IRA for the new Republican government. Following a meeting on 16–17 October 1922 the IRA declared that 'this executive calls upon the former President of Dáil Éireann to form a government which will preserve the continuity of the Republic.'[134] It was a token gesture, designed to placate de Valera, and it did not alter the imbalance of power between the republican party and the IRA. The new 'government' could 'do little more than issue statements on anti-Treaty policy from time to time.'[135] However, de Valera had achieved his objective of clarifying his position within the anti-Treaty organisation. He was President of the Republic, with his own government, and had secured, in theory, the subordination of the IRA to his control. As President of the Republic he appointed a Council of State composed of twelve deputies and, on 13 November, a government.[136]

De Valera's actions were prompted by two other separate but related factors: money and legitimacy. Joe McGarrity, one of the most ardent supporters of Irish republicanism in the United States,[137] had suggested that Irish-American financial support would be easier to procure if it could be channelled into a recognised Republican institution.[138] Existing funds donated by American citizens during the years 1919–21 and put in trust, in anticipation of an established Irish Republic, also had to be accounted for. De Valera was disinclined to allow such lucrative sources of money to find their way to a political organisation not under his control.

The Catholic hierarchy's condemnations also had to be contended with. The church's pronouncement on the Civil War, made known on 10 October and read out from all pulpits on 22 October, declared that 'in the absence of any legitimate authority' the anti-Treaty forces were guilty of 'murder and assassination.' According to the bishops, republicans were 'riff-raff, scum, looters, brigands and murderers,' inspired by 'vanity . . . greed for land, love of loot and anarchy.' Their actions contravened 'Divine Law' and 'Roman Catholic teaching regarding obedience to authority.' Henceforth the sacraments would be withheld from republicans and 'reserved for her worthy members.'[139]

Wounded by such condemnations, de Valera responded by forming a Republican government from the anti-Treaty second Dáil, thereby establishing a 'legitimate authority' in Ireland. The legal basis for this action rested on the fact that the Provisional Government had adjourned the second Dáil until 30 June 1922 and then postponed a reconvening indefinitely. De Valera and his supporters maintained that these actions had prevented the second Dáil from dissolving itself. Furthermore, it was claimed that the meeting of the Free State legislature on 9 September lacked the Republican mandate that could be conferred only by the proper dissolution of the second Dáil. It was maintained that the Free State parliament derived its validity from the British Parliament, while the republicans retained the legitimacy of the Republican Dáil Éireann, which was an independent, and all-Ireland, legislature.[140]

De Valera lost little time in adopting the symbolic trapping of a republic and enacting Republican legislation to negate the Treaty. An early example of this was a piece of legislation issued under the names of de Valera, as President of the Republic, and his Minister for Home Affairs, Patrick Ruttledge, which declared that the

> resolution passed by Dáil Éireann on 7 January 1922 purporting to approve of the instrument entitled 'Articles of Agreement for a treaty between Great Britain and Ireland' . . . be hereby rescinded and revoked . . . and that any act purporting to be done thereunder is void and of no effect.[141]

Having revoked the Treaty so effortlessly, the government of the Republic, under de Valera's leadership, continued its war of two fronts against the Provisional Government. The imprisonment and hunger strike of Mary MacSwiney (sister of Terence MacSwiney) provided de Valera with a powerful propaganda opportunity,[142] but this was negated by her release in November and overshadowed by an intensification of government efforts to crush Republican forces. On 23 November, Erskine Childers was shot by firing squad, despite the fact that an application for *habeas corpus* was pending. The ostensible justification for his death was the possession of a small pistol that was a present from Michael Collins and was of sentimental rather than military value.[143] On 8 December, 'without any pretence of legality,'[144] four prominent republicans—Liam Mellows, Rory O'Connor, Joseph McKelvey and Dick Barrett—were shot together by direct order of the Executive Council (as the Free State government was called).[145]

The Irish Free State had formally come into existence two days earlier, and the executions, facilitated by a conveyor-belt system of justice composed of military tribunals, announced the determination of the Treaty forces to secure a decisive victory.

Once the Civil War had begun in earnest, de Valera stayed on the periphery, though he remained the primary focus of government odium. While presenting an assured and determined public image, he vacillated in private. By July 1922, only weeks after the start of the Civil War, he committed to his diary the belief that the republican forces had no chance of military victory, and therefore he considered it his duty to persuade 'the men to quit—for the present.'[146] The IRA, on the other hand, would not countenance an unconditional ceasefire, while the Provisional Government demanded submission before negotiations could take place. The death of Collins and the summary executions of republicans made de Valera's position less tenable, and he appeared to revert to a more pugnacious stance.[147] On 5 February 1923 he wrote to J. J. O'Kelly, the official Republican emissary in America, declaring that 'it must be death or glory for us now.'[148] In private, however, he was indefatigable in his attempts to secure a ceasefire. Free State army atrocities, such as those at Ballyseedy Cross and Cahersiveen,[149] strengthened the resolve of the militants, but Liam Lynch eventually relented to requests for a meeting of the IRA Executive, which met in the Waterford mountains on 23 March. De Valera was forced to endure the humiliation of waiting outside the meeting while those inside debated whether to permit the 'President' to participate in the discussion. The decision reached demonstrated de Valera's subordinate position within the republican movement. He was permitted to speak in favour of the motion that continued resistance would 'not further the cause of independence' but could not vote on the issue.[150] Liam Lynch strongly opposed the motion, and it was defeated by six votes to five. The meeting was adjourned until 10 April, but events took a decisive turn when Lynch was killed on the day the meeting was due to reconvene.[151]

Lynch's replacement by a de Valera supporter, Frank Aiken, tipped the scales in favour of those advocating a ceasefire. Again there was a divergence between de Valera's private and public persona. In an address to Republican forces he declared that 'it is better to die nobly as your chief [Liam Lynch] has died than live like a slave'; their cause was immortal, and military defeats 'may defer but cannot prevail against its ultimate triumph.'[152]

Negotiations for a ceasefire foundered on the issue of surrendering arms to the Free State government,[153] but de Valera was determined to bring matters to a close. On 24 May, Frank Aiken, as chief of staff of the IRA, ordered republicans to dump their arms, as 'the foreign and domestic enemies of the republic have for the moment prevailed.'[154] De Valera's statement, issued the same day, gave the impression that the ceasefire was merely tactical and that hostilities could be resumed if conditions proved favourable.

> Soldiers of liberty! Legion of the Rearguard! The Republic can no longer be defended successfully by your arms. Further sacrifices on your part would now be in vain . . . Military victory must be allowed to rest *for the moment* with those who have destroyed the Republic.[155] [Emphasis added.]

De Valera's public views on democracy had become more qualified since the Treaty, and he had informed a Labour Party delegation that 'the majority have no right to do wrong.'[156] He also believed that the combined hostility of the church and the press meant that any verdict of the electorate was akin to the judgement of a court that had not been fully informed of the facts.[157]

The differences that emerged between de Valera the politician and the guerrilla leaders of the IRA were portentous. 'I am almost wishing I were deposed,' de Valera had written to McGarrity at the height of the Civil War, 'for the present position places upon me the responsibility for carrying out a programme which was not mine. The programme "Revise the Treaty" would be mine and I would throw myself into it heart and soul.'[158]

With the Civil War at an end, and with de Valera's most popular and militant colleagues dead, this policy of modifying the institutions of the Free State was the one that de Valera would attempt to introduce into Sinn Féin. The process would lead first to division and then to a split within the republican movement and would end with the establishment of Fianna Fáil.

Chapter 2 ~

REMOVING THE STRAITJACKET OF THE REPUBLIC, 1923–6

D e Valera's views in the immediate aftermath of the Civil War are difficult to ascertain, as he was arrested on 15 August 1923 while speaking on an election platform in Ennis. Though he was neither charged nor tried for any crime, he was to spend not just the election campaign but the next year imprisoned in Arbour Hill military prison, Dublin, and Kilmainham Jail.[1] But despite venomous personalised attacks on his character by the Free State government during the campaign,[2] he succeeded in retaining his seat in Co. Clare.

In the wake of military defeat, and with twelve thousand IRA members in prison, the possibility of republicans polling significantly seemed remote. Sinn Féin election meetings were broken up, canvassers and candidates were harassed and beaten, and posters were torn down by the Free State army and the new police force, the Garda Síochána. The republican organisation was in tatters, its leaders imprisoned, and on 18 August its national offices were raided and the director of elections imprisoned. Unable to get employment because of pervasive discrimination, many republicans had reluctantly taken the emigrant ship.[3] Moreover, the republican party was 'opposed by the entire press and the Catholic hierarchy.'[4]

In such circumstances the forty-four seats won by Sinn Féin, an increase of eight seats (22 per cent), was 'far better than anticipated even by the optimistic.'[5] The result compared very favourably with that of the new pro-Treaty party, Cumann na nGaedheal, which, assisted by extensive administrative resources and near-unanimous support from church and press, saw its representation increase by five seats (9 per cent) to sixty-three. Unlike Sinn Féin, it relied on paid rather than voluntary organisers during the election, reflecting 'a deficit of enthusiasm and energy which had characterised treatyite supporters and an overeagerness ... to compensate for this by throwing money at the problem.'[6]

The anti-Treaty forces remained a minority, and their support still resided mainly in the western part of the country,[7] but for Sinn Féin the forty-four seats 'heralded the first step back, proving that all the people had not turned from 1916 or swallowed whole the Treaty line.'[8]

The 'second Dáil' continued its activities in the absence of its President, de Valera. Imprisonment and fear of capture meant that meetings of the Republican government were poorly attended, with an average of fifteen present. Renewed momentum was given to the assembly's deliberations when de Valera was released from prison in July 1924, and on 7 August he presided over a meeting attended by fifty-five prominent republicans. De Valera's position remained unaltered from the one he adopted in October 1922; indeed 'he acted as if the Civil War had not been fought—or won!'[9] As President of the Republic he declared the second Dáil to be 'the *de jure* Government and Legislature,' while the Free State government was derided as 'the present junta.'[10] A new government was appointed,[11] and a new institution, Comhairle na dTeachtaí (council of deputies), was established. This was composed of those members of the second Dáil 'who remained faithful to the Republic' and all Sinn Féin deputies elected subsequently.[12] By this procedure the second Dáil was deemed to represent the legitimate Republican government of Ireland, while Comhairle na dTeachtaí was to provide the administrative government that would execute government policy. T. Ryle Dwyer has referred humorously to the complexities of such arrangements:

> In short, the second Dáil would be the *de jure* government, while Comhairle na dTeachtaí would, in theory, be the *de facto* one. Yet de Valera personally accepted the Free State Dáil as the *de facto* government of the country, with the result that what he was really saying was that Republicans should consider Comhairle na dTeachtaí as the *de jure de facto* government, and the Free State parliament at Leinster House the *de facto de facto* one.[13]

Sinn Féin enjoyed something of a revival, and the establishment of the Republican government coincided with a rejuvenation of the organisation. In June 1924 there were a thousand Sinn Féin branches throughout the country, representing a spectacular recovery from the fragmentation that had followed the Treaty.[14]

In November de Valera was arrested and was imprisoned for a month in Belfast when he attempted to defend his Stormont seat during the Northern elections.[15] This brief period of incarceration prevented him from attending the 1924 Sinn Féin ardfheis. Deputies were eager for a clear pronouncement on fundamentals to be made, but de Valera's statement on the oath appeared somewhat flexible and open-ended.

> The Oath was a barrier to entering those buildings. Other clauses were equally objectionable. He was not prepared to state his personal view, much would depend on the size of our majority.[16]

The 'other clauses' cited by de Valera numbered ten in all. Sinn Féin deputies pointed out that, apart from the oath (article 17 of the Constitution of the Irish Free State), there were several articles that recognised the King and thus made acceptance of the Free State impossible for republicans. Article 12, for example, stated that 'Parliament shall consist of the King and two Houses,' while article 24 mandated that 'Parliament shall be summoned and dissolved by the representative of the King.' That the oath was recognised as only a part of a larger constitutional entity was made clear by Kevin O'Higgins, who, when alluding to articles 12, 17 and 24, declared that they were 'vital and must not be altered.'[17] De Valera concurred with this reading of the Constitution when he claimed that these articles were 'equally objectionable.' His

intentions, should Sinn Féin secure a majority, were ambiguous, however, and provoked speculation that some republican deputies were entertaining notions of entering
the Free State parliament. On 18 March 1925 de Valera quashed these rumours.

> He believed the time had come when this rumour was hampering the cause. The
> question of entering with the Oath must be definitely closed. But the question is
> what if the Oath were removed? Even if we had a majority vote to-morrow and we
> wanted to take control we could not get in without taking the Oath. The thing
> would be to concentrate upon the removal of the Oath.[18]

Later in the same meeting he added that he 'did not believe that any Republican
representative could go up there and take the Oath even for the sake of taking over
control.'

De Valera was stressing the primacy of principle and was urging delegates not to
sacrifice ideological fundamentals for the allure of immediate power. Few noticed at
the time that a shift had occurred, a shift so subtle and deftly executed that it eluded
detection. To 'concentrate upon the removal of the oath,' as de Valera advocated, may
have appeared, in the light of previous statements, to represent a first step in
removing objectionable aspects of the Free State. But it would soon become clear that
de Valera privately considered such an objective to be the *only* step necessary to
facilitate entrance to the Dáil, despite his own previously stated conviction that other
aspects of the Constitution were equally repellent.

The results of nine by-elections in March 1925, in which republicans secured only
two victories, seem to have depressed de Valera considerably. He expressed his doubts
to Joe McGarrity, confiding that Sinn Féin's political programme was 'too high, and
too sweeping. The oath, on the other hand is a definite objective within reasonable
striking distance.'[19]

De Valera's colleagues in Sinn Féin were unaware of his private reservations, and
after a detailed discussion a majority of the delegates, including de Valera, voted in
favour of the principle of abstention from the Free State parliament. Not only was this
the first explicit policy decision of the second Dáil in favour of abstention but it was
also taken in the absence of Mary MacSwiney, who was on tour in America. These
facts conflict with a popular belief that de Valera had the policy of abstention foisted
upon him by MacSwiney.[20]

On 22 April the decision of the meeting was publicly announced by de Valera and
forty-three other Sinn Féin deputies.

> We the undersigned do not recognise the legitimacy of either the 'Free State' or
> 'Northern' Parliaments. The rumour, therefore, sedulously propagated, despite
> repeated official denials, that we, or any of us, propose (or at any time contem-
> plated) entering the Free State Parliament and taking the oath of allegiance to the
> British King, is without foundation.[21]

This statement not only denied the possibility of taking the oath but rejected the
legitimacy of the Free State parliament as an institution. It was a stance reiterated in

July in response to further rumours that divisions on strategy had emerged at a meeting of Comhairle na dTeachtaí on 28 June.

> There was no such division as that suggested. Every Republican TD was elected on the express policy of non-recognition of the Free State Assembly, which precludes the possibility of entering the Dáil with, or without, the oath. We believe in keeping our pledges to people. Besides it is a mistake to imagine that the oath in the Free State Constitution is the only part of that Constitution that Republicans object to. We are no less opposed to every Article in that Constitution which recognises either Partition, or the claim of England to dictate to the Irish people what their governmental institutions, or what their political relations with other countries, shall be. Our demand is that the Irish people shall be supreme and free in all these matters.[22]

In the light of subsequent events, statements such as these are of great importance, as they advocated the position that was in a very short time to be the subject of a fundamental split within Sinn Féin and that led to the foundation of Fianna Fáil as a rival republican organisation. Unknown to his colleagues, de Valera was privately exploring alternative avenues of movement. Since entering politics he had been

> acutely conscious of the power of the Catholic Church and had endeavoured to harness the Church's influence in his own interests. The condemnation in October 1922 by the Catholic hierarchy of the anti-Treaty side had gravely weakened the republican movement, and, as de Valera prepared for a new beginning, he badly wanted the support of the Church.[23]

Such backing could not be attained at home, where de Valera was *persona non grata* in most clerical circles. He therefore looked further afield for assistance, in particular to three people who had remained consistently supportive during the difficult years that followed the Treaty: Archbishop Daniel Mannix of Melbourne[24] and Monsignor John Hagan[25] and Monsignor Elias Magennis,[26] both of whom were in Rome. Disguised as a priest, de Valera travelled to Rome with his trusted colleague Seán T. O'Kelly and the 21-year-old Seán MacBride, who acted as secretary and interpreter. There de Valera secretly met his three friends of the cloth, and Mannix and Hagan paid a return visit to Ireland during the summer.[27] Hagan had provided de Valera with 'both a theological and historical explanation of how to enter the Dáil,'[28] while MacBride has claimed that during these 'very hush-hush meetings' de Valera

> had a great many talks with Mannix; very long sessions. They went on for three or four days. Mannix, I knew, was pressing him to recognise the Free State Dáil. I felt this was a turning point. I felt De Valera was trying to get political control of the State from within. The breach with Sinn Féin, was no surprise to me . . . It was really in these meetings that the whole plan of campaign for the future policy of Fianna Fáil and the dismantling of the Treaty was taken . . . The whole policy of

entering the Dáil by taking the oath as an 'empty formula', and of proceeding to dismantle the constitution of the Free State and Treaty was taken.[29]

De Valera never reported the meetings to the Sinn Féin Ard-Chomhairle or to the second Dáil.[30] Joe McGarrity received news of negotiations between Archbishop Mannix and a Free State representative with the knowledge and approval of both de Valera and Cosgrave, and he sent a message from America, through Mary MacSwiney, warning de Valera not to take steps towards a settlement without consulting the rank and file. 'Such action had led to trouble before and would lead to it again.'[31] Having passed on the message, MacSwiney added incredulously that 'it looks as if the Free Staters believe you have sent Dr. Mannix out to prepare the way for a surrender on our part.'[32]

De Valera kept his intentions close to his chest, and several actions were taken that could only have been interpreted as demonstrating a solid commitment to the republican movement. In June 1925 two of de Valera's closest allies—Seán Lemass, as Minister for Defence, and Frank Aiken, as chief of staff of the IRA—despatched an IRA delegation to the Soviet Union, 'obviously acting with de Valera's approval.'[33] The three-man delegation managed to secure a half-hour meeting with Stalin in Moscow but left empty-handed, as the Soviet leader doubted their professionalism and feared reprisals from Britain.[34]

The future careers of two members of the delegation are instructive and indicate the separate paths that Sinn Féin members were soon to take. Gerry Boland would follow de Valera into Fianna Fáil and would enjoy almost continuous ministerial office from 1932 to 1957. Seán Russell would remain in the IRA, becoming chief of staff in 1938. He was to die on a German submarine in 1940, while Boland, as Minister for Justice, distinguished himself for his zealous repression of those who continued to follow Russell's leadership. But for the moment the two men were united in common purpose under de Valera's leadership.

Further evidence of de Valera's continued support for IRA operations at this crucial time is provided by a letter from Lemass to O'Kelly. Writing on behalf of the Dáil government, of which de Valera was president, Lemass instructed O'Kelly, as the Republican minister in America, to raise more money for the IRA. Lemass wrote that they were 'endeavouring to maintain the Army as an effective force, capable of being brought into immediate action should the occasion arise that would justify or necessitate its use.'[35] In addition, de Valera's public statements did little to indicate a shift in policy. In October he reaffirmed his adherence to abstention when he addressed a 7,000-strong republican rally commemorating the deaths of members of the 3rd Tipperary Brigade. Referring to a recent by-election in which the Free State candidate had won by a large majority, de Valera was reported by the *Tipperary Star* as stating that

he had been asked . . . why they did not go into the Dáil and try, from within, to work for the Republic. He couldn't understand how any Irishman could ask that question. Even if the end was right, they must not stand in the way of a chance of achieving right by proposing wrong methods. 'We ask that every one of you demand that your representatives shall not take the oath of allegiance to a foreign king.'[36]

In spite of attempts to strengthen the IRA's position, and in spite of the un-equivocal nature of De Valera's public utterances, rumours persisted that he was considering a different course of action. As the Sinn Féin ard-fheis approached in November, de Valera found that he could no longer make plans for a new departure in secret, and he was forced to defend his position to his colleagues. When Comhairle na dTeachtaí met on 15 November he immediately raised the issue of the oath and stated that it was time 'to close the present chapter and begin anew.' He responded to the assembly's reluctance to discuss the issue by stating that he 'would not allow himself to be re-elected at the ard fheis without knowing where he stood.'[37] At a meeting the following day de Valera objected to an ard-fheis motion submitted by the Cahersiveen branch that represented a direct challenge to de Valera's plans. The motion read:

> Owing to the insidious rumours that Republicans will enter the 'Free State Parliament' if the Oath be removed, we call on Sinn Féin to get a definite state-ment from the Government that they will adhere to the policy of Cathal Brugha, Erskine Childers and their fellow martyrs, and enter only an Irish Republican Parliament for all Ireland.[38]

The motion, though firmly in line with Sinn Féin policy, caused de Valera considerable annoyance, and he declared that 'if held as a matter of dogma by the ard fheis he could not conscientiously go on.'[39] In response to this threat Mary MacSwiney devised a compromise proposal to replace the Cahersiveen motion, and the ard-fheis, which met in Rathmines, Dublin, on 17–19 November, eventually agreed that

> no change be made in the policy of the Sinn Féin organisation at this Ard Fheis; but it is agreed that no subject is barred from the whole organisation or part of it with the exception of the acceptance of allegiance to a foreign King and the Partition of Ireland.[40]

This resolution left more room for manoeuvre than the Cahersiveen motion it replaced. De Valera had a setback, however, when the IRA withdrew its allegiance from his 'government' on 15 November. He had attended the IRA's general army convention the previous day and had failed to convince it that he was not considering a break with fundamental policy. In response, Peadar O'Donnell's motion withdrawing alleg-iance to the Republican government obtained an overwhelming majority, and Frank Aiken was dismissed as chief of staff.[41]

In the midst of these events the republican movement was temporarily unified by the signing of a tripartite agreement by the Dublin, Belfast and London governments that copperfastened partition.

THE BOUNDARY COMMISSION

Sinn Féin had always doubted the virtues of the Boundary Commission, established by article 12 of the Anglo-Irish Treaty,[42] but it did not devote a degree of energy to the question comparable to that devoted to its internal wrangling on the oath.[43] When the *Morning Post,* a conservative English newspaper, published a leaked (and accurate) summary of the Boundary Commission report and revealed how limited the border adjustments would be, Sinn Féin republicans temporarily redirected their attention.[44] So damaging was the Boundary Commission report that the Free State negotiator, Eoin MacNeill (Minister for Education), resigned from the commission on 24 November. The Cumann na nGaedheal government panicked, and ministers, including Cosgrave himself, dashed to London to seek a face-saving deal. In the end the border remained unchanged. The Free State government secured some financial concessions to soften the blow, though these only exposed the Cosgrave government to the charge that it had 'sold' the Northern nationalists.[45]

Describing the Free State's handling of the Boundary Commission as 'one of the most elaborate confidence tricks ever played on the Irish people',[46] the IRA newspaper, *An Phoblacht,* argued that the commission had followed the path of least resistance. As the Unionist leader James Craig had threatened rebellion if any Northern Ireland territory was transferred to the Free State, and as Cosgrave had promised to abide by the decision of the commission, it was clear, the paper maintained, which claim would be taken seriously.[47] Mass rallies against partition were held in Dublin, and a committee was established that transcended party allegiance and sought to reverse the 'national setback'.[48]

De Valera's condemnation of the report was couched in pugnacious language that bordered on incitement. This entrenchment of partition had demonstrated 'how futile merely verbal protest is,' and there was no nation on earth, he believed, that would not have 'felt justified in shedding its best blood to prevent it.' He claimed that the southern states of the American union had a 'far better case' for secession than Northern unionists. Lincoln had faced four years of terrible civil war rather than permit them to leave the union, and 'the opinion of the world has justified him—and the results have justified him.'[49]

De Valera realised that Cumann na nGaedheal's difficulty could be his opportunity. It is clear, in retrospect, that he was seriously considering entering the Free State legislature before the Boundary Commission report, but government ineptitude on the issue of partition presented a key that might unlock the Dáil door.

De Valera revised his political career and implied that his break with the Treatyites had been because of the failure of the 1921 agreement to secure a united Ireland.

When I met Mr. Lloyd George in July 1921, the outstanding impression made in my mind by my conversations with him was that partition was his settled policy, settled by imperial motives. I broke with him on this policy of partition; and had Mr. Griffith acted as I had believed he meant to act, he too would have broken on partition.

De Valera paid particular attention to the position of Northern nationalists. He refused to acknowledge a unionist right of secession; and even if such a right did exist, on what grounds, he asked, could unionists justify holding on to nationalist areas in the North? Was it not, he enquired, the principal argument of the Treatyites that, through the Boundary Commission, nationalist communities would be liberated and that, through their liberation, partition in any form would be rendered inoperative? Six-county nationalists had been abandoned to the mercies of their enemies, de Valera concluded; and, worse still, it appeared that their fate had been decided by pecuniary considerations.[50]

Such comments have often been interpreted as suggesting that de Valera's fury at the Boundary Commission fiasco and his frustration at the general trend of Free State policies on Northern Ireland were major factors in his adopting a stance that would facilitate his entry into the Dáil. However, de Valera's decision to embark on a road that would end in his swallowing the bitter pill of the oath predated the boundary agreement by some time, and it was motivated by factors other than the plight of Northern nationalists in the new six-county state. Fear of becoming an irrelevant speck on the broad canvas of Irish politics was the catalyst that inspired his actions. As one historian has argued, de Valera was 'merely using the partition issue to cloak political expediency in the hypocritical garb of principle.'[51]

SINN FÉIN DIVIDES

Within a month of the boundary agreement de Valera summoned an extraordinary ard-fheis, which met on 9–11 March 1926. He claimed that no section of republicans favoured immediate entry to the Free State parliament and stressed that 'the oath of allegiance to a foreign power' was, and had always been, 'a barrier which no one may cross' and remain a member of Sinn Féin. The question, according to de Valera, was whether Sinn Féin would promise, in an attempt to unify the Irish people and to remove the 'national humiliation', that if the oath was eliminated they would take their seats in the Free State assembly. De Valera was adamant that they would continue to consider the Dáil of the Free State to be a 'non-sovereign subordinate twenty six county institution' but one that 'in fact' was in a position to control the lives of a large section of the people.[52] He included a motion on the ard-fheis agenda declaring that once the oaths of allegiance of the 26-county and 6-county assemblies were removed 'it becomes a question not of principle but of policy' whether or not republican representatives should attend these assemblies.[53]

This motion was contested by Father Michael O'Flanagan, who asked the ard-fheis to resolve that it was incompatible with the fundamental principles of Sinn Féin to send representatives to any 'usurping legislature set up by English law in Ireland.'[54] This motion was narrowly passed, by 223 votes to 218, and de Valera resigned as president of Sinn Féin. In his resignation speech he claimed that 'the "Free State" junta [was] solidifying itself as an institution' and that the people would fall in behind it unless a republican party entered the political fray.[55]

The official story propagated by de Valera in later years was that, after seeing his new policy rejected by the ard-fheis, he wished to return to the passive life of an ordinary citizen.

On that day in March 1926, I happened to be walking out of the Rathmines Town Hall with Seán Lemass. I had just resigned as President of Sinn Féin and I said to him, 'Well, Seán, I have done my best, but I have been beaten. Now that is the end for me. I am leaving public life.' Seán was shocked to hear me saying this, and he said: 'But you are not going to leave us now Dev, at this stage. You cannot leave us like that. We have to go on now. We must form a new organisation along the policy lines you have suggested at the ard fheis. It is the only way forward.' We discussed it further and at last I told him that I could not but agree with his logic and said I would do all the necessary things. But we were only a few people and we hadn't a penny between us.[56]

To say that de Valera was being economical with the truth in this recollection would be to understate the case. In reality he was relieved to have rid himself of some of his more doctrinaire colleagues, and he had connived at producing the desired split in the party with a view to establishing an organisation over which he would exert direct control. Lemass, who was indefatigable in his efforts to secure acceptance of de Valera's policy in Sinn Féin, later recalled that he was 'never sure whether de Valera wanted an adverse vote or not.' Of equal significance is his observation that he 'was not upset by his narrow defeat.'[57] Added to this is the manner in which de Valera's supporters advised delegates who had been converted to his policy on the oath but had been instructed by their cumann to vote against it. Instead of advocating that they obey their own conscience on the issue they were instructed to comply with their cumann mandate, thus ensuring that de Valera's motion would be defeated.[58]

It would appear that such delegates were so instructed on the understanding that once the issue was defeated they would be able to join a new party led by de Valera and that would be devoid of the 'galaxy of cranks' Sinn Féin had allegedly accumulated.[59] The ard-fheis result, therefore, did not come as a surprise to de Valera, and in fact he had already made contingency plans.

Long before the split de Valera had moved by stealth, carefully removing those faithful to their pledge to the Republic from positions of authority and replacing them with those personally loyal to him. The case of J. J. O'Kelly is instructive. While O'Kelly was in Australia during the election of August 1923, propagating the republican position on de Valera's instructions, his Louth seat was allocated to Frank Aiken, a loyal supporter. While O'Kelly pointed out that the move would 'give temporary justification to those who oppose our mission,' he acquiesced. After the split he looked at the event less charitably and bemoaned the fact that he had allowed his constituency to be 'annexed in the interest of Mr. de Valera's pliant instrument, Frank Aiken.'[60]

In July 1924 O'Kelly was removed from his position as Republican minister in the United States and replaced by another de Valera stalwart, Seán T. O'Kelly. This was an astute, if dissimulating, move on de Valera's part. If his new organisation was to thrive, a steady supply of money would be necessary, and America was by far the most lucrative source of finances for republicans. Father O'Flanagan, another strong opponent of de Valera's new policy, who remained in Sinn Féin, recalled bitterly that he and J. J. O'Kelly had been made tools of by de Valera for working up an organisation in America for the followers of de Valera's policy to profit by. As soon as he and Sceilig [J. J. O'Kelly] had gotten things well under way in the U.S.A. a slick little politician [Seán T. O'Kelly] was sent over.[61]

In January 1926, the same month in which de Valera had called the extraordinary ard-fheis, Aiken was despatched by de Valera to America, his brief being 'to retain for de Valera the financial support of the military element in America, especially that connected with Joe McGarrity.'[62] It is clear that de Valera was determined not to find himself and his supporters bereft of finances. Rather than being caught unaware by the ard-fheis decision and being eager to leave public life he had prepared for all contingencies and had laid his plans with remarkable care and skill, in a manner that does not sit well with his projected image of the sincere political neophyte. The story of his 'conversion' by Lemass is therefore certainly apocryphal, though the fact that he should present such an account reveals something of de Valera's character and political thinking.

Despite having resigned as president of Sinn Féin, de Valera remained 'President of the Republic' and head of the 'government' based on the second Dáil. To clarify matters in the wake of the ard-fheis, Comhairle na dTeachtaí met on the 28 March 1926, with an attendance of forty-six members. The chairman of the joint committees of Sinn Féin, Art O'Connor, informed the meeting that it had been established that 'no co-operation was possible on the proposal to enter the "Free State Parliament" in the event of the oath being removed.' In an effort to decide the matter, Mary MacSwiney proposed

> that the entry of any member of Dáil Éireann into the Free State Parliament, or any Parliament set up by British law in Ireland is incompatible with membership of the *de jure* Government of the Republic, and inconsistent with the principles and policies advocated by Republican Teachtaí and candidates since 1922.[63]

At de Valera's behest, two amendments were proposed. The first, which deleted the words 'principles and', was passed by 21 votes to 17, while the second, which urged the deletion of 'incompatible with membership of the de jure Government of the Republic, and', was approved by 23 votes to 21. These amendments were not motivated simply by pedantry or punctiliousness: if the motion was passed as stated it would have made de Valera's position untenable and his resignation unavoidable. The amended motion, which was passed comprehensively, by 26 votes to 15, declared that

> the entry of any member of Dáil Éireann into the Free State Parliament set up by British law in Ireland is inconsistent with the policies advocated by Republican Teachtaí and candidates since 1922.

After one deputy suggested that this vote be regarded as a vote against the President's policy, de Valera responded that 'the terms of the resolution were not sufficiently definite for him to regard it in that light and warranting his resignation.'[64]

Again, to clarify the issue, Mary MacSwiney proposed that 'this assembly does not approve of the policy as outlined by the President.'[65]

Echoing the Treaty debate almost five years earlier, de Valera had been defeated by his colleagues on an issue of policy; and, once again, the issue was simplified and reduced to one of confidence in de Valera personally. This time de Valera was defeated by one vote, 19 votes to 18, with several abstentions.[66]

The vote against de Valera by his peers in Comhairle na dTeachtaí is not surprising, given the admissions he made during this crucial meeting. As the substantive motion was being debated de Valera claimed that he had been considering entering the Free State parliament three years previously. He told members that before his arrest in Ennis in August 1923 he was prepared to tell his audience that he would enter the Dáil. 'If I had the chance in Ennis I would have said I was willing to go in.' This admission 'shocked most of the delegates,' for it meant that 'for three years de Valera had been presiding over a republican Dáil and a republican Sinn Féin while contemplating entry into the Free State.'[67] In essence, the self-proclaimed President of the Republic had been saying one thing and believing another. He had ruled out—as a matter of principle—acceptance of the Free State while secretly planning the smoothest and most credible entry route to Leinster House.

While this ambivalent condition may explain the discrepancy between de Valera's public words and his private deeds, it took most members of Comhairle na dTeachtaí by surprise. When asked bluntly by David Ceannt[68] if he was going to enter the Free State parliament, de Valera refused to reply. Another asked if he would be prepared to enter Leinster House with a party of ten, to which de Valera evasively replied that he could not say 'what I would do in all the circumstances.' A former minister of the Republican Dáil, Michael Colivet, then asked, 'How long will it be till the details are put before us?' De Valera's response—'probably not till the actual time of entry'— revealed that it was now a question of 'when' rather than 'if' he entered the Free State parliament. Realising the implications of what he had said, de Valera added that 'Count Plunkett and others will say I am accepting things,' to which Plunkett replied, 'We will.' (George Plunkett had been made a Papal count and was widely known by this title.) When Colivet concluded that it appeared that de Valera sought *carte blanche* to develop a policy in public that they had not seen 'in any shape or form,' de Valera declared that he had not come to the meeting to seek approval for his policy, and he urged them to vote against it if they wished.[69] It was against this background that he lost the debate within Comhairle na dTeachtaí and relinquished his title as President of the Republic.

The next meeting of Comhairle na dTeachtaí, which took place on 22–23 May 1926, sought to deal with the vacancy for the position of President.[70] By this time de Valera had already publicly announced his intention of establishing a new party, and those of his supporters who intended to enter 'either of the foreign-controlled partition "Parliaments" in Ireland' if the oath was removed were instructed by the Sinn Féin leadership to resign their seats—a request with which they refused to comply.

Curiously, considering his actions in establishing a rival organisation, de Valera was in attendance at this meeting and participated in the debate. Anticipating the leadership's intention of electing Art O'Connor in his place, he made the bizarre claim that he had never considered himself 'President of the Republic' since his resignation from the position in January 1922, at the end of the Dáil debate on the Treaty. The disbelief this statement aroused is exemplified by the response of David Ceannt, who declared that such a contention was unsustainable, as de Valera had consistently employed the title since 1922, including when he had issued the ceasefire order at the end of the Civil War. Ceannt concluded by asking de Valera whether he was suggesting that they had been wrong in calling their assembly 'Dáil Éireann' and that he had not been President of the Republic during the previous four years. De Valera's reply did not dispel the confusion.

> I was not President of the Republic from the time I resigned that position when the Treaty was passed. I do not know that I ever formally accepted the position. I was elected Head of the Emergency Government and I have always maintained that position as such . . . I would not have accepted the position as President of the Republic on this account. I was prepared to act as Head of the Revolutionary Government for the time being.[71]

This denial flew in the face of everything de Valera had been engaged in politically during the preceding years. He had adopted all the trappings of President of the Republic, including the letter-heads he used, on which was printed 'Dáil Éireann | Government of the Republic'; and it is difficult to conceive how he could have tolerated fellow-deputies referring to him as such if he did not believe he was the legitimate holder of the office. Only when he had been *denied* possession of the title did he suggest that deputies should desist from using the term.

While de Valera was eager that a new President should not be appointed, it was clear that he wished that his new party would enjoy some power within Comhairle na dTeachtaí. As a compromise he stated that he was prepared 'to propose Art O'Connor as Chief Executive provided that some arrangement as to a Coalition Cabinet could be come to.' His chances of achieving such a coalition were undermined, however, by his refusal to give a guarantee that Fianna Fáil members would not enter 'any foreign-controlled Parliament under an Oath-bound Ministry [government].'

Art O'Connor was proposed as 'President of the Republic and Príomh Aire [prime minister] of Dáil Éireann and Comhairle na dTeachtaí.' De Valera then raised a technical issue, pointing out that Comhairle na dTeachtaí was the *de facto* government, while the second Dáil had *de jure* authority—despite the fact that he had hitherto treated the two institutions as one and the same. Notwithstanding his protest that his opponents were 'going to set up a one-party Executive,' the motion was put to the assembly, and O'Connor was elected. 22 members voted in favour, while 16, including de Valera, did not register a vote.[72]

It is curious that de Valera continued to attend meetings of Comhairle na dTeachtaí while simultaneously organising a rival political entity. Many in Sinn Féin did not seem to have considered this situation anomalous but rather believed that essential republican unity could be maintained. De Valera's motivation cannot, however, be in doubt: it was money.

At the meeting of Comhairle na dTeachtaí on 23 May, the first issue raised by de Valera was that of the destination of funds raised in America. He wanted to know if American funds were 'going to be distributed to Sinn Féin and the Army [the IRA] and was his organisation going to be cut off?' He threatened to establish a rival American fund-raising mission if Fianna Fáil did not receive a sizeable portion of the funds contributed to the Republic. He also admitted that the Republican minister who had replaced Seán T. O'Kelly had been acting in his interests and that his contacts in America and Australia had indicated to him 'that monies were being forwarded to help the idea which I had, and that they were coming directly through the Envoy.'[73] This admission confirmed J. J. O'Kelly's and Father Michael O'Flanagan's interpretation of the reason for their being removed from the American mission.

What de Valera did not reveal was that Seán T. O'Kelly had been attempting, since 1924, to harness the resources of the American Association for the Recognition of the Irish Republic for the purposes of supporting de Valera's plans for a new departure. The AARIR was the most important Irish-American organisation, and it had been an invaluable source of financial assistance to the republican movement. To ensure the success of any new political venture, de Valera knew it would be imperative that he enlist the support of this influential organisation. What his colleagues in the second Dáil did not know was that he had contacted leading members of the AARIR, most notably the organisation's treasurer, John J. Hearn, in an attempt to divert funds to Fianna Fáil.[74] Many of the AARIR's leaders had welcomed de Valera during his American tour of 1919–20, and he had been careful to remain in personal contact with them and to keep them regularly informed of developments in Ireland from his own point of view.[75]

De Valera's political designs also received valuable assistance from Archbishop Mannix. He had already rallied Irish support for de Valera's position in Australia,[76] and with the establishment of Fianna Fáil he embarked on a tour of the United States to drum up support. De Valera was now cashing in on the clerical contacts he had carefully cultivated. The ostensible reason for Mannix's American visit was to attend a Eucharistic Congress in Chicago, but the timing of his visit, coinciding with the formation of Fianna Fáil, was fortuitous. While in Chicago he met Seán T. O'Kelly and delivered a speech tailored for an Irish-American audience, a skilful blend of pugnacity and unequivocal support for de Valera. The Free State government was portrayed as a collection of imperialist lackeys, with few friends except traditional pro-British elements and those who derived an income from the regime. Neither Pearse nor de Valera had fought for an oath of allegiance, he declared to loud applause, and Ireland's struggle remained a cause 'for which men died in 1916, and for which men are willing to die, if necessary, in 1926.'[77]

By linking militant republicanism exclusively with de Valera, Mannix was advocating that those who wished to end partition and to achieve full independence should support Fianna Fáil. He reiterated his message at a reception hosted by Seán T. O'Kelly at Carnegie Hall, New York, and at similar meetings in Philadelphia and Boston[78]—all important centres of AARIR activity.

Realising the importance of such clerical support, Fianna Fáil published a collection of Mannix's speeches for distribution in Ireland. The pamphlet also summarised the new party's policies as uniting the Irish people on the march towards an independent republic, abolishing the oath, replacing the Constitution of the Irish Free State with one 'freely framed by the Representatives of the Irish people,' and repudiating the partition of Ireland, using 'every effective means to bring it to an end.'[79]

The impact of Mannix's visit to the United States was recognised by those opponents of de Valera who remained in Sinn Féin. Arriving in America shortly before Mannix's departure, Art O'Connor noted that the archbishop's tour 'was more than a godsend to them [Fianna Fáil]: its influence on the places he spoke cannot be estimated.'[80] This influence and that of other de Valera acolytes sent to the United States can be gauged from the fact that the great majority of the AARIR swung behind de Valera, who for them had embodied the Presidency of the Republic since 1919. Little of the internal ideological debate within Irish republicanism had reached Irish America—a result of Sinn Féin inertia—and few could distinguish the differences between the opposing factions, a fact that favoured de Valera, probably the best known Irish politician in America. His success with the AARIR cut off a vital supply of money from Sinn Féin—estimated at £28,000 in 1924—which was diverted to Fianna Fáil.

Despite these manoeuvres, de Valera was present when Comhairle na dTeachtaí met on 18–19 December 1926 to discuss the forthcoming American bonds case that was due to be decided in the US courts. During the War of Independence the Dáil had raised an external loan in the United States for the purpose of achieving recognition for the Irish Republic. This effort had proved remarkably successful and had secured almost $6 million from half a million subscribers.[81] The terms of the bond read:

> This certificate is not negotiable, but is exchangeable if presented at the Treasurers of the Republic of Ireland one month after the international recognition of the said Republic, for one $................. Gold Bond of the Republic of Ireland.[82]

All but $2½ million had been transferred to the Dáil up to the time of the Treaty, whereupon the money became the subject of a legal wrangle.[83] The Free State government's claim was debilitated by the fact that it did not constitute the government of the Irish Republic, for which the bonds had been issued. Sinn Féin's case was stronger in principle, for, while the second Dáil was not internationally recognised as the government of the Irish Republic, it claimed, with some credibility, to be the legitimate heir of the independence movement formed to achieve the Republic. It had kept the faith, it argued, and so should keep the money.

At the instigation of the anti-Treatyites, the money had been placed in safe deposit boxes, which prevented the Free State from gaining access, and there it had stayed since 1922. The Free State government had attempted to retrieve the funds, and the culmination of its efforts was to be on 7 March 1927, when the American courts would decide on the appropriate destination for the money.

Having relinquished the office of President of the Republic the previous March, de Valera realised that Fianna Fáil's chances of securing a share of the American money had been impaired. Furthermore, he had denied that the position had existed since 1922. His opponents within the second Dáil and Comhairle na dTeachtaí had retained their claim to be the *de jure* government of the Republic, headed by a

President of that Republic. Clearly, if de Valera was to entertain any hope of getting a portion of the funds it was imperative that he maintain contact with the second Dáil. These considerations provide some explanation for his presence at the meeting of Comhairle na dTeachtaí convened to discuss the American bonds case.

At the meeting, de Valera agreed to give up every right to the office of President of the Republic and proposed the ratification of Art O'Connor in his place. (It is worth stressing again that de Valera had previously told the assembly that he did not acknowledge the existence of such a position.) In return for this gesture the new President proposed that de Valera's position as trustee of the bonds be confirmed; and it was agreed that de Valera should represent the second Dáil in the American courts.

The relationship between de Valera and the Republican government was not unlike Collins and Griffith's relationship with him when they were despatched to London in 1921. In theory, de Valera was representing the second Dáil in America, but there was no guarantee that he would act in a manner that would meet the approval of his superiors in Dublin. Austin Stack, who remained a minister in O'Connor's new Executive, declared confidently that 'Mr. de Valera will regard us as his principals in the course of litigation.' De Valera's reply—'I will give an understanding here that I will safeguard the Republican position'—was true to form.[84] He did not reply affirmatively to Stack's statement, and he left himself some room for manoeuvre in defining at a future date what constituted 'the republican position'.

De Valera devoted most of his time during the early months of 1927 to the American bonds case. On several occasions he denied the right of the Free State to the funds, declaring that they had been raised 'for the purpose of carrying on the Government of the Republic of Ireland.'[85] He claimed that 'to turn these funds over now to the usurping legislature . . . would be a reversal of the intentions of the subscribers and a betrayal of trust.'[86]

At the beginning of March, de Valera departed for America, leaving the Fianna Fáil vice-presidents, Patrick Ruttledge and Seán T. O'Kelly, to continue the work of the party at home.[87] He attended the proceedings of the New York Supreme Court, which opened on 9 March, and put forward his case before the arbitrator of the dispute, Judge Peters.[88] It was clear, however, that de Valera considered his brief to be wider than merely defending the republican position during the bonds case. Using the recently acquired support of the AARIR, he embarked on a national tour promoting the Fianna Fáil position.[89] He gave numerous interviews to the American press and addressed dozens of rallies. Such occasions were used to put forward the Fianna Fáil policy on the oath and to stress his determination to abolish partition.[90] Copies of these speeches were sent to Ireland, where they were published by the party and submitted to the national press.

In effect, de Valera's American tour was an Irish election tour, and it served the dual purpose of collecting money for Fianna Fáil in the United States and raising his prestige at home. The position of the second Dáil, whose interests he was ostensibly promoting, was never alluded to. Indeed the only occasion on which implicit reference to Sinn Féin was made was when he bemoaned the exclusion of 'forty-eight Republican TDs' from the Free State assembly.[91] As de Valera treated 'Fianna Fáil' and 'republicans' as interchangeable entities during his speeches, it is not unreasonable to suggest that the purpose of referring to the 'forty eight Republican TDs' (the majority of whom had no desire to enter the Free State parliament) was to give the impression that Fianna Fáil was larger than it was. In this way de Valera manipulated Irish-American ignorance of internal debates within Irish republicanism to the advantage of Fianna Fáil. Aided by such dubious statistics, he confidently predicted that Fianna Fáil would secure a majority in the forthcoming election.[92] To this end he announced shortly after his arrival in New York that he was launching a drive for election funds in the United States.[93]

Fearing that the court might decide in favour of the Free State, de Valera in 1925 had overseen the establishment of an Irish Republic Bondholders' Committee, representing fifty thousand subscribers. Seán T. O'Kelly was given the task of forming 'a representative committee' that would 'defend their own interests and exert their influence in supporting the claim of the Irish Republic' to the funds.[94] The committee dutifully submitted to the New York court that the money should not be given to the Free State authorities but should be returned to the subscribers, who could then individually decide its appropriate destination.[95] De Valera had covered his options well. Confirmed in his position of trustee of the funds for the 'Republic of Ireland', and selected as the official representative of the second Dáil, he had retained sufficient contact with that organisation to ensure that Fianna Fáil would receive a large portion of the money should the Republican government emerge victorious. In addition, legal counsel for the trustees of the Irish Republic were personally devoted to de Valera and not to the second Dáil.[96] If, however, the court decided in favour of the bondholders, de Valera's control of that organisation and his presence and status in America would give him the opportunity to secure most of the funds for his new party.

On 11 May, Judge Peters issued his long-awaited judgement, deciding that the money should be returned *pro rata* to the original subscribers.[97] On receiving the judgement, de Valera urged all bondholders to transfer their bond money to Fianna Fáil.[98] If anyone had detected some equivocation in de Valera's guarantee to the second Dáil 'to safeguard the republican position,' these suspicions were now confirmed; but it was too late.

De Valera informed American bondholders that Fianna Fáil was the republican party and that if they wished to ensure that the funds were used as originally intended the Fianna Fáil coffers were the only place for them. In this manner he siphoned off this vital supply of finances for the benefit of Fianna Fáil and to the detriment of the second Dáil, whose interests he had been formally representing. The *naïveté* of the members of the second Dáil in nominating de Valera as their representative provoked anguished responses from those in America who remained loyal to it and who recognised it as the *de jure* government of the Irish Republic.

The bond money that de Valera secured for Fianna Fáil was of inestimable value to the new party, then in a critical stage of development. It would also be significant for the establishment of the party's national paper, the *Irish Press*, in 1931.[99] De Valera's actions, while understandable in the party-political sense, are difficult to reconcile with his professed innocence of the *realpolitik* of political life. Having achieved his objective of harnessing all available American finances for the benefit of Fianna Fáil, he had little use for the second Dáil. His attendance at meetings of Comhairle na dTeachtaí ceased. He now ruled out any plans for co-operation between Sinn Féin and Fianna Fáil, despite having advocated such a *rapprochement* while the bonds case was pending.[100] Indeed, within three days of the Supreme Court judgement he rebuffed initiatives from Mary MacSwiney for a united approach and suggested a parting of the ways for the two republican organisations.[101]

When the second Dáil met on 10 December 1927 it expressed disapproval of 'Mr. de Valera's action in asking that the returned American bonds be handed over to Fianna Fáil, instead of urging, as Trustee for the Republic, that they be applied to their original purpose.'[102] It was a feeble response, reflecting the impotence of the republicans that de Valera had left behind without a steady source of revenue. De Valera had emerged victorious—the pragmatic having defeated the dogmatic—and he could present himself as leader of the only republican party with a future.

WAS SINN FÉIN DYING?
Organisational vitality and ideological change
A consensus has emerged in recent years about the series of events that led to the split in Sinn Féin and the establishment of Fianna Fáil. Though they have never been the subject of much academic study, the conclusion often reached is that the republican party was dying and that de Valera jumped from a sinking ship before it faced another electoral test.

The basis for this consensus is largely two lengthy articles by Peter Pyne published in 1969–70.[103] Pyne's analysis has provided the bedrock for much of the historical work on the vicissitudes of Sinn Féin from the end of the Civil War to the founding of Fianna Fáil. It was a ground-breaking study, and it has yet to be surpassed in many respects. The span of Pyne's investigation is 1923–6, and in it an attempt is made to document what is perceived to be the inexorable decline of what is called the 'Third Sinn Féin Party'. Taking that as his starting point, Pyne attempts to elucidate the 'factors contributing to [the party's] collapse.'[104]

Three criteria are employed for gauging the organisational health of Sinn Féin: the financial position of the party; the number of branches; and the support received in the various elections it contested.

Pyne records that Sinn Féin's income for the year 1923/4 was £26,000, which included a contribution of £20,000 from American supporters towards the cost of contesting the 1923 election. During the following year, 1924/5, income dropped by a third, to £17,000, the bulk of which consisted of American donations. Between 1925 and 1926 the party's finances 'plunged' to £3,800, and two-thirds of this was subscribed in the United States. In assessing these statistics Pyne points out that by 1926 Sinn Féin's income was only 15 per cent of what it had been two years previously. In addition, it is suggested that its reliance on American financial support is indicative of poor organisation and dwindling domestic support. He concludes that 'the financial position of the party was, therefore, one of rapid decline from 1924 onwards.'[105]

However, the position of Sinn Féin appears less unfavourable when it is compared with the experience of Fianna Fáil during its first three years of existence as an organisation. The honorary treasurers' report submitted to the 1927 ard-fheis reported that income for the previous eighteen months was £30,402, of which an incredible £29,782, or 98 per cent, had been contributed from abroad, mainly from the United States and Australia.[106] This figure compares favourably with that of Sinn Féin in the year after the Civil War. But it can be argued that the Sinn Féin figure of £26,000 is more impressive, as it covered a twelve-month period, as opposed to an eighteen-month period, and the money was raised to contest one election, while Fianna Fáil had contested two within four months and therefore sought and received further foreign donations. Had there been only one election in 1927 the figure would have been considerably lower.[107] The report also recalled that at the party's first ard-fheis the previous year it had been agreed that £4,370 would be budgeted for a 'normal year,' that is, a year in which an election did not occur. Moreover, a figure of £7,000 was projected as the amount necessary to finance activities for the coming year. Receipts received for the year 1927/8, however, revealed that the party could muster only £3,702 in the course of the twelve-month period.[108] Total income for 1928/9 increased to £6,792—though this was £607 short of expenditure—before falling again in 1929/30 to £5,156.[109] In 1931 the amount raised declined further to £4,252 before increasing on the party's assumption of power the following year.[110]

If we were to employ Pyne's logic to these statistics we might see a party heading for terminal decline—one whose immediate disposable income declined within a year to 12 per cent of its 1927 figure. Such an interpretation would, however, be misleading. What these statistics reveal is the artificiality of the figures for 1923 and 1927, both of which were election years. There is invariably an inter-election lull, and the party always finds it difficult to keep the machine oiled and members motivated.

The second criterion used by Pyne to demonstrate the decline of Sinn Féin, the number of cumainn, produces an equally inconclusive result. He argues that after an initial boom following the Civil War (and a corresponding mushrooming of cumainn) membership had levelled off by mid-1924 before going into irreversible decline thereafter. Between June and November 1923 seven hundred cumainn were established, and the party continued to expand into 1924. But, as Pyne notes, only 700 of the 1,025 cumainn were able to raise the affiliation fee for the 1924 ard-fheis, held at the end of the year. This number had declined to a little over 350 by July 1925. Pyne concludes by quoting the Sinn Féin honorary secretaries' report for 1925, which attributed the figures to poor organisation, and argues that it was obvious that the party was not adequately representing the republican population. This leads him to conclude that 'there can be little doubt that the Third Sinn Féin party was declining internally.'[111]

Let us compare these figures with those of Fianna Fáil during its early years. Throughout 1926 and 1927 the Fianna Fáil organisation expanded rapidly, so that by the party's 1927 ard-fheis 1,367 cumainn were registered.[112] By 1928, however, a somewhat different picture emerges. The honorary secretaries reported that, of 1,033 cumainn, only 354 had managed to pay the affiliation fee. These organisational deficiencies were starker in constituencies such as Cork West, which possessed only one affiliated cumann. (The city of Cork had three; Waterford and Dublin South each had four; and even a republican heartland like Co. Kerry could muster only ten affiliated cumainn.)[113]

The picture was not any rosier in 1929, during which the number of registered (as opposed to affiliated)[114] cumainn declined in all but five constituencies. In numerous areas the number fell by almost half during the year, and in two—Mayo South and

Monaghan—it fell by two-thirds.[115] The honorary secretaries were just as critical of these figures as were their predecessors in Sinn Féin. Their report attributed the decline to organisational weakness. 'It cannot be said that any county carried out the work systematically,' they complained. Furthermore, they argued that the figures indicated that the party was not adequately reflecting the republican population, as the number of cumainn had collapsed in areas where there was reportedly good support for Fianna Fáil policies.[116]

It is evident that a reliance on the number of cumainn as a barometer for organ-isational vitality and as an indicator of a party's potential could be defective. The period 1926–9 could be interpreted as indicative of a party suffering interminable decline; but it weathered the storm. The number of cumainn picked up in 1930 and 1932, reaching 550 and 759, respectively, and exploding in the period before the 1932 election and in the immediate aftermath of Fianna Fáil's assumption of power.

Pyne underestimates the organisational strength of Sinn Féin. For example, Jeffrey Prager claims that 'only when Fianna Fáil emerged as a political force did Cumann na nGaedheal more than triple its local branches from 276 in 1924 to 797 in May 1926.'[117] Yet Fianna Fáil was only established in May 1926, and the evidence cited therefore suggests that Cumann na Gaedheal was responding to the organisational challenge of Sinn Féin and not to that of the non-existent Fianna Fáil.

Pyne argues that election results between 1923 and 1926 demonstrate the organ-isational malaise within Sinn Féin.[118] However, Sinn Féin succeeded in augmenting its share of the popular vote during this period, increasing its representation from 44 seats to 48. As regards the five by-elections held in November 1924, the republican vote increased in all constituencies: in fact Sinn Féin gained more than 29,000 votes in these constituencies compared with its performance in the 1923 general election, an average increase of almost 6,000 votes per constituency.[119]

The same pattern was evident during the nine by-elections held in March 1925, when Sinn Féin again increased its vote in every constituency, leading Dorothy Macardle to comment that 'the tide had already turned; the ebb that had begun with the signing of the Treaty was already over and the flow, however slow and gradual, had begun.'[120] It should also be noted that by-elections traditionally favour the largest party. In the circumstances of the 1920s, Sinn Féin experienced the disadvantage of all transfers from conservative elements tending to go to Cumann na nGaedheal, which habitually portrayed such contests as life-and-death struggles for the continued existence of the state.[121]

Fianna Fáil would be confronted with the same problem during its formative years. The party contested nine by-elections before its historic victory in the 1932 general election. Of these it won only two, almost exactly the same proportion (four out of seventeen) that Sinn Féin won between 1923 and 1926. Three of the by-elections were occasioned by the death of Fianna Fáil TDs, but only one of those seats was successfully defended by the republican party. The failure to retain Markievicz's seat was particularly embarrassing. The constituency of Dublin South, though never a republican heartland, was the base of Fianna Fáil's rising star, Seán Lemass, who had already secured the crucial leadership positions of national organiser and honorary secretary. The combined vote of Fianna Fáil and Sinn Féin had been greater than that of Cumann na nGaedheal in the June general election, but the August by-election saw the government party extend its lead over Fianna Fáil from 900 votes to almost 4,500.

Pyne's analysis of the 'Third Sinn Féin Party' has been accepted without inter-rogation,[122] and it is not difficult to understand why. There is a simplicity and tidiness about the analysis that is tantalising. His conclusions, however, appear less impressive when a comparison is made with the first three years of Fianna Fáil.[123]

His starting point, 1923, was an election year, which distorts much of the sub-sequent analysis of membership and income. An authoritative conclusion could have been attempted only if Sinn Féin had remained intact for a few more years and had contested another election. De Valera, however, was not willing to wait that long, and Pyne is correct in pointing out the perception among members of the party elite that the party was in danger of dying. The data certainly does not support Pyne's trenchant conclusion that Sinn Féin declined 'from its position as the second largest party in the country to that of a very minor organisation on the fringe of the political scene within the space of three years.'[124]

What is clear from Pyne's study, and what cannot be contested, is that there existed within Sinn Féin a body of opinion, led by de Valera, eager to divest itself of the more doctrinaire and less election-focused elements within the party. This eagerness is made clear in a letter de Valera wrote to Joe McGarrity in 1925 to prepare him for the inevitable break.

> For over a year—since the nine Bye-Elections, I have been convinced that the programme on which we were working would not win the people in the present conditions. It was too high, and too sweeping. The oath, on the other hand, is a definite objective within reasonable striking distance. If I can mass the people to smash it, I shall have put them *on the march* again, and once moving, and having tasted victory, further advances will be possible.[125]

De Valera argued that the economic conditions in the Free State had demoralised republicans, most of whom were destitute, and that many of the party's best workers had been forced to emigrate. Though there was a general dislike of the Free State government, 'the people could only see us as offering them the fire as the retreat from the frying pan.' De Valera felt that this perception would change. People knew that Britain could not compel its representatives to take the oath unless a majority took it voluntarily and that once the people were determined to abolish it it would go. Such a public repudiation of the oath, he argued, would be 'only less than a redeclaration of Independence.' De Valera anticipated McGarrity in explaining why he no longer waited to force the issue.

> It is vital that the Free State be shaken at the next General Election, for if an opportunity be given it to consolidate itself further as an institution—if the present Free State members are replaced by Farmers and Labourers and other class interests, the national interest as a whole will be submerged in the clashing of the rival economic groups. It seems to me a case of now or never—at least in our time.[126]

In this regard de Valera's fears were not unfounded, for at the election of June 1927 the Labour Party secured its best result, taking 22 seats, while the Farmers' Party received 11, independents 14 and the National League 8. The combined vote of these sectional groups was considerably higher than that of either Cumann na nGaedheal or Fianna Fáil, which took 27 per cent and 26 per cent, respectively.

As for his fear of the Free State consolidating itself, no factor aided the stabilisation of the Free State more than de Valera's decision to enter the Dáil.

Chapter 3 ～

FIANNA FÁIL—THE REPUBLICAN PARTY

THE BEGINNING

De Valera had set about organising a new republican organisation with breathtaking speed, and by 17 April 1926 he was able to inform the press of the imminent establishment of Fianna Fáil. Paraphrasing Pearse, he claimed that the central conviction of the party was that 'in the heart of every Irishman there is a native undying desire to see his country politically free, and not only free but truly Irish as well.' It was not clear, however, whether he included unionists in this category.

Particular care had been taken in finding an appropriate name for the new party. De Valera explained that 'Fianna Fáil' was chosen

> to symbolise a banding together of the people for national service, with a standard of personal honour for all who join as high as that which characterised the ancient Fianna Éireann and a spirit of devotion equal to that of the Irish Volunteers from 1913 to 1921.[1]

The purpose of the organisation was to reunite the Irish people and to gather them together for the 'tenacious pursuit' of the party's ultimate objectives, the first being to secure 'the political independence of a united Ireland as a republic.' The party would use 'at every moment such measures as are rightfully available.'[2] On the issue of the oath, de Valera remained adamant that it was inconceivable that any republican could enter the Dáil while it remained. 'That oath no republican will take,' he insisted, 'for it implies acceptance of England's right to overlordship in our country.' The removal of the oath would allow republicans to co-operate with other elected representatives 'without having to forswear any of their principles.'[3]

On 16 May 1926 Fianna Fáil was formally established at a public meeting in the La Scala Theatre in Prince's Street, Dublin (later the Capitol Theatre). In his presidential address de Valera lamented that the national effort had become fragmented, making progress difficult and the triumph of 'the imperial forces' certain. He wished to see these divisions vanish and stressed that 'means must be found to bring the national forces together.'[4] He also regretted the separation from his former colleagues in Sinn Féin but believed that the attainment of their objectives would reunite these natural allies.[5] He then stated that it was only after power had been secured in the Free State that the oath could be removed and effective action against partition initiated.

The right way to proceed is obvious. We must first make good the internal sovereignty of the people of the Twenty-six Counties. That is a task well within our power . . . When we have established our right and strengthened our position in the Twenty-six Counties, then we shall be in a position to attack the problem of the Six with some chance of success. Meanwhile, we must make it quite clear that we are no parties to partition and that there will be no active co-operation between us and the foreign power that has been guilty of this outrage upon our country until partition is ended.[6]

It was clear that obtaining power in the Free State was seen very much as a means to an end and that the compromise of entering the Dáil could be justified only by the achievements that this act of *realpolitik* would bring.

However, those who remained in Sinn Féin believed that actions that were 'wrong in principle' would not achieve sacred ideals.[7] Mary MacSwiney believed that 'the policy now adopted by Fianna Fáil seems to be that which we refused four years ago.'[8] If such a policy was inappropriate for republicans in 1922, she asked, how could it be right in 1926? MacSwiney feared that the accession of Fianna Fáil deputies rather than dismantling the Free State, would stabilise it. Time would dilute the revolutionary fervour of the deputies, and the 'few faithful and honourable souls' who remained would be 'left high and dry.' She said of de Valera: 'I have no doubt that he means well . . . but so did 90 per cent of those who passed the Treaty.'[9]

Fears that expediency would dilute the fundamental principles of the republican movement and deflect it from its mission of securing a united republic were not confined to those who remained in Sinn Féin. Many of those who followed de Valera into Fianna Fáil voiced concerns for the future and sought assurances that there would be no weakening of the party's resolve to end partition. A private letter from Frank Barrett, former OC of the IRA's 1st Western Division, reflects the concerns of many who joined Fianna Fáil.

I don't know how to express exactly what I think of the New Movement. That there is a crying need for some move is evident, but is it a move? And if it is, is it a safe one? In my opinion it points to a *policy* that bristles with danger to Principle. If Ruttledge initiated this matter, and Dev opposed it, what would be its chances? Or even if Dev remained neutral, what would be the hopes of the new departure? . . . The future danger will be that Principle will be merged in policy, that will be the tendency, as it already is, in many quarters . . . The economic conditions prevailing, emigration and unemployment constitute a formidable argument in favour of a change of policy, and Dev would be entitled to a fair chance on his new scheme, so long as he can guarantee that there is no danger in it to Republicanism. He feels he can guarantee this, but personally I have fears . . . The old spark should be kept kindling as strong as possible. We must only hope that things will come alright in time—*in our time*. [Emphasis in original][10]

The letter, written three weeks after the inaugural meeting of Fianna Fáil, confirms the extraordinary influence that de Valera exerted over his followers, something acknowledged by those who parted company with him by remaining in Sinn Féin. The Sinn Féin TD Tom Maguire recalled that

> you had the virtual dissolution of this thriving organisation with its 44 seats in the South in order to create Fianna Fáil. That was almost inevitable, once De Valera had made his decision to take part, in view of the great personal magnetism of the man.[11]

De Valera had broken with Sinn Féin on a purely hypothetical point: whether or not the movement would countenance entry to the Free State parliament if the oath was removed. This had been done in the knowledge that it was highly unlikely that Cumann na nGaedheal would commit political suicide by removing the oath, so jeopardising its grasp of power. Barret's letter implies that were it not for the power of de Valera's personality it is doubtful that the initiative would ever have got off the ground.

NATIONAL AIMS

Every organisation, whether social, economic or political, has fundamental objectives for which it was established. For Fianna Fáil these were enshrined in the *córú* ('arrangement', i.e. constitution). The first national objective, 'to secure the unity and independence of Ireland as a Republic,' was central to the party's ideology and to its claim to be 'the Republican Party.' It was also Fianna Fáil's stated *raison d'être,* and it served the dual function of legitimisation and orientation. The second aim was 'to restore the Irish language as the spoken language of the Irish people' (as opposed to *a* spoken language): it was a policy of restoration, not of mere preservation.

Economic development was also part and parcel of the struggle for political independence.[12] The party's third national objective, 'to make the resources and wealth of Ireland subservient to the needs and welfare of all the people of Ireland,' owed much to the Proclamation of the Irish Republic (1916) and the Democratic Programme of Dáil Éireann (1919).

More specific was the fourth national objective, which was 'to make Ireland, as far as possible, economically self-contained and self-sufficing.' The policy of economic self-sufficiency had been an integral part of the Sinn Féin programme, espoused as such since its foundation by Arthur Griffith in 1905. Political independence, Griffith had argued, would not in itself secure independence, and 'in modern parlance he feared neo-colonialism as deeply as legislative dependence.'[13] Fianna Fáil had inverted the relative importance attached by Griffith to economic and political independence but, like him, believed them to be inextricably linked and mutually dependent. By promoting this policy Fianna Fáil acquired the additional advantage of possessing another ideological stick with which to beat Cumann na nGaedheal, which had opted for free trade within the British Commonwealth, thus silently repudiating Griffith.

The fifth and sixth national aims related to life in rural Ireland and complemented the ideal of a self-sufficient economy. The fifth aim was 'to establish as many families as practicable on the land,' while the sixth was 'by suitable distribution of power to promote the ruralisation of industries essential to the lives of the people as opposed to their concentration in the cities.' The inclusion of these objectives can partly be attributed to de Valera's own upbringing on a small farm in Co. Limerick, which gave him his vision of Arcadian frugality. His idealisation of rural life resembled the nineteenth-century German philosophy of cultural nationalism developed by such thinkers as Herder and Fichte. According to Gearóid Ó Crualaoich, such an idealisation has a marked tendency

> to lift 'the peasant' and traditional society in general out of history, regarding them both as changeless, as somehow not subject to the process of continuous trans-formation that is the actual lot of all societies in the real socio-economic world.[14]

Rural life was perceived as the embodiment of a traditional Ireland imbued with high moral codes: modesty, patriotism, industriousness and resilience. These virtues were considered an antidote to the evils attributed to industrialisation and urban-isation. The fifth and sixth national aims also complemented the traditional view, held by many in the party, that the 'Irish spirit' that had sustained the country's nationhood throughout the ages was largely due to the exertions of the poor.

It was the dedication to a united, independent Ireland that connected the dis-parate strands of Fianna Fáil's membership. The supremacy of this objective was encapsulated in the obligatory pledge taken by all Fianna Fáil candidates during its first electoral campaign in June 1927. The pledge, which received an entire page in the party's first election manifesto, was preceded by lengthy quotations from revolution-ary leaders of the eighteenth and nineteenth centuries, such as Theobald Wolfe Tone and James Fintan Lalor.

> I, ..., hereby undertake that if elected to the office of .... I will support Fianna Fáil (Republican Party) in every action it takes to secure the Independence of a United Ireland under a Republican form of Government, and, in accordance with its constitution, I will not take any position involving an oath to a foreign power and I further undertake that if called upon by a two-thirds majority of the National Executive of Fianna Fáil to resign that office, I shall immediately do so.[15]

It is interesting to observe how this pledge is worded. It suggested that a member had the right to refuse to implement a decision that they felt was not compatible with the attainment of a united Ireland. This flexibility was qualified somewhat by the stipulation that the National Executive could request the resignation of an elected party representative on any grounds, illustrating the hierarchical nature of the party and the importance attached to internal party discipline The provision on oaths was to be deleted after the pledge was broken *en masse* by the parliamentary party without reference to the rank and file, but the rest of the pledge was retained.

This quest for an Ireland united and independent under a republican form of government was crucial in legitimising the Fianna Fáil project in the eyes of many of its founding members. It also acted as an irresistible rallying call for the membership, depicting as it did the future society that the party sought to realise.[16] However, putting forward national aims was one thing, implementing them was quite another. Having identified what the objectives of the new national movement were, Fianna Fáil had to attain power to put them into effect. The party leadership set about building the most formidable political machine in the Free State. But before looking at the circumlocutions by which Fianna Fáil deputies entered the Dáil it is appropriate to consider the internal dynamics of the organisation.

FROM SOLDIERS TO POLITICIANS

When de Valera led his followers from the extraordinary ard-fheis of Sinn Féin in March 1926 he had almost half the Sinn Féin cumainn behind him, which immediately were transformed into branches of Fianna Fáil. Realising that they had perhaps only a year before their first electoral contest, the party leadership, under the capable direction of the honorary secretaries, Gerry Boland and Seán Lemass, set about expanding the new organisation in preparation for the inevitable Judgement Day. This task was undertaken with remarkable vigour and determination. A group of twenty to twenty-five regular speakers travelled around the country organising public meetings with a view to establishing a cumann in every parish.[17]

Travelling by road was a hazardous venture, and motor cars in the 1920s were very much a novelty. When a car could be procured it was packed with four or five speakers, who were let off at various points along the way to attend meetings organised by local supporters. Sometimes the car would stop merely to catch the crowd before they dispersed after Sunday Mass. Those, such as Gerry Boland, who were not in possession of motor transport would travel by train to the most central town of a county before disembarking with their bicycle, on which they travelled from village to village.[18]

On their arrival the real work began: convincing local republicans that it was worth their while to involve themselves in the new political venture. Such men (for men they largely were) were soldiers, not politicians, and they had an instinctive distrust of politics. In every parish there was at least one significant person who had to be won over if Fianna Fáil was to thrive in the district. Normally this person was the highest-ranking or the best-known and respected IRA officer in the region.

Having identified the principal local republicans, the Fianna Fáil organisers set about persuading them to assist in the new party's activities, a task that proved remarkably difficult. Gerry Boland's son Kevin, himself a future Fianna Fáil minister, has sketched the challenges and vicissitudes that his father encountered on these proselytising missions.

> Many of these 'keymen' were still, in a sense, active in the IRA or on the run. Most of those released from jail went home to try and reconstruct their lives bearing in mind the President's [de Valera's] promise that soon the people would be ready again and that their place would be 'as of old in the vanguard.' Some of the best had no option but to emigrate—they knew they were marked men. All of them knew they had been beaten electorally and in arms but all retained their loyalty to the Republic. In most cases, however, the attitude was that, however loyal they

might be, there was nothing that could be done now but they would be available when the new [military] effort was made. None of them were politicians. They were men of action, men of violence as historians and outside observers would describe them.[19]

Boland recalls men who required several visits, involving all-night arguments, before finally acquiescing and joining Fianna Fáil. For some, such as Seán Moylan and Oscar Traynor, the process of attrition took several months, and it took even greater exertions to persuade them to stand for election. But the efforts paid handsome dividends in accruing support for the new organisation. If the leader of an IRA company could be won over, his military subordinates often followed *en masse*.

Once a reliable and influential republican had been recruited he was entrusted with the task of building the organisation in his area and communicating with Fianna Fáil head office, which would send representatives to meetings to supervise the local organisation's development until it was firmly established and self-supporting.

One of the main tasks of the cumainn during this early period, apart from attracting the largest possible membership from the area, was to assist in the establishment of new cumainn in neighbouring districts. These in turn were directed to facilitate the formation of yet more branches; and so the process continued. By 20 February 1927, 571 cumainn had been established, rising rapidly to 777 by 10 April.[20] At the party's second ard-fheis, in November 1927, the honorary secretaries could announce that 1,307 cumainn had been established throughout the Free State.[21] The credit for these organisational advances has been rightly bestowed on Seán Lemass and Gerry Boland.

The crucial importance of organisation was demonstrated during the two general elections of 1927, in June and September, in which Fianna Fáil succeeded in increasing its parliamentary representation almost threefold while its competitors for the mantle of alternative government wilted under the organisational pressure.

The achievement in the September election is particularly striking. Cumann na nGaedheal must have believed that it had pulled off a master-stroke by calling a general election within weeks of the Dáil assembling. The assassination of Kevin O'Higgins[22] and the implementation of the bitterly contested Public Safety Act would provide Cumann na nGaedheal with its favourite platform on which to fight an election: the security of the state against the republican infidels. In addition, a snap election would allow it to capitalise on the confusion within the Fianna Fáil ranks after the parliamentary party had entered the Dáil and on the universal depletion of coffers among the opposing parties, which, it could only be presumed, had exhausted their financial reserves on the June contest.

De Valera had condemned the calling of 'an unnecessary election during the harvest season,' believing the action to be a devious ploy to scatter his party's resources. 'They will find, however, that Fianna Fáil is not quite as unprepared as they think.'[23] It was a telling remark. Fianna Fáil had succeeded in tapping into lucrative Irish-American support, and a steady stream of money had made its way to the party. In the period before the June election this stream became a flood as Fianna Fáil successfully mobilised support among the Irish emigrant community. During one week, 28 April to 5 May, the party received the extraordinary sum of £8,200 from the

American Association for the Recognition of the Irish Republic, and this was before the election had been formally announced.[24] Large donations from the AARIR continued throughout the election period, as did smaller sums from the weekly *Irish World* (New York). The endeavours of Archbishop Mannix in Melbourne also bore fruit in Australia, which, after America, was the largest foreign donor to Fianna Fáil's election fund.[25]

The health of party finances was such that Fianna Fáil was still in the black after June, and the same sources were harnessed for the snap election in September. The funds were smaller but still considerable, with Mannix proving the most consistent source: in two separate donations he provided the party with £1,500.[26] These contributions contrasted with the paucity of funds available to other parties. Impoverished and confronted with the electoral oath, Sinn Féin did not contest the election, so facilitating Fianna Fáil's monopoly of the republican vote. A similar fate confronted Clann Éireann, the Labour Party, the National League, the Farmers' Party and independents, all of whom suffered from post-election financial hangovers and, acknowledging their poor economic position, put up only a small fraction of the number of candidates submitted to the electorate in June. With the effective choice narrowed, the stage was set for a duel between Fianna Fáil and Cumann na nGaedheal, and the result was a triumph for both parties over their smaller rivals.

The divergent paths of Sinn Féin and Fianna Fáil demonstrated the professionalism of the the new party and its determination to make electoral strides within the Free State political framework. Despite the financial drain of two elections in four months, Fianna Fáil's honorary treasurers could report a surplus at the end of the year when they submitted the figures to the 1927 ard-fheis. The report, however, underlined the financial reliance on the Irish diaspora and the dearth of money raised locally. Of the £30,402 received, more than £29,782 came from foreign sources, mainly the United States and Australia.[27]

While such generosity on the part of the Irish abroad was welcome, the party elders were far-sighted enough to realise that it was a position that could not be allowed to continue indefinitely. The £620 raised in Ireland, representing 2 per cent of party income, would have to be improved upon if the party was to have a future. Furthermore, Irish-American support had been siphoned from its channel to Sinn Féin, and those finances could be redirected again if that party reorganised sufficiently in the United States.

Once election fever had subsided, the party leadership began to formulate plans for achieving a more healthy balance in party finances. An annual national collection was announced at the 1927 ard-fheis, and a target of £7,000 was adopted for the financing of party activities in a non-election year.[28] Meanwhile, as long as the Irish-American goose could be coaxed to pass some of its golden eggs Fianna Fáil's way, the party would use them for the expensive but long-term project of establishing a national mass-circulation party paper, while pressure would be applied on cumainn to stand on their own feet and to contribute to the maintenance of a professional party headquarters.

The period immediately before and after the two 1927 general elections marked the zenith of Fianna Fáil's organisational strength up to 1931. This is not surprising, as branch interest is easier to maintain during these short but intensive pursuits of power.

After the September 1927 election, however, Fianna Fáil faced the daunting task of keeping its newly created organisational machine well oiled for up to five years.[29] The inevitable decline came, and it was reflected most starkly in the ever-decreasing number of cumainn and attendances at ard-fheiseanna. A year after the elections, affiliated cumainn numbered only 354, while only 400 delegates attended the 1929 and 1930 ard-fheiseanna.[30] Morale and organisational activity were maintained during these difficult years by initiating projects aimed at keeping cumainn busy. For example, the party leadership instructed cumainn to continue collecting signatures for a petition to abolish the oath even after Fianna Fáil had entered the Dáil.[31]

The national collection, launched in 1927, also provided a focus for activity. Each year, on a Sunday chosen by the National Executive, the collection was held through-out the Free State. Each cumann was responsible for a particular area, and gross receipts were sent to party headquarters. The importance of this activity was emphas-ised by the punitive rule that any cumann that failed to participate in the national collection would automatically lose its right to be represented at the ard-fheis.[32] Even those that did participate were often subjected to public chastisement by the party hierarchy should the amount collected fall short of expectations.[33] Targets rose annually, keeping branches on their toes. A third device for maintaining local activity was the sale of *Irish Press* shares conducted between 1928 and 1930.[34]

Fianna Fáil learnt early on that if its cumainn were to thrive they would have to be more than debating forums: they would have to become focal points for social activity. At the 1929 ard-fheis the honorary secretaries' report stated that 'everything possible should be done to counteract the tendency in recent years among members to concentrate exclusively on purely political matters, and members should realise that work done to foster the Irish language, games and customs was useful work for the Fianna Fáil movement.'[35] Many of the proposed activities were social in content but also had a political dimension. For example, the National Executive decided to circulate, free of charge, a book containing 'national songs' in Irish, accompanied by a request that they be learnt so that 'when the occasion would arise for singing the songs, they would be rendered in Irish rather than in English.'[36] Members were urged to learn Irish, so that it could increasingly be used for internal administration.[37] In so doing Fianna Fáil tried to replicate the attraction of the old Gaelic League branches of the late nineteenth and early twentieth centuries, which had combined political and cultural activism with a strong social content. These activities took a number of forms, from the organising of céilithe[38] to the establishment of a republican swim-ming club.[39] By advocating a social dimension to cumainn the leadership hoped to bind its membership together: if members' social life was inextricably linked to the party branch they would be less inclined to countenance defection.

The combination of these organisational tasks and social gatherings did not prevent the party from declining in strength after 1927; but without them the decline would undoubtedly have been much sharper.

ELECTORAL RIVALS

Fianna Fáil was not, of course, the only political group in opposition to Cumann na nGaedheal. Parties and individuals of various hues presented themselves as alternatives to the status quo. Fianna Fáil's main achievement during this period was the manner in which it succeeded in polarising the political debate and consequently in squeezing out the minor parties as serious contenders for governmental power.

Clann Éireann posed an early if insubstantial threat to Fianna Fáil. To Cumann na nGaedheal supporters this group had betrayed the party at a vulnerable time and therefore were untrustworthy renegades. For republicans these deputies had lost ideological ground by having taken the oath, and their continuation of such a policy put them beyond the pale. An alliance was mooted in some quarters but was publicly repudiated by de Valera, who cited their acceptance of the oath as the primary obstacle.[40] This strategy paid dividends, as both Clann Éireann and the National Group disappeared from electoral politics, though many of their prominent leaders drifted into Fianna Fáil in time to contest the 1932 election.[41]

Another potential rival was the party within which most of the Fianna Fáil leadership had served their political apprenticeships: Sinn Féin. By the late 1920s, however, it had shrunk to a hard core of doctrinaires, whose sincerity was matched only by their impotence. By 1929 there were only seventy-one Sinn Féin branches in the Free State, and at that year's ard-fheis it was announced that party funds after expenses were only slightly more than £3.[42] The death of Austin Stack the same year deprived the movement of its most prominent leader.[43]

An IRA initiative to secure a common republican platform with Sinn Féin and Fianna Fáil before the 1927 election was torpedoed by both Sinn Féin and de Valera.[44] Having fought so hard to extricate himself from his more doctrinaire colleagues, de Valera had no intention of voluntarily aligning with them again. Sinn Féin became increasingly irrelevant, and the IRA had ceased to take it seriously as a political force. 'Even the police,' J. Bowyer Bell remarks, 'had given up worrying much about Sinn Féin.'[45] Republicans were joining the two organisations of action, the IRA and Fianna Fáil, so that 'Fianna Fáil Cumainn by day drilled as IRA columns by night.'[46] The two organisations eyed each other with suspicion, sympathy and respect.

During the 1920s the Labour Party was an obvious potential threat to Fianna Fáil's expansion.[47] However, by formulating a dynamic socio-economic programme couched in radical nationalist language Fianna Fáil succeeded in making the Labour Party's programme appear incomplete and insufficiently national. Fianna Fáil consciously aimed its policies at the working person, the underclass and those dispossessed by the government's free-trade policies. 'Speaking generally,' the party paper declared, 'the man-in-the-street, the labourer in the fields, the worker at his bench—these are the Irish nation. And these, if it will succeed, Fianna Fáil must satisfy, inspire, and lead.'[48]

Fianna Fáil maintained that the Labour Party's penchant for moderation and its fear of red-baiting had robbed it of any radicalism. Seán Lemass, for example, derided the party's timidity, claiming that its 'outstanding characteristic . . . is . . . that it is the most respectable party in the state. So long as they cannot be accused of being even pale pink in politics they seem to think they have fulfilled their function towards the Irish people.'[49] Another argument Lemass used within months of entering the Dáil was that 'long association' with the parliament had 'sapped the vitality of the Labour Party.'[50] The longer Fianna Fáil remained in the Dáil the less popular this argument became.

A registration drive—similar to that adopted by black American civil-rights activists several decades later—was started by Fianna Fáil with the aim of mobilising apathetic republicans disenchanted with the Free State and with politics generally. It sought to persuade the poor and first-time voters to go to the polling stations. This would be a crucial factor in Fianna Fáil's electoral triumph of 1932. Cumann na nGaedheal's vote would remain solid but would be submerged by an increased electorate and increased turn-out, both of which benefited Fianna Fáil exclusively.

DE VALERA, THE *IRISH PRESS* AND IRISH-AMERICA

Establishing a national daily newspaper under the control of Fianna Fáil was the biggest and most ambitious organisational exercise undertaken by the party between 1927 and 1931. During this period Fianna Fáil relied on its political weekly, the *Nation*, to convey its views to the public. Though the *Nation* took its name from the nineteenth-century radical nationalist newspaper edited by Thomas Davis, it lacked the punch and sophistication of its predecessor. The paper had been established to publicise Fianna Fáil's activities but also to avoid the unsatisfactory situation of having to rely on the IRA's newspaper, *An Phoblacht*, as the sole medium through which party policies could be communicated, which was Fianna Fáil's position during its first year.

With a circulation of about six thousand, the *Nation* was something akin to a peashooter when compared with the cannons of the national daily press. Nor did it compare well with the more dynamic *An Phoblacht*, weekly sales of which reached forty thousand,[51] an impressive figure considering that the average daily sales of the *Irish Times* was little more than twenty thousand.[52] Moreover, as a paper whose average reader was not as affluent as that of, say, the *Irish Times*, *An Phoblacht* probably had a higher circulation (as opposed to sales) than most of its contemporaries. It also contained articles of considerable literary interest and merit, particularly under the stewardship of Peadar O'Donnell, reflecting a cosmopolitanism that was rare in republican literature.

In contrast, the *Nation* was a more turgid party organ, which, while giving valuable insights into the political philosophy of Fianna Fáil, never attained a circulation that corresponded to the party's electoral support. The diversity of republican literature, combined with the pre-eminence of *An Phoblacht*, militated against increases in circulation. In any case, such was the perceived convergence of Fianna Fáil and IRA views that many Fianna Fáil members would, it seems, have been content with purchasing just one paper—*An Phoblacht*—in order to be informed of events from a republican point of view. This explains why Fianna Fáil was so sensitive to criticisms of its party in *An Phoblacht* and why it always sent prompt responses.[53]

The *Nation* was always considered a stop-gap for the benefit of the party faithful until a national daily paper could be financed. During de Valera's five years of parliamentary opposition no other object so consumed his attention as the promotion of this enterprise. Advertisements for a new national newspaper began to appear during 1928, and on 4 September, Irish Press Ltd was formally established. Hostility from the national media towards Fianna Fáil and republicanism in general was the argument most frequently used to emphasise the need for a republican daily newspaper.[54] 'Soldiers in battle do not conscientiously read enemy propaganda,' the party declared, 'and the same should be true in politics.'[55] The first advertisement (which was refused publication in the *Irish Independent*) announced that 'today the Irish people are given the opportunity to break the stranglehold of an alien Press.'[56]

What is of special interest is how Fianna Fáil managed to portray the creation of a party-political paper, owned and directed by the party leader, as a *national* enterprise. Quotations stressing the increasing encroachment of English papers on the Irish market accompanied literature promoting the *Irish Press*. Combined with the perceived anti-national bias of the mainstream Irish dailies, Fianna Fáil painted a picture of a people 'in a condition of mental bondage,' increasingly becoming 'England's slaves' in matters of intellect, taste and world view.[57]

The drive for shares in Ireland was inspired as much by organisational as by financial considerations; America was the real focus. The campaign for funds for the *Irish Press* was a concerted attempt by de Valera to harness the vast reservoir of Irish-American republicanism for domestic purposes. Between 1927 and 1930 he would spend nine months in the United States, engaged in the ambitious task of securing large-scale financial assistance during a world recession. Fortunately for Fianna Fáil, Irish America had been abandoned by the Free State government, which now confined visits largely to infrequent (and often ill-received) official trips.[58] De Valera had the advantage of having toured the United States as President of the Irish Republic in 1919–20, when he personified the struggle for independence in Irish-American eyes. During his visits to promote the sale of shares in his proposed newspaper de Valera conscientiously sought to retain this image intact and unsullied. But while he had represented the Irish nation in 1919–20, his return almost a decade later saw him engaged in a purely party-political exercise. This important difference was camouflaged by a consistently militant republican rhetoric that he reserved for Irish-American audiences. De Valera pandered to the sentiments of the crowds and accepted their militant greetings. 'So long as Ireland is unfree,' declared Frank P. Walsh, who presided over the New York mass meeting, 'there will be plenty of men willing to rise up and by any means whatever strike for Ireland.'[59] De Valera responded by adopting the militant posture expected of him.

> We have a point in front of us that the enemy cannot strengthen. We are strong enough in Ireland to break it down [applause], and when we have broken it down are you going to tell me that the conquering army is going to stop at that point? It is not![60]

Such defiant statements—and there were many—were aimed primarily at traditional Irish-American elements eager to part with their money to enable an armed assault on British power in Ireland. Foremost among the organisations representing this constituency was Clan na Gael, which had been instrumental in promoting and supporting rebellion in Ireland since it was founded in 1867. Its most prominent leader, Joe McGarrity, told de Valera that Clan na Gael was 'cold to the proposition which they consider a part of the political effort in which they have no faith whatever.'[61] De Valera, however, refused to accept that his mission to Clan na Gael would not bear fruit, and he replied to McGarrity in soothing tones, without acknowledging that there existed any fundamental disagreement between them.

I am sure you will understand how necessary a newspaper is for our present fight and that you will try to get our old friends to support the enterprise. To make any progress we must try to get co-operation between all the forces working for a free Ireland. The imperialist forces here are all co-operating. It is heartbreaking that we are not.[62]

During his visits de Valera did his utmost to reacquaint himself with Irish republicans in the United States, as both Frank Gallagher and Seán Moynihan, who accompanied him on his trips, recalled. 'The Chief has gone to Philadelphia to see Luke Gibbons,' Moynihan noted in a letter, referring to de Valera's attempts to contact the old Fenian dynamiter. 'I have also met several of the Kerry IRA lads. It has been worth coming to see them all.'[63] In addition, the services of noted republican veterans such as Ernie O'Malley were of great benefit in attracting militant support for the project, and they proved financially rewarding.[64]

Advertisements claimed that 'many subscribers in America are donating the value of their Bonds to the Independence movement, and for this purpose are assigning them to Éamon de Valera.' Readers were informed that assignment forms could be obtained from Fianna Fáil headquarters or from the *Irish World*.[65] The fact that de Valera was portraying Fianna Fáil as *the* independence movement, combined with his use of bellicose republican rhetoric, induced many Irish people in America to make donations to what they believed was part of a militant republican struggle. In fact their donations were destined solely for the party coffers of the 'slightly constitutional' Fianna Fáil. Even more secret were the details regarding the ownership and control of the *Irish Press*, which were vested not in Fianna Fáil but in de Valera personally.[66]

PARLIAMENTARY PARTY DISCIPLINE

Fianna Fáil's entry into the Dáil and its acceptance of the oath as an 'empty formula' meant that the Civil War was fought anew on a different battlefield.[67] Though the method of struggle had changed, parliamentary language would take some time to catch up, as Fianna Fáil sought to link constitutional politics with militant action. One example—an article from the party paper in 1928—complained of the Government's predilection for guillotining Dáil debates by comparing Civil War military executions to jousts with parliamentary procedure:

To move the closure is now the only defence of the Cumann na nGaedheal deputies against the vigorous onslaughts directed at them daily by the Republicans . . . The closure must be used with greater and greater frequency, but this fact in itself will help to expose the shamelessness of the gang of thieves who, to cling a little longer to their ill-gotten gains, would rob the people of rights for which the same unscrupulous clique shed so much Irish blood. In 1922 the Free State watchword was "Firing Squad, shoot." Today it is, "Ceann Comhairle, closure."[68]

Civil War animosities did not die easily, as is clear from a perusal of Fianna Fáil's parliamentary party minutes. On 29 November 1928 a motion put before the party claimed that conversations with Free State ministers in the corridors of Leinster House were 'unbecoming and demoralising,' and it urged that such meetings be prohibited.[69] Seán Lemass proposed an amendment that was stronger, clearer and less equivocal. This amendment, which was carried on a show of hands, declared that it should be the party rule that members 'should not conduct any business with Cumann na nGaedheal Ministers or deputies in the bar or restaurant and that fraternisation under any circumstances be prohibited.'[70]

This motion was followed some months later by another that declared that the Leinster House bar was 'definitely out of bounds' for members of the party.[71] While the principal motivation for this was to avoid the unsavoury prospect of being present in the same room as members of the government party, another factor may have been the prevention of the unedifying spectacle of party members being drunk during Dáil proceedings. A motion passed three months earlier, sponsored by the whips' department of the party, compelled members to name deputies who were 'visibly under the influence of drink in the Dáil' at the following party meeting.[72]

Whether motivated by fear of fraternisation with the enemy or of the demon drink, the party leadership was determined that deputies would not be permitted to wander around the corridors of Leinster House without their movements being monitored, a fact made clear by the following resolution:

> That the places where members of the Party may go in Leinster House, without notifying the Whips be: the Committee Room: the Restaurant: the Grounds, and the Library.[73]

The purpose of these orders, at once draconian and slightly comic, was to preserve party discipline and to create a strong, unified organisation. In line with this, deputies were instructed to attend all meetings of the parliamentary party,[74] and any absence from the Dáil would have to be accompanied by a credible excuse.[75] Also, the need for uniformity of views was stressed, and it was made clear that deviations from the party line would not be tolerated. Deputies were instructed 'not to speak on any question in the Dáil' without first consulting the whips.[76] In case any deputies contemplated feigning ignorance of party policy, it was made clear that if a deputy was not present at a party meeting when a particular issue was decided on he was prohibited from publicly articulating a view on that subject.[77] A standing order was also proposed by Frank Aiken that declared that all party members must support 'by speech and vote' a majority decision of the party on all issues 'vitally affecting our national status or the lives of the people.'[78]

The need to foster a unified and disciplined organisation was continuously emphasised.[79] The commitment required of deputies can be gauged from the fact that each TD and Senator was required to make a subscription to the party from their salary for the purposes of paying clerical staff and paying the bills incurred in maintaining the party headquarters.[80] In addition, the requirement that party members adopt a strict code of secrecy was stressed: a pledge was drawn up, compelling deputies not to divulge the internal discussions of the party, the penalty for violation being expulsion.[81] A similar pledge was formulated for members of the National Executive.[82]

ARD-FHEISEANNA

According to the Fianna Fáil constitution, the National Executive was 'the supreme governing body of the organisation' except during ard-fheiseanna, when that assembly assumed control of policy formation.[83] Special care was taken, however, to ensure that motions submitted 'spontaneously' by cumainn for consideration at the annual ard-fheis were strictly in line with the views of the party leadership.

One way of preventing the party faithful from supporting a motion unapproved by the party leadership was to ensure that it was never submitted for endorsement. In this way party unity could be preserved and differences papered over. Another method of evading awkward resolutions was to ignore them; at the 1928 ard-fheis, for example, delegates drew attention to the leadership's inertia on implementing resolutions passed at the previous ard-fheis.[84]

Such actions demonstrated the fundamental power imbalance—which only increased over time—between the party's rank-and-file supporters and the leadership. The Fianna Fáil hierarchy, like many ambitious leaders of mass political parties, quickly discovered that democracy and organisational unity were not only strange but incompatible bedfellows: ultimately one or the other had to be sacrificed. True democracy in determining party policy, they decided, was debilitating, constraining and time-consuming; instead they settled on their own form of democratic centralism, with the emphasis being on centralisation rather than democracy.[85] As the party progressed and matured, real power would move from the base to the apex as the leadership tightened its control on the party machine, while the ordinary member enjoyed the illusion of participation. Decision-making powers would become the preserve of a few, and ultimate authority would rest with only one.

This imbalance was nowhere more aptly demonstrated than in the party's evolving relationship with the oath of allegiance contained in the Constitution of the Irish Free State.

PRINCIPLE VERSUS ORGANISATIONAL SURVIVAL: THE OATH OF ALLEGIANCE

Fianna Fáil and the oath

How the oath of allegiance was transformed within a matter of months from 'an Oath to Partition'[86] and 'an impossible and unnecessary test'[87] into a mere 'empty formula'[88] is the story of the collision of principle and practical politics. Sinn Féin was divided on the purely hypothetical issue of how best to respond to the improbable scenario of the Free State government abandoning the oath. Orchestrated by de Valera, this had enabled him to establish a party within which he was the undisputed arbitrator of political strategy. The abolition of the oath was Fianna Fáil's 'immediate national objective,'[89] and the party applied itself vigorously to the task. Opposition to the oath was enshrined in its constitution, which declared that membership was

> open to all adults of Irish birth, parentage, or residence, who accept the Constitution of Fianna Fáil, save that no person who has taken an oath, or made any declaration, involving a recognition of British Authority in Ireland, shall be

eligible for membership, so long as he or she retains the position of office involving that oath or declaration.[90]

As the prohibition encompassed 'declarations' as well as oaths, it excluded people employed in the public service.[91] This stance was also enshrined in the pledge that all Fianna Fáil candidates were required to take before contesting parliamentary elections.[92]

As the government party, intent on retaining the oath and on considering it an integral part of an international agreement, Cumann na nGaedheal and its leader, William Cosgrave, were the target of most Fianna Fáil attacks. De Valera stated that 'only the Imperialists and the Cosgrave Party' wanted the oath,[93] as they were pursuing the policy of Lloyd George, proclaiming the Free State a sovereign political entity and threatening chaos if the remaining imperial manacles were removed.[94] Realising its vulnerability, Cumann na nGaedheal maintained a 'penal oath',[95] the sole function of which was to exclude the republican electorate from the parliament by demanding that they pass an impossible political test.[96] National unity was impossible, and the threat of renewed domestic strife remained, while the 'impossible and unnecessary oath' was in force.[97]

Taking an oath of allegiance to a British monarch had a historical dimension, which Fianna Fáil exploited. Such oaths, the *Nation* continually pointed out, had traditionally symbolised more than verbal acquiescence to foreign rule and represented the difference between victory and defeat in the centuries-old battle between the Irish people and their colonial masters.[98] In a series of articles, mostly written by the indefatigable Diarmuid Ó Cruadhlaoich, repeated reference was made to the significance of oaths in the various phases of the national struggle.[99] De Valera also adroitly employed certain facts of Irish history to bolster his position on the oath, conjuring up images of honest republicans being locked outside the gates of power, suffering for their espousal of the nation's rights. 'Long ago,' he reminded a rally in O'Connell Square, Ennis,

> on the walls of Bandon there was an inscription: 'Beggar, Jew, Atheist may enter here, but not a Papist'. Over the gates of Merrion Street [Government Buildings] the Free State Government has now inscribed: 'Unionist, Orangeman, Anarchist may enter here, but not a Republican'.[100]

The association with historical figures who had suffered for their beliefs complemented attempts to present Fianna Fáil as a movement that could not be compromised by the allure of power. Fianna Fáil policy, as articulated by de Valera, argued that the ideals for which the party stood transcended the narrow sectional interests represented by Free State parties. Accordingly, these pro-government organisations were depicted as parties that promised the electorate material rewards for participating in national self-denigration.

Fianna Fáil's pronouncements on the oath sometimes had a strong spiritual tone. Cumann na nGaedheal, it was claimed, had appealed to lawyers and casuists, but 'they forswear Ireland, and for them is reserved the doom . . . Honest men know that they have committed perjury and that their souls are dead.'[101] Fianna Fáil boasted that its message to the electorate was 'not material, no promise of comfort or relief, no bribe or trafficking,' but rather was 'the spiritual issue of the right of a foreign king to exact an oath of allegiance from Irishmen.'[102]

De Valera claimed that the oath would 'not be removed by any group or party acting within the Free State Assembly' but that the Irish people alone would be the instrument of its destruction.[103] The oath could be 'swept away by the people's vote,'[104] and if a majority of republican deputies were elected there would be no Irish repre-sentatives to impose the oath, rendering it 'a dead letter.'[105] Fianna Fáil admonished the entry of Dan Breen, the renowned IRA commander, into the Dáil in January 1927, and de Valera declared that 'many who voted for Mr. Breen would feel that he had broken faith with them.'[106]

Breen contended that once Fianna Fáil had stated its willingness to enter the Dáil it was obtuse to remain outside because of an oath that would go sooner or later.[107] De Valera, however, addressing a rally in Limerick, unequivocally rejected this.

> The suggested policy of taking the oath to break it is an impossible one for Republicans. If examined from the point of view of expediency alone, not to speak of principle at all, it could only lead to futility and disaster . . . As far as the Fianna Fáil party is concerned, if there are any people who think that I, or any of those associated with me will be brought to take the oath, they are deceiving themselves. Neither I, nor any member of Fianna Fáil will ever take that oath. That is final, and I hope it is clear.[108]

The party gained some comfort when Breen's bill to abolish the oath was defeated on its first reading in April.[109] Nobody was surprised, the *Nation* declared, that 'Messrs Cosgrave, O'Higgins and Co.' refused to remove 'the only prop upon which the Free Staters have to depend to keep them in office.' The paper expressed incredulity that Breen expected them to 'relinquish so easily the power they seized by armed force in 1922.'[110]

As the June 1927 election beckoned, Fianna Fáil intensified its campaign against the oath. By making it the issue of the election, the *Nation* claimed in an editorial, Fianna Fáil had not misinterpreted the feeling of the nation, nor had it misjudged the national interest. It knew that the people wanted the assembly that legislated for three-quarters of Ireland to be open to all whom they elected to it; that no barrier should be raised or maintained against any of their representatives; and, above all, that 'no oath to perpetuate a status of inferiority or subjection should be imposed on deputies.'[111]

In a one-page advertisement with the suggestive headline 'FIANNA FÁIL IS GOING IN,' the party claimed that it alone could provide a national government, as it was the only party whose members had not taken 'an oath to Partition.' It also claimed that only Fianna Fáil could provide a stable government, as it would not 'shut any party out of the National Assembly.'[112] The June election results, which saw the government party lose more than a hundred thousand votes and sixteen seats, were interpreted by de Valera as 'a signal defeat' for Cumann na Gaedheal, as it had been the only party contesting the election on a platform of retaining the oath.[113]

On 22 June, Fianna Fáil held its first parliamentary party meeting—an event significant in itself, considering that it was a party with no parliament to go to. At the meeting it was decided that the party's deputies would go to Leinster House and demand their seats in the Dáil. It was further resolved that if they secured entry, P. J. Ruttledge and Seán French would propose Seán T. O'Kelly for the position of Ceann Comhairle (chairperson). If they failed to gain admission a public meeting would be held in College Green to protest against their exclusion from the national assembly.[114]

Having made clear their intention not to take the oath, the deputies approached Dáil Éireann, to find it surrounded by police and the Free State army and to be informed that the doors to the assembly had been locked. In a vitriolic editorial, the *Nation* described the action as 'an outrage on democratic liberty', though its contention that de Valera's 'statesmanlike policy' had 'forced the Cosgrave-O'Higgins Imperialist party into a *cul-de-sac*'[115] obscured the dilemma Fianna Fáil continued to face.

Fianna Fáil tried a number of legal approaches,[116] the most promising being an attempt to put the issue to the electorate in a referendum, as permitted under article 48 of the Constitution of the Irish Free State.[117] But these endeavours came to an abrupt end with the assassination on 10 July of Kevin O'Higgins (Minister for Justice and vice-president of the government). On the day of the killing de Valera was in Ennis, where he told a large rally that he would

> never take an oath of allegiance to a Constitution forced on Ireland, and will never bow the knee to a foreign king. I will continue to refuse to take that oath even if there is not another man in Ireland who refuses.[118]

The government's immediate response to its member's murder, however, fundamentally altered the political environment in which Fianna Fáil would have to operate. Gardaí suppressed a Fianna Fáil meeting on the oath that was to be held on the night of O'Higgins's assassination.

Far more significant, however, was the announcement that the government was to introduce three bills whose combined effect could have led to Fianna Fáil's demise or to its being forced underground. As far as the oath was concerned, the Constitutional Amendment Bill and Electoral Amendment Bill would have far-reaching consequences. The former unilaterally removed the provision permitting referendums to be called by popular demand, while the latter compelled prospective candidates to swear that they would take the oath of allegiance if elected. If a candidate refused to subscribe to this new obligation their names could not appear on the ballot paper.[119] By removing all possible avenues whereby the oath could be peaceably removed, Cumann na nGaedheal had pushed Fianna Fáil into a corner, forcing it to choose between ideological purity and organisational survival.

Fianna Fáil's first parliamentary party meeting following O'Higgins's assassination took place on 18 July amid widespread rumours of the proposed legislation. Referring to moves that had been made and that would be made to 'get us to take the oath to the Free State Constitution,' de Valera asked: 'Is there any member of our Party who would be willing to take the oath of allegiance in the Free State Constitution?' There was no reply. At this point Patrick Belton claimed that he had 'no moral qualms about taking the oath,' but he added that he had given a pledge and would keep it.[120] However, on reading the proposed legislation Belton promptly reconsidered his position, and on 26 July he took the oath and entered the Dáil. During the previous day a specially convened meeting of the National Executive had unanimously called on the errant deputy to resign his parliamentary seat, as he had repudiated 'the principles and policy of Fianna Fáil.'[121] A similar resolution unanimously passed by the party's County Dublin Comhairle Dáilcheantair (constituency council) condemned 'in the strongest manner' Belton's 'flagrant violation' of the signed pledge by which he had obtained selection and election.[122]

Belton's expulsion, unanimously approved by the parliamentary party,[123] opened a Pandora's box, with de Valera and his erstwhile colleague becoming embroiled in a sparring match in the columns of the press. In a letter to the *Irish Independent* headed 'A challenge to Mr. de Valera', Belton asked him why he persisted 'in fooling the people in public about an oath of allegiance when he admits in private that it is only an undertaking.'[124] De Valera retorted that 'everyone who was not absolutely blind could see that Mr. Belton since his election has been manoeuvring for an opportunity to take the oath . . . He will be alone, however.'[125]

In public Fianna Fáil remained adamant that it would not compromise on so fundamental a principle. Responding to the new legislative proposals and to Belton's defection, de Valera made an authoritative statement that ruled out the possibility of the party reconsidering its attitude.

> As a party we have been elected on the distinct understanding that we would not take that oath. After the election and after our exclusion from the Free State assembly, the Party met and each member signed a statement reiterating his election pledge and stating that 'under no circumstances whatever' would we subscribe to such an oath. That was final . . . The fact that the Free State now propose to block every avenue by which the oath could be removed by political action will not alter the attitude of Republicans towards the taking of that oath . . . If Mr. Cosgrave's new legislation goes through, the effort Fianna Fáil has been making to secure national unity will undoubtedly be frustrated. Mr. Cosgrave's aim apparently is to secure that result and to force us to retire. Be it so.[126]

In this statement de Valera made explicit the stark choice facing Fianna Fáil: to submit or retire. As a last-ditch effort, he entered negotiations with the Labour Party to see if, together with the National League, they could form a coalition government.[127] The draft agreement negotiated by de Valera and approved by the parliamentary party on 26 July stated that if a coalition government could be formed and could secure the removal of the oath Fianna Fáil would not 'press any issues involving the Treaty to the point of overthrowing such Government during the normal lifetime of that Assembly.'[128]

There was an air of unreality about these deliberations. The question of how Fianna Fáil could enter the Dáil without subscribing to the oath still remained—a predicament exacerbated by the party's unanimous decision that it would not enter the Free State parliament on the day that the coalition government was to be formed.[129] It has been suggested that de Valera was not fully committed to his arrangement with Tom Johnson, the leader of the Labour Party, and that he merely sought to test his intentions and those of the government, with which Johnson was in regular contact.[130]

By the time Fianna Fáil met for its fifth parliamentary party meeting on 5 August a significant shift had occurred, as the party leadership, following de Valera's lead, began tentatively to speculate aloud about whether the oath might not, after all, be as insurmountable an obstacle as previously thought. As one member present at the meeting recalled, de Valera 'proposed that we go into the Dáil, fight the Government there and put a stop to coercion.'[131] This new reasoning is encapsulated in an extract from the parliamentary party minutes.

> A general discussion was entered into, which ranged over the present situation, the future prospects, the feeling in the country, the question as to whether our commitments were such that they precluded us even in the present emergency from deviating from our pledges with respect to non-subscription to the Free State formula for entry into the Free State Parliament. The general view was that if the question was put to the Constituency Conventions they would release the Party from their pledge at this time.[132]

The most significant feature of this influential statement was the absence of a single reference to the word 'oath'. No longer was it a penal oath taken by perjurers and those who had forsaken God and country: it was merely 'the Free State formula' required for entry into Leinster House. In this statement lay the seed that within a few days would flower into the oft-quoted 'empty formula', the carefully worded label that would release the party from this ideological hook. A rough draft of a resolution, which made 'absolutely clear the circumstances under which the decision was taken,' stated:

> Provided the Committee to be hereafter appointed recommends that there is a reasonable prospect of the Party being effective in defeating the measures which the Minority Government have introduced to provoke Civil strife to suppress rightful political activities, and to deprive the people of their common rights and liberties the Party hereby resolves to take the steps which it considers essential to defeat such measures and save the country from their consequences by taking their seats in the Free State Assembly before the adjournment of that body.[133]

The rationale behind the resolution is significant, as it suggests that the proposed action was determined solely by the national interest. It obscures the fact that the interests of the nation coincided with those of the party. De Valera told the meeting that they 'would not be required to take the Oath actually, but to sign a book which contained the printed form.'[134] And when the motion was put to a vote, all declared themselves 'in general agreement' with its contents, with two exceptions: James Victory and Kathleen Clarke—though both relented.

The composition of the committee appointed to examine 'whether there was a reasonable prospect of the Party being effective in carrying out the policy outlined in the above resolution' made it a foregone conclusion. De Valera headed the committee, assisted by his most ardent supporters: Seán T. O'Kelly, Seán Lemass, Gerald Boland, Seán MacEntee and Frank Aiken.[135] In an effort to spread responsibility for the proposed action, it was agreed that a special meeting of the National Executive should be held on 9 August 'to consider what action the Fianna Fáil TDs should take in relation to the present political situation.'[136] The decision, however, had already been taken, and with a large number of deputies represented on the National Executive the question of approval was never in doubt, only the margin of victory.

De Valera repeated his contention to the National Executive that there was 'no alternative between giving up political action and entry to the Free State Dáil.' He would not take an oath, but he claimed that 'it was being said that it was not being administered as an oath.'[137] One can only speculate about how de Valera discovered this important piece of information: probably Thomas Johnson allayed de Valera's concerns during their meetings. In any case, he told the National Executive that the only way to find out the exact procedure was to go to Leinster House. The choice confronting Fianna Fáil having been explained, a motion proposing that the party's elected deputies be given 'a free hand in the matter of entering the legislature or not' was passed by 44 votes to 7.

After a long discussion it was decided that an explanatory statement, drawn up by de Valera and signed by every Fianna Fáil deputy, would be issued to the press the following day. This historic document said that the Fianna Fáil deputies had given careful consideration to the situation arising from the 'National emergency' and had recognised that the proposed legislation 'may imperil the peace and cause widespread suffering.' Despite the fact that the legislation would disenfranchise all republicans who refused to give allegiance to the English Crown, the statement continued, the deputies had unanimously decided that they could not transfer their allegiance from the Irish people. The statement then proclaimed that it had been 'repeatedly stated, and it is not uncommonly believed, that the required declaration is not an oath' and that the Fianna Fáil deputies 'would certainly not wish to have the feeling they are *allowing themselves to be debarred* by nothing more than an empty formula from exercising their functions as public representatives.' (Emphasis added)[138]

On 11 August the special committee reported to the parliamentary party. Speaking on behalf of the committee, Seán T. O'Kelly read documents in which Thomas Johnson and William Redmond (leaders of the Labour Party and National League, respectively) declared their commitment to abolishing the oath, repealing the Public Safety Acts and re-establishing the constitutional provisions for popular referendums.[139] It was decided that on the following day Fianna Fáil deputies would present themselves to the clerk of the Dáil and sign the rollbook containing the oath of allegiance but would make it clear that they were acting in accordance with their public pledge and 'did not intend or wish it to be inferred that we intended to give allegiance to the English King.'[140]

With the meeting ending on this note, de Valera, accompanied by Frank Aiken and Dr James Ryan, travelled the short distance to Leinster House, where he presented the clerk, Colm Ó Murchadha, with the party's signed press statement and then read out a statement, of which the following is a translation:

I want you to understand that I am not taking any oath nor giving any promise of faithfulness to the King of England or to any power outside the people of Ireland. I am putting my name here merely as a formality to get the permission necessary to enter among the other deputies who were elected by the people of Ireland, and I want you to know that no other meaning is to be attached to it.[141]

Ó Murchadha replied that these remarks did not concern him and that he merely sought de Valera's signature in the relevant book, which he motioned towards him. De Valera's eye rested on another book, however. 'Then, what is this for?' he retorted, pointing to a Bible. Picking up the Bible, he brought it to the other end of the room, declaring, 'You must remember that I am taking no oath.' He then covered the words of the oath with some paper he had brought with him and signed his name, so allowing him to maintain that, having neither seen nor heard an oath, he had therefore taken no oath.[142] Everyone recognised, however, that the political landscape had dramatically changed.

Having complied with the provisions of article 17 of the Constitution of the Irish Free State, the Fianna Fáil deputies returned to the party office and decided to attend the next day's Dáil session.[143] Meanwhile the government was given notice of a motion of no confidence by the leader of the Labour Party, Thomas Johnson, and it was agreed that this would be debated on Tuesday 16 August.[144] When the Fianna Fáil deputies held their first parliamentary party meeting in Leinster House, on 13 August, they devised their strategy for dealing with this motion.[145] An alliance between Fianna Fáil, the Labour Party, the National League and the two independent republicans, Dan Breen and Patrick Belton, gave them a slight majority. If it was successful, Thomas Johnson would be proposed as leader of a coalition government of the Labour Party and the National League, with Fianna Fáil supporting the government without participating in it. One National League deputy, Vincent Rice, claimed that this would make the new government the pawn of Fianna Fáil and declared his intention of voting with Cumann na nGaedheal.[146] This defection still left the alliance with a majority of one over the combined strength of the government party, Farmers' Party and independents.

When the Dáil assembled, however, the non-attendance of the National League deputy John Jinks was noticed, and efforts to contact him proved fruitless.[147] His absence decided the result, and, on the casting vote of the Ceann Comhairle, the government defeated the motion of no confidence by 72 votes to 71.[148]

The democratic deficit that had developed between the Fianna Fáil leadership and the rank and file was clearly evident. Deliberations on the oath had been confined to a small number, consisting of party representatives elected on a policy of abstaining from the Dáil until the oath was abolished. According to Fianna Fáil's constitution, delegates at the ard-fheis defined policy, and the National Executive was not permitted 'to alter or amend any decision of the Ard Fheis.'[149] The ordinary members of the party, however, were not privy to the discussions that led to the taking of such a crucial action. Pity, for example, the staff of the *Nation*, who published the following on 13 August, the day *after* the entire Fianna Fáil parliamentary party had committed their names to the book containing the oath:

If all the Fianna Fáil TDs published tomorrow a signed declaration, that, in their opinion, the Oath in the Free State Constitution is an unsworn undertaking, the Oath would still remain an oath, and to swear it falsely would continue to be perjury.[150]

The article alluded to the plight of Galileo, who had been forced to abjure the heresy that the earth moved around the sun but who, according to legend, said afterwards that, his denial notwithstanding, it would continue to move. The point was that even if Fianna Fáil solemnly declared that the oath was not an oath it would continue to be an oath. The article's adamant tone was partly in response to Patrick Belton's much-publicised letters to the papers, in which he claimed that he had put it to de Valera that there was no oath of allegiance *per se* and that de Valera had 'agreed that all the Article demanded was an undertaking.' The *Nation* had rebutted such heretical notions and admonished the anonymous 'eminent theologian' from whom Belton had sought ecclesiastical endorsement, claiming that 'it takes a quick-witted race like us to distort the words "I swear" into meaning "I do not swear."'[151]

The actions of the quick-witted de Valera, who managed to sign a document beginning with the words 'I swear' and yet publicly claim that he had not sworn, caused considerable confusion within Fianna Fáil, not least among the staff of the *Nation*. A complete reversal of editorial policy was required. Some party journalists must have blushed when the very next issue of the paper contained an editorial dutifully declaring that the leadership's decision had given 'hope for Ireland's future, hope for the advancement of Irish Ireland, new hope and new heart to carry to victory the cause of the Irish Republic.' The editorial speculated that the decision to enter the Free State parliament 'must have caused much heart-burning to many Republicans,' but to those who questioned the essential wisdom of the move due weight would have to be given to the fact that 'this grave decision was *unanimously* agreed to by the Fianna Fáil Teachtaí.' The belief was confidently expressed that the vast body of Republicans would 'loyally accept the decision made in their name by their own elected representatives,' and for those who wished to withhold judgement time would convince them that the decision taken was best suited to achieving 'the final and complete liberation from foreign domination.'[152]

Having devoted months of research and acres of paper to demonstrating that there were no possible means whereby a Fianna Fáil deputy could subscribe to the oath while simultaneously retaining their political integrity—not to mention their soul—the intellectual resources of Fianna Fáil were again employed to trawl afresh through their sources and to discover arguments previously thought inapplicable. Diarmuid Ó Cruadhlaoich, who wrote more than a dozen theologically inspired articles condemning the oath and those who took it, admitted that he was not a theologian. 'Not in breaking, but in keeping it,' he now argued, 'would they, in my opinion, incur moral guilt.'[153]

Such comments were not only ideologically necessary but were also important in responding to calumniators. Speaking at a Cumann na nGaedheal meeting in de Valera's own constituency of Co. Clare, Canon O'Kennedy told those assembled that 'it was an oath, and the breaking of it was one of the gravest crimes against virtue and religion.'¹⁵⁴ It was statements like these that provoked political theologians within Fianna Fáil into action.

While noting that the Fianna Fáil leadership had decided to 'shift the ground of the present discussion completely,' the *Nation's* new expert on oaths, 'Sacerdos', argued that Fianna Fáil deputies remained 'free before God and Man.' Citing fourteenth-century canon law, the writer stated that an oath was to be defined 'according to the intention of the swearer.'¹⁵⁵ Then, after quoting the works of such theological authorities as Genicot, Lehmkuhl, Tanqurey and Prummer, he contended that in the 'empty formula' pronouncement there had been 'no perjury, no profanation, no scandal, no sin of any kind whatever.' The confusion the Fianna Fáil action had aroused was attributed to a deliberate or inadvertent misreading of the established body of theological works that dealt with the subject of oaths.

> Ecclesiastical historians, are, I think, agreed that nearly every heresy that has arisen in the Church has so arisen because of the over-emphasis of one aspect of a truth to the exclusion of each other. If anybody doubts this let him just glance through Volume I and II of such a work as Tiperont's *Histoire du Dogme* . . . To charge the Fianna Fáil delegates with perjury or irreverence can be nothing less than the unmitigated calumny . . . since the declaration of the Fianna Fáil deputies makes it absolutely unmistakable that in uttering the oath formula imposed on them, they promised nothing contained in it.¹⁵⁶

It was at this time that de Valera's highest-ranking supporter in the Catholic Church, Archbishop Mannix, dutifully entered the debate to give a more authoritative ecclesiastical endorsement of Fianna Fáil's *volte-face.* In a cable to de Valera, Mannix claimed that he (de Valera) had been left with 'no choice' and that 'desperate ills need desperate remedies.'¹⁵⁷ In reply de Valera expressed his gratitude to the archbishop. 'Your Grace's message shows how clearly you understand the situation . . . I hope all our friends will come to understand it equally well.'¹⁵⁸ To this end he sent copies of Mannix's cable to the party's Irish-American supporters, whose financial support would be crucial in assisting Fianna Fáil during the coming general election.¹⁵⁹

A small number of prominent members of Fianna Fáil quit the party as a result of the new stance on the oath. Dorothy Macardle wrote to de Valera, informing him that she had decided, 'very reluctantly,' to resign from the National Executive as a result of the adoption of a policy with which 'I could not co-operate, and against which it would be useless for me to contend.'¹⁶⁰ Hanna Sheehy Skeffington, considered the most likely candidate to contest the excepted by-election necessitated by the death of Constance Markievicz,¹⁶¹ also resigned from the National Executive, citing the 'complete reversal of policy' that made it 'impossible' for her to remain a member of Fianna Fáil.¹⁶²

There was then the position of the rank and file, who had devoted so much of their energies to establishing the new republican party on the basis of non-acceptance of the oath. The stated belief that party supporters would approve was never tested, with the question of summoning an extraordinary ard-fheis being explicitly ruled out.[163] This action contrasts with de Valera's earlier insistence that an extraordinary Sinn Féin ard-fheis be called to discuss the less important—and entirely hypothetical—question of what the party would do if the oath were removed.

It can be argued that there was insufficient time to organise such a representative gathering of the party; but throughout the long month of deliberations on this fundamental question there was little to suggest that the party hierarchy was particularly eager to submit the issue to the members for consideration.

Despite electoral success and the eclipse of Sinn Féin, Fianna Fáil's entry into the Dáil created considerable disenchantment among the party's rank and file. Presented with a *fait accompli*, the grass roots retrospectively endorsed the leadership strategy at the party's second ard-fheis on 24–5 November. The thousand delegates present, however, resolved that 'the furthermost limits in compromise have been reached'[164]; and John Bowman notes that the rank and file 'tolerated rather than supported de Valera's pragmatic lead.'[165]

Chapter 4

FIANNA FÁIL AND THE IRISH FREE STATE, 1927–31

THE ASSASSINATION OF KEVIN O'HIGGINS AND THE PUBLIC SAFETY ACT

Kevin O'Higgins's assassination[1] and the repressive legislation it provoked formed the tumultuous background to Fianna Fáil's entry into the Dáil, and they provide a useful starting point in any examination of the fundamental differences in attitude towards matters of security and state between Fianna Fáil and Cumann na nGaedheal. O'Higgins had been considered the 'strong man of the Government,'[2] respected rather than loved among Treaty supporters, hated and despised by republicans, including Fianna Fáil. Much of this odium was the result of the perception that he was primarily responsible for the executions of IRA members during the Civil War, including that of Rory O'Connor, who had been best man at O'Higgins's wedding the previous year.[3]

Considering O'Higgins's position as vice-president of the Executive Council, and his personification of the government's tough law-and-order policies, his murder was seen as 'the political assassination of a pillar of state.'[4] Cosgrave made it clear that he did not believe the killing was the act of private individuals but was the fruit of a steady, persistent attack against the state. Moreover, he implicitly linked the assassination to the activities of Fianna Fáil, arguing that those who had devoted their energies to discrediting the Free State were responsible for O'Higgins's death.[5] Other government supporters claimed that, regardless of de Valera's condemnation,

> a very large proportion of Mr. de Valera's followers ghoulishly gloated over the assassination of the Minister for Justice, and openly rebuked the people for describing it as a murder. They referred to it as the execution of Kevin O'Higgins, and regretted that it had not taken place long before.[6]

There is little doubt that the assassination did not occasion much shedding of tears within Fianna Fáil. Long the *bête noire* of the party, O'Higgins even in death could not evoke sympathy, and this was reflected in the response of Fianna Fáil leaders. P. J. Ruttledge, vice-president of the party, found himself unable to support a motion of Ballina Urban District Council (which he chaired) condemning the assassination. The motion, he claimed, was 'tinged with politics,' and 'anyone knowing his views knew he could not endorse it.'[7] In addition, the party paper, edited by the other vice-president, Seán T. O'Kelly, even implied that renegade Free State army personnel were responsible.[8] In a carefully worded statement, the IRA repudiated suggestions that it was responsible, pointing out that it had never refrained from accepting responsibility for any acts, however drastic, that had official sanction.[9]

De Valera was equally circumspect. Describing the act as 'murder' and 'inexcusable,' he stated his conviction that 'no Republican organisation was responsible for it.'[10] The use of the term 'Republican *organisation*' is significant, as it reflected de Valera's fear that, considering the overlapping membership of many in Fianna Fáil and the IRA, the perpetrators might have been members of his party.[11] His fears in this regard were justified: one of the three assassins, Tim Coughlan,[12] was indeed a member of Fianna Fáil. Fortunately for de Valera, Coughlan's participation did not come to light until decades later, and the matter appeared to end with his own death, in controversial circumstances, eight months later.

The Fianna Fáil parliamentary party did not escape suspicion, however, and, in the words of one prominent member, 'we were all suspect.'[13] The houses of Fianna Fáil deputies were raided by the police; one of them, Robert Briscoe, was advised by his raiders to sleep in his clothes, as, when they returned, they would 'take care of you as we did Noel Lemass.'[14] Lemass, the older brother of Seán Lemass, had been murdered by Free State personnel shortly after the Civil War, and his mutilated body was found in the Dublin Mountains some months later.

The government's legislative response to the O'Higgins assassination, the Public Safety Bill, proposed giving extensive security powers to the Free State government. It empowered the government to declare organisations unlawful,[15] membership of which would entail a maximum penalty of five years' penal servitude.[16] Possession of 'documents' connected to such organisations would be met with fines and terms of imprisonment.[17]

Of particular relevance to Fianna Fáil was the provision that an organisation could be declared unlawful on the grounds that it 'engages in, promotes, encourages, or advocates any act, enterprise, or course of action of a treasonable or seditious character, or encourages or advocates the attainment of any object of a treasonous or seditious character.'[18] As Fianna Fáil was advocating non-recognition of the Free State and frequently employed phrases such as 'the Cosgrave Gang' and 'the Free State Junta' to describe the government, a strict interpretation of the act could render the organisation unlawful. Indeed the editor of the *Nation*, Seán T. O'Kelly, would soon be prosecuted under the act for impugning the integrity of the judiciary.

The publication of any statement emanating from an unlawful organisation or 'calculated to aid or abet' such an organisation was also prohibited,[19] and, as Fianna Fáil literature regularly contained items meeting such a description, the act clearly put the party paper in jeopardy. Moreover, Fianna Fáil's continuing involvement in the land annuities campaign was also endangered by a provision that an organisation could be deemed unlawful if it advocated non-payment of money that the government was authorised to collect.[20]

From government speeches it was clear that the act had not been formulated with only the IRA in mind but was intended also to encompass the activities of Fianna Fáil.

Cosgrave set the tone of the debate when he began with a synopsis of developments within the anti-Treaty camp since the end of the Civil War. He noted that the forces that had nominally been under de Valera's control had never surrendered their arms, and that there remained a large body of 'disappointed and vindictive revolutionaries, who [had] sought, by every means in their power to subvert the State.'[21] He proceeded to quote extensively from documents seized from the home of Maud Gonne MacBride and from sources that related to recent abortive attempts by the IRA to obtain a basis of agreement with Sinn Féin and Fianna Fáil to facilitate a common political platform for electoral purposes.[22] While acknowledging that the Fianna Fáil leadership had cut its umbilical cord with the IRA, Cosgrave contended that many of the party's activities contributed to an environment conducive to violent revolution.[23]

As the debate developed, government ministers became more explicit in linking Fianna Fáil with the revolutionary endeavours of the IRA. Paddy Hogan, Minister for Agriculture, claimed that the state was under attack from two sources—Fianna Fáil and the IRA—and that the state had a duty to protect itself.

> This Bill is for the protection of the State, and not for individuals. Is there no connection between the murder of the Vice-President and the conspiracy that has been carried out by Fianna Fáil? Has not that party been endeavouring to wreck the Constitution for the last three years? Had that nothing to do with the assassination of the Minister for Justice? No deputy believes that it has not. To say there is no connection is absolutely wrong.[24]

The fact that Hogan characterised Fianna Fáil's activities as being part of a three-year campaign—despite the fact that Fianna Fáil had been in existence for only fourteen months—demonstrates that for many government members there was little to distinguish Fianna Fáil, Sinn Féin and the IRA. Fianna Fáil was considered a 'semi-constitutional body', and while it remained such 'so long will we have a body of young opinion recruited to the ranks of mistaken super-patriotism, and very little divided that from crime.'[25]

Perhaps the most stinging attacks were those made by Ernest Blythe, Minister for Finance and O'Higgins's replacement as vice-president of the government. He reserved his most vehement denunciations for a speech at a by-election meeting in support of the government candidate in Dublin, the late minister's constituency. Fianna Fáil, he asserted, was guilty of a violent attack on the Constitution, while its elected representatives 'spit upon the Constitution and the institutions of State [and] say that they will not soil themselves by going into the Parliament of this country.' The late vice-president was not a hard or a bitter man, and there was no vengeful spirit in him. 'Some slimy people spoke of his hands being stained with blood, but he had no more responsibility for any execution than any one of the rest of us.' He had been killed in the hope that the state would be killed and the Treaty destroyed.

It was then that Blythe made his most controversial claims. There had been ample opportunities for the assassination of O'Higgins before the June election, but the assassins 'did not want to injure the election prospects of Fianna Fáil, and it was held over.' If the voters of Co. Dublin refused to return the government nominee and elected the Fianna Fáil candidate, their action would constitute a 'qualified approval' of O'Higgins's murder and would aid the establishment of 'a tradition of political assassination.'[26]

In the event, Cumann na nGaedheal comfortably held the seat, with Gearóid O'Sullivan defeating both Robert Brennan (Fianna Fáil) and Dr Kathleen Lynn (Sinn Féin) by taking almost 70 per cent of the vote. On the same day Robert Briscoe failed to hold the party seat vacated in Dublin South following the death of Constance Markievicz.[27]

LAW AND ORDER

The Public Safety Act illustrated the major policy divergence between Fianna Fáil and Cumann na nGaedheal on internal security. These differences remained while Fianna Fáil was in opposition during the late 1920s and early 30s. Between 1926 and 1931 the Free State government launched a new security initiative every year, accompanied by additional repressive legislation. Personal antagonisms and a mixture of malice and incompetence—largely the product of inexperience—became the hallmarks of the relations of the police with the republican community. Republican disdain for the Garda Síochána, particularly the Special Branch, often boiled over into assaults and other provocations, thus creating a cycle of violent confrontation. In addition, the Gardaí were confronted with a long-established political tradition that viewed the act of informing as a breach of communal solidarity. Clashes between the Free State government and Fianna Fáil were most frequent and virulent on three issues: the police and army; the judicial system (particularly juries); and political prisoners.

THE POLICE

In 1922 the Provisional Government had started the difficult process of establishing a new police force, the Garda Síochána, to replace the Royal Irish Constabulary and Dublin Metropolitan Police. With no other models to emulate, and under time constraints, it is not surprising that the Gardaí differed little in structure from the RIC, with the vital exception that they were to be unarmed. Not surprisingly, this last feature could not be fully implemented during the Civil War without needlessly endangering the lives of the new recruits, and gardaí were initially heavily armed with an assortment of revolvers, hand grenades and the odd machine gun.[28] In general, however, they were kept away from the fighting, and their non-combatant status meant that, though obviously Free Staters, they were not on the anti-Treaty IRA's list of legitimate targets.[29]

Their membership was drawn in large part from IRA members thoroughly screened for any latent 'irregular' tendencies. Many of the high-ranking members of the new force, however, were former RIC officers, who, because of their experience and knowledge of policing, were needed to ensure efficiency.[30] Indeed the committee entrusted with drafting recommendations for a new police force contained no less than nine former RIC men, including three district inspectors and a head constable. On the advice of these RIC veterans the pro-Treaty leadership opted for a force controlled by the government through a politically appointed Commissioner. This meant that the Garda Síochána 'was to occupy a status in relationship to the government which was identical to that of the RIC to the old Castle administration.'[31]

More controversial was the establishment of the heavily armed Criminal Investigation Department, which had its headquarters in Oriel House, on the corner of Westland Row and Fenian Street, Dublin. It quickly gained a reputation for ruthless brutality and efficiency. Its head was Captain Henry Harrison, a former Home Rule MP who had been decorated for bravery with the British army in France, and the force itself was composed mainly of men with a British army background.[32] In September 1925 the CID was transformed into the Special Branch of the Garda Síochána (though Fianna Fáil, like most republicans, persisted in using the term CID to describe it).

During its formative years in opposition Fianna Fáil devoted a considerable amount of its energies to discrediting the Free State police force and in particular its anti-subversive branch. In the eyes of Fianna Fáil these were 'the paid *agents provocateurs* of the Free State Department of Justice,' and the party bemoaned that 'today in the Twenty-Six County area of Ireland, neither the home, the life nor the liberty of any Irish Republican is safe from the roaming crews of gunmen known as the c.i.d.'[33]

It was not that Fianna Fáil opposed the idea of a police force *per se*—the party dispelled this notion by stating that 'if Ireland were completely free tomorrow, and a Republican Government restored and functionally fully, a properly recruited, trained and equipped police force would be one of the first necessities.'[34] Rather, their objections were concentrated on the use of the police as a partisan force against republicans. As one party deputy, Patrick Little, put it in the Dáil, the Gardaí were not merely used for containing civil crime but 'every police barrack is a centre of information as to the activities of a certain section of the community. They are asked to gather information about the activities of Republicans in their areas.'[35]

The Gardaí were viewed as 'the successors of the RIC,' whose dual purpose was to bolster the regime and attack republicans.[36] The Minister for Justice, James Fitzgerald-Kenney, was frequently subjected to personal abuse, on the grounds that 'he is as ready to condone outrages on personal liberty as any Shortt or Hamar Greenwood.'[37]

Successive Fianna Fáil ard-fheiseanna considered a number of strongly worded motions on the Gardaí and in particular on the Special Branch. One motion at the 1929 ard-fheis condemned the refusal of the responsible authorities to hold inquiries into the conduct of gardaí when allegations of 'lawless and brutal conduct' were made against them. In addition, the motion advocated publicising the 'unwillingness or inability' of those authorities to enforce discipline among a section of the force. It concluded by instructing cumann secretaries to report 'all cases of illegal conduct by members of the Civic Guard [Garda Síochána] occurring in their areas' to their TDs or directly to Fianna Fáil headquarters,[38] a point reiterated from the platform by Seán Lemass.[39] Cases of brutality, harassment and ill-treatment against republicans would, the party declared, be brought to trial when Fianna Fáil came to power.[40]

These motions are all the more significant when compared with the absence of motions dealing with IRA actions, such as executions and drilling, which was illegal under Free State law. The intense hostility expressed towards the actions of the Special Branch against the IRA is reflected in the following resolution, whereby the ard-fheis prohibits all members of the Organisation from social fraternisation with members of the political detective forces of the Free State Government or their agents, refusal to observe this decision to involve expulsion from the Organisation.[41]

Such resolutions complemented the policy of ostracising the Special Branch that was advocated by the IRA in the columns of *An Phoblacht*. The predicament of republican prisoners and their treatment by members of the Special Branch became a standard part of every Fianna Fáil ard-fheis. At the 1930 ard-fheis de Valera caused a stir when he produced for delegates a confidential circular issued by the Commissioner that indicated that a policy was being pursued of hounding republicans out of employment. 'The letter created a sensation even at the press table,' the *Nation* concluded gleefully, 'and with that exposure of police methods a great ard fheis came to an end.'[42]

While Fianna Fáil's criticisms of the Special Branch were largely confined to its actions towards IRA members, they also included harassment and intimidation of the broad republican family, including Fianna Fáil itself. Robert Briscoe recalled that membership of the Dáil 'did not protect us from raids, both authorised and illegal,'[43] while Seán Lemass complained in the Dáil of gardaí who kept party members under constant surveillance and 'seem to think it is their duty to know everything that members of Fianna Fáil do.'[44] In his autobiography Briscoe provides a useful insight into the nature of these raids.

Lily [Briscoe's wife] telephoned me at the Dáil and said, 'Some people have dropped by. Use your own judgement about coming home'. I knew this meant a raid was taking place, and I was to stay in the Dáil; or go on the run if I thought it was necessary. Meanwhile the c.i.d. were ransacking my house . . . Lily did not lose her head. She realised that the c.i.d. might try to plant evidence against me so she followed them from room to room never letting them out of her sight.[45]

Eoin O'Duffy, appointed Commissioner of the Garda Síochána in August 1922 at the age of twenty-nine, possessed an ill-concealed hostility towards Fianna Fáil and anti-Treaty republicanism generally. In a report submitted to the Minister for Justice in 1931 and circulated to the entire Executive Council he described Fianna Fáil's contribution to the security situation since August 1927.

Since the entry into the Dáil of the Fianna Fáil party the situation has become worse. The Police have been made to learn that it is dangerous to impede the liberties and progress of these would-be murderers, a halo of righteousness surrounds them and their followers.[46]

During its period in opposition, Fianna Fáil could do little to prevent house raids save draw attention to individual grievances in the Dáil. According to Briscoe, however, a novel tactic was devised by Seán MacEntee to discomfit gardaí who attended Fianna Fáil political gatherings.

Pick out a particular Guarda [*sic*], and stare at one particular part of him, say his belt, while you're speaking. He will nervously feel his belt and other parts of his uniform. Other people will begin to wonder and stare at him, too. Pretty soon, he will be a nervous wreck, and you will be in command of the situation.[47]

According to Briscoe, it worked every time.

THE FREE STATE ARMY

The other significant security institution, the Free State army, did not play as public a role as the Gardaí.[48] This did not save it from persistent attacks from Fianna Fáil, which argued that, because of its anti-republican function, it existed 'for the same purpose that the British Army fulfils in the six Northern counties.'[49] This position was strengthened by the admission of the Minister for Defence, Desmond FitzGerald, that 'in the event of a general attack on these islands it is perfectly obvious that our army must co-operate with the British Army.'[50] As the Free State had little reason to antagonise any other power, it appeared that England's difficulty would become Ireland's difficulty too. Fianna Fáil maintained, therefore, that the government was training and supporting an army that might easily find itself 'fighting on England's side, in England's quarrel, under England's direct or indirect control.'[51]

In fact events bore out Hogan's contention that the purpose of the Free State army was to be an auxiliary to the Garda Síochána and therefore an instrument of purely internal security.[52] The size of the army progressively decreased during the later years of Cumann na nGaedheal rule, so that by 1932 it was smaller than the IRA, though much better armed and financed. Nevertheless Fianna Fáil continued to argue that the army's retention at its existing strength was a wasteful extravagance.

The army pension scheme was viewed (not unjustifiably) as an elaborate system of patronage, whereby loyalty to the state and to the governing party with which it was identified was financially rewarded. It was also contended that up to half those who obtained such benefits were not entitled to receive them and that the government, in an attempt to satisfy party supporters, had not subjected claims to rigorous examination.[53] Desmond FitzGerald's response—that while it was true that 'pensions may be got through perjury' it would not be 'in the interests of the State' to have the details published—did little to mollify Fianna Fáil's criticisms.[54] Indeed the Fianna Fáil paper went as far as to publish over a long period the names, area by area, of all Free State army pensioners and the amount they received.[55] The purpose of this campaign was never explicitly stated. Probably it was to draw attention to the amount of money involved in rewarding such men for past services in combating republicanism. However, in a divided environment following a civil war and when the embers of internal strife had not yet been extinguished, identifying former Free State army soldiers in each region might be considered a provocation that could even endanger the safety of those listed.

JUDGES AND JURIES

The legal system and its personnel had remained almost intact from the days of British rule, from the retention of the statutes to 'the absurdity of keeping "republican" judges and barristers in wigs and gowns.'[56] The Dáil courts were abolished, an action partly motivated by the fact that so many of the judges were anti-Treaty in sentiment.[57] But there was also an important symbolic aspect as yet another integral part of the revolutionary struggle was jettisoned. V. T. H. Delany notes that

> as far as the courts of the Irish Free State were concerned, the decrees of the Dáil Courts were regarded as being not only void, but also illegal; for there was no continuity, in law, between the courts of the revolution and those of the Irish Free State.[58]

George Gavan Duffy, a signatory of the Treaty, resigned from the government in protest against the abolition of the Dáil courts, but the force of his attack was blunted by his decision to accept an appointment to the High Court, which had replaced its more revolutionary predecessor.[59] The great majority of senior counsel had been opposed to the independence struggle,[60] but, with the exception of a few notables grafted on to the legal system,[61] these same legal luminaries provided the bulk of the judiciary in the new state. As they were trained by the British system and imbued with a strong colonial mentality, the political views that coloured their legal judgements remained unaffected by the change of government. Therefore it was not surprising that, years after the establishment of the Free State, Supreme Court judges were still handing down judgements that contained such insights as this one, delivered by Mr Justice Fitzgibbon:

> There is no ground for wonder if the ambitious among them turn their attention to the wider stage of the great Commonwealth of Nations. We know well that genuine Irish patriotism is not incompatible with distinguished service and exalted position in the colonies and dependencies beyond the seas . . .'[62]

As late as 1932 all but one of the ten judges of the Supreme Court and the High Court bore the initials KC (for king's counsel) after their names.[63] In discharging their duties the judiciary proved remarkably sensitive to the government's needs and were unobtrusive in implementing draconian legislation. Indeed when the first case under the Free State's Treason Act was brought before the Criminal Court in 1925 it was adjudicated by Judge O'Shaughnessy, who during the War of Independence had dutifully signed British proclamations declaring Sinn Féin, the IRA, the Gaelic League and Fianna Éireann to be 'dangerous associations.'[64] The role entrusted to Judge O'Shaughnessy and his peers had altered little, despite the revolutionary upheaval.[65]

The courtrooms were another battleground on which Free State and Republic came face to face. When republicans were brought before the courts they refused to acknowledge the legitimacy of the judicial institution.[66] This attitude infuriated the judiciary; but it was up to the juries to deliver a verdict on whether or not defendants were 'mute by malice or by act of God.' To save a republican defendant from imprisonment on the grounds of contempt of court, juries simply deemed themselves unable to decide whether such suspects were unable to speak or were refusing to speak. Neither the judiciary nor the government believed that the state was being challenged by an army of mutes—particularly as the defendants were often charged with making seditious speeches. The cumulative effect of seeing so many republican suspects walk free proved too much for one High Court judge, who castigated jurors for failing to agree a verdict in the case of republican prisoners who had escaped from Mountjoy Prison. By refusing to convict, the jury, according to Mr Justice O'Byrne, had 'acted in disregard of the Oath they had taken, and in disregard of the law under which they lived, and in disregard of the rights and well-being of the citizens of this State.'[67]

Such was the zeal with which Mr Justice O'Byrne was criticised in the *Nation* that its editor, Seán T. O'Kelly, found himself summoned before the High Court by the Attorney-General on the charge of contempt of court. The offending article, headed 'Judge's insolence to jurors,' compared the actions of such Free State judges to those who had operated under the British regime and had similarly admonished jurors for refusing to convict republicans.[68] Pleading not guilty, O'Kelly described himself in his affidavit as a member of 'the Republican Party, Fianna Fáil,' and said that he had been 'a convinced Republican since boyhood.'[69] After describing Fianna Fáil's view as 'radically at variance'[70] with the government, O'Kelly did little to endear himself to the court by repeating the substance of the article and drawing parallels between the Free State government and British colonial regimes.[71] He affirmed that Mr Justice O'Byrne had acted illegally in attacking the jurors and concluded by asserting that a jury was the only appropriate tribunal to assess his case.[72] The court decided that it was competent to decide whether O'Kelly was in contempt, found him guilty as charged, and fined him £100 and awarded costs against him.[73]

While the party incurred a minor financial loss, this was more than recouped in the publicity the case brought to its campaign against the secret jury system. The *Irish World* dutifully informed its Irish-American readership that

the Junta's latest is an attempt to impoverish one of the oldest workers in the cause of Irish Republicanism. Sitting opposite the Cosgrave gang, he has never lost an opportunity of reminding them of the blood of brothers still dripping from their hands.[74]

Such publicity in America reached the very readers who de Valera was exhorting to subscribe to his *Irish Press* project. Indeed the *Irish World's* address was the one to which American residents were requested to send their subscriptions.

It was clear that many jury members sympathised with the actions of those brought before the courts, and Fianna Fáil contended that the refusal of juries to convict republicans reflected a widespread antipathy towards the Free State's persecution of the IRA. Additional measures would be taken by republicans to ensure that juries returned the 'right' verdict. Squeezed between the demands of the government, the judiciary and the IRA, jury service was not the most popular of pastimes during the 1920s.

Fianna Fáil's ire was also provoked by the government's decision in 1927 to prohibit women from serving on juries. It trenchantly condemned the move, pointing out that the 1916 Proclamation and the Democratic Programme of the First Dáil had guaranteed equal rights for women. In legislating to withdraw from women the right to be tried by juries composed of women as well as men, and in denying all women the right to exercise an important civic function, the government had displayed 'a reactionary and anti-democratic spirit consistent with its record.'[75]

Women were of concern to the government in more ways than one. In 1929 the female wing of the IRA, Cumann na mBan, started an intensive campaign aimed at persuading jurors of their 'duty' to acquit republicans or, if that failed, at intimidating them. A taste of the messages sent to jurors is provided by the following Cumann na mBan leaflet, issued under the heading 'Ghosts':

> The enemies of Ireland are imprisoning the men and women who are carrying out the only practical programme to attain Irish freedom. Unfortunately some of Dublin's degenerate and slavish citizens assist them in this work. Last month the following: [twelve names and addresses]—helped Corrigan and the infamous 'Judge' Sullivan to send the Irish patriot CON HEALY to penal servitude for 5 years. These men are traitors to their country. (Death would be their fate in any free country in the world).[76]

If a threat of retribution was implied, it was not an idle one. On 23 January 1929 one of the jurors listed in this leaflet, John White, was fired on and seriously wounded. The following month a witness who had given evidence against republicans on trial for burning Union Jacks was shot dead.[77] A Fianna Fáil TD was interviewed in connection with the killing.[78] In response, the Dáil introduced the Juries (Protection) Bill. Jurors in political cases would henceforth be summoned by post, would give their name to a court official in secret and would receive a number by which they would be known for the duration of the trial. The trial would be held in secret.

Fianna Fáil vehemently attacked the 'diabolical plan', for a number of reasons. Trial by jury, it claimed, was the ultimate guarantee of civil liberty, and with the bill's implementation 'personal liberty will cease to exist' in the Free State. It was noted that in the past a prisoner had the right to challenge the composition of the jury selected to try him, and this 'ancient right' had been discarded. The possibility of 'packed juries' was, for Fianna Fáil, ominously likely.

> If this Bill passes into law it will be a terrible engine in the hands of some ruthless and unscrupulous men . . . Where there is secrecy there is the opportunity for injustice, and with opportunity the temptation. Many ephemeral tyrants plotted and planned the suppression of this right, but the Press, however anti-national it may have been in other respects, was always outspoken in defence of an open trial. When this measure is smashed as assuredly it will be, when it is relegated to some chamber of horrors with other outworn instruments of oppression, what will be said of the journalists of this time who remain silent . . .[79]

The act, however, proved incapable of securing its objective of obtaining republican convictions, and it would be replaced in 1931 by an amendment to the Constitution that abolished juries in political cases in favour of a military tribunal.

PRISONERS

Since the time of the Fenians the issue of republican prisoners has been central to any appreciation of Irish political history. The degradations endured by Jeremiah O'Donovan Rossa became the stuff of legend, and the Amnesty Association, established to demand the release of IRB prisoners, was an integral part of the mobilisation of political nationalism. Similarly, in the aftermath of the 1916 Rising prisons became an important battleground for the independence movement's legitimisation, with Thomas Ashe's and Terence MacSwiney's hunger strikes providing inspiration for a new generation of republicans, characterised by the triumph of endurance over adversity.[80]

When the guns of the Civil War fell silent the Free State government had fifteen thousand republicans in its prison camps, while scores of others had been put to death in military custody. The issue of political prisoners is important as a barometer of republican sentiment within Fianna Fáil and throughout the Free State generally. It is important also that the official Fianna Fáil position during this period be noted so that it can be compared with the party leadership's attitude on assuming power.

A flavour of Fianna Fáil's early position on IRA prisoners is provided by an editorial in the *Nation* written by Seán T. O'Kelly a few months after the party's deputies took their seats in the Dáil. It is worth quoting at some length, as it encompasses the main themes addressed by the party in its discussions of this issue.

The IRA were presented as upstanding members of the community, persecuted for their sincerity of purpose and their dedication to the cause of republicanism and callously abandoned by their erstwhile comrades.

> There are men kept in prison today who have every right to regard the heads of the State as tyrants . . . Their only crime is that they did not change their opinions when men jumped into the saddle of authority through backsliding—through the desertion of these, their younger friends and comrades, and the forsaking of the principles they had taught them to uphold. Their guilt is solely to have learnt their lesson of adherence too well—even though, perhaps, they learnt it from the lips of the defilers of nationality.[81]

Fianna Fáil's position on the incarceration of IRA members was inextricably linked to its attitude towards the legitimacy of the state and the IRA campaign to overthrow it. The IRA were 'Irish soldiers of freedom whom Cosgrave as well as his English friends . . . have forced from their homes.'[82] When the Free State released Seán Russell and Michael Price after their brief spell of imprisonment the party congratulated the IRA men and expressed the hope that 'the persecution of these two reputable citizens by the Free State and its hired thugs will cease.'[83] Personal friendships and shared exploits with many of those under lock and key also heightened Fianna Fáil's interest in the fate of republican prisoners. During one debate on prison conditions the future minister James Ryan told the Dáil, 'I know George Gilmore [a leading member of the IRA, then in Arbour Hill military prison] for a good many years and I am perfectly willing to believe anything he tells me.'[84]

The issue also featured regularly during meetings of the Fianna Fáil parliamentary party. After a meeting between the party leadership and the Prisoners' Defence League a parliamentary party sub-committee was established to monitor republican prisoners' grievances.[85] Four TDs, including de Valera, were nominated to act as party representatives.[86] The party also decided to ensure that there was a Fianna Fáil representative on the visiting committee of every prison, though a motion suggesting that the party should 'look for the right of every TD to enter any prison at any time' was defeated.[87]

When five women prisoners embarked on a hunger strike for political status, de Valera raised the matter at a meeting of the parliamentary party, and it was agreed that Fianna Fáil would introduce the issue in the Dáil and link this action 'with our objection to the reactionary Bills introduced by the Government.'[88] In the Dáil, de Valera argued forcibly for the rights of the women and claimed that the Executive Council, by pretending that there were no political prisoners, was pursuing a policy devised by the British colonial government. Sacrifices had been made in the recent past to compel the British authorities to distinguish political prisoners and common criminals, he argued, and the distinction was recognised internationally. The prisoners on hunger strike were 'fighting for a political principle, the principle of the Irish people to be completely free.'

Referring to the plight of Thomas Ashe, de Valera condemned the repeat

of the same inhumanities which were associated with the British system. It shows the position that we have been brought to when we find Ministers giving an excuse for their action precisely the same as given by Ian MacPherson, Shortt and Hamar Greenwood. I hope that Deputies here, who understand the basis of the fight that we put up against the British, are not going to follow the example of the Executive and pretend now that they do not understand what these women are fighting for or what is the principle at stake ... Now, these are Republican women, some of whose names are known to us personally. I know myself that in the home of Sheila Humphreys the Republican Cabinet met when the Black and Tan regime was in progress. With that home I associate many of the acts of that Cabinet, and nothing that this young girl is doing now is different from anything which was preached in that home by members of the Republican Cabinet, some of whom are now persecuting her.[89]

Not long after this speech the Executive Council capitulated and conceded the demands of the hunger-strikers. The mood in Fianna Fáil was euphoric but tinged with recrimination, as it deplored a situation in which republicans of honourable character and service were subjected to the pangs of hunger and the danger of ill-health for the right to be treated as political prisoners. The party paper noted that Thomas Ashe had been the first of 'our prisoners' to die for 'the same cause,' the cause that Cosgrave and his ministers had 'betrayed.' The paper concluded by expressing hope that 'even now' the Free State government 'has learned that there are still men and women left in Ireland who have kept their national principles and are prepared to make sacrifices— even to offer the supreme sacrifice—so that these principles may be made to prevail.'[90]

Another typical example is the following extract from an article published in the *Nation*, which illustrates the case of one republican who was allegedly given a severe beating by a prison warder. The article stated that a 'republican investigation' was being conducted to establish accountability in the matter.

> The psychology of the case is easy to understand. This Britisher thought he was doing a grand thing in 'beating up' an unarmed prisoner who had hauled down the British flag. He doubtless thought he was pleasing Mr. Fitzgerald Kenny who is also a Britisher, and that he might get a promotion for it; but he got a bit nervous when he reflected, or was reminded of the facts by some colleagues that all the Republican organisations, the IRA, Fianna Fáil, and Sinn Féin have pledged themselves to punish any warder who is proved to have ill-treated any Republican prisoner . . . He overstepped himself. If we do not publish his name today it is because the Republican enquiry is not closed. Certain responsibilities have yet to be established.[91]

As the IRA had killed and maimed a number of prison warders and gardaí, and as it would continue such activities sporadically in the coming years, Fianna Fáil was voluntarily linking itself to these punitive acts. The party leadership was more circumspect on other occasions and was careful to distance itself from individual executions; but when the half-hearted criticisms that accompanied these deaths were juxtaposed with comments such as those quoted above an element of hypocrisy is discernible. Talk of 'republican investigations' and punishment by an alliance of the IRA, Sinn Féin and Fianna Fáil can only have strengthened the credibility of those who considered arbitrary executions a natural and desirable system of justice. The party's spokesperson on finance, Seán MacEntee, 'pledged himself and his colleagues, when they came to power, to punish every official, from the governors of the jails to the humblest warder, who is proved guilty of acts of cruelty to Republican prisoners.'[92]

The *Nation* continually informed the party membership of developments within the prisons. Its reporting of the topic, continued for a time by its successor, the *Irish Press*, contrasted with that of the mainstream national papers, whose treatment of the issue was negligible. Every week the paper devoted a section to the plight of republican prisoners, compiled by the Political Prisoners' Committee or by Maud Gonne MacBride, whose indefatigable work on behalf of incarcerated IRA members was frequently applauded.

Articles relating to prisoners were rarely devoid of an emotive and polemical style. 'John Horgan is lying very ill in Maryboro [Portlaoise] Jail,' a typical report began; 'if he dies it will be one more murder due to the Free State prison system and to political vengeance.'[93] The issue of the prisoners was much more than news: it was a call to action and an invitation to members to show solidarity. Every week a full list of republican prisoners in Irish and English prisons was published, together with their offence and the duration of their sentence. And every week Fianna Fáil members were urged by the party paper to buy and use night-lights from the Green Cross, a republican prisoners' aid organisation, to help the prisoners.[94] A Prisoners' Dependants' Committee was established, and contributions could be sent directly to the *Nation* to assist the dependants of 'men imprisoned by the Free State junta on account of their activities in the National Cause.'[95]

It is also important to remember that in drawing attention to the predicament of IRA prisoners the Fianna Fáil leadership was merely reflecting the sentiments of the party rank and file, who annually vowed to reverse the Free State's anti-republican security campaign and to release all republican prisoners. As confrontations between the Special Branch and the IRA intensified during 1928, the Fianna Fáil ard-fheis of that year reaffirmed its determination 'to exert every means' to secure the release of the prisoners.[96]

The 1929 ard-fheis called on the National Executive to hold public meetings throughout the country at least once a month to protest against the ill-treatment of political prisoners and to continue these meetings 'until such time as there are no political prisoners in either English or Irish jails.'[97] The ard-fheis of the following year renewed its sympathy with the political prisoners, demanded their release and called on all TDs and members of local government bodies to 'do everything in their power' to press this demand.[98]

Fianna Fáil's concern for the welfare of political prisoners was underlined when de Valera himself was imprisoned in Belfast in February 1929. Throughout the 1932 election campaign the cry of 'Release the prisoners' became a potent rallying call, drawing all strands of republican opinion together for Fianna Fáil's electoral machine.

FIANNA FÁIL, THE IRA AND THE USE OF FORCE

During Fianna Fáil's formative years the conflict between the Free State and the IRA continued unabated. The problem that confronted the Free State government was not unlike that of successive British governments: they could not with ease distinguish between members of the IRA, an illegal military organisation, and Sinn Féin, a legal political entity. The fact that most ministers possessed first-hand experience of how the organisations operated was of little assistance within the confines of Leinster House and Dublin Castle. The existence of a new republican organisation, Fianna Fáil, only exacerbated matters, blurring further the lines that divided IRA militants from political activists. In many parts of the country 'there now were families who were represented in Fianna Fáil, Sinn Féin and the IRA . . . and the Gardaí were aware that there was some kind of collusion between all three.'[99] On every occasion, however, when the police raided the homes of Fianna Fáil members or arrested and interrogated party activists at their place of work Fianna Fáil deputies raised the cry of 'police intimidation' in the Dáil and compared the Garda Síochána to the despised Royal Ulster Constabulary in Northern Ireland.

The case of Timothy Coughlan, which in 1928 became a *cause célèbre*, demonstrated the difficulties caused by the overlapping in membership of republican organisations. Coughlan was a member of the IRA and was one of the trio that had assassinated Kevin O'Higgins (though this was not known at the time). He was also a member of Fianna Fáil, and his death, in controversial circumstances, reverberated throughout the party, leading to protests at the highest level.

On the night of 28 January 1928 Coughlan and another person awaited the return of a police informer, Seán Harling, to his home in Dartry Road, Rathmines, Dublin, after being dropped off by a Garda car. Like many republicans after the Civil War, Harling had found it impossible to find work to support his family, and in desperation he had accepted an offer to work as an agent for the Special Branch under David Nelligan.[100] The discovery by the police of an IRA arms dump aroused suspicions about Harling, and the task of executing him fell to the 24-year-old Coughlan. The assassination backfired when Harling saw the two men as he walked towards his house. When they began shooting, Harling returned fire, killing Coughlan instantly.

Fianna Fáil condemned those responsible for Coughlan's death, without regard for the circumstances. His funeral was attended by thousands of republicans, including many high-ranking members of Fianna Fáil, who placed wreaths on behalf of the party. Sympathy was expressed to Coughlan's widow 'on the death of her illustrious husband,'[101] while Seán MacEntee, a future Minister for Finance who would be noted for his strident denunciations of republicans, declared: 'We will avenge Tim Coughlan.'[102] He elaborated on this promise and linked a vote for Fianna Fáil to retribution for those responsible. 'This much is certain: when Fianna Fáil comes into power, the murder of Timothy Coughlan will not go unpunished.'[103]

The issue was discussed at meetings of the parliamentary party, which agreed to demand the establishment of a tribunal to investigate Coughlan's death and the activities of the Special Branch generally.[104] When the inquiry, composed of what Fianna Fáil described as 'the regular hacks of the Government,'[105] concluded that Harling had fired in self-defence 'after shots had been fired at him with intent to kill by Timothy Coughlan,'[106] the party condemned the verdict. 'We wonder,' the *Nation* asked rhetorically, 'if anyone in the country was so simple as to expect any other kind of verdict.'

> Of course, the Cosgrave Party will hail this as another vindication of their administration and will paint the Harlings and Redicans and the like as virtuous and innocent upholders of law and order, but those who have read the evidence given . . . will have their own views as to the dirty type of tools this Government is obliged to employ to keep in office. The general public will also know what to think of the moral standards of the members of a Government which keeps such discredited individuals on their payroll.[107]

Such statements—made about men helping the police to identify IRA members and to prevent further illegal acts—raise an important issue, crucial to understanding the character of Fianna Fáil during the six years before it came to power, that is, the attitude of the party to physical force as a means of achieving Irish freedom and ending partition.

A constant theme in the columns of *An Phoblacht* was the danger parliamentarianism presented to revolutionary struggle. Before this point is developed it should be noted that the paper did not claim to speak on behalf of any political party: instead it considered itself the voice of 'militant Irish Republicanism,'[108] a term that was shorthand for the IRA. Many in the IRA were openly derisive of Sinn Féin's efforts, and *An Phoblacht* refused to publish Sinn Féin's 'Constitution of the Irish Republic' on the grounds that it was insufficiently radical. Indeed if the paper's editorials were anything to go by it seemed to have a qualified preference for Fianna Fáil, whose singleness of purpose, and the momentum it inspired, was impressive.

It must be remembered that Fianna Fáil was a progeny of the same republican family, and that many Fianna Fáil members were slow to sever their connections with the IRA. As Fianna Fáil and the IRA drew their support from the same republican reservoir, each fed off the other. High-ranking Fianna Fáil members were regular contributors to *An Phoblacht*—in defiance of its suppression as a seditious publication. Despite such a cordial relationship, the paper did not shirk its self-appointed role as guardian of the revolutionary struggle. This in turn led to a questioning of Fianna Fáil's political strategy and to a pointing out of the perceived dangers of constitutional politics.

This attitude was eloquently described in an editorial headed 'Reform or revolution', which cast doubts on the ability of constitutional politicians, whatever their past revolutionary credentials, to achieve separation from Britain. According to this point of view the creation of two 'puppet parliaments' in Ireland was an obstacle to—rather than a vehicle for—complete liberation. *An Phoblacht* disclaimed any predilection for factionalism or criticism for criticism's sake; it did not 'snap at every passing heel,' its editors said, but rather bemoaned the forsaking of militant action by a large section of Irish people for 'the barren and devious ways of parliamentary agitation.' Moreover, the editors stated that,

> believing, as we did, that men, however honest of heart and sincere of purpose would inevitably become enmeshed in the imperial web into which the Constitution of the Irish Free State is woven, we opposed such 'constitutional departures'. It was Plato . . . who . . . said that politicians who promise to reform the Constitution are like quack doctors who, with their nostrums, suppress the outer symptoms of their patient's malady while inwardly he grows ever more diseased. It is a vain effort, he said, to reform the Constitution—it must be destroyed, for it as a whole, and not the ills or 'symptoms' arising from it, the disease which poisons the body politic . . . reform is impossible . . . it must be revolution.[109]

This article identified the dangers facing a party that traded revolutionary action for constitutional politics and the danger of institutionalisation; but, like many similar articles, its strength lay more in its ability to criticise existing realities than to provide blueprints for a future society. The call for militant action could be effective only if accompanied by a credible strategy, and it certainly could not be a substitute for one. As evidenced by the advent of Saor Éire in 1931, the IRA (or at least the section that assumed dominance within the movement) did possess radical socio-economic objectives—far more radical than anything contemplated by Fianna Fáil—but, even entertaining the unlikely prospect of the IRA attaining the means to implement them, power would still stop at the border. In effect the IRA seemed at most to be promising a short-cut to a republic that politically would be completely independent of Britain and economically would be administered in the interests of workers and small farmers.

Exactly what militant policy would be pursued in relation to the North was vague at the best of times, and in this respect the IRA and Fianna Fáil shared an unrealistic optimism. Many assumed that once *they* were in power the problem of partition would somehow evaporate when subjected to the heat of radical republicanism. Some of this muddled thinking can be attributed to the fact that both Fianna Fáil and the IRA devoted most of their energies to altering the status quo in the 26-county state. This is not to suggest that either organisation was not interested in the plight of Northern nationalists or did not seek reunification—far from it—but it is clear that both groups had given priority to certain of their objectives, the foremost being the destruction of the Free State. How they differed was in their assessment of the most appropriate tactic for achieving this, with the IRA advocating a revolutionary assault on state institutions, and Fianna Fáil preferring the evolutionary constitutional path (though drawing at times on a rhetorical commitment to revolution if necessary).

The attitude towards parliamentary democracy was also important. Fianna Fáil's method illustrated the need to secure majority support for its policies and obtain a parliamentary majority to implement them. The IRA, on the other hand, attached less importance to majority support than to the need to create revolutionary conditions from which a successful uprising could spring. This difference is reflected in the fact that none of Fianna Fáil's republican rivals contested elections and so had no accurate method of assessing the support that existed for their strategy. Attendance at rallies and commemorations and the 'general mood' of the population were considered the ways to gauge fluctuations in popular opinion.

The reference to Plato quoted above does not, in this context, appear entirely coincidental. Plato's instinctive distrust of the masses—susceptible as they were to populists, demagoguery and promises of material reward—would have found a receptive audience among many republicans. Republicans—who thought majority support a desirable (as opposed to a necessary) precondition for revolution and a new constitutional order—never adequately brought this thinking to its logical con-clusion. If a large minority of armed radicals took on the state, what leadership would emerge to dictate the pace of struggle? While all republicans were committed to free elections and majority rule, once an all-Ireland republic was established would not the leadership of Ireland during this transitional period of struggle fall to the IRA Executive?

The Fianna Fáil leadership claimed that its origins were in the 1916 Rising, and the party stressed on numerous occasions that they were the 'guardians of the 1916 tradition.'[110] Emphasis was also placed on the leadership's revolutionary credentials. Of the seven principal officers of the party,[111] five had participated in the Rising. All seven had taken part in the War of Independence and were on the Republican side in the Civil War. 'Such officers with such records,' it was claimed, 'are proof unanswerable of the unaltered aim and ideal of Fianna Fáil.[112]

The legacy of 1916, which was a manifestation of a much older tradition of armed resistance to British rule, provided Fianna Fáil with a ready-made 'glorious history' of armed combat. Dedication to the revolutionary ideal permitted the party to lay claim to a tradition far older than itself. It also enabled it to bridge a cultural gap between the ideals of the revolutionary generation and the reality of the Free State that Cumann na nGaedheal, tainted by compromise and coercion, had allowed to develop. Invocation of the Rising and commitment to its ideals provided an inspiring rallying call and united republicans who might otherwise have felt that the revolutionary cause was being abandoned.

However, it also posed problems for a party that had embarked on a path of constitutional agitation, particularly as there was a large body of IRA militants who enjoyed considerable support and claimed to be the true heirs of the same revolutionary tradition. The rebels of 1916, after all, had not received any popular mandate before taking up arms: they did not seek endorsement of their proposed actions by reference to the ballot box but had armed in secret. Similarly, when Fianna Fáil declared that 'the lesson of the Fenians must be well learnt by the men of today'[113] it was commending the actions of a clandestine movement that had, among other things, initiated a bombing campaign in England, again without ever having contested an election.[114]

The recent Civil War had also created martyrs, whose words were celebrated at annual commemorations, during which Fianna Fáil re-dedicated itself to the republican ideal. The commemoration at the grave of Liam Mellows near Arklow was one such occasion. Fianna Fáil, Sinn Féin and the IRA rubbed shoulders to pay tribute to the martyr who all claimed as their own. Liam's life, the *Nation* reported, could be summed up in the slogan 'Out to fight, not to run away.' A strong appeal was made at the 1928 commemoration to take up the legendary Fianna ideal so that the Irish people would 'again be brothers in arms against the old common enemy, until the whole thirty-two counties of Ireland were absolutely free.'[115]

Commitment to parliamentarianism and the desire to be associated with the revolutionary tradition led to conflicting statements. Speaking in January 1928, de Valera declared that Fianna Fáil was 'committed to a policy of political action rather than revolution to achieve its aim of an independent Ireland'[116]—a statement that seemed unambiguously constitutional in character. Four months later an editorial in the *Nation* suggested that Fianna Fáil's commitment to constitutional agitation was purely tactical and was dependent on the attainment of a united Ireland free from British influence. If its objectives could not be achieved peaceably, the editorial concluded, the party would be more than willing to take up arms.

> Fianna Fáil is not afraid of the word Constitutional as so many brave Irishmen would pretend to be: Fianna Fáil, if forced, having tried constitutional means of eluding England's grasp will not be afraid of Revolution either . . . What would the men of 1916 have said had they seen [our] tireless efforts today? Would they not have approved and applauded the men who do not wish to let the grass grow under their feet even between one Rising and the next? There may be no next. But there may be. If Fianna Fáil's programme of peaceful penetration into our own land is in any way blocked or interfered with by an outsider, then, if the occasion should arise, it will no more fear the cry of Revolutionary than it does today of Constitutionalist.[117]

As the annual commemoration at the grave of Wolfe Tone beckoned, the party rhetoric became indistinguishable from that of the IRA. Supporters were told that the party did not stand for piecemeal reform but for the complete liberation of Ireland.

Reforms were derided as sops designed 'to make our slavery more tolerable' and to quell revolutionary dissent. O'Connell's agitation for Catholic emancipation, the destruction of the foreign landlord and the restoration of Irish language rights were to be welcomed, it was argued; but progress in the fight for civil rights had not contributed directly to the cause of national liberation. Referring to such reformist victories, Fianna Fáil claimed that,

> weighed in the scales, any virtues such victories might have in the eyes of the Republican and Nationalist are more than counter-balanced by the cruel imposition by England of Partition in Ireland—Partition by which she retains for herself an Irish province on our small island. The great lesson of the last 130 years, however, is one of hope. The great lesson for those who wish to read is that such 'concessions' to Irishmen, as we have had, have not satisfied their aspirations or stifled their desire to be free. Individuals may settle down as slaves; indeed there were always a host of such people in Ireland. But as long as there are others—and they show a strange persistence—who prefer to die rather than acquiesce to slavery, the Irish nation cannot abdicate . . . We did not win. But all is well; for we have the same national creed as Wolfe Tone of 130 years ago. And the cause that is not lost is militant, and what is militant today is triumphant tomorrow.[118]

If reforms and concessions were of such little value one could be forgiven for questioning the purpose of Fianna Fáil's participation in the Dáil. The apparent inconsistency in the party's statements provoked an intellectual debate between the *Nation* and *An Phoblacht* during the later part of 1929. Its origins are to be found in an editorial in *An Phoblacht*[119] that accused Fianna Fáil of inaction after attacks by the Special Branch on republicans in Co. Clare.[120] Fianna Fáil took umbrage and challenged the accusation with such detail that *An Phoblacht* withdrew its criticism and commended de Valera's prompt and energetic response to the crisis.[121]

But a larger issue had been touched on by the paper's assertion that 'parliamentary agitation diverts the attention of the people from serious revolutionary efforts.' The *Nation* responded by stating that it did not favour revolutionary methods 'if by that is meant the speedy use of physical force,' as three-quarters of the electorate had demonstrated that they would not approve.[122]

The chief of staff of the IRA, Moss Twomey, and the *Nation's* new editor, Frank Gallagher, entered the debate, and their correspondence was published in both papers.[123] Twomey argued that while the problem of how to achieve Irish freedom was political in complexion it was essentially military in character, and, as had often occurred in other phases of Irish history, 'the political aspect has been over-emphasised to the detriment of the military.' Many people had been seduced into accepting the Treaty on the understanding that it would give republicans an opportunity to acquire arms and organise a better-equipped army. Faced with the threat of British force, this argument had found a receptive audience but has since proved spurious. The IRA, Twomey declared, was endeavouring to organise the most consciously national elements of the nation, around whom it was later hoped to rally the bulk of the population.

On behalf of Fianna Fáil, Gallagher stated that the party did not 'renounce the doctrine of physical force for achieving the freedom of Ireland' but believed that such a policy was inappropriate at the present time. The people were cynical and embittered, he claimed, and it would only break their confidence further to set them a task they could not fulfil. Twomey did not deny that there existed a strong sense of apathy among the populace but claimed that 'too often the alleged tiredness of the people is availed of for adopting weak national policies.' He also refused to accept that the people would not support a revolutionary programme or that by casting their votes they had approved of non-revolutionary objectives. If only a non-revolutionary programme was submitted to the electorate they might acquiesce; but that was not to say that they would not support a revolutionary programme if it were presented to them.

In my opinion, to judge national feeling, sentiment and desires by the results of elections is unwise and misleading. Judged by such standards, the Insurrection of 1916 had not popular approval. The Parliamentarians then sat in the British Parliament, and seemed content, and outwardly it could be claimed that the people acquiesced in their policy. It is easy now to judge whether at the time the Parliamentarians or the physical force movement more truly represented national desires or ideas.

It is clear from this debate that Fianna Fáil considered the Irish Republic to have been established *de jure* (if not *de facto*) in 1916, which placed the party in a difficult ideological position. Its desired association with revolutionary martyrs and its commitment, however qualified, to parliamentarianism made it vulnerable to charges of hypocrisy, and not only from *An Phoblacht*. The weekly paper *Honesty*, noted for its sympathy towards Fianna Fáil, had also begun to attack the 'pettifogging politicians,' 'pseudo-Republicans' and 'hypocritical piffle talked over the grave of Wolfe Tone.'[124]

Fianna Fáil took such claims seriously and went to great lengths to counter them. Rebuttals were not only published in the *Nation* but were forwarded for publication to the republican journal that had made the charge. This attitude was understandable, considering that Fianna Fáil supporters would have been regular readers of *An Phoblacht* and *Honesty*. Indeed at the 1928 ard-fheis the delegates had expressed their 'warm appreciation' to the editors and owners of both journals for their 'weekly fight, made against great odds . . . in the cause of Freedom, Nationality and Independence— both political and economic.'[125] As well as holding these journals in high esteem, Fianna Fáil members would be aware that *An Phoblacht* sold considerably more copies than the *Nation*.[126]

The constant need to clarify Fianna Fáil's attitude towards constitutionalism and physical force, in response to hostile republican editorials, was motivated by four separate considerations. Firstly, it was necessary for retaining the support of the rank and file, whose membership depended on the party adopting a strong republican position. Secondly, it can also be viewed as part of a strategy aimed at those who had 'hedged their bets' by retaining dual membership of Fianna Fáil and the IRA; the hope was that a blend of pugnacity and pragmatism might wean them from their association with the latter. Thirdly, the publication of Fianna Fáil policy in other republican journals, and its rejection of suggestions of weakness, might even entice the readers of those papers to abandon their exclusive allegiance to a non-Fianna Fáil brand of republicanism in favour of that advocated by the party. Finally, prompt clarification of differences could only help to foster a harmonious relationship between Fianna Fáil and the other members of the republican family. Hostility from rival organisations could only hinder Fianna Fáil's progress, while their qualified support helped internal party unity and ideological cohesion.

Such ideological confrontations were rare, and for the most part Fianna Fáil and the IRA enjoyed a cordial relationship. The party stressed its revolutionary credentials and paid tribute to those who continued to advocate force as a method of ending British rule in Ireland. These sentiments were encapsulated in an article that appeared in the *Nation* in January 1928. After describing the rebellious past of the Fianna Fáil leadership, the article continued:

> They are, therefore, men and women who, having proved themselves as soldiers, are not likely to under-rate the value of force as a weapon to be used as opportunity offers for the winning back of the complete freedom of Ireland. Neither are they likely to decry the Irish Republican Army or to have anything but the highest regard for those whose aim it is today to devote themselves solely to training and preparing Irishmen for the task of completing, by force if necessary, the final wrestling of Ireland from the control of the English invader . . . As we are all aware, there is in existence today, as there has always been, a physical force party. The Junta [Free State government] have for years tried to stamp out this party. They have brought in time after time the most vicious and savage legislation to deal with it. The attempt has failed. When the other day the Republican leader [de Valera] introduced the repeal of the Public Safety Act into the Dublin Assembly, he made a magnificent effort to win the deputies of that assembly to a proper attitude towards the IRA. Instead of that attitude being one of suppression and persecution, he urged with all his power that it should be one of understanding and sympathy.[127]

For Fianna Fáil, history had demonstrated the futility of attempting to quash armed resistance to British rule. As long as Ireland remained divided and bound within the straitjacket of the British Empire there would always be a sizeable section of dedicated volunteers who would seek to remedy the situation by force of arms. The party acknowledged therefore that it shared common ground with the IRA.

> In effect, the Fianna Fáil Party and the physical force party know that they share the same ideals . . . Nothing less than that full freedom will satisfy Fianna Fáil. While both parties travel their individual roads, the attitude of the Republican deputies will always be that the young men ready to give their lives for freedom are among the salt of the Irish earth.[128]

Such statements raise the question: what were the differences between Fianna Fáil, Sinn Féin and the IRA? Of the three, only the IRA was armed; but both Sinn Féin and

Fianna Fáil were supportive of its efforts, and all three favoured a vigorous campaign to secure the complete independence of Ireland. The essential difference, which Fianna Fáil acknowledged, was that the party was willing to secure whatever gains were possible in the Free State legislature.

THIRTY-TWO INTO TWENTY-SIX WON'T GO: FIANNA FÁIL AND PARTITION

The partition issue was not one discussed at parliamentary party meetings during this formative period of constitutional opposition. This can be partially explained by de Valera's ideological supremacy within Fianna Fáil, which was rarely challenged. Furthermore, ard-fheis delegates always vigorously debated partition, while de Valera made many public statements on the topic. It is curious, however, that Northern policy was not debated during parliamentary party meetings between the September 1927 and February 1932 elections.[129] The treatment of the partition question contrasted sharply with the extensive consideration given to other issues, such as the Irish language.[130] Despite attempts by other representative party institutions, such as the ard-fheis and the National Executive, to push partition to the forefront of party policy, it would seem that the parliamentary party—in practice the most powerful organ within the party structure—confined its deliberations to issues concerning the future of the 26-county state. This fact should also be contrasted with Fianna Fáil's constitution, which explicitly declared that the unification of the national territory as a republic was the party's principal objective.

The paucity of debate within the parliamentary party also contrasted with the generous coverage of the partition issue at public forums, not least in the columns of the *Nation*. Irish nationalists, Fianna Fáil maintained, had 'a right to their island home which a grasping neighbour has partitioned.'[131] Attention was devoted to the subordinate position endured by the Northern nationalist population, and the policies of the Free State and six-county governments were unflatteringly compared. The two governments were seen as pursuing a common objective of annihilating republicanism.

> In the North the minority was barely suffered to exist. Positions, other than those of the hewers of wood and the drawers of water, were denied them, unless they did violence to their convictions, religious and political. For the crime of protesting against the terrorist regime that was set up in Belfast in 1921 men, women, and children have been dragged from their beds at dead of night and murdered by paid agents of the Government. The sword of Justice in Belfast was given to the custody of one whose hands were quite uneven. In the South similar conditions have prevailed since 1922 . . . Today in the Twenty-Six County area of Ireland, neither the home, the life nor the liberty of any Irish Republican is safe from the violence of the roaming crews of gunmen known as the C.I.D.[132]

Partition punctured Cumann na nGaedheal's claims of sovereign independence, and Fianna Fáil suggested that the patriots of the pre-Treaty days who now controlled the 26 Counties had not only 'dropped the ideal of a separate island' but had 'sold the population of six of our Northern counties into slavery to the English enemy.'[133] The party decried the pervasive anti-nationalist discrimination in Northern Ireland, and the Nationalist Party leader, Joe Devlin, was praised for his 'courage and states-manship' in declining to lead nationalists into the Northern Parliament. The only qualification for office or public employment in the Six Counties, according to Fianna Fáil, was 'their ability to strike the big drum,' and a tradition had been handed down from father to son of 'making a living from the abuse of religion.'

As not a single Catholic was a member of the Northern Senate or judiciary, Fianna Fáil proclaimed that Catholics had received 'not a single crumb from the rich men's table' presided over by Craigavon and 'his select coterie of wealthy men.' These discriminatory practices were compared with Cosgrave's treatment of the Northern government's 'bosom friends and fellow-lodgemen in the South,' who were treated with 'overflowing-bumper generosity.' And, 'in view of what is happening in the North,' Cosgrave and his government had 'shown themselves to be spineless slaves.'[134]

The Fianna Fáil campaign against partition received a timely boost when, on 5 February 1929, de Valera was imprisoned by the Northern regime for entering Northern Ireland, thereby violating an exclusion order imposed by the Northern government. The incident galvanised the party at a time when sluggishness had permeated its local and regional levels. Protest meetings were called, motions were put down for local government bodies and copies of condemnatory resolutions poured in from all parts of the state.[135] North Tipperary County Council protested against 'the unjust, uncalled for, and tyrannical arrest and imprisonment of Mr. Eamon de Valera by the imperialistic clique presently holding usurping control of six Northern Counties of Ireland.'[136] Leitrim County Council condemned 'the action of the Belfast bigots' and 'the unnatural division of our country into West British dependencies to suit the exigencies of Imperialism and Freemasonry.'[137]

The affair raised de Valera's stature in the eyes of the Irish diaspora and did no harm to his attempts to maintain Irish-American interest in Fianna Fáil. While in prison he received many cablegrams from the United States congratulating him on his 'anomalous but glorious condition.'[138] In response de Valera described partition as 'perhaps the biggest of all the crimes that England committed against us' and claimed that while it lasted 'real national progress is impossible.'[139] The publicity generated by his imprisonment advanced his endeavours to raise funds for a Fianna Fáil news-paper. He made frequent references to partition at subsequent Irish-American fund-raising rallies, and he did so in a manner calculated to arouse an enthusiastic response from traditional supporters. During these meetings he adopted a belligerent posture and used language little different from that of the IRA. In one speech, made in 1930, he expressed support for the wish that English rule in Ireland would be defeated in a decisive military encounter like that inflicted by Brian Bórú on the Vikings a millennium earlier.

> As long as a British soldier remains in Ireland . . . so long as our country is partitioned, no Irishman can say that this is the final settlement of Ireland's nationhood . . . Every Irishman worthy of the name, no matter where he may be, lives in the hope that there will be a battle of Clontarf for the British as there was for the Danes.[140]

The circumstances in which de Valera came to be incarcerated could not have been more propitious for gaining the maximum amount of favourable publicity in republican circles at home and abroad. The purpose of his visit had been to open a bazaar established by Conradh na Gaeilge and jointly sponsored by the GAA. The party reminded members of the importance of Irish in the liberation struggle and praised the efforts of Conradh na Gaeilge in the Six Counties to maintain a vibrant language movement. The Archbishop of Armagh and Catholic Primate of Ireland, Cardinal Joseph MacRory, had travelled to the opening, a fact emphasised by Fianna Fáil, which extensively quoted his views on the value of Irish. Having established a unity of purpose among the Catholic Church, Conradh na Gaeilge and Fianna Fáil, the party argued that the reason for de Valera's imprisonment was his unyielding republicanism and his resistance to partition.

> Ireland is not conquered yet: the Irish question is not settled by the installation of the Free State with Partition. Belfast blurts this out, when without any specific charge against Éamon de Valera it locks him up. It locks him up out of pure vindictiveness for what he is—an uncompromising and unbought Irish Republican, who continues to say that Ireland will never be satisfied without her independence, who continues to tell England that she has 'settled' nothing by her 'Treaty' and her lop-sided Financial Settlement and her machined Partition. Éamon de Valera has shown the world what he is, what he stands for, what he has risked all and suffered for: a determination to free Ireland of English domination.[141]

Seán T. O'Kelly made a similar point when he claimed that de Valera had been imprisoned 'primarily because he is the most powerful and the most indomitable enemy of English power in Ireland.' He was hated by the 'Craig Junta' because 'he has never changed his principles and because he stands today as convinced and as ardently an Irish Republican as at any time since he so gallantly helped to raise the flag of the Republic in 1916.'[142] De Valera was presented as the personification of the republican struggle, leading the battle to abolish partition, and it was pointed out that by his imprisonment he had drawn attention to the existence and ramifications of the division of the country.

> It has borne in upon many minds for the first time the meaning of Partition. In our daily lives we are rarely brought in contact with the fact that this country has been cut in two. The arrest of Mr. de Valera impressed on every mind the reality of the dismemberment of this country.[143]

In case the message was still insufficiently impressed on the popular imagination, a mass meeting was organised in Dublin to protest against de Valera's incarceration, and it was attended by more than fifteen thousand people.[144] The main theme was that de Valera's imprisonment represented an insult to the nation and that the party was urged to redouble its efforts to abolish partition.[145] Calls for an economic boycott were mixed with more bellicose exhortations to forcibly destroy the Stormont

Government and to de-Anglicise the country. Seán MacEntee, who as a Belfast man was not unacquainted with Northern realities, spoke in particularly strident terms.

> The people of the Free State who have stood against the guns of Maxwell, and of French, are not going to bow to Craig. We will not rest content until we have the Republican flag floating not alone over Cave Hill, but on Stormont. There was a time in 1920 when we had the Belfast garrison fighting for their existence—now they are enthroned in power. I appeal to those here to enter into a communion with their fellow-Nationalists in the North to bring that about. Northerners come to the Free State every day, and the people of the South trade with them and help to make them mighty. Let the grass grow in the streets of Belfast, let the mills of Belfast be silent as the mills of the Twenty-Six Counties, and we will have no partition problem. The people who built up Belfast were not Irish, but English and Scottish settlers, and they will not be Irish until the people of the South show them that they are stronger than they.[146]

This kind of threatening rhetoric was complemented by that of Seán T. O'Kelly, who stated that the incident, apart from bringing international attention to the injustice of partition, had dramatically refuted the contention that the Northern government sought a better understanding with the rest of Ireland. They now knew exactly what the sentiments of the 'Northern bigots' were towards them and wouldn't 'waste any time blathering about restoring the unity of Ireland with soft talk.' Indeed, according to O'Kelly, it would take 'more than soft soap and soft talk to abolish Partition and to abolish the Six-County Parliament.'[147]

The pugnacity of this speech, characteristic of many made at the time by Fianna Fáil speakers, hinted at a militant approach and the rejection of the politics of persuasion in favour of coercion of an ill-defined nature. Fianna Fáil did not take up arms, and to this extent it seemed that it was merely replacing 'soft talk' with a tougher vernacular. There were, however, several initiatives that it could have adopted in an effort to weaken partitionism. Foremost among these was the proposal to actively organise within the Six Counties and to establish Fianna Fáil cumainn there.

This proposal had received particular attention at the party's first ard-fheis. Supporters considered it paradoxical that a party whose professed *raison d'être* was to reunite the Irish people should refuse to organise in the North. This anomaly was accentuated by the fact that the party Fianna Fáil had split from, Sinn Féin, was actively organising on an all-Ireland basis. Moreover, as Fianna Fáil's constitution permitted membership to all those 'of Irish birth, parentage, or residence,'[148] a decision not to organise in the Six Counties would be tantamount to excluding those living in Northern Ireland from these categories.

The Fianna Fáil honorary secretaries' report of 1926 acknowledged that the general organising committee 'had not attempted actively' to organise the party in the North but stated that contact had been established with republicans in various centres. However, the report claimed that Fianna Fáil was anxious to avoid 'unnecessary division', and therefore the 'existing organisation had not been interfered with.'[149] De Valera argued that while Fianna Fáil was 'intended to be an all-Ireland organisation' it had to recognise the differences between the political environments in the two parts of the country. The time to organise in the Six Counties, he claimed, 'would depend on the conditions there¹⁵⁰; but the imprecision and obvious hypocrisy of this stance aroused protests from delegates.

Eventually a compromise was reached whereby the matter was referred to the National Executive for consideration—and there it rested. The party hierarchy had successfully circumvented criticism on this issue that was crucial for its organisational future. However, the question was merely postponed, and it would re-emerge at successive ard-fheiseanna, piercing the conscience of party leaders.

In response to pressure from Fianna Fáil's grass roots and to numerous communications received from Northern nationalists, this issue received detailed treatment at the 1928 ard-fheis. During the year the party had been requested by influential Northern nationalists to extend its organisation to the Six Counties and to contest the forthcoming Stormont elections. On behalf of the party Seán T. O'Kelly and Seán Lemass visited Northern Ireland in February 1928, ostensibly to examine the situation and to receive first-hand information from all sections of nationalist opinion. In their report they noted that 'many individuals are anxious that Fianna Fáil should take the initiative and actively organise the area from Headquarters,' but they claimed that 'the general view amongst Republicans is that an essential step to the realisation of national unity will be a political victory in the South.' The report declared that the Northern republicans consulted believed 'that it will be wise policy not to divert our energies from that object until it has been attained.'¹⁵¹

It appears a little too convenient that these views coincided perfectly with those of the Fianna Fáil leadership. Indeed the report bears the hallmarks of a political strategy conceived by it rather than by Northern nationalist opinion. Details of the content of the discussions Lemass and O'Kelly held with the Northern nationalists is limited to the selected sound-bites referred to in the report, and it is likely that the report does not reveal the full picture but gives only a partial and highly selective account.

From the beginning the Fianna Fáil leadership had been unenthusiastic about organising the party in Northern Ireland, and as time passed and as governmental power in the Free State was secured, resistance to the idea only increased. As for the position in the late 1920s, Fianna Fáil's primary aim was to secure power in the Free State—all the more gratifying if this partitionist objective could be presented as the desire of the party's 'separated brethren' in the Six Counties.

Fianna Fáil's explanation for 'postponing' expansion into the Six Counties—that it would 'divert' the party from its primary aim of securing power within the Free State—is credible up to a point, but there is a wider context that must be considered. To be executed in a coherent and professional manner the establishment of cumainn in the North would have required the talents of the honorary secretaries and of other Fianna Fáil leaders. Time-consuming speaking tours like those required to form a vibrant organisation in the South would have to be repeated.

On the other hand, these disadvantages would have to be set against the benefits of a recruitment campaign in the Six Counties. The practice encouraged by the Fianna Fáil leadership and implemented with unparalleled professionalism was that local branches would not only be self-financing but, through the national collection and other activities, would contribute to the upkeep of party headquarters and the organisation generally. Therefore, after the initial drain on time and resources the Northern cumainn would be a lucrative source of income for Fianna Fáil. Equally important would be the propaganda value of possessing a truly national organisation; what better way to demonstrate the anomaly of partition than to have elected public representatives of the same anti-partition party on both sides of the border?[152] Fianna Fáil's position appeared all the more strange when contrasted with the Organisation Committee's report to the same ard-fheis, which indicated that efforts were being made to establish 'strong cumainn' in England and that Lemass had travelled to London for that purpose. The report argued that the party could be 'improved considerably' in Scotland, and it recommended that the National Executive give the matter its attention.

In an effort to get a policy adopted by the National Executive in time for the 1929 ard-fheis, the Lemass and O'Kelly trip was followed by a visit by Gerry Boland the following September. Boland's conclusions differed little from those of the previous delegation, and his report persuaded the National Executive to rule that it 'would not be in the best national interests' to contest the forthcoming elections in Northern Ireland. While the National Executive promised assistance for any local attempts by Northern republicans to organise themselves, it believed that such endeavours were more likely to be successful if they 'originated in that area than if originated in Dublin.'[153] In other words, Fianna Fáil would adopt a low-key organisational strategy for the Six Counties, leaving the initiative and work to local activists without devoting the resources of the party.

Such a policy contrasted sharply with that employed within the 26 Counties, where nothing was left to chance in matters of organisation. Party organisers toured the constituencies, establishing contacts with local republicans, ensuring the formation of cumainn in all parishes, combined with follow-up meetings and regular updates on their progress, development and expansion. The different approaches reflected a general neglect of Northern nationalists, whose plight was capitalised on for anti-Free State political propaganda but who received little practical assistance.

The honorary secretaries' report to the 1928 ard-fheis recommended that the incoming National Executive 'continue to give this question their closest attention.' Few developments emerged between then and the following ard-fheis. The 1929 report noted that a general election had taken place in the North but that, in accordance with the decision ratified at the previous ard-fheis, Fianna Fáil had not contested it.[154] In fact two elections had taken place within days of each other.

The Stormont elections in May were conducted for the first time under the straight-vote system. In an effort to consolidate his position as Prime Minister, James Craig had abolished PR with the single transferable vote, which had been used in both parts of Ireland since 1920, as a result of which nationalist representation dropped from twelve seats to eleven. Three days later, elections for the British Parliament returned two nationalist MPs for Cos. Fermanagh and Tyrone.[155]

Despite de Valera holding the Northern Ireland seat for Co. Down since 1921, and despite the fact that Fianna Fáil had made much of this fact during his incarceration earlier in the year, he refused to stand for re-election to the Belfast Parliament. The report presented to the 1929 ard-fheis declared that the situation in the Six Counties had 'not changed materially since our last report,' and, while noting 'a revival of national spirit in that area,' it reiterated that organisational success could best be achieved through the efforts of local republicans. Rather feebly, it concluded with the same words as the previous year's report, recommending that the new National Executive 'give the position their closest attention.'[156]

In contrast to the downbeat tone that marked the summary of Northern organisational matters, the section of the report devoted to de Valera's month-long imprisonment in Belfast Prison was exuberant.

In laying bare the foundations of force and repression on which the present order in Ireland rests . . . the affair reacted to the advantage of the Republican movement and brought a substantial accretion of strength and prestige to Fianna Fáil.[157]

The incident had boosted de Valera's profile and Fianna Fáil's organisational strength in the South. Indeed de Valera's interest in the plight of Northern nationalists was less defined by the assistance that could be rendered—for he made it clear that little could be done in the immediate future—than by his eye to the Southern elector-ate. When it came to Fianna Fáil's relationship with Northern nationalists, principle was considered incompatible with organisational success. One successful ard-fheis resolution that combined organisational decentralisation and anti-partitionism, by advocating that the ard-fheis be held in rotation in Dublin, Cork, Galway and Belfast, was never implemented.[158]

It should be noted that 1929 was not a good year for the party's organisational activities in the 26 Counties. Disappointment was expressed with the level of finance achieved through the national collection,[159] and the number of registered cumainn had declined dramatically.[160] This organisational lethargy—the leadership was adamant that it did not reflect a diminution in support—was reflected in the poor attendance at the ard-fheis. Only four hundred delegates were present, and the unsatisfactory organisational statistics were attributed to 'the uneventful nature of the year, in the matter of election activities.'[161]

In such circumstances it is perhaps understandable that the leadership wished to consolidate the party's organisational base and confine its activities to the Free State. This is unlikely to have been the primary reason for the party's organisational inertia within the Six Counties, but it does at least provide a credible justification. At the very least the party had postponed organisational commitments north of the border until government power had been secured in the South. Only when that was achieved could its nationalist rhetoric be tested against the advantages of near-permanent institutional power in a truncated Ireland.

FIANNA FÁIL, THE STATE AND THE THREAT OF INSTITUTIONALISATION

The five years that Fianna Fáil spent in the Dáil as parliamentary opposition provided it with a useful introduction to parliamentary procedures and values, so that by 1932 it had become, as Cosgrave hoped, constitutionalised. Despite its early reluctance to enter the Dáil on ideological grounds and its initial taciturnity (only Seán T. O'Kelly spoke during the party's first day of attendance), the parliamentary party soon adjusted to the legislative process. This increased adaptation is reflected in the number of questions put to the government by Fianna Fáil deputies. Between August and December 1927 the party asked 302 questions, rising to a staggering 826 between February and July 1928.[162] This demonstrates that the party was determined to justify its presence in the Free State assembly by proving to the doubters inside and outside the party that it was getting important business done on behalf of its constituents.

Between October 1927 and July 1929 Fianna Fáil deputies asked forty-six questions on the adjournment, of which the following is a representative sample:

2 November 1927: Seizure of Fianna Éireann handbooks
17 November 1927: Compensation to Northern nationalists burnt out in pogroms
24 November 1927: Illegal payments of land annuities to Britain
29 February 1928: Shooting of prisoner in Roscommon
11 March 1928: Payment of dismissed republican teachers
22 March 1928: Death of a prisoner in Co. Kerry
9 May 1928: Wounding of a prisoner
30 May 1928: Tariff Commission: Report on flour millers' application
31 May 1928: Kellogg Anti-War Pact
1 June 1928: Petition to set referendum on oath in operation
7 June 1928: Prisoners on hunger strike
8 June 1928: Division of lands in Co. Cork
13 June 1928: Treatment of a prisoner
21 June 1928: Condition of republican prisoners in Mountjoy Prison
28 June 1928: Arrest of Peadar O'Donnell
11 July 1928: Land division in Co. Mayo
19 July 1928: Drainage of the River Barrow
25 October 1928: Embargo on imported barley and malt
2 November 1928: Congestion in Co. Mayo
8 November 1928: Floods in Co. Leitrim
22 November 1928: Unemployment benefit claim
20 February 1929: Arrest of Deputy de Valera
21 February 1929: The sugar beet industry
27 February 1929: Distress in west Cork
28 February 1929: Vesting of judicial holdings on the tenant
6 March 1929: Continuation schools
10 April 1929: Arrests of republicans in Dublin
17 April 1929: Outrages by the Special Branch in west Cork
24 April 1929: Special Branch outrages in Co. Clare
25 April 1929: Special Branch assaults in Glanmire
15 May 1929: Infection from second-hand clothing
27 June 1929: Entertainment tax in Cork
4 July 1929: Dáil loan subscribers in Sligo
31 July 1929: Special Branch activities in Co. Clare

The list illustrates Fianna Fáil's political priorities during this period and the parliamentary party's desire to prove to the republican constituency that it was actively seeking to ameliorate their position from within the Dáil. The most idealised gloss put on Fianna Fáil's participation in the Dáil was that it was part of a two-front strategy: the IRA and Fianna Fáil applied pressure from the outside, while on the inside the parliamentary party eroded the morale of the Free State and ensured that Cumann na nGaedheal could not deliberate behind closed doors but was confronted face to face with the unabating opposition of its critics. The number of questions also reflected the party's willingness to take up issues on behalf of constituents, so building up a political clientele and acquiring a reputation for publicising local grievances.

Despite increased participation, many in Fianna Fáil remained intoxicated by the illusion of the 'empty formula' ritual and continued to talk like revolutionaries while acting like politicians. Seán Lemass's oft-quoted Dáil speech demonstrated the extent to which Fianna Fáil was prepared to retain this comforting double-think on the issue of constitutional politics.

> Fianna Fáil is a slightly constitutional party. We are perhaps open to the definition of a constitutional party, but before anything else we are a Republican party. We have adopted the method of political agitation to achieve our end because we believe, in the present circumstances, that method is best in the interests of the nation and of the Republican movement, and for no other reason. Five years ago we were on the defensive, and perhaps in time we may recoup our strength sufficiently to go on the offensive. Our object is to establish a Republican Government in Ireland. If that can be done by the present methods we have, we will be very pleased, but, if not, we would not confine ourselves to them.[163]

Successive Fianna Fáil leaders have attempted to distort the sentiments expressed in this speech. In 1994 the former Taoiseach Charles Haughey stated that by using the term 'slightly constitutional party' Lemass was merely asserting that Fianna Fáil did not fully accept the legitimacy of Constitution of the Irish Free State and that the speech had been misrepresented as articulating an ambivalent approach to the use of force for political ends.[164] When the speech is considered in full, however, it is obvious that Haughey, like many others, was merely refashioning history to suit contemporary realities.

It is clear from Lemass's speech that, according to official Fianna Fáil rhetoric, politics was not an end in itself but was rather a means to achieving an independent republic. The party's adoption of constitutional methods was clearly described as merely tactical and the result of military weakness. Should those methods prove ineffective in attaining the party's objectives, or should republicans acquire additional military resources, constitutional politics could be dropped as quickly as it had been embraced. In essence, the door to violent revolution was, rhetorically at least, left ajar, if only to soothe the collective party conscience.

De Valera also continued to question the state's legitimacy. He told the Dáil in 1929:

I still hold that your right to be regarded as the legitimate government is faulty. There must be somebody in charge to keep order in the community and by virtue of your *de facto* position you are the only people who are in a position to do that. But as to whether you have come to that position legitimately or not, I say that you have not come by that position legitimately. You brought off a *coup d'état* in the Summer of 1922 . . . My proposition [to Sinn Féin] that the representatives of the people should come in here and unify control so that we could have one Government and one Army was defeated, and for that reason I resigned. Those who continued on in that organisation which we have left can claim exactly the same continuity that we claimed up to 1925.[165]

Shortly after de Valera's speech O'Kelly put forward the official Fianna Fáil position on the Free State government in an editorial in the *Nation*.

We entered a faked parliament which we believed in our hearts to be illegitimate and we still believe it; and we faced a junta there which we did not regard as the rightful government of this country. We did not respect, nor do we now, such a government or such a parliament; and we entered the latter with the utmost distress in our hearts . . . Our presence in the 'Dáil' of usurpers is sheer expediency, nothing else.[166]

The 1929 ard-fheis resolved that Fianna Fáil TDs and senators were prohibited from attending social functions promoted by Free State ministers.[167] The original motion had gone further, seeking to prevent party representatives from being present at any event at which Free State ministers were present. De Valera, however, had protested that Fianna Fáil could not be responsible for the presence of others and that if a project was a worthy national one they must be free to express their support for it.[168] Nevertheless, an instinctive disdain for the Free State and its functionaries persisted. Senior civil servants were viewed, in the words of one prominent Fianna Fáil member, as a 'crowd of Free State bastards,'[169] while the Free State itself was habitually referred to as the 'Slave State' or the 'Freak State'.

It was also noted that 'Independence Day' had hitherto 'not only passed off quietly, but uncelebrated, unnoticed and unknown,' and Fianna Fáil feigned surprise that the government had not declared the day the 1921 Treaty was signed, the 6th of December, a national holiday.[170]

In the eyes of membership and leadership alike, Fianna Fáil was not a party: it was a national movement. The most frequently used term was 'organisation', illustrating Fianna Fáil's instinctive dislike for 'parties', which were associated with the ills of 'politics'. Despite its organisational fervour, the party recognised the threat that organisational growth and participation in the Free State parliament might pose to ideological purity and revolutionary integrity. In response to editorial broadsides from *An Phoblacht*, Fianna Fáil acknowledged that the word 'politics' was a word of ill repute in Ireland and attributed this attitude to the historical experience of the Irish people. Politics had excluded 'real Irish nationalism, which is and always was separatism.'

Even when an extended franchise had led to the establishment of a home-rule party and had allowed a more representative sample of politicians to develop, it had also created, with few exceptions, 'men of no very fixed principles.' Long residence in London had weakened their resolve further, and their faith in progress had been stultified by participation in an alien parliament where they were permanently out-numbered. In more recent times 'politics' had led to the Treaty debacle, the Boundary Commission fiasco and the financial surrender of the nation's resources—all threaded together with 'the black cord of continual Coercion Acts.' For Fianna Fáil, history had provided ample testimony of the omnipresent threat of corruption and deradicalisation, and the political set-up in the Ireland of the 1920s was merely an old story with new characters.

> Men who seemed honest, modest mortals, brought into the limelight by what Lloyd George called the fortunes of war and what we call an infamous betrayal, have never recovered from their vertigo: a few hundred pounds a year, a few high-sounding titles of ministers, presidents and the like and they have lost their heads (their swelled heads); and they imagine they are sitting among the gods of the earth who are beyond good and evil. Success has been confused in their minds with honesty and victory with holiness. Might and right were never more mixed up. But their pride in their good conscience will be shaken by their loss of power. Downfall and adversity are great harbingers of clearer insight into the soul.[171]

Despite the failure of previous efforts at political agitation, Fianna Fáil was 'endeavouring to turn the machinery of that Parliament to national uses . . . in so far as that can be done.' Politics, it was argued, could be a benign vocation, and the party hoped to 'take its corruptions away.' Fianna Fáil trenchantly claimed, however, that it would not succumb to deradicalisation, as it was aware of the dangers and treated politics only as a means to an end.

> In this country, or in any country situated as ours, political action can only be a means to an end—simply one of the ways by which the independence of Ireland can be advanced. Parliamentary action is useful to the same degree. While the people wait for the moment when they can free themselves, it is well that one party at least should stand guard over their true national and material interests.[172]

According to one high-ranking party member, Fianna Fáil 'did not want any spoils of office as such' but instead wished 'to clear the honoured name of Ireland and Irish citizenship from the dregs which now dared to speak in Ireland's name.'[173]

The theme of self-sacrifice and honest public service formed an integral part of many Fianna Fáil speeches, particularly at election time. Cumann na nGaedheal was presented as a loose collection of status-obsessed careerists bound together by a common desire to exalt themselves. Fianna Fáil, in contrast, was portrayed as a body of men and women with a record of national service inspired only by a desire to serve and honour Ireland. Party election literature often concluded with the cry 'You are not a jobber or a self-seeker. Vote Fianna Fáil.'[174]

This type of propaganda emphasised the personal characteristics of candidates, and it was peppered with statements claiming that the candidate was someone who had 'ignored the allurements of a lucrative practice in a professional capacity'[175] or whom 'the lure of office and power did not attract... when others wavered.'[176] Elections were never presented as mere contests between rival parities seeking governmental office but involved struggles between 'the bureaucrats and the people' or 'dictatorship versus popular control,'[177] with a vote for Fianna Fáil being a blow 'for Nationalism against Imperialism.'[178]

These statements sought to allay fears that Fianna Fáil was only concerned about creating a new political class whose sole *raison d'être* was to gain office rather than to achieve national objectives. As one editorial in the *Nation* put it,

> on rare occasions only does a subject country get a real opportunity to free herself by arms. In between those rare occasions the independence movement has to strengthen itself by political and economic action, and such action can often bring great gain both to the country and to the cause. The chief danger in using the weapon of politics is that it may come to be regarded by those who use it as an end rather than a means. That would be fatal politically and nationally. But Fianna Fáil is not solely, or primarily even, a parliamentary movement. Politics is not its aim; political life is not its ambition. It is primarily a Republican Party working towards the independence of the whole nation. Its deputies have a greater duty outside the Free State Parliament than in it . . .[179]

It is clear that during its formative years Fianna Fáil displayed ambivalence towards the Free State; it was in the Dáil but not of it. Despite its claim to be 'the Republican Party' it was acutely aware of past precedents and of the predilection of political parties to become institutionalised, no matter how radical their origins or how daring the past revolutionary exploits of its personnel. Fianna Fáil was determined to avoid such a fate but realised that it would have to be vigilant if history was not to repeat itself.

| ELECTION TIME, 1931–2

BODENSTOWN AND THE KILDARE BY-ELECTION

Many in Fianna Fáil expected 1931 to be an election year, and the party would have to tread carefully to appear both republican and responsible, to mobilise and to mollify.

At the end of January, just before a general army convention, the IRA shot Patrick Carroll, a mid-ranking member of its organisation in Dublin. At first no claims of responsibility were made, until eventually, after a number of weeks, the Gardaí broke the silence by announcing that Carroll had been a police informant. Alive to the possibility of suppression orders, *An Phoblacht* had begun a series of articles relating to the fate of informers historically, from 1798 to the Black-and-Tan war, but then merely reported, on 28 February, the admission by the Gardaí of Carroll's work as a police informant.[1] His premature death cut off an important source of information for the Special Branch, which intensified its campaign against republicans.

Days after Carroll's death Superintendent Seán Curtin brought a treason case against IRA members in Co. Tipperary, who were apprehended while drilling.[2] Their acquittal did little to raise spirits amongst the Tipperary Gardaí, and on 20 March Superintendent Curtin sat down to write a report for the head of the Special Branch. He concluded that it would be 'useless to have anything in the nature of a political case ever tried again in this South Riding of Tipperary' and suggested that the jury system be abolished for similar offences.[3]

Two hours after finishing the report Curtin was shot dead outside his house by IRA members.[4] Shock waves reverberated throughout the Garda Síochána, as each member believed that he was a potential victim of 'men who could strike and be reasonably assured of mute witnesses, highly sympathetic juries, and armed colleagues.'[5]

As they had done in the case of Patrick Carroll, Fianna Fáil observed a studied public silence on the killing of Curtin and declined to issue a public condemnation. This stance changed suddenly when the party was subjected to attack from the government and its supporters. At a Cumann na nGaedheal meeting in Mallow Town Hall the Minister for Defence, Desmond FitzGerald, implied that de Valera and Fianna Fáil shared responsibility for Curtin's death.[6] This attack was more bluntly put at the same meeting by a Catholic priest, Archdeacon Corbett, who, on the subject of Fianna Fáil in general and de Valera in particular, declared that

I have no hesitation in saying that by their silence and public defence in the Dáil and at public meetings of various kinds of criminals that they are giving encouragement to it, and so far they are responsible for these murders. I say to the people of Mallow that when the General Election comes round, they should remember what has taken place in these years, and remind Mr. de Valera and his leading followers that he and they are responsible, and that the ghosts of Michael Collins, Kevin O'Higgins and Superintendent Curtin will haunt them at the General Election.[7]

The mention of a general election aroused the Fianna Fáil paper, which in its next edition put forward the most strident condemnation of an IRA action ever articulated by a party organ.

Every Irishman who loves his country and cherishes her honour, every Christian who acknowledges the authority of Divine Law and is conscious of the sacredness of human life, must deplore the murder of Superintendent Curtin. It was not merely an appalling crime; it was an act of utter cowardice.[8]

The editorial questioned Desmond FitzGerald's 'insinuation' that the murder was politically motivated; but, if his claim was true, the act was, 'in its social aspect, all the more heinous and all the more insane.' It then proceeded to make an enigmatic pronouncement on the relationship of politics to physical force.

Political aims have often in history been attained by criminal methods; but always the ultimate consequences, even on the material plane, have been evil.

The implications of such a statement, suggesting as it does a radical reappraisal of past rebellions, are obvious. Although the editorial confined its comments to the post-Treaty period, citing Free State actions against republicans during the Civil War as sole examples of its argument, the ambiguity remained. After stating that crimes such as those committed against republicans at Ballyseedy, Co. Kerry, in 1923 had facilitated the establishment of the Free State, the editorial concluded that

murder, by whomever committed and in whatever cause, will always bring such results in its train. Independence achieved by crime would prove not a blessing but a curse.

This editorial suggested a shift, albeit a subtle one. The IRA was mentioned not once by name: it was the government ministers who were considered the only 'defenders of murder' in the state. Possibly the fear of a snap election had jolted some within the party. Moreover, a crucial by-election was to be held in Co. Kildare within a couple of weeks. This was widely believed to be the last such contest before a general election, and a victory for Fianna Fáil was considered essential in order to raise morale.

The party attempted to widen its potential support, though in the process it risked losing some of its older followers. At the beginning of February, Lemass stated that

Fianna Fáil 'could not be accurately described as either pro-Treaty or anti-Treaty,' its policy being 'to utilise whatever tactical advantages might have been given by the Treaty to secure complete freedom.'⁹ To *An Phoblacht*, such sentiments had a familiar ring. It claimed that the pro-Treaty side had made similar pronouncements during the 1922 election immediately before the 'armed attack on the Republic.' Lemass's updated description of Fianna Fáil policy was unfavourably compared with a speech made on the same day in Navan by Ernest Blythe, who had told his audience that the demand for an Irish republic in 1918 had not been a matter of principle but of expediency.[10]

Any signs of acrimony between Fianna Fáil and the IRA quickly dissipated as Easter approached, with its commemorative gatherings around the country. Two thousand members of the Dublin Brigade of the IRA marched through the city, led by Oscar Traynor of Fianna Fáil, who was accompanied by 'officers from the period 1916–1931.'[11] This was followed by the highlight of the republican year, the parade to the grave of Irish republicanism's founding father, Theobald Wolfe Tone, in Bodenstown, Co. Kildare.[12] Bodenstown was also a time for meeting old friends, a time of reflection and of rejuvenation.

Despite the recent condemnations, Fianna Fáil members were present *en masse* at the Wolfe Tone commemoration of 1931. 'Every Republican must be there,' the *Nation* proclaimed, and over four weeks the times of the special trains to Sallins (the station for Bodenstown) were published in the paper. Members were urged to form local commemorative committees and to contact Michael Price, then on the IRA Army Council, for further information.[13] In a message to all Fianna Fáil cumainn the honorary secretaries, Seán Lemass and Gerry Boland, stressed the importance of securing a large attendance at the republican demonstration.

> As all Cumann Secretaries have already been informed, it is intended to make the demonstration this year an outstanding event in the history of the Republican movement. The attendance and demeanour of a large contingent of Fianna Fáil members will clearly demonstrate that the cause to which Wolfe Tone devoted his life still claims the unswerving allegiance of the patriotic manhood and womanhood of the country, and that our determination to win victory for that cause has, if possible, merely grown stronger with the passage of the years.[14]

The IRA also called for a mobilisation of republicans throughout the country and noted with satisfaction that the cumulative effect of the organising committees' work was 'to strike terror into the Cosgrave Government.'[15]

The preparations did indeed worry government ministers, who feared that the event might be the launching-pad for an all-out assault on the state. On the night before the commemoration Desmond FitzGerald issued a written order to the Great Southern Railways Company demanding the cancellation of all trains to Sallins. Then, between midnight and one o'clock, the Special Branch arrested the secretary of the Wolfe Tone Commemoration Organising Committee, Michael Price, and the IRA adjutant-general, Seán Russell, who was to give the oration.[16] Railway stations were occupied by the army, and there was a strong police presence at Bodenstown. Despite these measures, ten thousand people managed to make their way to Wolfe Tone's grave, overwhelming the police contingent.

Considering subsequent developments in relations between Fianna Fáil and the IRA, a glance at the order of procession, advertised in Fianna Fáil literature, is enlightening. The march was led by the 1st Battalion of the Dublin Brigade of the IRA, followed by the Workers' Union of Ireland Brass and Reed Band. Then came the 2nd, 3rd, 4th and 5th Battalions of the Dublin Brigade, followed by battalions from eighteen counties, accompanied by Cumann na mBan, Fianna Éireann and the Women's Prisoners' Defence League.

Amid all these IRA battalions and ancillary groups was a sizeable Fianna Fáil contingent led by Éamon de Valera.[17] The IRA leader Peadar O'Donnell—an unlikely substitute for Russell, given his decidedly socialist leanings—delivered a fiery grave-side oration, the tone of which J. Bowyer Bell has vividly captured.

> O'Donnell, the greatest agitator of his generation, gave them what they wanted to hear. To those who listened, Cosgrave and the Treatyites seemed to have entered the twilight, for the dawn of radical Republicanism was at hand. The country could take no more of the safe men—unemployment had soared, wages were low, emigration was no longer a solution, and somehow, the walk from Sallins to Bodenstown would be continued on up the high road to the Republic. Off to one side, listening to the soaring words of O'Donnell and testing the seething enthusiasm of the crowd, stood de Valera and the Fianna Fáil delegation, 'waiting in the wings.'[18]

The machinery of state, north and south, O'Donnell declared, was fulfilling a common objective: beating down the masses to 'make them the slaves of the exploiting interests of our imperial masters.' The condition of workers, the suppression of republicanism and the poverty of farmers forced to pay the British government for the right to till their own land were evidence of the malign character of the state, which was composed of 'bailiffs, jails, thugs, touts, police [and] soldiers.' Their state was a machine that republicans had to destroy. 'All the power that is in their hands we must take into our hands, and in that final phase we must be prepared to meet force with force.'[19]

The reins of power were indeed slipping from Cumann na nGaedheal's grasp, and within months they would be eagerly taken up by a Fianna Fáil government. What de Valera thought of O'Donnell's characterisation of the state machine that Fianna Fáil would soon control is a matter of conjecture. The party did, however, describe the occasion as 'one of the greatest tributes ever offered to Wolfe Tone's memory,' and it berated the government for blocking the trains to it.[20] The Free State government, of course, also paid homage to Wolfe Tone and claimed to be the political heir of the United Irishmen; but the *Nation* contrasted the government and republican commemorations and claimed that Wolfe Tone would have preferred the one attended by the common people.[21]

Solid evidence of increasing support for Fianna Fáil came in the form of a by-election victory in Co. Kildare shortly after the Wolfe Tone commemoration. The condemnation of Curtin's murder was modified greatly in 'Kildare's opportunity', a remarkable by-election editorial. Cosgrave's government was accused of creating 'mythical dangers' in the form of the IRA, from which it was necessary to protect the people, when it was the government's anti-national policies that constituted the 'very real dangers.' Referring to the IRA, it continued:

> If there is anything which Irish history has placed beyond all doubt it is that there will always be Irishmen prepared to do all and to risk all to achieve the independence of their country. When Pearse said that there would be no peace without freedom, it was no empty rhetoric but the literal truth . . . In the future, as it has done in the past, it will destroy every party that opposes or ignores it. Mr. Cosgrave and his colleagues, in defiance of their tradition and their personal experience, have set themselves against this force. Assuredly, it will break them.[22]

During the election campaign Cumann na nGaedheal concentrated again on the constitutional *bona fides* of Fianna Fáil. Ernest Blythe spoke of midnight murders, of terrorism during the coming general election and of the 'Mexican regime' that would follow a Fianna Fáil victory.[23] Meanwhile the June issue of the Cumann na nGaedheal paper, the *Star*, attempted to draw comparisons between the republican government of Spain and the likely nature of a Fianna Fáil government in Ireland.[24] These claims had been strengthened by the conveniently timed discovery of an arms dump in the Kildare constituency, which received considerable publicity and was used to demonstrate the dangers confronting the Free State. To Fianna Fáil it appeared that 'all the old stage props' had been dragged out for the election, with 'the "terrorist" bogey and the British bogey' taking pride of place.[25]

Fianna Fáil stressed the revolutionary credentials of its candidate, who had marched from Maynooth to participate in the 1916 Rising.[26] Moreover, its paper pushed to the forefront the twin issues of the land annuities and political prisoners.[27] For these reasons Fianna Fáil presented the election as something much more than a contest of party candidates. 'The contest in Kildare is not one of parties nor of political organisations, it is a conflict of two opposing ideas, a struggle between two fundamentally different philosophies.' This contest was simplified into a struggle of 'dictatorship versus popular control.' When the party candidate, Thomas Harris, emerged triumphant, Fianna Fáil interpreted the vote as a victory of 'Nationalism against Imperialism' and felt that for Cosgrave it was 'a notice to quit from a long-suffering people.'[28]

SAOR ÉIRE AND THE GOVERNMENT RESPONSE
During the later part of the 1920s the republican leadership shifted progressively to the left. This can be partly explained by the dire economic circumstances endured by the traditional republican supporters: small farmers, farm labourers and petty bourgeoisie. The global recession that followed the Wall Street Crash of 1929 hit the poorer sections of Irish society disproportionately. Economic hardship was exacerbated by an American embargo on immigrants in 1929 (Ireland's emigration rate was among the highest in Europe, and more than 80 per cent of emigrants opted

for the United States).[29] Those who entered the United States between 1929 and 1932 often found that economic opportunities were no better in the 'land of the free' and returned home, bitter and disillusioned. The circumstances that existed between 1929 and 1931 were not unlike those during the First World War, when traditional emigration routes were cut off, resulting in increased militancy among those who remained and contributing to the revolutionary climate that culminated in the 1916 Rising.[30]

The most important example of political cross-fertilisation between Fianna Fáil and the IRA was undoubtedly the land annuities campaign. Under Peadar O'Donnell's powerful guidance the IRA had involved itself in a concerted campaign aimed at withholding the land annuities collected by the Free State and paid to the British as a 'debt of honour'.[31] The poorer western counties were the focal point of the agitation, and throughout the summer of 1928 O'Donnell was in and out of prison, the victim of an elaborate cat-and-mouse operation. When the Gardaí eventually preferred charges against him, O'Donnell told the jury that, as the land annuities campaign was part of a vast IRA conspiracy, he should be acquitted, which he duly was.

In Galway the IRA seized the government files on annuities defaulters, thus blocking the progress of seizures. Senator Maurice Moore was the first prominent Fianna Fáil member to throw in his lot with the campaign,[32] and he was followed by the TDs Frank Fahy and Hugo Flinn in Galway. Resolutions calling for the retention of annuities were adopted by numerous county councils (those dominated by Fianna Fáil).[33] Many ordinary Fianna Fáil members threw themselves into the campaign with barely contained enthusiasm, while party elders realised that if they could stay on the right side of the law there was much to be gained. 'Don't you see,' Lemass told O'Donnell, 'that we stand to gain from your organisation so long as we cannot be accused of causing the turmoil.'[34] The electoral advantage to be derived from the issue was also emphasised. 'We are confident,' the honorary secretaries told the 1929 ard-fheis, 'that the Free State Party will be defeated on this single issue.'[35]

The reasons for Fianna Fáil's agrarian radicalism and the pivotal role of small farmers in de Valera's Arcadian vision were not solely ideological. Defeat in the Civil War meant that

> the hopes and dreams of radical land reformers, the articulate leaders and the desperate landless men of the west and south-west, could not be realised. The reality was the Free State, with the Cumann na nGaedheal government in office.[36]

Like Sinn Féin in 1923, Fianna Fáil's electoral support in its first general election in June 1927 had come mainly from the west, where small farmers were most numerous.[37]

Some of de Valera's most ardent supporters believed passionately in the cause of land distribution, which would deprive 'ranchers' of their large estates devoted primarily to cattle-rearing. Agrarian radicals believed that this system, whereby a relatively small number of people enjoyed the luxury of 'watching cows' tails grow,' was wasteful and should be replaced with more labour-intensive tillage. Accordingly, the *Mayo News* declared:

The spoken and written statements of Éamon de Valera, our great chief, openly and candidly convey to the ranchers that this state of things which keeps our people in poverty must end, as a consequence they are putting forth every effort to defeat him. Those men who lock up God's storehouse have the acres, but they have not the votes.[38]

The 1932 election was to demonstrate the truth of this maxim.

Allied to the IRA's leftward shift was the fact that a significant part of the republican leadership was becoming more internationalist in outlook.[39] The supposed link between the IRA and the Soviet Union caused the government most anxiety and constituted the main justification for tougher security legislation.

The link with communist, 'atheistic' Russia went back further than most Free State ministers would probably have cared to recall. The first Dáil, after all, had sanctioned a visit to Soviet Russia in 1920 by Patrick McCartan, who took the pro-Treaty side in the ensuing division.[40] In 1925 an IRA delegation comprising Gerry Boland, Seán Russell and Pa Murray travelled to Moscow (with forged passports) in an effort to procure weapons, though to no avail. Despite this setback the IRA army convention of 1927 resolved that in the event of a war between Britain and the Soviet Union—which was considered possible at the time—the IRA would support the USSR. It is unlikely that this decision altered Stalin's assessment of the military odds confronting the Soviet Union, nor is it likely that the resolution was influenced by an ideological solidarity between the Soviet Union and the IRA, as 'outside the few articulate men of the Left, the major factor was that any enemy of Britain's was a friend of Ireland's.'[41] In the summer of 1928 the IRA reached an agreement with the Soviet government, which promised to train thirty officers, an arrangement vehemently condemned by the Clan na nGael leader, Joe McGarrity. Once again the initiative came to nothing, as British intelligence was alerted to the plan. Eager to avoid a conflict with the western powers, the Soviet government sent home the few IRA officers who had made it to the Soviet Union.[42]

So much was made of these tenuous links between the IRA and the Soviet Union that the government gave the impression that when Stalin awoke each morning his first thoughts were of how to subvert the small Catholic Irish Free State. Interestingly, Cosgrave had also refused to entertain private plans to give Trotsky political asylum in Ireland.[43]

A secret Department of Justice report compiled in August 1931 gives a fascinating insight into government thinking and reveals its determination to intensify the confrontation with the republican movement.[44] The report, which stated that the IRA 'asserts itself to be the Government of the State,' estimated the organisation's strength at 1,300 officers and 3,500 rank and file (a distinction that did not really exist in the IRA). The Gardaí knew the names, addresses and ranks of all the principal IRA figures, but they found themselves unable to 'bring them to justice.' Recognising the IRA's continuity, the department noted that 'this organisation is the direct descendent of the armed forces that opposed the Free State Army in 1922/3: the succession of Headquarter Officers has never been broken.'[45] The IRA had become increasingly audacious and tended 'to emerge from hiding and to establish itself in the public eye as an open rival to Government authority.'[46]

Implicit in the report's synopsis on the banned Bodenstown commemoration was a strong criticism of Fianna Fáil's performance.

> Elaborate advertisements of a parade of i.r.a. troops, to be held at Bodenstown on 21 June last, with military nomenclature and in military order, appeared in the public press, and the Government's decision to prevent this open breach of the law was criticised in certain circles as if the authorised Defence Forces of the State and the i.r.a. were merely rival bodies equally entitled to parade in public and between which it was unfair for Government to draw any distinction.[47]

As a reprisal for the government's attempts to ban the Bodenstown gathering the IRA had attempted to prohibit meetings that it considered undesirable, such as athletic meetings organised by the Gardaí. These efforts, which also included interference with Orange Order meetings in Cos. Cavan and Leitrim, were 'mainly successful,' according to the report.[48] The document contrasted the 'leniency of the Government policy' with that of its opponents, who only sought to exploit such latitude to further undermine the state.[49]

The report also noted unfavourably that IRA drilling had been resumed with increased vigour and publicity and that newspapers had been guilty of augmenting their reporting of these activities. In particular, the public drillings were provocatively reported by *An Phoblacht,*

> which encourages and defends the activities of the Irish Republican Army (including murder) and denies the authority of the Government set up and maintained by the people of the Free State in accordance with the Constitution and by the exercise of the free votes of the entire adult population. It refers to that Government as a usurping Government of British Ministers, in league with the British Government against the Irish people, and it treats the police as unscrupulous men hired to suppress Irish national feeling and to persecute patriots. This paper is bought and sold openly in newspaper shops and is largely read by young people. It is impossible to realise the cumulative force of its constant incitements to violence . . .[50]

The activity of various women's organisations also merited attention, as did a number of communist groups, many of whose members were considered to be also IRA members. The report cited evidence of a widespread intimidation campaign that had put the police in a 'hopeless position'. Because of the non-cooperation of the civilian population they could not obtain any evidence in court, and on the rare occasion on which they could jurors refused to act on it. In the areas worst affected, such as Cos. Kerry and Tipperary, people were 'afraid to be seen speaking to the police.'[51]

Information—the essential tool of any counter-insurgency campaign—had dried up. Republican suspects refused to answer questions under interrogation, and this was a policy 'which ordinary citizens imitate through fear.'[52] The only source of information was that obtained from police informers within organisations, who could not be produced as witnesses in court lest their lives be imperilled and their usefulness ended. In essence, the report bemoaned, 'any person charged with con-spiring to overthrow the State by violence who refuses to plead and adopts a contemptuous attitude to the Court is practically certain of acquittal.'[53]

When the police had sought to pre-empt operations through surveillance and the frequent searching and detention of well-known IRA figures, this policy was defeated when suspects appealed to the courts (which they otherwise did not recognise) to secure their rights as citizens of the state that they were dedicated to overthrowing.[54] Inevitably, this situation led to frustration. While the report stated that 'to enter on an unauthorised and secret system of reprisals' could not be countenanced, it felt that the situation prevailing, which included the killing of members of the police with impunity, 'must impose an undue strain on the discipline and self control of their comrades.'[55]

Everything in the report suggested the need for a fundamental revision of security legislation. The statistics were at the ready—only the timing was in question, and that was decided when, the following month, a new IRA-sponsored body, Saor Éire, announced its formation.

In retrospect it is interesting to note that the report devoted only fourteen lines to those organisations whose object was 'the bringing about in this country of a revolution on the lines of the Russian Revolution . . . a "working class republic".' As the ostensible reason for the government's security campaign from October 1931 up to the general election the following February was the threat of a communist takeover, it appears that this section was magnified and exaggerated for effect. In inaugurating yet another anti-republican crusade to protect the state, Cumann na nGaedheal was selling a familiar but somewhat stale product. By painting the product red and attach-ing to it a new name—Saor Éire—it could hope that the campaign might awaken the public to the revolutionary threat in its midst while revitalising the electoral prospects of the now-faltering Cumann na nGaedheal.

Saor Éire held its inaugural congress on 26–7 September at the Iona Hall in Drumcondra, Dublin, having had its previous bookings at the Peacock and Abbey Theatres cancelled at very short notice (a whisper in the proprietors' ear being as effective as an official order).[56] The conference elected a National Executive[57] and issued a declaration, delivered by Seán MacBride, which stated:

> All those who have passed into the services of the State machine have betrayed the Irish cause. We must build on those alone who are being crushed by it and who alone have the will and the power to smash it. It will not be dismantled from the top: it cannot be geared to explode slowly: a change of drivers is no good, for it is the same machine with the same nature and the same tasks. On the ruin of their State we must build ours . . .[58]

As Saor Éire was dedicated to fulfilling the aims of James Connolly, it was appropriate that among the 127 delegates were one of the executed leader's daughters, Nora, and his son, Roddy. A detailed policy document was produced, which dealt with such issues as the distribution of agricultural workers, banking, industry, fishing, emigration, housing, unemployment and social conditions.[59]

Almost immediately rumours began to circulate that the government intended introducing new legislation to counteract the activities of republican and communist organisations. The *Irish Independent* reported that several members of the Oireachtas had been warned by visitors to their homes that they would vote for the bill at their peril.[60] Whatever the truth of the matter, Cumann na nGaedheal seized on the reports, claiming that they only bolstered the government's case for introducing tougher legislation.[61] Ministers, parliamentary secretaries and others identified with the main-tenance of government functions had for many years been under the protection of a special corps drawn from the Free State army. Now the government ordered every deputy and senator considered to be at risk from subversive intimidation to be afforded police protection.[62] It was also reported that steps were taken to reinforce the Special Branch, and a number of former army officers were invited to join.[63]

Represented among those condemning the new legislation were members of the artistic community, including the writers Austin Clarke, Liam O'Flaherty and Francis Stuart. Jack B. Yeats described 'the proposed Coercion Bill' as 'both hateful and stupid.'[64] A number of county councils and other public bodies passed condemnatory resolutions.[65]

Fianna Fáil was to the forefront in proposing votes of censure during meetings of local authority bodies. A flavour of these debates can be found in the deliberations of the Westmeath Board of Health, assembled to discuss a motion protesting against 'the Coercion Bill, which is threatened to be imposed on this country' and would lead to 'universal turmoil.' Having failed to have the motion ruled out of order, the Cumann na nGaedheal TD Patrick Shaw asked members whether they agreed that 'there must be only one army under State control' and that such legislation was necessary to deal with 'extremists . . . determined to take up arms.' The chairman of the board, M. J. Kennedy TD (Fianna Fáil), replied that 'so long as Ireland is not free men will be found to fight for freedom, and no Coercion Bill will stop them.'[66] Such statements led one government deputy, Dermot 'Gun' O'Mahony, to claim that Fianna Fáil constituted the greatest threat to the institutions of the state,[67] while another enquired whether it was the case that 'all these protesting councillors have secret armouries and are afraid of being found out, their arms confiscated, and themselves locked up.'[68]

The Constitution (Amendment No. 17) Act (1931) inserted a new article 2a in the Constitution of the Irish Free State, which established the Constitution (Special Powers) Tribunal—commonly called the military tribunal—composed of five army officers not below the rank of commandant appointed by the Executive Council.[69] Every sitting of the tribunal would be attended by three of these officers, and majority decisions would be adequate for the passing of sentences.[70] The tribunal would not be bound by the sentences prescribed by ordinary law but would have the power to impose greater punishment, including the death penalty, 'if in the opinion of the Tribunal, such greater punishment is necessary or expedient.'[71] No order, conviction or sentence of the tribunal could be appealed, nor could their validity be challenged by any other court.[72] It declared that 'no coroner's inquest shall be held in relation to a death occasioned by the execution of a sentence of death pronounced by the Tribunal.'[73] No action, civil or criminal, could be taken against any member or official of the tribunal 'for any actions taken in the performance of duty.'[74] In case all possible contingencies had not been adequately covered, it was stated that if the new article conflicted with any other article of the Constitution the new one would prevail, so sheltering the government from any challenge through the courts.

The act became a detailed addition to the Constitution; indeed the new article 2a was longer than all other articles of the Constitution combined. In every aspect the new legislation followed the logic of the Department of Justice report two months earlier. Moreover, it gave Eoin O'Duffy, the Garda Commissioner, the powers he had long sought to launch an all-out campaign against republicans, without the restrictions that constitutional niceties imposed. As O'Duffy and his political masters saw it, the IRA and republicans generally were bent on overthrowing the state but had been protected by the rights afforded them under the Constitution. O'Duffy had put forward a simple plan to the Executive Council in his most recent report: 'The Oireachtas can assist the police by legislation and the Bench can assist by exemplary punishment—by making an example of any person before it.'[75] The plan had now been put into operation, and the gloves were off.

The number of organisations outlawed by the act—twelve in all, including Saor Éire and the IRA—illustrated the breadth with which the description 'anti-state' was being applied.[76] Provision was made for additions to this list, and it was declared that 'the opinion of the Executive Council' would be 'conclusive evidence' in determining whether or not an organisation was an unlawful association. It was clear also that the wide application of the powers to include so many groups under the title 'illegal organisation' was aimed as much at quashing political opposition as it was at thwarting anti-state revolutionaries. The Women's Prisoners' Defence League, headed by the 87-year-old Charlotte Despard, according to the Department of Justice's secret report had only twenty members.[77] It took a highly sensitive government to believe that such a body had to be outlawed to protect the state.

FIANNA FÁIL OPPOSITION WITHIN THE DÁIL

When putting the new bill before the Dáil, Cosgrave said that it had been the aim of his government to devote its energies to the urgent task of economic reconstruction but that this task had been rendered almost impossible 'because of the existence in this country of the menace, never altogether removed, of unconstitutional action and revolt.' Cosgrave's depiction of the alternatives to the bill had a Hobbesian quality to them: the government must have the powers it sought or anarchy would prevail. Responding to suggestions that the proposed legislation was unnecessary, he claimed that one had only to read

the principal organ of the conspiracy, the weekly paper calling itself 'An Phoblacht' which, week in and week out, preaches the doctrines of the conspirators; that the true Government of the State is vested in the Army Council of the Irish Republican Army; that the Oireachtas is a mere cover or instrument for British usurpation; that the police and the Courts maintained by us have no moral authority, and that the murder of any State servant is a perfectly proper procedure, and is, in fact, the only immediately practicable step towards a Republic. These doctrines are preached with a directness, with a continuous incitement to violence and crime, which I do not believe has a parallel in any other State in the world.[78]

It was the aims of organisations such as the IRA and Saor Éire, as much as their specific activities, that perturbed the government. That an armed organisation was actively dedicated to overthrowing political institutions was the only justification that any government required. This point was later echoed by the Minister for Education, Prof. John Marcus O'Sullivan, who said that it was not the number of crimes that was the issue but the fact that they were the product of a conspiracy aimed at destroying the state.[79] Cosgrave quoted extensively from various issues of *An Phoblacht,* noting that it boasted a readership three times that of any other weekly paper, and he claimed that 'it is certain that it has a considerable circulation among young men.'[80] He also devoted particular attention to Cumann na mBan, which he claimed had taken 'a large part in the campaign of terrorisation and in the breakdown of the judicial system.'[81] Its systematic attack on the courts had been 'a complete success,'[82] and affiliated to Cumann na mBan were 'various other organisations of women with the same general objectives.'[83]

At times the debate deviated considerably from contemporary matters, and the embers of Civil War bitterness were fanned by both sides. The Vice-President of the Executive Council, Ernest Blythe, made little of the seventy-seven IRA men executed during the Civil War and claimed that 'if the matter had been dealt with anything like according to rule, there would have been ten or twenty times that number.'[84] Referring to the same policy, Cosgrave turned to the Fianna Fáil benches and said that 'there are a great many people over there who are very lucky.'[85]

Fianna Fáil's objections to the bill took many forms. It claimed that there was no crisis, that if there was it was the government's fault, and that the government was introducing the legislation to manufacture a climate of fear so as to secure re-election. Several speakers, including de Valera,[86] denied that the IRA was a secret organisation, though the counter-argument was one unlikely to appeal to the government.

> There is no secret conspiracy to overthrow existing institutions. Everybody in this house and everybody in the country knows just as well as the President and his Ministers that there is an organisation in this country whose object is to achieve the independence of Ireland through arms. It is not a secret organisation. It has never pretended to be. It has been an open organisation all along.[87]

De Valera admonished the government for dealing with what he called the results rather than the causes of political strife. He argued that the ordinary law was 'quite sufficient' and that there were already on the statute book six Public Safety Acts, three Firearms Acts, three Enforcement of Law Acts, four Jury Acts, a Treasonable Offences Act and a Protection of the Community Act—all introduced on the pretext that they would finally quell insurrectionary republicanism. He believed that the Executive Council knew the proper way to proceed but that it 'preferred to imitate the activities of Hamar Greenwood.'

> The Ministers opposite know only one way . . . Anyone who gets in your path, 'Squelch them, by God, squelch them,' as Carlyle said of Ireland. That is the only

policy apparently that the Executive Council knows how to put into operation . . . Force is the easy remedy to take: take a stick to hit somebody on the head who doesn't agree with you . . . That method would be successful for a time. The British Government had been successful for a time, but it never ultimately succeeded. The arguments that would be put up to young men to join the organisations mentioned would be a repetition of those put by Mr. Blythe and Mr. Mulcahy when they were asking the young men of the country to join the IRB. They were then asking these young men to stand up against the constituted authority. The British had maintained that they were the constituted authority, and these two gentlemen had bound themselves to oppose this established authority of the day.[88]

These statements contrasted with others made by de Valera during the opening day of the debate. Amid the condemnations he slipped in a passage that diverged greatly from previous statements. With the confidence of one who was merely repeating long-standing policy, he declared that

we here on these benches have never been slow to point out that we do not stand for crime. We have never been slow to point that out. I said long before we came into the Dáil that whatever might be said there was no authority outside this house that was entitled to take human life. We said that and we hold by that. We go even further and say that if there is no authority in this house to rule then there is no authority in any part of the country to rule—I mean in any part of the Twenty-six Counties.[89]

He claimed, somewhat audaciously, that his views on the Dáil's legitimacy had been misrepresented and that he was clarifying his position for the benefit of those who had misinterpreted his statements. He also put a new retrospective gloss on the reasoning behind Fianna Fáil's entry to the Dáil in 1927. 'Our principle was that majority rule by the elected Parliamentary representatives of the people was to be accepted. We stand by that. There was no other policy.'[90]

These statements were qualified somewhat by his depiction of the government as the benefactors of a *coup d'état*,[91] despite the fact that it had succeeded in securing majority support in the Dáil after four consecutive elections. When reminded by one government deputy of his maxim, declared during the Civil War, that the majority had no right to do wrong, de Valera replied that he still maintained that 'the doing of wrong is never right, no matter by whom it is done.'[92]

The Minister for Justice, James Fitzgerald-Kenney, spoke for many when he described de Valera's statement on the Dáil's authority as 'new' and 'remarkable.' If earlier speeches made in the Dáil had been misinterpreted they had been mis-interpreted by every member, and it was a pity that de Valera had allowed that 'misinterpretation' to go unchecked and unchallenged, though it had, according to de Valera himself, been quoted in the Dáil on several occasions.

I am glad now that Deputy de Valera has made it perfectly clear and definite that this Oireachtas here is the sole law-making power in this State, that this Oireachtas has got the authority of the people and that no persons outside have got any moral justification in challenging the right of the Oireachtas.[93]

Others were less sure where exactly de Valera stood. One deputy claimed that in the course of his speech de Valera leader had taken 'one step forward and then the other foot back.'[94]

One of the most militant contributions from the Fianna Fáil benches was that of Tommy Mullins, a future general secretary of the party, who announced that he was a member of four of the organisations the government proposed to outlaw.[95] He began by claiming that the Dáil was participating in 'the funeral of the Constitution.' He then quoted from that week's copy of *An Phoblacht*, which stated in its editorial that 'the enemy want a rising. Only thus can they behead the rising struggle and get a new lease of office.' *An Phoblacht*, Mullins claimed, had answered 'clearly and lucidly every allegation of the President and other Ministerial speakers.' He recalled that in October 1922,

> when it was in the interests of this Government to suppress opposition to the existing institutions . . . a most significant meeting of the Catholic Hierarchy was held in Maynooth and two days after this Execution Bill was passed by the Provisional Government to execute the bodies of those who stood out against it in arms, a similar Execution Bill was passed by Maynooth to execute their souls.[96]

Mullins claimed that the Free State government was 'adopting the very same methods and instruments as the British government adopted in this country for nearly three hundred years,' and he asked in strident terms:

> Has the Government not learned any lesson from the experience of the super-coercionists who ruled for Britain directly here for the last three hundred years? Have they not taken note of the ultimate result of their policies? Have they not taken the lesson that the more Coercion Bills are introduced, the more attempts are made to kill the spirit of Irish liberty, the more determined that spirit will be, the stronger the backbone will become and the more dangerous that ideal of one Ireland and free will become to the existing institution? Has not the Government taken any notice of that, or do they think that they are such supermen that they can crush what seven hundred years of British rule failed to crush? You will never kill by secret courts the desire in the hearts of the young men of this country to achieve its freedom.[97]

Mullins concluded by reiterating Fianna Fáil's conviction that the proposed legislation was a thinly veiled attempt to create a political environment conducive to securing the re-election of Cumann na nGaedheal. It had no right to create a panic, he declared, nor had it the right to use its power 'to destroy the idealism of these young men . . . The ideal of an Irish Republic will outlive you, and those who believe in that Republic will outlast your political careers.'[98]

With de Valera recoiling, perhaps, from an endorsement by such a person as Fitzgerald-Kenney, his speech on the second day of the debate was marked by his praise for—and understanding of—the position of armed republicans. He was not, even at this late stage and with an election on the horizon, able to overcome the ambivalence towards the IRA that permeated Fianna Fáil. As far as the calibre of IRA volunteers was concerned, he declared that while they were 'misguided and unreasonable, if you like,' they were 'at least brave men, and let us not deny them the respect that we should have for the brave.'[99]

> Every one of us who was in that movement—I am not talking of some of these men—this man today [Patrick McGilligan] who talked of himself as a democrat first: he admitted that he was in the national movement by accident. I am not appealing to these men. They have never felt the sentiment. I am talking to the men who understood it, who went out and braved everything in order to try and achieve the things that were intended, who tried to arm themselves when there were just the very same appeals for order, the very same appeal for respect for established authority. When all these appeals were made these men went out. They stood against it all. They were outcasts in their own country. They stood against it all because they hoped that some day those arms might be useful to win, as they put it, a crown for Dark Rosaleen. It is the same thought that is at the back of the minds of the young men who are driven mad by the attitude or want of understanding [by the government].[100]

Not content with victory, the government, de Valera maintained, was attempting to make the IRA 'pass under the yoke . . . to humiliate them.' Animated by 'mean motives,' they would not be content until they had forced the IRA into submission.

> These are the men who are being hounded, these are the men who are being driven, without the slightest attempt to understand their motives . . . which are, in themselves, noble and good—the desire to have the complete independence of their country . . . These men are to be condemned to death, condemned to the treatment we have been told of by Deputy Boland and to the treatment we know was served out to a number of other such people during the [Civil] War. They are to be taken into those secret tribunals and maltreated and nobody is to hear a word about it, and nobody is to be allowed to raise his voice in protest. That is the situation.[101]

De Valera also sought to defend the executions of spies and collaborators within the republican movement. Though an organisation open to all who accepted its aims, the IRA had by necessity to operate at some level in secret. The government, he declared, had sent *'agents provocateurs'* into the IRA, who suffered the retribution of those 'who were unfaithful to the promises or to the pledges of secrecy.'[102]

De Valera's sidestepping of both constitutionalism and physical-force republicanism attracted the attention of government ministers. What did he mean, they asked, when he compared the methods of the Free State government to those of the British regime if he did not mean that people were entitled to overthrow the Free State as they had the British government? Fitzgerald-Kenney rebuked Fianna Fáil for defending the IRA.

They can come out and say boldly, 'We will have no more of this gun work.' But deputies opposite make excuses for gunmen and say, 'We do not regard them as criminals: they do not regard themselves as criminals.' What are they? Crime is not a subjective thing. Crime does not consist of what a man thinks. Crime is the breaking of the law of the country, just the same as the breaking of the law of God. It is no use for a person to say, 'I am not sinning' when he is. Sin is not a subjective thing. The breaking of the law is sin.[103]

Fianna Fáil contested this definition, along with Fitzgerald-Kenney's claim that Fianna Fáil's duty was to plead with armed individuals to hand in their weapons. They would be handing in their arms 'to the gunmen,' a Fianna Fáil deputy replied.[104]

Desmond FitzGerald described de Valera's speech as 'one of the most dishonest, blackguardly and subversive' he had ever heard. The government, he claimed, had received its authority 'not from the people but from God.'

We have the power of life and death because God has given it to us. He has not given it to the people outside any more than He gave it to Deputy de Valera from 1922 to 1926 . . . There are arms all over the country in dumps, many of them placed by Deputy de Valera and his friends . . .[105]

But it was the duality of de Valera's statements, their inherent ambiguity, that Fitzgerald-Kenney found most infuriating.

I know his way of making two speeches in one and challenging anybody who quotes him at any time during the debates that that was not the meaning of the speech but it had another meaning. If one of the murderers had been in this house while Deputy de Valera was speaking he would be moved with emotion and sentiment at his own heroism in continuing these murders. There were other times when if somebody had just come into this house he would have thought that Deputy de Valera was the arch-supporter of constitutionalism . . .[106]

Paddy Hogan also decried what he felt was de Valera's duplicity. 'No-one knows what he means,' Hogan asserted during a heated exchange before describing de Valera as 'the most inveterate pettifogger that ever troubled this country.'[107] He claimed that de Valera had followed a consistent line since 1921.

On the one hand he will play up to the gunmen and on the other hand he will mouth vague morality . . . Remember this . . . bacteria will breed in a fetid atmosphere only. It is that sort of pettifogging, double-dealing, confusing morality, confusing moral constitutionalism and physical force, that has created the atmosphere that makes it possible for that sort of bacteria to breed that was responsible for the murder of Curtin and Ryan, and if there is one man in this country more than another responsible for these murders it is the leader of the party opposite.[108]

As de Valera had talked of being the next leader of government, Hogan declared, 'the country was entitled to know beforehand which set of principles he was going to adhere to when he was challenged by the gunmen.'[109]

After listening to de Valera's contribution to the debate one was likely to be confused about where exactly he stood on fundamental issues, and it was a confusion reflected in the discordant sounds that came from the Fianna Fáil benches. A multiplicity of views was expressed by different deputies, from Gerry Boland's new-found abhorrence of 'gunmen' to Tommy Mullins's fulsome praise. There was a duality in the contradictory positions of deputies on republicanism, constitutionalism and armed resistance to the state. This dichotomy stemmed from the fact that de Valera had two audiences, and his tune changed abruptly according to which audience he hoped was listening. The IRA, which was dedicated to the destruction of the Free State, was composed of people 'animated with honest motives,'[110] and he spoke highly of 'those beautiful sentiments and honourable ambitions of these young men.'[111] However, during one brief passage he had stated without equivocation, for the first time, that the Dáil Éireann that met in Leinster House was the only legitimate power in Ireland. Armed with the knowledge that an election would be called soon, de Valera was eager to attract the largest possible constituency.

None who participated in the Dáil debate ever felt that the result was in doubt. The bill passed all stages in three days. Immediately after the Seanad's approval, on 17 October 1931, the Executive Council met, and the President announced that the bill 'had received the King's assent and was now law.'[112] Accordingly, the government declared that parts II to V of the act were in force, as 'circumstances existed which rendered it expedient.'[113]

The legal formalities having been disposed of, it was now time for the Catholic hierarchy to take centre stage.

THE PASTORAL LETTER

Some weeks before the formal establishment of Saor Éire, Cosgrave had been assiduously cultivating the Catholic hierarchy with a view to securing its endorsement of the planned anti-republican crusade. On 18 August 1931 he spoke in some detail to Cardinal MacRory and outlined his fears of an impending communist revolution that would destroy both church and state. This memorandum was personally handed to Cardinal MacRory in Armagh on 11 September, accompanied by a letter from Cosgrave that implored the cardinal to use the influence and authority of the church to aid the state in its latest endeavour.

Cosgrave claimed that the Executive Council was now confronted with 'a completely new situation' with the spread of new subversive doctrines, and he believed that 'the influence of the Church alone will be able to prevail in the struggle against them.'[114] He also felt that the church could bring powerful influence to bear on those who, 'by unreasonable or uninformed criticism of State institutions and State servants,' had contributed to 'preparing the ground for the spread of the doctrines mentioned.' The government also sent a copy of the memorandum, coupled with a personal plea, to every Catholic bishop and archbishop in Ireland.[115]

The hierarchy dutifully responded and instructed its flock to respect the supremacy of the established order and, on 18 October—the day after the bill became law—issued a joint pastoral letter signed by the entire Catholic hierarchy.

The bishops declared that they could not remain silent in the face of growing evidence of 'a campaign of Revolution and Communism, which, if allowed to run its course unchecked, must end in the ruin of Ireland, both body and soul.' The IRA and Saor Éire had arrogated to themselves the right to terrorise and even kill public officials and conscientious jurymen in an attempt to intimidate honest citizens who wished to help the established authority. The two organisations aimed 'to impose upon the Catholic soil of Ireland the same materialistic regime, with its fanatical hatred of God, as now dominates Russia and threatens to dominate Spain,' by infecting their disciples with 'the virus of Communism' and by creating 'social disruption by organised opposition to the Law of the Land.' This campaign represented 'a blasphemous denial of God, and the overthrow of Christian civilisation.' Moreover, it would entail class warfare, the abolition of private property, and the destruction of family life.

> You cannot be a Catholic and a Communist. One stands for Christ, the other for Anti-Christ. Neither can you, for the same reason, be an auxiliary of Communism.[116]

The letter concluded by appealing to teachers to urge children to join in a crusade of prayer and by directing all Catholic priests to exert every effort 'to keep young people from secret societies, and diligently instruct them on the malice of murder, and the satanic tendencies of Communism.'

The government sought to capitalise on the pastoral letter by extracting the maximum amount of publicity from it for the new security campaign. Soon after article 2a had come into force the government received a number of protests from the United States, and in its reply to each one it sent a copy of the pastoral letter.[117]

In spite of the church pronouncements, large protest meetings were held in Dublin and Cork, with Fianna Fáil representatives prominent among the speakers. However, the joint church and state offensive dealt a fatal blow to the embryonic Saor Éire from which it never recovered. Having 'moved out of the shelter of "national rights" into the exposed ground of "social rights" . . . [they] were bombarded by everyone.'[118]

The IRA Army Council was at one with Fianna Fáil in its analysis of what had inspired the new church and state battle against republicans. It believed that the new legislation was intended to help Cumann na nGaedheal retain and extend its period of office and, by provoking a state of war and turmoil, to create a pretext for 'a great onslaught on Republicans, particularly [IRA] Volunteers.'[119]

The introduction of article 2a did undoubtedly lead to an intensification of coercion. The office of An Phoblacht was frequently raided, and its printer, Fodhla Printing Works in Kilmainham, Dublin (owned and managed by the Fianna Fáil TD Oscar Traynor), was a regular target.[120] The new military tribunal suppressed four consecutive issues, and the paper ceased publication,[121] to be replaced on 28 November by Republican File, a cut-and-paste publication similar to the famous Scissors and

Paste, designed by Arthur Griffith to evade a suppression order imposed by the British regime. But, like its predecessor, *Republican File* was suppressed and its editor arrested. The *Irish Press* was also hauled before the military tribunal for articles relating to the activities and judgements of the tribunal itself.[122]

However, in spite of the increased level of state repression, the IRA Army Council reported in January that 'the first shocks of the attack have been absorbed' and 'the worst of the storm has blown over, tension and speculation have died down.'[123]

'THE GUNMEN AND THE COMMUNISTS ARE VOTING FIANNA FÁIL'

Expectations of an early election had been high since the introduction of article 2a. On 29 January 1932 Cosgrave ended the speculation and called a general election for 16 February. In a letter that illustrates the intimacy of government ministers and senior civil servants, Patrick McGilligan, Minister for Industry and Commerce, had written to the Secretary of the Department of External Affairs, Joe Walshe, the previous September to put the case for an early election 'on consideration of the Irregular and Bolshie situation alone.'

> When I do go on to consider other things—falling revenue, increasing demands for services, falling prices, increasing unemployment, absence of emigrants' remittances and almost entire failure of dividends from foreign investments—I feel it would be sheer madness to think of trying to operate repressively throughout a miserable and poverty-stricken twelve months.[124]

Despite the early election, economic issues did creep into the electoral contest,[125] but, as planned, these were overshadowed by the security debate and the omnipresent threat to the state. It was a clever plan—a master-stroke even; and it had worked before. Other factors believed to favour the government included the gathering of Commonwealth states in Ottawa for the Imperial Conference and the much-anticipated Eucharistic Congress.[126] The government and its supporters argued that a strong renewed mandate was needed to meet the challenges presented by these events. The recently negotiated Statute of Westminster was not emphasised, as might have been expected; though it was repeatedly claimed that the Free State enjoyed the same freedoms as any other state in the Commonwealth, including Britain.[127]

The choice presented on Cumann na nGaedheal's election platforms was 'between Cosgrave's Government and no Government at all,'[128] and Cosgrave trenchantly argued that the people 'could not have a change of Government without it being a violent one.'[129] On another occasion he claimed that since 1922 the Irish people had not had 'any alternative, only the alternative of disturbance, and the Irish people do not want a change of this kind.'[130] Another government representative declared that 'constitutionalism is the big issue in this election,' and until the people could get 'another Constitutional Party, prepared to carry on constitutionally, they had no right to change.'[131] Fitzgerald-Kenney declared that 'two great political principles' had been espoused during the previous ten years in the Free State; Cumann na nGaedheal had urged 'that the majority of the Irish people were entitled to be masters in Ireland,' while Fianna Fáil had advocated 'that any person who so desired might impose his will on the majority.'[132] Fianna Fáil's policies would 'inevitably lead to the end of the present peaceful and orderly conditions.'[133] Powerful elements within the Catholic Church also weighed in, condemning 'secret societies' and Fianna Fáil's indulgence of 'gunmen'.[134]

Fianna Fáil's electoral strategy was less defensive and proved to be an effective synthesis of ideology and organisation. Its land annuities policy was popular, as was its promotion of industrial protection, which was much more attuned to the economic *zeitgeist* than was the government's rigid adherence to free trade. Since the Wall Street Crash most industrialised states had adopted protectionist policies, including one traditional republican *bête noire*, the British Conservative Party.[135] Fianna Fáil's demands proved a perfect blend of politics and economics, irresistible to those concerned with national pride as well as to the small farmer eager to keep a few extra shillings in the pocket. In a time of economic recession, attacks on 'waste and extravagance' were also guaranteed vote-winners.[136]

The party had consistently advocated a reduction in the number of Dáil deputies from 153 to 100,[137] and de Valera's dictum that 'no man is worth more than a thousand pounds' was likely to attract all those who earned a small fraction of this figure. The importance of constitutional issues was emphasised by the fact that the first promise in the Fianna Fáil manifesto was the removal of the oath of allegiance, which was described as a barrier to national unity. The security legislation enacted to combat the IRA would be repealed, while at the party's monster meeting on the eve of the election in College Green, Dublin, those assembled were told that 'Fianna Fáil would make no apology to anybody for the fact that if returned they would release all political prisoners.'[138]

From the beginning of the campaign the government attempted to limit the debate to the consideration of the constitutional legitimacy of Fianna Fáil, whose election would result in the destruction of the state and the triumph of terrorism, communism and anarchy. It spoke of 'De Valera's capacity for attracting and encouraging the mob' and asserted that 'the mob' and 'international Communism . . . are working for him in this election.'[139] It was noted that de Valera had travelled to the Bodenstown commemoration, sponsored by the IRA, and had rubbed shoulders with all sorts of revolutionaries, and that the IRA had 'issued an order to vote for de Valera at the coming election.' Under the slogan of 'Show me your company,' attention was drawn to the communist sympathies of such individuals as Charlotte Despard and Peadar O'Donnell, who in turn were connected with Fianna Fáil.

Considering the ideological chasm between the two sides, confrontations between speakers and hecklers were to be expected, and none more bitter than those between Charlotte Despard and Desmond FitzGerald, which took place over a number of days in Co. Kilkenny. At Graiguenamanagh, Despard set up a portable platform only yards from the minister's lorry. In addition to condemning Despard as a communist (which she was), FitzGerald claimed that she was an associate of the 'murder gang' that controlled de Valera. In response Despard reminded FitzGerald that she had intervened on his behalf when he was imprisoned by the British in the Curragh, and she questioned him on his present policies towards political prisoners.[140] Such reminders did little to impress FitzGerald, who, according to the *Irish Independent*, appealed to the people to give the Government a mandate, and not Mrs. Despard, Mrs. MacBride and those who were trying to bring in Soviet conditions. 'If we are elected,' Mr. FitzGerald said, 'we are going to put down people like these and put them in prison, and if they persist, and if it is necessary, we are going to execute them.'[141]

Republicans responded by publishing this quotation on the front page of *Republican File* juxtaposed with a photograph of the frail-looking Despard, then in her eighty-ninth year.[142]

James Fitzgerald-Kenney claimed that the IRA was composed of people 'who had refused to obey the bishops or the Ten Commandments,' and that de Valera would allow them to 'do anything they like.' He warned that 'the people should remember . . . that Fianna Fáil is in close alliance with gunmen, who are ready to terrorise the people and to set aside the laws of God and man.'[143] De Valera's promise to release political prisoners and to repeal the anti-IRA legislation vindicated such assertions. The Public Safety Act, it was argued, had brought peace and contentment to the country, and to illustrate the point one government deputy, Batt O'Connor, claimed that two days before the bill was due to be passed two hundred 'Russian agents' had left the country.[144] One front-page advertisement declared that Fianna Fáil was attempting to achieve the same end in 1932 as it had in 1922: to give 'a free hand for the Communists and Terrorists at home and a new quarrel about nothing with England.'[145] Others claimed that Fianna Fáil's rule would mean 'turmoil and disorder and the ascendancy of a small junta of armed desperadoes,'[146] and that de Valera believed that 'young men must be allowed to drill, arm, and do anything they like.'[147]

Paddy Hogan declared that 'government by Fianna Fáil is government by the rowdy and the blackguard.' Commenting on the Fianna Fáil campaign against the state, he said the people could see what Fianna Fáil could do unarmed, 'so they could imagine what they would do if armed.'[148] These allegations were echoed constantly in Cumann na nGaedheal election posters, which sought to portray de Valera as a Kerensky-like figure, the mask behind which lay the face of anarchy and bloodshed.

In the welter of accusation and counter-accusation about the IRA and communism, the issue of partition was submerged. It did, however, emerge occasionally as a stick with which to beat the government. In the republican heartland of Co. Kerry, de Valera described partition as the government's 'greatest national crime.' He claimed (erroneously) that the Treaty had provided for local plebiscites that would have permitted nationalist areas to register their protest against the imposed border, before declaring that the government 'ran away even from the Treaty and allowed themselves to assent to the partition of the country.'[149]

On another occasion de Valera told his electorate in Co. Clare that he had broken with Lloyd George in July 1921 because he (de Valera) 'would not accept any settlement involving the partition of the country.' The reason he had not gone to London was that he felt that if negotiations had broken down a second time a section of the people would have been 'ready to cry out, "De Valera will never make peace."' In what was a rare admission of error he said that 'events had proved him wrong,' implying that he should have conducted the Treaty negotiations himself.[150]

Seán T. O'Kelly promised that when Fianna Fáil was elected it would 'clear away all the obstacles in the path to the attainment of complete freedom, not for twenty-six counties but for the whole Irish nation . . . [by] peaceful and constitutional means.'[151]

The partition issue, however, did not feature highly in the party manifesto, which claimed that Fianna Fáil would 'never cease to protest against the iniquity of the partition of our country ruthlessly cut in two against the wishes of the people, and shall by every peaceful means strive to bring it to an end.'[152] In other words, the policy was one of expressing outrage against the iniquity of partition without developing a clear strategy for bringing it to an end.

Cumann na nGaedheal openly courted the Ancient Order of Hibernians, the National League, and former members of the old Irish Party. In Co. Monaghan an advertisement appeared in local papers signed by forty-seven of the county's best-known followers of these organisations.[153] Co. Monaghan's most prominent government representative, Ernest Blythe, Minister for Finance and Vice-President of the Executive Council, emphasised 'the claim of Cumann na nGaedheal, as the Constitutional Party, to the support of the old Constitutional Party.'[154]

William Redmond (son of John Redmond) was one of Cumann na nGaedheal's most prominent acquisitions, and he was paraded around a number of constituencies in an effort to capture the old home rule vote.[155] Forgetting his own willingness to align with de Valera in 1927 when a ministerial post was in the offing, Redmond now declared that only Cumann na nGaedheal could 'be trusted with the future welfare of Ireland,' and he described Fianna Fáil's policy as one of 'political humbug and financial ruin.'[156] On another occasion he claimed that 'if there was one man in Ireland who by a policy of spite and hatred, and by proposals of non-cooperation with Britain, had kept this country partitioned it was Mr. de Valera.'[157]

The National League formally merged with Cumann na nGaedheal, and a number of former members contested the election under the government banner.[158] Alderman Alfie Byrne, the populist Lord Mayor of Dublin and a former Irish Party MP, responded positively to a letter from Cosgrave, which claimed that circumstances had rendered it 'imperative in the National interest' that he should stand for election in support of the government.[159] Byrne dutifully told the electorate that only a Cumann na nGaedheal government could prevent Ireland from becoming another Russia or Spain.[160]

If the government was anxious to link Fianna Fáil with the IRA and communism, Fianna Fáil proved equally adept at raising the issue of Cumann na nGaedheal's solicitation of ex-unionist support under the banner 'Who rules?' Before the campaign was formally begun, the Irish Press, launched by Fianna Fáil in October 1931, had published a copy of a confidential letter issued by Cumann na nGaedheal supporters seeking donations from affluent former unionists, on the grounds that it was 'essential in the interests of the country as a whole that the anti-Treaty forces should be defeated.'[161]

Most former unionists had by this time joined Cumann na nGaedheal, but those who retained the independent tag requested that their supporters give their preferences to the government party.[162]

Throughout the election the *Irish Press* warmed to this theme, producing a series of cartoons implying that Cumann na nGaedheal was dependent on unionist assistance for survival.[163] Probably the most evocative of these was a cartoon on the eve of the election purporting to show a post-election meeting of former unionists. The room was filled with corpulent, monocled men in jovial form surrounded by Cumann na nGaedheal posters of 'the shadow of the gunman' variety. Addressing those assembled, a man, described simply as 'ex-unionist', proclaimed that even though Cosgrave had not been returned to power their money had been 'well spent.' Motioning to the posters on the wall, he continued: 'As you will see, it has been employed by Cumann na nGaedheal to defame the natives far better than we used to do it.'[164]

Prof. William Thrift, who, along with Sir James Craig and Prof. Ernest Alton, represented the unionist bastion of Trinity College, told supporters in Dalkey, Co. Dublin, that they 'had abandoned their policy as Unionists and accepted the Free State,' as it had retained a 'certain link with Great Britain,' which republicans proposed to sever.[165]

The government's attempts to depict a society threatened by anarchic violence received a timely boost when Patrick Reynolds, a Cumann na nGaedheal candidate, and Detective-Garda Patrick McGeehan were shot dead in Co. Leitrim two days before the election. They were returning from a party meeting in Carrick-on-Shannon when they stopped at the house of an RIC pensioner to solicit his vote.[166] A row ensued, and when the two men departed with a Cumann na nGaedheal organiser the pensioner fired two shots from a shotgun, killing both Reynolds and McGeehan.[167]

Despite the fact that the motive for the killings was not political (according to the accused, who was himself a government supporter, the deputy had threatened to cut off his pension), various attempts were made to attach political significance to them. Fianna Fáil expressed sympathy for the bereaved, but de Valera felt that some sought to 'make political capital out of the tragedy.'[168] On hearing of the incident Cosgrave had declared that 'the people are determined that this sort of work shall be stopped, and every right-thinking man and woman in the country wish, in God's name, that it be stopped'—implying that the deaths were part of a continuous campaign.[169]

Deploring any attempt to link the deaths with the election, de Valera said that 'everyone knows the issues in this election, and they have nothing to do with this tragedy.'[170] The day after the double shooting the newspapers reported the claim of a Cumann na nGaedheal candidate that his car had been fired on by unknown individuals.[171] This incident, combined with the deaths in Co. Leitrim, prompted the *Daily Herald* (London) to proclaim in its front-page headline: 'Gunman terror sweeps Free State on eve of election.' Though the Gardaí publicly announced that the report of the car attack was without foundation, most newspapers failed to publish the correction.[172]

Throughout the election Cumann na nGaedheal had identified itself so closely with the state that they seemed almost indistinguishable.[173] Addressing a crowd of thirty thousand people in College Green, Dublin, on the eve of the election, Cosgrave drove home the theme of danger to the state. Referring to a poster that exhorted voters to give Fianna Fáil a chance, he said:

Do Fianna Fáil accept the institutions of the State? They have tried to destroy the institutions of the State, and they said that if it was not done by election there would be a revolution to destroy it.[174]

On his arrival in his home constituency of Carlow-Kilkenny that evening Cosgrave reiterated the point more forcibly when he told his audience that Fianna Fáil called his Public Safety Bill a 'Coercion Act', while he believed that 'the shooting of a man without authority, the taking out of a poor labouring boy and riddling him with bullets,' was what really constituted a coercion act.[175]

To the end, the government portrayed Fianna Fáil as the instigators of a communist revolution under the guise of patriotism. A Cumann na nGaedheal front-page advertisement boldly declared: 'The gunmen are voting for Fianna Fáil. The Communists are voting for Fianna Fáil. How will you vote?'[176] Similarly, on election day the *Irish Independent's* editorial warned voters that 'the very life of the State' was at stake, and that should they choose Fianna Fáil the verdict of the world would be 'suicide during temporary insanity.'[177]

THE POST-MORTEM

A number of records were broken on 16 February 1932. Apart from being the quietest polling day in memory, with no serious incidents, the election also had the highest turn-out of voters, more than 75 per cent; in some places it exceeded 90 cent.[178]

With 45 per cent of the vote, Fianna Fáil emerged as the largest party and the clear winner of the election, with seventy-two seats. Its share of the vote increased by 9 per cent, a figure all the more impressive considering the dramatic increase in the turnout. Cumann na nGaedheal's vote remained remarkably solid but was swamped by the increased turn-out: its share of the vote dropped to 35 per cent, and its parliamentary representation fell to fifty-six seats. Its performance is less respectable, however, when account is taken of the absorption of the National League and a number of independents before the election. Its traditional allies, the Farmers' Party and independents, won five and twelve seats, respectively—not enough to keep Cosgrave's government in power. The role of king-maker, therefore, fell to the Labour Party, whose Dáil representation was almost halved, to seven seats, its support having evaporated in the Fianna Fáil sun.

This was the election in which the trojan organisational work supervised by Seán Lemass and Gerry Boland during the lean years of opposition paid off. The ethic of organisation and discipline was no more amply demonstrated than in Co. Kerry, where Fianna Fáil took five of the seven seats. Not only did its candidates obtain the five highest first-preference votes but only 708 votes separated the first and last-placed candidates.[179] It obtained an absolute majority in another seven constituencies: Clare (59 per cent), Meath (56 per cent), Galway (55 per cent), Mayo (54 per cent), Roscommon (54 per cent), Longford-Westmeath (52 per cent), and Tipperary (50 per cent).[180] In most other constituencies the Fianna Fáil vote was within a few points of the national average, with the important exception of the densely populated counties on the eastern seaboard, which stayed with the government. In Louth, Fianna Fáil received only a third of the vote, in Dublin County and Wicklow a little over a quarter.[181]

The government party lost because its 'institutional rigidity, free trade economics and lack of political party organisational structure all undermined the position of the Cumann na nGaedheal leadership.'[182] Its organisational deficiencies were particularly apparent when compared with Fianna Fáil's electoral machine. Part of its difficulties stemmed from its unorthodox genesis. The personnel who led the new state had formed a government before having the time to establish a party: they had been in power for more than a year before forming Cumann na nGaedheal. The leadership also displayed a patrician disdain for the mundane work of party organisation, preferring the duties of statesmen.[183]

A semi-official history of Fine Gael noted that while Fianna Fáil 'realised the need of a strong organisation to win power, Cumann na nGaedheal felt no such need—it was, after all, in office—and it tended to lose touch with the electorate.'[184] Richard Mulcahy later referred to a clique around the leadership afflicted with what he termed the 'Ballsbridge complex', a pernicious disease from an organisational point of view that manifested itself in a snooty disregard for grass-roots opinion. The establishment and maintenance of local branches was seen as a bothersome distraction.

How much truth was there in the much-publicised claim by Cumann na nGaedheal that 'the gunmen and the Communists' voted for Fianna Fáil? At the IRA's general army convention in January 1929 an order had been made forbidding members to work or vote in elections for either of the two parliaments in Ireland. However, on 12 January 1932, with an election in the offing, the Army Council temporarily reversed this decision in response to a feeling 'throughout the Army' that that order should be reviewed so that 'those at present in control of the 26 Counties should be deprived of power.' As the increased anti-republican activity of the state precluded the holding a general army convention before the election, the Army Council took the decision on its own initiative to suspend the prohibition. Instead, members and supporters were advised to 'vote against the candidates of the Cumann na nGaedheal party and other candidates who actively support the policy of that party.' As Sinn Féin was not contesting the election, this recommendation could only be interpreted as a vote for Fianna Fáil.

Obviously aware of this inference, and apprehensive of its potential ramifications, the Army Council was at pains to make it clear that, while they were recommending that volunteers should vote, 'it must be clearly understood that Óglaigh na hÉireann [the IRA] do not accept or approve of the policy of any of the parties contesting the elections.' Moreover, it stated that volunteers could not become candidates in the election, nor could they speak on the platform of any party. The document concluded by urging caution.

Realising the natural urge to end the rule of a party which has been responsible for such national disaster and economic distress, the Army Council would, however, emphasise to Volunteers that while advocating voting at these elections, our objects cannot be achieved by the methods or politics of the parties seeking election. This fact should be borne in mind by Volunteers throughout the elections.[185]

It is interesting to note that the name Fianna Fáil was not used once in this seminal document; yet the entire text, and the momentous decision it communicated, was inspired by the need to secure a Fianna Fáil electoral victory. This was necessary to reverse the perceived national catastrophe caused by the apostasy of the erstwhile republican leadership of Cumann na nGaedheal. It was also expected that a Fianna Fáil government would fulfil its promise to release political prisoners and to abolish the array of anti-republican legislation enacted during the previous decade. Finally, it is clear from the document itself that throughout the IRA there was a sentiment that republicans were being presented with an opportunity to advance the struggle for an all-Ireland republic by ousting the hated government party.

Harry White recalled the active participation of many Northern IRA members in the election campaign and the euphoria that Fianna Fáil's victory generated north of the border.

> When De Valera was elected in the south, there was great excitement, the news being conveyed by bulbs on to the front of the Telegraph building in Royal Avenue. People came in throngs to watch the final hours. *A Republic will be declared,* they said. Some of them were for marching up the Shankill there and then, which would not have done at all, so we contented ourselves by cheering, whistling and singing songs. We were excited because many of the lads had gone from Belfast to help in his [de Valera's] election and we saw his victory as one up for us.[186]

It is probable that the Army Council sought to assert its authority over its members by agreeing to reverse the decision of the 1929 convention, so pre-empting mass unauthorised work on behalf of Fianna Fáil. Fianna Fáil was rewarded for its court-ship of the IRA, and the most disciplined political party received the assistance of the most disciplined non-governmental organisation, united under the slogan 'Put them out.'[187] The recollections of Seán MacBride—then a member of the Army Council—give an insight into the level of IRA participation and suggest that the directive was not strictly adhered to and that flexibility was tolerated by the higher echelons of the organisation.

> We did all the usual things for Mr. de Valera's party in the 1932 election. We canvassed from door-to-door, we ferried people to vote. We organised groups. We even spoke at meetings and, of course, we heckled.[188]

It would appear that many IRA volunteers and Sinn Féin activists made a significant if covert contribution to Fianna Fáil's election campaign. This assistance varied greatly between different regions; but J. Bowyer Bell points out that, in Dublin, Seán Lemass oversaw co-ordination between the IRA and Fianna Fáil.[189]

Fianna Fáil's victory alarmed some senior civil servants. When it became clear that the government had been defeated the Secretary of the Department of Finance, J. J. McElligot, called a meeting of all departmental secretaries and 'advised them to remain calm.'[190]

Much has been made of the smooth transfer of power between the erstwhile Civil War rivals less than a decade after the formal cessation of hostilities.[191] Some, like Eoin O'Duffy, may have considered establishing a military dictatorship, but this was an option never seriously entertained by Cosgrave.[192] Had O'Duffy's instincts been acted on, Ireland might have faced a situation not unlike that in Spain four years later, when a democratically elected republican government found itself confronted by established interests, military, political and ecclesiastical. In the Ireland of 1932, republicans—now mobilised more than ever—would probably have emerged victorious, so long as there was no British intervention. On the other hand, if Cumann na nGaedheal had managed to stay in office as the benefactor of a coup it would have entered a political cul-de-sac, having destroyed the Free State institution it had so ardently defended.

Cosgrave, however, did not intend becoming a dictator, and, while defeat was unexpected, the blow was softened by the belief that Fianna Fáil would not remain long in power—a belief strengthened by its status as a minority government dependent on the support of the Labour Party. Few if any could have predicted that another six elections would come and go before Fianna Fáil would be ousted, fewer still that it would take an alliance of Richard Mulcahy and Seán MacBride to achieve it.

Chapter 6 ∽

FIANNA FÁIL IN POWER, 1932–8

'A FUSION OF FORCES'

Between 16 February 1932, when the election result was announced, and 9 March, when Fianna Fáil formed a government, high-level discussions took place between Fianna Fáil and the IRA. The purpose of the meetings, in the words of the Fianna Fáil representative, was to achieve 'a fusion of forces' in the face of imperialism. The two organisations 'have at bottom the same national and social outlook,' the Fianna Fáil representative wrote to the IRA chief of staff, Moss Twomey; 'there is really less friction between them today than often exists within one organisation.' The letter warned that 'all the usual reactionary forces will be whipped up' in an effort to force Fianna Fáil into coalition with the Labour Party, and that the impending Eucharistic Congress, declining Anglo-Irish relations and world depression would be exploited to dislodge Fianna Fáil from power. 'We will be on the defensive', the letter continued, 'and may fail to secure the reins of government unless you come to the national rescue by showing that you will accept our authority wholeheartedly when the oath is removed . . .' If such a 'fusion of the national forces' could be achieved there could be cultural, social, and economic rejuvenation, the Fianna Fáil agent argued, and he appealed to the IRA 'to clear the way by making the announcement *at once* that you are prepared to accept and act up to the principles which the men who fought the civil war agreed upon.'[1]

This correspondence has de Valera's fingerprints all over it, and indeed the initiative could not have taken place without his personal approval. We will probably never know how likely the Fianna Fáil leadership considered a breakthrough, but it was clear that, if such a fusion could be negotiated, maximum leverage could be exerted during the three weeks before Fianna Fáil took office.

De Valera's scrutiny of the correspondence is evident in the covering note he sent to the Army Council along with the 1923 IRA ceasefire proposals. In fact his emphasis on the terms of the 1923 ceasefire reflected his wish to appear at all times consistent with previously articulated republican doctrine. This yearning for consistency in the face of what appeared to be embarrassing ideological U-turns was to become a significant feature of de Valera's handling of the IRA in the coming years.

Despite the IRA's refusal to be absorbed into the Free State army, Fianna Fáil kept its election promise and released all republican prisoners. Few histories reveal the actual number of those released. In fact, only seventeen were incarcerated in March 1932, because of their opposition to the 'despotic' Free State regime, and in this sense it was largely a symbolic act. Frank Aiken, now the Minister for Defence (with control over the army that had defeated his IRA forces less than a decade earlier), travelled to Arbour Hill military prison, where he had a long discussion with George Gilmore and formally released the prisoners. A statement issued by the prisoners thanked the Irish people for their 'unceasing efforts' to secure their release and praised the Fianna Fáil government for the promptness with which they had acted.[2] The following day a monster meeting of thirty thousand people was held in their honour in the centre of Dublin.

Three months later, on 19 June 1932, republicans from all corners of the country made the annual pilgrimage to Bodenstown. A section of the procession was again reserved for members of Fianna Fáil. An estimated twenty thousand people attended, including ten thousand members of the IRA, described by *An Phoblacht* as 'the most imposing muster of the IRA since 1922.'[3] In his graveside oration Seán Russell condemned the enforcement of the Treasonable Offences Act (1925) by the 'anti-national' Special Branch and predicted that any negotiations with Britain would not result in 'an honourable settlement for Ireland.'

At the previous year's Bodenstown commemoration a high-ranking delegation led by de Valera had taken part, but in 1932 the Fianna Fáil leadership was noticeable by its absence. There was a sign of things to come when, shortly after the republican commemoration, Frank Aiken led the Free State army to Bodenstown for an official commemoration. This event was advertised as 'the annual commemoration ceremony in honour of Wolfe Tone,' a curious description, considering that Fianna Fáil had never attended it before. Michael Price, secretary of the Wolfe Tone Commemoration Committee, denounced as hypocrisy Aiken's placing of a wreath on behalf of the Free State army and challenged the Fianna Fáil leadership's presentation of the ceremony as the official commemoration.[4]

During the early 1930s de Valera was responding to the expectations of two constituencies, and as a result he assumed a dual responsibility. As the head of an elected government, armed with the authority of the state, he had a responsibility to the electorate as a whole; but he was also eager to preserve the image of de Valera the insurgent, President of the Republic and trenchant opponent of the Free State. While he longed to satisfy both images, he would ultimately discover that they were irreconcilable.

CREATING A DURABLE STATE NATIONALISM
Speaking in April 1933 at the graves of the executed leaders of the 1916 Rising in Arbour Hill military cemetery, de Valera told those assembled that the time had not yet come for the Republic and that

> we must content ourselves with the declaration that it is for that goal we strive and that we shall not rest until we reach it . . . Let it be made clear that we yield no willing assent to any form or symbol that is out of keeping with Ireland's right as a sovereign nation. Let us remove these forms one by one, so that this State that

we control may be a Republic in fact and that, when the time comes, the proclaiming of the Republic may involve no more than a ceremony, the formal confirmation of the status already attained.[5]

In this speech is to be found the most succinct and accurate explanation of the constitutional policies pursued by de Valera throughout the 1930s. He would adhere rigidly to this blueprint; and the first bill that the new government put before the Dáil was for the removal of the oath of allegiance. During the 1932 election campaign MacEntee had declared that when the oath was removed 'George Gilmore would march under the banner of Mr. de Valera.'[6] Fortunately for Fianna Fáil, Gilmore had been unavailable for comment, as he passed his days in Arbour Hill military prison; but when he was released he showed little inclination to fulfil this prediction.

Regardless of the IRA's scepticism, the progressive dismantling of the Treaty was necessary to demonstrate to Fianna Fáil supporters the fruits of constitutional endeavour. Introduced to the Dáil on 20 April, the Constitution (Removal of Oath) Bill consisted of three main sections. The first section would repeal article 17 of the Constitution of the Irish Free State to remove the provision that made the oath obligatory for members entering the Dáil. The second section would remove article 2 of the Constitution of the Irish Free State (Saorstát Éireann) Act (1922), which made the Constitution subordinate to the Treaty. This provision, known as the 'repugnancy clause', complemented the British view of the Treaty as a final settlement—the end of the 'Irish question'. The third section would delete the provision of article 50 of the Constitution, which compelled the government to introduce amendments to the Constitution only that were within the terms of the Treaty. The relevant section in article 50 had the same effect as article 2 of the 1922 act, and de Valera was eager that there would not be a 'back-door method of getting the same results as you get in Article 2.'[7]

Coinciding with de Valera's bill to remove the oath was the fulfilment of the other major election pledge, to retain the land annuities in Ireland. The British Government responded by imposing a 20 per cent *ad valorem* tax on imports from the Free State, a measure that provoked a similar levy on English exports.

The 'Economic War' of 1932–8 refers merely to the weapons employed in what was essentially a political dispute. The dire economic circumstances of the 1930s, which resulted from world depression, suggest that a protectionist policy was not an imprudent one. Indeed protection was increasingly adopted in the industrialised countries, including Britain and the United States. Moreover, the Economic War provided de Valera with the opportunity of promoting one of his most cherished objectives, the old Griffithite policy of economic self-sufficiency.

Fianna Fáil also adopted a policy of non-cooperation with the King's representative in Ireland, the Governor-General, James MacNeill.[8] Within a month of taking office the Fianna Fáil ministers Frank Aiken and Seán T. O'Kelly made a much-publicised exit from the French Legation when MacNeill arrived for a reception.[9] When MacNeill complained to de Valera, the latter described the incident as 'unfortunate and regrettable' and asked that he be informed of MacNeill's future social engagements. This confirmation that his ostracising was government policy did little to mollify MacNeill, who was to endure a series of snubs over the coming months aimed at demeaning his office.[10] After being subjected to considerable pressure, and despite some vacillation, he eventually resigned on 3 October, four months before his official retirement date.[11] Several alternatives were toyed with before de Valera settled on appointing Domhnall Ó Buachalla, who had unsuccessfully contested the 1932 election on behalf of Fianna Fáil.[12]

The last of the major constitutional initiatives that paved the way for a new basic law was the Constitution (Amendment No. 27) Bill and the Executive Authority (External Relations) Bill, introduced in December 1936 amid the confusion arising from the British monarch's abdication. In one fell swoop de Valera removed all references to the King from the Constitution and also took the opportunity to abolish the Seanad. The office of Governor-General of Ireland was another casualty of the legislation. As the Constitution of the Irish Free State was flexible, there was no need to refer the delicate matter of the Free State's relationship with the British Commonwealth to the electorate, and both bills were pushed through within twenty-four hours.

In Fianna Fáil's 1932 election manifesto it had given a commitment not to go beyond its original mandate without first putting the matter to the people, and during the Dáil debates of 11–12 December this apparent *volte-face* was pointed out by opposition deputies. The main result of this initiative was that the role of the King disappeared from Irish constitutional law, though his diplomatic functions on behalf of the Free State remained largely unchanged. De Valera never tired of pointing out in later years that the Executive Authority (External Relations) Act was a statute that could be repealed at any time should the Oireachtas consider it necessary or desirable.

FIANNA FÁIL AND THE IRA, 1933–6

De Valera's attempts to create a durable state nationalism and his relationship with the IRA were inextricably linked. His efforts to dismantle the Treaty conformed to his own desires and those of his followers, but it was also hoped that they would promote his much-vaunted objective of 'national unity'. In many ways this was shorthand for reconciling the IRA to the Free State, in much the same way that de Valera himself had done after his electoral triumph. The release of prisoners and the lifting of the ban on the IRA and *An Phoblacht* ushered in a short-lived honeymoon; but some feared de Valera's long-term strategy. 'If the Oath goes,' *An Phoblacht* asked, 'will there be an offensive against the Revolutionary Movement?'[13] The answer, quite simply, was yes.

Despite some mutual sniping, the honeymoon endured for the first nine months of Fianna Fáil rule. When de Valera called a snap election in 1933 a general army convention of the IRA was called on 8 January, which issued a 'Manifesto to the Irish People', calling on the electorate to return the Fianna Fáil government to power.[14] Fianna Fáil went to great lengths to woo the IRA, even taking out full-page advertisements in *An Phoblacht*.[15] Once it was safely ensconced in office with a comfortable majority, however, there was a noticeable decline of tolerance towards the republican movement.

The advent of the Blueshirts shortly after Fianna Fáil's rise to power presented de Valera with a perfect opportunity to consolidate his control over the more militant grass roots of the party and to enhance Fianna Fáil's credibility with moderate recruits within the IRA. Officially called the Army Comrades' Association, later the

National Guard, the Blueshirts were paramilitary and fascist in form, with drilling and uniforms (mimicking the Italian Blackshirts and German Brownshirts) and fascist salutes and slogans. The organisation was militantly anti-communist, and membership was confined to Christians of Irish parentage. Ostensibly established to protect Cumann na nGaedheal speakers from republican intimidation, the Blueshirts rapidly developed a mass, quasi-military character. Their leader, Eoin O'Duffy, had played a significant role in building up the Garda Síochána during the 1920s, but he had become increasingly eccentric and authoritarian. His dismissal from his post as Commissioner immediately after the 1933 election relieved him of the task of serving under a Fianna Fáil government, and his organisational talents were harnessed by the Blueshirt movement. But when he announced a 'March on Dublin' in August 1933, which would pass Leinster House, de Valera (remembering Mussolini's 'March on Rome' a decade earlier) banned the meeting.

Soon afterwards the organisation was outlawed, but its members were absorbed into Cumann na nGaedheal, leading to the foundation of a new party, Fine Gael, which also absorbed the National League.[16] O'Duffy was made president of Fine Gael, while Cosgrave was demoted to leader of the parliamentary party. However, O'Duffy's increasingly unconventional and inflammatory behaviour led to his resignation in 1934, and from then on he took a back seat in Irish politics, resurfacing briefly to lead an Irish Catholic contingent to fight for Franco against the Spanish government forces (which were assisted by a body of mostly IRA volunteers led by Frank Ryan).

The Blueshirts put many of the more militant elements within Fianna Fáil, those most sympathetic to the IRA, into the position of defending the state. The state that they had sought to destroy was considered a prize that their defeated foes, vanquished at the ballot box, now sought to seize back for their own malevolent ends. By presenting the state as being under threat from the Blueshirts, de Valera also succeeded in enticing many members of the IRA to join the Special Branch. The new Special Branch, nicknamed the Broy Harriers (after Ned Broy, appointed Garda Commissioner to replace O'Duffy, and the Bray Harriers, a well-known hunt), could be relied on in any military conflict with the Blueshirts.[17] There was 'the inevitable scramble for jobs as soon as word got around that recruitment into the Guards had been set aside for the Fianna Fáil faithful.'[18] The unit provided many Civil War veterans with a gun, a salary and an opportunity to patrol their old adversaries. The first two hundred members had been hastily recruited in the forty-eight hours before O'Duffy's threatened march on Dublin. Another two hundred were recruited after the crisis was averted and were given a mere three days' training before being despatched to various parts of the country. The Harriers were ill-trained and ill-disciplined (often refusing to accept orders from non-Harrier Garda officers), but over time they developed into a cohesive anti-IRA force. Blueshirt activities also allowed de Valera to reintroduce the repressive legislation that Fianna Fáil had condemned in opposition when employed against republicans, in particular article 2a of the Free State Constitution.

As it turned out, the Blueshirt threat was a transient one, but the legislation was retained for use against the IRA. As the Blueshirt threat subsided, the net was slowly extended to take in an increasing number of IRA members. By then many republicans had been sucked into the paid service of the state machinery through employment in the Free State army, the police and the civil service. The introduction of pensions for those who had fought on the republican side in the Civil War had a similar effect. In March 1935 Frank Aiken revealed that 100,000 application forms had been printed for pensions under the Military Service Pensions Act (1934), of which 57,000 had already been circulated.[19] Such initiatives were instrumental in absorbing as many of the IRA into the state machinery as possible by giving them a financial stake in the system.

Relations between Fianna Fáil and the IRA became increasingly strained throughout 1933. Fianna Fáil's safe parliamentary majority undoubtedly emboldened the leadership in its attitudes towards the IRA, but the continued existence of the Blueshirts papered over the ideological cracks, as both organisations directed their odium at O'Duffy. Following O'Duffy's resignation from the Fine Gael leadership in 1934 that party sought to pressure the Fianna Fáil leadership into using the article 2a to combat the IRA, its original target. Frank MacDermott TD (Fine Gael) asked in 1935 whether the IRA would be declared an unlawful organisation under the article and commented that perhaps the main strength of such organisations was derived from the belief that 'in their hearts the majority of the Fianna Fáil Party approve of their existence.' De Valera responded by saying that that belief, if it existed, was 'without foundation.'[20]

With the success of state pensions for republican Civil War veterans and of recruitment to the Volunteer Force, a new army reserve, combined with a haemorrhage of left-wing members, who established the Republican Congress in 1934, IRA numbers were shrinking.[21] At the same time what had begun as a trickle of republicans being imprisoned soon became a deluge, prompting disquiet among some Fianna Fáil backbenchers over the treatment of political prisoners.[22] Even such republican legends as Tom Barry now found themselves behind bars, charged with a compendium of crimes, including sedition, unlawful association, refusal to answer questions and contempt of court—charges that had been brought against them under three different regimes.

Away from the glare of publicity de Valera secretly met the IRA leader Seán Russell in April 1935. Russell promised co-operation with Fianna Fáil 'in every way' for five years if de Valera would reciprocate by promising to declare a republic for all Ireland at the end of that period. De Valera was unimpressed. 'You want it both ways,' he told Russell, and with that 'de Valera angrily dismissed him.'[23]

The deteriorating relations between the Fianna Fáil and IRA leaderships was also evident in the government's changing attitude towards An Phoblacht, the primary republican organ since its foundation in 1925. Prominent Fianna Fáil members had been regular contributors during their years in parliamentary opposition, and until October 1932 An Phoblacht continued to be printed by Fodhla Printing Works, owned by the Fianna Fáil deputy Oscar Traynor. After that it was printed by the Longford Printing and Publishing Company and published by the Republican Press in Dublin. No explanation for the change in printers was given in An Phoblacht, though it is possible that it was connected with a strike at the Irish Press during this period. If this was the cause it was fortuitous, for it provided an opportunity for An Phoblacht to procure an alternative printer without an unseemly confrontation. It also relieved

Fianna Fáil of the potential embarrassment of being linked to a paper that was to be proscribed by government order.

On 11 April 1935, as the paper prepared to report on the annual commemorations of the 1916 Rising, armed members of the Special Branch broke into the Longford Printing Works, seized eight hundred copies of *An Phoblacht* and four laid-out pages of type, and took them to the local Garda barracks. No warrant was produced. Returning later, they destroyed four other pages of type with knives. One of the photographic blocks destroyed contained scenes of the recent unveiling of the memorial to Liam Lynch in the Knockmealdown Mountains. The home of the owner of the printing works was ransacked, and all trains and buses leaving Longford were searched to ensure that no copies of the paper left the town.

The National Union of Journalists condemned the raids[24]; but it was clear that the ideological war between Fianna Fáil and *An Phoblacht* had now entered a new phase. Aided by the machinery of state, de Valera was always going to have the upper hand in this battle, which ended with the formal suppression of *An Phoblacht* the following year as the paper prepared to report on the Bodenstown commemoration, which was itself banned.

Until its formal banning in June 1936 *An Phoblacht* was to be subjected to constant interference from the police. It was not uncommon for an issue to be delayed for long periods while detectives pored over its contents and demanded deletions before finally authorising a bowdlerised version. Such actions were not conducted within any known legal framework. Publishers were left in the position of trying to guess what might be considered 'seditious' by policemen, whose views varied from one week to the next.[25]

During their years in opposition to the British and later to the Free State regime, those in charge of Fianna Fáil had refused to recognise the legitimacy of established institutions. Instead they sought to deprive state institutions of legitimacy by refusing to attend them and by creating and maintaining alternative structures and symbols. Now in power, de Valera adopted the reverse of this policy by formulating government-sponsored alternatives to established republican institutions. Instead of banning the Bodenstown commemoration it first boycotted it and created its own Fianna Fáil ceremony (in addition to the Free State one attended by Fianna Fáil deputies). Attendance at the commemoration sponsored by Fianna Fáil, however, never exceeded five thousand, while the traditional republican one attracted annually three or four times that number. And while the government was able to cite ostensible security considerations for its decision to ban the republican commemoration at Bodenstown, one cannot but suspect that the move was partly—perhaps primarily—motivated by a desire to monopolise republican ideology.

A similar policy of duplicating existing structures that the Fianna Fáil leadership refused to recognise was adopted in relation to the sale of the Easter Lily, the traditional republican badge for fund-raising and for commemoration of the 1916 Rising. While in opposition, Fianna Fáil had condemned the harassment of those selling this emblem, citing it as indicative of how far Cumann na nGaedheal had strayed from the republican fold. However, in 1935 the Fianna Fáil leadership announced that party members would no longer be permitted to sell Easter lilies, as they were the symbol of 'an organisation of whose methods they disapprove.'[26]

Simultaneously a rival badge, the 'torch', was launched to coincide with the Easter commemoration of 1935. It was described as the 'emblem of freedom and remembrance.'[27] De Valera urged Fianna Fáil parliamentarians to ensure that the new emblem and the national collection were a success, adding that it was 'necessary that we should make it clear to the people that the Fianna Fáil Organisation [is] the Premier Republican Organisation in the country.'[28]

Discussions with other groups, including the 'Old IRA' (the name given to veterans of the War of Independence and the Republican side in the Civil War), failed to secure a basis of agreement because of what Fianna Fáil said was 'a rejection by other organisations of the proposal that there should be one emblem, and that the proceeds be used for activities of a benevolent nature.'[29] As the torch failed to supplant the Lily even among Fianna Fáil supporters, the leadership began to promote the torch more intensively while simultaneously prosecuting those selling Easter lilies. The Special Branch was permitted to renew its activities against the sale of Easter lilies, for much the same reasons offered by the previous regime. As with Bodenstown, the alternative failed to catch on, and in this case it was quietly discontinued; but the precedent of using government resources to intervene in the ideological debate between Fianna Fáil and the IRA was set.

During the eighteen months before the IRA was formally proscribed, republicans were responsible for the death of three people—the same number that had led Cumann na nGaedheal to outlaw twelve organisations, including the IRA, and to introduce its controversial amendment (article 2a) to the Constitution. The first killing, of Richard More O'Farrell, resulted from a local land dispute. In response to the threatened eviction of 121 tenants, the Edgeworthstown Town Tenants' Association had passed a resolution on 5 November 1934 inviting the intervention of the IRA in the Sanderson Estate dispute. Two weeks later it announced that the IRA had accepted the invitation, and a further resolution was passed inviting the IRA to hold a public meeting in Edgeworthstown. The meeting, which took place on 2 December, was the scene of venomous attacks on the landlord's agent, Gerald More O'Farrell. An attempt on 9 February 1935 to intimidate the land agent got out of hand: a scuffle ensued, during which Richard More O'Farrell, the agent's son, was fatally wounded. Four men were charged with the murder the following month but were acquitted by a jury in December.[30]

The other two deaths occurred within a month of each other in 1936. On 24 April, Vice-Admiral Henry Boyle Somerville was shot dead when he answered a knock on the door of his house in Castletownsend, Co. Cork. His 'crime' was providing information and references to local men who wished to join the British navy. The second death was that of John Egan, shot dead in Dungarvan after conviction by an IRA court-martial of passing information to Free State forces.[31] The government responded with alacrity. Known republicans were rounded up under article 2a, and the IRA leader Mick Conway was sentenced to death by the military tribunal, though the sentence was later commuted.

On 17 June, Gerry Boland—who had temporarily replaced P. J. Ruttledge as Minister for Justice—told the Dáil that if at any time they felt it necessary to make an order banning the IRA they would not hesitate in doing so. The reason the IRA had not been banned was that 'it was, itself, on the face of it, an illegal organisation.' The minister said that it had been collecting arms for three years and would continue to do so. If people knew where arms were being hidden and did not inform the government out of a sense of civic spirit, the government would provide them with 'some other inducement.' Anyone who informed would be given 'a full reward for the information.' In giving the reasons for the destruction of the Blueshirt movement Boland assured opposition deputies that he would be equally ruthless with republican organisations: 'We smashed them and we are going to smash the others.'[32]

Two days later a decision was taken by the Fianna Fáil government to proclaim the IRA an illegal organisation and to ban the Wolfe Tone commemoration at Bodenstown. At 10 p.m. journalists were summoned to Government Buildings, where the decision was announced. The statement declared that 'the Government warns all citizens to avoid visiting the neighbourhood of Sallins and Bodenstown on Sunday next.' All police leave in Dublin was cancelled. Roadblocks were placed on all points of entry to the Bodenstown area and outside all large towns. An *Irish Independent* reporter captured the scene.

> Bodenstown yesterday was an armed camp! About 1,000 troops, with full war equipment, and supported by aeroplanes, were quartered in the vicinity of the cemetery and Sallins, and about 500 Gardaí were also on duty . . . For a radius of twenty miles the countryside was in a state of siege. Only under the strictest surveillance was it possible to get within two miles of the little churchyard where the body of Wolfe Tone lies buried.[33]

Seán Hales TD resigned from Fianna Fáil, but among the party's parliamentarians he was alone in his protest.[34] Despite Seán MacEntee's defence that 'those who founded Fianna Fáil came into public life as soldiers, not as assassins,' there is evidence that not everyone within the party accepted this *volte-face*. Speaking in Co. Offaly, the Minister for Education, Tom Derrig, was challenged by Fianna Fáil members when he refused to consider a motion asking the government to explore every means of coming to an arrangement with the IRA and demanding the release of the prisoners.[35]

Shortly after the banning of the Bodenstown commemoration Fianna Fáil was questioned about the arrest and imprisonment of the IRA leader Mick Conway. When asked by the leader of the Labour Party, William Norton, why he believed it right to arraign a man on a capital charge before the military tribunal when he had vehemently opposed such a tribunal being given such powers in 1931, de Valera's reply was illuminating. His views in 1931, he said, were determined by the fact that 'I did not trust the Executive Council of the day with these powers,' the implication being that the powers were not repugnant in themselves and that Fianna Fáil, but not Cumann na nGaedheal, could be trusted in using them. The second reason offered was that the Fianna Fáil government, unlike its predecessor, had 'tried to make it possible for all sections of the community to be represented freely in the Parliament without any appeal to force to settle the political differences between them.'[36] Cumann na nGaedheal, of course, had also felt that it presided over a political regime in which all Irish citizens could participate.

There was a sequel to Bodenstown that further exacerbated relations between Fianna Fáil and the IRA and that was symptomatic of a new determination to break republican prisoners. Twenty-year-old Seán Glynn had been arrested while travelling from his home in Limerick to the Wolfe Tone commemoration in Bodenstown. Without any trial, he was put in solitary confinement for several months in Arbour Hill military prison. Refusing to accept criminal status, Glynn, with fifty-six others, was subjected to the 'silent treatment', whereby not the slightest noise or human contact was permitted, to the extent that prison warders wore rubber-soled shoes. Deprived of any mental stimulation, Glynn became insane and was found hanging in his cell. Another republican, Christy Aherne, had made a suicide attempt some months earlier.

Joe McGarrity, previously de Valera's greatest supporter in the United States, wrote in his diary that Glynn's death was 'the last straw for me,' and he made his first public criticism of de Valera, who, he declared, was 'selling out his former friends and repressing all freedom of thought in Ireland with the ruthlessness of a dictator.'[37] The veteran activist Maud Gonne MacBride wrote that 'in my long experience, I say deliberately that I have never known prison conditions so terribly calculated to destroy mental and bodily health as those being enforced on Republican prisoners in Arbour Hill today.' In the prison cells there was 'solitude and silence, accomplishing the same dread work on living men's minds as quicklime on dead men's bones.'[38]

PARTITION

The partition issue in general and the position of Northern nationalists in particular continued to dominate the minds of many Fianna Fáil members. Northern nationalists had adopted a more moderate stance than many of their Southern counterparts during the revolutionary period. In 1918 Sinn Féin had eclipsed the Nationalists in what would become Northern Ireland and had taken their seats in the first Dáil. However, to prevent a split vote, eight seats had been divided between the two parties, which saved the home-rulers from greater embarrassment. In 1921 the two parties obtained six seats each in the new Belfast Parliament, though Sinn Féin's vote was significantly higher.[39]

The majority of Northern nationalists accepted Collins's optimistic interpretation of article XII of the Treaty, which provided for a Boundary Commission,[40] and this was reflected in the Nationalist Party's ascendancy after the 1924 election.[41] The fiasco of the Boundary Commission report (the 'damned good bargain' in Cosgrave-speak) fatally weakened nationalists' confidence in the Cumann na nGaedheal government, and they 'switched their hopes to de Valera.'[42]

Northern nationalist expectations rose further after Fianna Fáil's accession to power.[43] A central figure in harnessing anti-partitionist sentiment in Fianna Fáil was Éamonn Donnelly, an abstentionist MP at Stormont between 1925 and 1929 who joined Fianna Fáil in 1927 and was elected to the Dáil in 1933. Donnelly 'thought the south quiescent, even polite,' on the subject of partition and was 'incensed at de Valera's refusal to extend Fianna Fáil across the border.'[44] In early 1933 he suggested that the Nationalist Party in the North should simply rename itself Fianna Fáil, while at the Fianna Dáil ard-fheis in November he heckled de Valera, forcing him to defend the apparent inconsistency of his policies on partition.

De Valera's defence was received enthusiastically in the North, and the *Irish Press* published a 'sensational report' that revealed that the entire Fianna Fáil government had been invited to stand as abstentionists in the Six Counties. Only de Valera accepted a nomination, for South Down; the rest of the government remained aloof, ostensibly on the grounds that Fianna Fáil's aim was 'to consolidate, not to divide, northern nationalists.' This was a somewhat dubious justification, as the nomination of prominent Fianna Fáil ministers as abstentionists was more likely to unite nationalists than to divide them. John Bowman has suggested that the week-long speculation orchestrated by the *Irish Press* 'was in fact a kite being flown by Donnelly.'[45] If so it was a kite that the Fianna Fáil leadership allowed to float harmlessly by.

A complementary policy option advocated by a considerable section within Fianna Fáil was that elected representatives from the Six Counties would be permitted to attend Dáil Éireann. Northern Sinn Féin MPs had participated in the first Dáil and had been disenchanted with their exclusion after the Treaty. De Valera had condemned that exclusion but now had the power to rectify the situation by reverting to the pre-1921 position and admitting Northern MPs to the Dáil. Such a policy would have united the disparate strands of republicans, legitimising the Dáil by providing for the attendance of all elected representatives who wished to participate in the national parliament.[46]

In February 1933 Cahir Healy and Joe Devlin, two leading Northern MPs of a moderate hue, approached de Valera privately and requested that they be permitted to take their seats in the Dáil. De Valera not only ruled out the suggestion but refused to advise them on the most appropriate strategy for Northern representatives. Without a lead from Fianna Fáil, two other Northern organisations were established, National Unity and the Irish Union Association, which sought to pressure de Valera into assuming a more determined stance on the partition issue.

By 1936 Fianna Fáil had been four years in power, and, much to the disappoint-ment of Northern nationalists and the more fervent anti-partitionists within the party, no serious initiative on partition had been undertaken. The Treaty was being systematically dismantled, and the Economic War affirmed Fianna Fáil's commit-ment to an economically self-contained state; on the partition front, however, there was little to show, and Northern nationalists were increasingly frustrated at the lack of progress. In September, Éamonn Donnelly wrote to Cahir Healy, declaring in exasperation that 'Partition is now in operation for fifteen years and we are worse today than when we began.' If the present situation continued for another ten years, he complained, they might as well 'chuck in,' and their generation would be remembered as 'a lot of weaklings who saw what to do and who didn't do it.'

Donnelly's plan was simple: the time had gone for mere resolutions and delegations to Dublin; Nationalist MPs should leave Stormont and demand admission to the Dáil. Donnelly believed that they would 'carry all Ireland on this' and that such a strategy would unite Northern nationalists, accelerate the pace of anti-partition agitation and make the question of the reunification of Ireland 'practical politics again.'[47]

Motions for the 1936 ard-fheis gave Donnelly reason for optimism, and he believed that one in particular contained the solution to partition. The motion stated that 'this ard fheis demands that a clause be inserted in the new Constitution enabling the elected representatives of North East Ulster to sit, act and vote in Dáil Éireann.'

Despite Healy's and Donnelly's agitation, de Valera succeeded in having the motion withdrawn while maintaining party unity on the issue. He argued that, as the proposed constitution was in gestation, it was premature to pass any resolutions on the matter. The most that could be extracted from him was an assurance that 'there would be no words in the new Constitution that could possibly place bounds on the march of the nation.'[48] In reality this was a spurious defence, as there was nothing incompatible in a resolution that bound the party leader to include certain provisions in his proposed constitution.

There are several possible explanations for de Valera's desire to defer discussion on the issue. Firstly, it is clear that he wished to maintain full control over the formulation and drafting of the constitution. As he did not feel the need to have a discussion among his government colleagues on the details, it was not out of character for him to be reluctant to promote a discussion among mere party delegates at an ard-fheis. Secondly, he may have been genuinely concerned that an impression might be created that the constitution, which was intended to serve the interests of the whole country, was merely the result of internal party resolutions. Finally, the decision to circumvent the motion may simply have reflected de Valera's antipathy for its content. This was arguably the most decisive factor, borne out by the absence of such a provision from any of the drafts prepared during the months before the the completion of the constitution and its endorsement by the electorate.

On 21 December 1936 Donnelly put a motion before Fianna Fáil's National Executive calling for a special ard-fheis in early February to discuss the new constitution, 'with special reference to Partition, and that Republicans from North-East Ulster be asked to attend.' He suggested that the personnel of the republican representation be decided by a special sub-committee of the National Executive, comprising MacEntee, Aiken and Donnelly (all TDs of Northern origin) and the honorary secretaries of the party.[49]

While de Valera was keen to keep the drafting of the constitution within his own exclusive control, Donnelly's motion can be interpreted as an attempt to widen the debate on what constitutional provisions were intended to meet the challenge of partition. With the calling of a special ard-fheis to discuss the most appropriate provisions for combating partition, the issue would be submitted to the party rank and file for consideration. This suited Donnelly's purpose perfectly, as it was obvious from the mood of successive ard-fheiseanna that grass-roots sentiments were more militantly anti-partitionist than those of the leadership. By suggesting the presence of Northern representatives at the ard-fheis Donnelly was ensuring that delegates would be informed of Northern nationalists' views before deciding on the most desirable course of action. Northern nationalists would also feel that they had been consulted in a manner that contrasted with their treatment during negotiations for the Treaty and the 1925 Boundary Agreement.

It can only be assumed, in the absence of any action on the contents of the motion, that de Valera, not unnaturally, considered the suggestion an ideological trap. Though he was an enthusiast for special ard-fheiseanna while in Sinn Féin (when he was eager to gain approval for his policies on the oath of allegiance), his experience in power had awakened him to the dangers of delegating authority to the rank and file. If Donnelly's motion was entertained, not only would it force him to rebuff the proposals of some of the party's most ardent supporters but the ard-fheis would be heavily influenced by the presence of Northern delegates, who, no doubt, would advocate the inclusion of strongly worded provisions in the constitution—and not least their right to be represented in Dáil Éireann.

De Valera would not relish explaining to the party faithful why the leader of the self-professed republican party would not adhere to the wishes of those with whom it sought ultimate unity. He could argue that he had not formulated the provisions of the Treaty or the Boundary Agreement, nor had they ever received his assent. The problem with Donnelly's motion was that the constitutional provisions contemplated were entirely within de Valera's gift. To publicly reject the suggestions of the 'interventionist wing of the party,'[50] now bolstered by Northern republicans, would have weakened de Valera's supremacy within Fianna Fáil as the authoritative source of anti-partition policy. This could only produce a questioning of de Valera's ideological orthodoxy. So Donnelly's call for a special ard-fheis went unheeded, though the substance of his motion—that a stronger anti-partition policy was required—would have to be discarded with the maximum of care and the minimum of fuss.

On 4 January 1937 Donnelly's motion at the National Executive was seconded, but discussion was postponed, as it was deemed necessary to hold a special meeting of the National Executive to consider the issue.[51] This meeting did not take place until the beginning of February, a fact rendering obsolete the principal recommendation of the motion, an ard-fheis in early February.[52] After a brief discussion on an unrelated motion dealing with Easter Week commemoration ceremonies, the meeting adjourned for an hour and a half. When it reassembled de Valera was present (he had not been present during the earlier part of the meeting) and took the chair; and it can only be assumed that the meeting was adjourned after so short a time to facilitate his participation. Since Fianna Fáil had taken power, de Valera's attendance at National Executive meetings had become ever more infrequent.[53] His decision to attend this special meeting can be seen, therefore, as demonstrating the importance of the issue for him, and it may also have resulted from a fear that without his intervention the National Executive might adopt a policy that was embarrassing for the leadership.

Donnelly asked permission to withdraw the motion as submitted and to substitute for it the following:

> That an all-Ireland convention be called before the Constitution is introduced and that steps be taken to approach the question of the re-unification of Ireland on the basis as adumbrated in President de Valera's letter of the 19th July 1923.[54]

Some months later Donnelly would describe in the Dáil the content of de Valera's proposals in 1923.

> Derry city and the greater parts of the Counties Tyrone and Fermanagh as well as South Armagh and South Down would be represented directly in the National

Parliament. On no plea could the 'Ulster' minority [nationalists] demand anything more.[55]

Donnelly's proposal was an adroit challenge to de Valera's ideological orthodoxy. It defied him to translate opposition rhetoric into affirmative action when in power. The minutes of the National Executive reveal nothing of the content of the discussion, merely noting that Donnelly's motion was defeated by 21 votes to 4, 'after a long discussion.'[56]

De Valera was vulnerable to pressures from within his party to adopt a strong, if ill-defined, line on partition, and during the 1937 election and referendum campaign his cautious approach wavered considerably, as John Bowman has noted.

Those voters whose support for de Valera was based on their belief that only he could solve 'the national question,' might have noticed the range of opinion within Fianna Fáil, not only on how Partition might end, but also on when. Two weeks before polling day, de Valera admitted that unity might not come within 'a short time,' a prediction which may have caused misgivings in the party because during the rest of the campaign, he gradually changed his emphasis. He first predicted unity 'long before twenty years,' then 'before a very short time,' then within a 'relatively short time,' and, finally, on polling day, 'soon.'[57]

Despite de Valera's attempt to formulate a constitution that would remove the basis of republican objections to the state, it did not go far enough even for some members of his own party. The more republican wing of Fianna Fáil had called for the abolition of partition in the new Constitution, a stance supported by Northern nationalists. The most radical alternative open to the Fianna Fáil government, and the option preferred by the most ardent anti-partitionists, would have been the retention of article 2 of the Constitution of the Irish Free State without the *de facto* acknowledgement of partition as a temporary phenomenon in article 3, and with seats in the Dáil for Northern MPs.[58]

Shortly after the ard-fheis on 8 November the indefatigable Donnelly submitted a motion to the newly elected National Executive that emphasised the need for a new departure after the new constitution came into effect in December. The motion stated that 'as the present phase of National Politics definitely ends on 29 December,' Fianna Fáil should be

remodelled and made applicable to all Ireland under its present title, or, if necessary, under another name, with a view to recommending:
(a) Contesting all Parliamentary seats in Northern Ireland at coming General Election.
(b) Holding a General Election in Southern Ireland on same date.
(c) The formation of an all-Ireland National Party under the leadership of Mr. de Valera with Headquarters in Dublin.[59]

The motion was first tabled before delicate Anglo-Irish talks, and it has been suggested that Donnelly's agreement to defer it may have been at de Valera's urging.[60]

At the next meeting of the National Executive, on 22 November, Donnelly asked permission to postpone the motion until the following meeting.[61] Illness prevented him from attending subsequent meetings, and the motion was never considered.[62]

THE 1937 CONSTITUTION

The Constitution of Ireland, enacted by the Dáil in 1937 and then endorsed by plebiscite, 'completed the reconciliation of sovereignty with majority rule,'[63] and it is de Valera's most enduring legacy. The Constitution of the Irish Free State, which remained flexible throughout its short life, had been amended no less than twenty-seven times,[64] and there were objective merits in starting afresh. The principal motivation for drafting a new constitution, however, 'had less to do with inaugurating a brave new world than with bringing an old—and from de Valera's viewpoint—desperately unhappy world to a close.'[65] De Valera was determined to rid the state of the stigma of having an imposed constitution, and he wanted to ensure that the new constitution would be seen to have originated in Ireland and to have been approved by its people. He declared that the Constitution was designed as 'the framework within which a united Irish State could be rebuilt.'[66]

The Constitution of Ireland made a clear distinction between the concept of the state, which referred to the 26-county entity under the *de facto* control of Dáil Éireann, and that of the nation, which encompassed the entire population resident in the whole of Ireland. The primacy of the nation was established at the beginning of the document, as the preamble remembered with gratitude the 'heroic and un-remitting struggle to regain the rightful independence of our Nation' and stressed the need to promote the objective of seeing 'the unity of our country restored.'[67] The preamble is followed by the first two sections of the Constitution, entitled 'The Nation' (articles 1–3) and 'The State' (articles 4–11). Article 1 affirmed the 'inalienable, indefeasible and sovereign' right of the Irish *nation* to govern itself. Article 2 then defined the territorial limits of the nation, and article 3 sought to reconcile the claim that Ireland constituted the entire island with the reality of partition.

Article 2.
The national territory consists of the whole island of Ireland, its islands and the territorial seas.

Article 3.
Pending the re-integration of the national territory, and without prejudice to the right of the Parliament and Government established by this Constitution to exercise jurisdiction over the whole of that territory, the laws enacted by that Parliament shall have the like area and extent of application as the laws of Saorstát Éireann and the like extra-territorial effect.

The distinction of nation and state was maintained throughout the constitution. Article 9.2 declared that 'fidelity to the nation and loyalty to the State are fundamental duties of all citizens.'[68] Even articles that were devoid of any strong political emphasis contained the same distinction. Article 41.1.2, for example, stated that 'the Family' is the basis of social order and is 'indispensable to the welfare of the Nation and the State.' The prospect of the Belfast Parliament retaining its legislative independence but transferring authority from London to Dublin was explicitly provided for in article 15.2.2, which determined that provision could be made for 'the creation or recognition of subordinate legislatures.'

Despite the overt republican ethos of the constitution, most explicitly articulated in articles 1, 5 and 6,[69] the Constitution stopped short of declaring a republic. To the disappointment of some supporters, article 4 did not proclaim the state to be Poblacht na hÉireann or Republic of Ireland but instead asserted that the name of the state was Éire, 'or in the English language, Ireland.' De Valera's reluctance to declare a republic stemmed from his belief that only a 32-county Ireland, united as a political entity, would merit such a description. He also expressed the hope that the retention of a connection with the British Commonwealth, however tenuous, might facilitate reunification.

All fundamental rights enumerated in the Constitution were comprehensively qualified,[70] while the Government's security powers were stated without equivocation. Article 40.6.1 (i) declared ominously that

the education of public opinion being . . . a matter of such grave import to the common good, the State shall endeavour to ensure that organs of public opinion, such as the radio, the press, the cinema, while preserving their rightful liberty of expression, including criticism of Government policy, shall not be used to undermine public order or morality or the authority of the State.

It was not clear from this formulation at what stage criticism of Government policy became detrimental to the authority of the state or to the preservation of public order and morality. Where was the line that divided the two, and how did one know when one had crossed it? If a Government introduced security legislation with the expressed intention of preserving order, and this legislation was vehemently denounced by the news media, could the proponents of this view be deemed to be threatening the preservation of order? The Government subjected to criticism was to be the final arbitrator.[71]

The *pièce de résistance* of the Constitution's security provisions was undoubtedly article 28.3.3, which in one sweep denuded the Constitution of any effective guarantees protecting civil liberties. Under the provisions of this article the Government was empowered to pass any law, no matter how repugnant to the Constitution, 'which is expressed to be for the purpose of securing the public safety and the preservation of the state in time of war or armed rebellion.' It thus negated totally the provisions of article 15.4.1, which stated that 'the Oireachtas shall not enact any law which is in any respect repugnant to this Constitution or any provision thereof.' The article ran into difficulties when Seán MacBride challenged the constitutionality of legislation used to intern suspected republicans.

In response, the Government took advantage of the provision allowing it to amend the Constitution by an act of the Oireachtas for a three-year period. This period of constitutional flexibility was originally intended to facilitate minor and technical adjustments to the Constitution, but the two amendments to article 28.3.3 introduced in 1939 and 1941 were anything but, and they differed substantially from the version put to the electorate in 1937. The first amendment declared that the state need not be a participant in an armed conflict for the Oireachtas to be of the opinion that a state of emergency existed affecting the vital interests of the state. While this addition was occasioned by the outbreak of world war, it permitted the Government, in theory at least, to declare a state of emergency as a result of any external conflict, no matter how distant or extraneous to the daily life of the state.[72] As Basil Chubb has remarked, the amendment represented the first step taken 'on a road that could make a mockery of constitutional guarantees and rights.'[73]

The 1941 amendment undermined constitutional rights further and had even more far-reaching implications. It permitted the Government to extend the state of emergency beyond the cessation of actual hostilities. The combined effect of the two amendments meant that the Government could, theoretically, suspend all constitutional rights in response to a localised war that broke out on the other side of the globe and that was no longer taking place. It was for this reason that the amendment was described by one deputy, John Marcus O'Sullivan, as the 'formal wiping away of what is left of constitutional guarantees for personal liberty.'[74]

Having reduced the Constitution to an irrelevance in the sphere of constitutional rights, the Government was able to introduce the Offences Against the State Act. The state of emergency declared in September 1939 continued undiluted in its constitutional implications until September 1976, when it was rescinded, only to be replaced by a new state of emergency, introduced in response to developments in Northern Ireland. A plethora of reasons was given after the end of the Second World War to justify the retention of such draconian provisions. The Cold War and the advent of nuclear weapons were cited throughout the 1950s and 60s.[75] After 1969 the seemingly interminable conflict in Northern Ireland provided the Government with a cast-iron reason for making what was intended to be a temporary expedient a permanent reality.[76]

Numerous other provisions in the Constitution reflected de Valera's preoccupation with security matters. The exclusive right of the Oireachtas to raise and maintain armies was enshrined.[77] Provision was made for the establishment of special courts, the composition of which would be determined by the Oireachtas whenever it believed 'that the ordinary courts are inadequate' to secure effective justice and preserve order.[78] The effect of these provisions was to legitimise the establishment of military courts, which denied a defendant the right of trial by jury.

While retaining in substance the parliamentary system inherited from the British, de Valera Gaelicised his own constitutional position by creating the new title of Taoiseach for the head of the Government (as the executive was now called).[79] A position of deputy head of government, that of Tánaiste, was also established, but it did not come with any substantial powers save when deputising in the absence of the Taoiseach.[80] A directly elected President was now entrusted with a small number of constitutional functions and a larger number of ceremonial ones, many previously carried out by the British Governor-General.[81] A second chamber was reintroduced with the establishment of a sixty-seat Seanad. This was indirectly elected (though eleven members were to be appointed by the Taoiseach) through procedures corresponding to the vocational corporatist model popular in 1930s Europe.[82] Collectively the Seanad and the Dáil, together with the President, constituted the Oireachtas.

While in opposition de Valera condemned every move to curtail the right of the electorate and the individual to challenge government policy. Fianna Fáil particularly prized the provision of article 48 of the Constitution of the Irish Free State that allowed citizens to organise petitions, which, if they contained the signatures of 5 per cent of the electorate, compelled the government to hold a referendum on a particular issue. When the Free State government abolished this provision in response to Fianna Fáil's efforts to force a referendum on the oath of allegiance, the party denounced the move as 'reactionary' and 'anti-democratic' and pledged itself to obstruct government business in the Dáil.[83] During the 1932 election campaign Fianna Fáil had promised to restore the referendum initiative,[84] but after taking power the leadership displayed little enthusiasm for resurrecting the provision, and de Valera omitted it from the Constitution of Ireland.

On 1 July 1937 Fianna Fáil lost its absolute majority, with sixty-eight deputies (a loss of eight) returned to a Dáil reduced in number from 153 to 138. The Constitution fared somewhat better, obtaining the approval of 56 per cent of the valid votes cast, though, uniquely in the history of Irish referendums, almost 10 per cent of voters spoiled their ballots, an act many interpreted as signifying hostility to the proposal. De Valera was disappointed with the result and complained that 'a written constitution, to be completely understood, required to be explained to the people over a long period. They were pressed for time, as the general election was due.'[85] As Joseph Lee points out, this argument was disingenuous, as the only reason for an election being due was that de Valera had called one, six months before the government's term expired. Had he put aside his wish for a summer election more time could have been devoted to discussing the intricacies of the Constitution. Also, there was no compelling reason why the election should have been timed with the constitutional referendum, apart from saving money and a desire to link the fortunes of the party with those of the new basic law.

Few quibbled with the need for a new instrument of government, given how discredited the 1922 constitution had become and given the number of changes imposed on it; but, despite protestations to the contrary, the decision to submit the fate of the party and the Constitution to the electorate at the same time clouded the debate and unnecessarily politicised the new Constitution.

IRISH POLITICS IN THE TWILIGHT OF THE THIRTIES
Not long after the ratification of the new Constitution, de Valera entered into negotiations with the British Government aimed at addressing the myriad of issues that strained Anglo-Irish relations. For many the 1938 negotiations with the British Government—the first of their kind since Fianna Fáil had taken office—were believed to constitute a rare opportunity for ending partition. The fact that the meetings were the first face-to-face negotiations on fundamentals between de Valera and a British Prime Minister since July 1921 also raised expectations. The more optimistic Fianna Fáil supporters felt that the provisions of the Treaty, and partition, were back on the

agenda. However, what was thought to be a unique opportunity to end partition became instead the crowning glory of 26-County sovereignty.

That the dismantling of the Treaty had dominated politics throughout the 1930s was a natural development, as frustration at the lack of progress regarding partition could easily be redirected into a drive to attain the maximum independence possible for the new state. Though Britain remained intransigent on the issue of partition, de Valera tended to 'insist on linking Partition with the wider questions in Anglo-Irish relations.'[86] Deirdre McMahon has argued that labouring on the unresolved question of partition was to de Valera's advantage during the 1938 Anglo-Irish negotiations, as his 'sounding of the Partition trumpet put the onus of concession on Chamberlain.'[87] Once partition had been raised, de Valera moved on to negotiating less contentious issues.

As Clare O'Halloran succinctly put it, 'both sides contented themselves with a restatement of their entrenched positions and then turned to more amenable questions.'[88] John Bowman has claimed that such pragmatism demonstrates the questionable nature of de Valera's dedication to the eradication of partition and that the most striking feature of the 1938 agreement was that 'de Valera's primary concern was not Partition, which he believed intractable in the short term, but the return of the Treaty ports, thus facilitating southern neutrality.'[89] However, this should be seen in a broader context. There were twin tenets of faith in orthodox nationalist ideology: a commitment to ending partition and the achieving of the maximum degree of independence from Britain. As the former seemed unobtainable in these negotiations, facilitating Irish neutrality was a logical extension of the latter. More immediately, de Valera's experience in the League of Nations had alerted him to the danger of an imminent European war, and there were very practical reasons for considering the return of the ports to be of primary importance.

De Valera finally concluded an agreement with the British Government on 25 April 1938. The land annuities issue that had helped bring Fianna Fáil to power six years earlier was finally put to rest with a payment of £10 million to the British exchequer, a small fraction of what was 'owed'. De Valera said that the sum could be described as 'ransom money' and that if justice prevailed reparations would be paid 'in the opposite direction.'[90] Not only did the amount represent only two years of payments but de Valera managed to normalise trade relations with Britain and, most importantly, secure the return of the three naval bases retained by the British since 1921 at Cóbh, Castletown Bearhaven and Lough Swilly.[91]

Although de Valera successfully played the role of international statesman, some of his colleagues could not resist the temptation to interpret the significance of the agreement for the party faithful in rather colourful language. The Tánaiste, Seán T. O'Kelly, employed his oratorical skills to the full when he told an election rally in Dublin that

> in the past six years look how we whipped John Bull every time. Look at the last agreement we made with her. We won all round us, we whipped her right, left and centre, and, with God's help, we shall do the same again.[92]

Whether under the influence of O'Kelly's rhetoric or not, the agreement was very popular, and Fianna Fáil obtained its largest absolute majority at the snap election called for 17 June 1938, thus reversing the losses sustained in the 1937 contest. It was the only occasion on which de Valera managed to obtain a majority (52 per cent) of the vote,[93] showing how Fianna Fáil had moved closer to the political centre and attracted some erstwhile sceptics (or even opponents) to its banner.[94] Particularly in Dublin, Fianna Fáil courted the Protestant ex-unionist vote, which, while less power-ful than it used to be, was not insubstantial and could be vital in securing extra votes in marginal constituencies.

One of the most astonishing converts was the *Irish Times*, previously a mouth-piece for unionist opinion that still fervently defended the British connection during the 1930s. Commenting on the Fianna Fáil landslide, the paper described the results as 'eminently satisfactory . . . we are glad that he [de Valera] has been returned to power.'[95]

Fianna Fáil's election tactics had by now settled into a smug assertion that only it could rule effectively. The opposition was disunited, and the Labour Party and Fine Gael could unite only to deprive the people of de Valera's leadership (but not to legislate, as they were poles apart ideologically). A vote for either party, Fianna Fáil literature continually asserted, would mean deadlock, stagnation, chaos, and another election. In appealing to those who had rejected the party in the past Fianna Fáil portrayed itself as the party of business and the defender of the proportional representation electoral system that favoured minorities.[96]

One election address made in 1938 shows how Fianna Fáil had expanded its support considerably from the small farmer, petty bourgeoisie and ex-IRA electoral base. In a message delivered to all homes in the Dublin Townships constituency the Fianna Fáil candidate, William Black, declared that 'I have many new supporters representative of commercial success, of intellectual thought, and of academic scholarship,' and their point of view was expressed in an enclosed copy of a letter from R. G. L. Leonard KC, described as 'a staunch and leading spokesman of the "Southern Minority".'[97] Leonard's letter, addressed 'My Dear Black,' championed a vote for the Government on behalf of those who 'may be described as . . . "ex-Unionists".'[98] That Fianna Fáil could hope to attract votes from these constituencies is testimony to its ideological flexibility. But, while it was presented as a virtue in 1938 that the party was attracting all manner of people to its fold, it was conveniently forgotten that only six years earlier Fianna Fáil had mocked and berated Cumann na nGaedheal for soliciting ex-unionist votes and money. The difference, from the point of view of the Fianna Fáil leadership, was that Cumann na nGaedheal had been beholden to these unchanged unionists, mere pawns of British imperialism and the old elite, whereas Fianna Fáil had converted unionists to its cause without deviating from its republican principles.

Protected by tariffs, Irish big business increasingly threw in its lot with Fianna Fáil during the 1930s. During the 1937 election campaign in the Dublin Townships, Fianna Fáil spent £1,210 on promoting its two candidates (only one of whom was elected). This can be compared with the combined sum of £106 spent by Fine Gael on its two successful candidates and £218 spent by that party on four candidates in Co. Dublin. The Labour Party spent £350 on its candidate in the Dublin Townships.[99]

During the early years of its existence Fianna Fáil was wary of large domestic political donations, most of which in any case went to Cumann na nGaedheal. Presenting itself as the 'small man's party', Fianna Fáil instead initiated highly successful church-gate collections, though the majority of its funds came from republican sympathisers in America and Australia.[100] Once in power, Fianna Fáil would attract less money from its traditional financial supporters and would depend more on a smaller number of wealthy donors. Shortly after the election of a Fianna Fáil government in 1932 a donation of the 'undreamed-of amount' of £500 arrived. It was an unsolicited donation from Joe McGrath, formerly a well-known supporter and financial backer of Cumann na nGaedheal, who oversaw the operation of the Irish Hospitals Sweepstakes. Fianna Fáil's general secretary was aware of the party's policy on large donations, and he brought the matter to the attention of Gerry Boland, one of the party's honorary secretaries, who instructed him to send the cheque back. Seán Lemass, the party's other honorary secretary, raised the matter at a party meeting,[101] and it was decided to accept the donation.

In his highly personal review of Fianna Fáil's evolution, Kevin Boland (Gerry Boland's son) goes to considerable lengths to argue that the objection was not based on McGrath's political affiliation but on the belief that the acceptance of such a large donation was incompatible with the party's ethos. He was convinced that

> the acceptance of this subscription was a major decision, which I suppose, helped the development of the party—it certainly made decisions to call elections easier—but it was a new beginning and, certainly, not all the party realised the dangers involved to fundamental principles. It is, at least, an arguable proposition that this decision contained within it the seeds of the parasitic growth which eroded the Fianna Fáil ethos . . .[102]

Irish-American money did not dry up entirely, but influential republican supporters, such as Joe McGarrity, continued to back the IRA. As the years went on, the Irish diaspora tended to put hand in pocket for more militant brands of republicanism than that offered by de Valera's party.

Fianna Fáil election literature emphasised the skill and virtues of its leader. The 1938 agreement with Britain was presented as something that could never have been negotiated without de Valera's participation, and, as one election letter cautioned, it would be impossible to derive the fullest benefit from the settlement 'unless the Statesman who made the Agreement is permitted to carry on his good work un-hampered by misrepresentation.'[103] The same letter crowed that de Valera had 'given the country good Government . . . He restored domestic peace, and has inculcated respect for law and order which did not exist before he came to power,' without recognising in any way Fianna Fáil's part in discrediting the Free State's security policies before 1932.

Throughout the 1930s the IRA's fortunes declined, bedevilled by splits, arrests and lack of engagement with the electorate. Differences between left and right and between militants and constitutionalists were played out among an ever-decreasing number of adherents. Seán MacBride was instrumental in persuading other members of the IRA leadership to make another stab at supporting an abstentionist electoral venture, Cumann Poblachta na hÉireann. The party performed poorly in the 1936 local elections and in two by-elections, despite putting forward some veteran republican luminaries. Seán MacEntee welcomed the opportunity to confront the IRA party, which he challenged to spell out what kind of republic it envisaged. 'Was Mr Hayes's Republic to be communistic in essence?' he asked (with reference to the candidate Stephen Hayes), 'with a constitution based on the teachings of Marx and Lenin but misusing the names of Pearse and Connolly to commend it to the people?'[104] As Cumann na nGaedheal had done before him, MacEntee painted a dark picture of life without Fianna Fáil, one of arbitrary administration and open disrespect for the law. It was emphasised that constitutional evolution rather than violent revolution was the way forward, and that, in contrast to its pro-IRA rivals, Fianna Fáil did not talk idly about its ideals but worked tirelessly to bring them into effect.

The derisory number of votes cast for Cumann Poblachta na hÉireann only strengthened the conviction of those in the IRA, such as Seán Russell, who wished to dump electoral experiments for a decisive military campaign against Britain. A veteran of 1916, the War of Independence and the Civil War, Russell represented the traditional military wing that longed for a second round with Britain to achieve the republic denied them in 1921.[105] Another militant, Frank Ryan, though ideologically far to the left of Russell, was also frustrated with the lack of action, and he had taken a sizable section of the IRA to Spain, where, in the ranks of the International Brigades, they had fought to defend the republican government against Franco's fascists.[106] By 1939 Russell was in the ascendant within the IRA and had gathered around him a coterie of veterans with the expressed aim of launching a bombing campaign against England. His proposal aroused opposition and hostility from much of the IRA leadership but was popular with many ordinary members, as J. Bowyer Bell eloquently explains.

For years the army had drifted along in the wake of events, pulling small stunts and talking of a future Armageddon. The young and the active had been alienated. Russell had come back from America determined to strike out and no one high or low had produced a decent alternative. Whether or not the campaign was technically feasible, it was emotionally desirable. Russell and the Army Council were far from mad but they were angry. Despair, drift and delay had at last been put aside. If the odds were steep, so had they always been. For centuries in the marrow of their bones Irishmen had felt that in each generation someone, somewhere has to strike the first blow. Russell had offered his fist and the army voted to follow him.[107]

Chapter 7 ∿

REVOLUTIONARY CROCODILE, 1939–40

All we can say now, however, is that you appear to have run the full cycle of revolutionary movements as we know of them in history. Long ago, the various stages of revolutions were described, as when, in the French Revolution, it was pointed out that after passing through one or two stages of a revolution, a third stage is reached when certain people who had used the guillotine were being brought to the guillotine themselves because others had become successful in the meantime, and the revolution was then described as having reached the stage where the crocodile was swallowing its young. Well, the party opposite have reached the stage of revolutionary progress where the crocodile is swallowing its young. Very well; make a good meal of it—make a grill of it—but remember that we, in our time, helped to grill these people for you. We grilled a lot of these people, and we would have grilled some of you also if you had not changed your tune in the meantime.

PATRICK McGILLIGAN (DÁIL ÉIREANN, 2 MARCH 1939).[1]

THE REPUBLICAN CROCODILE SWALLOWS ITS YOUNG

Mr. Ruttledge: A lot has changed in this part of the country since 1932.
Mr. Davin: You have changed yourself.
Mr. Ruttledge: I have not changed.
Mr. Davin: Of course you have.[2]

The enactment of the Constitution of Ireland was a central event in legitimising the Fianna Fáil leadership's stance towards the IRA, and its introduction was swiftly followed by a raft of new legislation aimed at curbing militant republicanism. On 17 May 1938 the Government authorised the drafting of legislation along the lines of a proposal submitted by the Department of Justice for the establishment of a Special Criminal Court.[3]

The IRA and its republican allies were also active. In the dying months of 1938 the remnants of the second Dáil (composed of members elected at the last all-Ireland elections in 1921 who continued to present themselves as the legitimate government) had been induced to confer their 'authority' on the IRA. This demonstrated the desperation of the IRA, which during the 1920s and most of the 1930s had viewed the 'second Dáil' as something of a joke.

Secretly the IRA had been planning a bombing campaign in Britain, and the chief of staff, Seán Russell, had recalled many veterans of the War of Independence for active service. Paddy McGrath trained a younger generation in the use of explosives, Moss Twomey travelled to Britain, and Jim O'Donovan devised a blueprint for the campaign, which the IRA called the S Plan (S for sabotage).

Armed now with the 'authority' of the second Dáil, the IRA sent an ultimatum to the British Government that threatened 'appropriate action without further notice' if a statement of intent to withdraw from Ireland was not made within four days.[4] In fact the IRA had spent the previous six weeks organising and transporting explosives to England, and when its demands were not immediately acceded to the bombing campaign was started. The campaign, perhaps best remembered for the writings of one young IRA recruit, Brendan Behan, suffered a tragic setback in August 1939, when the first bomb exploded in Coventry, killing five people and injuring sixty.[5]

With world war looming, de Valera was anxious to avoid provoking Britain into encroaching on the Government's intended policy of neutrality. An Emergency Powers Bill was drafted in January 1939, and the Offences Against the State Bill was introduced on 10 February.[6] Simultaneously a new Treason Act, based largely on the 1925 act, was ratified.

By June 1939 the Offences Against the State Act had become law, and it conferred on the Government all the powers contained in the various Public Safety Acts enacted by the Cosgrave government and so vociferously denounced by Fianna Fáil while in opposition. (Comparisons with the Special Powers Act in the North were obvious.)[7] A more interesting and symbolic provision was the prohibition placed on newspapers using the name IRA to denote any organisation except that known affectionately to the Fianna Fáil leadership as the 'Old IRA'.[8] Section 30 permitted any member of the Garda Síochána, without warrant, to stop, search, interrogate or arrest any person 'whom he suspects of having committed or being about to commit or being or having been concerned in the commission of an offence under any section or sub-section of this Act'.[9] On this very broad definition a suspect could be detained for up to forty-eight hours without charge. During this period any garda could interrogate, search, photograph or fingerprint the detainee.[10]

Defending the proposed legislation, Frank Aiken told the Dáil that there was

a lot of claptrap about coercion. It takes two sets of people to make a war, and if one section starts to coerce, the other will have to try coercion too . . . Coercion is the use of force to obtain a desired object . . . Force is no argument, in my opinion.[11]

In responding to criticisms from Fine Gael, Aiken drew attention to article 2a of the Constitution of the Irish Free State, introduced by Cumann na nGaedheal in 1931. 'It is exactly the same as article 2a . . . Read article 2a for you own enjoyment,' he told John Marcus O'Sullivan, to which O'Sullivan replied: 'Very good; you are re-enacting article 2a, and I have no objection to that . . .'[12]

The Fine Gael TD Paddy Belton (who had spent a brief period in Fianna Fáil) declared that the bill vindicated Arthur Griffith and Kevin O'Higgins, and that it constituted 'a vindication of the living—the leader of this party. I hope we will not hear any more talk about secret agreements and about the treachery of the Cosgrave Ministry.'[13] He concluded: 'I venture to say that the people who were set free and who carried the minister shoulder-high down Blackhall Place are some of the men he has in mind to put in Arbour Hill again.'[14]

One Labour Party deputy, William Davin, declared himself happy to hear MacEntee claim

> that the Fianna Fáil Party and the Fianna Fáil Government, as now constituted, does not stand for revolutions. Is this not like an act of contrition for past political sins, to hear a statement like that coming from our Minister for Finance? As far as I can see, this bill, if passed in its present form, will certainly carry out the final execution of the republic that up to now, we understood, the Minister for Finance and those who think and talk with him, stood for.[15]

Patrick McGilligan (Fine Gael) said that de Valera was 'now trying to direct by forceful means into the paths of rectitude people whom you assisted to stray from these paths,' and while it was proper that he should do so he was fortunate that 'we will not go bad on you the way you would have gone bad on us. From our experience of government we know what these things mean.'[16] John A. Costello raised a similar point, claiming that 'the cycle that the present Government party have yet to complete is to find themselves once again in opposition here' and to support an alternative government confronted with similar circumstances.[17] A number of deputies also claimed that the bills would only justify anti-republican actions by the Northern government and embolden it to intern nationalists there.[18]

Perhaps the most embarrassing aspect of the debate was the sharp reminder of Fianna Fáil's past views on emergency legislation and, indeed, on the legitimacy of the Dáil. When Cumann na nGaedheal had introduced article 2a in 1931 it had been vehemently opposed by Fianna Fáil, whereas the Offences Against the State Bill incorporated thirty sections of it verbatim. William Norton quoted a speech made by de Valera in 1929 in which he said: 'I here and now declare that the Oireachtas is not the law and the legislature of Ireland, Saorstát Éireann, Republic of Ireland or any part of Ireland.'[19] In referring to the recent IRA proclamation, Seán Mac Eoin declared that 'the names may be the names of Plunkett and Russell but the words are the words of de Valera and Ruttledge.' He went on to mention the 'astonishing fact' that if one of the proclamations signed by those two ministers were now found in the pockets of someone it would render them guilty of an offence under the new measure.[20]

Dr T. F. O'Higgins (Fine Gael) claimed that the Government had a far greater responsibility to justify the proposed measures, because 'the present Government are the men who fought ruthlessly and relentlessly with every weapon against powers such as are asked for in this bill, and they did that in dangerous times.' He concluded by saying that 'people may say that the present government introducing a bill such as this are in the position of a schoolmaster who punishes the pupil for having learnt his lessons just too well.'[21] It was a theme that Fine Gale leaders warmed to. McGilligan declared that 'it may be that you will temper justice with a little mercy when you remember that some of these people you have misled by yourselves.'[22]

Fianna Fáil's replies differed in tone but were the same in substance. Previous statements by party leaders denouncing similar legislation had been made 'in quite different circumstances' (Aiken)[23] or in 'very different circumstances' (Ruttledge)[24] or, in de Valera's words, 'were misrepresented or misunderstood.'[25] How those circumstances differed was more difficult to deduce. Fianna Fáil's response to criticisms from the Labour Party was much the same as that of Cumann na nGaedheal in 1931 when it was subjected to hostile criticism of its legislation from both Fianna Fáil and the Labour Party. Concern for civil liberties was met with crude innuendoes that implied that the Labour Party was allied, in some ill-defined way, with the IRA. Aiken claimed that 'from certain phrases used by the Labour Party here, it will be taken that they favour a certain armed organisation continuing.'[26]

The section dealing with 'seditious documents' had an immediate impact. *Republican Review*, which, with the *Wolfe Tone Weekly*, represented a modest effort to fill the vacuum in republican literature after the suppression of *An Phoblacht*, bowed out rather than conform to the new wave of censorship. In its last editorial it described the provisions of the Offences Against the State Act and declared that *Republican Review* was by definition a 'seditious document', as it had always endeavoured to undermine the authority of the state, which it did not consider legitimate. The new act demonstrated the 'utter impossibility' of criticising the 26-County Government from a republican point of view, and 'all criticism of this nature must in future be printed and circulated secretly in the same manner as the Anti-Nazi journals are kept in existence in Germany.'[27]

EMERGENCY AND NEUTRALITY

The Government's legislative response to the outbreak of the Second World War was to introduce a wide-ranging amendment to the Constitution giving itself dictatorial powers for 'securing the public safety and preservation of the State in time of war' under article 28.3.3.[28] Taking advantage of the three-year flexible period during which it was not necessary to have amendments ratified by referendum, the Government summoned the Dáil by telegram, and all stages of the Emergency Powers Bill were rushed through on 3 September 1939, the day Britain declared war on Germany. Apart from extending the definition of 'time of war', as defined in article 28.3.3, the act allowed the Government to rule by decree by means of Emergency Powers Orders, which could be issued with immediate effect and without reference to the Oireachtas.[29] Seán MacEntree responded to the challenge that when the Cosgrave government had sought similar powers in 1931, and on much the same grounds, he had vehemently resisted giving such powers, declaring:

> Looking back at it now—and I think that we have got to have the courage in this country at the present time to confess our mistakes—if I made very ill-judged speeches, the fact that I am here tonight making a speech on behalf of this bill . . . is, at any rate, an admission that those measures were necessary then, and that those measures are necessary today.[30]

He was congratulated on behalf of Fine Gael by James Dillon, who described the declaration as courageous and said that the two parties had 'now arrived at common ground.'[31] The Labour Party provided the only opposition, carving out for itself the position of being the only consistent defender of civil liberties within the parliament since the 1920s.[32]

A Government Committee on Internal Security was established, headed by de Valera (who, in addition to his usual practice of keeping the posts of Taoiseach and Minister for External Affairs, had also taken on the portfolio of Education).[33]

De Valera was obsessed with avoiding the fate of his old rival John Redmond, who had dug his political grave by supporting Irish participation in the British army during the First World War. The turbulent years of 1914–18 provided ominous parallels and a cautionary tale for any party leader.[34] The Irish Party had dominated the political stage for almost fifty years and had been a powerful force in the British House of Commons. It had possessed an unprecedented and unrivalled organisation, extending to every parish. In comparison, de Valera's Fianna Fáil had been in existence for only thirteen years, and its political supremacy was never unrivalled—it had, after all, been in opposition for five years and had twice been a minority government dependent on Labour Party support. If the demise of the Irish Party had been sudden and exceptional, Fianna Fáil's position was in many ways more precarious.

But at other, more important levels Fianna Fáil was far more secure. One crucial difference was that de Valera had the power of a sovereign government at his disposal: an army, a police force, a civil service and a host of supporting institutions. Redmond had had none of these and was therefore relatively impotent, vesting his political future in the hope that his support for the British war effort would be reciprocated with the speedy delivery of the promised legislature in Dublin. Lack of competition had resulted in the organisation of the Irish Party becoming less active and flexible at the local level, as the majority of its seats were uncontested, whereas post-Treaty Civil War party politics necessitated constant organisational endeavour to stay ahead of rivals in local and national elections.

The position of the IRA in 1916 and in 1939 was also analogous, up to a point. Redmond led a party whose policy had been endorsed at successive elections, while armed republicans were but a tiny minority. De Valera had entered politics in 1914 as a member of the Irish Volunteers and, taking advantage of British involvement in world war, had participated in an armed rebellion that had little prospect of military success. His early release (after having been condemned to death) had allowed him to capitalise on Redmond's increasing unpopularity. Like the IRB of the late nineteenth and early twentieth century and in particular the period 1914–16, the IRA of the 1930s and 40s armed and organised, waiting for the appropriate moment to strike. During both wars it made contact with Germany to further its endeavours and received funds from America, in particular through Joe McGarrity.

While de Valera had decided on joining a rebellion in Dublin to capitalise on British attention elsewhere, the IRA in 1939 had reverted to the Fenian tactic of a bombing campaign in England. Redmond had to watch as the British Government executed republicans in the most public way. As Seán Cronin has pointed out,

de Valera would never forget the example of John Redmond who had been driven from the political stage by his own generation of 1916 rebels. He made sure that it would not happen a second time.[35]

With the assistance of pervasive censorship, and without the odium attached to being a foreign power, the Fianna Fáil leadership would also execute IRA leaders and would allow republican prisoners to die on hunger strike. There would be no retrospective endorsement of the IRA.

Military neutrality was the only logical option for any government in the circumstances in which Ireland found itself. The army was in a poor state, capable of dealing with internal subversion but with little else. Participation in the war would not only have thrown up the very real prospect of invasion but would have exposed unprotected urban centres to the whims of the world's most sophisticated air force, which would have extracted a heavy price for Irish involvement. Such destruction would be for nothing, as the Irish forces would be unable to render effective assistance. And Ireland's entry into a war of such magnitude would have had not the slightest effect on the outcome. The existence of partition, as de Valera never tired of pointing out, also rendered a military alliance with the British impossible and politically suicidal.

Neutrality enjoyed cross-party support and created a political consensus that was unique in post-Civil War Ireland. Even the IRA, despite its reckless high-risk strategy, supported neutrality, and most observers seem to accept that it would have fought to defend it should the occasion have arisen. However, throughout the war Fianna Fáil did its utmost to present neutrality as an exclusively Fianna Fáil concept, and Government-sponsored censorship was used to promote this view. It was understandable and natural that the opposition parties would want to portray their support for neutrality as the product of an independent appraisal of the political situation rather than as the blind following of a Fianna Fáil consensus.

Sensitivities on both sides reached a peak towards the end of 1942, as all parties knew that the Government was constitutionally obliged to hold an election early the following year. A Labour Party advertisement in November 1942 that stated 'Labour's foreign policy: Labour is the keystone of the national arch of neutrality' was changed by the censor to 'Labour's foreign policy: neutrality.' Another advertisement that stated simply 'Labour policy is the people's policy of strict neutrality' was stopped altogether.[36] On the face of it such an advertisement could be interpreted as depicting a disciplined people united under the banner of neutrality. The Labour Party was merely stating that it reflected the will of the people, but this was obviously unacceptable: neutrality, according to the censor, was Fianna Fáil's policy.

While de Valera constantly declared that the state was in imminent danger and proclaimed the intrinsic value of neutrality, he resisted appeals by Fine Gael and the Labour Party to form a coalition. Joseph Lee notes that these parties 'despite their staunch parliamentary support for neutrality were treated as virtual pariahs.'[37]

The idea of a wartime national coalition government, like that created in Britain, was anathema to de Valera, who was always unwilling to share his party's hard-won power. His answer was to create the National Defence Conference, a forum in which opposition politicians could meet Government ministers to 'offer advice on the problems arising from the war.'[38] It had no powers and did little to mollify opposition leaders, such as Richard Mulcahy, who complained of being treated contemptuously and of having to grub for information 'like hens scratching.'[39]

OFFERS OF IRISH UNITY

The actions of the de Valera Government during the Second World War have been the subject of considerable analysis, with some attributing partitionist motives to the South's neutrality policy. Roy Foster has argued that de Valera rebuffed offers of reunification in return for Southern entry into the war because 'the principle of neutrality was too closely bound up with Irish identity and Irish sovereignty to be easily relaxed.'[40] There is an element of truth in such arguments, but they do not capture the complexity of what exactly was on offer. This argument is most cogent in relation to the offer made by the British Prime Minister, Neville Chamberlain, in May 1940. With Britain fearing for the future, the British Cabinet began for the first time since partition to seriously consider the possibility of Irish reunification, in this case as a means of extracting military concessions. Suddenly, the adage that Britain's difficulty was Ireland's opportunity appeared to hold true.

The revised terms of Britain's final offer were conveyed to de Valera on 26 June. The British Government would issue an immediate declaration accepting the principle of a united Ireland and would give a solemn undertaking that unity would become an accomplished fact at an early date, from which there would be no turning back. A joint body composed of representatives from the Northern and Southern governments would be established immediately

> to work out the Constitutional and other practical details of the Union of Ireland. The London Government was willing to assist in this work with the common objective of establishing 'at as early a date as possible the whole machinery of government of the Union.'

In return, a North-South Defence Council would be set up immediately, and the Irish Government—which would be provided with necessary military equipment from Britain—would invite British naval vessels to use ports under its jurisdiction. British soldiers and planes would co-operate with the Irish army at certain points, to be agreed by the two governments, for the purpose of increasing the security of the 26 Counties so as to avoid the fate of the other neutral states that had been overrun by Germany. The Irish Government would intern all German and Italian nationals and 'take any further steps necessary to suppress Fifth Column activities.'[41]

Malcolm MacDonald, who was Secretary of State for Dominion Affairs during much of the later 1930s and Secretary of State for the Colonies from 1938 to 1940, later recalled that when he was on his own de Valera would confide that even if he assented his Government would not agree. MacDonald assumed that de Valera meant Frank Aiken, who had swapped the Defence portfolio he had held for seven years for the position of Minister for the Co-Ordination of Defensive Measures.[42] John Redmond's shadow also loomed, and his legacy of supporting the British war effort for the unfulfilled promise of home rule was undoubtedly an inhibiting factor. De Valera had admitted as much some months earlier when he told Chamberlain that 'his position might rapidly come to resemble that of Mr. Redmond in the Great War when the latter lost the support of the majority in Ireland through his loyalty to the empire.'[43] And the memory of the Treaty's promise of a judicious improvement on the existing partition boundaries cannot have been far from de Valera's mind.

Perhaps even more influential for de Valera—definitely so for Aiken—was the idea that Britain would lose the war, and that the Government was being asked to align itself with a lost cause for which there would no doubt be retribution from the victorious Germans.

Churchill's proposal to de Valera eighteen months later was far less tangible. A cryptic telegram delivered at 2 a.m. on 8 December 1941 made reference to Ireland having the chance to become a 'Nation Once Again.'[44] De Valera interpreted this to mean a united Ireland, while Churchill subsequently interpreted it as meaning that 'by coming into the war, Ireland would regain her soul.'[45] Churchill thus made it possible for de Valera to reject his offer with an ease of style and clarity of conscience that had not accompanied his deliberations on the earlier Chamberlain proposals.[46] He admired and trusted Chamberlain but felt no such sentiments for Churchill.[47]

Since coming to power Churchill had sent a stream of threatening missives to the Irish Government, aimed at frightening it into supporting the British war effort.[48] In this they were gauchely if sometimes effectively assisted by the US minister plenipotentiary to Ireland, David Gray. Only a month before Churchill's enigmatic telegram Gray had warned the Taoiseach that 'Americans could be cruel if their interests were affected and Ireland should expect little or no sympathy if the British took the ports.'[49]

CENSORSHIP AND THE IDEOLOGICAL WAR

The reach of the censor's talons was pervasive throughout the war years as Fianna Fáil continued its battle with republican rivals, with the defence that this was being done to better protect the country. This standard explanation—that Fianna Fáil's repressive policies were a result of the national emergency—can be challenged by placing these policies in context. Fianna Fáil had experienced the heavy hand of censorship in 1931 when the *Irish Press* was hauled before the military tribunal for questioning the Garda Síochána's interrogation techniques. On assuming power, however, the Fianna Fáil leadership were if anything more sensitive to censure and eager to stifle criticism in the media.

Early in 1932 an acrimonious correspondence developed between de Valera and the Governor-General of the Irish Free State, James MacNeill, concerning perceived snubs of the King's representative in Ireland during the Eucharistic Congress. When MacNeill released the letters for public consideration de Valera responded by going to extraordinary lengths to prohibit their publication by any newspaper in the Free State. When MacNeill released the correspondence to the newspapers in Northern Ireland and Britain, de Valera stopped the Northern papers at the border and the British papers at Dún Laoghaire. In the end the episode was reduced to a farce, and, realising that the ban had proved ineffective and counterproductive, de Valera released the papers himself. But behind the absurd drama lay a serious issue. A news item critical of de Valera was equated with a threat to the state. The state, however, had not been damaged, only Fianna Fáil—and, more particularly, its leader.

In the correspondence de Valera had responded to MacNeill's accusation that he had censored the *Irish Press* by admitting that 'any particular item of news would, it is true, be suppressed were I to issue an express order to that effect,' before quickly denying that he had abused this position of authority with the paper. However, such formal censorship was not necessary most of the time, as the *Irish Press* staff was recruited from Fianna Fáil supporters, and the editor, Frank Gallagher, was a long-time follower of the party president[50]—not to mention that the de Valera family owned the paper. Government power meant that Fianna Fáil control went much further than the offices of the *Irish Press*, and when it was considered necessary—as in the MacNeill case—a blanket ban on all newspapers could be imposed.

As Minister for Posts and Telegraphs in the early 1930s Gerry Boland was highly sensitive to criticism. Despite his assiduous efforts to minimise the amount of jazz transmitted on Radio Éireann, the secretary of Conradh na Gaeilge, Seán Óg Ó Ceallaigh, had criticised the Minister for Finance, Seán MacEntee, for displaying what he considered insufficient zeal in this regard. Ó Ceallaigh, who was due to embark on a series of broadcasts, was promptly banned from Radio Éireann by Boland. Defending his action, the minister said that 'if he wants to make a personal attack on a Minister, he can [not] do it over the radio if I can help it.' As Rex Cathcart has pointed out, this ban was 'purely vindictive,' as Ó Ceallaigh would have been speaking from a script submitted some time before for examination.[51] He might have added that Ó Ceallaigh's lectures, devoted to 'the Gaelic heritage', did not contain any criticism of the Fianna Fáil government.[52] In effect the Government was punishing Ó Ceallaigh for criticising a Fianna Fáil minister.

Such notions of censorship also extended to literature, and, as John A. Murphy records, there existed 'a widespread feeling that the indecent and obscene label was only a pretext for getting at unorthodox views and at authors who did not serve the cause of Catholic nationalism.'[53] Seán Ó Faoláin—who had written a biography of de Valera, entitled *Unique Dictator*—joined the host of literary victims of censorship when, in 1936, his novel *Bird Alone* was banned. This situation would continue after the war, when Ireland was described as having 'the fiercest literary censorship' in western Europe.[54]

During a Dáil debate on the proposed Constitution of Ireland, de Valera had elaborated on what he considered the basis of censorship policy in the Free State.

> I say that the right of citizens to express freely their convictions and opinion cannot, in fact, be permitted in any state. Are we going to have anarchical principles, for example, generally propagated here? I say no . . . You should not give the proponents of what is wrong and unnatural the same liberty as would be accorded to the proponents of what is right.[55]

The primacy of state interests in matters relating to censorship was clear, as was the fact that the Government would assume the role of arbiter. Less clear was how one was to distinguish between 'right' and 'wrong' ideas. These statements, however, made well before the outbreak of world war and in a relatively tranquil political climate, indicate that the Fianna Fáil leadership's censorious mentality was established before 1939, and it is in this context that later events should be understood.

During the war years press censors were working constantly from 9 a.m. to 3 a.m. to ensure a uniform presentation of the 'facts' as understood by the Government.[56]

A memorandum prepared by the Censorship Board for Frank Aiken before the debate on the defence estimates in the Dáil in February 1940 declared that it was 'the right and duty of the Government to avail of information obtained in the public interest. That is what Censorship is for.' It was contended that the state was entitled to use any information that it could obtain for 'the common good,' whether this information related to criminal offences *or otherwise*. Demonstrating the degree of sophistry perfected on security-related matters, the memorandum concluded that the imposition of censorship

> is the very negation of secrecy. Censorship and secrecy are incompatible—the one excludes the other—and as the object of censorship is to enable the authorities to know what is going on it is foolish to expect them not to use this information—in the interests of the State of course—when they obtain it.[57]

In short, there could be no secrets from the state. Every sentiment expressed was to be examined to ensure conformity, and those not fully appreciative of the state were suspect. Letters were opened and examined for politically (and sometimes even morally) deviant tendencies. Letters addressed to specific individuals were divided into three categories: the 'black' list, the 'white' list and the 'watching' list. The black list comprised those whose correspondence was required for examination by the Military Intelligence Section of Army Headquarters or by the Censorship Office; the white list consisted of individuals whose correspondence was exempt from censorship (such as heads of state and heads of diplomatic missions); and the watching list consisted of those whose correspondence was temporarily scrutinised. These letters were given to the chief political censor or his deputy, who would decide on the most appropriate response. The remainder was distributed to the sorters, who examined approximately two thousand letters a day, looking for objectionable passages. Letters considered suspicious, objectionable or merely possibly objectionable were brought to the attention of the supervisor, who, if they required additional consideration, referred the matter to their superiors, up the hierarchy to the deputy chief or chief censor.[58]

According to the Controller of Censorship, T. J. Coyne, 'the staff quickly acquired an almost uncanny instinct for picking out the potential trouble-makers.'[59] All those employed in the Postal Censorship Section were investigated by Military Intelligence and the Gardaí to assess their suitability; some were fired when it emerged that suspected republicans were among their acquaintances.[60]

Letters that aroused suspicion sometimes led to surveillance. The continuity of anti-republican surveillance was illustrated by the fact that one Military Intelligence man employed to monitor republicans had previously been assigned to following Frank Aiken before he became Minister for Defence in 1932.[61]

The ideological basis of the censorship was explicit. 'There is a public interest to be preserved,' the Controller of Censorship told the editor of the *Standard*, 'which requires that nothing should be published at the present time which would encourage the idea that the so-called IRA of today is in apostolic succession to the pre-truce or even the pre-1931 body.' He therefore ordered that there should be no publication of 'anything which could give anyone an excuse for supporting the so-called IRA of today.'[62] The addendum 'at the present time' was a subterfuge, as it suggested that the situation would be different in circumstances other than those prevailing during the national emergency. The aim was to break the continuity of the IRA in the public mind, an objective that predated the emergency and would outlive it.

Some IRA leaders of the 1940s, such as Seán Russell and Jim O'Donovan, had worked with Michael Collins, and the IRA leadership contained numerous War of Independence veterans, such as George Plant and Paddy McGrath. The reference to the 'pre-1931' IRA suggests that the IRA had operated with a degree of legitimacy before Fianna Fáil's rise to power. The essential continuity of the IRA leadership had been acknowledged by Cumann na nGaedheal; but that party had had a vested interest in linking the IRA and Fianna Fáil leaderships.[63] No such interest now existed for the Fianna Fáil hierarchy.

As part of this ideological war the reporting of republican commemorations, particularly those commemorating the 1916 Rising or of Wolfe Tone at Bodenstown, was censored. Many of these gatherings were banned; only reporting of the official Fianna Fáil commemorations was permitted. When Detective-Sergeant Dinny O'Brien of the Special Branch was shot by the IRA in a premeditated attack in 1942 the press censors were instructed to stop the word 'gunmen' being used and to substitute 'murderers'. The *Irish Independent* responded by omitting the passages of its report that contained the substitution, while the *Evening Herald* refused to publish any report of the incident. The refusal of the papers to describe the killing as murder was partly motivated by the fact that only the previous week the press had been discouraged from describing as murder the execution of the IRA man Tom Williams by the Belfast government.[64]

The justifications of 'national security' and 'preserving neutrality' were repeated mantra-like but were selectively employed. All reporting of executions carried out in the 26 Counties was suppressed, and for reprieve campaigns it was denied. By way of contrast, reporting pertaining to the executions carried out by the governments in the North (of Williams) or in England (of Barnes and McCormack) was permitted. Reprieve campaigns established to save the lives of IRA men sentenced to death by those regimes were afforded press coverage during the emergency period, though it could have been argued that such publicity promoted anti-British sentiment and so endangered neutrality. Similarly, all matters relating to the imprisonment or intern-ment of republicans in the South was suppressed, while similar information relating to the North was permitted. For the public a picture was painted that only the old enemies of Irish republicanism, the Ulster unionists and the British government, killed IRA men.

Republicans had few means of contesting the official interpretation. Shortly after the declaration of the emergency the Censorship Board contacted Government departments seeking information on any matters 'which it is desirable to prohibit from the point of view of the welfare and protection of the State.'[65] The *Wolfe Tone Weekly* was the first casualty, ceasing publication on 30 September 1939; its proprietor and deputy editor, Joseph Clarke, a 1916 veteran, was interned.[66] At that time the eight-page journal was the only republican publication in circulation.[67] *War News* was produced clandestinely in December 1939 but ceased publication after its second issue seven months later. Another publication, *Republican News*, was issued sporadically throughout 1942 and 1943. The title was hand-drawn, and it was typed rather than printed. It was distributed free of charge and was difficult to circulate. Readers were asked to pass their copy on to a friend or to leave it in a tram, bus or train when they had finished reading it.[68]

THE GERMAN CONNECTION

The existence of an alliance between the IRA and the Nazi government was central to the case presented by the Fianna Fáil leadership to justify drastic anti-republican measures.

What was the German connection? It was more ephemeral than enduring, and it was similar in many ways to the 'German Plot' of 1918 and the 'Russian Plot' of 1931–2, manufactured by the British and Cumann na nGaedheal governments, respectively. The German authorities were divided over the desirability of links with the IRA. The Foreign Office had sought the advice of the head of the German legation in Dublin, Dr Eduard Hempel, who advised against such links, arguing that the IRA was militarily weak and that German interests could best be served by not allowing the British any excuse to invade Ireland. The Nazi Foreign Minister, Joachim von Ribbentrop, had agreed with this assessment but wanted to ride two horses, tolerating Irish neutrality but also supporting the IRA. The matter was resolved by the Under-Secretary of the Foreign Office, Paul Woermann, who, in a memorandum of 10 February 1940, argued that in essence the IRA and Fianna Fáil wanted the same thing: the reunification of Ireland; the only difference between them was their choice of methods, he claimed, and he noted that most Irish Government members were themselves former IRA leaders. Therefore, he concluded, 'by reason of their militant attitude towards England, the IRA is Germany's natural ally.'[69]

To this end a German agent, Hermann Görtz, had been sent to Ireland shortly after Seán Russell's arrival in Berlin. His presence was known to both British and Irish Military Intelligence, but, despite their fears, the German-IRA alliance never posed a serious threat. The IRA and Görtz distrusted each other,[70] and most of Görtz's time in Ireland was spent on the run. Even SS Col. Edmund Veesenmayer, the Foreign Ministry official most intimately involved in German intelligence operations in Ireland, was forced to concede that 'the value of his activity in Ireland has sunk to nil.'[71] By the end of 1943 Military Intelligence had captured twelve German agents, including Görtz, and by April 1944 the Allies were satisfied that they 'could find no flaw in G2's [Military Intelligence] arrangements and [were] sure that the D-Day preparations would not be leaked via Dublin.'[72]

A number of factors militated against the IRA attaining any substantial gains from its relationship with Nazi Germany. Firstly, there was the efficiency of Military Intelligence and the police. Also, German interdepartmental warfare, combined with a general ignorance of Irish affairs, diluted the quality of support rendered to the IRA. However, it was the general disorganisation of the IRA itself that was the decisive factor. The S-Plan was doomed from the start. The first paragraph of the plan argued that 'in order to exercise maximum world effect, the diversion must be carried out at a time when no major war or world crisis is on,' conditions that could certainly not be said to exist in 1939. Either the IRA leadership had not got its finger on the pulse of world trends or the initial rationale was abandoned in favour of the more traditional attraction of exploiting 'England's difficulty' to further republican objectives.

PRISON LIFE AND THE QUESTION OF POLITICAL STATUS

During the years of the Second World War more than 1,500 people were incarcerated without trial in No. 1 Internment Camp in the Curragh, a name rapidly replaced in popular currency with 'Tintown'. Not since the Civil War had there been so many political prisoners, a comparison that did little to warm the hearts of Fianna Fáil ministers, all of whom had been subjected to imprisonment for politically inspired actions against the established authority.

The use of prisons as agents of political control had been documented for many years in Ireland. While the prison system aimed to break the will of political dissidents—political prisoners suffered much greater deprivations than ordinary prisoners—they survived because of their commitment to the sustaining ideology of Irish republicanism. As the majority of the IRA members were imprisoned during the emergency period, so the battle was joined anew in the prison camps. J. Bowyer Bell noted:

> For most IRA men Mountjoy and Arbour Hill, the coldest prison in Europe, were way stations on the road to the Curragh Camp. Caught by surprise by the need for a concentration camp, they [the Government] had neither the time nor the inclination to set up an elaborate establishment but had cordoned off an area of bleak wooden huts with a barbed wire fence. Sanitary and kitchen facilities were primitive, the huts nearly derelict, and recreation possibilities remote.[73]

In such a stimulus-deprived environment republicans fiercely resisted attempts to be converted, holding ideals they often felt to be more important than remaining alive. Prison was used as a social control agency in which prisoners were constrained at all levels and were stripped of autonomy. Their self-image was challenged, as they were refused recognition as political prisoners, even though everything about their predicament could be traced to political events, domestically and internationally.

The prisons became the battleground for contesting ideologies. For republicans, to permit the Government to treat them as criminals was to allow the state to determine the nature of their struggle. For the Fianna Fáil leadership, to acknowledge the political character of their actions would be to risk undermining their own claims to ideological purity and republican legitimacy. While the Government held the upper hand, the determination of republicans to refuse to co-operate at least denied the Fianna Fáil leadership an undisputed victory.

The fate of Barney Casey, shot dead without cause by military police on 14 December 1940, provided a striking example of the vicissitudes of the internment camps.[74] Following the killing the Minister for Justice, Gerry Boland, issued an order under the Emergency Powers Act to the Kildare County Coroner that jettisoned the jury normally assembled for an inquest. Only the identification of the victim and medical evidence was to be heard. All that would be established was what was already known: that Barney Casey had died from injuries consistent with those resulting from gunshot wounds. When Seán MacBride tried to cut through the veil of secrecy with one piercing question—'Why was Barney Casey shot in the back?'—the inquest was adjourned at once, never to reassemble. MacBride did manage, however, to force the authorities to put it on record that 'the entrance wound was at the back and the exit wound at the front.' The more fundamental question of 'why' has never been answered.[75]

The vindictiveness that characterised the treatment of republican prisoners is all the more stark when compared with the comparatively luxurious treatment afforded to the other internees held during the war. Captured soldiers and airmen of the Allied and Axis forces were interned in No. 2 Internment Camp, or the 'K Lines', as it was commonly called. Only a mile from Tintown, the K Lines were another world. These internees were housed in large huts that were divided into six rooms, each with electric light, wardrobe, chest of drawers, mirror, bed, table, chair, curtains and mat. Large washrooms were attached, in each of which there were two toilets, three hand-basins and two showers, with hot water available for almost fourteen hours a day. Because of the large number of soldiers stationed at the Curragh, the camp was equipped with the country's most modern recreational facilities, and 'the internees were offered the run of these.' The facilities included a fully equipped gymnasium, an indoor swimming pool, squash, handball and tennis courts, and a number of playing fields for various outdoor sports. Most popular was the eighteen-hole golf course, where Allied internees passed many an afternoon with former British officers or serving Irish ones.[76] Nightly inspections were discontinued, and the prisoners were given a weekly allowance that was enviable in austere wartime conditions—£3 for officers, £2 for others—as well as £5 each for the purchase of civilian clothes.[77] Such facilities were afforded despite the fact that many Allied internees were committed to escaping and rejoining the war effort, which they sometimes succeeded in doing.

THE 1939 HUNGER STRIKES

Repressive policies towards the IRA soon became politically embarrassing and a source of dissent within Fianna Fáil. When the new Minister for Justice, Gerry Boland, ordered the internment of suspected IRA members, the first batch included Paddy McGrath, a well-known veteran who had fought in 1916 and been seriously wounded by British forces during the War of Independence; indeed a number of bullets remained in his body. Imprisoned in Mountjoy, McGrath led republican prisoners on a hunger strike in protest against their imprisonment without trial. As J. Bowyer Bell has pointed out, the use of the traditional weapon of hunger strike by a man whose republican credentials were impeccable posed serious political and ideological problems for the Government.

> To concede too quickly would soon empty the prisons and make a mockery of the law. To wait too long would engender the wrath of a people all too familiar with their heritage of heroes who had sacrificed themselves for their beliefs . . . [McGrath's] 'crime' was loyalty to the ideals once held by the men imprisoning

him and his means no different than theirs had been in the past. Times may have changed but McGrath had not. Yet his release would be a public sign of weakness and the first step toward the collapse of public security.[78]

On 31 October 1939 the Government considered the case of the four hunger-strikers and decided that they should not be released. The grounds of their decision was that the powers of arrest and detention had been lawfully conferred on the Government by the Dáil and that the Government 'could not permit the State Authorities to be deprived of these means by the policy of the hunger-strike.'[79]

A week later de Valera and Boland met a deputation from the National Association of the Old IRA, who intervened on behalf of the hunger-strikers and whose support the Government was eager to secure during the emergency. In response to press enquiries, a statement was issued saying that the delegation had been informed that the Government had already considered the matter and reached its decision.[80] Letters and telegrams flowed in from the United States from traditional Fianna Fáil and republican supporters. Petitions were also received from Margaret Pearse,[81] sister of Patrick and William, who had represented both Sinn Féin and Fianna Fáil, had launched the *Irish Press* and was now a Fianna Fáil senator. The leader of the Army Mutiny of 1924, Liam Tobin, who appears to have been friendly with de Valera, also had a private meeting with him on the issue.[82] The Parliamentary Labour Party unanimously called for the immediate release of the hunger-strikers, describing internment without charge or trial as 'a grave breach of the liberty of the citizen' and claiming that resorting to such methods was not 'calculated to promote peaceful and harmonious conditions so much to be desired at this critical time.'[83]

In response to such appeals de Valera made an authoritative pronouncement on 9 November 1939, describing his position on the hunger-strike tactic and its impact on the security of the state. The IRA (not mentioned by name) had 'definitely proclaimed itself as entitled to exercise the powers of government here.' He did not wish to see the men die, but the Government, having found itself confronting 'the alternatives of two evils,' had chosen the lesser one, and 'the lesser evil is to see men die rather than that the safety of the whole community should be endangered.' He predicted that if the hunger-strikers were released every prisoner the Government sought to detain would follow suit until the prisons were emptied. Unless the Government faced up to the lesser evil of letting men die on hunger strike it would be unable to rule. 'Not merely would we be abdicating as a Government but we would be making it impossible for any other government to govern.'[84]

In the end the Government managed to see the affair resolved without losing face. On 1 December, Mr Justice George Gavan Duffy decided favourably on a *habeas corpus* application on behalf of Séamus Burke of Co. Mayo, who had been interned in Arbour Hill military prison.[85] The judgement declared that part VI of the recently enacted Offences Against the State Act was in conflict with the Constitution, as the minister's power under the act to order the detention of a person when he was 'satisfied' that it was necessary was a usurpation by the executive of powers reserved by the Constitution for the judiciary. He ruled the act unconstitutional and invalid, and ordered the immediate release of Burke. An appeal to the Supreme Court failed to reverse the decision, as the court held that it had no jurisdiction to hear an appeal against the granting of an order of *habeas corpus*.[86]

On 2 December the Government was forced to release fifty-three IRA men from Arbour Hill, including Paddy McGrath, then on the forty-second day of his hunger strike. Not for the first time, the judiciary had saved the Government from a potentially explosive situation. In a sense, the Fianna Fáil leadership had had the best of both worlds: McGrath had been released without any concessions, and the Government was able to say that it had been legally compelled to act as it did. On the other hand, the Fianna Fáil leadership had learnt some important lessons and could now introduce new legislation making its security powers watertight and resistant to legal challenge.

De Valera told the Seanad on 4 January 1940 that the Government had been 'taken by surprise', as the 'instrument for preserving the safety of the public was broken in their hands by the court's decision.'[87] But what was broken could easily be mended, in the form of the Offences Against the State (Amendment) Act (1940), which was upheld by a majority of the Supreme Court. Wounded by the fact that he had not secured unanimous endorsement, de Valera introduced the Second Amendment of the Constitution Act (1941), inserting article 34.4.5, which required that only one judgement be given by the Supreme Court while deciding on the constitutionality of any post-1937 law.[88] Even within the judiciary no disunity was permitted.

D'ARCY AND MCNEELA

The issue of political status did not go away, however. Six prisoners—Jack Plunkett, Tomás Mac Curtáin, Thomas Grogan, Seán (Jack) McNeela, Michael Traynor and Tony D'Arcy—demanded that three men who had been sentenced to five years' penal servitude and who were now in Mountjoy Prison be afforded the same status as other convicted republican prisoners. The prisoners' view was that, having been brought before the military tribunal and having thus been deprived of a civil trial, these men had the right to be treated as military, not civil, prisoners. When this demand was not conceded the six men embarked on a hunger strike, thus raising the stakes in the ideological battle between Fianna Fáil and its republican critics.

Two letters to the national press illustrated the nature of this contest. Relatives of the leaders of the 1916 Rising executed by the British signed the first. Kathleen Clarke, widow of Tom Clarke, was Lord Mayor of Dublin and still a member of Fianna Fáil, though her relationship with the party might best be described as one of 'external association'.[89] Áine Ceannt, Roddy Connolly, Neans Uí Rathgaille, Maud Gonne MacBride and Donagh MacDonagh added their names to the appeal.[90] A second letter was signed by the relatives of those who had died on hunger strike between 1917 and 1920 in their fight with the British colonial regime for political status.[91]

Because of the censorship procedures the Government was given advance notice of the letters, and the Government Information Bureau submitted a statement by Gerry Boland to be published in response. Most of the statement dealt with the attempts to draw parallels with political prisoners of the past, in particular with those incarcerated as a result of the 1916 Rising. As required by the Offences Against the State Act, the IRA was never referred to by name in the statement, but on the particular issue of the hunger strikes all Boland would say was that 'the responsibility for any consequences must rest not with the Government but with those who engage in the hunger strike and with those who thoughtlessly or recklessly encourage it.'[92] He evaded reference to the question of political status for republican prisoners, and so the central issue remained unresolved.

Despite the urgency of impending deaths, the hunger strike was not discussed by the Government at its meetings on 16 or 23 April, with predictable results. On 16 April, 31-year-old Tony D'Arcy died after seven weeks without food. He was described by the *Connacht Tribune* as 'a well-known figure in the West.' His family had been involved during the War of Independence, and his brother Louis had been shot dead by British soldiers in 1920. Tony D'Arcy had been arrested on 17 February and sentenced to three months' imprisonment in the Special Criminal Court for refusing to give his name and address and for refusing to account for his movements.[93] Addressing the jury, Seán MacBride attributed D'Arcy's death to the 'the intolerance of the Government and those in power who allowed a man with only a few days of his sentence to go to die on hunger strike.'[94] On behalf of the state, J. A. McCarthy KC said that everyone regretted the death of Tony D'Arcy, but the executive authority 'could not surrender to the demands made,' as 'such a surrender would have amounted to a negation of their own authority.' The jury took the unusual step of adding a rider to their verdict that urged 'immediate action' with regard to the remaining five hunger-strikers, and it expressed 'sincerest sympathy' with D'Arcy's widow and family. Coverage in the national press was negligible, but it did receive a quarter page in the *Connacht Tribune*, which reported that Galway Borough Council had voted sympathy with the relatives of Tony D'Arcy.[95] Galway County Council, Galway County Board of Health and Galway Harbour Board all voted sympathy and adjourned their meetings as a mark of respect.[96] The sympathy seems to have extended to members of the state forces, and it was reported that when D'Arcy's coffin, draped with a Tricolour, was being removed from St Bricin's Military Hospital in Dublin 'military police, soldiers and Gardaí, at intervals, stood at the salute.'[97]

When it had become clear that the men were going to die, the Government had begun to prepare for limiting the damage. The day before D'Arcy died the Department of Justice drew up a memorandum for the Government on the issue of inquests for those who died as a result of hunger strike. It claimed that it had been suggested to the Minister for Justice (by whom it did not say) that it would be worth considering an Emergency Powers Order to the effect that in the event of the death of a hunger-striker no inquest would be held, provided that the medical officer certified that the cause of death was attributable to the refusal of the deceased to take food.[98]

The Government did not issue the order at this time, perhaps because D'Arcy died the day after the memorandum and the draft Emergency Powers Order had been prepared, and there may have been insufficient time. However, some aspects of the proposal were to be applied. In an act that would be charged with emotive and symbolic resonance, under the draft order the body of a dead hunger-striker was to become the property of the state, and 'power is given as to the disposal of the body of the deceased.'[99] Such power was necessitated by 'the danger of the burial being made an excuse for inflammatory demonstration.' De Valera, more than most, knew the incendiary potential of graveside orations: it was, after all, Pearse's 'inflammatory' speech over the grave of O'Donovan Rossa in 1915 that provided the rallying call for de Valera's generation of republicans.

During the hunger strikes the issue at stake was not, as the Government some-times suggested, the release of prisoners, or that of better treatment: it was that all republican prisoners sentenced by the military tribunal should be afforded political status and be treated as political prisoners.[100] Throughout the years of the emergency the Government persistently evaded this issue.

In quintessential de Valera fashion, civil servants were instructed to research the position of political prisoners internationally and to consult textbooks for the precise definition of what constituted insurgency and political status. The first draft of an internal Department of Justice document on the subject was submitted to the secretary to the Taoiseach, Maurice Moynihan, on the night before Jack McNeela died. It stated that 'under the system as we inherited it from the British regime and as it still exists there is no recognition of "political prisoners".'[101] However, it was noted that under the Offences Against the State Act the treatment of persons convicted by the Special Criminal Court was 'almost entirely within the discretion of the Minister for Justice, demonstrating that the withholding of political status was motivated not by legal considerations but by politics and ideology. The research undertaken by the Department of Justice revealed that, while most countries did not provide for 'political courts', 'political prisons' or 'political treatment', some countries, including Sweden, Belgium, Portugal, Spain and Argentina, recognised certain crimes as political offences.

The most remarkable feature of this research is that it was undertaken at all. In attempting to produce a scholarly international study the Fianna Fáil leadership tried to distance itself from what was, from an Irish point of view, an emotional and in-tensely ideological issue on which many in Fianna Fáil had campaigned before coming to power.

Finally, and perhaps influenced by D'Arcy's death, an outside visitor, Father O'Hare, was permitted to visit Mountjoy Prison on 19 April, and he succeeded in persuading the four other prisoners to end their protest. But it came too late for 22-year-old Jack McNeela, who died four hours later.

The close-knit nature of the broad republican family was evident in the fact that McNeela was a nephew of Michael Kilroy, a prominent IRA veteran who had repre-sented Sinn Féin and then Fianna Fáil in the Dáil between 1923 and 1933 and at the time of McNeela's death was chairman of Mayo County Council (and who attended McNeela's inquest and funeral).[102] Kilroy was officer commanding the IRA prisoners in Mountjoy Prison in 1923 when thousands of republicans went on a mass hunger strike, which ended with two deaths.[103] This strike in 1923 had not been for political treatment but for unconditional release, and the memory of those hunger-strikers was revered and commemorated within Fianna Fáil. Gerry Boland had also participated in that strike and had gone for forty days without food.[104]

The ubiquitous Seán MacBride again represented the family of the dead hunger-striker, and his style of questioning bordered on an inquisition of the Minister for Justice.[105] The jury returned a verdict in accordance with the medical evidence—that death was due to inanition (i.e. loss of vitality resulting from lack of food and water) and cardiac failure—and added the following rider:

> We are of the opinion that permission should have been granted to Father O'Hare to visit Mountjoy Prison at an earlier date. We are further of the opinion that criminal status should not be accorded to political prisoners. The jury desire to express their sincere sympathy with the parents and relatives of the deceased.[106]

In this first fatal battle of wills between the Government and the IRA during the emergency years, it was not clear who had been victorious. The Fianna Fáil leadership had stood firm, as had the IRA, which now had two martyrs, and their memory quickly became another arena of struggle. On 22 May plain-clothes police raided the Irish Book Bureau in Dublin, operated by Joe Clarke, and seized all available copies of two publications: *Tony D'Arcy and Seán MacNeela: The Story of their Martyrdom* and *Imaginary Happenings*. The booklets had been published some weeks earlier and had been advertised in the *Irish Press*.[107]

Though Gerry Boland had hinted at McNeela's inquest that the people of Co. Galway would have an opportunity to express a verdict on Fianna Fáil at the forthcoming by-election, the party leadership tried hard to prevent one from taking place.[108] When the new rural party, Clann na Talmhan ('Children of the Land'), announced that it would be putting up a candidate, one Fianna Fáil minister, Tom Derrig, declared that

> clearly they do not believe in national unity in [the] face of difficulty and danger. Is it that they are looking for support to those who would disunite the country and weaken the national Government in a time of grave emergency? . . . Our opponents must declare to the electorate on which side they take their stand. Do they stand for maintaining internal peace or do they prefer to allow a state of disorder to be brought about by weakening the Government's hand?[109]

An alliance of interests between Clann na Talmhan and the IRA was heavily implied, though (as security legislation demanded) the IRA was not referred to by name but as 'the small band . . . who have no real backing among our people.' While these statements were characteristic, they were given added force by the hunger strikes that had immediately preceded the by-election, and it was likely that Clann na Talmhan would have tapped into local disaffection on the issue, which, though heavily censored at the national level, had obtained some publicity in Connacht.

Despite living outside the constituency, and being without funds or an organisation, Michael Donnellan of Clann na Talmhan surprised observers by taking more than a third of the vote in an election to which Fianna Fáil had devoted a great deal of ministerial energy and party finances, including a tour by de Valera himself. This trend of steadily declining popularity was emphasised in the 1943 election, when the Fianna Fáil share of the vote plunged by 26 per cent from its 1937 level. Donnellan topped the poll in his home constituency of East Galway, while the Fianna Fáil vote dropped by 13 per cent since the previous election. These figures suggest that the desire for uncontested by-elections was motivated by factors other than those relevant to neutrality. Claims that the issues transcended party politics were weakened by the fact that Fianna Fáil sought a free run in constituency by-elections even when the previous incumbent had been a member of a rival party.

THE SPECIAL BRANCH AND THE IRA

For most of the emergency years Chief Superintendent Seán Gantly led the Special Branch in a sustained and bitter campaign against the IRA. An IRA veteran himself, he had taken the pro-Treaty side when he joined the Garda Síochána at the age of twenty-one and was promoted to superintendent by the Cumann na nGaedheal government. Under Fianna Fáil rule he transferred to the Special Branch, and shortly before the outbreak of war in 1939 he was appointed to the Dublin Metropolitan Division, entrusted with the task of reorganising the Special Branch in Dublin Castle.[110] This branch had acquired, according to J. Bowyer Bell, a 'shoot-first-and-ask questions-later reputation,'[111] and Gantly

> had a new levee [levy] of detectives, few inhibited by republican principles, and plenty of money to pay for information . . . All sorts of people were willing to keep their eyes open for a chance to protect neutrality and turn a profit without earning the traditional informer's stigma. In the country the swollen Army and the local defence men were everywhere.[112]

The reward offered for wanted IRA men, dead or alive—£5,000—encouraged an unhealthy competition within the force, and 'most policemen had personal interests in wiping out the IRA.'[113]

One event in particular, the murder of Detective-Sergeant Dinny O'Brien, merits special attention, for several reasons. Firstly, it was the only time during the emergency that IRA members sought to assassinate a member of the police or army. Secondly, O'Brien's death resulted in the hanging of the IRA chief of staff, Charlie Kerins. Finally, O'Brien's personal history illustrates well the complexity of overlapping loyalties within the republican family and the journey travelled by many, including those in the Fianna Fáil leadership, from anti-state IRA revolutionaries to upholders of the constitutional order.

Along with his two brothers, Dinny O'Brien, then only seventeen, had participated in the 1916 Rising, stationed at the Marrowbone Lane garrison. The three brothers took part in the War of Independence, and they took the republican side in the Civil War, all fighting in the Four Courts. One of the brothers, Paddy, who had been officer commanding the Four Courts in 1922, was shot dead by Free State soldiers in Enniscorthy later that year. Dinny stayed on in the IRA throughout the 1920s and after Fianna Fáil took office. It was only in 1933 that he was persuaded by de Valera to join the Special Branch to fight the Blueshirts.

Within a few years O'Brien was hunting down his erstwhile comrades with the zeal of the convert. Harry White, who on more than one occasion came within a hair's breath of being shot by O'Brien, recalled that 'he was fighting and hunting his own, as rapacious as the most dyed in the wool [Free] Stater.'[114] According to Conor Foley, O'Brien had built his reputation by hunting down former comrades with a zeal which shocked even his police colleagues. He was well-known for brutality in the interrogation room and his trigger-happy attitude during raids.[115]

O'Brien would lead the raid that ended in the death of two Special Branch men and the resultant executions of Paddy McGrath and Tom Harte. McGrath and O'Brien were old acquaintances, having fought in the IRA and having been imprisoned together. O'Brien had also led the raid on a clandestine IRA broadcasting station in Ashfield House, which led to the imprisonment of Jack Plunkett and Jack McNeela, both of whom almost immediately went on hunger strike. (Plunkett was a brother of the 1916 signatory Joseph Plunkett, under whom O'Brien had fought in 1916.)

O'Brien's favoured strategy was to keep a hideout under surveillance for a time and then to attack it, guns blazing. Such a strategy was always likely to incur casualties on both sides. Gardaí were killed or injured, and IRA men, such as Charlie McGlade and Liam Burke, were 'shot while resisting arrest,' while Liam Rice retained two bullets in his lung received from O'Brien's revolver.

O'Brien's technique of 'heavy interrogation' on the Wexford IRA leader Michael Devereux led to Devereux's death and consequently to the execution of George Plant. Few of the major incidents of the war between the Special Branch and the IRA occurred without the participation of Dinny O'Brien somewhere along the line.

On the morning of 9 September 1942 O'Brien was shot dead in a gun battle outside his home in Rathfarnham, Co. Dublin. The impact of the killing was felt at the highest level of Fianna Fáil. (O'Brien was the brother of Seán Lemass's secretary.)[116] On the level of political security it appeared to be a direct challenge, confirming—if confirmation was needed—that the IRA was out to wreck the state. Yet the fact is that O'Brien's killing was the only premeditated murder of a state representative since Kevin O'Higgins's assassination fifteen years earlier. (One of the four men who shot O'Brien, Archie Doyle, had been responsible for Kevin O'Higgins's assassination in 1927, when O'Brien was still active in the IRA.)[117] According to Conor Brady, 'there was little grieving for Dennis O'Brien even in the Special Branch, for he was over-zealous even in the eyes of his own colleagues.'[118]

The decision to kill O'Brien deviated from IRA policy—formalised six years later as standing order no. 8 but already understood by all members—which demanded that volunteers avoid clashes with 'Free State forces' in order to concentrate on operations in Northern Ireland. It was for this reason that the leaders of the IRA's Northern Command, particularly Seán McCaughey, were enraged by the assassination, which they considered a serious tactical error. Ostensibly the motive for the killing was strategic, in that it would remove an arch-enemy of the IRA and might deter others from pursuing republicans with the same vigour.[119] Vengeance no doubt also played a part.

In fact the Special Branch campaign against the IRA intensified with O'Brien's death. Paddy Dermody, the IRA commander for the North Leinster-South Ulster region, was attending his sister's wedding on 30 September 1942 at a farmhouse in Co. Cavan when a large number of Special Branch men surrounded the house and opened fire. In the ensuing gun battle Dermody was killed. Harry White, who was injured, managed to escape with the assistance of the soldier who discovered him.[120]

Jackie Griffiths, who had escaped with four others from Mountjoy Prison on 1 November 1942, was cycling in Lower Mount Street, Dublin, on 4 July 1943 when he was spotted by a Special Branch car. Pushing a machine gun through the window, they opened fire, killing Griffiths in a hail of bullets.[121]

A similar fate awaited IRA members in the North. On 30 August 1942 Gerry O'Callaghan died in an ambush while inspecting an arms dump at a farmhouse in Co. Antrim, while Séamus Burns, who had been interned in the Curragh and imprisoned in Co. Derry, was 'shot while trying to escape,' following his arrest on 12 February 1944. Several republicans died while in custody, north and south.[122] The joint efforts of the Dublin and Belfast governments made such an impact on the IRA that by 1943 'the struggle had fizzled to extinction,' and 'north and south there was not a kick left in the organisation.'[123]

Chapter 8 ～

| THE SHOWDOWN, 1940–46

'THE VERY ERRORS THEY HAVE CONDEMNED': STATE EXECUTIONS, 1940–42

Between 1940 and 1942 the Belfast, Dublin and London governments executed more than half a dozen leading IRA men. The self-professed Republican Government executed more republicans during the wartime emergency years than the unionist and conservative governments combined, culminating in the execution of the IRA chief of staff, Charlie Kerins, in December 1944.

The first executions, those of Peter Barnes and James McCormack,[1] were carried out by the British Government and resulted from the explosion in Coventry that killed five people. Barnes and McCormack were found guilty under the 'common purpose' rule, a provision in English law whereby two or more people in a combination or conspiracy who are deemed to have committed a dangerous felony resulting in death are all considered guilty of murder.[2] The sentencing in December 1939 prompted an intensive reprieve campaign in Ireland,[3] and de Valera tried hard to save the lives of the two men. In a personal appeal to the Secretary of State for Dominion Affairs, Sir Anthony Eden, de Valera wrote that

> each succeeding generation of your countrymen have deplored the unwisdom of their predecessors and themselves fallen into the very errors they have condemned. Ought you not to make sure that you avoid doing likewise . . . It will matter little that Barnes and Richards [the pseudonym used by McCormack] have been found guilty of murder. With the background of our history and the existence of partition many will refuse to regard their action in that light. They will think only of the cause these men had in mind to serve.[4]

De Valera predicted that the execution of Barnes and McCormack would 'give rise to new and bitter antagonisms' between Britain and Ireland, which other countries might try to exploit. To reinforce his message he wrote a letter to the Prime Minister, Neville Chamberlain, that urged clemency and cited the 'long-time policy' of securing better relations between the Irish and British peoples.[5]

> I have received your decision with sorrow and dismay. The reprieve of these men would be regarded as an act of generosity, a thousand times more valuable to Britain than anything that can possibly be gained by their death. The latter will be

looked upon as an act fitting only too sadly into the historic background of our relations. Almost superhuman patience is required on both sides to exorcise the feelings which the knowledge of centuries of wrong-doing have engendered. I hasten with a final entreaty that this execution be not permitted to take place.[6]

De Valera's efforts were complemented by those of the general public. Every local authority registered its protest. Within Fianna Fáil, parliamentarians addressed mass meetings organised by the Reprieve Committee, and local cumainn also contributed to the call for clemency. The reprieve campaign enjoyed cross-party support as well as support from religious leaders of all denominations[7] and various republican organisations, such as the Old IRA.

These efforts failed, however, to induce the British Government to spare the lives of Barnes and McCormack. On the eve of their executions (6 February), the Irish High Commissioner in London, John Dulanty, met the Prime Minister for twenty minutes and was in telephone contact with de Valera to keep him up to date.[8] Chamberlain's message to de Valera acknowledged 'how deeply you feel on this matter' and stressed his continuing wish to promote Anglo-Irish relations. He concluded, however, by stating that 'for reasons which appear to us to be of overwhelming force . . . we have felt unable to act as you wish.'[9] At nine o'clock the following morning Barnes and McCormack were hanged in Winson Green Prison, Birmingham, by four executioners, including Thomas Pierrepoint and his nephew Albert.[10]

The executions led to monster meetings throughout Ireland. Cinemas and theatres were closed, workers downed tools, and most sports fixtures were postponed. Representative bodies passed condemnatory resolutions, and flags on most municipal buildings were at half mast.[11]

Two days after the executions the Offences Against the State (Amendment) Act (1949) was signed into law, and almost immediately the internment camps began to fill again.[12] While the Government appealed for the lives of Barnes and McCormack, the fate of one of their comrades was being deliberated on by the Irish courts.

TOMÁS MAC CURTÁIN

The vicissitudes experienced by Tomás Óg Mac Curtáin were similar to those endured by many republicans during Fianna Fáil's time in power. The only son of Tomás Mac Curtáin, the IRA leader and Lord Mayor of Cork murdered by the British army in 1920, Tomás Óg was continually harassed and beaten by Free State police during his formative years. Scheduled to speak at a 1916 commemoration in 1937, he had evaded arrest amid a hail of bullets. He eventually became commandant of the Cork No. 1 Brigade of the IRA—the same position his father held at the time of his death.

After several narrow escapes the 22-year-old Mac Curtáin thought he had met his end when, on 3 January 1940, he was attacked by five armed men while walking through Cork.[13] In the scuffle a shot was fired, and one of the men fell to the ground. The man who lay dead was Detective-Garda John Roche, and Mac Curtáin faced the military tribunal on the capital charge of murdering a garda.

Following the inevitable imposition of the death sentence, Cork was the scene of frantic activity aimed at securing his reprieve. There were formal and emotional appeals from the Lord Mayor, James Hickey.[14] Despite the very short period of three weeks between the sentence and the proposed date of execution he managed to collect several thousand signatures in Cork alone requesting clemency,[15] and it was generally felt that had there been more time a massive petition campaign could have been organised.[16] Protests were also received from Cork City Council, Cork County Council, Cork Harbour Commission and the Cork Old IRA, all of whom added their names to the petition.[17] Similarly, the Lord Mayor of Limerick and Fianna Fáil members of Limerick City Council cited the 'gravity of the present situation as it affects our country' and claimed that 'the importation of a foreign hangman would shock the conscience of the Nation.' The Limerick City Comhairle Ceantair (district council) of Fianna Fáil added their names to the representation.[18] The county council in de Valera's own constituency of Clare also unanimously appealed for Mac Curtáin to 'be saved from the degradation of suffering the death penalty.'[19] A greater source of worry to the Fianna Fáil leadership must have been the number of party cumainn and comhairlí ceantair that also passed condemnatory resolutions. Fianna Fáil's embarrassment was complete when the Lord Mayor of Dublin, Kathleen Clarke—widow of the executed 1916 leader Tom Clarke—used the Mansion House as the headquarters of the reprieve campaign.[20]

Protests were received from a variety of organisations and individuals. Most mentioned the 'illustrious career' of Mac Curtáin's father, the need for national unity, the fact that the killing had not been premeditated, the innate 'wrongness' of executing republicans and the past actions of Fianna Fáil's leadership. Telegrams were received from the 1916 Veterans' Association and numerous brigades and battalions of the Old IRA. The 1st Battalion of the Dublin Brigade of the Old IRA argued that 'the unity of 1921' could be restored, but not if Mac Curtáin was executed. Many Old IRA men had joined the Local Security Force to help defend the country from possible invasion and had therefore given a republican blessing to de Valera's initiative, but the number of condemnatory telegrams sent by LSF units suggested that this support was in danger of crumbling. Numerous protests came too from a plethora of Irish-American organisations, from Cumann na mBan, trade unions and county boards of assistance.

A deputation of relatives of those who had been killed by British forces in Co. Cork during the years 1920–21 also travelled to Dublin.[21] Accompanying them was an appeal from Youghal Urban District Council and a petition from parents and immediate relatives of those killed in action or executed during the period 1918–23.[22]

The Government met the day before the proposed execution and issued Emergency Powers Order No. 32, which allowed the Government to defer the execution of sentences imposed by the Special Criminal Court in capital cases,[23] and it postponed Mac Curtáin's execution for eight days, until 13 July.[24] By this time the English hangman, Pierrepoint, had already arrived in Dublin. So late was the announcement that rumours had begun to circulate that Mac Curtáin had already been hanged.

On 10 July the Government met and decided to advise the President to commute the sentence of death to penal servitude for life.[25] According to one source, Peadar O'Donnell had met Gerry Boland and had made a personal appeal for Mac Curtáin's life.[26] If this was the crucial factor it would be a remarkable illustration of the intra-republican camaraderie that still bound some members of the IRA and Fianna Fáil. It is an unlikely explanation, however, as O'Donnell had made similar appeals, and would again, to no avail.

According to Robert Fisk, there is evidence that de Valera's act of clemency may have been inspired by 'more than compassion.' The British Government had been kept informed of developments by RUC officers who were in communication with a senior Garda contact. When an RUC officer arrived in Dublin in July he found his Garda contact upset at Mac Curtáin's reprieve. According to the RUC officer he had begun the conversation

> by reminding my host that on my previous visit he was very busy . . . making arrangements for what he then described as 'a hanging match.' To this indirect question he replied, 'Sure, I had the grave dug and all, and Pierpoint in the gaol forby.' It was quite obvious that he felt somewhat hurt at McCurtain's reprieve, and seeing this I saw an opportunity to develop the subject. After some preliminary sparring I hinted that perhaps the IRA and De Valera had made a bargain about McCurtain, but this was denied 'so far as I know.' He told me that the Church and public opinion and 'chiefly politics which has always been the curse of the country' was responsible for obtaining the reprieve.[27]

Aware of the martyrdom tradition, the Garda informant consoled himself in the knowledge that Mac Curtáin 'would have been a far bigger man dead than he'll be alive.' In this he was correct, though it would exert little influence on the Government in future cases. Equally interesting is the Garda officer's claim that after Mac Curtáin's reprieve

> the Government had let it be known throughout the Defence Corps [the Volunteers] that in repayment for this act of grace, they expected all Volunteers who were in illegal possession of firearms or ammunition, or knew where such weapons were, to at once surrender them to the police.[28]

A promise was given that any person complying with this request would be immune from prosecution, and according to the Garda informant the response was good—so much so that the arms surrendered 'had greatly assisted in arming the new Defence Corps.'[29] If this was true it was indeed remarkable that a Government would ask members of its own Defence Forces to surrender their IRA weapons in return for Mac Curtáin's reprieve, and then use them to arm the same Defence Forces. As for Mac Curtáin, he might have wondered if death was a better fate than what awaited him. He was to spend the next four-and-a-half years in solitary confinement, naked, with only a blanket, bereft of human contact or indeed of any form of distraction, confined in a space of five square metres.

PADDY MCGRATH AND TOM HARTE

While we may never know what motivated the decision to spare Tomás Óg Mac Curtáin from the firing squad, the record shows that Fianna Fáil was bent on a policy of executions. Two months after Mac Curtáin's reprieve IRA men again faced the death penalty. Early in the morning of 16 August a force of Special Branch men attacked a shop in Rathgar, Dublin, that they had had under observation for some time, firing indiscriminately through the doors and windows. In an effort to escape, those inside— members of IRA GHQ and Cumann na mBan—returned fire and made their way to the exit at the rear. As the others made their escape, Tom Harte fell to the ground, seriously wounded. Noticing his absence, Paddy McGrath returned to the shop. Unable to carry the injured man, he stayed with him until they were both arrested.

During the raid a detective had been shot dead and another was fatally wounded, dying a few days later. No inquest was ever held on the detectives, and the results of an internal inquiry were suppressed, on the instructions of Gerry Boland, giving rise to a belief that the bullets that killed the detectives were not fired by the IRA.[30] Certainly no attempt was ever made to establish whether either McGrath or Harte had fired the fatal shots.

McGrath, who had been on hunger strike for forty-two days the previous November, knew the authors of his destruction well. Interned with his two brothers by the British in Frongoch internment camp in Wales during the independence struggle, he had come to know Gerry Boland, who now signed his death warrant, and Detective-Sergeant Dinny O'Brien, who had hunted him down and effected his arrest.[31]

After McGrath and Harte were sentenced to death on 20 August, the Government met at noon the following day to discuss their next move. For an hour and a half they deliberated, before deciding 'to decline to remit or commute the sentences.'[32] Two days later the Government met again and, after a discussion lasting more than two hours, issued Emergency Powers Order No. 45, which allowed the Government to postpone the execution of sentences imposed by the military tribunal in capital cases.[33] After this was agreed it was decided to postpone the executions.[34] Incredibly, it was only on Thursday 2 September that the Harte family in Lurgan, Co. Armagh, received news of their son's pending execution, and even then it was not from a Government source but from a family friend, who said that he had heard rumours that a man called Harte was to be executed on Sunday.[35]

During the afternoon of 4 September the Government met for three-quarters of an hour. It was at this meeting that the Fianna Fáil leadership made what was, in relation to their own party and personal histories, a momentous decision, though this is not captured in the dispassionate language of the Government minutes.

> In accordance with the terms of Article 4, Sub-Article (3) of the Emergency Powers (No. 45) Order, 1940, it was decided to direct the Adjutant-General that the sentences on Patrick McGrath and Thomas Green (alias Francis Hart) who were convicted and sentenced to death on the 20 August, 1940, by the Military Court constituted under the Emergency Powers (No. 41) Order, 1940, should be executed on the 6 September, 1940.[36]

With this order Fianna Fáil completed the attempt made by the British in 1920: the British bullet lodged near Paddy McGrath's heart was to be joined by those of the Irish army. Fianna Fáil had crossed the Rubicon.

The night before the executions Kathleen Clarke contacted Gerry Boland and pleaded with him for a reprieve. Boland replied that the matter was out of his hands, as it was a Government decision. 'It crossed my mind at the time,' Clarke recalled, 'that Fianna Fáil were showing as little mercy to those who opposed them as the Cosgrave Government had, and Fianna Fáil had denounced them in no uncertain terms.' To demonstrate her sympathy with the relatives and her disagreement with the Government's action, Clarke ordered the blinds in the Mansion House to be drawn and the flag to be flown at half mast and instructed the city manager to have the flag flown over City Hall at half mast. It was a remarkable and defiant gesture, for which Clarke believes she was 'never forgiven' by the Fianna Fáil hierarchy.

> McGrath's execution to my mind was a crime, and I had to make a protest. I never could see why as a member of a party or organisation I was bound to approve of everything the leaders did; I could not put Party interests before my ideas of right and wrong. I don't claim I am always right, but I act in accordance with what I believe to be right. It seemed to me that in executing men like McGrath, the government were carrying out the old British policy of killing or exterminating in one way or another all the best of our people.[37]

Press coverage was negligible, because of censorship. The *Irish Independent* had a one-line reference in the middle of page 8. Neither was editorial comment permitted; on the day of the first state executions of IRA men since 1923 the paper editorialised on 'Problems of the postman.'[38]

Shortly afterwards Fianna Fáil announced that its ard-fheis was being postponed to an unspecified date. While it is possible that the exigencies of the emergency influenced this decision, Fine Gael and the Labour Party went ahead with their conferences, so the ard-fheis may have been deferred because of internal party dissent.[39]

RICHARD GOSS

Almost a year elapsed before the next state execution, that of 26-year-old Richard Goss. The son of a veteran IRB man and trade unionist, Goss had followed in his father's footsteps in becoming an officer in the Dundalk Branch of the National Union of Shoe and Boot Operatives. In 1933, at the age of eighteen, he joined the North Louth Battalion of the IRA, and in March the following year he was sentenced to three months' imprisonment by the military tribunal for refusing to account for his movements. In 1938 Goss, by this time an explosives expert, was called to Dublin by Seán Russell to prepare for the sabotage campaign in England. Interned in Arbour Hill military prison during the initial swoop, he was released on 2 December 1939 with the fifty-three other internees as a result of the successful *habeas corpus* application by Séamus Burke, and he went on the run.

On 18 July 1941 in Co. Longford two lorry-loads of soldiers surrounded the house of Matt Casey, whose son, Barney, had been killed in the Curragh Internment Camp some months earlier. (Goss had led the IRA firing party at the funeral.) Shots were exchanged, after which Goss and two others escaped on foot for several hundred yards. Finding themselves surrounded, they surrendered. They were taken to Arbour

Hill, where Goss was singled out and sent to Collins Barracks, where the military tribunal sat.

Charged with shooting at members of the Defence Forces with intent to evade arrest, Goss's fate was decided by three army officers who were without any legal training and were bound by no rule of law. Despite an ardent defence by Seán MacBride, who argued that Goss's intention 'was not that of evading arrest but of self-preservation,' he was found guilty as charged on 1 August and sentenced to death by firing squad.[40]

On the morning of 5 August, MacBride telephoned the Department of the Taoiseach to inform de Valera that a deputation from Co. Louth was in Dublin and wished to meet him regarding the death sentence imposed on Goss. The deputation included Lawrence Walsh, a Fianna Fáil TD and Mayor of Drogheda, and James Coburn, a Fine Gael TD. The inclusion of Walsh indicated the unease within Fianna Fáil, and meant that the only Louth deputy who was not publicly appealing for clemency was Frank Aiken, who, as a member of the Government, was unlikely to depart from the decision it reached.

Aiken's republican comrades in the Old IRA differed in opinion from their former commander, however. Other members of the delegation included the Fianna Fáil chairman of Dundalk Urban District Council, the chairman of Dundalk Trades Council, the secretary of the Dundalk Council of the Boot and Shoe Operatives' Union, and the chairman of the Dundalk Building Trades Operatives' Union.[41] When the matter was submitted to de Valera he told his secretary that he 'was not prepared to receive the deputation' and that the 'proper procedure' was for the body to post any written submission they might wish to make.

When the message was passed to MacBride he asked if it would be possible for the secretary to meet the deputation; but, despite taking the petitions, the secretary reiterated de Valera's message and made it clear that he was not authorised to hear any representations. The deputation handed in a petition with almost two thousand signatures, including those of many members of Dundalk Urban District Council, collected at short notice, and a further 2,500 that had been forwarded to MacBride. In their hastily written letter to the Government they appealed as 'public representatives of County Louth' for clemency for Richard Goss. They also pointed out that this was the first occasion since the Civil War on which anyone was sentenced to death in respect of an offence not involving loss of life.[42]

The secretary of the Dundalk cumann of Fianna Fáil wrote that his cumann 'unanimously beseeched' the Government to reprieve Goss.[43] The former Fianna Fáil TD (and now abstentionist MP for Armagh) Éamonn Donnelly also telegraphed de Valera, describing the proposed execution as a 'serious mistake' despised by Irishmen, which would 'create revulsion against government.'[44] Telegrams were also received from trade unionists and from the Louth Brigade of the Old IRA, who declared that the execution of Goss was 'abhorred by all old IRA in area,' and that 'in the name of freedom of Ireland we call for a commutation of sentence.'[45]

Perhaps the most poignant plea came from Cissie Harte, sister of Thomas Harte, who had been executed with Patrick McGrath the previous September. Her letter to de Valera read:

Dear Sir,

    I would ask you to spare the life of Richard Goss, who is under sentence of death and also save his dear mother the bitter sorrow which my dear mother endured some months ago and from which she will never recover.

    Pray his life spare,

    Cissie Harte.[46]

All pleas fell on deaf ears. On 7 August a terse statement issued by the Government Information Bureau upheld the decision of the Military Court, and the execution was set for 9 August.[47]

From early in the morning the Goss family stood outside the gate of Arbour Hill military prison to be near when the fatal volley was fired. However, at 6 a.m. an official came out and attached a notice to the gate that stated that Goss had been shot fifteen minutes earlier, thirty-five miles away, in Portlaoise. During the night, and unknown to his family, he had been taken there by car, behind an army lorry that carried his coffin. There he was shot and then buried within the prison walls in an unmarked grave.

There is an intriguing epilogue to Goss's execution. On 15 August, Patrick Ruttledge resigned from the Government, ostensibly on the grounds of ill-health. Despite Brian Farrell's claim that there are 'no grounds' for disbelieving the official reason for the resignation,[48] this interpretation is not satisfactory, not least because Ruttledge continued to represent Mayo in Dáil Éireann until his death in 1952, while also taking up the position of Solicitor-General to the Wards of Court. Double-jobbing is hardly a remedy for ill-health. One explanation is that offered by Patrick Lindsay, whose memoirs contain a one-line reference in which he states his belief that Ruttledge was 'glad to get out of the cabinet because he wanted an even tougher line against the IRA than was being pursued by the de Valera Government in the 1940s.'[49] Lindsay offers no explanation for this belief, and it should be noted that his relationship with Ruttledge was tenuous, the connection being geographical rather than ideological or occupational. (He was an unsuccessful Fine Gael candidate for Mayo North.)

For the first time, Fianna Fáil had executed IRA men and allowed prisoners to die on hunger strike. What tougher line Ruttledge could have desired is difficult to imagine. A quite different and perhaps more cogent explanation is that Ruttledge's premature departure resulted from his distaste for the recent spate of executions.[50] To support this view, Ruttledge's militant republicanism of earlier years may be cited. It might also be considered relevant that Ruttledge was replaced as Minister for Justice by Gerry Boland just as the tough decisions were to be taken. He had retired for a number of months during 1936, being replaced by Boland, and it was during this period that the IRA was outlawed and the Bodenstown commemoration proscribed. Shortly after these punitive actions, aimed at curbing militant republicanism, Ruttledge returned to his position as Minister for Justice. However, in early September 1939—the month in which the Emergency Powers Act was introduced—he again stepped down from Justice and moved to Local Government and Public Health, to be replaced by Boland.

J. Bowyer Bell remarks that Boland had 'proved himself a suitably hard man' during his brief tenure in Justice in 1936, and he claims that it was assumed that Ruttledge was 'too gentle to grasp the nettle of coercion.'[51]

GEORGE PLANT

George Plant, a Co. Tipperary Protestant, was a veteran of the War of Independence and the Civil War who had emigrated to America during the 1920s, when anti-republican repression was rampant, but he returned at Seán Russell's request to participate in the S-Plan. Arrested with five other people on 3 December 1940, Plant had been sentenced to two years' imprisonment for possession of documents with IRA letter-heads and for refusing to answer questions.[52] In 1941 he was arrested with Joe O'Connor and charged with the murder of the IRA informer Michael Devereux.

The state's case rested on the confessions of two IRA members, Michael Walsh and Patrick Davern, which had been extracted under duress. When the men retracted these statements and refused to testify, on the grounds that they had been beaten into signing them while in custody, the prosecution case collapsed.

After this a bizarre series of events ensued. The legal principle of double jeopardy was discarded, for, after his case was dismissed, Plant was rearrested in the court and held in Arbour Hill. Then the Government issued Emergency Powers Order No. 139, the terms of which made it possible for the prosecution to read *retracted* confessions as evidence and for the military tribunal to act on such statements. Remarkably, the order went on to issue the tribunal with a *carte blanche* of breathtaking proportions, stating that 'if a military court considered it proper on any occasion during a trial that it should not be bound by the laws of evidence, whether of military or common law, then the court should not be bound by such a rule.'[53] The court, in effect, could make up the law as it went along.[54]

The legal goalposts having thus been moved, Plant, along with Walsh and Davern, was put on trial before the Military Court.[55] Seán MacBride argued that it was the first time in Ireland, England or America that a man had stood trial for a number of days and was then discharged by a court of competent jurisdiction only to be put on trial again for the same offence. It was also the first time that any court had been asked to forfeit the lives of men on unsworn statements not backed by evidence given on oath. There was not, he concluded, a shred of evidence against Plant except what was contained in the unsworn statements which—according to the evidence of the people who gave them—were untrue.[56]

However, the powers the Government had given itself in the form of the Emergency Powers Orders enabled it to overcome any legal obstacles.[57] On the morning of 5 March 1942 George Plant was shot by firing squad in Portlaoise Prison and buried within the prison walls.[58]

TOM WILLIAMS

On the night that Britain declared war on Germany the Northern Ireland Minister of Home Affairs, Richard Dawson Bates, ordered the internment of forty-five alleged members of the IRA.[59] By 1942 more than 800 IRA suspects were interned, 450 in Crumlin Road Prison, Belfast, and the remainder on the prison ship in Strangford

Lough supplied by a British Government greatly appreciative of the zealous pursuit of suspected republican activists.[60] Captured IRA members were arraigned not only on specific charges but also for 'treason felony', an offence created by the Treason Felony Act (1848) to combat the Young Ireland rebellion of that year and that was now unearthed to meet the contemporary republican challenge. In language similar to that employed by de Valera, the Northern Ireland Minister of Public Security, John MacDermott, argued that the 1848 act was appropriate at 'the present time when the . . . protection of our own State require that those who sustain the [IRA] movement should, on conviction, receive sentences of an exemplary nature.'[61]

By 1942 the long-planned IRA offensive in the North had begun in earnest, a campaign mostly remembered for the fate of one young man whose body lay within Belfast Prison for almost six decades. On 5 April six IRA men fired on an RUC patrol car in an effort to draw the police away from the banned 1916 commemoration that was being held on the Falls Road in Belfast. What was to be a diversionary attack developed into a full-scale gun battle as the IRA men were pursued into a house in Cawnpore Street. An RUC constable, Patrick Murphy, was killed, while the leader of the IRA unit, Tom Williams, was wounded. The unit was captured, and three months later all six were sentenced to death by Lord Justice Murphy.

Two days before the executions the Governor of Northern Ireland reprieved five of the six, but in the case of Tom Williams it was affirmed that 'the law must take its own course.' It was generally felt by nationalists, north and south, that the nineteen-year-old Williams had taken full responsibility out of a sense of loyalty to his comrades and that this responsibility had not been borne out by evidence produced at the trial. It was also pointed out that there had been no proof of premeditation in the killing of Constable Murphy.

The Reprieve Committee declared that 'in the event of the authorities persisting in making young Williams the victim, Ireland will make it known to the world that his execution has not the sanction of the Irish people by observing Wednesday as a day of national mourning as already announced.' Two days before the execution date the Lord Mayor of Dublin, P. S. Doyle, travelled to Belfast to meet his counterpart, William Black. He appealed to him and to Belfast City Council to add their voices to the campaign. Protests in Dublin and Sligo were reported that night, and Dublin Fire Brigade (which had travelled to Belfast the previous year to put out fires caused by the German blitz) also made an appeal to the Northern Government and to their colleagues in the Belfast Fire Brigade on behalf of the condemned man.[62]

Though tensions were running high within Fianna Fáil, there was little if any self-analysis. When Kathleen Clarke delivered a passionate address in O'Connell Street, in which she declared that there would be a march on the border if Williams was executed, one man shouted 'What about George Plant?' and was nearly lynched for his troubles by the mainly Fianna Fáil audience.[63]

The impending executions figured prominently in meetings of various representative bodies, a flavour of which can be obtained from a perusal of the censored reports of meetings held by the Fianna Fáil-dominated Thurles and Cashel Urban District Councils. The AGM of Thurles Urban District Council met to discuss a motion submitted by the newly elected chairman, Thomas Stapleton, which respectfully requested the Secretary of State for Foreign Affairs, Anthony Eden, to use his influence to secure a reprieve for the 'six young Irish boys' under sentence of death in Belfast. Seán Gleeson 'could not agree' with the terms of the communication, as 'no nationalist in the Twenty Six Counties ever crawled to a British statesman and he did not see why they should crawl to Mr. Anthony Eden today.' He disagreed with 'the appeal tone' of the communication and said that they should demand rather than request the reprieve of the condemned men, who were 'fighting a good cause.' J. Butler concurred, as did John Murphy, who declared that 'Pearse and Connolly never thought of making an appeal' and that if the six Belfast men had to face the executioner they 'would be in the company of good men.' This point was reiterated by William Ryan, who noted that the condemned men were not begging for their lives: 'The condemned men were being held against the will of the people of the South of Ireland as well as the North.' Councillor Tracey made the final comment:

> The 1916 men sacrificed their lives for Thirty two counties and not for Twenty six counties. The condemned men were also ready to sacrifice their lives for a great principle and until that great principle was established there would be no freedom. The people of the Six Counties would want to rise up and the sooner they did it, the better.

In the end the council changed the 'request' to a 'demand,' and it was decided that the Reprieve Committee in Dublin was to be contacted to inform it that the council joined in the reprieve effort.

The debate in Cashel Urban District Council was conducted on much the same lines, with the discussion centring again on whether they should request or demand a reprieve and whether they should also send a resolution to the Belfast government, which, according to one member, 'will only throw [it] in the wastepaper basket.' Introducing the motion, Councillor Feehan urged those present to join with the other public bodies petitioning the Northern Ireland government, as 'we don't want a repetition of the Manchester Martyrs.'[64] Colonel Carew recalled that there had been executions in the 26 Counties 'of young men claiming to be members of the same organisation as those six young Belfast men and [the] Council did not call for a reprieve.' He thought the council would be weakening the position of the men 'if there was any begging or cringing for mercy from a foreign Government'; instead he claimed that it was for the Taoiseach to take the matter up with the Northern government. 'An Taoiseach has an army of a quarter of a million behind him,' he said, and 'that was a more effective argument than the sending of any petition to the Northern Ireland Government.' Eventually the council decided that resolutions would be sent to both the Dublin and Belfast governments.

The articles relating to these discussions were to appear in the *Tipperary Star* but were stopped in full by the censors.[65] Indeed the censors continued to delete statements that they felt were prejudicial to the security of the state; but the operation of the censorship was far less rigid than during the executions authorised by Fianna Fáil. All references to the Censorship Board, however, continued to be purged.

An article on Ireland by the future British Labour Party minister Aneurin Bevan, which reported that 'though the Censorship is strict and little of the popular clamour for a reprieve finds its way into the newspapers feelings run high', was edited to 'feelings run high.'[66] Similarly, when the head of the Belfast Reprieve Committee, Éamonn Donnelly, MP for Armagh and a former Fianna Fáil TD, publicly requested that Frank Aiken 'remove the censorship so that the people of Éire could get to know the true state of affairs in the North,' his request went unheeded and unpublicised.[67] When Jim Larkin told a meeting of Dublin City Council that 'in the campaign for reprieve they had not been able to use the Press or the Radio because they were censored,' he found his point well illustrated when his own remark was excised from the record.[68] All references to the condemned men being members of the IRA were expunged, as were numerous reports of meetings from around the country.

Shortly before 8 a.m., the time fixed for the execution, a crowd knelt outside the gates of Belfast Prison in the Crumlin Road to recite the Rosary for the repose of the soul of Tom Williams. They had barely begun when a group of loyalists appeared and began jeering. The RUC had cordoned off the prison, keeping people away from the immediate vicinity. As the warder pinned the notice to the gate announcing that the execution had been carried out, prayers were again recited, with the rival group singing 'God Save the King' in an effort to drown them out. The streets were cleared, though a party of young women carrying black scarves marched in procession through the city.

It was understood that American soldiers were under strict instructions to keep off the streets of Belfast that day. Despite this, 'wild and ugly' scenes were reported.[69] Gun battles broke out in nationalist areas, prompting the authorities to impose a curfew. In Co. Tyrone an RUC constable and a member of the B Specials (part-time RUC reserve) were shot dead.

In Dublin all flags on private buildings were flown at half mast, and a crowd of several thousand assembled in O'Connell Street. Outside the GPO a large crowd gathered, and women admonished the authorities for not flying the Tricolour at half mast. Arrangements had been made for the closure of all shops, offices, factories and other places of work throughout the 26 Counties from eleven in the morning until noon, the period fixed for the hour of mourning by the Prisoners' Reprieve Committee.[70] An international news report stated that 'in all cases the employers have fallen in with the wishes of the workers.'[71] Throughout the country special Masses were offered, including one in the Pro-Cathedral at eleven o'clock attended by the Lord Mayor of Dublin and members of the city council. The appeal by the Lord Mayor of Cork for three minutes' silence before midday was also observed in the city.[72]

MAURICE O'NEILL

Two months after Tom Williams's execution, and in spite of the ardent defence offered on his behalf, another republican prisoner was sentenced to death on 5 November. This time, however, it was Fianna Fáil rather than the Ulster Unionist Party that was sanctioning the execution.

On 24 October 1942 Maurice O'Neill and Harry White had been fired on during a raid at their hideout in Donnycarney, Dublin, and when they returned fire down a blind passageway a member of the Special Branch was fatally wounded.[73] O'Neill, a

25-year-old native of Cahersiveen, Co. Kerry, was captured and tried before the Military Court for the murder of Detective-Garda George Mordaunt,[74] though it would appear that he had not fired the fatal shot.[75] Little time was lost in ruling out the possibility of clemency, and on 8 November the Government Information Bureau laconically stated that the Government had considered the case and had conveyed to the Adjutant-General its decision not to remit or commute the sentence of the Military Court.[76]

At a meeting of the Fianna Fáil parliamentary party some days earlier a motion noting the 'growing dissension and antagonism within the Old IRA Organisations to the Government' was discussed. The minutes of the meeting do not reveal the substance of the motion, suggesting that it was a sensitive issue and may have included an appeal to commute the death sentence on O'Neill. All that is stated is that the motion was not pressed to a vote after 'a lengthy discussion in which all the arguments now familiar to the members of the Party were advanced in support of it.'[77] At the same meeting the question of the procedure employed by gardaí when raiding the houses of suspects was raised. The minutes record simply that the Minister for Justice 'explained that the raids were planned and carried out by the most experienced officers of the Special Branch.'[78]

In a news item suppressed by the censors, the *Irish Independent* reported a large public meeting in Cahersiveen on 8 November to support appeals for clemency on behalf of O'Neill. The attendance of county councillors, members of the clergy, trade unionists and representatives of the Old IRA was reported, as were resolutions appealing for mercy passed by the Irish Farmers' Association, the South Kerry Workers' Union, Fianna Fáil, the INTO, the Old IRA, the GAA and the Local Defence Force. Petitions were signed outside all churches in south Kerry.[79]

On 12 November 1942 Maurice O'Neill was shot by firing squad.[80] The execution was marked by a one-line announcement in the newspapers, but even this caused problems. A heading 'Death sentence carried out' was altered to 'Donnycarney shooting case: Sentence carried out' by order of the censor.[81] A one-line report that stated simply that 'Kerry County Council adjourned its quarterly meeting yesterday as a mark of sympathy with relatives of the late Maurice O'Neill' was suppressed.[82] A paid one-line Mass notice was allowed, though the phrase 'who was shot at Mountjoy on the morning of the 12th November' was deleted by the censor.[83]

A HUNGER STRIKE AND TWO ELECTIONS

Having spent years in prison camps, without charge or trial, internees in the Curragh embarked on a hunger strike in 1943 but were met with the now-standard response of the Minister for Justice, Gerry Boland, that 'if these men are prepared to die I cannot help it.'[84] Responding in the Dáil to a call by the Labour Party for Government intervention, de Valera said that he had received a similar appeal from the Labour Party four years earlier and felt that his response on 9 November 1939 was equally appropriate on this occasion. He read out his 1939 statement in full, stressing the importance of the Constitution of Ireland, which was 'the people's Constitution,' passed by the people and permitting every section of the people to advocate any policy they chose. Suggestions that prison conditions for republicans were inadequate were firmly rejected, and Portlaoise Prison was described by the Department of Justice as 'the most up to date in the State . . . run on lines that challenge comparison with the prison regime of any country.'[85]

The hunger strike coincided with a general election. As Fianna Fáil's term expired, the leadership tried unsuccessfully to persuade the opposition to agree to the post-ponement of the election 'in the national interest' and then grudgingly called an election for 23 June. A similar request had been made to postpone the local elections in 1942. Though these elections were supposed to be held every three years, none had been held since 1934, and the opposition, smelling blood, were in no mood for another deferment. Kathleen Clarke, who was nominated for Fianna Fáil in the Dublin North-East constituency, refused to accept her nomination and resigned from the party on 3 May 1943. She wrote to de Valera, in his capacity as president of Fianna Fáil, tender-ing her resignation and stating her reasons for doing so after their long association.

> I held on so far in the hope that you would eventually make an effort to carry out the Fianna Fáil policy or that the Organisation would assert itself and force you to do so. That hope is now dead. You are going farther and farther away from the Fianna Fáil policy. I regret having to part from a group I worked with and to whom I gave faithful service, a group I had such a high opinion of and who I thought appreciated integrity, honour and straight forwardness.[86]

Seán McCool, interned in the Curragh and four weeks into a hunger strike, contested the election, but by order of the censor he was denied all publicity.[87] The only clues we can get of the mood at the hustings are from censored reports of Fianna Fáil election meetings, now in the files of the Department of Justice. They show that Fianna Fáil meetings were occasionally interrupted by hecklers who voiced concern for the fate of republican prisoners, but these were swiftly removed by gardaí.[88]

By 1943 the Labour Party appeared to be the radical alternative in constitutional politics, not so much because of any communistic tendencies, as some in Fianna Fáil tried to imply, but simply because Fianna Fáil, previously the champion of the under-dog, had moved so much to the right and had become the establishment party. The Labour Party had shown signs of unprecedented growth during the war years: the number of branches mushroomed, from 174 to 750, between 1941 and 1943.[89] The party's policies in 1943 were more or less the same as they had been during the previous two decades. It professed itself the enemy of preventable poverty, mass unemployment and emigration—all social ills that stemmed 'from following blindly alien methods and ideals.' Quoting illustrious patriots of the past, it defined Irish freedom as a time when 'the people would be lord and master in their own land,' and it adjudged that, by this definition, Ireland remained unfree. It pledged itself to 'the reconquest of Ireland by and on behalf of the Irish people.'[90] By 1943 the Labour Party had also become the only party in the Dáil to consistently express concern for civil liberties in the face of a barrage of emergency legislation.

Equal to the threat posed by increasingly disenchanted workers and farmers, now flocking to the ranks of a revitalised Labour Party and Clann na Talmhan, Fianna Fáil concentrated its campaign on economic issues.[91] However, much of its platform rested on expectations of rewards for their achievements while manufacturing apocalyptic visions of the consequences should power slip into the hands of its rivals. From a Fianna Fáil point of view, the mere fact that the opposition *opposed* was a threat to national unity and thus jeopardised neutrality and invited invasion.

Fianna Fáil's case to the electorate was simple: as the only organisation able to offer a single-party government (which was considered to be synonymous with stability), Fianna Fáil was the only bulwark against anarchy. (Slogans ranged from 'Don't change horses while crossing the stream' to 'If you vote Fianna Fáil, the bombs won't fall').[92] Fianna Fáil had already drifted steadily towards authoritarianism, and, as Dónal Ó Drisceoil has noted, the national emergency created a situation in which 'a single party government effectively became the sole arbitrator of the national interest, and the lines between government and state were blurred.'[93]

Seán MacEntee was one of the most visible of the ministerial campaigners, and his crusading brand of electioneering combined contempt for the opposition (or indeed for any opposition) with the arrogant self-assurance that Fianna Fáil was the only party capable of governing. In language not dissimilar to that used by Cumann na nGaedheal during the 1920s, MacEntee told his audiences that

> there undoubtedly are a number of simple, foolish folk, such as one finds in every community, who will vote against the Government, despite all we have done for them and the country. They will be the victims of our opponents' propaganda . . . But sane and sensible people and responsible people will vote for us, because they know that if the country is going to be brought in safety and in peace to the end of this war the government of the State must be in the hands of sane, sensible and responsible men.[94]

In MacEntee's world, Fianna Fáil was an oasis of reason and sanity surrounded by the incompetent, the irrational and, most ominously, the treasonous; the party was opposed by the agents or dupes of Moscow or Berlin. The inoffensive Labour Party leader, William Norton, was transformed into 'the figurehead of the Communist elements,'[95] while even the unmistakably rural appeal of the Clann na Talmhan leader, Michael Donnellan, was dismissed as the populism of 'Herr von Donnellan.'[96] The Labour Party was accused of wishing to 'set class against class, employee against employer, farm labourer against farmer, country against town.'[97] According to this view, the Labour Party had been thoroughly infiltrated by communists, so that Norton enjoyed only titular leadership over what was in essence a Moscow-inspired conspiracy. The Fine Gael leadership was dismissed as people who had 'set themselves to overthrow our democratic system' and 'embarked on a reckless campaign to establish a totalitarian state here.' Among Fine Gael's crimes were its failure to advocate neutrality in the Spanish Civil War and that 'they opposed the enactment of our democratic Constitution.'[98]

The most outlandish declarations from Fine Gael's Blueshirt days were unsparingly reproduced,[99] and it was asked rhetorically whether Chamberlain would have handed back the ports to a Blueshirt government, or whether Ireland could have remained out of the war had the leaders of Fine Gael succeeded in establishing a totalitarian government. This capitalising on Fine Gael's flirtation with fascism was almost a decade out of date and was reminiscent of Cumann na nGaedheal's attempts to win the 1932 election by citing the most imprudent remarks made by de Valera in 1922.

MacEntee also lashed out at what he vaguely described as 'groups with sinister aims': new, menacing organisations that had formed since the outbreak of war and were 'lavishly supplied with funds.'

> For what purpose have they been organised? Who is behind them? . . . Their appearance in such a period as this is sinister; they do not believe in democracy; they do not believe in neutrality; their members are not to be found in the Defence Forces; they are a menace to the peace and security of the State; and they are inimical to the rights of its citizens. Deal with the candidates of such parties as they deserve.[100]

He was probably referring to Córas na Poblachta, a small militant republican party formed in 1940, and Ailtirí na hAiseirghe, a right-wing cultural nationalist party established by Gearóid Ó Cuinneagáin in 1942.[101] Neither made an impact on the electoral landscape in 1943.

During the campaign it became obvious that MacEntee's vicious attacks on the Labour Party were backfiring. Seán Lemass wrote to him saying that a number of Fianna Fáil candidates had contacted him to suggest that the party should 'modify our attacks on Labour. They say that Labour is gaining by them and not the reverse.'[102] But MacEntee's anti-communist ranting had succeeded in planting a seed of doubt in the labour movement, which would soon produce a rich electoral harvest for Fianna Fáil.

Lemass and other ministers had viewed with alarm the Labour Party's extra-ordinary rise in the 1942 local elections, in which it trebled its representation on county councils, doubled its representation on urban district councils and increased its representation on Dublin City Council from two seats to twelve, becoming the largest party in Dublin and taking the mayoralty from Fianna Fáil in the process.

Considering the fact that the election occurred during the emergency, Fianna Fáil's performance was extremely disappointing: it lost 110,000 votes—10 per cent of the first-preference vote—and ten seats. Fortunately for Fianna Fáil, the index of proportionality (the degree to which the number of seats accurately reflects the proportion of votes) was higher than anything achieved before or since, at 115, giving it nine 'bonus seats'.[103] Only Fine Gael fared worse, losing 122,000 votes and thirteen seats. These mainly went to the Labour Party, which achieved its highest share of the first-preference vote (16 per cent) since the party was founded, increasing its vote by 80,000 and almost doubling its Dáil representation to seventeen. The 1943 election also saw the first concerted electoral outing of Clann na Talmhan.

With no unified opposition, however, Fianna Fáil remained in power, and the experience of 1932 and 1937 suggested that de Valera would not wait long before attempting another bite at the cherry.

It is often assumed that the 1944 election was called in response to the 'American Note' (by which the US government, with Churchill's blessing, requested the closure of the Axis legations in Dublin), which appeared to threaten Irish neutrality.[104] The reality was more mundane, however, with the immediate cause of the dissolution being a defeat in the Dáil by one vote on 9 May. The issue was a minor one, and it bore all the hallmarks of a premeditated act. The opposition parties had combined on the Transport Bill (which would nationalise a number of railway and bus companies and establish CIE), not to defeat it but merely to have it deferred for further consideration. De Valera could easily have secured a vote of confidence, but he chose instead to call an election and so make a renewed effort to gain an absolute majority.

Seán MacEntee again whipped up anti-communist hysteria, describing William Norton as 'the Kerensky of the Labour Party,' who, despite his innocuous rhetoric, was in reality 'preparing the way for the red shirts.'[105] The fatal blow, however, came from within the Labour Party itself, which had obligingly split early in 1944. The nomination of Jim Larkin as a candidate was followed by bitter agitation from William O'Brien, general secretary of the Irish Transport and General Workers' Union, the country's largest union. Members of ITGWU leadership took up Fianna Fáil's claim that the Labour Party was being overrun by communists, and when the party leadership refused to expel Larkin the ITGWU disaffiliated from the party on 7 January 1944. Five of the eight deputies sponsored by the ITGWU broke away to form the National Labour Party.[106]

In an effort to save the reputation of his party, Norton was forced to abjure all forms of radicalism and assert that the Labour Party 'proudly acknowledges the authority of the Catholic Church in all matters relating to public policy and public welfare.'[107] During the 1944 election the two Labour Parties were too busy attacking each other to land many blows on de Valera and his Government.

Fine Gael's vote had plummeted since the early 1930s and hovered just above 20 per cent. Cosgrave resigned as leader early in 1944, to be replaced by Richard Mulcahy, who had lost his seat in the 1943 debacle. So bad was Fine Gael's predicament that 'not only observers, but even some leaders of the party seem to have felt that Fine Gael was nearing the end of its life.'[108] Indeed the selection of Mulcahy as Cosgrave's successor indicated a continuation with the failed image of the past rather than a brave new departure. Many Fine Gael deputies, immersed in lucrative business or law practices, were only part-time parliamentarians. The central planks of Fine Gael's policy—the Treaty and the Commonwealth—had been rendered obsolete by Fianna Fáil, and the departure of Cosgrave suggested to many that he and his party had fulfilled their mission of consolidating the fledgling Free State and could now retire honourably.

Neutrality had been taken for granted during the 1943 election, and many voters were not persuaded of the need to further strengthen de Valera's position. But this sense of security was 'rudely disturbed' on 21 February 1944 by the American Note. Though it proved to be 'wholly pacific in style and intention,' it enabled the Government to present neutrality as under threat from the Allied powers.[109] James Hogan has pointed out that the effect of the American-British *démarche* 'was in the long run to strengthen Mr. de Valera's prestige at home, and to contribute to his victory at the forthcoming election.'[110]

From this viewpoint it would appear that the US government's initiative rebounded; but that would be to misunderstand the motivation behind it. The US minister plenipotentiary to Ireland, David Gray, an amateur diplomat and passionate Anglophile, believed that de Valera would seek to raise the partition issue in America after the war. Despite diplomatic assurances from the Assistant Secretary of the Department of External Affairs, Frederick Boland, that de Valera intended 'to let sleeping dogs lie,' Gray believed that the exploitation of American opinion would be the only anti-partitionist strategy open to the Government should the Allies win, and he thus sought to damage de Valera's reputation in the United States.[111] Gray interpreted the Taoiseach's portrayal of the American Note as an ultimatum and as a prelude to an invasion as 'characteristic of de Valera's political dramatics.'[112]

Despite Gray's pivotal role in the crisis, most of the odium was directed at the traditional enemy, Britain. De Valera rallied nationalist opinion around him, extolling the pre-Treaty virtues of unity and resilience against a common foe. He declared that the Irish people might be called 'at any moment . . . to defend our rights and our freedom with our lives,' a claim that Gray criticised as a 'calculating attempt to arouse and unify the country . . . against the alleged perils threatening it from without.'[113] Despite repeated assurances from the US government that no retaliatory measures were contemplated, de Valera 'generated a crisis which he exploited to his own political advantage.'[114] But even he could not prevent Gray from achieving his primary objective of pushing American opinion away from de Valera.[115]

On a reduced turn-out of 65 per cent, the 1944 election gave Fianna Fáil a majority of 14 in a Dáil composed of 138 deputies. With a civil war brewing within the Labour family and with Fine Gael in disarray, Joseph Lee's judgement that Fianna Fáil's victory reflected 'despair in the opposition more than confidence in the government' seems appropriate.[116] Gerrymandering also played a part: though Fianna Fáil regained fewer than half the votes lost in 1943, the existence of fifteen three-member constituencies— a product of Fianna Fáil's electoral manipulation—resulted in a disproportionate allocation of seats. Had the distribution of seats been strictly proportionate to votes cast, Fianna Fáil would have been denied an absolute majority.[117]

Censorship was maintained in full force throughout the 1944 election campaign.[118] Most active republicans were still interned, while those on the outside were not organised electorally. There is evidence, however, that some of the anti-Fianna Fáil republican sentiment was channelled into Clann na Talmhan, which had made a significant impact in both the 1943 and 1944 elections.

Clann na Talmhan has traditionally been viewed as merely a farmers' party—and it is true that it successfully challenged support for both Fianna Fáil and Fine Gael among the rural population. A close examination of its election literature, however, shows that it saw its mission as much broader. Its rhetoric reflected a growing dis-illusionment with party politics.[119] It argued that national unity was impossible if it was to be based on the existing system of political parties, as these had a vested interest in keeping the people divided, and yet without national unity progress was blocked. Contrasting contemporary factionalism with united movements of the past, Clann na Talmhan denounced the 'party bosses in Dublin' who had turned democracy into 'a veiled dictatorship.'[120]

Since it appeared that Fianna Fáil had vacated the republican high ground, Clann na Talmhan reclaimed much of the original Fianna Fáil rhetoric. It described itself as 'a non-political organisation . . . the only organisation in this country which can claim to unite in a common bond of friendship for the realisation of National Unity and Independence every patriotic and honest-minded citizen.' It claimed that 'politicians were responsible for the fact that six of our counties were torn away from us,' and it advocated 'a firm attitude in our bargaining with "John Bull".'[121]

Clann na Talmhan's total vote, which averaged approximately 10 per cent in both the 1943 and 1944 elections, is somewhat misleading, as the party did not contest most constituencies. Instead it concentrated its efforts on those areas in which Fianna Fáil had traditionally done well. In Galway East, Michael Donnellan topped the poll, taking 28 per cent of the vote, while the party vote there rose to 39 per cent in 1944. It took two seats in Mayo North in both elections, with an average vote of 35 per cent. In Roscommon it took two of the three seats in 1943, but despite increasing its vote from 37 to 40 per cent it narrowly lost one of these in 1944. Patrick Finucane was elected in Kerry North in both elections, securing 26 per cent of the vote on both occasions and topping the poll in 1944.

Other constituencies where Clann na Talmhan won seats in both elections were Tipperary, Waterford, Wicklow, Cork North and Cork South-West.[122] A seat was won in Kilkenny in 1943 but lost the following year, while the reverse happened in Cavan. In Donegal East, William Sheldon took a seat for Clann na Talmhan in 1943 but had switched to being an independent farmers' candidate by 1944. Standing in Kerry South for the first time in 1944, the party candidate took 24 per cent and missed the third seat by 149 votes.

Despite its impressive election performances, Clann na Talmhan never challenged Fianna Fáil's position as the natural party of government, not least because of limitations in leadership and organisation. Michael Donnellan, a former Sinn Féin and Fianna Fáil councillor, lacked charisma and avoided nurturing a leadership cult. In 1944 he was replaced as party leader by Joseph Blowick, who, though a solid constituency man, 'under stress of extreme excitement sounded like a tape recorder played backwards.'[123]

More importantly, perhaps, Clann na Talmhan was not a party in the conventional sense of the word, lacking as it did an organisation and a national headquarters. In many ways it was an agrarian flag of convenience for many of those disenchanted with the status quo, a loose collection of individuals bound by little but their common disillusionment. Fianna Fáil's loss of support to Clann na Talmhan among the small farmers in the west and to the Labour Party among the urban proletariat was compensated by its rising vote in the east and among the middle class.

'THE IRA IS DEAD, AND I KILLED IT': THE EXECUTION OF CHARLIE KERINS

Shortly after the 1944 election the services of a British hangman were to be called on again. On 15 June 1944 Dublin Castle learnt that the IRA chief of staff, Charlie Kerins, was staying at the home of Dr Kathleen Farrell in Rathmines, Dublin. At five o'clock the following morning Kerins awoke to find himself surrounded by Special Branch men armed with machine guns. A 26-year-old native of Tralee, Kerins had been appointed chief of staff after the capture of Hugh McAteer in October 1942.[124] During that month his adjutant-general, Michael Quille, was captured by the RUC in Belfast and handed over the border, where he was tried for the killing of Detective-Sergeant Dinny O'Brien and acquitted.[125] On 2 October 1944 Kerins was brought before the Military Court in Collins Barracks and charged with the same crime. Refusing to recognise the court, he declined to plead or to call witnesses.[126] During the six-day trial he sat in silence as others deliberated his fate.

The state case relied totally on circumstantial evidence, and even this was inconclusive. However, as J. Bowyer Bell notes, though the state could not be sure that Kerins had fired the shot, as chief of staff of the IRA he could be considered responsible, 'so no one was too fussy about the details of his case.'[127] As expected, he was sentenced to death.

Kerry County Council led the way in the campaign to save Kerins from the firing squad. It 'respectfully and unanimously' requested the Government to commute Kerins's sentence. Its campaign, however, immediately fell foul of state censorship. In an effort to garner support, telegrams signed by fifteen prominent Kerrymen, including Cormac Breathnach TD and Senator Donnchadh Ó hÉaluighthe of Fianna Fáil, were sent to other local authorities, urging them to support the campaign. All telegrams, however, were stopped from reaching their destination.[128]

Unable to get the message across in the press, the campaigners organised a public meeting in the Mansion House, and it was attended by a delegation led by the chairman of Kerry County Council and other local representatives.[129] The Lord Mayor of Cork, Seán Cronin, made a personal appeal to the Government for clemency and declared that anyone who wished to be associated with the reprieve campaign could get reprieve forms from the Lord Mayor's Office at City Hall.[130] All publicity for such activities in Cork and Dublin was again stopped by the censors. A Reprieve Committee was established, which met daily at the Mansion House. Paid advertisements asking citizens of Dublin on behalf of Kerry County Council to attend the Mansion House meeting were to run for a number of days, but they never appeared. Similar paid advertisements for meetings elsewhere in the country were also prohibited.[131] Even the following small notice was banned by Government order:

A CHIARRAIGHIGH [PEOPLE OF KERRY]
A MEETING OF ALL KERRY MEN AND WOMEN WILL BE HELD TO-MORROW NIGHT
(THURSDAY) AT 7.30 P.M. IN CLEARYS, O'CONNELL STREET.

Evidently any gathering of Kerry people at this time was suspect. This was not altogether surprising, as a precedent of sorts had been set when Maurice O'Neill had been sentenced to death in 1942. When an *Irish Press* heading, 'Three Kerrymen convicted,' had been passed, the Controller of Censorship, T. J. Coyne, told the press censors that

the use of headings which appeal to local patriotism in connection with lawbreakers and misdemeanants is something which is repugnant to man and most hateful to God and the Minister says he will chop the head off the next member of staff to pass a heading of this kind.[132]

The lesson was well learnt, and no heads rolled. All references to Kerins omitted allusion to Co. Kerry or Tralee. Even his age was edited out by the censor—anything, indeed, that endowed Kerins with a personality.

Because all letters to papers advocating a reprieve were suppressed,[133] and all advertisements and news items were stopped,[134] Kerry County Council and its supporters had to rely largely on word of mouth to further their campaign.[135] Despite these setbacks, two thousand people packed into the Round Room of the Mansion House, while more than three thousand congregated outside, unable to gain admission. A motion was proposed by the Lord Mayor of Dublin and seconded by the Lord Mayor of Cork

> that this mass meeting, summoned by the Kerry County Council and representing citizens of all Irish counties, urges the Government to commute the sentence of death passed on Charles Kerins by the Special Criminal Court.[136]

The campaign to suppress public interest by means of censorship was complemented by the harassment and arrest of those involved in the reprieve campaign. During the fortnight before the execution gardaí arrested several people who were engaged in collecting signatures or reciting the Rosary.[137]

As the Kerins family made their way to Dublin, forty men, described as 'actively connected with efforts to secure the reprieve of Charles Kerins,' were arrested. Some were captured during raids on the Reprieve Committee rooms in the Mansion House, others while seeking signatures for the reprieve petition or while putting up posters advertising the Mansion House meeting. The police tore down copies of the poster from walls and hoardings. A car fitted with loudspeakers was stopped by the police on Saturday as it was setting out to tour the city. The *Irish Times* reported that during all of Friday and Saturday nights police cars with dimmed lights slipped through the streets of Dublin, stopping and questioning passers-by. All these incidents were reported by the newspapers but were expurgated when submitted to the censor.[138]

On 28 November, Con Lehane, the solicitor nominated to act on behalf of Kerins, handed in a petition to the Government. With it was a memorandum signed by the three barristers who had appeared for Kerins in the Court of Criminal Appeal. Given that the Reprieve Committee had less than two weeks in which to organise the petition, the number of signatures obtained—77,000—was impressive, and the organisers claimed that thousands of reprieve forms did not reach their office in time for inclusion.[139] Among those who signed the petition were Noel Purcell, Seán Ó Faoláin, Austin Clarke, numerous clergymen, including the president of St Patrick's College, Maynooth, two dozen members of the Oireachtas and veterans of the War of Independence.[140]

The Government considered the matter that day,[141] the minutes simply recording that it decided it would 'not be justified' in advising the President to exercise the prerogative of mercy and that 'the law must take its course.'[142] The execution was fixed for 1 December.

Some of the most bitter exchanges since Fianna Fáil's entry to the Dáil took place on the eve of Kerins's execution, 30 November 1944.[143] When the order of business was announced, Jim Larkin rose from his seat, saying that he had given notice of raising on the adjournment a matter of urgent public importance, and he asked if he now had permission to speak. The Ceann Comhairle replied that, having considered the matter, he felt that the issue raised, while definite and of public importance, was not sufficiently urgent to warrant a debate. When Larkin challenged the judgement as arbitrary, a row ensued that almost came to blows.[144] Eventually Deputies Jim Larkin, Dan Spring and Michael Finucane were named by de Valera and were suspended from the Dáil. Discussion then resumed on the more urgent matter of a Drainage Bill, and this was followed by a discussion of mental hospitals and sundry votes for departmental services.

Letters and telegrams to de Valera continued to pour in from Fianna Fáil cumainn, Labour Party branches, the GAA, trade unions, army units and a disparate group of representative bodies and individuals. The fact that de Valera himself had been sentenced to death, only to be reprieved, did not escape the notice of many letter-writers.[145] Scores of letters from republican veterans expressed their disenchantment with Fianna Fáil's policy on political prisoners. The Old IRA, whose support Fianna Fáil had previously used to legitimise its brand of republicanism, called on 'all national elements still remaining' to express their 'abhorrence and detestation at this proposed legalised crime.'[146]

On the eve of Kerins's execution Kevin Barry's mother[147] sent a telegram to de Valera that read: 'The English hanged my son Kevin for murder. Which is your tradition—his or theirs'?[148] She received no reply or acknowledgement. Perhaps the irony suggested in the song 'Kevin Barry', written in 1920, was uncomfortably clear: 'Why not shoot me like a soldier? / Do not hang me like a dog.' Barry's death in Mountjoy Prison had prompted Michael Collins to declare that there would be 'no more lonely scaffolds'; and as President of the Republic during the Civil War de Valera had enjoyed the hospitality of the Barry household in evading capture and almost certain death at the hands of Free State forces. Now, twenty years after Barry's death, another lonely scaffold was erected in Mountjoy, with an English hangman paid to execute the leader of the Irish Republican Army. The wheel had turned full circle.

Shortly after the execution the Dáil adjourned for eight weeks, resuming on 24 January. Boland's and de Valera's depiction of the Charlie Kerins Reprieve Committee as an IRA front during the adjournment debate provoked a stern reply from the committee.[149] A letter denying the charge was shown to de Valera, and he instructed that no reply was to be sent.[150] The letter was also sent to the national press, but it was suppressed.[151] Masses for the repose of the soul of Kerins were censored,[152] as were the cross-party resolutions of local authorities extending sympathy to Kerins's family.[153] English journalists who were concerned about 'a big political crisis which had developed in Eire' were assured by the chief press censor, to whom all such queries had to be directed, that 'there was no foundation for the story.'[154]

SEÁN MCCAUGHEY
Long before Kerins's execution the IRA was a spent force, militarily and politically. Most of the principal leaders were imprisoned or dead, and 'there was nothing, outside the prisons, but a handful of demoralised and isolated individuals.'[155] By 1945

the IRA, J. Bowyer Bell writes, 'was not exactly dead but the signs of life were few and fragile.'[156]

With the formal termination of hostilities in Europe, official censorship was lifted, though its effects lived on, and the persecution of militant republicans and the vindictive treatment of political prisoners continued unabated. Proof, if any was needed, that the criminalisation policy was not linked to a threat to neutrality was starkly and poignantly provided by the experience of one man whose death would set in train the events leading to the most serious and concerted challenge to Fianna Fáil's claim to the republican mantle.

Under the alias John Dunlop, Seán McCaughey had been sentenced to six months' imprisonment in December 1939 for refusing to give his address to a garda and to a further six months for failing to give an account of his movements.[157] He had also played a central role in the bizarre Stephen Hayes episode,[158] for which he was arrested and charged with 'assault and unlawful detention.' Under common law, this offence carried a maximum sentence of two years' imprisonment; but the military tribunal sentenced McCaughey to death. Saved from the gallows by Seán MacBride, McCaughey was forced to endure an exceptionally harsh prison regime because of his refusal to conform to the criminalisation policy for republican prisoners. (The prison governor, Major Barrows, had been a prison officer in Belfast and Derry before being appointed to Portlaoise Prison by the Government in 1937. His father had also been governor during British rule.) After four years of solitary confinement, clothed only in a blanket and deprived of daylight and of any communication with the outside world, including access to reading material, McCaughey announced that he was going on hunger strike in an effort to secure an unconditional release.

Numerous meetings took place throughout the country in support of McCaughey, but all received minimal coverage.[159] The *Irish Independent* reported in a tiny notice that five hundred turf-cutters who had gone on strike had participated in a demonstration against President Seán T. O'Kelly, on his way to Arbour Hill military cemetery for the official commemoration of the 1916 Rising and to pay homage to the state-approved martyrs, while those of the non-approved variety languished within earshot of the presidential entourage.[160]

When Deputy Oliver Flanagan asked in the Dáil why he was unable to visit Portlaoise Prison (which was in his constituency), the Minister for Justice replied that he would be able to go there 'when he is somewhat more mature,' saying in effect that he would have to wait until he had adopted a less hostile attitude towards Government policy. While acknowledging that republican prisoners were 'having a hard time of it,' Boland claimed that it was 'all their own fault,' as 'they want to be treated as other than criminals.' When questioned on his own prison experiences, Boland admitted that he had participated in a prison break-out on one occasion but added that he 'did not enjoy doing it,' and indeed he was 'ashamed of it.'[161]

At 3 a.m. on Saturday 11 May, Seán MacBride was awakened by a phone call from the Secretary of the Government, Maurice Moynihan, who told him that Seán McCaughey had died an hour previously. He had been on hunger strike for twenty-three days and on thirst strike for the last seventeen. MacBride recalled:

He said the Chief [de Valera] had told him to phone me. It may have been moral anxiety. I never understood why.[162]

An insight into de Valera's thinking is provided by the notes taken by Sir John Maffey, the British representative in Ireland, to whom de Valera sometimes confided, of a private meeting shortly after McCaughey's death. He told Maffey that 'state censorship during the war had had the effect of keeping would-be martyrs in check,' but 'now that publicity was again available he feared there would undoubtedly be successors to McCaughey.' Revealingly, he said that the 'only reason' his Government, mostly 1916 veterans, were able to act firmly against the IRA was because of their national record, though this created difficulties for them, given that they too detested partition.[163]

Seán MacBride acted on behalf of the McCaughey family at the inquest in Portlaoise Prison, which was to become something of a *cause célèbre*. The state, despite vehement protests, limited the inquest so that no question regarding conditions in the prison could be raised. When MacBride tried to call one of the prisoners, Tomás Óg Mac Curtáin, as a witness, the prison governor refused on the grounds that, as he had worn nothing but a blanket for five years, Mac Curtáin was insufficiently dressed to be presented before a jury.

Unable to put any questions to the governor, MacBride concentrated on the prison doctor, Dr Duane. Putting his papers to one side, MacBride looked directly at the doctor and asked if it was true that during McCaughey's four-and-a-half years in the prison he had never been out in the fresh air or sunlight. The doctor acknowledged that this was so, and also confirmed that McCaughey had been in solitary confinement and had been prohibited from speaking or associating with any other human being. MacBride then asked: 'Would you treat a dog in that fashion?' At this point the coroner tried to intervene, but MacBride persisted and repeated the question. 'If you had a dog, would you treat it in that fashion?' After a pause, and in a voice that was barely audible, Dr Duane replied 'No.' MacBride turned to the jury. 'The answer is "no," gentlemen, in case you did not hear it.'[164] MacBride was prevented from asking further questions, and he walked out in protest, followed by his junior counsel, Noel Hartnett, and McCaughey's solicitor, Con Lehane.

Recriminations followed McCaughey's death and inquest, not least within the Oireachtas. Throughout the five hours of debate the atmosphere in the Dáil was tense. The *Cork Examiner* reported:

It is quite a time since so much interest was evinced in the business before the House on the part of the Deputies, no less than the public. The Visitors Gallery was thronged, and—not unusual in the circumstances—I noted the presence of quite a few prominent members of our Special Branch detectives.[165]

During one particularly vitriolic exchange about prison conditions the Minister for Justice, Gerry Boland, addressing the Clann na Talmhan TD Michael Donnellan, said, 'If I got Deputy Donnellan in, I would teach him something.'[166]

Owen Sheehy Skeffington, a future Trinity College professor, refused to accept condolences from Fianna Fáil on the death of his mother, Hanna, who had been involved in the formation of the party. Writing to the Rory O'Connor Branch of Fianna Fáil on 18 May, he said:

I received your letter of sympathy on the morning that the papers carried the account of McCaughey's inquest. I can accept no official sympathy from Fianna Fáil, nor would my mother want me to. She had nothing but contempt for the party who so assiduously carried on the British tradition in its treatment of prisoners, and so consistently betrayed the ideals for which it was founded.[167]

Echoing earlier Fianna Fáil rhetoric, Prof. Liam Ó Briain told a crowd in Eyre Square, Galway, that 'these men hadn't been bought by pensions and jobbery, as some had.'[168] Expressing such sentiments had its repercussions, however, and those found making 'seditious speeches' following McCaughey's death were promptly arrested.[169]

In June 1946 a new republican paper, *Resurgence*, appeared, but it was banned after six issues when it condemned the handing over the border of Harry White for imprisonment.[170] White was sentenced to death but was saved from Pierrepoint and the gallows on appeal through the legal dexterity of Seán MacBride.[171]

Seán McCaughey's case is significant because it demonstrates that the official attitude towards political prisoners was not coloured by the wartime emergency, as claimed by the Government and its supporters. From the case of Seán Glynn in 1936 to that of Seán McCaughey in 1946 the same policy was evident. The war and the emergency intervened, but the policy of criminalisation, and sensory deprivation, predated them and continued after them. Indeed the Government proved even less tolerant of such cases than its unionist counterparts in Belfast. During the month in which McCaughey died the Belfast government unconditionally released a republican prisoner, David Fleming, after he had been on hunger strike for more than fifty days.

The death of Seán McCaughey also led to the estrangement of an erstwhile de Valera supporter, Noel Hartnett, an event that was to contribute to the first serious assault on Fianna Fáil's electoral position since it took power in 1932. A long-time member of Fianna Fáil, Hartnett had assisted Seán McBride at the inquest into McCaughey's death. In addition to his work as a barrister, Hartnett worked for Radio Éireann as a broadcaster and contributor, best known for presenting the station's most popular quiz programme, 'Question Time'.[172] Shortly after the conclusion of the McCaughey inquest Hartnett was informed by the Minister for Posts and Telegraphs, P. J. Little, that he was banned from further participation in the state broadcasting station. It is questionable whether this decision was made on the sole initiative of the minister, a mild, scholarly man presiding over the 'wooden spoon' of portfolios. It has been suggested that the hidden hand of Boland or de Valera was most likely steering events,[173] though this can not be established conclusively.[174]

As in the case of Seán Óg Ó Ceallaigh, Hartnett was being banned not for anything he had said while broadcasting but for activities unrelated to the state radio service and connected only with his main source of work. He was being punished for choosing to involve himself as a barrister in a legal case that Fianna Fáil considered prejudicial to its party interests. More sinister, perhaps, was the spin put on the banning by de Valera. 'Anyone can express any political opinion,' de Valera claimed, 'provided he does not advocate force against the will of the people.' With that innuendo left hanging, Little claimed that Hartnett had taken part in 'a very vehement and dangerous political controversy.'[175]

Hartnett's reaction was equally indignant. In a letter to the *Cork Examiner* he produced an eloquent critique of the Government case for purging him from the broadcasting service.[176] He assumed that the 'dangerous political controversy' alluded to was his advocacy of an inquiry into prison conditions, for which he owed 'no apology to him or to Mr. de Valera.' He challenged the minister to produce any statement of his that advocated 'the use of force against the will of the people' and extended the challenge to include the period before 1932, 'when I stamped the crossroads in company with the Minister and his colleagues, and ofttimes boggled at the intemperateness of their own declarations.' He also disputed the minister's attempt to equate radio announcers and comperes. The former, Hartnett argued, was a state servant, the latter a programme artist.

The most damaging comments, however, were those relating to how Fianna Fáil so selectively found involvement in politics and broadcasting to be incompatible. He challenged the minister to deny that he had been a member of the National Executive of Fianna Fáil when he was a radio announcer. Was the rule to which his purge was ascribed in existence then, or was it only in more recent times, when another radio personality had spoken in P. J. Little's constituency on behalf of the minister? If de Valera and Little were attempting to portray him as untrustworthy it was a view inconsistent with their previous dealings with him. The most important programmes had been, as a matter of policy, assigned to Hartnett, and shortly before his call to the bar he had been approached by a colleague and informed that the Fianna Fáil Publicity Committee had arranged with Little for a weekly or monthly broadcast of selected proceedings from the Dáil, and that Hartnett had been chosen by the committee to take charge of it. For Hartnett the 'single truth of the matter' was that he had criticised the Government and that Radio Éireann was considered by it to be a party monopoly. Despite Hartnett's challenge, no further comment was made by de Valera.

Hartnett's expulsion provoked Seán Ó Faoláin—whose own literary works had been banned and who had long ceased to broadcast on Radio Éireann—to enquire 'what sort of broadcasting can now be expected except the safe, the sycophantic, the innocuous, the unadventurous?'[177]

But the censoring of Noel Hartnett had a more enduring impact, as he was to become the director of elections for a new party that was to pose the most serious threat to Fianna Fáil hegemony since it took power in 1932.

Chapter 9

A NEW REPUBLICAN RIVAL, 1946–8

IDEOLOGICAL DECLINE AND THE RISE OF CLANN NA POBLACHTA

T hat Fianna Fáil's anti-republicanism was becoming electorally damaging was evident in 1945 in the results of the first presidential election. In a three-way battle the Fianna Fáil candidate, Seán T. O'Kelly, received 537,965 votes, only five thousand short of an absolute majority. Seán Mac Eoin garnered 335,539 votes for Fine Gael. But the real surprise was the vote secured by Dr Patrick McCartan, the republican dark horse of the campaign, who received a respectable 212,834 first-preference votes. While McCartan's first-preference vote (20 per cent of the total) concerned Fianna Fáil, the distribution of his transfers was also alarming: 117,886 votes (55 per cent) transferred to Mac Eoin, while only 27,200 (13 per cent) went to O'Kelly. The remaining 66,000—slightly less than a third of McCartan's vote—were non-transferable.

What these statistics suggest is that hostility towards Fine Gael, associated in the republican mind with the betrayal of the Republic and the killing of the 'Seventy-Seven', was less intense than that towards the self-proclaimed republican party. In essence, the 'misdeeds' of Fine Gael were far less vivid (and further in the past) than those of Fianna Fáil, which were associated with recent executions and hunger strikes.

A new republican party, Clann na Poblachta ('Children of the Republic'), was launched on 6 July 1946 (to little public acclaim) by Seán MacBride, within weeks of Seán McCaughey's death. That month Fianna Fáil took a by-election seat in Cork. Describing Fianna Fáil as 'the only alternative to political chaos,' Seán Lemass had hinted that a by-election defeat might precipitate an early general election, despite the fact that the seat had been held by an independent.[1] In a contest in which the War of Independence veteran Tom Barry stood as an independent, Fianna Fáil had an ideal candidate in the former Lord Mayor of Cork, Paddy McGrath, himself a veteran of the independence struggle and chairman of the Cork Old IRA Association.[2] When the result was announced, Barry declared that the election had demonstrated that those dissatisfied with the existing parties could not hope to win as independents but should instead either form a party of their own or not contest elections at all.[3] The logic of Barry's assessment did not go unheeded, and within days Clann na Poblachta was established.

The first year was one of quiet and patient organisational activity, and it was not until the local elections of June 1947 that it began to make significant inroads into Fianna Fáil's support.

Clann na Poblachta drew its support from the 'republican university,' those men and women who had emerged embittered from the prisons and internment camps in which they had endured tremendous hardships. In this it did not have to start an organisation from scratch; but, despite the presence of a large number of politicised republicans, most of them had little practical experience in electoral politics. Republicanism of the IRA variety had reached its lowest ebb and, in the absence of a clear policy, rallied around the call of 'Release the prisoners.' Like the Fenians before it, the IRA of the 1940s was better known for the political agitation aimed at releasing prisoners than for any military endeavours.[4] The resurgence had reached a peak with the campaign to save the life of Seán McCaughey, but the formation of Clann na Poblachta resulted in a split in the Republican Prisoners' Release Association. The majority went against the Clann na Poblachta leaders and accused them of using the association to establish an electoral base within the republican community.[5]

The difficulty in getting prominent IRA figures, new and old, to join Clann na Poblachta was reminiscent of Fianna Fáil's endeavours twenty years earlier. Patrick Kissane, a veteran of the War of Independence from Co. Tipperary, decided to run for Clann na Poblactha. His wife recalled his initial reluctance, though he was subsequently elected to the Dáil:

> Some of the members of the party came down to see Paddy. He didn't give his consent at that time. Seán MacBride had come himself then. And after that he didn't even consent . . . so it took another while before he decided.[6]

The provisional executive of Clann na Poblachta 'sounded like a roll-call of the 1930s IRA,'[7] with at least twenty-two of the twenty-seven members having been active in the IRA at some point in their lives.[8] Among them were two former chiefs of staff, Seán MacBride and Michael Fitzpatrick, and two former adjutants-general, Jim Killeen and Dónal O'Donoghue. One executive member, Michael Ferguson, had been released from prison only three months earlier for his part in the bombing campaign in England. The morning after Clann na Poblachta's inaugural meeting a prominent committee member said that the establishment of the new party indicated that 'a significant number of what you might call the IRA were taking constitutional action.'[9]

The formation of Clann na Poblachta coincided with a bitter and prolonged strike by members of the Irish National Teachers' Organisation, which even the intervention of Archbishop John Charles McQuaid could not resolve.[10] A conference of Fianna Fáil teachers passed a resolution in April 1946 declaring that while in the past they had given 'unflinching support' to Fianna Fáil their position in that party 'may soon become untenable.'[11] The Government refused to budge, its autocratic streak apparent in the depiction by the Minister for Education, Tom Derrig, of the strike for better pay as 'a definite challenge to the authority of the State.'[12] Teachers had always provided vital support for Fianna Fáil, and many of the disaffected transferred their allegiance to Clann na Poblachta.

BY-ELECTIONS

The first serious opportunity for Clann na Poblachta to put a dent in the Fianna Fáil electoral machine came in October 1947, when three by-elections were held on the same day in Dublin, Tipperary and Waterford. The by-elections were a big organisational test for the new party: despite generating much enthusiasm, it had only a skeletal organisational structure compared with the major parties. The big contest was considered to be between the Clann na Poblachta leader, Seán MacBride, and Tommy Mullins, Fianna Fáil's general secretary.

Clann na Poblachta had an ideal figurehead in Seán MacBride for challenging Fianna Fáil's and de Valera's brand of republicanism. Everything about his life appeared, at least to his supporters, to have been leading to that point. The son of an executed 1916 leader, John MacBride, and the veteran republican Maud Gonne, he enjoyed an impeccable republican lineage. The veteran Fenian John O'Leary agreed to be his godfather, and his birth generated widespread interest in France, Britain and the United States, with greetings being sent to the 'Future President of Ireland.' One family friend sent a letter to the Pope announcing that 'the King of Ireland has been born,' while one of MacBride's biographers notes that 'many people regarded his stock so highly that he was spoken of as though he was an Irish prince, destined to have a major impact on the future life of the Irish nation.'[13] His parents did little to discourage such notions: throughout her life Maud Gonne MacBride kept a photograph of Seán as a child over which she had written *Man of Destiny*.[14] MacBride's early life in France had given him a pronounced French accent and endowed him with a certain exotic quality, which was 'an additional attraction in an Irish political chief.'[15]

In Tommy Mullins, Fianna Fáil had put forward one of its most experienced party stalwarts.[16] Conscious that Fianna Fáil would seek to attack MacBride's past connections with proscribed organisations, Clann na Poblachta set about exploring Mullins's radical past. It didn't have to look far. During his trenchant condemnation of article 2a of the Constitution of the Irish Free State, Mullins had casually announced to the Dáil that he was a member of four of the organisations that were to be outlawed.[17] This statement was dug up by Clann na Poblachta publicists, who, in an advertisement printed in the *Irish Times* on the eve of the election, asked mischievously, 'Which four?'[18]

Fianna Fáil pulled no punches, and Seán MacEntee wrote a series of long letters to the *Irish Times* and the *Irish Press* impugning the reputation of Clann na Poblachta generally and of Seán MacBride in particular by linking them to communist Russia and fascist Germany.[19] More pointedly, MacEntee accused 'MacBride and his friends' of attempting to involve Ireland in a war with Britain and the United States, something vehemently denied by MacBride.[20]

Two days before the election MacEntee's allegations received a timely boost from the Federated Union of Employers, whose president declared that 'today a bad service is being rendered to the national cause by the injection of political poison into the industrial life by partisan oratory,' and that 'tendencies towards social revolution are developing rapidly here.' The forces of labour, he continued, were being used by international organisations 'chiefly backed by Moscow,' and the method employed was the magnifying of grievances 'to such an extent as would ensure the embarrassment of existing Governments and the undermining of law and order.'[21] These statements were symptomatic of the strong alliance between Fianna Fáil and big business. Enriched under the shelter of protection, these employers now saw Fianna Fáil as the bulwark between them and the free market.[22] Fianna Fáil's castration of the unions and its fixing of prices had earned it much admiration among the business class.

The by-election results provided Clann na Poblachta with a surprise breakthrough: MacBride took Dublin County and Kissane the Tipperary seat, while Fianna Fáil retained its Waterford seat. The transfers indicated that a new alliance was developing, with both Fine Gael and Labour Party voters transferring heavily to Clann na Poblachta and with Fianna Fáil relying on a high first-preference vote to take a seat with the minimum of transfers. The comparison with Waterford—where the Clann na Poblachta candidate had finished last and lost his deposit—suggested that victories would depend very much on organisation.

Sensitive to how the electoral reversals might be interpreted, the defeated Fianna Fáil candidate in Tipperary said that Fianna Fáil 'had never deviated from their old principle as far as Ireland was concerned, and the organisation was still sound in matters of principle,' and that they 'claimed to be as good republicans as any other body in the country.'[23] Others saw Clann na Poblachta's success as proof that Anglophobia was alive and kicking: in its post-election editorial the *Irish Times* lamented that 'it is an unhappy fact that there is still a section of the Irish people that will support any appeal to anti-British sentiment.'[24]

THE 1948 ELECTION: THE RED SCARE REVISITED

De Valera kept his word—or carried out his threat, depending on how one looks at it—and announced that he would be seeking a dissolution of the Dáil 'as soon as practicable,' with a view to holding a general election early in the new year.[25] Every party was now on an election footing.

On the surface there seemed little reason for an election. The nearest thing to an explanation came from Frank Aiken, who told an audience in Co. Monaghan that while Fianna Fáil could have carried on for another eighteen months they had decided on an election because 'they did not want it left in the mouths of any foreigner or Irishman to say that the Government could not speak during the next five difficult years with the authority of the Irish people.'[26] Another Fianna Fáil deputy claimed that the party had been 'unable to carry out their programme fully because they lacked a clear overall majority,' and 'now that the war was over the electorate should give that majority to enable them to complete their work.'[27]

Neither of these reasons is convincing. Fianna Fáil had lost, in effect, only one seat. With a majority of fourteen—impregnable by Dáil standards—and forty-nine seats more than the nearest rival, the party had governed unimpeded and untroubled by a fragmented and ineffective opposition. From Fianna Fáil's point of view, however, the need to nip the new republican party in the bud was evident. In the dreary climate of the late 1940s, time could only aid the growth of a radical party armed with a barrage of grievances with which to bombard the Government. De Valera, perhaps remembering the circumstances that had allowed Fianna Fáil to thrive while in opposition, followed his instinct and opted for a snap election, and there were none in the Government who dared disagree.[28]

The election announcement was followed by frenetic activity within Clann na Poblachta. On 30 November the party held its first ard-fheis. 372 delegates attended, representing 252 craobhacha (branches), which makes it clear that the party was still in the throes of elementary organisational endeavour. A recruiting leaflet issued shortly before the ard-fheis announced:

> Instead of flag waving, 'national records', and personalities what is needed is a policy based upon realities. Instead of recriminations and self-glorification based upon past events, the need is vision and planning for the future.[29]

The party also committed itself to 'an end to Political Corruption, Quibbling, Jobbery and Graft.'[30] The Electoral (Amendment) Act (1947) was cited as an example of such dubious political practices. Despite a fall in population since 1935 (when the previous revision had been undertaken) the number of TDs was bumped up from 138 to 147 to alleviate an anticipated drop in Fianna Fáil's support. Twenty-four constituencies were altered in all, and the number of constituencies increased from thirty-five to forty, in part as a result of the desire to increase the number of three-seat constituencies from fifteen to twenty-two. As three-seat constituencies invariably load the dice in favour of the larger party, Joseph Lee has accurately described the result of the 1947 act as 'one of the most delicious pieces of fiction ever devised by even a harassed electoral cartographer to frustrate the will of the people.'[31]

Despite this rather crude attempt at electoral manipulation, de Valera declared that, 'with all our strength,' Fianna Fáil was going to find it 'very difficult' to obtain an absolute majority.[32] Clann na Poblachta's arrival on the political stage made the election the most fiercely contested yet, with more than 400 candidates seeking to take one of the 147 Dáil seats.

STRONG GOVERNMENT VERSUS COALITION

The kernel of Fianna Fáil's case for staying in power was that coalition governments were inherently bad and that, correspondingly, only a unified, disciplined and coherent government could meet the challenges of post-war life. De Valera believed that the opposition parties were united only in a destructive purpose—the defeat of Fianna Fáil—and that they had nothing constructive to offer, nor were they in a position to present a united policy to the electorate that could be judged against that of Fianna Fáil.[33] However, the arguments used to explain why the stability of the state demanded an experienced Fianna Fáil government could be used *a fortiori* five years later, when another election would be due: for if the opposition lacked experience in 1948 they would be even more ill-prepared for office in 1953. In short, the argument advocated that Fianna Fáil should rule in perpetuity.

For much of the election campaign Fianna Fáil fell back on the de Valera personality cult as a substitute for policies. Speakers declared that 'there [was] no other leader except Éamon de Valera,'[34] and they cautioned the people against placing their destinies in the hands of 'lesser men.'[35] The people could either help de Valera complete the centuries-old struggle or 'they could, if they wished, be renegade Irishmen and knife Éamon de Valera in the back.'[36]

De Valera had created the holy trinity of leader, party and country: while three distinct entities, they were really one and the same. One large Fianna Fáil advertisement placed in all national papers declared: 'Ní tír gan Taoiseach—Ní Taoiseach gan de Bhalera' ('There can be no country without a chief—There can be no chief but de Valera').[37] Clann na Poblachta attempted to turn this argument around, claiming that the party system as understood by Fianna Fáil was the will of one man. 'Why then bother about "yes" men, who would have to vote as directed?' MacBride asked rhetorically. 'It would be simpler to elect a dictator and have done with it.' De Valera, he claimed, was 'neither eternal nor infallible.'[38]

Despite the obvious temptations, MacBride went out of his way to challenge the politics of personality so ingrained in Irish politics. 'We do not want "Up this" or "Up that",' he told one crowd that had been inclined to shout 'Up MacBride!'[39] On several occasions he had refused the epithet of 'chief', something that only added to his prestige. He also sought to challenge the traditional reliance on a 'national record', attained thirty years earlier, as a necessary qualification for high office. The fact that a man had been on the 'right side' in 1916 or 1921 'did not necessarily make him a good administrator.'[40]

Fine Gael, for its part, claimed that Fianna Fáil was led by 'an individual who built himself up as a "leader" but who could only maintain this position by surrounding himself with a body of "yes" men.'[41] It criticised the Government for 'moulding an idea of the State which is completely totalitarian and one party in its nature.'[42] The *Irish Times* argued that, in a country in which there were 'no violent differences in ideology' between the parties, the ideal government was one as broadly representative of the people as the Dáil. 'The idea of a "strong" Government is a snare and delusion,' the editorial concluded: 'in fact, it is a euphemism for political dictatorship.'[43]

As part of his campaign to promote the concept of 'strong government' de Valera continually inveighed against the proportional representation system that the state had used since its foundation.[44] Having concluded that a parliamentary majority for Fianna Fáil was unlikely, he had surmised that only the abolition of PR could provide the necessary stability. Fine Gael and the Labour Party both opposed the proposal,[45] as did the *Irish Times*, which proved the most trenchant defender of the electoral system.[46]

The call for the abolition of PR was not new: only its advocates were. De Valera had long been an ardent supporter of PR. During the September 1927 election he had declared that those advocating the abolition of PR 'will get no support from me,' as the system guaranteed the representation of minorities.[47] He had also reminded voters that when the British Government had first introduced PR to stymie the electoral advance of Sinn Féin, he had, as president of Sinn Féin, accepted the system because it was just. Cumann na nGaedheal's leaders had also changed their minds about PR during their decade in office. Frustrated at their inability to obtain an absolute majority, they had claimed that the 'fundamental evils' of the 'non-democratic' electoral system had to be confronted.[48] For both parties the alleged interests of the nation and the real interests of the party had simply been merged.[49]

THE BATTLE FOR THE MANTLE OF REPUBLICANISM

Underlying much of the election rhetoric was the battle between the old and the new, particularly in the sphere of republican ideology. Fianna Fáil had entered government on the back of a republican resurgence in 1932, but its radical image and republican credentials were tarnished, its *raison d'être* openly questioned. One paper claimed that the McCaughey episode had emphasised that on the issue of law and order—as on most issues—Fianna Fáil had merely inherited the policies of Cumann na Gaedheal, illustrating 'a continued alienation of Fianna Fáil from its dreams of 1932.'[50] Disorderly scenes at public gatherings were common (though, unlike the 1933 election, the great majority of interruptions were verbal, not physical).[51]

As in 1932, emigration was a hot political topic, and it was another way the 'youth' issue manifested itself. MacBride accused de Valera of actively encouraging emigration, a charge that had more truth than he perhaps realised.[52] De Valera did little to counter these charges, describing emigration as 'a national evil' but adding that there was 'a limit to the number of people who could be maintained in reasonable comfort in this country, because, as an island, we could not expand.'[53]

Clann na Poblachta also made populist attacks on centralisation and bureaucracy reminiscent of early Fianna Fáil rhetoric, and it claimed that the Government had 'taken from the people every vestige of personal freedom to an army of bureaucrats.'[54] It also courted the women's vote, urged them to take a more active role in politics,[55] and asked them to remember de Valera's 'reactionary, undemocratic and anti-feminist attitude' when introducing the Constitution of Ireland in 1937.[56]

Fianna Fáil increasingly turned to the issue of the Irish language to simultaneously demonstrate its republican credentials and dismiss opponents as inferior Irishmen and Irishwomen.[57] At a time when Fianna Fáil appeared to be bereft of distinguishing policies and in which it was unable to realise its first national aim of ending partition, this was an important device for securing intra-party loyalty to a national ideal that was unmistakably identified with Fianna Fáil.

As well as the republican luminaries on the Clann na Poblachta executive, the party attracted candidates such as Michael Barry, brother of Kevin, and Ruairí Brugha, son of Cathal and son-in-law of Terence MacSwiney.[58] This ensured that Fianna Fáil would not be able to monopolise the republican card, nor could it present the republican background of Clann na Poblachta as 'only' those of the 'new IRA'—the term loosely applied to anyone who had participated in the IRA after Fianna Fáil's rise to power.

Equally disconcerting for Fianna Fáil was the manner in which Clann na Poblachta succeeded in attracting such well-known Fianna Fáil malcontents as Kathleen Clarke and Aodh de Blacam. As in the Civil War, some families were divided. In Co. Meath, for example, the main Fianna Fáil candidate, Michael Hilliard, had been a member of the IRA Executive until 1934, when he joined Fianna Fáil, and he subsequently held a number of ministerial portfolios, including Defence.[59] Standing against him under Clann na Poblachta's banner was his brother James, also a veteran of the War of Independence, who had already secured election to Meath County Council as an independent republican.[60]

De Valera dismissed the defectors with eloquent paternalism. 'Of course, most of you have seen a good chisel with chips flying off,' he said. 'Many a chisel has lost chips but did you ever see anybody collecting the chips to make another chisel out of them'?[61] According to de Valera, Clann na Poblachta was 'purely an artificial movement' that had been forced to 'make up a programme by taking bits and scraps and tying them together.'[62]

During the campaign de Valera was sensitive to aspersions cast on the republicanism of his party. In response to one heckler in Ballina he declared that 'we can say "Up the Republic" because we have established an independent republic here in the twenty-six counties.'[63] Three days before the election he elaborated on this point:

> No matter what people say, Fianna Fáil is a republican organisation, and the whole of the Opposition parties could not produce a republican government like the present Government. Is there any party, or combination of parties, that can produce a government that is as republican as our Government? We have brought this country to freedom as a republic, and those people who talk about being a republican party may be the children of the republic [i.e. Clann na Poblachta], but all of us are children of the republic. If you look at them you will see that they cannot compare with Fianna Fáil as a republican party.[64]

On another occasion de Valera claimed that 'when the division came in 1922 we took the part we took because we were loyal to the original objectives with which we entered public life,' and he predicted that if they were returned it would be because

> we have been constantly loyal to these objectives and have never swerved from the road to the attainment of these objectives. We intend to be equally loyal until we have secured freedom for the whole of our people and not for part.[65]

Like Fianna Fáil in 1932, Clann na Poblachta played down constitutional issues and emphasised its commitment to radical socio-economic change. However, just as Fianna Fáil had emphasised the oath of allegiance, Clann na Poblachta hinted that, if elected, it would repeal the Executive Authority (External Relations) Act, thus breaking the last constitutional connection with Britain.[66] Candidates expressed the hope that 'this new Republican party' would 'bring to fulfilment the hope and aspirations of 1916.'[67] But Erskine Childers (a Fianna Fáil TD, son of Erskine Childers shot by the Free State in 1922) claimed that Clann na Poblachta members 'talked as though they had lately emerged from the ranks of the IRA and preached what was almost revolution.'[68] Such accusations, reminiscent of Cumann na nGaedheal's negative campaigning in 1932, were symptomatic of another significant feature of the election: the resurrection of the Red Scare.

RED SCARE TACTICS

Before and during the election Fianna Fáil employed the same material that Cumann na nGaedheal had used against Fianna Fáil during the late 1920s and early 30s to damage the reputation of Clann na Poblachta and the Labour Party. Since the by-election campaigns in October, Seán MacEntee had been amassing security files compiled by civil servants under the Cumann na nGaedheal and Fianna Fáil regimes.

Early in the new year he wrote a letter marked 'private and confidential' to Tommy Mullins, general secretary of Fianna Fáil (and the candidate in the Dublin County by-election defeated by MacBride). The letter was accompanied by a secret security file that documented the activities of the Communist Party of Ireland between 1942 and 1943, information that MacEntee was sure Mullins would find 'useful and interesting.'[69]

What was clear from the file was that Fianna Fáil, through intelligence agents, had infiltrated the CPI at the highest level and was privy to its every move. But all that the files revealed was that the party had decided that it could employ its talents most effectively by encouraging its members to join the Labour Party to promote CPI policies—hardly a life-threatening prospect. Much of the material was extremely dated, and it was clear that some of the old Cumann na nGaedheal files had been dusted down. One 'shocking' item that caught MacEntee's eye was a letter from Jim Larkin junior in Moscow, who had sent fraternal greetings to the *Workers' Voice* in 1930 and promised to forward an article on 'unemployment in the Soviet Union' some time in the future.[70] The letter was hardly a secret, as it had been printed in the 26 April 1930 issue of that paper.

Despite the dearth of reds threatening to undermine the state, the temptation to fall back on anti-communist scare tactics was too great. Rational, constructive arguments were replaced by abusive sloganeering as candidates occupied themselves with formulating charges of communism while their opponents devised appropriate defences. For the *Irish Times*, MacEntee had reverted to his favourite role of political Don Quixote, 'tilting gaily at Communist windmills, and smelling Bolsheviks behind every bush.'[71] The paper wondered why the minister devoted so much time and industry to 'this silly crusade against a non-existent threat to the national security,' concluding that 'Mr. MacEntee seems to have Bolshevism on the brain.' Communism in Ireland was 'utterly negligible,' the editorial concluded, and 'what Seán MacBride did or said in 1931 is just as irrelevant to actual issues as the physical or spiritual whereabouts of any given politician on the morning of Easter Monday, 1916.'[72]

The president of University College, Cork, Dr Alfred O'Rahilly, also intervened in the debate and asked whether de Valera was claiming 'that some of his rivals are tainted with Communism, or, as the Tánaiste [Lemass] put it in Carlow, that the first object of the forces hostile to a Christian democracy is the destruction of Fianna Fáil'?[73] In response MacEntee depicted Dr O'Rahilly as a 'political hypnotist' and communist stooge.[74]

At times MacEntee's accusations bordered on the absurd. Russian films shown by the Irish Film Society were deemed 'not incapable of being used for propagandist purposes,' to which the society's secretary replied: 'I think Mr. MacEntee has demon-strated that very clearly.'[75]

To drive the point home, Fianna Fáil took out expensive half-page advertisements in national and local papers headed 'A Plan for Safety.' It warned of forces working for the overthrow of democracy, 'disguised . . . perhaps even under names in the Irish language.' Their methods would be 'to destroy confidence in the motives of the Government, and, if possible, by slander and abuse of political leaders, to weaken public faith in the democratic system.'[76] The advertisement concluded in apocalyptic terms by claiming that the free election that would bring 'the enemies of Christianity and democracy' to power 'is always the last free election ever held.' Predicting that the revolutionary danger was 'on the horizon,' the advertisement made explicit what had hitherto been heavily implied: that a vote for the opponents of Fianna Fáil would signal the end of Christianity and democracy in Ireland and the triumph of revolutionary communism.

> The 'cells', whose task it is to exploit temporary causes of public discontent, and to promote social unrest are at work. The chance of destroying the Fianna Fáil Government, which the General Election gives them is being fully used … Fianna Fáil means safety. It means the preservation of democracy … which is the alternative to dictatorship. This is why these elections in Ireland are so important. That is why Fianna Fáil must win.[77] [Emphasis in original.]

It was a remarkable argument for voting Fianna Fáil, and it demonstrated the long road the party had travelled since 1932, when Cumann na nGaedheal had attempted to stay in power with the slogan 'The Gunmen and Communists are voting for Fianna Fáil today: How will *you* vote?' De Valera's supporters presented him as the man who had kept Ireland out of the war, and, just as Portuguese citizens had erected a monument in thanks to the dictator Salazar, the Irish people 'needed him [de Valera] to keep them out of the war that was certain to come again in a short time.'[78]

The witch hunt, soon to be replicated in McCarthyite America, was contagious, and it instilled fear in all candidates lest they be considered even mildly left-wing. They vied with each other to exonerate themselves from the heinous charge of communism. The leader of the National Labour Party, James Everett, accused the Labour Party leader, William Norton, of harbouring avowed communists in the highest levels of his organisation, two of whom had been educated in Russia.[79] Norton hotly denied the accusations and promised that the Labour Party would employ 'all its strength to ensure that Communism will not stain the political and the religious life of the Irish people.'[80]

Clann na Poblachta also felt obliged to vehemently deny all charges of communism (as Fianna Fáil had done in 1932); it was keenly aware of the potential electoral damage should any of the red mud stick. In Co. Clare, MacBride declared that there were 'no Communists in Clann na Poblachta and no one who has ever been a Communist.'[81] The party repeatedly claimed that its policies were based on the teachings of the Papal encyclical *Rerum Novarum* and on the social plan of the Bishop of Clonfert, Dr John Dignan.[82]

PARTITION

Partition was mentioned sporadically throughout the campaign, but, according to the *Irish Times*, it was 'not a real issue in the election.' The paper editorialised that de Valera had gone into the contest 'dangling the carrot of a united Ireland before the noses of the voters,' but it noted that the issue had receded, as 'neither Mr. de Valera nor anybody else can offer a solution.'[83] This was evidenced by the lack of original ideas on partition thrown up during the campaign. Fine Gael rarely spoke on the matter, and Labour Party policy—to 'work for the abolition of partition by raising *our* living standards and social security schemes'—was old and insular.[84] While all parties had advocated this policy at one time or another, it was essentially a 26-County policy covered in attractive anti-partitionist wrapping paper.

Clann na Poblachta was the party most associated in the public mind with an agitational approach to partition. The former internee and hunger-striker Seán McCool told an audience in Co. Donegal that the party had established many branches in the Six Counties and that it was getting 'handsome contributions' from that area.[85] A significant anti-partition initiative was promised, which would make extensive use of radio to establish worldwide interest.[86] Clann na Poblachta also stressed the importance of the parity of economic prosperity and social services as a means of eroding the border, but it placed a much greater emphasis on this policy than did the Labour Party.[87] Seán MacBride pointed out that the North was able to maintain a population of 275 people per square mile, compared with 112 in the South, and that the marriage and birth rates were higher in the North and infant mortality much lower.[88]

For Fianna Fáil, Clann na Poblachta and the Labour Party were making cheap political capital out of anti-partitionist sentiment. Erskine Childers described Clann na Poblachta's proposals as 'shameful,' and he said that his belief that Northern nationalists 'could not be bought by higher social services'[89] was supported by the public representatives of that community.[90] Like most of the Fianna Fáil leadership, Childers had missed the point. Nationalists might not be induced by higher social and economic standards in the South; but the proposal was aimed at enticing unionists, who had added disparities in services to their arsenal of reasons for rejecting Irish unity. The dismissal of the proposal also flew in the face of de Valera's earlier declarations, in which he argued as early as 1933 that 'the only policy for abolishing partition' that he could see was to create conditions in the South that would 'make the people in the other part of Ireland wish to belong to this part.'[91]

The debate on comparative social services aroused the interest of the Northern Minister of Home Affairs, Edmund Warnock, who said he had been 'surveying the progress of the election campaign.' He took solace from de Valera's realisation of 'the impossibility of uniting North and South, and it was not unfair to say that, recognising that fact, he had not made any real attempt to alter the position.' Northern nationalists, he continued, could expect little from a man who was 'too long in the head to do anything more than talk about the problem.' Warnock also believed that Northern nationalists had received 'a nasty shock' from de Valera's advocacy of abolishing proportional representation and from his concurrence with Unionist Party opinion that this electoral system promoted instability and led to weak governments. Nationalists had long campaigned for the restoration of PR, but 'his condemnations would probably kill Nationalist agitation.'[92]

Warnock's intervention had an immediate impact on the Fianna Fáil leadership, which was fearful that the charges might gain currency among the electorate.[93] Seán Lemass, eulogised today for his pragmatism, reverted to a classic statement of republican orthodoxy.

The unshakeable faith of every Irish nationalist was that partition would end. So deep was that faith that the passage of time could not weaken it. The determination to end it was not being lessened by internal political dissension, much as the governing faction in the Six Counties might desire it. Nor was it being overshadowed by preoccupation with urgent economic and social matters, important though they were.[94]

Lemass asked 'Mr. Warnock and his friends' why, if they were so sure of their position, 'did they have to gerrymander their elections to win security for their clique?'[95] However, just as Fianna Fáil's criticisms of the Northern government's jettisoning of PR had been weakened by de Valera's advocacy of its abandonment in the South, so too were criticisms of gerrymandering undermined by Fianna Fáil's Electoral (Amendment) Act, which also sought 'to win security for their clique.'

Throughout the campaign Clann na Poblachta candidates attacked Fianna Fáil's performance on partition. According to Aodh de Blacam—one of the many prominent former Fianna Fáil members who had switched allegiance to Clann na Poblachta—Fianna Fáil now had 'no plan to end partition' and was guilty of 'a terrible desertion from the principles of 1932.'[96] The main parties were accused of paying 'lip service' to partition, while the 'abandonment' of Northern nationalists was described as 'the outstanding disgrace of our generation.'[97] MacBride claimed that during the previous twenty-five years 'vested interests on both sides of the border had been allowed to grow and develop, so that their existence depended on the continuation of partition.'[98]

Clann na Poblachta's most original and dynamic proposal for weakening partition advocated the invitation of MPs from the Six Counties to attend Dáil Éireann. It also promised that it would use existing constitutional provisions to nominate Northerners to the Seanad. MacBride claimed that these provisions were 'not generally known', despite having been in force for a decade, and that the powers had been 'utilised solely [by de Valera] to nominate his own henchmen from his own party.'[99] When the *Irish Press* criticised the first proposal on the grounds that Unionist MPs might take up the offer, if only to obstruct parliamentary business, MacBride expressed the hope that they would take their seats, as 'the moment that happens, it is the end of partition.' He would welcome Unionist MPs 'with open arms,' as 'we have no enmity against our fellow-countrymen in the Six Counties, and we are willing at all times to extend the hand of friendship.'[100]

The debate about whether members of the Ulster Unionist Party would or would not accept such an invitation was, however, in the realms of fantasy, and it is doubtful if many realistically expected Basil Brooke to give up his position of Prime Minister to sit on the back benches of Leinster House. Clann na Poblachta was confident, however, that Nationalist MPs would attend, and it castigated de Valera for rebuffing deputations that had sought to exercise their 'right' to attend the national parliament. It was also suggested that independent Unionist and Labour members of the Northern Parliament would agree.[101] The propaganda value was stressed: when they came 'we would say to the world, are you going to permit a foreign power to occupy the territory from which these men come?'

Gerry Boland dismissed the plan as 'completely foolish'; and Seán MacEntee, despite Clann na Poblachta's insistence that the road to Irish unity would be constitutional,[102] claimed that if Northern MPs acquired full voting rights in the Dáil 'it would follow logically that the Government, which was responsible to the Dáil, should undertake the task of extending the authority of the Oireachtas over all Ireland, even by force of arms.'[103] Clann na Poblachta rejected as 'a downright lie' Fianna Fáil's claim that 'we will use the gun and march on the North, and that we will involve the country in a war.'[104]

Fianna Fáil did not make any specific policy proposals aimed at ending partition. Instead its main approach was to argue that only it was competent and experienced enough in the nuances of diplomacy to take advantage of any opportunity that might present itself.[105] 'We know it is a difficult task,' said de Valera, and he cautioned against methods of securing unity that would 'make the final result worse than the first position.' Confident that the injustice of partition could not endure, he promised that, 'day in and day out, we will never lose sight of that objective, and will avail ourselves of every opportunity to secure it.'

The return of the Treaty ports in 1938 was cited as the clearest example of how Fianna Fáil could seize opportunities. De Valera pointed out that before the return of the ports he could not have anticipated how they were to be retrieved, but retrieved they were.[106]

Just as Cumann na nGaedheal had made the mistake in 1932 of living on the distant triumph of the Treaty while ignoring contemporary realities, Fianna Fáil's trumpeting of the return of the ports was but an echo of previous achievements, attained a decade earlier and already rewarded in the 1938 election. By 1948 the electorate was more concerned with the cost of living, emigration and the scourge of TB—grievances seized on by Clann na Poblachta.

By the end of the campaign, de Valera—possibly in response to Clann na Poblachta's declarations on the issue—hinted at intensifying the struggle to end partition as he addressed an election rally in Sligo. Citing partition as the 'one remaining matter between Great Britain and ourselves,' he claimed that 'the foundations of an advance towards dealing with the question were already well laid' and that if Fianna Fáil was returned the pressure of the Irish people around the world would be harnessed to this end.[107] This statement was interpreted by some as suggesting that de Valera 'knows there is something in the air in which bargaining may play a part,'[108] but in fact de Valera had admitted in the Dáil some months earlier that no formal approach on partition had been made to the Labour Government in Britain since it had come to power in 1945.[109]

ELECTION RESULTS

On 3 February 1948 twenty thousand people wandered between the GPO and College Green, where Fianna Fáil and Clann na Poblachta, respectively, held their final rallies on the eve of the election. Clann na Poblachta's processions to the rally were diverted by a police cordon at the Parnell Monument in Upper O'Connell Street, following rumours that 'warfare' between the parties was expected. While Noel Hartnett was speaking on the Clann na Poblachta platform the fire brigade came rushing through the crowd, bells clanging, for what turned out to be a false alarm.

De Valera used the occasion to deliver a bitter attack on Clann na Poblachta, which, he said, if it lived long enough to be mentioned in Irish history would be regarded as an organisation which was most contemptible in its foundations. We had the organisation known as Ailtirí na hAiseirghe; it was crazy politically, but there were at least some ideals behind it, but there are no ideals in the programme or actions of these people. I would be sorry for Dublin if Dublin were deceived by them, and I hope the Dublin people are wise enough to see that these people are not trusted with their votes.[110]

De Valera contradicted MacBride's accusations of fraud and corruption before returning to the theme of the innate contemptibility of Clann na Poblachta, which had selected a name 'to which they are no more entitled than the so-called IRA during the war.' For de Valera,

the men who came with me tonight are the IRA and entitled to call themselves that. The others have simply got a hotch-potch policy—a collection of things which have been rejected by every person who has examined them. Fianna Fáil do not want to turn the island into a primeval forest, and that is what some of our opponents want to do.

The Irish people were entering 'a very critical time,' which might be 'the turning point in our history,' and he appealed for an absolute majority for Fianna Fáil. As for the suggestions that 'we have outlived our usefulness and that I should pass off the stage,' when that happened he would be satisfied that there were 'many magnificent Irishmen in Fianna Fáil—from the Tánaiste down—who will take my place.' This theme was taken up by Lemass, who claimed that 'these enemies of Fianna Fáil' who were 'trying to spread the idea that the organisation had outlived its usefulness, and must now die,' would receive their answer on polling day.[111]

This was the answer: Fianna Fáil, 549,000 votes, 68 seats; Fine Gael, 262,000 votes, 31 seats; Clann na Poblachta, 175,000 votes, 10 seats; Labour and National Labour, 139,000 votes, 19 seats; Clann na Talmhan and Farmers' Party, 102,000 votes, 11 seats; independents, 81,000 votes, 8 seats.[112] If the electorate had sent a message to the parties it was difficult to interpret, and it was far from conclusive.

Most eyes focused on Clann na Poblachta's performance. Several explanations can be offered for its disappointingly small number of seats. Organisationally Clann na Poblachta, as de Valera expected, was playing catch-up throughout the election campaign, and many election meetings coincided with the establishment of new party branches. These provided a presence for Clann na Poblachta for the first time in many areas; but they were starved of resources and were entrusted with the onerous task of dislodging local political hierarchies that had existed for almost a quarter of a century. Many writers have attributed the failure of Clann na Poblachta to make the vital breakthrough to the fact that it put up so many candidates, its panel of ninety-three being second only to that of Fianna Fáil. But the evidence to support this view is far from conclusive. The splitting of the party vote between candidates was not ideal, and it undoubtedly played some part in the failure to take the last seat in no less than ten constituencies; but, generally speaking, candidates transferred well, and only a small proportion of later preferences strayed outside the party ticket.[113] The effect of Fianna

Fáil's Electoral Amendment Act should not be underestimated, and the increase in the number of three-seat constituencies acted to the disadvantage of Clann na Poblachta, as intended.

Putting forward so many candidates also contributed to the general lack of finances at the disposal of the party. Clann na Poblachta had to advance almost £10,000 just to pay the deposits necessary for contesting the election. As a new party, organisationally stretched and with not enough time to consolidate its position, it spread its money too widely, and, in retrospect, it might have been wiser to concentrate resources on crucial constituencies in which the party might realistically have expected to gain at least one seat, and possibly two. This, however, would have deprived Clann na Poblachta of its image as a national party capable of taking the mantle of government from Fianna Fáil, and it would have bolstered de Valera's argument that there was no alternative but an *ad hoc* coalition.

The relative inexperience of Clann na Poblachta candidates was obvious, and this was best captured by the *Irishman's Diary* columnist, Quidnunc (probably Séamus Kelly), who found himself captivated by the memory of 'a Clann na Poblachta orator in Clare, standing gaping in front of a microphone—his face frozen, as if some Fianna Fáil supporter at the back of his audience had held up the Gorgon's head.'[114] Armed with enthusiasm but with little experience, Clann na Poblachta had to contend with existing loyalties, organisational machines that had existed for more than two decades, and even older established interests.

That the curiosity value of Clann na Poblachta did not translate into votes was clear from the fact that in Dundalk, for example, more than four thousand people turned out to hear MacBride speak, but his party secured only two thousand votes from the whole of Co. Louth in the election. Even in de Valera's constituency, Clare, MacBride managed to draw bigger crowds than the Chief; but, despite narrowly falling short of a seat, Fianna Fáil still outvoted Clann na Poblachta there by more than five to one. MacBride's urgings to 'break the habit' of voting for de Valera proved as optimistic as de Valera's exhortations to the electorate to give up smoking. MacBride's efforts were not assisted by his strategy of playing down his leadership role, and his refusal to portray himself as an alternative 'chief' may have rebounded in a political culture noted for its authoritarianism and its deference to leaders and established institutions.[115]

It is difficult to gauge precisely what impact the Red Scare had on Clann na Poblachta. It certainly frightened off the more conservative elements of society, and as Clann na Poblachta candidates were often less well known than their rivals, who had been engaged in public life for many years, it was easier to depict them as shady. It is also likely that emigration played its part in limiting the party's electoral inroads. Since the Great Famine, emigration had tended to hit hardest those most disenchanted by the status quo: the poor, the radical and the young. It also made a significant contribution to the renowned conservatism of Irish politics, which traditionally favoured the established parties and militated against radical new departures.[116]

Finally, and perhaps most importantly, Clann na Poblachta's defeat had as much to do with unreal expectations as with performance. During the campaign the optimism and euphoria was sometimes difficult to contain, despite MacBride's best efforts. One candidate claimed that 'the Fianna Fáil swan song had been sung and the victory song of Clann na Poblachta will soon be sung in every corner of Ireland,'[117] while another confidently predicted that Fianna Fáil would lose between forty-five and fifty seats.[118] On the eve of the election Clann na Poblachta's director of elections, Noel Hartnett, declared that the Government was 'going to get its greatest pasting ever,' and he expected that his party would take at least forty-five seats, at most seventy-five—a figure that would give the party an absolute majority at the first attempt.[119]

Clann na Poblachta's actual performance was very solid, achieving the highest share of the vote for a new party in Irish electoral history, with a figure that has not yet been surpassed.[120] The scale of this achievement was obscured by the fact that, despite taking more votes than the combined total of the Labour, National Labour and Farmers' Parties, these groups received 22 seats to Clann na Poblachta's 10. Similarly, Clann na Poblachta attained more 60 per cent of the Fine Gael vote but less than a third of its parliamentary representation. There is no denying, however, that Clann na Poblachta's failure to meet even its most modest of predictions, combined with its going into government with Fine Gael, seriously damaged its credibility among many supporters and delivered a blow to morale from which it never recovered.

Fianna Fáil's slogan for the election, 'Play safe', encapsulated what the party had become: a safe, middle-of-the-road party with little to inspire except loyalty to its leadership and local candidates. Erskine Childers claimed that Fianna Fáil TDs had been 'careless, shockingly briefed and a very large number contented themselves talking up Dev and down with coalition.' They had underestimated Clann na Poblachta and the quarter of a million voters between twenty-one and twenty-five 'who do not believe that there is any substantial difference between us and FG [Fine Gael].' Childers agreed with this view, saying that, except for the Irish language, there was 'no policy difference' between Fianna Fáil and Fine Gael, and he concluded sadly that those who had chosen Fianna Fáil had done so because of 'Dev and other personalities.'[121]

The scale of the 1948 defeat, however, can be overestimated. Fianna Fáil achieved exactly the same share of the vote as in 1943, namely 42 per cent, which was less than 1 per cent below what it attained when it first came to power in 1932. It still had one more seat than the combined strength of the opposition parties, but this time there were twelve independents.[122] Such a situation had always produced a Fianna Fáil minority Government in the past, and many a seasoned observer, such as Lord Rugby (the former Sir John Maffey), thought that Fianna Fáil would retain a precarious grasp of government. However, it now faced a united opposition that possessed an unprecedented will to power.

In 1932 the catch-cry of republicans—Fianna Fáil, Sinn Féin and the IRA—was 'Put them out.' Sixteen years later, all sides united under the same slogan. Up to the inaugural meeting of the new Dáil, Fianna Fáil leaders assumed they would be re-elected, believing that the National Labour Party would find it impossible to align itself with Clann na Poblachta and its despised rivals in the Labour Party.[123] But they underestimated the allure of office. The National Labour Party was to be offered a seat at the Government table, while the best that Fianna Fáil could offer was to permit the party to fulfil its patriotic duty to support the Government from the back benches, with no influence on policy formulation.

Crucially, Clann na Poblachta's Ard-Chomhairle defeated a motion not to take office under any Fine Gael nominee, by 18 votes to 12. On the proposal of Noel Hartnett (seconded by MacBride) the Standing Committee narrowly voted in favour of accepting either Sir John L. Esmonde or John A. Costello as Taoiseach. Esmonde got one more vote than Costello but was unacceptable to his own party. The republican character of Clann na Poblachta was stressed by a unanimous vote to review its position after one month if all republican prisoners were not released.[124] Accusations of opportunism and betrayal proliferated, and there were some prominent resignations. One of the lesser-known members who parted company was twenty-year-old Seán Sabhat, who was to die in an IRA attack on a RUC barracks nine years later.[125]

During the heady days of electioneering, most Clann na Poblachta members thought that, failing to secure an absolute majority, the party would ally itself with the other parties of the underdog: the Labour Party, National Labour Party and Clann na Talmhan—to form a Government. While such an alliance seemed a distinct possibility at the height of the campaign, post-election parliamentary arithmetic forced an uncomfortable reappraisal of party strategy. Before the election the thought of an alliance with the erstwhile Blueshirts, with whom many Clann na Poblachta supporters had clashed, was unthinkable. The Civil War record of the Fine Gael leader, Richard Mulcahy, was particularly unpalatable.[126]

MacBride's approach to the question of a coalition was 'pragmatic rather than militant or revolutionary.'[127] Having fought the election under the slogan of 'Put them out,' MacBride felt he had a duty to fulfil this objective if at all possible. Clann na Poblachta had attempted to transcend Civil War divisions and to attract supporters from throughout the political spectrum, an aim encapsulated in the slogan 'We don't care what shirt you wore.' It could hardly say now that it *did* care, and cared so much that it was unwilling to share the responsibilities of power.

Fortunately for Clann na Poblachta, Fine Gael was in a mood for compromise. With its vote dipping below 20 per cent for the first time, the threat of extinction induced an accommodating attitude among the party hierarchy. Mulcahy stepped aside in favour of Costello, who was without a Civil War record and who was a colleague of MacBride, Hartnett and Lehane at the bar. Also, much of the Clann na Poblachta manifesto was incorporated in the ten-point programme announced by the new inter-party Government. The unexpected merger caught Fianna Fáil by surprise, and its defeat in the Dáil was followed by a hasty gathering up of departmental papers.

| DRIFT, 1948–59

The new Government was a patchwork of all organised non-Fianna Fáil parliamentary opinion. John A. Costello was a competent but far from imposing figure,[1] chosen more for who he was not than for who he was. The structural limitations of the inter-party arrangement ensured that Costello could not adopt a presidential style of governmental leadership, like that of his predecessor.[2] The fact that he was not the leader of his own party and that he presided over a five-party coalition resulted in a general relaxation of procedural norms, most notably the principle of collective responsibility. Government departments often became the autonomous bailiwicks of individual ministers, and Costello could do little to contain the deluge of conflicting policy statements emanating from the various departments notionally under the Taoiseach's control.[3]

Seán MacBride's presence in the Government in the pivotal position of Minister for External Affairs was a potential cause for concern for the British Government; but, despite his initial charismatic dominance witin the Government, he could not overcome the numerical weakness of his party. Lord Rugby, impressed with MacBride and possibly recalling de Valera's career, noted optimistically that 'it would not be the first time that a reputed fire-brand turned out to be a pillar of the State.'[4]

In some ways the Government's attitude towards the IRA echoed that of Fianna Fáil when it had first come to power sixteen years earlier. All republican prisoners were released in 1948, while the remains of those IRA men executed by Fianna Fáil governments were handed over to their families. As preparations were made for the reburials the *Waterford Standard* reported that some of the prison graves of recently executed IRA men had been subjected to a policy of callous neglect.

Plant's grave was in a shocking state. Refuse and dirt had been allowed to accumulate on top of it, and whether or not one shared the slightest sympathy with the man and his beliefs, the condition of what, seemingly, was to have been the final resting place could not but be regarded as a mockery of Christian burial. A member of Government, who visited Maryborough [Portlaoise] this summer, described Plant's grave with horror in his voice. A patch of weed-choked, refuse-littered earth was pointed out to him by a prison official who kicked a piece of corrugated iron with his boot. 'That's Plant,' was the laconic comment. 'My God,' said the Minister, 'it's not possible that a human being lies under that.'[5]

The Gardaí stayed away as the IRA gave the executed men military honours, and prominent Clann na Poblachta TDs attended the reburials.[6] Such gestures reflected a higher tolerance of IRA activity than had been permitted during the later years of Fianna Fáil's rule. The general policy of the inter-party Government towards the IRA seems to have been that unnecessary displays of state force were counterproductive and unnecessary in the current tranquil political climate. This became clear when Frank Aiken asked the Minister for Justice whether he was aware that the Army Council 'of the so-called IRA' had posted a manifesto in Dublin, and that arms had been illegally carried and used publicly at funerals in Cos. Clare and Dublin. When he asked if it was the Government's intention to take any action, the minister replied that he considered that 'in the present peaceful state of the country it is best to ignore these incidents.'[7] It may also have been believed (naïvely, as things turned out) that the Government's plan to repeal the Executive Authority (External Relations) Act (1936) and to adopt a concerted anti-partition campaign might, in the words of J. A. Costello, take the gun out of Irish politics.[8]

THE REPUBLIC

De Valera's concept of an 'external relationship' with Britain, as embodied in the 1936 act, had become increasingly open to criticism. The act provided useful ammunition for republican taunts, and it was a recurring source of discontent within Fianna Fáil, which resolved at the 1948 ard-fheis that it should be repealed.[9] When de Valera quoted defensively from five dictionaries in the Dáil in an attempt to prove that Ireland was in fact a republic, the act's anomalies were only revealed further.[10] If it was a republic, his critics asked, why did the King of England sign the letters of credence for Irish representatives abroad? De Valera also claimed that he had implemented and retained the act because it enabled 'an association to be maintained which, I think, is valuable both materially and from the point of view of the ending of partition.'[11]

The material benefits stemmed from Ireland's preferential economic relationship with Britain and the other dominions within the British Commonwealth, an advantage that was also emphasised by Fine Gael. However, in enticing unionists to reconsider their attitude towards a united Ireland it had proved a dismal failure, a fact that de Valera privately acknowledged. Unionists openly derided the 1936 act, seeing it as a subterfuge and believing that the British connection would not be maintained in a united Ireland. In October 1947 de Valera instructed the Attorney-General to draft a bill to repeal the act, and this was completed shortly before the general election in February.[12]

Costello's unilateral declaration of his intention to repeal the act surprised many of Fine Gael's long-standing supporters. Up to the 1940s the party had continually voiced its support for membership of the Commonwealth, primarily on the grounds of economic advantage.[13] Many Fine Gael supporters felt they had been misled, even betrayed[14]; but those with an emotional attachment to the Commonwealth were a shrinking constituency, and some now believed it politically expedient to reappraise the party's position.

While the *Irish Times* condemned the Taoiseach for what it considered a 'flagrant breach of faith'[15] and characterised 'his sudden conversion to dyed-in-the-wool

As partition is imposed, anti-Catholic pogroms prompt refugees to stream across the border. Meanwhile the new 'Free State' descends into civil war. (*Corbis/Bettmann*)

Éamon de Valera is arrested by Free State soldiers while addressing an election rally in Ennis, Co. Clare. (*National Library of Ireland*)

De Valera, 'President of the Irish Republic,' spends a year (1923–4) in a Free State prison with other prominent republicans, such as Austin Stack (*right*). Stack, who undertook a 41-day hunger strike during this period, refused to join Fianna Fáil, and died prematurely in 1929. (*National Library of Ireland*)

Fianna Fáil TDs elected in the June 1927 election. They are a parliamentary party with no parliament to attend, as they refuse to take the obligatory oath of fidelity to the British monarch. Two months later the Fianna Fáil deputies entered the Free State legislature *en masse*. (*UCD Archives*)

Why Wouldn't They?

The Free State Ministers are Enthusiastic Upholders of the "Treaty"

WHY WOULDN'T THEY BE?

Since they came into power they have netted the following sums in personal salaries:—

Mr. COSGRAVE	£12,500
Mr. O'HIGGINS	8,500
Mr. BLYTHE	8,500
Mr. FITZGERALD	8,500
Mr. J. J. WALSH	8,500
Mr. FINIAN LYNCH	8,500
Mr. EOIN MacNEILL and Prof. O'SULLIVAN, between them	8,500
Mr. JOS. McGRATH and Mr. McGILLIGAN, between them	8,500
Mr. RICHARD MULCAHY and Mr. P. HUGHES, between them	8,500
Mr. P. HOGAN	8,500
Mr. J. J. BURKE	8,500

If the jobs secured by both Ministers and Deputies for their relatives and friends are added, we need not wonder at the eagerness with which these men appeal for re-election nor at the bitterness with which they malign all who stand in their way.

Vote for the Fianna Fáil Candidates

and

End this Colossal Jobbery!

Printed by Mellifont Press, Ltd., Dublin and published by Fianna Fáil, 34 Lower Abbey Street, Dublin.

In its early years Fianna Fáil adopted a populist, anti-corruption stance. By the 1960s, however, many in Fianna Fáil had abandoned frugality, and the party offered dinners with Government members to wealthy businessmen for £100. (*National Library of Ireland*)

HOW WILL YOU VOTE TO-MORROW ?

- THE GUNMEN ARE VOTING FOR FIANNA FAIL
- THE COMMUNISTS ARE VOTING FOR FIANNA FAIL

THEY WANT A FREE HAND IN IRELAND

The Danes are Hoping that you will Vote for Fianna Fáil.

They Want a Free Hand in the British Market.

They Would Like to See Ireland Losing Her Ten Per Cent. Preference.

IRISHMEN

who want Peace and Prosperity At Home and Peace, Friendship and Increased Markets Abroad, will

VOTE FOR THE

GOVERNMENT PARTY

The front page of the *Irish Independent* on the eve of the 1932 election, which saw Fianna Fáil emerge as the largest party in the Free State. (*National Library of Ireland*)

WILL YOU VOTE FOR FIANNA FAIL?

THE so-called I.R.A. of the present day is a conspiracy against the people and its programme is murder. It wants Fianna Fáil in power because Fianna Fáil is afraid of it. If a Fianna Fáil Government once took office, future Elections would be won not by argument and persuasion but by NAKED TERRORISM. Fianna Fáil needs your Vote to put it into power. IT WOULD NOT NEED YOUR VOTE TO KEEP IT IN POWER. THE GUN-BULLIES WOULD DO THAT.

A Fianna Fáil victory, followed by the operation of that Party's policy of non-co-operation with great Britain, seizure of the Land Annuities, and high tariffs, would put the farmer into an economic position worse than existed when the power of landlordism was at its height. It would lose the Free State the advantage of the newly-given Dominion preference and so reduce the price of our agricultural produce. It would raise the cost of all other necessities of life. It would force the farmer to pay his Land Annuity twice over, firstly to Mr. de Valera, and secondly to Great Britain through the medium of special taxes levied on Saorstat cattle, butter, eggs, bacon etc., at the Border or at British Ports.

The result of it all would be the BANKRUPTCY OF THOUSANDS OF FARMERS, AND INDIAN MEAL PORRIDGE all year and every year for most of the others. And there would be no way out; for THE NEW ASCENDANCY OF GUN-BULLIES WOULD KEEP THE GRIP.

Published by Standing Committee of Cumann na nGaedheal.

A typical Cumann na nGaedheal anti-Fianna Fáil advertisement. (*National Library of Ireland*)

The first Fianna Fáil government, 1932. *Back*: Seán MacEntee, Seán T. O'Kelly, Joseph Connolly, Seán Lemass, Gerry Boland. *Front*: Frank Aiken, P. J. Ruttledge, Éamon de Valera, Jim Ryan, Tom Derrig, James Geoghegan. (*TopFoto/AP*)

Freed IRA prisoners address a rally in Dublin, March 1932. The Fianna Fáil government released republican prisoners incarcerated in Free State prisons, but within a few years thousands more would be imprisoned, with some dying on hunger strike or facing execution. (*Getty Images/Central Press*)

Óglaiġ na h-Éireann
(IRISH REPUBLICAN ARMY)

A CALL TO YOUNG IRISHMEN

In the name of our Great Dead who gave their lives in asserting in arms the right of Ireland to be a free Nation, the Army Council calls to the youth of Ireland to enroll in the Irish Republican Army.

It is appropriate to issue this call at Eastertide, as at Easter 1916 the Sovereign Independence of Ireland was asserted in arms, and the Republic of Ireland proclaimed.

IT IS THE DUTY OF YOUNG IRISHMEN TO JOIN THE IRISH REPUBLICAN ARMY :-

1. Because this Army has pledged itself to make the Republic of Ireland, proclaimed in 1916, effective.

2. Because it is pledged to end England's centuries-old political servitude and economic exploitation of Ireland.

3. Because, as history proves, it is only when Irishmen are organised, trained and disciplined, and armed as soldiers that British aggression can be successfully defeated.

4. Because the I.R.A. is the National Army of Ireland.

5. Because the I.R.A. is true to the teachings of Tone, Emmet, Mitchell, Lalor and Pearse.

6. Because it is the duty of young Irishmen to be true to these teachings, and to help to break the connection with England, and to enthrone the Republic of Ireland, one and indivisible.

Intending recruits should see the provincial newspapers for addresses, in their districts, to which they can report.

Issued by the Army Council,

APRIL, 1933.

Óglaiġ na h-Éireann.

An IRA recruitment poster, 1933. (*National Library of Ireland*)

Charlie Kerins (1918–44), chief of staff of the IRA. After being tried by a non-jury military court he was executed in Dublin by the British hangman Albert Pierrepoint.

Revolutionary woman: As Lord Mayor of Dublin, Kathleen Clarke (née Daly, widow of the executed 1916 leader Tom Clarke) spearheaded reprieve campaigns aimed at saving IRA prisoners from execution. She subsequently left Fianna Fáil, though she received a state funeral in 1972. (*Courtesy of Helen Litton*)

The veteran republican agitator Maud Gonne MacBride casts her vote in the 1948 election for Clann na Poblachta, the party established by her son, Seán (seen here standing by her side). Chief of staff of the IRA during the 1930s, Seán MacBride went on to become Minister for External Affairs, 1948–51, a founder of Amnesty International, and a winner of the Nobel Peace Prize, 1974. (*Corbis/Bettmann*)

Fianna Fáil consistently emphasised the party's past association with militant republicanism. The Torch was a short-lived attempt to replace the republican Easter Lily. When the initiative failed, the Torch was quietly abandoned, while sales of Easter Lilies were banned. (*UCD Archives*)

The 1950s witnessed a crisis of legitimacy as almost half a million people emigrated and the state's population dipped below 3 million. A Fianna Fáil election poster of the time tries to translate past freedom struggles into a language understandable to a generation living in very difficult socio-economic conditions. (*UCD Archives*)

HOW MUCH IS FREEDOM WORTH ?

(Some thought it worth Dying for)

WILL YOU VOTE WITH YOUR HEAD UP - OR YOUR HAND OUT ?

Stand up to the Future with

FIANNA FÁIL

A PLAN FOR
SAFETY

.

THE "COLD WAR"

A "cold war" in Europe, says the U.S. Secretary of State. What is the character of this war? "The Nations are living in anxious expectation of an uncertain future," said His Holiness the Pope. Is there danger, and, if so, what is it? Is there need to plan for our Safety?

ENSLAVEMENT OF FREE PEOPLES

All over Eastern Europe, free peoples are being enslaved. They are being subjected to the rule of Governments they did not choose, to policies they do not want, to tyrannies which deprive them of elementary rights to freedom of speech and association. There is an organisation which is planning the extension of this slavery to Western Europe, to Italy, to France, and to Ireland.

CAN IT HAPPEN HERE?

How can it happen? How do free peoples get into a position in which they are saddled with Governments they cannot remove, forced to accept laws and policies they resent? Could it happen here?

THE PLAN AT WORK

Have no doubt that it is being planned to happen here. We may not be the first on the list for attack, but the preliminary steps are being taken, the plan is at work. First, the propagation of social unrest; second, the weakening of national solidarity by the promotion of political discord; third, the intensification of bitter class strife. That is the plan. Said His Holiness: "Not by stirring up discord, not by unrest and rebellion, not by shedding fraternal blood can the misery of nations be mastered and the lost well-being regained." But it is by spreading discord and unrest that the organisers of international revolution expect to prepare the way for the seizure of power.

REVOLUTION IN DISGUISE

The forces working for the overthrow of democracy do not march under their true colours. They will appear in Ireland disguised as groups of apparently well-meaning people concerned only with social improvement, perhaps even under names in the Irish language. Their propaganda will be insidious. Their preliminary task will be to create the atmosphere of social unrest required for a more vigorous campaign, to promote sectional strife, to destroy confidence in the motives of the Government, and, if possible, by slander and abuse of political leaders, to weaken public faith in the democratic system. That is how they have worked elsewhere. Here, as elsewhere, these agitators will hope to be assisted by many people who will not realise the purposes for which they are being used.

A WEAK GOVERNMENT—THE FIRST STEP

A strong Government, which believes in Christian principles, is an obstacle which must be removed. A straight election victory for the forces of revolution is not possible, therefore, the Government must be destroyed otherwise. The plan is to promote a welter of minor parties with nothing in common except a desire to replace the Government in office, and to work for the creation of a multi-party coalition, which would elect a weak Government. In such a political arrangement the only effective force would be the disciplined and directed minority group, skilfully led by experts in the tactics of destroying Christian democracy. The stage could then be set for the next act.

CONSTITUTIONAL SAFEGUARDS?

Do not think that your constitutional rights will prove a protection. You may say that if the Government in office does not act as you would wish you could always remove it. That is what many people in the enslaved European States thought. But when the time came they found they could not remove the Government they did not want. These enemies of Christianity and democracy do not play according to rules. They change the rules to suit their own ends. The free election which gives them power is always the last free election ever held.

WHEN?

This danger is not yet at hand in Ireland. But it is on the horizon. The "cells," whose task it is to exploit temporary causes of public discontent, and to promote social unrest, are at work. The chance of destroying the Fianna Fáil Government, which the General Election gives them, is being fully used. The plotters do not care who destroys it or even who replaces it, provided they are, as they must be, weak and divided.

DEMOCRACY IS SAFE WITH FIANNA FAIL

FIANNA FÁIL means safety. It means the preservation of democracy as the accepted method of conducting public business. Democracy has, perhaps, a better opportunity in Ireland than elsewhere of showing its superiority over any other system, of demonstrating the practicability of achieving efficient national administration, and material and social progress, through the understanding and co-operation of free men of all classes, which is the alternative to dictatorship. That is why these elections in Ireland are important. That is why FIANNA FÁIL must win.

PLAY SAFE
Vote FIANNA FÁIL

By the time of the 1948 election, Fianna Fáil had become a mirror image of the Cumann na nGaedheal party it had been established to replace, viewing itself as a bulwark against revolution, communism and instability. There was little separating Cumann na nGaedheal's 1932 election slogan, 'Safety first,' with that of Fianna Fáil sixteen years later, 'Play safe.' (*National Library of Ireland*)

Frustrated with the consolidation of partition, the IRA, now largely composed of members born after the 1921 Treaty, initiated a 'border campaign' (1956–62). Though the campaign was directed exclusively against the Northern Ireland state, Fianna Fáil introduced an anti-republican internment policy to complement that pursued by the Stormont regime. This photograph shows the funeral of Seán Sabhat, an IRA member killed in action during the campaign on 1 January 1957. (*Getty Images/Fox Photos*)

Functional co-operation signalled a thawing of the cold war between Stormont and Dublin, but it delivered little beyond photo opportunities and served to further alienate Northern nationalists, whose lot did not improve under O'Neill, despite his ostentatious liberal rhetoric. *From left*: Jack Lynch, Terence O'Neill, Frank Aiken, Seán Lemass (Dublin, 9 February 1965). (*Irish Times*)

By the 1960s a new generation of activists emerged from the Northern nationalist community who were unwilling to accept pervasive anti-Catholic discrimination. *Centre*: Bernadette Devlin, Westminster MP for Mid-Ulster, 1969–74. (*Irish Times*)

Initially welcomed by many Catholics, British troops quickly came to be viewed as a force mandated to prop up the Stormont Unionist regime. The Falls Road curfew of July 1970 decisively ended any British army honeymoon in Northern Ireland. (*Getty Images /Wesley/Keystone*)

The 1969 Government photographed a month before renewed 'Troubles' in Northern Ireland. *Back row*: Patrick Lalor, Pádraig Faulkner, George Colley, Brian Lenihan, Charles Haughey, Joseph Brennan, Seán Flanagan, Jim Gibbons, Colm Condon (Attorney-General). *Front row*: Mícheál Ó Móráin, Neil Blaney, Jack Lynch (Taoiseach), Éamon de Valera (President), Erskine Childers, Kevin Boland, Dr Patrick Hillery. In May 1970 nine changes were made to this Government to accommodate sackings and resignations arising from the Arms Crisis. (*Irish Times*)

The imposition of one-sided internment in Northern Ireland forced thousands to seek refuge in the South, though Dublin was often ill-equipped to accommodate them. (*Irish Times*)

COMMEMORATION
OF THE
TRUCE
JULY, 1921

DAN BREEN

"... NO MORE FEARLESS FIGHTER FOR IRISH FREEDOM..."

"... THE GOVERNMENT'S ABSOLUTE OPPOSITION TO VIOLENCE AS A MEANS OF ENDING BRITISH RULE..."

Nick

The struggle between an invigorated IRA and the British army brought apparent inconsistencies in Fianna Fáil's position on armed struggle into closer focus. A cartoon by Nicholas Robinson from the *Irish Times*, 1971. (*Nicholas Robinson*)

A visibly wearied Jack Lynch prepares to defend his Northern Ireland policy to the 1971 Fianna Fáil ard-fheis. (*Irish Times*)

De Valera in old age, again President of the Irish Republic (until 1973) but not the one for which he took up arms in 1916. In the background a Seán Keating painting, *Men of the South*, depicts an IRA flying column waiting to ambush British troops. (*National Library of Ireland*)

republicanism' as 'one of the most remarkable and baffling events in Irish history,'[16] it seemed curiously unaware of the political advantages that would accrue to Fine Gael. The timing of the 'announcement' of the Republic and the passing of the Republic of Ireland Act (1949) was calculated to achieve the maximum advantage for Fine Gael 'in the conflict . . . as to who were the better Republicans.'[17] It 'stole Fianna Fáil's Sunday suit of constitutional clothes' and also had the advantage of 'stealing McBride's thunder,' as Clann na Poblachta had been to the forefront in advocating the repeal of the act.[18]

Fianna Fáil was unsure how to respond[19]; and while Seán MacEntee made the audacious claim that the decision to repeal the 1936 act was due to the 'communist pressures' exerted on the Government,[20] most critics contented themselves with pointing out the inconsistency of Fine Gael's position.[21] When the idea had been first mooted in August 1948, de Valera had challenged the Government to 'go ahead,' as 'you will get no opposition from us.'[22] In the light of de Valera's own plans to repeal the act, Fianna Fáil could hardly have said otherwise.

De Valera's official biographers offer two explanations for Fianna Fáil not participating in the celebration on Easter Monday 1949.[23] Firstly, de Valera claimed that Fianna Fáil had undertaken constitutional changes 'in our usual way, without fanfares.' This was not strictly true, for a party that does not advertise its achievements is unlikely to survive long, and Fianna Fáil had not proved wanting in this regard.[24] The second reason offered was that Fianna Fáil had 'strong feelings' against celebrating any political or constitutional event short of the reunification of the whole country as a republic. In this it may have been more in tune with nationalist sentiment in the Six Counties. One unidentified retired academic related:

It was the biggest watershed in my own life. I was in Dublin, at a GAA meeting. They were all celebrating and I felt very emotional. I went home by myself and went to bed—it had nothing to do with me. They weren't thinking about us in the North at all. I think that was when I decided I might as well try to make something of living in this place.[25]

It has been argued that the repeal of the 1936 act epitomised a partitionist attitude, in that it put sovereignty before unity. Thomas Hackey has contended that had the Government chosen to combine the status of a sovereign republic with membership of the Commonwealth, as India had done, 'the practical obstacles to unification would be less formidable.'[26] Joseph Lee, on the other hand, has argued that remaining in the Commonwealth, or retaining the act, 'would not . . . have advanced unification by one day,' for the act was 'despised by unionists'; and if they had refused to contemplate unity to persuade the Irish state to enter the war in 1940 they were unlikely to do so simply because it chose to remain in the Commonwealth.[27]

What is not in doubt is the British response to the severing of the last tenuous link between the two states: the adoption by the British Parliament of the Ireland Act (1949). The manner in which Costello announced his intention to repeal the 1936 act has been a source of considerable (if inconclusive) debate,[28] but it is clear that the failure to notify Britain in advance did little to win favour in London. The retaliatory

Ireland Act stated that 'in no event will Northern Ireland or any part thereof cease to be part of His Majesty's dominions and of the United Kingdom without the consent of the Parliament of Northern Ireland.'[29] Reciprocating what it felt had been Costello's lack of courtesy, the British Government gave no formal notification to Dublin that it was adopting such a course. The Ireland Act was considered an attack on the Irish people, and, to applause, Costello told the Dáil that 'we can hit the British government in their prestige and in their pride and in their pocket.'[30] The new act was also vehemently condemned by de Valera, who seemed to imply that force might be necessary to resolve the problem of partition.

> If this thing is done to our country, I say for myself that then feelings will be back to what they were in 1919 to 1921. If these people are to tell us that our country can only be united by setting us an impossible task, we hope another way will be found that will not be impossible. We had hoped for something different than that.[31]

The official parliamentary response was a unanimous declaration by Dáil Éireann on 10 May 1949, adopted on the joint proposition of Costello and de Valera.

> Dáil Éireann,
> SOLEMNLY RE-ASSERTING the indefeasible right of the Irish Nation to the unity and integrity of the national territory,
> RE-AFIRMING the sovereign right of the people of Ireland to choose its own form of Government and, through its democratic institutions, to decide all questions of national policy, free from outside interference,
> REPUDIATING the claim of the British Parliament to enact legislation affecting Ireland's territorial integrity in violation of those rights, and
> PLEDGING the determination of the Irish people to continue the struggle against the unjust and unnatural partition of our country until it is brought to a successful conclusion;
> PLACES ON RECORD its indignant protest against the introduction in the British Parliament of legislation purporting to endorse and continue the existing Partition of Ireland, and
> CALLS UPON the British Government and people to end the present occupation of our Six North Eastern Counties, and thereby enable the unity of Ireland to be restored and the age-long differences between the two nations brought to an end.

The resolution is significant in that it is the only declaration of policy regarding partition adopted unanimously by Dáil Éireann since 1922.[32]

On the same date the Dáil ordered that the declaration be transmitted to the parliament and government of all countries with which Ireland had diplomatic relations.

On 23 July, Costello told the Dáil that 'for the first time since 1922, this cabinet will, by its policy and its actions, give some hope of bringing back to this country the north-eastern counties of Ulster.'[33] Lavishly produced anti-partition pamphlets were distributed, and the Irish News Agency was established as a statutory body to present an Irish view of the news, particularly in relation to partition. (Hitherto, most news on Ireland received by an international audience came from British sources.)

In January 1949 the All-Party Anti-Partition Conference (sometimes called the Mansion House Conference) had set up a fund for anti-partition candidates in the North. Though de Valera participated in the work of the committee, he was un-enthusiastic about the venture, 'given [his] lack of enthusiasm for involvement in any anti-Partition strategy which he was not controlling.'[34] In an attempt to put the spotlight back where he felt it belonged, he embarked on an extensive tour of America, India, Australia, New Zealand and Britain, ostensibly to internationalise the issue of partition and to put 'an anti-partition girth around the world.' The campaign was launched with the declaration that

> the phrase 'Partition must go' must henceforth be on every Irishman's lips, to be used on every appropriate occasion, that is, in season and out of season, until the continuing crime against our country shall have ceased.[35]

One English journalist remarked sardonically that de Valera 'found more to say about the iniquity of partition during his two months out of office than during the whole sixteen years he was in.'[36] Though he was touring a world strangely uncaring about partition in the aftermath of the Second World War, Joseph Lee and Gearóid Ó Tuathaigh claim that this 'didn't really matter,' as the tour was 'essentially an Irish election tour, not a world tour except in a purely geographical sense.'[37]

In what seems a bizarre usurpation of authority, the Secretary of the Department of External Affairs, F. H. Boland, asked Lord Rugby to get the American minister in Dublin, George Garrett, to persuade de Valera not to make the trip to America. Boland's fear, according to Rugby, was that anti-partitionists there might trap him 'into taking a false position that might easily be harmful to the success of the European Recovery Programme' (the Marshall Plan).[38] Garrett duly had a talk with de Valera, who assured him that he would do 'the right thing.' This private talk may have been influential in de Valera's decision not to mention partition when he met President Truman during his visit.[39] However, on the rest of his American tour he talked of little else, delivering his message to massive crowds throughout the United States. He told them what they had come to hear: 'The struggle is not over . . . the British are still occupying six of our counties . . . We are asking the people of America, those of good will, to help us in that fight.'[40]

During this period de Valera made a number of statements that constituted an important shift in his position on the North. He demanded that, 'in all fairness and justice,' the areas contiguous to the border that possessed nationalist majorities should be 'given back to us.' As Taoiseach he had studiously avoided making such demands, as a matter of principle and of political tactics. In principle such a demand would be incompatible with the ideal of a united Ireland, and it could be represented as an acceptance of the unionist veto. It could then be argued by political opponents that Fianna Fáil's objection to partition was not based on the concept of an imposed border but rather was a quibble over the size of the area excluded from the jurisdiction of the Irish Government.

The tactical rationale for opposing partial transfers of territory was the belief that if the majority of Northern nationalists came under the rule of Dublin the remaining nationalist rump would constitute a tiny minority in a new Northern state. In such circumstances the strength of anti-partition opinion in the North would be substantially reduced and the cause of unity debilitated, perhaps irrevocably. Traditional Fianna Fáil policy, as articulated by de Valera, appears to have viewed Northern nationalists as essential pawns in the Anglo-Irish diplomatic game, and successive Fianna Fáil Governments 'were quite content to leave them as hostages in the hope that they might eventually help to secure Irish unity.'[41]

It is difficult to understand why de Valera, in opposition, should alter his position on an issue as fundamental as this. Any attempt to rationalise his actions can only be speculative, as he did not attempt to explain this apparent *volte face*. Instead, in quintessential de Valera style, he did not acknowledge that any change of policy had taken place and presented this changed stance as traditional Fianna Fáil policy. It was clearly at variance, however, with his firmly held opinion espoused while he was holding the reins of power. One possible explanation is that he simply wished to adopt a different position from the coalition Government and to articulate a policy distinguishable from Clann na Poblachta, which steadfastly opposed partial transfers of territory, for reasons similar to those previously defended by de Valera. Alternatively, he may have been motivated by a genuine frustration at the lack of progress on the issue, and, infused with a desperate realism, sought to secure some territory immediately rather than no territory at all. If so, the desperation evaporated on his assuming power again. And he did not have to wait long for such a reversal of fortune.

During the 1948 election Noel Hartnett—listing a number of Fianna Fáil bills that the Supreme Court had declared unconstitutional—referred to the Public Health Act, which he said 'interfered with the Catholic principles governing the rights of the State and of the family.'[42] Attempts by Noël Browne to resurrect the substance of the 1947 act ran into difficulties with the medical profession, the Catholic Church, the coalition Government and Clann na Poblachta itself.[43] Though the Government actually fell on the issue of milk prices, most observers have attributed its demise to the ill-fated Mother and Child Scheme. It was a disappointing end to a Government that had promised so much.

THE 1951 ELECTION

Fianna Fáil had undergone a significant overhaul of organisation while in opposition, under the direction of Seán Lemass. The party invested a lot of money in advertisements for the election, taking out half-page notices in all local papers for two weeks. These contained a message from de Valera that concentrated on the alleged virtues of single-party government. Fianna Fáil was presented as a 'broad national organisation embracing all classes within the State', while the alternative was 'a number of sectional groups . . . in temporary alliance on the basis of present expediency but each expecting ultimately to overreach the other.'[44] In essence, an intra-party coalition rather than an inter-party coalition was promoted. Biographical profiles in election literature continued to emphasise the pre-1921 revolutionary exploits of Fianna Fáil candidates, as well as their membership of the Air-Raid Precautions

Service during the war. Interestingly, their actions during the Civil War were not alluded to.[45]

Fianna Fáil was sensitive to the fact that the inter-party Government had declared a republic and adopted a more stridently anti-partition stance. De Valera attempted to argue that it was merely copying Fianna Fáil policy and that it was a late convert to republicanism. Speaking in Achill, Co. Mayo, he outlined Fianna Fáil's 'sixteen years of achievement,' which had been attained 'despite the bitter opposition of many of the people who pretended that they were good republicans'—a clear swipe at Fine Gael. Listing Fianna Fáil's constitutional initiatives from 1932 to 1938, de Valera asked rhetorically whether it could be said 'that Fianna Fáil were idle during the first six years of their sixteen in office.'[46]

The concentration on these early breakthroughs, however, only served to illustrate indirectly the relative paucity of achievements in the latter ten years of Fianna Fáil's rule. Admittedly, the five-year national emergency occasioned by the Second World War was not a time for radical policy innovations, though it did allow Fianna Fáil to intensify its policy of self-sufficiency (while exposing its limitations). The emergency years, however, disguised the fact that by 1938 Fianna Fáil had exhausted its original programme for constitutional reform. With the enactment of the Constitution of Ireland and the procurement of the Treaty ports, de Valera had taken the final step on the journey to external association.

This might explain why (as in 1948) Fianna Fáil's election campaign was largely defensive and negative—defensive in that it rejected criticisms of its republicanism and countered these with a rendition of its achievements from 1932 to 1938, negative in that it relied almost entirely on the alleged iniquity and ineffectiveness of coalition government. Responding to assertions that the inter-party Government was representative of the different sections of the nation, de Valera claimed that

the last election had proved that Fianna Fáil represented the great body of the Irish nation. They represented all sections of the nation. They were the only national organisation in existence. The others were sectional organisations but Fianna Fáil represented the broad centre of the nation.[47]

Concentration on the *form* of government revealed that, in the new political environment, ideology had ceased to be a factor. With the declaration of a republic, the last important cleavage in Irish party politics evaporated, and the political debate now centred on the more mundane issue of whether a single-party government was more effective than a coalition. Despite the fact that they were 'all republicans now,' an attempt was made to mask the lack of difference between the contending parties. It was no longer a case of fundamentally opposed philosophies: it was merely a competition to gain office. Neither side in the political debate suggested that it would implement anything different from what was proposed by its opponents. This might explain the conspicuous concentration on the achievements of years past, particularly 1932–8, and on the previous anti-republican stance of Fine Gael. For example, one piece of Fianna Fáil election literature quoted James Dillon as saying in the Dáil:

I will not stand up when you play the Soldier's Song [Amhrán na bhFiann], because I detest it and it is associated in my mind with horrors . . . If the Executive Council proceeded to outlaw me because I was not prepared to raise my hat to the Soldier's Song and kow-tow to the Tricolour I should resent it.[48]

The date for this statement was not given; it was, in fact, made twenty years earlier, in 1932. The statement was quite dated, and by using it Fianna Fáil revealed a desire to keep alive a division that no longer existed. In this it was merely echoing the earlier electoral tactics of Cumann na nGaedheal, which, during the 1927 and 1932 elections, quoted extensively from de Valera's speeches of 1922. When Fianna Fáil came to power it had expressed the hope that it could facilitate the unity of the nation, the healing of old wounds and the overcoming of barriers created by the Civil War. Now, in 1951, it was erecting barriers where there were none.[49]

The election results were a disappointment for Fianna Fáil, which gained only one seat, five short of a majority. Disunity and acrimony within and between other parties, however, facilitated de Valera's return to power as head of a minority Government. For the first time the Department of External Affairs got a full-time Fianna Fáil minister, Frank Aiken. De Valera had previously kept this portfolio himself, and his decision to relinquish External Affairs may have been due to his advancing years (he was now sixty-nine). It may also have been a recognition of the higher profile that the department had enjoyed under MacBride, and that de Valera believed that the main constitutional objectives of Fianna Fáil had been achieved and that it was safe to hand the job over to someone else. But he remained the sole spokesperson on the North, which, as a matter of principle, officially remained within the remit of the Department of the Taoiseach, being ostensibly a domestic issue. However, by a 'delightfully ironic application of the doublethink which pervaded these matters,' Northern Ireland questions were sent to the Department of the Taoiseach only to be automatically forwarded to the Department of External Affairs.[50]

The new Fianna Fáil Government relegated the issue of partition to the periphery of policy considerations. Conor Cruise O'Brien, one of the civil servants who had enjoyed a meteoric rise while working with Seán MacBride on the anti-partition campaign, recalled being summoned to Aiken's office. There he was told that he would continue to work as before, but 'the spirit of his instructions' would be very different.

There would be no more of what his colleague Seán MacEntee called the 'sore thumb', always going on against the British about the injustice of partition and generally making trouble for them.[51]

Cruise O'Brien claims that Aiken 'didn't want to attack partition, as such,' though he did wish to draw attention to anti-Catholic discrimination under the Northern regime. A suggestion of producing a film on discrimination in Co. Derry was mooted (before being dropped), and for the subsequent three years that Fianna Fáil was in power the sole effort made to challenge partition seems to have been the directing of visiting journalists to Northern nationalist politicians.

Cruise O'Brien also recounted a conversation with Aiken in which he related an incident involving Dan Breen, Oscar Traynor and Aiken himself while they were on the run along the new border during the Civil War. Having listened to the minister, Cruise O'Brien concluded that 'by the period of his life when I knew him, Aiken had become virtually a pacifist, but all the same this reminiscence of his bellicose youth seemed somehow to cheer him up.'[52]

Indeed it might be accurate to use this as a description of most of the revolutionary generation who found themselves in the Fianna Fáil Government. Pacifism is a noble political philosophy, but in some cases it can be used as a mask for inertia. It now became clearer that the enthusiasm generated by de Valera's international tour had been for electoral gain.

Frederick Boland, who was Irish ambassador to Britain from 1950 to 1956, recalled that, diplomatically, the issue of partition was 'not active at all' during those years.[53] Northern nationalists reacted with dismay as the anti-partition campaign was deprived of funds and political interest before being quietly wound up. Neither Aiken nor de Valera thought it necessary to refer to partition when introducing their departmental estimates, the traditional occasion on which important policies were reviewed.[54]

REPRESENTATION FOR NORTHERN MPS

This policy of inertia on the partition question appears to have been the result of a new paralysing pessimism that engulfed the Fianna Fáil leadership. When an outline was sought in the Dáil of what policy on partition de Valera intended to pursue there was little evidence of the confidence of his international tour.

If I am asked, 'Have you got a solution for it?' in the sense 'Is there a line of policy which you propose to pursue, which you think can, within a reasonable time, be effective?' I have to say that I have not, and neither has anybody else. All I can do is choose the methods which seem most likely to produce the best results.[55]

The deputy who posed the question, Jack McQuillan (independent), claimed that de Valera's policy was one of 'hoping for a miracle', and it seemed that he was doing just that. Despite his refusing to give a clear lead, there were some policy options that might have deepened links between North and South.

One method that, for de Valera, was unlikely to produce results came before the Dáil on the same day as his fatalistic assessment of the situation regarding partition[56]: whether Northern representatives should enjoy a 'right of audience' in the Dáil. Seán MacBride was the deputy who put two motions before the lower house that, if passed, would have allowed Northern MPs to address the Dáil. It was believed by its supporters that such a right would would be of immense symbolic importance and would boost nationalist morale in the North, considering that participation in the Belfast Parliament had done little to advance the nationalist cause.

All parties allowed a free vote on the question, except Fianna Fáil. The matter was personalised by its being linked to the vote on the Office of the Taoiseach, thus making it something like a vote of confidence in de Valera. Furthermore, de Valera was the only Fianna Fáil deputy who spoke on the motion. He said he had considered the issue 'time out of mind' and had come to the conclusion 'many years ago' that it would not help towards solving partition. It was not, as had been suggested, that his mind was made up on the issue,[57] and if conditions changed, or if a new situation arose in which it was clear that the proposal would be a step forward, he would then be in favour of it. Characteristically, he did not give any indication of what new circumstances or new situation would occasion a reappraisal of the merits of the proposal.

Responding to the point that the first Dáil had been an all-Ireland body,[58] de Valera said that that had been 'quite right in the circumstances of that particular time,' but that 'a lot of things have happened since.'[59] They now had a representative democracy and a functioning parliament in a state that was 'completely free.' De Valera then steered the debate to the impracticability of attempting to exercise jurisdiction over the Six Counties. This was, in fact, largely irrelevant, as the issue was the mere right of audience; but MacBride took the bait and entered into a brief verbal exchange. When he pointed out that the Constitution claimed jurisdiction over the whole country, de Valera responded that 'if claiming was going to solve it, then there was not any difficulty. The fact is to make good our claim.' MacBride countered by asking if the Taoiseach rejected the idea of holding plebiscites within Northern Ireland, only to be told that no machinery was available for carrying out such an exercise. When MacBride pursued the issue he succeeded only in giving the impression that his arguments, however well intentioned, were grounded in abstruse legal concepts rather than in political realities.[60]

Having shifted the debate to the question of actual representation for Northern MPs, de Valera summarised why the proposal should not be entertained. Firstly, they would 'have people here able to cast their votes on the matters that come up for decision with a feeling very different from that of other members.' They would thus be in a privileged position, enjoying representation without taxation. Also, the Northern MPs would not obtain any advantages, as the Dáil did not exercise jurisdiction over the areas they represented. Within 'a very short time' they would probably 'take sides, and that would mean that certain antagonisms would be created.' Northern MPs were 'very often at sixes and sevens themselves regarding what policy they should pursue,' and their presence in the Dáil 'would create antagonisms and difficulties between themselves too.'[61]

The phrase 'would create antagonisms' was the key to de Valera's rebuttal, and it was used on more than half a dozen occasions during his contribution. He devoted a considerably shorter time to the actual proposal—a right of audience in the Dáil. This, he argued, would be 'almost as bad' as full representation:

When will that right be exercised? People can, by arguments and speeches, create antagonisms almost as effectively as by their votes. Again, antagonisms would be created. We have nothing to gain. The only argument I saw put forward was that there would be a closer relationship between the people here and the people of the Six Counties.[62]

The possibility of consultations with Northern nationalists outside the Dáil had been raised by J. A. Costello. An organisation representative of anti-partitionists in the North could appoint an executive body that the Government might consult regularly. De Valera replied that if he was on the opposition benches and Costello proposed such a thing he would support him, but, from where he stood now, 'I have not any great hopes of what might be secured by it.' He expressed the fear that 'they would hold that we are not doing what they think we should do and what we believe it is not possible for us to do.'

This was probably the factor most keenly felt by de Valera. Access to the Dáil, however tenuous, would afford Northern nationalists the opportunity of arguing in a very public way that Dáil Éireann was not devoting enough energy to its professed aim of reintegrating the national territory. This would not only have ramifications for internal party unity but would also debilitate Fianna Fáil's ability to speak authoritatively to the 26-County electorate on the issue.

MacBride had been hoping that the proposal would be unanimously accepted, but as it was clear that this would not be possible a division was called, and the motion was defeated by 82 votes to 42.[63] Patrick O'Donnell, a Northerner, concluded sadly that 'we are going to leave it to the people of the Six Counties to settle the question of Partition for themselves.'[64] MacBride refused to put the second related motion to a vote, 'as I do not want to expose the people of south Armagh and Mr. McGlennon to further insults from this House.'[65]

Shortly after the defeat of MacBride's proposal de Valera met a Northern anti-partition deputation comprising two MPs and two senators, who made a case for the token nomination of one or two Northern representatives to the Seanad. According to the Government minutes, de Valera explained 'at length' the difficulties inherent in the proposal, which, he said, were of the same kind as existed in the case of the admitting of Northern MPs to the Dáil.[66]

The policy of non-admittance of Northern nationalists—even to address the Dáil—was pursued consistently throughout the 1950s. In January 1952 de Valera vehemently rejected a suggestion made by two members of the British Parliament from Cos. Fermanagh and Tyrone that they should be permitted to take seats in the Seanad. He could offer little advice for an alternative, having claimed that they should abstain from the House of Commons. Even though this meant that the two MPs would receive no remuneration, de Valera rejected suggestions that the Dáil should reimburse them for their lost salaries so that they could devote themselves to constituency work. To the bewilderment of the MPs, he then issued a stern lecture on how much he 'resented statements' that he had done nothing to end partition. A 'steady policy in the direction of re-unification had been, and would continue to be, pursued,' he said, though he did not elaborate on what this policy was.[67]

De Valera met another delegation in August 1952, this time led by the Derry MP Eddie McAteer (brother of the IRA leader Hugh McAteer).[68] He reiterated his belief in abstention as a policy, but again he rejected any suggestion that Northern nationalists should get representation of any form in the Oireachtas. Perhaps in response to de Valera's attitude, McAteer watered down the delegation's proposal to one of 'symbolic' attendance—a 'right of audience of some kind.' This too was rejected by de Valera, who feared that 'symbolic representation' would be followed by demands for 'fuller representation' and that 'the idea of representation in the Twenty-Six Counties' would be raised. Nationalists would not be permitted to get their foot in the Dáil door lest it become unhinged. The delegation was sent home empty-handed.[69]

Frank Aiken's presence at these meetings, while justifiable on the grounds that he was the Minister for External Affairs, may have been to bolster de Valera's position, psychologically and symbolically. Aiken was, after all, from south Armagh, the same constituency as Charlie McGlennon, the most persistent and vociferous of those seeking admission to the Dáil, who had been elected on a platform of taking his seat in the Oireachtas.[70]

The issue was raised in the Dáil on several occasions in 1952 and 1953, only to be met with a standard response that nothing had happened since de Valera's statements in 1951 to change the Government's position.[71] Alfie Byrne made the point that members of Dublin City Council, of which he was a long-serving member, had had the right to present themselves before the bar of the British House of Commons, and that this right had been exercised on a number of occasions.[72] He argued in favour of allowing Northern representatives to come regularly to speak before the bar of the Dáil 'in order to have on the records of this house what they want done. We could then base our arguments in the future on what the representatives of the Six Counties tell us.'[73] This was what Valera was most eager to avoid. Representations were also made by a number of county councils, including that of de Valera's home constituency of Clare, and other local authorities.[74]

Shortly after the 1954 ard-fheis of Fianna Fáil the Dáil debated yet another proposal: that all elected parliamentary representatives of the people of Northern Ireland should be given a right of audience in the Dáil or Seanad.[75] Taking the opportunity, Eddie McAteer asked for what he called a 'courtesy audience' in the Dáil to put forward the view of nationalist representatives on the question of 'the right' of Northern representatives to be heard in the national parliament. The circumstances were similar to those of 1925 (if considerably less dramatic), when nationalist MPS travelled to Dublin in an unsuccessful attempt to address the Dáil on the report of the Boundary Commission. Now the Northern representatives were again left in the corridors while the Dáil deliberated, only to turn down the request. In a letter to Costello, McAteer wrote that 'it is not at all unreasonable that the people vitally concerned in the matter be given a brief hearing.' He commented bitterly that 'evidently the two main parties in the Dáil are determined that no reproachful voice from the North will disturb their Kathleen Mavourneen policy on partition.'[76]

De Valera's contribution to the debate was short and to the point. He admitted that he had 'for a moment played around with the idea' when it was first mooted many years previously, but now he believed that no 'thinking person' could agree with the proposal. 'What is the point of people coming in here and taking about partition?' he asked. 'We know only too well that partition exists.' He conceded that they 'did not know all the details' of circumstances in the North, just as the Northern representatives would not be as intimate with events in Co. Roscommon as would the deputies who represented that constituency; but they had the means to consult representatives from the Six Counties, and they were 'always glad to discuss *their* problems with them.'[77] There was little to suggest that de Valera considered the problems facing Northern nationalists to be the concern of the Irish Government.

De Valera was being less than frank when he claimed that he had 'played around with the idea' for 'a moment,' having championed the proposal during the 1920s. When the third Dáil was convened, de Valera had seized on the expulsion of Northern representatives from the chamber as evidence that the Dáil was not the successor of the parliamentary body established in 1919. Indeed he made it a precondition in 1922 for legitimising the Free State Dáil in the eyes of republicans.[78] During his time as president of the underground 'government', Comhairle na dTeachtaí, de Valera had insisted that the right of elected Northern representatives to enter the Dáil 'was the symbol of the unity of the country.'[79] Once Fianna Fáil was established, de Valera refused to be bound to such a strategy.[80]

An ancillary issue was whether or not Fianna Fáil should organise in the North, and it was continuously hinted that the matter would be sympathetically considered once the party attained power in the Free State.[81] Once this happened, in 1932, the issue was raised regularly by delegates at the annual ard-fheis, but by then the party leadership appeared less sympathetic, and it argued that the matter would be pertinent only in the context of a new constitution—effectually postponing the issue. When preparations for the Constitution of Ireland were being made, the issue returned, and firm proposals were made at the 1936 and 1937 ard-fheiseanna and in the National Executive.[82] There was considerable disappointment in Fianna Fáil circles that a provision was not included, and a strong motion was put forward at the 1938 ard-fheis demanding that a clause be inserted in the Constitution enabling 'the elected representatives of North East Ulster to sit, act and vote in Dáil Éireann.'[83] This continued to be discussed in the National Executive, but it was put on hold by the wartime emergency period.[84] It re-emerged when Clann na Poblachta made it a central plank of their electoral platform in 1948,[85] and the party did fulfil its promise of appointing Northern nationalists to the Seanad.

Up to this point Fianna Fáil had used the eleven Taoiseach's nominees to appoint party hacks, and some prominent Clann na Poblachta leaders were disgruntled when this tradition was abandoned. The issue of *ad hoc* Seanad nominations, however, was different from the *right* to representation in the Dáil. When the issue was raised at the Government level in March 1949 the Attorney-General, Cecil Lavery, decided that such claims were 'natural and proper' but that a constitutional amendment would be necessary.[86] It is not clear why such an initiative was not carried out. It may have been because a fully fledged anti-partition campaign was already in operation; or perhaps Clann na Poblachta's numerical weakness in the coalition may have blunted the extent to which it forced the issue.[87]

Tim Pat Coogan has interpreted the rejections as demonstrating that de Valera 'did not want the Northern Nationalists making a substantive issue which he might have to act on, as opposed to securing electoral kudos for mere verbal republican-ism.'[88] John Bowman has suggested that de Valera may have feared that the implementation of the proposal would increase support for those within Fianna Fáil who advocated the extension of the Dáil's sovereignty to nationalist areas in the Six Counties and who argued that the Dáil should seek the support and allegiance of local authorities controlled by nationalists in the North,[89] a proposal first developed by Michael Collins.

The other significant proposal that raised its head at consecutive ard-fheiseanna during the 1950s, that of extending Fianna Fáil's organisation to the Six Counties, also proved a source of embarrassment for the party leadership, and de Valera found himself consistently opposing or postponing discussion on the matter. This proposal had also been actively considered by the party leadership during its formative years.[90] In response to grass-roots pressure, a high-level party delegation had travelled North to meet local republicans, but in the end they concluded that the first 'essential step to the realisation of national unity will be a political victory in the South.'[91]

Despite springing from a party that organised throughout the country, Fianna Fáil decided to consolidate its support in the 26 Counties in order to take control of the Free State before embarking on a vigorous organisational and anti-partition drive in the North.[92] On assuming power, however, de Valera actively discouraged discussion on the matter at successive ard-fheiseanna, and he fended off attempts in the National Executive to establish Fianna Fáil in the Six Counties.[93] The matter had been raised again in the form of a motion put forward at the 1949 ard-fheis, but de Valera countered it by saying that

> considered opinion had always been against the extension of the organisation to the Six Counties, although it might at first seem desirable. It might cause a considerable amount of damage. In the Twenty-Six Counties they could make the laws for themselves because they could form a government to carry out their policy. The people of the Six Counties had similar problems but, having been put in an impossible position by the gerrymandering of our country, they were not in a position to carry out their programme at all. The danger was that they would cause confusion because their problems were not precisely the same kind, although one thing they had in common was the desire to bring about the unity of the country. The result would be the introduction of confusion where they wanted unity.[94]

It was this policy of non-intervention that de Valera consistently pursued throughout the 1950s. The Nationalist Party representatives who met both Costello and de Valera had emphasised the importance of gaining access to the Oireachtas to demonstrate to their electorate that there was an effective constitutional alternative to militant republicanism. The question of enhanced nationalist rights in the Dáil— whether in the form of actual representation or a mere right of audience—was alive during 1955, but it seems to have disappeared suddenly. There were two reasons for this. Firstly, after several refusals the Nationalist MPs finally accepted that the matter was closed for the foreseeable future. Secondly, the rise of Sinn Féin as a serious electoral threat eclipsed the issue.[95]

DRIFT AND DIVISION: FIANNA FÁIL, 1951–6

Fianna Fáil's rhetorical commitment to a united Ireland was undiluted on regaining power in 1951. Speaking at the ard-fheis in November, de Valera told delegates that our political aim is to secure the independence of the whole of the country—and as a Republic. The people of the Twenty-Six Counties are united and the Nationalists of the Six Counties are united, and I am sure that if we follow our own policy the reunification of the country will be secured. As a Government we will do everything possible to secure our aim. It can be done by our saying that it is our national duty to do it and to make whatever necessary sacrifices are entailed in the effort.[96]

De Valera's message to the ard-fheis the following year was equally vague. According to the *Irish Times*,

the Taoiseach concluded his message by stating that he had not dealt with the problem of partition, not because it was not uppermost in his mind and in the mind of every member of the Government. The ard-fheis knew their views, and everyone could feel assured that whenever it appeared that any fruitful steps could be taken to bring partition to an end they would be taken.[97]

It was this sort of woolly thinking that characterised the Fianna Fáil leadership's approach to partition between 1951 and 1954 (and, indeed, throughout the 1950s). De Valera was sure that partition would go, provided that Fianna Fáil policy was diligently followed. Everybody knew what Fianna Fáil's *aim* was: it had been articulated at every ard-fheis since the party's foundation. But few had any idea of what *policy* would be pursued to achieve that aim. It was not sufficient to say that a united Ireland would be attained simply 'by our saying that it is our national duty.' Little recognition was given to the setbacks since the party's foundation—such as the Ireland Act (1949)—or to how the policies of successive governments might have reinforced partition.

Economic nationalism had reduced cross-border trade to a trickle. The policy of restoring Irish had raised the question of how unionists would be able to adapt in a united Ireland. Differentials in incomes and social welfare benefits had reduced further the attractiveness of a united Ireland, even to some Northern nationalists, as would, for unionists, the influence of the Catholic Church, which had been demonstrated from the Eucharistic Congress to the Mother and Child Scheme fiasco. Examining the effects of Government policy in different spheres in relation to partition might not have occasioned the changing of a single domestic policy, but it may have been sobering for party members to acknowledge how few of the 'necessary sacrifices' they were prepared to make to secure the allegiance of Northern unionists.

Policy differences among delegates manifested themselves at ard-fheiseanna during the annual debate on partition. There was a general frustration that no movement had been made on achieving the party's first national objective, a united Ireland. One such motion, which proposed that the Government break off negotiations with Britain in order to bring the partition issue to a head, advocated that force be used to end partition. The sponsor of the motion, Joe Dowling,[98] claimed that we have been paying lip-service to the idea of unity, when what we want is the sort of active service by which we have won the freedom of this country. The only way we can solve this problem is by the gun. We don't want the British troops in Ireland; the only British troops we want here are dead ones.[99]

When confronted with such motions, the general practice was for the party leadership to dedicate itself again to the national aim and to introduce an amendment that urged the Government to take all practicable steps to end partition. The motion, now reduced to a simple call for the abolition of partition, would be passed without dissension, and the issue would be shelved for another year. The futility of such motions is clear from the fact that delegates of strongly opposed views were able to vote for the same motion, thus creating a façade of a united approach to the issue.

As the party was bound by its constitution to unite the country, general anti-partition motions were entirely superfluous. It was not the aim that was in contention but the means. Such motions merely papered over important divisions, as questions of policy were submerged in an annual avalanche of rhetoric. The leadership—de Valera excluded—often acknowledged the lack of progress and promised to intensify efforts; but the issue remained frozen until the next ard-fheis. While the use of force was rejected, there were few practical proposals for ending partition. Modest efforts to open contact with Northern counterparts were often met with indignation from speakers who saw unionist ministers as usurpers who should be treated accordingly.[100]

After three inconspicuous years in power as a minority Government, Fianna Fáil could point to no achievements on partition since regaining power in 1951. The 1954 election campaign was one of the dullest and the longest (ten weeks) in the history of the state. An air of despondency followed MacEntee's austere deflationary budgets, and few believed that Fianna Fáil had a realistic chance of winning the election.[101] Much of the debate, such as it was, dealt with socio-economic issues, though some could not resist dragging in old ghosts. The Minister for Health, Dr James Ryan (a founder-member of the party), told a Fianna Fáil convention in Enniscorthy that Fine Gael had 'departed from their allegiance to the Republic in 1921' and sought to impose an oath of allegiance to the English monarch. He also made reference to the fact that Kevin O'Higgins had travelled to London in the mid-1920s to propose that the King of England be made King of Ireland in a ceremony in Dublin, in which he would be formally crowned by the Catholic and Protestant Archbishops of Dublin. 'The type of people running the Fine Gael party . . . bitterly opposed the enactment of an Irish Constitution framed in Dublin and wanted to retain one in which a foreign king was mentioned twenty-three times.'[102]

De Valera made reference to the Blueshirts and their 'allies' in Germany and Italy. He said of Fine Gael: 'They believed in dictatorship, it appeared at the time. Did they believe in dictatorship today?'[103]

The issue of partition received less attention than it had in any previous election. Clann na Poblachta made its familiar proposal of opening the doors of Dáil Éireann to Northern MPs, of internationalising the issue and of making it economically and politically unprofitable for Britain to 'use her political, financial and military power to maintain Partition.'[104] De Valera did not put forward any proposals, contenting himself with the traditional assertion that national unity had always been 'one of their foremost objectives.' He admitted that 'neither he nor anyone else' could say how unity would be attained but claimed (once again) that 'the unity of the country would come if only they were true to their ideals and persevered in their claims to the right of the Irish people to govern their own country.'[105]

The primary issue for Fianna Fáil was again that of coalition versus single-party government.[106] In a private report to the Secretary of State for Commonwealth Relations, the British Ambassador in Dublin remarked that the election had

> demonstrated the sterility of party politics here—Fianna Fáil speakers confining themselves to pious platitudes and ancient history, and Fine Gael to destructive criticism of the present administration ... The election is once again merely, as my predecessor put it, a struggle between ins and outs.[107]

It was a depressingly accurate assessment. Fianna Fáil lost four seats and dropped to its lowest parliamentary strength since 1927. A minority coalition Government was formed, with Costello again at the helm, though this time Clann na Poblachta's three TDS declined to participate, preferring to give external support. Fianna Fáil licked its wounds and embarked on another intensive reorganisation campaign.

De Valera's Northern policy was challenged again at the 1954 ard-fheis as delegates argued that the ineffectiveness of constitutional anti-partition agitation was dis-illusioning the youth, who were seeking other means.[108] While the National Executive was full of living legends who had fought for independence, the argument that the country was therefore in safe hands and that Irish unity was assured was beginning to wear thin. Some argued that the party had become increasingly conservative and needed an infusion of new blood to reinvigorate the republican spirit; for 'people who have held office for so long a period, this question of organisation becomes merely a matter of routine.'[109] Lemass met the issue head on.

> We are not, perhaps, living up to our responsibilities as a national movement. Fianna Fáil is the architect and custodian of national policy whether in govern-ment or in opposition. Its duty to defend national aims is all the greater when it is in opposition. National policy can never be static, it must be livened and rejuvenated by a flow of ideas from the people ... It is, perhaps, inevitable that during the years when Fianna Fáil was in office, the organisation should tend to become a mere political machine rather than a national movement. The time has come to take stock of the party's position and get back to the status and functions in mind when the organisation was started. Even the election machine is less efficient in some constituencies than it should be. The re-organisation campaign has started. It is a big task, but there is no reason to think that it will not go ahead.

Lemass adroitly linked the fulfilment of Fianna Fáil's republican aims with the organisational vitality of the party. Organisational survival and aggrandisement were equated with increased dedication to the founding aims of Fianna Fáil, though experience had demonstrated the opposite to be the case.

Shortly after the 1954 ard-fheis yet another Anti-Partition Committee of the National Executive was established, this time a 'permanent' one.[110] The timing of this initiative was a response to recent events in the North and was to head off increased frustration within Fianna Fáil at the party's lack of progress. It also reflected an anxiety that the country's youth were becoming disillusioned; a flight from Fianna Fáil to militant republicanism was feared. These concerns are reflected throughout the committee's deliberations, and the submissions received demonstrate that fundamental divisions existed within Fianna Fáil over the most appropriate anti-partition policy to adopt.

While de Valera did not participate in the committee, he appointed its members,[111] thus ensuring that the report would not deviate greatly from his own thinking. The committee contained many of the party's founding fathers, and these were assisted by some less experienced members. Among the party elders were Seán Lemass (who chaired the committee), Gerry Boland, Seán Moylan, Frank Aiken and Seán MacEntee (both natives of the North). The younger generation was represented by forty-year-old Liam Cunningham TD, first elected for Donegal in 1951, Lieutenant-Colonel Matthew Feehan, and a 29-year-old Charles Haughey, who had already unsuccessfully contested two general elections.

Two submissions in particular convey the chasm in the party regarding partition. Feehan devised a number of practical measures to induce unionists to abandon their pro-partition stance as well as some ideas for using the media, public debates and lecture tours to promote the idea of a united Ireland, echoing tactics already tried with gusto by the defunct anti-partition campaign.[112] His submission was heavily influenced by what he characterised as a rising sentiment within Fianna Fáil and in the country generally that constitutional means for challenging partition should be abandoned in favour of physical force. He lamented that this sentiment was also articulated by party representatives at all levels, including the Dáil, 'raising doubts as to the correctness of our methods [and encouraging] the false idea that our approach has been wrong and those who believe in force are right.'[113] A new generation was emerging that was 'unable to distinguish between the physical force tradition and the national tradition,' as evidenced by the 'widespread sympathy' for convicted IRA members. As the 'true Republican Party,' he concluded, Fianna Fáil 'must endeavour to win over the young IRA' and to 'convince our own rank and file that our approach is not wrong,' and he suggested that IRA veterans now loyal to Fianna Fáil might be used for this purpose.[114]

Feehan's fears of rising militancy in the grass-roots organisation were not unjustified, if the submission of the Tomás Ó Cléirigh Cumann was in any way representative.[115] The cumann stated that many 'honest nationally-minded members of Fianna Fáil' felt bound to make 'every effort' to end partition, and it warned that unless the party adopted an 'active policy' these people 'will find themselves unable, in conscience, to continue to give allegiance to the Organisation.'[116] They argued that

> our present position, while it is a wonderful achievement in itself, is, when viewed from a national point of view a poor thing, resulting from national disunity when victory was within our grasp; that it is not something to which we must cling and

defend, and that the only honourable use we can make of it is to use it as an opportunity to regroup and remarshall all our forces for the complete expulsion of the British from our territory. It seems to us that if we have become so soft and self-indulgent in our enjoyment of freedom, that we are not prepared to stake all in our effort to free our country, as our fathers did, then we are not worthy of our freedom, and deserve to be brought under foreign domination. We regard the argument of 'saving the Twenty-Six Counties' as being selfish and utterly unworthy of Irish nationalism.[117]

The submission also raised the question of 'the use of our regular armed forces in the Six Counties.' In this connection the document drew attention to the actions of the Egyptian Government, which had unofficially organised a liberation army consisting of irregular volunteers, mainly drawn from regular army units. The cumann demonstrated a somewhat exaggerated view of the potential militancy of the Fianna Fáil leadership when it advised that if similar groups had already been secretly organised by the Irish Government their existence should be publicised immediately with a view to alerting the British Government that Dublin was in earnest when it sought to end partition. It was also believed that such an announcement would bolster the morale of Northern nationalists and help Fianna Fáil with 'the more irresponsible members of the younger generation who believe that we have washed our hands of Partition.'

While there was a 'reasonable hope that negotiations could be forced before the necessity for military action arose,' the submission claimed that it would be 'criminally negligent' not to prepare for every possible contingency.

In this connection, we advocate the laying in of the greatest possible stocks of arms and ammunition suitable for guerrilla warfare, the closest possible study of British military installations likely to be of particular importance in relation to the areas in which the campaign will be carried out, the organisation of local forces to work in conjunction with the Army in making simulated and diversionary attacks on British military installations if required, plans for the destruction of official British and Stormont records in regard to rates and taxes in the selected areas etc.[118]

There were obvious reasons why the Fianna Fáil leadership would not be attracted by such a proposition. A statement of intent would most probably stiffen British and Unionist resolve to meet the threat while further endangering the position of the Catholic community in the North. To organise a military force clandestinely would— quite apart from precipitating a civil war in the North—lead to the possibility of the Government's role being discovered, thus embroiling the South in a war that could undermine the very existence of the 26-County state. As it turned out, the leadership adopted neither of the policies advocated in the two submissions, and it was not until the Lemass-O'Neill *rapprochement* a decade later that elements of Feehan's argument were implemented, though other—arguably more important—aspects were neglected.[119]

RENEWED ARMED CONFLICT IN THE NORTH

Militant sentiment among Northern nationalists increased during 1955. At the British general election in May, Sinn Féin secured the biggest anti-partition vote since 1921, obtaining more than 150,000 votes and winning seats in Fermanagh-South Tyrone and Mid-Ulster.[120] However, the two victorious republicans, Tom Mitchell and Phil Clarke, were serving ten-year prison sentences for their part in an arms raid at St Lucia Barracks, Omagh, the previous year. Another by-election in August merely extended the republican margin of victory, at which point the British Labour Government deemed Clarke and Mitchell to be ineligible to be elected and awarded the seats to the defeated Unionist candidates.[121] Naturally these events did not enhance the confidence of nationalists in the political process, nor did they demonstrate the advantages of pursuing a constitutional path to attain political objectives.

Since the IRA's raids for arms on British army barracks in Armagh and Omagh, harassment by the RUC and B Specials had intensified, occasionally spilling over into shootings. In March a B Special patrol had shot dead an eighteen-year-old man and wounded his girl-friend as they returned from a dance in Keady, Co. Armagh. A long, hot summer followed, in which Orange Order marches were forced through Catholic areas while nationalists were prevented from marching through their own towns. On 12 July 1955 fifteen thousand Orangemen, led by three prominent Unionist MPs, paraded twice through the Longstone Road in Annalong, Co. Down, shepherded by the RUC. The previous day three bombs had damaged the road, but this had been promptly repaired by police and soldiers.

Two weeks later, in stark contrast, a parade in connection with the Newtownbutler feis in Co. Fermanagh, in an entirely nationalist town, was banned, and a large force of RUC and British soldiers was drafted into the area. A serious riot ensued, during which water cannons were used for the first time. A dozen civilians were injured, and two members of Clones Urban District Council were among those arrested.[122]

At this time there was very little armed republican activity. The IRA refused to engage in any overt activity, and armed actions were the preserve of two tiny break-away organisations, Saor Uladh ('Free Ulster') and Laochra Uladh ('Ulster Heroes'). Saor Uladh was the more significant of the two, and it reflected a new pragmatism among some sections of Northern republicans. It enjoyed a particularly close relationship with Clann na Poblachta in the South; its leader, Liam Kelly, was a friend of Seán MacBride. Kelly and his supporters recognised the legitimacy of the 26-County state and sought to make the Constitution's definition of the national territory a reality by force of arms.[123]

The drift towards militancy among Northern nationalists was made clear when Kelly successfully took a seat from the Nationalist Party in Mid-Tyrone. The electorate had been left in no doubt about Kelly's policies for ending partition. 'I do not believe in constitutional methods,' he had told one election gathering. 'I believe in the use of force; the more the better, the sooner the better.'[124] Shortly after his election Kelly was imprisoned for making a 'seditious speech', but he found himself made a member of Seanad Éireann while incarcerated. Fianna Fáil had been removed from office in the interim, and Kelly was appointed by the Taoiseach, J. A. Costello, on the recommendation of Seán MacBride.

The IRA still held back from engaging in an armed campaign, and there were very few violent incidents in the North. Two arms raids and a premature explosion outside Stormont on 2 July, killing a Laochra Uladh member intent on destroying the Stormont telephone exchange, were the only armed republican activities between January and November 1955.[125] These events did not go unnoticed in the Republic, however, and the local elections in June had 'provided evidence of substantial Sinn Féin strength.'[126] A number of resolutions were passed by local government bodies condemning the activities of the British and Northern Governments. One such resolution, passed by Kerry County Council, condemned the British Government for sentencing two IRA members for their part in an arms raid in Berkshire. Supporting the motion, John O'Connor, a Clann na Poblachta TD, declared that

> all the major political parties have failed to give a lead on the partition issue. Successive governments have given it the brush off with the result that full blooded young men will go out and attempt to do things which the Government of the country failed to do.[127]

At the 1955 ard-fheis de Valera, while acknowledging the fundamental injustice of partition, refused to endorse armed actions to abolish it. Indeed he challenged the coalition Government to take stern measures against republicans but suggested that they 'would be unable to take a course that might be unpopular as they might be divided among themselves.'[128] In this he was in accord with the British Government, which had expected 'drastic action' to break up a resurgent IRA, only to find that Costello could not generate sufficient support, publicly or politically, for such an assault.[129]

Ideological flexibility was the central theme of the honorary secretaries' report, read by 25-year-old Brian Lenihan, who in the following decade would become associated with the mohair-suit wing of the party. He stated with satisfaction that the reorganisation campaign that had been carried out throughout 'the country' had resulted in the registration of 1,787 cumainn during the year—ninety more than the highest total achieved during the previous twenty years. His message was of interest to those who adhered to traditional Fianna Fáil policy: 'Our policy planners should be completely uninhibited, and opinions, however dearly held, should be ruthlessly cast aside if they are not of value today.' This statement opened a floodgate of criticism as delegates argued that the party had become opportunist, attracting those who did not share the traditional 'national outlook.'

Seán Lemass, as ever with his finger firmly on the pulse of the party, sought again to quell fears of ideological decline by linking success against partition to organisational regeneration. 'The purpose of the reorganisation,' he assured delegates, 'has been to attract those young people with the national position.' If the party was to retain its republican soul more cumainn would have to be established. Those who were concerned with partition and the overall direction of Fianna Fáil could reverse any decline by helping to create a larger and more successful party.

On 26 November, two weeks after Fianna Fáil's ard-fheis, the RUC barracks at Roslea, Co. Fermanagh, was subjected to a bomb and gun attack.[130] No organisation claimed responsibility, though the IRA was widely suspected; it was in fact the splinter group Saor Uladh.[131] In January 1956 the Government received an *aide-mémoire* from the British Government that alleged 'a total unwillingness' on the part of the Gardaí in assisting the RUC with information or in co-operating to identify the perpetrators. The document strongly urged collaboration between the RUC and the Garda Síochána and claimed that in March 1955 the Gardaí and the Government had been told of IRA training activities in Scotstown, Co. Monaghan, 'yet it appears that the men were allowed to continue with their illegal activities without interference.' In February 1956 the British Government received a rebuff from the Department of External Affairs, which left the British in no doubt that they could except little co-operation on the matter.

> Briefly, the attitude is that the Government could not allow information to be furnished about Irishmen already apprehended, or being actively sought in connection with armed political activities and could not accept any responsibility or commitment in regard to the intentions of unlawful organisations which are, by their nature, secret.[132]

Costello had already responded to British and Unionist demands for extradition by arguing that armed republicanism was a product of partition and of British and Unionist misrule.[133] In relation to republican attacks on the Northern state he spelled out future Government policy on extradition.

> I must ... emphasise, in order to prevent any future controversy or discussion on this point, that there can be no question of our handing over, either to the British or to the Six-County authorities, persons whom they may accuse of armed political activities in Britain or in the Six-Counties.[134]

With buoyant election returns in the North, and a higher degree of tolerance in the South, Sinn Féin was displaying increased confidence. Addressing an audience of two thousand people in Ennis, the Sinn Féin leader Séamus Sorahan declared that 'the younger people are looking for an anchor-sheet where men could not be tempted by bribes or office to turn their backs on the national ideal of a free Ireland of 32 counties.'[135]

When the IRA began an organised campaign in December 1956 with a series of attacks on border installations, de Valera's calls for firm anti-IRA measures became more difficult for the Government to resist.

FIANNA FÁIL AND THE BORDER CAMPAIGN

During a private meeting with Sir John Maffey in 1946 de Valera confessed that 'if he were a young man in Northern Ireland today he felt that he would be giving his life to fight the existing order of things.'[136] Despite this, and despite the ambivalence of others in Fianna Fáil during the 1950s,[137] de Valera rarely wavered from public opposition to the use of force for undermining Unionist rule. During 1956 a number of Fianna Fáil TDs successfully petitioned him to participate in a secret meeting with an IRA delegation, during which the IRA asked de Valera 'to assist in their attacks or at least connive at them.' They received no encouragement from de Valera, who was 'extremely forthright' in saying that their actions were destined to end in failure, causing great suffering without any visible weakening of partition.[138]

With or without de Valera's approval, the IRA was wedded to a renewal of an armed assault on the Northern state, and Sinn Féin's election successes had encouraged an unrealistic optimism. Even before the announcement of the beginning of the IRA campaign the Catholic hierarchy had used its ecclesiastical and moral weight to issue the usual pastoral letter that accompanied any whiff of subversion. On 18 January 1956 it declared it a mortal sin for a Catholic to be a member of an organisation or society that 'arrogates to itself the right to bear arms or to use them against its own or another state.' It declared it sinful for a Catholic 'to co-operate with, or express approval of, or otherwise assist any such organisation or society, and that if the co-operation or assistance be notable, the sin is mortal.'[139] A strict interpretation of the phrase 'express approval' could have condemned a number of TDs to eternal damnation.[140]

On New Year's Eve 1956 a botched raid on an RUC barracks in Brookeborough, Co. Fermanagh, left two IRA men dead, Seán Sabhat and Fergal O'Hanlon.[141] As was so often the case in Irish history, an act of inconsequential military importance was transformed into a major political event. The funeral of Seán Sabhat was something of a national procession. As the coffin made its way from Monaghan to Dundalk and Drogheda, thousands of workers left their jobs to join the mourners. Shops were closed in Dublin as the hearse made its way through the city flanked by an IRA guard of honour. On the same night Dublin County Council passed a resolution extending sympathy to the relatives of the two men who had 'lost their lives fighting for Ireland.'[142]

The funeral procession made its way through a number of towns in which people had waited for hours in driving rain to catch a glimpse of the coffin. Local members of the Old IRA formed a guard of honour in each town. Thousands, including the Fianna Fáil Lord Mayor, braved the inclement weather as the hearse entered Limerick at midnight. The funeral was the biggest in the city since 1921, with more than fifty thousand people making their way to the city cemetery, where the republican plot was opened for the first time in thirty-four years. It was attended by the chairmen of a variety of representative bodies in Co. Limerick, by neighbouring county councils, members of the Catholic clergy, and the GAA and Conradh na Gaeilge (of both of which Sabhat was a prominent member). Among the public representatives present were the Fianna Fáil TDs J. J. Collins and Donogh O'Malley.[143]

Apart from the latent republican sentiment, which had never quite evaporated, popular attitudes were also influenced by international events. Nationalists in Hungary had attempted to overthrow communist rule, and, condemning their suppression, Seán MacBride attempted to use his influence in the Council of Europe.[144] The other issue he raised there, that of Cyprus, had already attracted considerable attention in Ireland. Many saw EOKA, the paramilitary group that fought for the liberation of Cyprus from Britain and its unification with Greece, as a Cypriot IRA fighting a malign British regime that now openly talked of partition as a solution to the crisis.[145] During the first week of 1957 several hundred people had been killed in British air attacks in Aden (Yemen),[146] while British forces the previous year had been engaged in a war with

Egypt following the nationalisation of the Suez Canal. British imperialism was clearly still active, and some viewed events in the North in that context.[147]

Members of the Catholic hierarchy also drew international parallels. Citing Poland and Hungary as examples of how communism had allegedly destroyed Catholic countries, the Bishop of Clogher told a congregation in Roslea, Co. Fermanagh, that 'we have a number of communists who will certainly take this opportunity to destroy us.'[148] He reaffirmed the stance adopted the previous year, saying that it was a mortal sin

> to take part in any way [in] the occurrences that had taken place recently. It is not these upstarts that are appointed to rule the Church of God, or to lay down the law in regard to the Commandments of God . . . it is the bishops of the country, under the Pope.

He urged his flock to 'beware of those who go about in sheep's clothing but, inwardly were ravening wolves.' It is clear, however, that this position was not universally shared within the Catholic Church if the large number of clergy who attended the funeral of Seán Sabhat the previous day was anything to go by.[149]

Motions of sympathy for the relatives and friends of Sabhat and O'Hanlon were passed by dozens of county councils and other local bodies and almost always with unanimous support.[150] Many called for the matter to be raised at the United Nations and for a UN force to be sent to the North. Other resolutions were more militant, such as that of Sligo Corporation (town council), offering 'congratulations to the resist-ance forces in the Six Counties in their struggle against British Imperialism and extending best wishes for success.'[151]

One example of the divisions within Fianna Fáil can be found in the local organisation's response to a motion proposed by the Fianna Fáil chairman of South Tipperary County Council, which urged the Government to release all republican prisoners and to 'give the Republicans fighting the common enemy the full support of our army and police force.' He added that if Dáil Éireann believed that it needed a new mandate to pursue such a policy it should dissolve itself and put the matter to a popular vote. Supporting the motion, Councillor Ahessy (also Fianna Fáil) declared that 'when Seán Tracey started to fight for freedom people thought him insane, but they thought different now and cherished his name.' Several Fianna Fáil councillors openly questioned the wisdom of constitutional agitation on the issue of partition. For example, Councillor J. J. Kearney declared that

> he believed that there was no hope of ever achieving the unification of the country peacefully, so that it was up to the people to take a hand. They were listening to rumours and talk for hundreds of years and they were as far away as ever by peaceful methods. It was about time that support be given to the men who had the courage to use arms.

Similarly, Councillor Gerard Meskill said that it was his belief that 'constitutional means would not solve the partition problem' and that 'the time was ripe to do something about it, and the sooner the better.'

When it was pointed out by a Fine Gael councillor that de Valera was, 'if anything, stronger in his condemnation of violence than An Taoiseach,' he was told by Councillor Tom Hogan that 'we have got our own opinions.' One Fianna Fáil councillor, who voted against the motion, confessed that if he were an independent member he would be in favour of the motion, but as a Fianna Fáil member he had to follow his leader, 'who had asked for something different.'

Reflecting these internal party divisions the motion was supported by seven Fianna Fáil councillors but opposed by four. Fine Gael voted *en masse* against the motion, while the Labour Party, whose members said that they were reflecting official party policy, supported it.[152] Alderman Seán Tracey of the Labour Party expressed pride in the fact that he had witnessed this patriotic upsurge and added that, because of the IRA actions, 'this generation of Irishmen would not pass away in shame.' Such assertions did not appear to be politically debilitating: Tracey became the Mayor of Clonmel later that year and contested the general election in February for the Labour Party, before embarking on a parliamentary career spanning thirty-six years.[153]

Some of the Fianna Fáil criticisms were opportunist. They claimed that the Government had not got a mandate for its actions and should therefore dissolve the Dáil and leave the matter for a decision by the people (thus implying that a vote for Fianna Fáil would mean an end to the imprisonment of republicans). Few realised that the Government's life had almost expired. The independent deputy Jack McQuillan and the Clann na Talmhan TD Patrick Finucane made a formal request to the Taoiseach, urging him to recall the Dáil immediately to discuss 'two motions of grave national importance.'[154] The motions read:

> That Dáil Éireann is of the opinion that, as the situation in the Six Counties is on a parallel with that obtaining in Hungary, Egypt and Cyprus, our permanent delegate to the United Nations should be instructed to demand of the Secretary-General the immediate despatch of UN observers to the occupied part of the national territory.
>
> That Dáil Éireann is of the opinion that the Government should discontinue immediately the use of the Irish Army and the Gardaí Síochána as instruments of British policy in helping to maintain partition; and that the men recently taken into custody as a result of such use should be released forthwith.

In a letter to McQuillan, Costello said that he had 'no intention' of prematurely summoning the Dáil to consider motions that would invite it to 'abrogate its own authority in favour of persons who have set themselves in defiance of the Dáil itself and of the Government.' He also denied the 'unfounded and mischievous' suggestion that the Army and Gardaí were being used as 'instruments of British policy.' They were employed solely for the purpose for which they were established, to 'defend the rights of the people and the democratic institutions of the State.'[155]

In a radio broadcast Costello sought to clarify his position regarding recent events. The speech did not address circumstances within the North but rather concentrated on the implications for the 26 Counties. In particular he sought to dissuade people from encouraging the activities of the IRA—which, as the law prescribed, was never mentioned by name but was referred to as 'minority groups' that sought to defy the institutions of the state. According to Costello, a 'heavy responsibility' rested on those who were in a position to influence public opinion, particularly public representatives and the press. It was necessary for people to be on their guard against false comparisons with the past.

> We rightly honour those who rose against British rule in other times. Many of them are to be found among members of the Government and of Dáil Éireann today, and they are the first to recognise the fundamental differences between circumstances of the past and those that obtain today.

The difference, he asserted, was the fact that they now had an independent state and a freely elected parliament entrusted to take decisions on national policy. Those who defied these institutions, which had been 'established with so much labour and suffering,' could 'surely claim no reflected glory from the men whose efforts made the creations of those institutions possible.' No Irish government could permit 'the rich achievements of past generations to be squandered at the hands of ruthless and reckless men.'[156]

The speech was immediately welcomed by the Northern Ireland Minister of Home Affairs and the Attorney-General, both of whom professed a hope that words would be matched with 'real action.'[157] De Valera also declared himself to be in 'entire agreement' with the sentiments expressed in the Taoiseach's broadcast. Partition could not be solved by force, and were force to be used it could only be under the authority of Dáil Éireann. To allow any military body not subject to the Dáil to enrol, organise and equip would lead to 'anarchy and ruin.' No government could permit it, and 'no thinking person' could support it.[158]

Costello's speech, however, did little to mollify growing disquiet within Clann na Poblachta, on whose support the Government depended for its survival.[159] Fresh from her surprise by-election victory, Kathleen O'Connor associated herself with a resolution passed by her local branch that condemned 'the Government attitude in garrisoning the Border with military and Gardaí [and] the capturing and imprison-ment of patriotic Irishmen, who are prepared to risk and suffer so much for their ideals.' The resolution claimed that the Government was acting as an 'accomplice' of the Brookesborough regime, and it called on the party's Dáil deputies to force the Government to withdraw the army and police from the border and to release all IRA men unconditionally.[160]

Similar motions from other branches flooded in, with some calling for an immediate withdrawal of support from the Government and for a special meeting of the Ard-Chomhairle to be convened to consider their position now that the Government had 'embarked on a policy of repression against Republicans, and is employing the forces of the State to maintain the border.'[161]

Just before Christmas, MacBride had been asked by the Fine Gael minister Tom O'Higgins to propose a vote of confidence in the Government, which he did. When O'Higgins visited MacBride at his home he found him 'charming and concerned with the problems of the Government.' The official response to the deaths of Sabhat and O'Hanlon quickly changed all that, and O'Higgins concluded that in politics

MacBride 'ended up having the extreme republican views he started with.'[162] Privately, MacBride considered any move to withdraw support from the Government headed by Fine Gael to be tactically unwise. He had personal experience of de Valera's attitudes towards militant republicanism, and he knew that he would embark on a much harsher anti-IRA policy than had been pursued by the Costello Government.[163]

This was something that the Ard-Chomhairle of Clann na Poblachta was perhaps less quick to appreciate. Filled with indignation at the Government's refusal to support (or at the very least tolerate) the republican assault on the Northern state, it instructed its three TDS, as was its prerogative under the party constitution, to put down a motion of no confidence in the Government. Many members of the Ard-Chomhairle served on local government bodies and may have been impressed by the stance of local Fianna Fáil representatives. Rather than face the prospect of defeat, Costello sought, and received, a dissolution of the Dáil and called a general election.

THE 1957 ELECTION

For the first time in thirty years Sinn Féin put forward a selection of candidates, and it presented itself not merely as a political party but as 'a national movement with a policy.'[164] Its policy, however, was fanciful in the extreme. The party was unequivocally and unapologetically abstentionist, and it was repeatedly stated that it would not take its seats in either of 'the partition parliaments.'[165] According to the election manifesto,

> Sinn Féin candidates will not enter Leinster House as a minority group. Given a majority they are prepared to assume governmental control of the area, not through the present partition machinery, but through the Republican Government constituted of elected or selected representatives.

Whatever credibility such a policy enjoyed was seriously weakened, if not negated, by the fact that Sinn Féin submitted only twenty candidates to the electorate, despite needing seventy seats to secure an absolute majority.

The reference to 'selected representatives' was not incidental. The manifesto acknowledged that it was unlikely that Unionist MPs would take their seats in the new all-Ireland assembly. However, representatives from the areas affected could be 'selected through constituency conventions or other agreed machinery.'[166] Fortunately for Sinn Féin, few of its party advertisements dealt with these provisions of the manifesto. Rather, candidates were described as, for example, 'a young man of courage and principle who played his part in the revolt against the British Occupation in Northern Ireland,'[167] and it was asserted that the Sinn Féin candidates had 'one allegiance and one only—Allegiance to the ideals of Pearse, Connolly and MacDermot.'[168]

At times one might have wondered whether it was 1957 or 1927 as de Valera raked over old controversies—something also taken up by opponents of all shades. During the campaign he contradicted 'the lie that had been sedulously propagated' that Fianna Fáil had ever taken an oath of allegiance to the British monarch when its deputies first entered the Dáil. 'I have seen in the Oxford Dictionary Fianna Fáil put down as a party who took the Oath,' he said, before declaring that there was 'no truth whatsoever' in the claim.[169] Such protestations may have been symptomatic of a realisation by the 75-year-old de Valera that this might be his last election as leader of Fianna Fáil, and they may have been motivated by a desire to clarify the historical record and reaffirm Fianna Fáil's claim to be the standard-bearer of republicanism. There had not been a day while he was in office, he claimed, on which he had not kept the idea of a united Ireland fully before his mind. 'I am convinced,' he stated, 'that the method we were using at the time [in office] was the only method that gave any hope of success.' (Characteristically, he did not attempt to define what this policy was.) Recalling that Fianna Fáil had been founded to reunite the divided republican forces, he said that

> we did resume the march towards the ideals of 1916 and 1917 to 1921, and politically we have been successful as far as five-sixths of the national territory is concerned. If we make sure that the five-sixths is made really Irish we will have the preservation of the Irish nation in our hands. Time will settle the other thing.[170]

Advertisements for the final election rally in College Green emphasised that a 'Guard of Honour for the Chief' would be formed by veterans of the War of Independence.[171]

Fianna Fáil made its now familiar denunciation of coalition government and claimed that 'we cannot afford any more experiments in the art of government.'[172] Confidence had been 'scraped out of the Nation by three years of Coalition Government,' and should Fianna Fáil prove unable to secure election 'the damage may be irreparable.'[173] From Donegal to Dingle the messages from the posters were on the same theme. 'The dilly-dally decade has ended,' declared one, while another stated vaguely that 'ten years ago you knew what you wanted and you didn't get it.'[174]

Despite the fact that the IRA was engaged in the most concerted military assault on the six-county state since the 1920s, future policies on the North received little attention. Seán Edmonds has described the 1957 election campaign as

> a classic example of massive political camouflage. As best they could, the parties contesting seats in the Dáil side-stepped questions about their attitude towards the militants and the fight in the north. And this was the question everyone was asking.[175]

Cornelius O'Leary concurs, claiming that both Fianna Fáil and Fine Gael 'tried to avoid the delicate problem of what policy to adopt in regard to the IRA after the election.' The election campaign was conducted 'in an atmosphere resembling that of 1933 and earlier,' as the IRA raids 'had aroused the latent patriotic feelings of many of the electorate.'[176]

Fine Gael lost more than 100,000 votes, while the size of the Fianna Fáil majority suggested that it would be four or five years in opposition. Given the political fluidity of the 1950s, few would have believed that the best part of two decades would elapse before it got another taste of power. The problem, as always, was organisation. Fine Gael was still a party of amateur gentlemen who spent much of their time either in the Law Library or on the farm. The leaders of Cumann na nGaedheal had 'remained indifferent to the very notion that they should soil their hands in cultivating anything as soil-encrusted as grass roots.'[177] Things had improved since then, but the process was gradual, and old habits died hard. Fianna Fáil's first national collection had been held within three years of its foundation. Fine Gael, on the other hand, waited until 1949—twenty-six years after its establishment—to mimic this most lucrative source of funds.[178]

The big surprise of the election was the relative success of Sinn Féin, which took four seats: Kerry South (25 per cent of the vote), Monaghan (19 per cent), Sligo-Leitrim (16 per cent) and Longford-Westmeath (15 per cent). Three of these were gained at the expense of Fianna Fáil, the fourth from an independent. The national party vote averaged 5½ per cent, though in the nineteen constituencies contested the average was 11 per cent.[179] It is probably fair to depict such a vote as one of sympathy as much as of solid support. Despite a manifesto that covered many socio-economic issues, Sinn Féin was perceived as a one-issue party and wedded to abstention. In its post-election editorial the *Irish Press* claimed that the Sinn Féin vote could be interpreted as 'an expression of "no confidence" by a large body of the people in all the parties that constitute the Dáil' and that, while it obtained 65,000 votes, 'it is clear that a much stronger voice would have been raised for the party had it sought an opinion in more than nineteen constituencies.'[180]

Combined with the recent vote in the North, Sinn Féin now had garnered 220,000 votes in Ireland as a whole. The question that remained was what attitude the new Fianna Fáil Government would take.

Some clues about the kind of people active in the IRA can be found by looking at those prisoners sentenced to more than three years imprisonment in Belfast between 1953 and 1960.[181] They ranged in age from seventeen to fifty-one; 29 per cent were from the South, the great majority from either Dublin or Cork, with a small number from Cos. Galway, Kerry, Limerick, Monaghan and Louth. By occupation, 18 per cent were labourers and 22 per cent were tradesmen, with carpenters the largest sub-group, constituting a third of all tradesmen. Other categories included factory machinists (6 per cent), clerks (5 per cent) and bricklayers (4 per cent). Civil servants, bakers and bus conductors found themselves in the company of a marine engineer, a freelance journalist, a publican and a fisherman.

The rampant emigration of the 1950s was probably a significant factor in Fianna Fáil's campaign against the IRA. Almost half a million people left the country during the decade, most of them young; had they stayed in Ireland, probably some of these would have channelled their disenchantment into militant republicanism.

The IRA attempted to persuade de Valera to stand aside, at the very least, in a battle between republicans and the Northern regime. Part of this hope rested on an addition to the IRA's standing order no. 8 that sought to convince the Dublin government that armed republicanism was aimed solely at the Northern state and posed no threat to the 26-County authorities. It now stated:

1.   Volunteers are strictly forbidden to take any militant action against 26-Co. Forces *under any circumstances whatsoever.* The importance of this Order in present circumstances especially in the Border areas cannot be over-emphasised.

2.   Minimum arms drill shall be used in training in the Twenty-Six County area. In the event of a raid every effort shall be made to get the arms away safely. If this fails, the arms shall be rendered useless and abandoned.

3.   Maximum security precautions must be taken when training. Scouts must always be posted to warn of emergency. Volunteers arrested during training or in possession of arms will point out that the arms were for use against the British Forces of Occupation only. This statement should be repeated at all subsequent Court proceedings.

4.   *At all times* Volunteers must make it clear that the policy of the Army is to drive the British Forces of Occupation out of Ireland. [Emphasis in original.]

At a massive rally in College Green on 12 January 1958 Tomás Mac Curtáin told those assembled that the IRA would not even return fire should it come into contact with forces of the 26 Counties.[182]

Despite consistent remarks by de Valera to the contrary, some believed that Fianna Fáil would adopt a softer line on the republican campaign in the North.[183] This perception was quickly dispelled. Within days of taking office the new Government decided to suspend without pay all civil servants, officers and employees of local bodies and employees of state-sponsored bodies found guilty of an offence under the Offences Against the State Acts (1939 and 1940).[184] A similar decision was made for employees imprisoned by the authorities in the Six Counties.[185] It was also decided that public employees should sign the following statement, with refusal to sign leading to permanent dismissal:

I, ..., undertake to uphold the Constitution of Ireland and its laws, and I declare that I am not and will not become a member of, or assist, any unlawful organisation.[186]

What was to be de Valera's last Government was still very much dominated by those of the revolutionary generation. There were three newcomers (though two, Boland and Blaney, were the sons of prominent Fianna Fáil revolutionaries): Kevin Boland (Minister for Defence), Neil Blaney (Minister for Posts and Telegraphs) and Jack Lynch (Minister for Education). The British Government was happy with the Fianna Fáil victory. It had been heartened by de Valera's ard-fheis speeches while in opposition and believed that his large majority would embolden him to act decisively against the IRA.[187]

Shortly after the formation of the Government on 20 March the new Minister for Justice made it clear that there was no question of the premature release of republican prisoners, among whom were two of the four Sinn Féin TDs.[188] On 5 July the Government went one step further by using the provisions of the Offences Against the State Act to reintroduce internment. Within three months 130 people had been placed in the Curragh under ministerial warrants, adding to the 120 interned in the North since December.[189]

The issue of the republican internees was raised in the Dáil on several occasions during the Border Campaign. In one of the more colourful debates the independent deputy Frank Sherwin declared:

> I am a good student of history. I know as much of the history of the country as the Taoiseach does, and he knows a lot. I know the whole origin of partition; I know the situation in the North was brought about by physical force, but I am not aware that anything brought about by physical force can be undone except by physical force. The Taoiseach himself admits that he has no policy on partition. The Government's argument is that they will not permit those people to challenge the authority of the State. I am not aware that they do. Those people have gone across the border, and in the area in which we have no jurisdiction they have committed certain acts. I am not aware that they ever tapped the noses of our Guards. On occasions when the Guards met them they surrendered their weapons, and by doing that, in my opinion, they were guilty only of having weapons illegally. They believe a certain method is the right method, and I believe it too. My attitude is that they might give the authorities there so many headaches that some responsible people in Britain would start taking about partition, which they are not prepared to do now.[190]

De Valera took up the challenge, and his reply suggests a somewhat selective view of his own history of anti-state activity.

> They talk about past history. They choose to misread past history . . . There can be but one government and one army in this country if it is going to last. We have done nothing but what was absolutely necessary, and despite the things that have been done we still have recurrences of these incidents which result in loss of life. Even when we, away back in 1922, took up a position that authority at that time had been usurped by those who got into power, we still believed and held it as a basic theory that we had not the right to take life. Human life is very sacred.[191]

With internment on both sides of the border, the IRA had nowhere to hide. Even its most optimistic strategists had based their hopes on enjoying a safe haven on the Southern side of the border, from which attacks could be launched and to which activists could retreat. By the time of de Valera's retirement, in June 1959, the Border Campaign was over in all but name. The Government began releasing internees unconditionally at the end of 1958, and by March the following year the Curragh Internment Camp was closed.

In his final address to a Fianna Fáil ard-fheis, in October 1958, de Valera told delegates to 'take off your coats and end this dangerous system.'[192] He was not, however, referring to the Stormont regime but to proportional representation. Indeed he did not refer to partition at all but was preoccupied with the future of his creation, Fianna Fáil, which, having been weaned on a cult of leadership, could not envisage a Fianna Fáil without the 'Chief' at the helm.

The abolition of PR was intended to be de Valera's parting gift to Fianna Fáil, which he had established thirty-three years earlier. As in 1937, a national election and a referendum were held on the same day, this time with the slogan 'Vote Yes and de Valera.' The electorate said Yes to de Valera but declined—by a narrow margin—to endorse his proposal to abolish PR. De Valera stepped down as Taoiseach and as leader of Fianna Fáil, though he waited until all the presidential votes had been counted. His departure marked the end of an era for Fianna Fáil.

Chapter 11 ~

APPROACH TO CRISIS, 1960–69

THE 1961 ELECTION AND THE END OF THE BORDER CAMPAIGN

The 1961 election has been described with considerable justification as 'the dullest on record.'[1] This was despite the fact that the three major parties had new leaders contesting their first general election. The *Irish Times* commented: 'There has never been an election campaign that made so little impact on the people.'[2] The turn-out dipped below 70 per cent for only the second time since 1927 (the other being the snap election in 1944, a time when wartime rationing made it difficult to travel).

The general lack of interest resulted partly from the fact that the Labour Party had made it clear it they would not participate in any coalition. Its stance was based on the belief—not unjustified by recent experience—that coalitions succeeded only in bolstering the larger party electorally, to the detriment of the Labour Party. It was also felt by party strategists that Fianna Fáil would be weakened by de Valera's departure, while Fine Gael—bereft of any substantial policies that distinguished it from its larger rival—would disappear from the political landscape.

The logic of this analysis was that the existing party system, based on the Treaty split, was coming to an end. Its demise was assured, so long as the Labour Party did not intervene and throw a lifeline to either Fianna Fáil or Fine Gael to help them secure power. The party would wait patiently on the sidelines, therefore, in expectation of the inevitable collapse of Civil War politics, ready to play a pivotal role in a new left-right party system.[3] This way of thinking would dominate Labour Party policy on coalitions throughout the 1960s.

Though the IRA Border Campaign had not officially ended, Fianna Fáil did not raise the issue of partition at all. Instead electors were presented with 'the simple issue' of either a Fianna Fáil party 'inspired by [the] brilliant and dynamic Seán Lemass' (de Valera's successor as leader of Fianna Fáil) or 'the only alternative,' which was 'another coalition foredoomed to failure.'[4] This emphasis was made clear in an internal party booklet entitled 'Notes for Speakers', which advised candidates to emphasise that 'a Fianna Fáil majority is the only safeguard against another disastrous Coalition.' Throughout its nineteen pages candidates were told how to deal with issues as diverse as drainage, turf, grass-root and drinking hours; but there was no reference to partition.[5]

Sinn Féin's vote was cut almost in half, from 65,000 to 35,000. The party had done little to build on its electoral breakthrough four years earlier,[6] and its amateur approach to electoral politics was reflected in the way it conducted its campaign. In areas in which it had done well in 1957 it put up different candidates,[7] while some of its best performances were in constituencies it had failed to contest in 1957, suggesting that its approach in 1957 had also left much to be desired.[8] In 1961 areas in which it had done well in 1957 were not contested, while constituencies in which it had made less of an impact or that it had not contested at all in 1957 were selected, with predictable consequences.[9] In the event it secured 5½ per cent of the vote in the twenty constituencies contested, 3 per cent altogether.[10] Proportionally, it should have secured four seats,[11] and its failure to retain even one demonstrated that its support was spread too thinly. In fact the combined vote of Clann na Talmhan and the National Progressive Democrats was less than the Sinn Féin vote, yet each succeeded in getting two deputies elected.[12] Michael Mullen (who had been a member of the IRA during the 1940s) was elected for the Labour Party in Dublin North-West. De Valera's fears about proportional representation had proved justified: Fianna Fáil went from enjoying the largest majority since 1922 to becoming a minority Government dependent on independents.

The IRA campaign could still be lethal. The killing of an RUC man in November was condemned by the Taoiseach, Seán Lemass, who declared that 'no sane person could think that such murderous activities serve any national purpose.'[13] On 22 November he reconstituted the Special Criminal Court and authorised it to try offences under the Offences Against the State Act. Lemass revealed that, in addition to the army, more than six hundred gardaí were engaged full time in connection with the Border Campaign, at a cost of £400,000 per year.[14] In the Dáil, Jack McQuillan criticised the fact that the military officers who comprised the Special Criminal Court had no legal expertise, and he argued that 'these tragic events flow from the state of frustration and disillusionment of our youth today at the failure of our Government to take steps to end partition.'[15]

The Border Campaign, however, was staggering to its inexorable end, and the IRA officially ceased fire on 26 February 1962. It had lasted little more than five years and resulted in eighteen deaths: six RUC men and twelve republicans (all but two of whom had been killed accidentally).

Two factors hastened its end. The joint security measures of Dublin, Belfast and London proved too much for a guerrilla army with few resources and little active support. It was internment that had really debilitated the campaign, and the reactivation of the Special Criminal Court was the *coup de grâce*. The second factor was that, as the results of the general election confirmed, the campaign had failed ultimately to capture the public imagination: implicit in any campaign led by a vanguard is that a much wider section of the public will join its struggle. The ascendancy of the socialist wing of the IRA was also beginning to make itself felt and would pull the IRA away from armed activity and towards socio-economic agitation for the remainder of the 1960s.[16] What had kept the campaign from success according to the IRA itself was 'the attitude of the general public whose minds have been deliberately distracted from the supreme issue facing the Irish people—the unity and freedom of Ireland.'

LEMASS AND O'NEILL

The logic of Lemass's new economic policy suggested that stronger ties should be developed with Ireland's nearest trading partner, Britain, and, more controversially, with Northern Ireland. Lemass had attempted to meet the Northern Prime Minister, Lord Brookeborough, but the latter rebuffed all efforts at formal conferences or economic co-operation. Tariff walls had reduced North–South trade to a trickle. In 1963 the South exported £34.6 million of goods by land to the North while importing £21.8 million.[17] Lemass sought a comprehensive trade agreement with the British Government; and a *rapprochement* with the Northern Government was a logical step in that direction.

In his initial declaration of policy as Taoiseach, Lemass had defined the problem of restoring national unity as one of 'breaking down the barriers of suspicion, antagonism, prejudice and misunderstanding' that divided 'a minority in the north east from their fellow countrymen.'

> Anything which tends to break or lower these barriers is good; anything which tends to raise or strengthen them is bad. I think it is as simple as that, and certainly that outlook will continue to settle our policy and determine our actions.[18]

This was a clear articulation of a policy based on common sense and neighbourly co-operation. The contradiction that neither Lemass nor his successor, Jack Lynch, managed to reconcile was that, by this new criterion, drawing attention to the legitimate grievances of the Northern nationalist community served also to antagonise the Unionist regime and to raise the barriers dividing the Dublin and Belfast governments. Thus, in an effort to ingratiate itself with the Belfast Government and promote comprehensive economic arrangements it de-emphasised the plight of Northern nationalists during these vital years in which an early resolution of the civil rights issue might just have defused the time bomb that was to explode in 1969.

Lemass had put his faith in the EEC, and, possibly in an effort to popularise this idea, he said that, after joint membership by Ireland and Britain, partition would 'become so obviously an anachronism that all sensible people will want to bring it to an end.'[19] The Northern Minister of Finance, Terence O'Neill, had countered by saying that 'Northern Ireland will no more become part of the Irish Republic if Éire joins the Common Market than Yorkshire will become a German province.'[20]

Shortly after O'Neill's election as Prime Minister, Lemass repeated his 'willingness to meet at any level without preconditions,'[21] and he made the following declaration, which was nothing short of an invitation:

> I do not think there can be any misunderstanding regarding my willingness to meet the Prime Minister at any time to discuss practical problems of common interest and methods of co-operation to solve them and I would welcome an indication that Captain O'Neill would be prepared to talk over such matters.[22]

Possibly Lemass's most important speech was one made in Tralee in which he argued that 'a new situation would develop' from 'the extension of useful contacts at every level of activity,' and that, in essence, 'the solution of the problem of partition is one to be found in Ireland by Irishmen.' In the same speech he demonstrated a growing impatience that, after O'Neill had been in power four months, his overtures were not finding a response.

> The efforts which appeared to be developing spontaneously for contact and discussion are now being countered by a new gimmick called 'constitutional recognition.' That this is just a gimmick—an excuse for inaction—is, I am sure, recognised by those who use it.[23]

O'Neill, for his part, responded in roughly the same quantities of respect and derision. He called for an end to 'public statements either in Ireland or abroad about the "ultimate reunification of our country," the "evil of partition," the "Six County area" and similar subjects.' He remonstrated: 'Talk will not of itself change things . . . There is more to the winds of change than hot air.'[24] On another occasion he claimed that 'the people of Londonderry and the people of Ulster would do very ill to exchange their hopes of prosperity for a tattered green banner and a snatch of an old song carried away by the wind.'[25] However, he appeared to leave the door open to possible constructive dialogue, but he insisted that 'only in mutual respect and absence of recrimination and an atmosphere of true friendliness can any real progress be made.'[26]

On the surface, things appeared to take a turn for the worse during 1964, and there seemed to be a return to the megaphone diplomacy that had characterised the exchanges of North and South for decades.[27] But behind the scenes both T. K. Whitaker, Secretary of the Department of Finance, and his Northern counterpart, Jim Malley, worked diligently at securing a common basis for a meeting of their respective prime ministers. Some signs of a new departure were evident in statements issued on New Year's Eve 1964 by Brian Faulkner (Minister of Commerce and Production) and Jack Lynch (Minister for Industry and Commerce), who had professed an interest in meeting each other to discuss trade barriers.[28]

Two weeks later Lemass accepted an invitation by O'Neill to visit Stormont to participate in what would be a historic meeting between the two leaders.[29] In a confidential document prepared for the British Government, the Secretary of the Northern Government, Cecil Bateman, stated that the discussion was 'conducted in a most amicable atmosphere.' Political and constitutional questions were 'not at issue,' and this was 'fully accepted' by both sides. The theme was rather 'the possibility of co-operation on purely practical matters, particularly in the economic field.' Given that the official meeting took less than an hour and covered almost a dozen issues, it is not surprising that it was a purely cursory exploration of possibilities. Indeed Bateman noted that 'no final conclusion' was reached on any of the issues raised and that the discussion was a 'preliminary *tour d'horizon*.'[30]

After the talks the prime ministers issued a two-line statement that declared that they had 'discussed matters in which there may prove to be a degree of common interest.' The talks 'did not touch on constitutional issues.'[31] O'Neill had greeted Lemass by welcoming him 'to the North,' thus avoiding any embarrassment that might arise from being welcomed to 'Northern Ireland'. The most revealing exchange, however, occurred when Lemass confided to O'Neill that he would 'get into terrible trouble for this,' to which O'Neill promptly replied: 'Oh, no, Mr. Lemass, it is I who shall get into trouble for this.'[32] Events were to prove him right.

Lemass's initial public response to the event was cautious. The meeting was 'significant,' though 'its significance should not be exaggerated.'[33] Such was the public acclamation that accompanied the visit, however, that by the following day it was considered to be of 'tremendous significance,' and Lemass claimed that 'things can never be the same again.'[34]

As the weeks passed he became more audacious. In a speech to a Fianna Fáil cumann in Dún Laoghaire he reaffirmed that 'our aim is to reunite the Irish people in one nation and one state,' and 'our method is to remove the barriers of misunderstanding and prejudice which have divided the Irish people in the past.'[35]

In an interview with the *Irish Times*, O'Neill countered suggestions by some people that the meeting was a step on the road to reunification.

> I have already made it clear that the constitutional position of Northern Ireland is not open to discussion. It is quite ridiculous to think that, because I meet someone on a friendly basis, we intend to leave the United Kingdom . . . I think it is important that this is accepted in Dublin. The sooner it is accepted and understood the better, for I would not like to see erroneous impressions formed down there.[36]

When asked whether North-South relations would be improved if censorship regulations in the South were eased and the prohibitions on birth control and divorce were lifted, O'Neill replied that

> moves such as those would be welcomed here as indications of a liberalisation of attitude, but I would not like anyone to think that they would make Northern Ireland leave the United Kingdom. I seem to keep on stressing this point, but you see, the inference in questions like this is that if the South makes certain changes, we will be encouraged to unite with it. Well, it is complete and utter rubbish to think that the border is going to fall suddenly like the Walls of Jericho . . . I found Mr Lemass most realistic about this.

O'Neill was equally unimpressed by suggestions that the North might enter a federal relationship with the Republic should it rejoin the Commonwealth. He stressed the importance of the British welfare state and said that he could see 'no economic advantage in joining with Éire.'

Functional co-operation had been contemplated in 1925 when the governments in London, Dublin and Belfast signed a tripartite agreement following the report of the ill-fated Boundary Commission. Since that time there had been sporadic contact between the Northern and Southern governments, though the Foyle Fisheries Authority, a cross-border body established in 1952, stood as a lone and innocuous example of what such co-operation could achieve. Other proposals in the field of tourism and transport had met with political rather than economic objections from the Unionist Government.[37]

A proposal to make the two parts of Ireland a free-trade area was discussed by the Northern Government throughout 1959, but it also came up against hard-line resistance.[38] In his latter years de Valera had made it clear that he would be willing at any time to have talks with the Stormont Government, but not on the basis of recognising Northern Ireland.[39] Terence O'Neill's incumbency in 1963 provided the catalyst, as O'Neill did not insist on this precondition but was quietly satisfied that the visit constituted *de facto* (if not *de jure*) recognition. O'Neill told the Northern House of Commons that, as he attached less importance to pieces of paper than to action, he had come to the conclusion that 'if Mr Lemass was prepared to drive through the gates of Stormont and to meet me here as Prime Minister of Northern Ireland he was accepting the plain fact of our existence and our jurisdiction here.'[40] He said that 'the benefits for which I look are not entirely, or even mainly, practical': instead he hoped that the exchanges would alter 'many of the myths about Northern Ireland current in the South,' which were 'misconceptions based on ignorance.'[41]

In Lemass's Government, only Neil Blaney argued that Stormont had been legitimised.[42] The issue was largely glossed over in the media, though Sinn Féin claimed that the visit constituted both *de facto* and *de jure* recognition.[43] Speaking to the College Historical Society of Trinity College, Dublin, on the motion that 'the Easter Rising stands betrayed,' Hugh McAteer, a former IRA chief of staff, described 'the long-sought recognition of Stormont' as 'the greatest betrayal of all.'[44] The diplomatic correspondent of the *Irish Times* wrote that 'whatever the feeling in Dublin, it will certainly be accepted in Belfast that some form of recognition has been granted.'[45] It was also considered significant that the Government Information Bureau's official statement referred to O'Neill as the 'Prime Minister of Northern Ireland'.[46]

There was one immediate, tangible result that O'Neill could present to his supporters. The leader of the Nationalist Party, Eddie McAteer, had travelled to Dublin to be urged by Lemass to agree to the Nationalist Party assuming the role of official opposition in Stormont.[47] Though McAteer supported Lemass publicly,[48] it was with more resignation than optimism that he agreed that Nationalist MPs would become the official opposition for the first time. (It is worth noting that these MPs had taken an oath of allegiance not dissimilar to the one that had caused such consternation within Fianna Fáil decades earlier.) McAteer recounted that

in my role as leader of the Nationalist people, I made many trips to Dublin, some publicised, some private, for talks and consultations with Dublin ministers. I got hospitality but little real support. There was less than enthusiasm to get involved. The Unionists, not knowing that, again missed the chance to woo us. When I returned home after my post-O'Neill talk with the Taoiseach I was more worried than ever. I got neither the encouragement nor understanding of our position that I expected. Lemass said that it appeared to him that Catholics in the North were just as intractable as the Protestants. It was hardly the reaction I expected from a Taoiseach with his Republican background to the representative of the oppressed Irish minority in the six counties. The Taoiseach expressed the opinion that industrial progress in the twenty-six counties would help bring the Unionists towards a united Ireland. I did not share his optimism and was surprised to hear such a naive opinion from a man who had been born into revolution. I came away with the conviction that as far as Seán Lemass was concerned, the Northern Irish were very much on their own.[49]

Brian Feeney has used the term 'unrequited love' to describe the relationship between Northern nationalists and their fellow-countrymen in the South.[50] Despite nationalist criticisms of the Government's performance on partition, Fianna Fáil was spared public censure because of a desire to maintain Northern nationalists' morale. 'There was a feeling, certainly in the fifties,' Feeney recalls, 'that you shouldn't be criticising the Irish Government.' Such public criticisms left one open to recriminations within one's own community and gave succour to the Unionist government.

> You could criticise it privately but you didn't wash dirty linen in public . . . No one knew unless they visited the Republic how little people cared, and hardly believed it when they found out . . . Eddie McAteer would go down to Dublin in the fifties, or for that matter in the early sixties to speak to de Valera or Seán Lemass and be told 'Well there's nothing we can do about it. You'll just have to find ways of managing up there.' . . . When the northern nationalists came down to remind [de Valera] that 'England's difficulty is Ireland's opportunity' . . . de Valera said, 'No it isn't. There is nothing I would do to damage the integrity of the 26 County State.' So you knew that was the case, and it was disappointing, but you tried to pretend that it wasn't true, that really the Government and the people there were interested and wanted to do things for you.[51]

For some, such as a young Paddy McGrory, the need to believe that the Irish Government took an active interest in the plight of Northern nationalists was strong.

> I went to Dublin feeling a great pride that this was our capital. I would have listened to the Easter speeches [in Belfast] and believed [them] . . . The average nationalist identified with all of that, that they really cared about us. It was important. Without it, I don't know what would have happened. Either you would have been driven into the arms of the IRA, or you would have become so disillusioned as to say, 'Oh well, if that's the way it is, let's *be* British, at least we'll get a job out of it.' It had a greatly sustaining effect on Northern Nationalism.[52]

The belief in a vigilant Dublin Government actively promoting the rights of its separated brethren was a comforting one. As one former editor of the *Derry Journal*, Frank Curran, recalled, Northern nationalists

> scrupulously projected, for Unionist consumption, the view that Dublin automatically sided and sympathised with them. The assumption that Dublin identified with the Northern minority was a telling factor in bolstering Catholic morale, while ensuring Unionist caution about what would happen if their extremists ever

launched an all-out assault on the Catholic community. In fact, this Dublin 'guarantee' of Northern minority rights was no guarantee at all. It was a myth, pure and simple.[53]

The new *détente* between Fianna Fáil and the Northern Government exacerbated existing difficulties for the Nationalist Party. Moderate nationalists had always had to fend off the challenges of more radical elements within the Northern nationalist community. As the avenues for effective constitutional action were greatly circumscribed by anti-nationalist prejudice and unionism's built-in permanent majority, the Nationalist Party had traditionally looked to Dublin for support. Now it was confronted with a Fianna Fáil Government that viewed it as a burdensome liability in its efforts to secure new economic alliances and to enhance relations between Dublin and Belfast. The Nationalist Party's obvious impotence made it increasingly vulnerable to being outflanked by an emergent civil rights movement that used more direct and radical means to forward its objectives.

In the aftermath of Lemass's visit to Stormont there was an intense but brief flurry of inter-governmental meetings. Brian Faulkner travelled to Dublin, again in complete secrecy, to meet Jack Lynch and Erskine Childers (Minister for Transport and Power).[54] A week later the Ministers for Agriculture, Neil Blaney and Harry West, also met.[55] In between the two visits Lemass and O'Neill met again, this time in Dublin; Jack Lynch and Frank Aiken (Minister for External Affairs) were also in attendance with their departmental secretaries.[56]

Despite the choreography, functional co-operation created little of enduring value. Though they were considered historic at the time, the most significant effect of these meetings was to undermine further the leadership of Terence O'Neill and to set in train events that would lead to open conflict in 1969.

Basking in popular acclamation, Lemass called a general election within a month of O'Neill's return visit to Dublin. After the rather unassured performance of 1961, Lemass was now considered an electoral asset, and the campaign was highly personalised, suggesting that he had the magic touch. The title of Fianna Fáil, 'the Republican Party', was replaced with a new description: Fianna Fáil, 'the Party of Reality'.[57] On 7 April, Lemass did not get the absolute majority he had hoped for, but he had the support of exactly half the members of the new Dáil, which was enough to carry on.

The 1965 ard-fheis in mid-November did not dwell on partition. There was the traditional resolution reaffirming that 'the territorial re-unification of Ireland' was 'the primary aim of national endeavour',[58] but Lemass devoted his speech to economic matters, in particular to the EEC and to the new free trade agreement with Britain.[59]

'THE CORKMAN'S BURDEN'

The campaign slogan of the 1965 election, 'Let Lemass lead on,' was deceptive, as Lemass had no intention of leading for much longer and was turning his mind to the thorny issue of the leadership succession, the first that would not involve a representative of the revolutionary generation. When Lemass took office, eight of the thirteen members of the Government had fought in the Civil War. In six years this number had been reduced to three: Aiken, MacEntee and Lemass himself. While there were many pretenders to the throne, none of the possible candidates commanded universal support within the party. Lemass had fostered a Government laden with new ministerial talent, and their competence was equalled only by their ambition. As befitted the Taoiseach who introduced competitiveness to the Irish economy, Lemass encouraged and rewarded ambition, thus promoting a sense of competition among his ministers. He frankly explained this policy and the difficulties it inevitably presented when the question of his successor arose.

> If the Taoiseach begins to indicate whom he wants as successor then, of course, it could be discouraging to a lot of people who felt that they could grow to take the office. This is a very difficult decision to take; to sort of indicate who was going to be the choice of the retiring Taoiseach as successor, because everybody's entitled to feel the office is open to him, providing he works hard enough, providing he's good enough.[60]

Jack Lynch also noted this feature of the Lemass style of leadership.

> He had frequently spoken of Government Departments as 'development corporations', which in itself implied a degree of independent initiative. He had also wanted to create the opportunities for ministers to show their individual flair and enterprise prior to the change of leadership which he, almost alone, knew was in the offing before it was generally expected.[61]

Lemass, therefore, never discouraged any of his younger ministers from harbouring aspirations to the highest office in the country. This policy, while paying dividends in ministerial performance, produced a Government with almost as many potential leaders as members. It also encouraged the formation of factions, some of which were ideologically irreconcilable. Lemass was not oblivious to these facts, and in an effort to promote unity within the party he approached Jack Lynch in mid-September, eight weeks before his retirement, and asked him whether he would be interested in succeeding him. Lynch emphatically rejected the offer, and he believed that Lemass accepted and understood this decision. However, some weeks later he was again summoned to the Taoiseach's office, this time in the company of Charles Haughey and George Colley. Lynch reiterated that the position of party leader held no appeal for him; but he recalled that the other two ministers 'seemed to indicate that they were interested.'[62]

Lynch would be approached on several occasions after this meeting, but he steadfastly refused to entertain ambitions for the leadership. Lemass leaked the news of his imminent retirement to Michael Mills of the *Irish Press* in the hope that an atmosphere would be created in which a natural successor, preferably Lynch, would 'emerge' before his official announcement.[63] It failed to produce the desired result; instead the parliamentary party was thrown into panic, and the Government was forced to deny the story; Mills was even pressured to retract it.[64]

When, a week later, Lemass announced his retirement, Haughey and Colley immediately declared their interest. They were very much products of the Lemass period, though they differed greatly in personality and political outlook. Neither enjoyed the confidence or support of a clear majority of the party. Haughey's campaign manager, Donogh O'Malley, was another of the Fianna Fáil young bloods who oozed flamboyance and bonhomie in the same quantity that Haughey displayed intellect and aggression. Jim Gibbons, who had yet to carve out a niche within the party, nominated and managed Colley. Had the contest remained a two-horse race it seems unlikely that Lemass would have made any further efforts to entice Lynch to seek the nomination; however, Kevin Boland was unhappy that there was no 'republican' candidate. He distrusted Haughey's acquisitiveness and personal ambition but found little in Colley to recommend itself.

Despite Colley's and Boland's shared sense of traditional values and their support for the use of Irish, Boland thought that Colley had insufficient interest in Fianna Fáil's 'first national aim.' He therefore approached Neil Blaney and persuaded him to let his name go forward while offering his services as campaign manager.[65] Blaney's intervention changed everything, including O'Malley's loyalty to Haughey, and he promptly switched his allegiance to Blaney.[66]

There were now three powerful ministers in the contest, each representing an influential faction within the party, and it was a distinct possibility that the new leader could be elected without obtaining the formal approval of a majority of parliamentary party deputies. Lemass summoned Lynch once again to his office. Three delegations of party elders, mainly from Munster, had visited both Lemass and Lynch and stressed the importance of maintaining party unity, arguably Fianna Fáil's greatest electoral asset. According to Lynch, the deputies 'strongly pressed the case for getting me to stand as the sole contender, saying that I had clear majority support . . . that as I had remained aloof from the fray I was not a divisive force within the party.'[67]

Lemass was eager to see a smooth transfer of power to the post-revolutionary generation, and this time he was not willing to accept Lynch's apathy and self-deprecation. When Lynch made his anticipated refusal Lemass pointed out that he 'owed the party a duty to serve, even as leader.' He told Lynch that he had spoken to the other three candidates and that they had agreed to withdraw in Lynch's favour. Still Lynch equivocated. He promised Lemass that he would consider his proposition, but he would first have to ask his wife. According to Lynch, he went home to his wife, and they decided 'after a long and agonising discussion that I would let my name go before the party.'[68]

Haughey and Blaney immediately withdrew; but Colley decided to stand in opposition to Lynch. As Fianna Fáil had never conducted a leadership contest before, the rule book laying down procedures had to be consulted. The votes were counted in a green shoe-box that the chief whip, Michael Carty, had picked up from a shop.[69] There were 52 votes for Lynch, 19 for Colley.

The new leader took up office 'knowing he didn't have anything like the same stature as his predecessors.'[70] According to Brian Farrell, Lynch appeared 'an inert government leader' who adopted 'a passive approach to leadership.'[71] He was perceived by many of his Government colleagues as a weak leader—someone who, as Neil Blaney put it, 'should never have been where he was.'[72] The attitude of the more charismatic hard-liners, such as Blaney and Boland, was akin to that of 'powerful medieval barons when faced by a rather weak monarch.'[73] Unlike de Valera and

Lemass, Lynch 'never achieved a position of dominance in the party,' and it seemed to many observers that 'he was unable to impose authority on the cabinet, and that Ministers were taking advantage by pursuing their own, often unwise, pet schemes.'[74]

Lynch's succession also marked a radical departure from collective responsibility, and it began a process whereby the Taoiseach presided over what was virtually a coalition Government—a change that would have serious consequences for its Northern policy.

LYNCH'S FIRST ARD-FHEIS

Within a few days of his election as Taoiseach, Lynch faced the challenge of addressing his first ard-fheis as party leader. As few rank-and-file party members were aware of his views on a wide range of policy areas, the ard-fheis presented a perfect opportunity for him to ingratiate himself with the grass roots and to present his vision of what Fianna Fáil represented and how it would achieve its objectives.

Lynch's presidential address contained all the elements that had made Fianna Fáil Ireland's archetypal *volkspartei*. It was 'the only real farmers' party this country has ever had,' but it was also the party of industry, and it was the friend of the trade unions and pledged to serve 'the special interests of workers.'[75] It was, in fact, the friend of everyone, pledged to serve the interests of every section of the population, no matter how conflicting those interests might be. It was 'the party of development, the party of ideas, the party which has been, and intends to remain, in the vanguard of progress in every sphere.'

Lack of progress in Fianna Fáil's national aims was not attributed to a dearth of ideas but to the intrigues of those who did not share the party's national vision. There were the 'enemies of the language' (Irish), who had taken succour from Fine Gael's recent policy document, which had been interpreted as 'a signal of retreat.' Indeed Lynch derived great mileage from the issue of Irish, despite the fact that in his entire address only one sentence of Irish passed his lips.

A similar divergence between rhetoric and reality was illustrated by Lynch's treatment of 'the other unrealised national purpose,' that of restoring Irish unity. The Lemass-O'Neill meetings represented a 'real breakthrough,' he said, and confirmed Fianna Fáil's reputation for 'exploring new paths, probing new ideas and breaking new ground.' Again this brief section was marked more by platitudes than by a description of how the recent 'breakthrough' could be consolidated, or surpassed. There was no attempt to ascertain why Fianna Fáil had so conspicuously failed to achieve its first national aim after thirty years in power.

For those who thought his election as Taoiseach would mark a new departure from the policies of de Valera and Lemass on the North, Lynch had this to say:

> My election as Taoiseach, it has been said, marks the end of an era. Perhaps in a sense it does. But if there are any who think that for Fianna Fáil it will mean a slackening off or a slowing down they would do well to think again. Let us here tonight, together rededicate and pledge ourselves anew to accelerate and intensify our efforts to keep Fianna Fáil in the van of the nation's advance and so take another great leap forward . . .

James Connolly was then quoted, and the conference was over. Few of the party faithful could dispute Lynch's assertion that Fianna Fáil had 'set forth its aims with clarity and simplicity' or could have doubted the merits of his exhortation to 'work without rest or hesitation or doubt for their fulfilment.' There were not many, however, who could claim that they had been armed with instructions for how these elusive national aims could be attained and could cease to be aspirations to which they would merely rededicate themselves annually.

The *Irish Times* in its editorial recognised the tactical nature of Lynch's speech, with its transparent aim of demonstrating his republicanism to the party organisation: it was 'an obvious congress speech, it consolidates his base, it proves that he is well grounded in all the party tenets; he has reinforced his image as a solid man with nothing new-fangled about him.'[76] The constant predictions of impending breakthroughs, combined with the ill-defined nature of Fianna Fáil's policies, provoked the satirical John Healy to encapsulate Fianna Fáil policy as 'the corner around which everything lies.' The party was always on the brink of a great achievement, despite the exertions of opportunists and 'West-Britons'. The widening chasm between concept and execution was never acknowledged; instead the party pledged that it would fight to retain the right to fight for its national aims.

FUNCTIONAL CO-OPERATION

Despite the frequently declared urgency in fulfilling the first national aim, the policy of functional co-operation that Lemass had inaugurated was not pursued with noticeable alacrity by his successor. During his first press conference, on 17 November 1966, Lynch had expressed a wish to meet Terence O'Neill whenever such a meeting was convenient. Lynch's belief in O'Neill's integrity and good intentions was unmistakable.

> I think he is a most enlightened man who is striving hard for co-operation among all the people of the North. He is a man who does not approach questions in an emotional way but in a rational and intelligent way, and this should make for progress.[77]

When asked about anti-Catholic discrimination in the North, Lynch replied that he was aware that there had been discrimination, but he was confident that steps were now being taken to rectify the situation. This view was not substantiated by reference to a single piece of legislation that had been enacted to challenge—let alone eliminate —discrimination or by any reference to the collective effect that the Lockwood, Wilson and Matthew Reports had had in entrenching discrimination. It appeared that Lynch, like many of his contemporaries, had erroneously equated visits to Catholic schools with the removal of institutionalised discrimination. A more benign interpretation, however, would be that Lynch was aware of O'Neill's internal party difficulties and did not want to press him on the issue of civil rights. To present civil rights for nationalists as the price that would have to be paid for cross-border co-operation might strengthen unionist opposition to the policy of functional co-operation and would therefore be counter-productive.

Lynch was careful to sidestep some of the more contentious questions regarding Northern policy. When asked if he would raise the issue of partition during his forthcoming meeting with the British Prime Minister, Harold Wilson, he replied that he could not reveal his agenda. This satisfied party supporters, but it did little to assuage the fears of unionists who believed that Taoisigh used such meetings to obtain secret commitments from disinterested British prime ministers to 'hand over' the North. With a Labour Prime Minister these fears were heightened.

On the question of seeking UN intervention in the North, Lynch employed a similar tactic of coy evasion: he did not rule out such a possibility, but he suggested that Frank Aiken, as Minister for External Affairs, would be better able to judge its merits. This response was illuminating, as it suggested that Lynch would not be the one to formulate such an important aspect of Northern policy. However, by refusing to deny that such a proposal was an option he once again satisfied party activists while causing unnecessary fears to develop among unionists, as the idea of raising the issue of partition at the United Nations had never been considered within the Government during the 1960s.[78]

There was one question that Lynch had little difficulty in rejecting as an unrealistic proposition: the inclusion of Nationalist members of the Northern Parliament in the Dáil—an issue that had plagued de Valera but had become a non-starter by the 1960s. Lynch was careful, however, to couch his refusal in terms that suggested that his objection was based not on principle but on practical difficulties that would be impossible to overcome. He also expressed his willingness to meet Nationalist MPs; to emphasise the point, he revealed that he had already met the Derry representative Patrick Gormley earlier the same day. Lynch believed that membership of the Common Market would help break down barriers between North and South. He welcomed the Nationalist Party's decision to become the official opposition in the Northern Parliament, arguing that this would ameliorate inter-community relations.

Somewhat naïvely, Lynch did not agree that his declared aim of Irish reunification would act as a barrier to cordial relations with his Northern counterpart. 'We know that . . . O'Neill has not changed his attitude,' Lynch declared, 'and he knows that we still maintain our position that the Border is unnatural.' Journalists described Lynch's first press conference as a success and noted that on the North the new Taoiseach 'remained probably even more doctrinaire than Lemass on fundamental attitudes.'[79]

The biggest obstacle to securing a 'mutually convenient' date for a meeting between the two prime ministers was truculence within the O'Neill Cabinet. Some unionist ministers believed that until the Republic reduced trade tariffs there was little on the economic front to discuss, while the more obdurate among them suggested that Lynch would have to renounce his ambition to abolish partition before a further meeting could be considered.[80] As this was as likely as O'Neill abjuring his unionism, such suggestions sought in effect to scupper the cross-border talks. O'Neill would have to move cautiously in attempting to consolidate the cross-border co-operation process without alienating his support. He sought advance approval for a meeting with Lynch, and when the decision was collectively agreed it was left to O'Neill to choose the most propitious date.

However, the first meeting between Lynch and O'Neill did not take place until 11 December 1967, more than a year after Lynch's election as Taoiseach and almost three years since the previous meeting with Lemass.[81] Because of criticism over the secrecy that had surrounded Lemass's visit, O'Neill released news of the visit as Lynch crossed the border. The news travelled quickly, and when his car passed the statue of Edward Carson at Stormont it came under a sustained snowball attack from Ian Paisley and a handful of Free Presbyterian ministers.[82]

Lynch was accompanied by the Secretary of the Department of Finance, T. K. Whitaker, and the Secretary of the Government, Nicholas Nolan, but no Dublin ministers were present. O'Neill, for his part, had made the astute move of including in the meeting his main Cabinet rival, Brian Faulkner, to stymie any attempts by Faulkner to claim that he had not been privy to decisions reached. James Chichester-Clark also participated, as Minister of Agriculture, to discuss the problem of foot-and-mouth disease.

All O'Neill's ministers were invited to the informal lunch with Lynch that followed the meeting. The discussion ranged over such issues as tourism, electricity supply and trade (though the *Irish Times* reported that 'undoubtedly the most urgent topic is the foot and mouth threat').[83] Lynch claimed that the meeting was 'a very useful, successful and happy opportunity to talk about various matters.' O'Neill declared that the discussions had taken place in an 'extremely happy' atmosphere. Before leaving for Dublin, Lynch assured reporters that there had been no discussion of *de jure* recognition of Northern Ireland by the Republic, to which O'Neill added: 'We never talk about that sort of thing.'

The meeting was generally welcomed in the South, though enthusiasm was tinged with disappointment that it had not occurred earlier and about the extremely limited scope of the discussions. The consensus among the opposition parties was that it was no longer sufficient to establish a formal point of contact, as this was a bridge that had already been crossed by Lemass: the time had come to move beyond symbolism and to address substantive issues in a more rigorous fashion. Opposition parties were adamant that, irrespective of the economic benefits of functional co-operation, the issue of anti-Catholic discrimination should not continue to be ignored. Liam Cosgrave (leader of Fine Gael, son of W. T. Cosgrave) and Brendan Corish (leader of the Labour Party) were vociferous on this point, with Cosgrave declaring that the cross-border discussions should not 'push into the background or under the carpet the very serious infringements of democratic rights of those who are broadly described as the nationalists of the Six Counties.'[84] Speaking on behalf of the Labour Party, Michael O'Leary accused the Government of abdicating its responsibility for defending nationalist rights and of applying insufficient pressure on the British and Northern Governments to ensure equality of treatment and freedom from arbitrary discrimination. He felt that

> there is nothing extreme in our request that ordinary democratic rights should be the equal possession of every citizen in the Six Counties. If we do not get results through this so-called liberal wave that is supposed to be swamping the Unionist Party, then we have our remedy in going to the British Government.[85]

In December 1967 Lemass made a speech in Queen's University, Belfast, in which, much to the consternation of nationalists, he criticised politicians on both sides for relying on the religious affiliation of constituents rather than on social and economic policies; he also criticised the 'narrow attitudes' of the Nationalist Party.[86] It was a particularly infelicitous remark, symptomatic of the 'one side is as bad as the other' view that now seemed to colour official Fianna Fáil thinking on the North. Partition had institutionalised a sectarian division and had made normal politics impossible. The Nationalist Party could, and did, put forward economic and social policies, but interest in these issues was diluted by the certain knowledge that the party would never be in a position to implement them, being condemned to permanent subordination. Even in local government, gerrymandering and disenfranchisement deprived nationalists of seats; when privately questioned by the British Government, Unionist leaders claimed that they 'did not accept [that] universal franchise was necessarily the best method of voting.'[87]

The Northern Government—which, under permanent one-party rule, set the political agenda—never encouraged discussion of socio-economic issues lest they blur the supremacy of the constitutional question, which guaranteed Unionist power in perpetuity. Indeed proportional representation had been unilaterally abolished in 1929 so as to polarise Northern politics and to prevent the emergence of any third force, such as labour parties or rival unionist parties. When labour movements attempted to inject a dose of economic thinking into the stale constitutional debate they were condemned as crypto-republicans, communists or traitors. Similarly, during the brief moments when Catholics and Protestants united to combat economic deprivation, as in 1932 and 1935, the regime assiduously promoted the division by stressing constitutional issues and the advantages of a sectarian labour aristocracy.[88]

For decades the Fianna Fáil leadership had understood all this; but now Northern nationalists were being told that they were just as culpable as unionists (the British Government curiously escaped responsibility) for the sectarian structure of Northern Ireland. The criticism of relying on sectarian support was also ironic, coming from a party that for many years had promoted elections as occasions for reaffirming old loyalties rather than as opportunities for appraising conflicting economic policies.

The Nationalist Party leader, Eddie McAteer, travelled to Dublin to make his views known on the drift between the Irish Government and the Northern nationalist community; but it was symptomatic of the new North-South axis that he was unable to meet Lynch and had to content himself with meeting a civil servant. He confided to the Secretary of the Government, Nicholas Nolan, that he would be 'greatly disturbed' if Lemass's speech reflected official Government policy. He had come to express his concern at 'the widening gulf that seems to exist between the South and Nationalists in the Six Counties' and at the fact that 'the Nationalists feel that they are now nobody's children.'[89] It was disheartening for nationalists, he said, to read of a stream of ministerial meetings between Dublin ministers and their Northern counterparts while similar encounters with nationalist representatives were rebuffed.

The remedial action he proposed was very modest. It amounted to occasional meetings between McAteer and the Taoiseach; the Nationalist Party would also appreciate courtesy invitations when Dáil ministers visited their counterparts in

Belfast for a meeting—a proposal most probably aimed at renewing contacts but also at giving Dublin ministers the opportunity to hear nationalist concerns after they had participated in a meeting with exclusively Unionist representatives. McAteer also suggested that the initiative for meetings with the Taoiseach should come from Lynch, 'as the bigger man.' This was probably motivated by a desire to avoid the embarrassment of petitioning the Taoiseach for a meeting only to be spurned on arrival in Dublin. In the case of Government ministers travelling to Stormont there was the added factor that such excursions had been conducted in secrecy, and a minister could have departed for Dublin without the visit coming to the attention of the Nationalist Party, so making a formal request from their side impossible.

However, McAteer's attempt to rebuild the bridge between Northern nationalists and the Irish Government came to nothing. When Lynch brought the issue to the attention of the Government on 8 December he decided, without encountering any dissent, that if McAteer wanted to meet him he should take the initiative. There the matter rested.

Whereas popular sentiment united most Irish people with their kin in the North, and partition remained an emotive issue never far below the surface, there was a new relationship of power between the Dublin and Belfast governments. Northern nationalists, powerless within Northern Ireland, found that they had no place in this new arrangement. Not only had McAteer not been told in advance of the Lemass-O'Neill meeting but the rationale for rapprochement with Stormont had not been spelt out. McAteer was disappointed too that, after persuading the Nationalist Party to take up the role of official opposition in Stormont (with no tangible rewards from the Unionists), he was not offered a separate meeting. At the very time when nationalists' frustration was rising, their party leaders were ignored by Dublin (as well as by the usual deaf ears in Belfast). A new generation would soon push McAteer and the old Nationalist Party aside, and it would insist on being heard.

Coinciding with Lemass's speech in December 1967 was another significant event that largely escaped the notice of the public and the media: the Report of the Committee on the Constitution. The report was largely a device to push through a recommendation to abolish proportional representation[90]; but as Kevin Boland sat down to read it on Christmas Eve his attention was drawn to a recommended change in article 3 of the Constitution. This article read:

> Pending the re-integration of the national territory, and without prejudice to the right of the Parliament and Government established by this Constitution to exercise jurisdiction over the whole of that territory, the laws enacted by that Parliament shall have the like area and extent of application as the laws of Saorstat Éireann and the like extra-territorial effect.

The committee stated that it had given 'careful consideration to the wording of this provision,' and it felt that it would 'now be appropriate to adopt a new provision to replace Article 3.' The suggested replacement was:

1.   The Irish nation hereby proclaims its firm will that its territory be re-united in harmony and brotherly affection between all Irishmen.

2.   The laws enacted by the Parliament established by this Constitution shall, until the achievement of the nation's unity shall otherwise require, have the like area and extent of application as the laws of the Parliament which existed prior to the adoption of this Constitution. Provision may be made by law to give extra-territorial effect to such laws.[91]

To Boland the Constitution of Ireland had not been a hastily conceived document but was the fruit of five years of Fianna Fáil's efforts to replace the provisions of the Anglo-Irish Treaty of 1921. In particular, articles 1–3 were considered to be a repudiation of the Report of the Boundary Commission (1925), and they represented a direct challenge to the British Government's claim to jurisdiction over Northern Ireland. To unilaterally remove the provision in article 3 that referred to the right of the Dáil to legislate for the whole country would, Boland believed, be tantamount to recognising the British claim to the North. His suspicions were aroused by the fact that—unlike practically every other recommendation—no reasons were offered for the proposed change.

Boland's misgivings were accentuated by the fact that the proposed change to article 3 did not appear in the advance copies of extracts from the report that were circulated to the media. These copies contained the extracts that the committee considered important, and whatever media and public comment there was had concentrated on those elements. Boland suspected that the committee was attempting to put forward the proposal surreptitiously and with a minimum of public debate.

According to Boland, the Fianna Fáil members of the committee were 'very raw' and, with the exception of George Colley, were 'complete novices.' Colley was himself only a 'minor solicitor', and Boland believed that the delegation was overawed by the legal expertise of other members, such as T. F. O'Higgins, a former Fine Gael presidential candidate and a future Supreme Court judge.[92] On his retirement from the Fianna Fáil leadership Lemass had joined the committee, but by this time most of the substantive deliberations had been completed, and he was eager to secure agreement that would pave the way for a referendum. The fact that, in their zeal to preserve Fianna Fáil's electoral supremacy by abolishing proportional representation, they were willing to contemplate tinkering with article 3 came as a shock to Boland, who considered the report to be 'the first formal public indication of the departure from basic Republican principles within the party.'[93]

Boland telephoned the secretary of Fianna Fáil's Ballyfermot comhairle ceantair on Christmas Day, informing him that he wished to make a public disavowal of the report, and they agreed that 2 January 1968 would be the earliest possible date. A Government meeting was due the morning before, and he decided to first raise the matter there. Accordingly, he gave a copy of his script to Lynch, adding that he believed it would be better if the Government as a whole rejected the recommendation. In his paper Boland stated that

the first thing this Committee recommend is that the people should be asked to formally renounce this claim. Members of Fianna Fáil, whose ard-fheis almost every year unanimously passes a resolution reaffirming the Nation's indefeasible right to the whole of the national territory have, I know, found this an amazing suggestion. Even more amazing, in my opinion, is the fact that—although the Committee in all other cases appear to have given reasons for their recommendation—no reason whatever is advanced as to why it is considered that now in 1967 the Irish people should formally renounce their historic claim to the whole national territory. It almost appears as if the Committee were naive enough to hope this proposal would slip through unnoticed, because instead of referring to it we have fifteen lines of claptrap about the Continental Shelf . . . No one, of course will object to the sentiment that 'its territory be re-united in harmony and brotherly affection between all Irishmen'. Fianna Fáil has always tried to bring about a 'union of wills' and it is generally accepted that it is by the promotion of harmonious relations and by mutual co-operation that progress will be made. That is, however, a long way from saying that we have arrived at a position where it is necessary or desirable that our claim to our national territory should be abandoned.[94]

Lynch was 'appalled at the prospect of one Minister publicly rejecting what had been recommended by another Minister.'[95] Indeed the potential embarrassment could hardly be more acute, considering that a former party leader had also participated in the committee's work. Boland in the end agreed to modify the tone of his statement while retaining its essence. Several hours were spent revising the script. He retained his position that the report only indicated that four Fianna Fáil TDs and two senators held these views, that nothing was known of the views of the rest of the party, and that there was 'no commitment whatsoever on our part to the views expressed in the report.' Though no explicit reference to article 3 was made, Boland concluded his speech by stating that 'our members' minds will be set at rest if they bear in mind the Aims of the party as laid down in the Corú and the many resolutions unanimously passed at successive ard fheiseanna.'

In the coming months Boland continued, in a number of carefully worded and carefully timed speeches, to remind party members of Fianna Fáil's fundamental aim and to repeat the importance of articles 2 and 3 for the constitutional expression of republicanism. For him article 3 was 'probably the most important article in the Constitution': it was 'an inherent principle of Fianna Fáil and if this was changed the Party would in effect be disestablished and there would be an immediate need for a new party.'[96]

Cross-border meetings continued in the month after Lynch's visit to Stormont. On 15 December 1966 James Chichester-Clark travelled to Dublin to meet Neil Blaney, and the two ministers for agriculture discussed precautionary measures against the spreading of foot-and-mouth disease from Britain.[97]

On 8 January 1968 O'Neill made his expected return visit to Dublin, which yielded many photo opportunities but few hard decisions.[98] Among the issues discussed were tourism, tariffs, the introduction of the metric system and exchanges of art collections. The subsequent communiqué conveyed the ceremonial and superficial nature of the discussions: 'It was agreed . . . that the utmost effect would continue to be given to the policy of co-operation in all these spheres.' O'Neill ruled out a tripartite meeting with the British Prime Minister, and he said that, while no plans had been made for further meetings, these could be arranged when necessary.[99] Neither Lynch nor O'Neill probably realised that there would never again be a bipartite meeting between prime ministers representing North and South.

THE CIVIL RIGHTS ASSOCIATION IN ACTION

While O'Neill and Lynch exchanged platitudes, the political temperature in the North was reaching boiling point. The organisation most associated in the public mind with the articulation of nationalist grievances was the Northern Ireland Civil Rights Association. Founded in January 1967, the NICRA initially concentrated on relatively passive activities, such as compiling statistical data and sending letters to political representatives. Its first eighteen months were uneventful, and only seventy people attended the organisation's first AGM, of whom almost half were known republicans or IRA members.[100] Realising that the NICRA's impact on Stormont was negligible, the association devised more radical initiatives. In February 1968 the Derry Housing Action Committee was established, and it adopted more radical means of drawing attention to the housing issue. The 'Caledon Affair' of 13 June 1968, when a large Catholic family was evicted from a council house in Caledon, Co. Tyrone, to make way for a nineteen-year-old single Protestant woman who was secretary to a local Unionist councillor, while by no means unique, received widespread publicity and gave renewed impetus to the civil rights campaign, not least because the Nationalist MP Austin Currie was then induced by local republicans to squat in the house. (He was removed by a member of the RUC who was the brother of the Protestant woman.)

Ciarán Mac an Ailí, a founder-member of the NICRA who practised as a solicitor in Dublin, had made a study of the tactic of civil disobedience so successfully employed in the United States by Martin Luther King Jr, and he had suggested as early as 1966 that this could be usefully applied in the North.[101] The strategy received endorsement in August 1968 when the NICRA Executive agreed to a protest march on 24 August from Coalisland to Dungannon. Ian Paisley immediately announced a counter-demonstration for the same date, and threatened violence if the march entered the Market Square in Dungannon. The chairman of the gerrymandered Dungannon Urban District Council, Senator William Stewart, and the local MP, John Taylor, demanded that the procession not be permitted to enter the centre of the town, and the RUC dutifully rerouted the march. Paisley mobilised 1,500 'Ulster Protestant Volunteers', many of them B Specials, who occupied Market Square during the day; but the anticipated confrontation never occurred.

The march of three thousand people, with approximately seventy republicans acting as stewards, halted at the RUC barrier. The speeches were moderate and of immediate relevance, and they were followed by a rendition of the American civil rights anthem 'We Shall Overcome'. The marchers dispersed peacefully, and there were no incidents. In 1969 the official inquiry into the causes of disturbances in the North, the Cameron Commission, would refer to the march as a historic event, and it emphasised the significance of the fact that

> this first Civil Rights march, unaccompanied by any provocative display of weapons, banners, or symbols was carried out without any breach of the peace. It

attracted considerable public attention and was also regarded as proof in certain circles that many elements in the society in Northern Ireland whose political purpose differed in very marked degree could co-operate in peaceful and lawful demonstration in favour of certain common and limited objectives.[102]

The NICRA had proved capable of mobilising significant numbers for direct action. More marches were planned, with greater numbers and with greater publicity. Sensing that nationalists were mobilising in opposition to the state, unionists redoubled their efforts in getting Stormont to act. O'Neill would come under tremendous pressure, squeezed between the demands of the civil rights protesters and his Cabinet ultras, now led by his erstwhile colleague William Craig. O'Neill reflected that,

> had we all known it, that unreported Civil Rights march was to be the start of something which would shake Northern Ireland to its foundations, split the ruling Unionist Party, and initiate more reforms in two years than I had thought possible in ten. Moreover, Westminster, our sovereign Parliament, had Northern Ireland thrust on its plate as never before since the Government of Ireland Act of 1920.[103]

The next march was planned for Derry, the most notorious site of unionist discrimination. Derry would be different.

THE END OF FUNCTIONAL CO-OPERATION

On 5 October 1968 two thousand civil rights supporters marched through the centre of Derry. At the front of the march were Eddie McAteer, Austin Currie, Gerry Fitt (Republican Labour MP in Stormont and Westminster) and three members of the Campaign for Democracy in Ulster, all of them British Labour Party MPs. The march was surrounded by the RUC, who then, in the words of the Cameron Commission, 'used their batons indiscriminately.'[104] The commission also found that both Fitt and McAteer, who were seriously assaulted (along with almost a hundred others), had been batoned 'wholly without justification or excuse.'[105]

Though events such as these were not uncommon in the history of Northern Ireland, it was now possible for them to become international news because of the intervention of television, which beamed the realities of a police state to incredulous audiences in Britain and the Republic. This fact also cemented nationalist unity in the North, as that community developed a greater awareness of the pervasiveness of their plight—indeed it has been argued that the televised images on 5 October 'did more in a few hours for the minority in the Six Counties than the Republicans had been able to in fifty years.'[106] Two weeks later Eddie McAteer announced that the Nationalist Party would no longer act as official opposition in the Northern Parliament, ending the brief experiment promoted by Seán Lemass.

For Jack Lynch the disturbances in Derry were an unwelcome intrusion into domestic political affairs. He was in the middle of a referendum campaign in which Fianna Fáil was seeking to replace proportional representation with the 'first past the post' system, as used in Britain. The motivation behind this was obvious to supporters and opponents alike. Since 1948 Fianna Fáil had been unable to secure an absolute majority in the Dáil. This had been attributed to PR, which encouraged a multi-party system, as it enabled the voter to choose candidates of different parties, thus permitting small parties to establish and maintain themselves. The result of adopting the British system would have been to enhance Fianna Fáil's prospects of forming majority governments to the detriment of minority interests, such as the Labour Party.

Because of the recent events in the North, the opposition parties compared Fianna Fáil's actions to those of the Unionist Party, which had abolished PR in 1929 to minimise nationalist participation in state institutions. The comparison is not as facile as it may at first appear. Fianna Fáil had been in continuous power for eleven years, and had been the party of government for thirty of the previous thirty-six. To opponents the referendum appeared to be symptomatic of a naked desire for permanent power. At a time when the Unionist Government was being accused of manipulating the electoral system—a grievance that formed a central plank of the civil rights platform—superficial similarities exploited by Fine Gael and the Labour Party during the referendum campaign proved embarrassing.[107]

Lynch's response to the violence in Derry was inconsistent, and it reflected Government divisions on the root cause of the disturbances and on the best policy for ameliorating the situation. There were those, such as Lynch, who believed the issue to be one of civil rights and who saw functional co-operation with Stormont as the most effective way of remedying the political ills that had brought the civil rights movement into existence. However, there was an influential minority who attributed the trouble to partition and who favoured bilateral talks with the British Government to confront it with its historic responsibility for the division of Ireland and to seek a declaration of its intention to withdraw from the North. Lynch's initial response to the recent violence reflected his own inclinations and preferred strategy. Addressing an audience in Kilkenny on 6 October, he expressed the hope that

> the root cause of such disturbances would soon be eliminated, so that people of different religious beliefs and political convictions would be treated as equals in every respect, and would be permitted to live with each other in peace and harmony, free to enjoy their lawful democratic rights.[108]

This statement was an unambiguous reiteration of Lynch's belief that the lack of civil rights was the fundamental issue. However, when addressing a referendum meeting at Clonmel two days later he put forward an entirely different argument, stating that 'partition is the first and foremost cause' of the conflict in Derry. He stated that 'partition arose out of British policy' and that 'the methods necessary to maintain Partition against the wishes of the vast majority of the Irish people . . . could not be maintained without the political and the huge financial support received from Britain.'[109]

This dramatic *volte-face* was most probably the result of the influence of traditionalists within the Government, who had had the opportunity to express their views during the Government meeting earlier that day (the first such meeting since the events in Derry). That such divisions existed was made evident by a speech by Neil Blaney on 11 October in Milford, Co. Donegal, in which he declared that the border was 'the basic cause of all the troubles in Derry.' He claimed that the Government was endeavouring to 'get the British Government to begin to undo the wrong of Partition for which it is solely responsible.'[110] This speech unequivocally rejected the central tenet of the Lemass approach to the North, favoured by Jack Lynch: that the problem resided almost exclusively within Ireland and could be resolved only through a *rapprochement* with the unionist tradition.

The ascendancy of the Government's traditionalist wing was further illustrated by the official announcement that Lynch was to travel to London to inform the British Prime Minister of 'the views of the Irish Government in relation to the recent civil rights protest in Derry and to indicate to him that we regarded the partition of our country as its root cause.'[111] Lynch met Harold Wilson in the House of Commons on 30 October for an hour-long meeting. He said afterwards that Wilson had made 'no positive comment' in response to his views on the 'root cause' of the events in Derry.[112] The initiative had been a predictable failure, but it was a sign of the conflicting pressures to which Lynch had to respond. He had been forced to make a reversal of policy, and he was now attempting to articulate the sentiments of a minority of the Government with whom he had a fundamental difference of opinion.

Lynch's visit to London and its purported justification were a victory for those in the Government who were sceptical of the merits of functional co-operation and who sought to circumvent this policy by negotiating directly with London, thus bypassing Stormont. What Lynch was forced to realise was that the policies of functional co-operation and of pressuring the British Government were mutually exclusive. The success of functional co-operation had depended on confining discussion to economic and social matters, to the exclusion of the constitutional issue. Unionists had to be convinced that there was no hidden agenda in pursuing a policy of neighbourly co-operation. Pressuring the British Government to 'hand over' the Six Counties was not conducive to establishing or maintaining cordial and constructive relations with the Unionist regime. While Lynch's meeting was aimed at placating the traditionalist wing in the Government, it also served to alienate O'Neill, who had his own dissident wing to contend with.

It was not surprising, therefore, that Lynch's actions precipitated a return to the megaphone diplomacy of the pre-Lemass era. O'Neill deplored Lynch's 'quite unwarranted intervention into our domestic affairs'[113] and his reversion to 'the old, but somewhat moth-eaten, war horse of anti-partition activity.'[114] It is clear that O'Neill also feared the reaction of his own Cabinet hard-liners. Just as Fianna Fáil ultras considered functional co-operation to be tacit recognition of Northern Ireland's legitimacy (which entrenched partition), there was a suspicion among the more recalcitrant of O'Neill's Cabinet that it weakened the Union and represented the first tentative steps towards a united Ireland. Persistent references to partition by Southern politicians increased the qualms of those within the Unionist Cabinet who feared that North-South co-operation was considered by Dublin as a means to an end rather than as an end in itself. O'Neill moved quickly to dispel the suspicion that the constitutional question was a secret item on the North-South agenda, and on 31 October he publicly affirmed that there is no member of the Unionist Party, let alone of the unionist government, who wants to have anything to do with changing the constitutional position of Northern Ireland. Mr. Lynch knows that I have always refused to discuss Ulster's constitution . . .[115]

Ironically, the strategy adopted by O'Neill for mollifying the dissidents was almost identical to the one pursued by Lynch. He met Harold Wilson and the Secretary of State for the Home Department, Jim Callaghan, in London on 4 November, and he was accompanied by the two ministers most strongly identified with the traditional unionist wing, William Craig and Brian Faulkner.[116] In a joint statement the two prime ministers declared that they had discussed the local government franchise, housing, the Special Powers Act and the events in Derry. More importantly for O'Neill, Wilson reaffirmed Clement Attlee's pledge that 'no changes should be made in the constitutional status of Northern Ireland without Northern Ireland's free agreement.'[117] Both the Taoiseach and the Northern Prime Minister had now consulted the oracle in Westminster, and a definitive judgement had been handed down: partition was to stay.

Anxious to repair any damage done to the process of functional co-operation, Lynch declared that he had no wish 'to engage in any recriminatory battle of words with Captain O'Neill.'[118] He reiterated his conviction that O'Neill was 'a reasonable man,'[119] who was 'anxious to promote civil rights.'[120] Even while in London, ostensibly to confront the British Government with its responsibility for partition, Lynch clearly did not believe in the ideological position that he had been despatched to express. While addressing the Anglo-Irish Parliamentary Group in the House of Commons immediately before his meeting with Wilson he said it was his earnest hope that 'the ultimate solution of the problem of partition can be found in Ireland by agreement between Irishmen, North and South.'[121] Immediately after his meeting with Wilson he confronted another republican sacred cow by declaring his satisfaction that the British Government had 'no particular interest in maintaining partition,' and 'if the Irish found a solution, then the British Government would not be likely to object.'[122] By professing a belief in the neutrality of the British Government, Lynch demonstrated that he was at odds with many in Fianna Fáil who argued that the British were the principal obstacle to reunification.

Lynch's intention of reverting to the policy of functional co-operation (after a very brief lapse) was articulated in greater detail on 7 November during a Dáil confidence motion. He argued that his policy of establishing a *détente* with the Unionist Government was not a new departure, and he claimed there was a continuity in Northern policy by stating that 'it has been the aim of this Government, and its predecessors, to promote the reunification of our country by promoting and fostering a spirit of brotherhood, mutual understanding and good will among all sections of the Irish people.'[123] He reiterated his conviction that O'Neill

is a reasonable and fair-minded man. That being so, I am convinced that he is anxious to ensure that all the people within his jurisdiction will get a fair deal. Therefore, I believe the spirit of brotherhood to which I have referred can eventually prevail not only in the northern part of our country but throughout the whole country and that this could lead to a new approach to the solution of the main political problem.[124]

The speech was a classic restatement of the merits and desirability of functional co-operation. It firmly reiterated Lynch's contention that reconciliation would have to come before reunification, and not the other way around (which was the belief of his Government rivals). Equality of treatment for Northern nationalists, combined with the social, economic and psychological benefits that would accrue from closer North-South co-operation, was presented as the first step on the road to national reconciliation and, hopefully, to ultimate unity. The role of the British Government in this was not that of 'perfidious Albion' but rather that of the passive facilitator of any agreement reached between the Dublin and Belfast Governments.

Lynch's speech was a public rejection of the views of the Government's republican faction, and it did not go unchallenged. Within twenty-four hours Neil Blaney retorted with a controversial speech to an audience of the Fianna Fáil faithful in Letterkenny. Rather than attributing honourable motives to O'Neill, as Lynch had done, Blaney accused him of attempting 'to set himself up as the exclusive spokesman for the historic province of Ulster, when in fact he can only speak for a mere bigoted junta in six of its Counties, a junta that has made his liberal image a shameful sham.'[125] It was a far cry from Lynch's assertion that O'Neill was 'a fair-minded man,' eager to implement reforms. But Blaney's attack went much deeper. His dismissal of all cross-border discussions as a 'futile exercise' questioned the entire basis of the Government's Northern policy. He implicitly rejected the notion that the problem resided primarily within Ireland by asserting that 'the partition of Ireland was imposed by Britain and it must be undone by Britain.'[126]

Séamus Brady, a journalist from Derry and a close associate of Blaney's, has described his speech as an attempt 'to try and force the leadership of the Fianna Fáil Government . . . into adopting a stronger and what he considered traditional Fianna Fáil policy in relation to the deteriorating situation in the Six Counties.'[127] This speech, therefore, can be seen as an attempt to counteract what Blaney perceived as an undesirable shift from the traditional policies of Fianna Fáil on the national question. By stressing O'Neill's alleged dishonesty, the futility of North-South co-operation and Britain's culpability, he at one stroke sought to undermine the entire foundation of Lynch's Northern policy.

The speech was obviously intended to be a direct challenge to Lynch's authority. Blaney had copies of his statement circulated to the press, but not to the Taoiseach, who was traditionally regarded as the only legitimate spokesperson for the Government on Northern policy. Blaney attempted to reassure those within the party, particularly at the grass-roots level, that Fianna Fáil's traditional policy remained intact, and he rebuked Lynch for adopting a misguided policy and requested that he articulate the views of the traditionalists, who were a minority within the Government but probably a majority of the party as a whole.

Lynch's reaction to Blaney's speech, made in his address to the National Executive on 11 November, was typical of his approach to leadership and of his personal style when under pressure: he pretended that there was no crisis, and if there was it would somehow go away. Instead of rebuking his errant subordinate he justified Blaney's intervention by acknowledging that partition continued to arouse 'deep feelings and emotions.'[128] He attempted to present a united front on partition. Accordingly, he attributed Blaney's broadside to a feeling of disappointment that 'the practical co-operation which has taken place in recent years has not led to greater progress and given more tangible results.'[129]

Lynch illustrated the precarious state of functional co-operation by imposing conditions, for the first time, on the resumption of cross-border talks. Two weeks earlier he had told the Dáil that there was 'no question' of conditions being attached to the resumption of such talks[130]; now he said that 'clear evidence of sincere intent' to speedily implement reforms would be necessary before contact between Belfast and Dublin could be resumed.[131] He probably felt that by conceding this point and attempting to understand the dissidents' motives he would paper over the cracks in the Government and present a united front to the electorate. In reality he was under-mining his own position as Taoiseach. The message to the dissidents was that they could publicly challenge Lynch's right to formulate and execute Northern policy with impunity. Speaking at a party function in Listowel, Co. Kerry, on 11 November (the same night as Lynch's address), Blaney decided to raise the stakes by making his most controversial speech yet. He told those assembled that 'the recovery of the Six Counties . . . by whatever means possible . . . is the foremost plank in the platform policy of Fianna Fáil.'[132] The assertion that Fianna Fáil would end partition 'by whatever means possible' suggested a flexibility towards the use of force that unsettled those less bellicose in their approach to Northern policy.

The opposition parties concentrated on the speech's ambiguities and forced Lynch to respond. His defence was more assured and assertive this time, possibly because he felt it easier to reject force than to defend functional co-operation. He stressed that Blaney's speech had been made without his approval, and he insisted that his own speech to the National Executive should have 'left nobody in any doubt as to what the Government attitude was on north-south relations and towards partition generally.' He reiterated his adherence to a policy that would eliminate past dissensions, so facil-itating, ultimately, a reappraisal of partition when these barriers were removed. He concluded trenchantly that 'that will continue to be the Government's attitude. I have spoken on behalf of the Government, and that is what the Government think.'[133]

Despite this more confident statement, Lynch's approach was still tempered by a tendency to excuse Blaney's actions. He suggested that Blaney had made his speech off the cuff, and that he may not have been aware that the press were present[134] (sug-gesting that Lynch did not mind his Government colleagues disavowing his policies before the party faithful so long as the media were not involved). He conceded that his policy of functional co-operation was not universally accepted within the Government, and he declared that the merits of the cross-border talks were 'capable of subjective assessment'; he acknowledged that there could be 'differences of opinion, even within the cabinet as to how valuable they were.'[135]

The success of functional co-operation necessitated governments in Dublin and Belfast willing to participate. Support for O'Neill in the Unionist Party was being continuously eroded, diluting the prospects for renewed cross-border talks. O'Neill's position was similar to that of Lynch. O'Neill was considered an outsider in unionist circles, both in background and in outlook. Educated in England, he lacked an appreciation for the nuances of unionist sentiment. Though he was a member of the Orange Order and of other related organisations, his enthusiasm for anti-Catholic rituals was lukewarm; he lacked the crude sectarianism that had been the basis of those organisations. He did not cultivate close friendships within the party, and he was a rather aloof political figure, which accentuated his vulnerability in times of crisis. Most importantly, he refused to believe, unlike many of his colleagues, that the civil rights movement was devoid of any independent or legitimate *raison d'être* but was merely a front for republican subversives.

However, O'Neill's immediate political problems did not stem from 'Southern irredentism' (though this was always in the background): they were from what many unionists termed 'British interference'. At their meeting on 4 November 1968 Wilson had pressed O'Neill strongly on the need to introduce reforms in the local government franchise to ensure 'one man, one vote' as quickly as possible. While sensitive to O'Neill's vulnerability within the Unionist Party, Wilson hoped that reforms could be imposed without recourse to drastic measures—not excluding a fundamental reappraisal of relations with Northern Ireland.[136] O'Neill responded with alacrity and introduced a batch of reforms that conceded many important civil rights demands, but there was still no movement on the crucial demand of 'one man, one vote,' and this gesture meant that O'Neill's initiatives did not receive the universal approval of the nationalist community. Their objections paled into insignificance, however, compared with the consternation that the reforms aroused among members of O'Neill's Cabinet and the Unionist Party.

On 9 December, O'Neill decided to go over the heads of his opponents and appeal directly to the people of Northern Ireland in a radio and television address.[137] Ulster, he solemnly informed his audience, stood at a crossroads between the forces of law and the forces of anarchy. Emboldened by the positive response to his address, O'Neill sacked Craig and secured a vote of confidence from his party.[138] His honeymoon, however, was short-lived. At Burntollet Bridge, a few miles outside Derry, a small, peaceful civil rights march organised by People's Democracy, a group of leftist Queen's University students, was ambushed by a loyalist mob, which included more than a hundred B Specials in plain clothes. The RUC, which had colluded with Paisleyite stone-throwers throughout the progress of the five-day march, watched as marchers were severely beaten with nail-embellished cudgels before moving in to arrest the victims.[139] News of the marchers' plight reached Derry, and when the students reached the city they received a tumultuous reception in Guildhall Square. That night a large force of RUC men rampaged through the Bogside, a Catholic district of the city. A commission established by the British Government some months later reported what happened next.

We have to record with regret that our investigations have led us to the unhesitating conclusion that on the night of 4/5 January, a number of policemen were guilty of misconduct which involved assault and battery, malicious damage to property in streets in the predominantly Catholic Bogside area giving reasonable cause for apprehension of personal injury among other innocent inhabitants, and the use of provocative and sectarian political slogans.[140]

O'Neill's response, however, was to blame the marchers. 'Enough is enough,' he declared. 'We have heard sufficient for now about civil rights; let us hear a little about civic responsibility'[141]—a statement that only damaged further his already shaky reputation among Northern Catholics.

Meanwhile, Unionist Cabinet divisions were re-emerging. On 24 January, Brian Faulkner resigned as Deputy Prime Minister, giving as his reason O'Neill's decision to establish an independent commission to investigate the civil right disturbances. Two days later William Morgan, Minister of Health and Social Services, also resigned over the Government's handling of the controversy. On 30 January thirteen dissident Unionist MPs formally demanded O'Neill's resignation. With his authority ebbing, O'Neill decided to throw the political dice one more time by seeking a new mandate from the electorate. After an affirmative party vote, he called a general election for 24 February.

The election result was not as decisive as O'Neill would have liked, and on 28 April he resigned as Prime Minister, making way for his cousin, James Chichester-Clark.[142] O'Neill's political demise put the whole functional co-operation programme on ice, despite Lynch's best efforts to afford him the maximum support it was politically possible for a Taoiseach to give. Lynch had softened his position once again after Blaney's speech in Letterkenny, and he attempted to facilitate the resumption of cross-border talks. Sensing O'Neill's increasing isolation, he removed his pre-condition that progress in civil rights was a prerequisite for the continuation of North-South talks. Three days after the Northern election Lynch told the Dáil that he was eager to see 'the North-South talks resumed at an appropriate time which would be mutually convenient.'[143]

However, there was a widening gulf within the Government about the value of efforts to preserve functional co-operation or of supporting O'Neill's endeavours. On the eve of the Northern election Blaney exhorted 'the Irish people of the Six Counties . . . [to] withhold their votes from all those candidates who stood for the Union with Britain.'[144] Blaney remained fearful that the thirst for civil rights might induce moderate Catholics to endorse O'Neill, and he cautioned them not to prostitute their nationalism for the promise of reform. According to Blaney's confidant Séamus Brady, the minister 'had waited until the eve of the election in the hope that Lynch would speak out and give some guidance to minority voters in what was for them a perplexing election.'[145]

It was only after Lynch had failed to say anything that Blaney took the initiative and addressed the nationalist people on behalf of the Government. It was for this reason, as Brady points out, that the remarks were not included in the prepared statement that was circulated in advance by the Government Information Bureau. A less understanding reading of events might suggest that Blaney had given his speech to Lynch for approval, as requested, only to alter its content afterwards, thus circumventing any veto Lynch might attempt to impose. It was patently obvious to someone like Blaney, endowed with sensitive political antennae, that Lynch had no intention of making a speech on the lines sought by himself. It was clear also that even if Lynch could have been induced to make a speech on the subject its tone and content would have been markedly different from those of Blaney. Blaney had probably waited until the very last moment to make his speech, safe in the knowledge that Lynch would not have an opportunity to rebut his remarks until the election was over. His statement, by default, would be the only authoritative pronouncement on the election made by a member of the Government.

Lynch refused to admonish Blaney for his ill-disguised usurpation of the Taoiseach's authority to be the sole enunciator of Northern policy. Instead he told the Dáil that Blaney's speech accorded fully with Government policy,[146] and he rejected suggestions from the opposition that Blaney's remarks were 'catchcries.'[147] While it could not be demonstrated that Blaney's speech offended any aspect of Government policy, its whole tone was inimical to Lynch's efforts at securing a *rapprochement* between North and South. References to 'the sham democracy that is the Six Counties' and 'the specious offerings of an Irish-Britisher' were calculated to undermine O'Neill, on whom the success of Lynch's Northern policy depended.

Lynch's predicament exposed the difficulty of reconciling a policy of functional co-operation with the necessity of advocating the eventual destruction of the Northern state. The problem that Blaney's periodic attacks created was not that he was opposing Fianna Fáil policy: in fact it was the reverse. By advocating the traditional anti-partition policies of the party Blaney was impairing Lynch's ability to formulate Government positions on the North, and his actions placed an ideological straitjacket on Lynch. There were few issues closer to the heart of Fianna Fáil than partition, and it would be an audacious Taoiseach who would try to deny its fundamental injustice. The problem was that Lynch's approach entailed co-operation with a state whose right to exist was not recognised by his party. While Lemass had the revolutionary and party background to square this ideological circle, Lynch had not. He hoped to pursue his policies surreptitiously and endeavoured to steer Government policy away from the sterile anti-partitionism of the past towards a gradual and minimalist strategy. The shift in emphasis did not go unnoticed. The more orthodox party members attempted to test Lynch's commitment to functional co-operation by challenging him to deny the veracity of traditional policy, knowing that Lynch would refuse to fall on his own political sword in order to defend his heretical ideas.

In response to the Derry riots of 19–20 April 1969 the Government met in a day-long emergency session. Two decisions were made, both of which represented a victory for the republican faction within the Government. It was resolved that Lynch would seek an immediate meeting with Wilson; and it was decided that the Minister for External Affairs, Frank Aiken, would visit the UN Secretary-General, U Thant, in New York to 'advise him of the situation.'[148] Boland and Blaney suggested these initiatives,[149] and the dual strategy conformed neatly to their traditional anti-partition policy. It was at their goading that Lynch had travelled to London in October, and he was once again being despatched to confront the old enemy. This move had put the whole functional co-operation policy in jeopardy the last time it was attempted, and with O'Neill fighting for his political life in Stormont the initiative would constitute a fatal blow to North-South co-operation.

The UN initiative was unprecedented, and it was a clear break from established Government policy. Though Ireland had joined the United Nations in 1955, in the thirteen years since then it had never formally raised the question partition.[150] Indeed, such was the silence on the issue that one journal commented sarcastically that Ireland's UN delegation 'might as well have emanated from Lapland.'[151] This policy, as Aiken later explained, had been the result of the fact that 'none of our Governments was convinced that during its period of office the adoption of a United Nations resolution would contribute to the restoration of Irish unity.'[152] A UN initiative was attractive to Boland and Blaney because it provided the opportunity to mobilise world opinion against the British Government. It was a partial repetition of the 'sore thumb' policy of the 1948–51 Government, which had sought to gain maximum exposure for partition by raising the matter in international forums in an effort to embarrass and pressure the British Government. This strategy was, of course, totally incompatible with functional co-operation. It would also make a meeting with Wilson less likely to yield results, as this policy had not endeared itself to British Governments in the past.

In the Government, Frank Aiken expressed serious reservations about a UN visit, and he was extremely reluctant to meet U Thant to discuss the crisis.[153] Considering the options open to the Government at the United Nations, the initiative was of a very limited nature. The issue was not raised in the General Assembly or the Security Council; instead it was confined to a meeting with the Secretary-General, the weakest UN institution.

Aiken's meeting with U Thant took place on 23 April, and his replies at the press conference in New York and in the Dáil emphasised the merely cosmetic nature of the exercise. Aiken agreed that he had 'just told him of the situation,'[154] and that he did not 'request the Secretary-General to take any action.'[155] In addition he told the Dáil that the Government had no intention of tabling a formal motion at the United Nations, to which Brendan Corish retorted: 'In other words, the Minister is going to do nothing.'[156]

The Government did not believe that a visit would make any difference to the political situation; rather it hoped that the exercise would silence critics within Fianna Fáil who believed that the Government was pursuing a policy of inertia in response to deteriorating circumstances in the North. Contrary to popular belief, the Government had not made 'a radical departure from [its UN] policy,'[157] as the *Irish Times* claimed, but instead made a minor adjustment to traditional policy to meet immediate pressures. Aiken made it clear that the Government believed 'the best way, the way most preferable to everybody, is to settle this [problem] between ourselves.'[158] Civil rights were of immediate importance, he said, and 'if the present situation can be kept under control, if the Paisleyite groups are suppressed from interfering and attacking the anti-Unionist section, by degrees a peaceful arrangement can be made.'[159] Aiken had not discussed partition with the UN Secretary-General; he had confined the discussion to the impasse in the O'Neillite reform programme.[160] It is clear that despite the concession to the Government dissidents Aiken was determined to use the opportunity to espouse Lynch's policy of functional co-operation; he was also determined not to berate the British or Northern Governments, as desired by the republican wing of the party.

The most transparent illustration of Lynch's reluctance to pursue the traditional policy of the dissident faction was the manner in which he prosecuted the decision to seek an 'immediate' meeting with Wilson. On 29 April, Lynch told the Dáil that 'a definite date for the meeting has not yet been fixed,'[161] while on 20 May he informed the Dáil that 'no definite date has yet been fixed for my visit to Mr Wilson.'[162] Two months (and a general election) later he again told the Dáil on 15 July that 'no definite date has yet been fixed for a meeting.'[163] Finally, on 22 October, two-and-a-half months after the outbreak of the Northern conflict, he declared that 'no arrangement for such a meeting has yet been made.'[164] His reluctance to pursue this particular Government decision is easy to understand, and the method he employed to circumvent it is symptomatic of his style of leadership. It meant, however, that the Dáil fiddled while Belfast burned.

1969 is also significant because it was perhaps the last year in which the Government could participate in national or republican commemorations without the attendant controversy caused by violence in the North. It was the fiftieth anniversary of the first Dáil, an event that all shades of opinion could unite in remembering. As in 1966, there were many references to how far 'the country' had advanced over the decades. However, the event was not so distant that there did not remain survivors of the era who scorned the Government's commemorative efforts and who demonstrated the gap between the aspirations of 1919 and later failures. As de Valera opened his address he was interrupted by the veteran republican Joe Clarke: 'The programme of the old Dáil has never been implemented. This is a mockery. There are people on hunger strike in Mountjoy. The housing of the people . . .' At this point, the *Irish Times* reported, 'Dáil Éireann ushers grappled with the disabled veteran.' They moved him to the outer door, where they gave him his crutches and released him. (Ironically, Clarke had been usher-in-charge at the first Dáil.) De Valera, whose voice 'seemed to be directed towards that part of the hall where sat the Fianna Fáil deputies and the cabinet . . . carried on as if unhearing.' The *Irish Times* correspondent, Liam Mac Gabhann, remarked that it had not been a

> triumphant jubilee, though everything went (almost) according to plan. Allegiance had been pledged anew to a dream that nobody was claiming had altogether come true.[165]

THE 1969 ELECTION

The Fianna Fáil ard-fheis was timed to coincide with the celebration of the first Dáil, though its main task was to prepare for a general election, which was held in June.[166] 373 candidates contested the election, the largest number since 1948.[167] Superficial comparisons with the 1948 election can be observed. Fianna Fáil had enjoyed a long spell of uninterrupted tenure in office, and the opposition was desirous to 'put them out.'[168] The Labour Party, with the slogan 'The seventies will be socialist,' was cast in the mould of Clann na Poblachta, providing the radical alternative and injecting some ideological vitality into the debate. But there the similarities end. Whereas the 1948 election had elected six parties and twelve independents to the Dáil, the political situation had become less diverse, and the 1969 election produced only three parties and one independent. Since the 1950s 'turbulent issues and charismatic personalities had tended to fade from Irish politics,'[169] leading to the extinction of smaller sectional parties and their absorption by the major organisations.

The increased burden of financing an election, with its attendant advertising costs, accentuated existing imbalances and accelerated the process of streamlining. The crucial factor that distinguished the two elections, however, was the absence of a unity of spirit among the opposition parties. The Labour Party had ruled out the possibility of coalition, citing ideological incompatibilities with both of its larger rivals.[170] This left Fine Gael in the unenviable position of having to portray itself as a realistic alternative government, despite having failed to gain a majority of seats in any election since the foundation of the state. The extent of the task facing both the Labour Party and Fine Gael to convince the electorate that they could replace Fianna Fáil was reflected in the number of candidates presented to the electorate. Fine Gael put forward 125, while the Labour Party put forward 99—colossal figures, unprecedented in either party's history.[171] Fianna Fáil contented itself with 121 candidates, and Neil Blaney noted with satisfaction that 'the lost deposits will be falling so fast that they will help to pay a fair share of the cost of the election.'[172]

Opposition criticism of Fianna Fáil centred on a few themes, and they were reiterated throughout the campaign: corruption, arrogance and an obsequious deference to affluent vested interests. Justin Keating declared that 'Fianna Fáil has now become the party of big business and is fundamentally opposed to democracy.'[173] In the case of Charles Haughey these allegations became quite personal. The attack was led by Conor Cruise O'Brien, contesting his first election in Haughey's constituency, who saw Haughey as a manifestation of 'the Fianna Fáil speculator-orientated oligarchy.'[174]

The controversy centred on the rezoning of land attached to Haughey's home in Raheny, Dublin, which had secured for him more than £200,000, enabling him to purchase the Georgian mansion and 400-acre estate of Abbeville in north Co. Dublin.[175] Haughey was repeatedly challenged by Cruise O'Brien to debate 'the morality of the land sale,' as this was a 'vitally important public issue.'[176] Citing the 'widespread feeling amongst the public that he may have used his position in the cabinet to further his own personal interests,'[177] the Labour Party adroitly linked the issue with the resignation of the Northern minister Harry West over an alleged conflict of interest concerning a land deal in Co. Fermanagh.[178] The implication was that Fianna Fáil could not accuse the Unionist Party of corruption when it tolerated similar 'improprieties', and the issue was picked up by Fine Gael's spokesperson on finance, Gerard Sweetman, who claimed that Haughey might have been liable for income tax on the sale of his home had he not recently amended the Finance Act (1965).[179] Haughey was compelled to publicly defend his position,[180] in which he was supported by the Attorney-General[181] and the Revenue Commissioners.[182]

Much of the opposition's energies were directed against Taca ('support'), a Fianna Fáil fund-raising organisation established in 1966, which to some was the negation of the party's spiritual values and the repudiation of Fianna Fáil's tradition of supporting the economically marginalised. Taca was a rather amateur attempt at imitating American-style fund-raising by eliciting financial support from the expanding business community. Annual membership was £100 (a huge sum), and in return businessmen were afforded the opportunity to meet and socialise with Government ministers. While Lynch claimed that 'no member of Taca has benefited in any way from membership,'[183] the public perception was somewhat different, and the seemingly organic link between Fianna Fáil and big business perturbed those more inclined to traditional values. During the election campaign Luke Belton of Fine Gael referred to the 'frantic efforts being made in Taca to ensure that Fianna Fáil would remain in power,' and he declared that the organisation was 'a special prop for those individuals who in return for large subscriptions have staked their claim to a seat in Dáil Éireann . . . In this election there is more at stake than a change of Government.'[184] Prof. John Kelly joined this chorus and noted 'the willing collaboration' of the Fianna Fáil leadership with 'narrow interests of wealth and speculation.'[185]

With corruption came its companion vice, arrogance. The previous four years may have produced Europe's youngest government, according to Fine Gael's spokesperson on agriculture, Mark Clinton, but it had also become 'the most arrogant and dictatorial cabinet in any European democracy.'[186] Gerard Sweetman warned of the 'jackboot methods of Fianna Fáil,'[187] and, in case the inference was lost, two Fine Gael speeches went so far as to make explicit connections with the Nazis.[188]

The 1969 election also brought the return of the Red Scare as a theme in Irish politics. The Labour Party had temporarily overcome its phobia about the word 'socialism' and boldly entered the election asking the people to 'peel off the tattered rags and battered image of the old Republic of the conservative Civil War politicians.' Instead electors were exhorted to vote for 'the new Republic,' a land of community responsibility, full employment and equal opportunity.[189] Few could imagine a more unlikely standard-bearer of socialism than Brendan Corish, who throughout the 1960s had displayed a greater knowledge of Papal encyclicals than many a parish priest. Fianna Fáil portrayed Corish as the prisoner of the Labour Party, in the thrall of Marxist intellectuals eager to seize power and eradicate civil liberties. (In retrospect, one of the more amusing aspects of the election was the fact that Conor Cruise O'Brien was endorsed by the Republican Congress veterans Peadar O'Donnell and George Gilmore, who urged that he be given the support of republicans in his constituency.[190])

Fianna Fáil's response was to answer with counter-allegations. The ace up its sleeve was the claim that there was no alternative to a continuation of the present Government. Haughey claimed that a defeat for Fianna Fáil would be 'a serious national setback,'[191] a variation of the party's familiar election chant (encapsulated by John Healy in 'Don't let them muck it up').[192]

In keeping with traditional policy, Fianna Fáil did not issue a manifesto. In practice this was to allow the party the maximum flexibility after taking office, but Haughey, as director of elections, offered a new ideological pretext. 'Manifestos,' he claimed, 'have a Marxist ring about them.'[193] The veteran red-baiter Seán MacEntee entered with characteristic gusto, claiming that the Labour Party stood for Lenin, Stalin and the 'red flames of burning homesteads in Meath.'[194] In full-page advertisements in the national newspapers, the traditional argument espousing the virtues of a united single-party Government (i.e. Fianna Fáil) as against a divided coalition of irreconcilables was extensively employed. Particular emphasis was given to those in the Labour Party who constituted a 'group of extreme left-wing socialists . . . preaching class warfare and who want total state control and all that goes with it.'[195] Neil Blaney warmed to this subject, accusing the Labour Party of promoting the 'failed system of atheistic socialism' of the Soviet Union, Cuba, North Korea and Vietnam, where 'the freedom of man is a myth, where democracy has been trampled down and brutal dictatorship is supreme.'[196] Lynch claimed that by voting for Fianna Fáil the people would demonstrate 'that they prefer the reality of progress and prosperity to the Cuban myth.'[197]

Anti-intellectualism was also much in evidence. Mícheál Ó Móráin, the Minister for Justice, condemned the 'left-wing political queers from Trinity College and Telefís Éireann,'[198] while another candidate, Joe Dowling, declared that 'the intellectuals had never done a day's real work in their lives.'[199] Blaney struck an Orwellian note when he claimed that the Labour Party's programme was not for 1969 but for 1984.[200]

Despite the political upheaval that had led to Terence O'Neill's resignation, and despite increased civil rights agitation, the North did not figure at all as an election issue. References to republicanism, on the brief occasions when they were made, were usually of the Civil War variety.[201] In its editorial on the eve of election the *Irish Times* declared that 'we are polling today to set the scene for a genuine confrontation, to end Civil War politics, which, in spite of all statements to the contrary, are still firmly embodied in the two main parties. Almost nothing else divides them.'[202]

The election returned 75 deputies for Fianna Fáil, 50 for Fine Gael, 18 for the Labour Party and 1 independent, giving Fianna Fáil a comfortable majority of 6. The 'Bolandmander', which increased the number of three-seat constituencies, had played its part in Lynch's first election victory. In Dublin, Fianna Fáil's share of the vote fell from 47 per cent in 1965 to 39 per cent, though its share of the seats dropped only from 52 to 48 per cent. Similarly, in Connacht the party's vote rose slightly, from 48 to 51 per cent, while its share of seats jumped from 52 to 62 per cent.

It was a personal triumph for Jack Lynch, who confounded his critics by attaining the absolute majority that had eluded his predecessor, Seán Lemass. He had under-taken an American-style tour of the country by helicopter—a high-risk strategy, as a defeat would have been considered a personal rebuff. In this victory he had acquired a mandate and an authority that he had previously lacked.

Having won another election with exceptional ease, Fianna Fáil settled down for another five years in office. One minister, Kevin Boland (who within two months of the election would tender his resignation on the issue of the North), captured the atmosphere within the party.

Fianna Fáil had now been over twelve years continuously in office. They were now starting on another five years uninterruptible term and there was no sign of an alternative. We had permanent jobs—and we liked them. We could sit back and run our (twenty-six county) departments while our parliamentary colleagues— Fine Gael and Labour—went through the motions of opposition. But first, we had to have the holidays we had earned by our herculean efforts to retain our seats and our jobs. The post-election belligerence of the Opposition evaporated with the

advent of the good weather so that with their co-operation the Dáil adjourned ...
We had an over-all majority; therefore the 'country' was stable and the
Government went on holiday for the month of August.[203]

But there were storm clouds on the political horizon. Within weeks the members
of the new Government would be called back to confront their greatest challenge as
the mistakes of the past returned to haunt them. Things would never be the same
again.

Chapter 12

'THE MOMENT OF TRUTH,' 1969–71

ARMS AND THE MEN

On 1 August 1969 the Minister for External Affairs, Dr Patrick Hillery, had a secret meeting in London with the Secretary of State for Foreign and Commonwealth Affairs, Michael Stewart, with the object of getting the British Government to pressure Stormont into implementing reforms and, most urgently, into banning the Orange parade in Derry planned for 12 August.[1] Stewart's response would set the tone for British policy during the early period of the Northern conflict: he questioned Hillery's characterisation of Stormont's reform programme as ineffective; he expressed confidence in the ability of the Northern and British governments to handle the matter; and he made it clear that Northern affairs were no business of the Irish Government but were a purely internal matter for the United Kingdom. At one point Stewart remarked, 'You accept, of course, that responsibility for this area rests with the Stormont and London governments and not with your government.' Hillery accepted that the British were now in control, but he drew attention to the danger of things spilling over into the Republic, stating that 'if things were to go wrong, he would have reactions in his country, with which it would be necessary to deal, possibly with very serious repercussions.' When Hillery asked incredulously whether Stewart was really not expecting any trouble to arise, Stewart replied 'very firmly' that he was not, and he returned to the theme of putting the Irish Government in its place by saying that 'there is a limit to the extent to which we can discuss with outsiders—even our nearest neighbours, this internal matter.'[2]

The day after this meeting an Orange march clashed with residents of the Unity Flats in Belfast, and the ensuing riots were the worst the city had experienced in thirty-four years.[3] Chichester-Clark returned from his holiday in Switzerland, and an emergency Cabinet meeting sought and received assurances from London that British soldiers would be supplied if matters got beyond Stormont's control. For the benefit of the RUC and the B Specials, the Northern Government empowered the Minister of Home Affairs to 'feel free to interpret in a less restrictive way existing conditions applying to the use of CS gas [a powerful tear gas].'[4] A statement issued after the meeting announced that the Northern Government would 'not shirk from any measure, however firm or exceptional, which may be necessary'; people were urged to support the army and the police and to remain indoors.[5]

Ian Paisley's reaction was to announce the 'greatest possible loyalist parade' in the predominantly Catholic town of Newry. The dreadful harvest of O'Neillism was being reaped, he said, and Stormont's 'appeasement policy' was encouraging and condoning the actions of the IRA, People's Democracy and 'CRA front organisations.' He urged the Government to cease its capitulation to 'the never-to-be-satisfied demands of those in this country who are out for total destruction.'[6]

The Northern Government's actions revealed the folly of having a unionist government—bigoted, hegemonic and in power for half a century—decide on matters pertaining to Orange marches. The Unionist Party and the Orange Order were inextricably linked (a third of the seats at Unionist Party conferences were reserved for members of the Order, and all Government members were Orangemen), and the Government preferred to permit an almost certain confrontation, with a clear risk of death or injury, than to interfere in the 'traditional marching rights' of their Orange brethren.

The British Government was in recess and issued no statements. Several Labour MPs made representations requesting that impartial observers be sent to the North and for the British Government to assume control of the RUC, but these requests went unheeded, as did a demand for the recall of Parliament.[7] Chichester-Clark met Jim Callaghan on 8 August. The Prime Minister, Harold Wilson, was unavailable, having departed on his summer holiday the previous night. No formal statement was issued after the two-hour meeting, but Chichester-Clark confirmed that the deployment of British soldiers had been discussed, and he reassured his followers that Orange marches due to take place the following week would not be banned. He concluded by saying that the situation in the North was 'not critical, but not stable either.'[8]

The Irish Government, also on holiday, made no official response, and individual ministers were unavailable for comment. The *Irish Times* prophetically assessed that, should widespread violence erupt in the North,

> the Government here could then be faced with a Republican demand for militant action. Such demands could lead to a Government request for United Nations observers to be sent to the North, or even request for action by a UN force. Should the minority in Belfast and elsewhere encounter incidents like those of the 1920s and 1930s then the Government would be in a dilemma if any unofficial militant action were to be taken by militant Republicans. The general feeling would be that somehow the Nationalists of the North would have to be defended.[9]

The atmosphere in Derry was apocalyptic. In Celtic Park, on 10 August, Eddie McAteer made it clear that, should nationalists be attacked, support from the South would be sought.

> If this is indeed our hour of trial at hand, if we are to be ground in this city as a helpless minority then I pray to God that our watching brethren will not stand aside any longer.[10]

On 12 August the Northern state, a powder-keg since its inception, finally exploded. Embittered and disillusioned by the failure of the Northern Government to deliver reforms, nationalists were further incensed by the provocative march of the 'Apprentice Boys' through Derry. It resulted in rioting, and when unionists, aided by the RUC and B Specials, attacked the nationalist ghettoes of the Bogside and Creggan (a new housing estate specifically for Catholics), barricades were thrown up. The defence, which was to last for more than forty-eight hours, has gone down in history as the Battle of the Bogside.

At 12:30 a.m., as petrol bombs began to be traded for CS gas, Neil Blaney was contacted by phone by anxious nationalist leaders in Derry, and shortly afterwards a similar plea for assistance came from Dungannon. According to Séamus Brady, their message was unambiguous: the Bogsiders 'had no weapons, but they had their backs to the Irish border and they felt the South must come to their aid.'[11] Blaney rang Jack Lynch and the Tánaiste, Erskine Childers, at their homes, but there was no reply. Blaney later admitted that he did not wait too long to receive a response, as this allowed him greater flexibility to fashion events as he saw fit.[12]

A Government meeting was called for 13 August, and, according to Brady, 'the first question at issue was the use of the Irish Army in crossing the Border.'[13] Blaney, Boland and Haughey were the most vociferous in advocating the movement of the army to alleviate the plight of nationalists and to force UN intervention. This argument assumed that Britain would then have to acquiesce to demands for negotiations on the constitutional future of the North. Brady claims that the troika were among those who were aware of 'the political realities of a situation in which the entry of a mere company of soldiers . . . would have brought Britain to the conference table for the first time in half a century on the basic question of the partition of Ireland.'[14] It was, for Boland, 'the moment of truth for the Fianna Fáil party, the time for the solution to the final problem.'[15] Blaney remembers arguing that 'we had the same right to protect any citizen of the Six Counties as we would have had if it had happened in Cork. I mentioned Cork deliberately because Jack Lynch came from Cork.'[16] Lynch countered by arguing that pogroms in Belfast against beleaguered nationalists would be the result if the army crossed the border. In this analysis he was supported by Childers and George Colley.[17] The rest of the Government 'took no side in the discussions,' said Boland, 'but knew on which side their bread was buttered.'[18]

Hillery, who as Minister for External Affairs was a vital actor in the process, missed the meeting. He was on Achill Island on a painting holiday, and the Government and its officials were unable to contact him, as the boarding-house where he stayed had a fixed rule that painters could not be disturbed.[19]

Lynch had arrived at the meeting with a prepared statement, possibly hoping that by producing it as a *fait accompli* he could avoid a detailed discussion on the issue.[20] Blaney, Boland and Haughey expressed extreme displeasure at the moderate tone of this document,[21] which Boland has described as 'civil service gobbledegook.'[22] However, while Boland's and Blaney's criticisms were to be expected, they were surprised to find an unexpected ally in Haughey.

Haughey's position is curious, because until that meeting he was not known to have any views on the North, let alone hard-line ones.[23] The assault on Lynch's document, which had been largely composed by the Secretary of the Department of External Affairs, Hugh McCann, precipitated a general discussion, and Haughey was entrusted with the task of drafting a modified statement.[24] The 'amended' document that emerged bore little resemblance to the one that Lynch had submitted earlier that day.[25] The statement was not put to a vote but was unanimously approved after a discussion of its contents.[26]

Lynch made his way to the RTE studios in Donnybrook, Dublin, to make what was quickly (and inaccurately) dubbed the 'we won't stand idly by' speech.[27] While stating that 'the reunification of the national territory can provide the only permanent solution to the problem,' he declared:

> It is evident also that the Stormont Government is no longer in control of the situation. Indeed the present situation is the inevitable outcome of the policies pursued for decades by successive Stormont Governments. It is clear also, that the Irish Government can no longer stand by and see innocent people injured and perhaps worse.[28]

This speech was interpreted by some members of the British and Northern Governments as a threat—and by many nationalists as a promise—that the Government was actively considering military intervention of some kind if matters did not improve. Such perceptions were reinforced by the announcement that the army was moving to the border to establish field hospitals 'in Co. Donegal adjacent to Derry and at other points along the Border where they may be necessary.'[29] According to Blaney, the use of the term 'field hospital' was merely a sop to international opinion.

> It was the view of myself and others that we had to send our troops to protect the people and it was agreed to send the army to the border, under the cover of Field Hospitals. But as it turned out, the deviousness of certain minds thereafter utilised the 'good cover' as just that. But the Field Hospitals idea we went along with: I didn't give a goddam how they went up as long as the army went up and were there to go in. And that is what was on the minds of, I'd say, the majority of the Cabinet that day.[30]

The atmosphere that the speech created is perhaps most evocatively described in the front-page story of the *Evening Press* of 14 August.

> The people are hopeful that aid in some form will arrive from somewhere. Their eyes are turned chiefly to the Border only five miles away where they have heard Irish troops are building up. The news spread through the Bogside this morning like wildfire. It is one of the things that keeps men at the barricades, gives them the courage and strength to hurl stones and bombs at the police and the bravado to stand while tear gas bombs are bursting all around them. But, why don't they come? Why didn't they come last night?[31]

The British Government was at a loss to explain Lynch's vehement speech and the implied threat that the Irish Government would not remain passive should the situation deteriorate. The consensus in London was that Lynch had been pushed over the edge, as Jim Callaghan recalled.

Everybody was in a very jumpy state. I was on holiday and the Home Office rang me up late one night after he'd made this speech and said, 'We think you ought to come back. We don't know what Prime Minister Lynch is going to do.' Well, I knew Jack Lynch as a very sensible Minister of Finance when I'd been Chancellor of the Exchequer before, and it seemed to me to be out of character with that rather reserved and self-controlled personality that I knew. But the situation was such in Northern Ireland—we hadn't experienced anything like it for years—that I thought I'd better go back to the Home Office. I went up that night and we said, 'What on earth is Jack Lynch thinking about? He can't really mean he's going to invade Northern Ireland. He couldn't be so stupid.' And of course he wasn't. He backed off.[32]

General Sir Anthony Farrar-Hockley, who in 1970 became commander of British army land forces in Northern Ireland, believed that whatever military designs the Irish Government may have entertained they would have been ineffective and easily repelled.

In terms of intervention, as things stood, it was impossible at the time. Derry was the nearest large area of course for them to come in to. But I cannot myself believe that the British Government could have permitted any such incursion and they would therefore had to have been called upon to withdraw, governmentally, and if they'd not been withdrawn they'd have to have been pushed out. Now their numbers were simply *tiny* [smiles] compared with the resources of the British Government at that time and it would have been an extremely unpleasant and unhappy event to have taken place. And so I do not believe that it was a practical operation whatsoever.[33]

There is little reason to doubt Farrar-Hockley's assessment. The Irish army had been neglected over the previous twenty-five years, and its full-time strength of 8,000 was a third below the establishment (the figure officially provided for) of 12,000.[34] To make matters worse, a 400-member unit was in Cyprus on peace-keeping duty. Equipment was poor, and, as Tim Pat Coogan has commented, the Government had at its disposal 'four obsolete Vampire jets and three ancient corvettes (one of which actually sails) to back up this shamrock rattling.'[35]

An unsatisfactory substitute was the second-line reserve, the FCA, with a paper strength of 30,000, of whom 20,000 could have been mobilised in an emergency. The Government was well aware of these deficiencies: Boland recalls that during the meeting of 13 August 'our opponents in the Cabinet kept on talking irrelevant nonsense about the inadequacy of our Army as opposed to the British Army. We would be wiped out in the first few hours, we were told.' Boland emphasises, however, that 'no one contemplated war with the British Army.'[36] What was intended was internationalising the partition issue, as the lives of Northern nationalists were jeopardised and as Britain continued to claim that Northern Ireland was a domestic affair. As James Downey has reasoned, 'the argument in favour of military intervention . . . was not really a military one at all, but a call for an "internationalisation" of the question, forcing some kind of UN intervention.'[37]

Tim Pat Coogan has revealed that an emissary of one Government minister briefed him that, 'in order to bring the matter to UN attention,' the army was going to be used to cross the border to seize 'even a football field.'[38] Blaney, on the other hand, wanted the army to 'go straight off into the west bank of the Foyle where the thing had really caught fire.'[39] The rationale of those advocating military intervention in the immediate aftermath of the Battle of the Bogside was that there was no military presence behind the barricades, and if the army was to move in behind them a temporary ceasefire could be negotiated, during which Dublin and London could discuss the issue. That the pressure existed for such an initiative was not in doubt: Vincent McDowell, vice-chairperson of the NICRA, called on the Government to send its soldiers in to establish joint British-Irish peace-keeping patrols, pending UN intervention. 'A war of genocide is about to flare across the North,' he declared. 'The CRA demand that all Irishmen recognise their common interdependence and calls upon the Government and people of the Twenty Six Counties to act now to prevent a great national disaster.'[40]

A Government decision was postponed as Hillery dashed to London for an unannounced meeting with his British counterpart. He was not favourably received.[41]

> The British wouldn't talk to me . . . I was sitting in the embassy in London and it was embarrassing for them to have the Irish Minister sitting in the embassy waiting to be seen and they not wanting to see me. Finally, they arranged a meeting with the Junior Minister. It was quite unsatisfactory. They said it wasn't any of our business.[42]

The meeting with Lord Chalfont (a minister in the Foreign and Commonwealth Office) and Lord Stoneham (a minister in the Home Office) was tetchy and adversarial. Hillery, furious that his earlier warnings had been ignored, was alarmed by the plight of Northern nationalists and the threat of the conflict spilling over into the Republic. The RUC was, 'at best, not an impartial force,' he said, and the B Specials were a 'partisan, armed mob, such as is found only in dictatorships.'[43] Throughout the meeting the British looked for a guarantee that the Irish soldiers who had amassed at the border would not cross into Northern Ireland, but Hillery refused to give one, saying, 'I did not come here to give assurances but to seek them.' The British responded by protesting 'in the strongest terms' about the large crowds that had gathered outside the British embassy in Dublin and that had taken the Union Jack down from its flagstaff. Attacks like this, Chalfont said, would 'not help matters, are very provocative, and will have a profound effect on people in Britain.' At this point Hillery retorted that

> such incidents are not as serious as people being shot and terrorised. Northern Ireland is part of Ireland. Our people do not accept that it is part of the United Kingdom. It is not a separate island. It is Ireland, our island.[44]

The British emerged more successfully from the battle: they held most of the cards, and Hillery left London with nothing. Despite repeated requests, Chalfont and

Stoneham ruled out a meeting with Harold Wilson. Moreover, the Foreign and Commonwealth Office had issued a swift rebuttal of Lynch's television speech, reaffirming their commitment to remaining in Northern Ireland as long as the majority there wished it and further claiming that 'the border is not an issue.'[45]

In turning down with such alacrity the Irish side's request for early talks, the British had put the ball back in Dublin's court. The Government met on the morning of 14 August; at 5 p.m. the same day the British army rolled into Derry. There was confusion at first among the B Specials: when they saw British soldiers in green fatigues moving past they mistook them for the Irish army. Nationalists also thought the Irish army had arrived, but disappointment quickly turned to relief and rejoicing, as the British commander, Lieutenant-Colonel Bill Todd, ordered the RUC and B Specials to withdraw.

The fact of British soldiers on the streets of Derry and Belfast brought a new dimension to the problem facing the Government. After all, Lynch had claimed in his television address that their deployment would be 'unacceptable' and not conducive to restoring peace, 'certainly not in the long term.'[46] The British army had also played a controversial role during the burning of Bombay Street in the Catholic area of Clonard in Belfast, adding urgency to the Government debate regarding the Irish army's role. Boland felt it imperative that the army should achieve a state of maximum preparedness for all contingencies, and to this end he demanded the immediate withdrawal of the Irish peace-keeping unit from Cyprus and the calling up of the first-line reserve (former members of the regular army). Boland believed that any UN initiative would not bear fruit unless it could be demonstrated that the Government viewed events in the North with gravity and was in earnest about taking action. When his request was not acceded to, he informed the Government that he was resigning, and he stormed out of the room. 'After a few days' interminable wrangling,' Boland later reflected, 'it became apparent to me that the policy of "to preserve what we have down here" and "to restore normality up there" had prevailed.'[47]

With an emotional atmosphere pervading the country, Lynch realised that there might be a serious political crisis. It was also obvious that the resignation of a Government minister of Boland's standing would be politically calamitous for a party whose *raison d'être* was the reunification of the national territory. Lynch immediately set about inducing his errant minister to return to the Government. No effect was given to Boland's resignation, which had been submitted verbally; instead, he was bombarded with phone calls, and party elders were despatched to his home, but to no avail. With all avenues exhausted, the services of President de Valera were enlisted, and he eventually convinced Boland not to publicly resign (with the argument that, at this critical juncture concerning the national question, it was imperative that Fianna Fáil and not Fine Gael be in power). Boland later regretted his decision to return, and he believes that had Fine Gael been in power Fianna Fáil could have been mobilised, as, 'if the collaboration had started from that end it wouldn't have been tolerated.' However, with 'the Republican Party' in power, Fianna Fáil was complacent, and the party's 'origin and past history facilitated the confidence trick planned by the Leadership.' Boland agreed to attend future Government meetings, though he refused to take an active part in discussions relating to Northern Ireland.[48]

Lynch desperately needed to produce a strategy that would keep the dissidents on board and maintain party unity. At the Government meeting of 16 August a Northern Ireland sub-committee was established, the composition of which illustrated how much control the republican clique exercised during the deliberations. In addition to the republican doyen Neil Blaney and Charles Haughey, who was by now also synonymous with hard-line republican views, it included Pádraig Faulkner and Joseph Brennan, both representatives of border constituencies. At this critical time Lynch was delegating Northern policy to ministers with whom he had fundamental differences of opinion. The sub-committee had ill-defined terms of reference, and it met only once. A propaganda unit was also created, headed by Blaney's friend Séamus Brady, and a large-scale PR initiative was agreed. It was also decided that a sum of money, the amount and distribution of which would be determined by Haughey, would be made available 'for the victims of the current unrest in the Six Counties.' This was the money that would be used for the procurement of arms, leading to a series of events that would rock the foundations of the Southern state.

Within a few days of the Government's 'field hospital' directive the army had come up with a shopping list of items required to fulfil its mission.[49] The items sought showed that the mission the Government envisaged went far beyond providing humanitarian assistance on the Republic's side of the border. It included large quantities of 25-pounder and 120-mm ammunition, as stocks were considered insufficient for prolonged 'duration of fire at combat rates.' (25-pounder ammunition was for artillery, 120-mm ammunition was for large mortars, both offensive weapons.) Other supplies requested were anti-tank and anti-aircraft weapons, a variety of high-powered machine guns, five thousand sleeping bags and ten thousand gas masks. Plans for secret war games were devised, to be carried out by the Military College 'to study, plan for and rehearse in detail the intervention of the Defence Forces in Northern Ireland in order to secure the safety of the minority population.'[50] The quartermaster-general stressed the need to diversify sources of supplies, 'since the main source is British.'[51] This recommendation was reinforced in a message from the Secretary of the Department of Defence informing the minister, Jim Gibbons, of the need to stockpile arms, as, in the event of hostilities, 'normal channels of supply would be interrupted by blockade and . . . our regular Continental suppliers would, through diplomatic or other pressure, be prevented from fulfilling contracts for the defence forces.'[52]

By 27 September, six weeks after the Battle of the Bogside, the army had produced an interim report based on Government directives outlining four different scenarios in which Northern nationalists might be threatened and how best they could be assisted. Firstly, in a situation in which the Catholic minority was attacked by Protestant extremists, and the Northern police were unable to cope, conventional operations could take place in Derry and Newry, a wide range of unconventional operations could be undertaken in any part of Northern Ireland 'to draw forces off the area of direct conflict,' and arms, ammunition, equipment and medicine would be supplied to the Catholic population. In the second scenario—a conflict between the Catholic population and the police and British army on civil rights issues—the response was more or less the same, except that the attack would be directed at the British army, with appropriate diversions and the arming of Catholics. The third scenario was perhaps the most interesting, as it envisaged a conflict between 'Republican-Nationalist elements,' possibly supported by 'illegal elements from South of the border,' and the British army and the police. In such an event the same combination of conventional attacks and unconventional diversionary attacks was foreseen, as well as the arming of those in need. In addition, training for republicans and nationalists would be required. The fourth scenario—a conflict between Protestant extremists and the police and British army, not directly involving the Catholic population—was perhaps the least likely. The proposed response was the infiltration of 'elements armed and equipped to [organise], train and advise Catholic and Nationalist groups' in vulnerable areas far from the border, such as Belfast. Additionally, sub-units, up to company level (approximately 200 men), would be sent across the border to keep routes open for refugees fleeing south.

Given the existing resources and the retaliatory potential of British forces, unilateral strikes against Northern Ireland were thought militarily unsound, but conventional operations at the company level or smaller-scale unconventional operations could be contemplated, subject to the necessary organisational changes. The report concluded that operations by the Defence Forces could involve

(1) organising and conducting military training in the Republic for nationalists living in Northern Ireland.
(2) supplying arms, ammunition and equipment in accordance with availability to nationalist elements in Northern Ireland.[53]

The extensive road network connecting the two parts of the country would facilitate cross-border operations, though the modern surveillance techniques available to the British army meant that 'guerrilla operations in Northern Ireland would be difficult to conduct over a protracted period.' Derry, Strabane, Enniskillen and Newry were considered the most suitable targets for military operations, in view of their proximity to the border and their political significance. The report noted that the majority of the North's vital installations, such as the international airport, television studios and docks, were in the greater Belfast area, and 'any military operations conducted against these should preferably be of the unconventional type.'[54]

On 13 October the Council of Defence met to review the situation. Those present included the Minister for Defence, Jim Gibbons, the parliamentary secretary, Des O'Malley, and the Secretary of the Department of Defence, Seán Ó Cearnaigh, together with the chief of staff and quartermaster-general. Gibbons reiterated the need for military plans for extreme contingencies in the North, while the chief of staff reminded the politicians that increased army strength, equipment and training would be essential for such an operation. The army produced its shopping list, and the minister decided that the chief of staff should submit a programme for procurement, for intensive training for the personnel necessary for such an operation and for special courses of continuous trainings for 'elements of the FCA.'[55]

After the Battle of the Bogside a steady stream of nationalist representatives, including several MPs, made their way to Dublin to seek arms from Government ministers. Representative of these was a delegation on 16 August composed of three

Stormont MPs—Paddy Devlin (Northern Ireland Labour Party), Paddy O'Hanlon (independent) and Paddy Kennedy (Republican Labour)—who crossed the border as the Ardoyne district of Belfast was under heavy attack from unionist extremists, including B Specials. After a spontaneous rally in O'Connell Street, at which they publicly appealed for arms, the delegates told Government officials that the situation developing in Belfast was mild in comparison with Derry. Fearing a massacre, they demanded firm action from Dublin. 'If Irish troops would not be sent in to the North,' they said, they wanted guns to protect Belfast's Catholic population. When their attempts to meet Hillery and Lynch failed, Devlin's anger was such that an official phoned Rathmines Garda station to ensure that the armed guard protecting the Taoiseach's house was increased.[56]

Many delegations were received, however, and they were assured that assistance would be rendered. With British soldiers now on the streets of Northern Ireland, and initially welcomed by besieged Catholics, the focus shifted to preparing for a 'doomsday' situation in which Northern nationalists would be in danger of large-scale attack, with no force willing or able to defend them.

On 2 October, Haughey held a meeting at his home with the Director of Intelligence, Colonel Michael Hefferon, and another Military Intelligence officer, Captain James Kelly. They discussed a forthcoming meeting in Bailieborough, Co. Cavan, at which Kelly was to sound out various members of the Northern Defence Committees, and Haughey arranged for £500 to be paid to Kelly, through Hefferon, to cover expenses for the meeting and for any follow-up meetings.[57] The Bailieborough meeting was to be of historic significance, being, in the words of Kelly, 'the genesis of the plan to import arms.'[58]

On 6 October, Captain Kelly submitted a report on the Bailieborough meeting to the Director of Intelligence. The meeting concluded that the acquisition of arms for defence was essential and that the training of nationalists in the use of arms should resume as soon as possible. Under the direction of the Minister for Defence a number of Derry republicans had been trained with the FCA in Fort Dunree at Buncrana, Co. Donegal, but the attention of the local and national media had forced Lynch to call it off. Kelly had explained this to the Northern representatives, who accepted the reasoning behind the 'postponement' of the operation but emphasised that it should be resumed under some other guise.[59]

The need for secrecy, and a rivalry between Military Intelligence and the Special Detective Unit (the former Special Branch), had left the Department of Justice and the Gardaí in the dark. When the head of the Special Detective Unit, Chief Superintendent John Fleming, informed the Secretary of the Department of Justice, Peter Berry, of the forthcoming Bailieborough meeting on 4 October both thought it was without Government sanction. Berry, who was in hospital awaiting an operation, attempted to contact the minister, Mícheál Ó Móráin, and Lynch, but both were away. He then phoned Haughey, who had previously been his minister, and a meeting was arranged for that evening at the hospital. Haughey feigned ignorance of the Bailieborough meeting but was 'intrigued about the sources of this information and pressed Berry on these.'[60] Berry was shocked to learn subsequently of Haughey's meeting with Kelly and Hefferon two days previously.[61]

On 16 October, Fleming visited Berry again and told him in some detail of what took place at the Bailieborough meeting, after which Berry promptly arranged a meeting with Lynch for the following morning. His diary describes his meeting with Lynch.

> I told him of Captain Kelly's prominent part in the Bailieboro meeting with known members of the IRA, of his possession of a wad of money . . . and of the sum of the money—£50,000—that would be made for the purchase of arms. I remember a conjecture of the Taoiseach as to where they could possibly get it and my suggestion that perhaps Mr. Y or Mr. Z, two millionaires of the Taca Group and the Taoiseach's observation that those boys don't give it up easily.[62]

Lynch consistently claimed that he did not learn of the arms plot until 20 April 1970, six months after this meeting with Berry. There is further evidence that challenges Lynch's claims. A few days after the Lynch-Berry meeting, Gibbons received a briefing on the Bailieborough meeting from Hefferon, and it may be assumed that Gibbons reported back to Lynch. At the subsequent hearings of the Public Accounts Committee, Hefferon related that

> Mr. Gibbons asked me to see him and told me that the Taoiseach had had a report from Mr. Berry that Captain Kelly had attended a meeting at Bailieboro . . . at which there were IRA people present, that he had waved a wad of notes around promising money to them.[63]

This evidence shows that, in addition to Blaney and Haughey, both Gibbons and Lynch were aware at an early stage of the Bailieborough meeting and its implications. Mícheál Ó Móráin and Kevin Boland were also informed of the meeting.

Haughey had met a Northern delegation in late September, which included Paddy Kennedy MP and John Kelly, a member of the Belfast IRA and chairman of the Central Citizens' Defence Committee, which had been established to co-ordinate the defensive efforts of the nationalist community. The question of arms arose, and Haughey promised that money from the Relief of Distress fund would be provided for the use of the delegation.[64] On 12 November an account was opened by the delegation at the Munster and Leinster Bank in Baggot Street, Dublin, and two days later two subsidiary accounts were opened in the fictitious names of George Dixon and Anne O'Brien. The Dixon account was to finance the purchase of arms, and the O'Brien account was for the propaganda paper *Voice of the North*, edited by Séamus Brady. Both subsidiary accounts were financed by the main account.

The first indication that Kevin Boland received from an official source that arms were being procured for nationalists came from Charles Haughey. (It should be borne in mind that Haughey consistently denied that he was in any way involved with the importing of weapons destined for Northern insurgents). Boland recalled:

> He came in to me at about eight o'clock in the morning . . . 'In case you didn't know,' he says, 'I wanted to tell you what is being done,' and he gave it to me specifically that a cargo of what they call machine pistols and flak jackets were

coming in. And the only thing I said to him was, 'Are you sure that you have a reliable chain of command, that these will only be used in a defensive situation?' . . . 'Oh, yes, of course,' he says, 'of *course.*' And I knew immediately that was a lie. And I know [laughs] that when he's most authoritative like that and pushes it aside, that's when he's telling a lie. 'Not at all, not at all' [impersonates Haughey accent]. And he gets away with it. But he came in to tell me, and the only reason for that was in case I might think Blaney was doing it.[65]

Boland's interest in the chain of command for distributing the guns stemmed from his belief that weapons should remain under Government supervision and direction unless a 'doomsday' situation developed, when the supply of weapons to nationalists for defensive purposes would prevent their massacre. He later concluded that Haughey's participation in arms procurement was motivated by a desire to enhance his republican credentials within Fianna Fáil. Boland believed that, at a time when the national question had assumed primary importance, and when Lynch's vulnerability on the issue was detectable, Haughey was laying the groundwork for a heave against Lynch. His main rival for supremacy of the republican wing of the party was Blaney, and Haughey sought to outflank him by becoming intimately acquainted with the issue of nationalist defence, and was determined that his role in this venture would not go unacknowledged.[66]

After unsuccessful efforts to procure arms in England, John Kelly and his colleagues went to Blaney to try again. Kelly had been wary of attempting to obtain arms in England, as 'you didn't know what types they were, MI5, MI6 or whatever,' so when Blaney asked Kelly to identify the safest place from which to arrange a shipment he suggested the United States, as 'you were dealing with your own people . . . people who had a tradition of republicanism.'[67] Blaney agreed, and in December, John Kelly and Seán Keenan travelled to the United States, where they met the former senator Liam Kelly, who had been instrumental in getting arms for the IRA Border Campaign during the 1950s. Having obtained a sizeable quantity of sub-machine guns, assault rifles, grenades, flak jackets and gas masks, Kelly arranged through the International Longshoremen's Association (the New York dockers' union) to have the consignment shipped to Ireland.

Kelly and Keenan returned to Ireland shortly after New Year's Day, 1970, pleased with the consignment and content in the knowledge that the arms could be distributed to the North expeditiously. However, on arriving home they were informed by Captain Kelly that Blaney had changed his mind and that arms would now be brought in from the Continent. Captain Kelly informed the two IRA men that Blaney had arranged an alternative deal with an arms dealer in Hamburg through his friend Albert Luykx, a Belgian businessman now domiciled in Ireland. Blaney's ostensible reason for this sudden change of plan was that he felt that arms could be obtained with greater speed in Europe. John Kelly was disappointed with the decision, as it entailed cancelling all the arrangements in America; but, as he pointed out,

we had no alternative. They had the money. They were providing the finances. Again, had the Irish-Americans been organised in New York or in Boston,

Chicago, Los Angeles, San Francisco, as they had been two years later, after internment ... That's the reason that we had to run with the Irish Government for the arms, for the money for the arms. As I say, if we'd not been in that situation we would have done it ourselves, but that's the way it was. We felt obliged going back. So when Blaney says, 'No, that's not the place to go,' we were beggars, we couldn't be choosers. So we had to go by his instructions.[68]

Blaney had now assumed a pivotal role in the arms importing, and henceforth he was in direct control of all operations to procure arms on the Continent. The move to Europe and away from the United States was to have fatal consequences for the entire effort. Attempts to obtain arms in Europe were to drag on for months and, according to John Kelly, were 'a total disaster.'[69]

While the Government deliberated on how best to protect Northern nationalists, some people were taking defence into their own hands. At public gatherings, spontaneous collections were taken to buy weapons. On 28 September, at a large meeting in Dublin addressed by several Northern notables, a collection was taken up to buy machine guns and revolvers, 'so that we will not be unprepared when the Paisleyites attack us and burn us out of our homes.'[70]

Trouble was brewing too within the republican movement. The IRA's inability to protect nationalist enclaves had led to the leadership of the IRA in Belfast being deposed in September. So deep had the ideological fissure become that when an extraordinary army convention was held in mid-December there was no representation from Belfast. The convention voted to end the long-standing republican policy of not participating in the 'partition parliaments' of Dublin and Belfast or the British Parliament in London. For some traditionalists and militants this was the final straw. Led by Seán Mac Stiofáin, the dissidents walked out and formed the Provisional Army Council. All this went unnoticed outside republican and state security circles.

The first public indication of a split came a few weeks later at the Sinn Féin ard-fheis of 11–12 January 1970. The split between 'Provisionals' and 'Officials', now irrevocable, was based on a number of fault-lines. Provisional supporters tended to be older, more right-wing and more militant, while officials were, as a rule, younger and left-wing and advocated a broad political front rather than the traditional weapon of force as the means to end partition.[71] More particularly, the official wing

no longer wanted to be a movement, with all the outmoded clutter that that entailed. They wanted to be a *party*. For that reason the division, when it came, was as much the wish of the Goulding camp as it was of the traditionalists.[72]

The IRA convention and the Sinn Féin ard-fheis merely formalised a position that had existed for several months.[73] It also made it easier for traditional Fianna Fáil supporters and militant Irish-Americans to channel money to the republican movement. The Marxist rhetoric of the Dublin IRA leadership under Cathal Goulding found little favour within Fianna Fáil: it was certainly not going to arm individuals and supply them with money if there was the slightest possibility that they would be used against the Southern state.

In the Provisional IRA, Blaney and others could see kindred spirits—rough and ready defenders of embattled communities, fighting for unity, and no 'Marxist non-sense'. When asked years later about the destination of the weapons being procured, Blaney said that 'they'd have gone into Ballymurphy and to whoever was capable of handling, using and directing their organisation.' He concedes that they would 'very probably' have gone to the newly formed Provisionals, and there was 'no way' that they were going to be distributed to the Officials.[74]

THE 1970 FIANNA FÁIL ARD-FHEIS

The Fianna Fáil ard-fheis of January 1970 provided the first opportunity for party members to appraise events in the North since the outbreak of the conflict. Blaney's trenchant anti-partitionism was enthusiastically received, so much so that Lynch amended his presidential address that morning; further amendments were made while Boland was making his secretary's report.

Lynch had to walk a delicate line, as the principal dissidents, Boland and Blaney, were also senior establishment figures in Fianna Fáil. Their organisational endeavours, particularly those of Blaney, had resulted in several successive by-election victories. The Organisation Committee had met on eighteen occasions during the year, with Blaney in the chair. Boland's work as honorary secretary saw the number of cumainn climb to 2,240[75]; Blaney's work as treasurer resulted in the party's coffers reaching a record of £42,000.[76]

In the honorary secretaries' report, Boland sought to reaffirm what he believed to be Fianna Fáil's policy on the North. Success at the polls in 1969 had been

> quickly overshadowed by the outbreak of violence and terrorism to which a large section of the people in our six north-eastern counties were subjected. While the lives and property of our fellow Irishmen and women were in grave and imminent danger, it was starkly made clear that the major crime of the settlement accepting the 1920 'Partition Act' was that these many thousands of our people were made hostages as a security against re-unification.
>
> In so far as the Fianna Fáil party is concerned it can at least be said that the events in the Six Counties—producing as they did renewing British declarations guaranteeing the inviolability of Partition—served to remind us, at this time of transition, that we must never become so pre-occupied with Twenty-Six County politics as to forget the fundamental reason for the existence of our Party.

The adoption of the honorary secretaries' report provided the first opportunity for the militant section of the membership to express their criticisms of Government policy since the outbreak of violence in August. Seán Sherwin, the Fianna Fáil candidate in the forthcoming Dublin South-West by-election, spoke of 'the feelings of frustration within the party at the failure to render effective assistance to our countrymen in the Six Counties,' who were 'as much the concern of the Government as the people of Dublin, Cork or Galway.' The violence in August had caused a reappraisal of attitudes. 'It is only in extreme circumstances that we could give help, but these circumstances were very new last August,' Sherwin declared, and 'there would certainly have been no shortage of volunteers.'[77]

Dónall Mac Giolla Buíoll, a delegate from Bandon, believed that the Government would have to be prepared to take sterner action during the coming year if necessary. He predicted that Northern republicans would revolt during 1970, and 'it was up to the Fianna Fáil party to give them every support necessary, both moral and physical.' A delegate from Tullamore said they were 'in danger of forgetting the primary objective of Fianna Fáil,' while Nóirín Ní Scolláin asked if they had become so concerned with economic issues that they had 'forgotten republicanism.' She felt 'deeply ashamed' that they had given 'a monopoly of republicanism' to relative newcomers, such as Bernadette Devlin, who was 'able to criticise Fianna Fáil, which was in fact the Republican Party. We should now see if we went wrong and show the people in the North that we have not forgotten them.'[78]

Of a dozen speakers on the subject only one deviated from the Boland-Blaney line. Dermot Ryan, a Taca millionaire and Lynch loyalist and a member of the National Executive, said that those who advocated force were weakening the Government's position, as it 'had to say that force was not proposed.'[79]

Boland's ard-fheis speech provided a detailed critique of partition, with the responsibility firmly pinned on the British Government. He concluded by saying that

> our main objective must continue to be 'to secure the Unity and Independence of Ireland as a Republic,' and every situation that arises in either part of the country must be assessed as to how it may affect this objective and must be handled accordingly—unhampered by pre-conceived ideas or pre-determined conditions as to the methods to be used.

Boland believed he was supporting Blaney's position, expressed some months earlier, in which he declared that force could not be ruled out and was not contrary to Fianna Fáil policy. In one of his autobiographical books Boland accused Lynch of duplicitous conduct during this ard-fheis: by refusing to contradict Boland's and Blaney's speeches and by reaffirming his adherence to traditional Fianna Fáil policy, Boland contends that Lynch gave delegates the impression that he agreed with his two ministers. 'The truth was that he didn't agree with a word of what I had said, and he knew that I knew this, but in the circumstances of that ard-fheis he daren't disagree overtly.'[80]

Lynch's address contained traditional shibboleths regarding the inherent iniquity of partition, aimed at reassuring delegates. Partition, he declared, was 'a deep, throbbing weal across the land, heart and soul of Ireland, an imposed deformity whose indefinite perpetuation eats into the Irish consciousness like a cancer.' On the question of force, Lynch was unequivocal. Military action might appear 'a heroic, romantic and decisive master-stroke,' but it would be allowing the heart to rule the head. The 'naked reality' was that the Government did not possess the capacity to 'impose a solution by force,' and even if it did it would not be a desirable policy to pursue, as it would not achieve real unity.[81]

In this regard, Boland's assessment of Lynch's address is misleading and unfair. Far from obscuring the fundamental issue, Lynch was also putting out his stall and challenging the dissidents to repudiate his pronouncements on the use of force.

Neither side repudiated the other but both contented themselves with restating their positions, which often appeared to delegates merely as differences of emphasis rather than of substance. Neither side advocated force as a solution to partition; indeed Boland argues that no-one adhered to such a view. Neither side denied that partition was undemocratic, nor did they fail to stress their desire to promote reunification. The essential divergence was between those who pinned the responsibility for the situation in the North on Britain and those who advocated a *rapprochement* with the Northern Government.

But these divisions were papered over in Lynch's closing remarks, which emphasised the essential continuity of Fianna Fáil policy.

Fianna Fáil was founded to unite and not to divide. Fianna Fáil was founded to uphold the Irish Republic and not to disestablish it. To secure the unity and independence of Ireland as a Republic—that has been the primary aim of Fianna Fáil since May 16, 1926. Our commitment to the attainment of that objective is as firm and resolute now as it was on that historic day.

Lynch's speech was enthusiastically received by the British government, which focused on his attitude towards the use of force. The British ambassador, Sir Anthony Gilchrist, who had received an advance copy, described the address as 'remarkably friendly and sensible.' He reported to London that Lynch 'told me that he intended to take another step forward in the education of his party . . . but he has gone much further than I expected.'[82] A message from the British Government to Lynch was passed on secretly by Hillery. It commended Lynch, saying that 'we recognise and value the courage and realism of this speech.'[83] Gilchrist suggested something similar from Stormont, recommending that Chichester-Clark should make 'some vague but immediate welcoming gesture' to encourage Lynch in his line of thinking, and he produced a draft for the purpose.[84]

The morning after the address Lynch and Hillery met Gilchrist, who told them he was 'pleased to see how well he [Lynch] was succeeding in his object of educating public opinion.' Lynch said he had felt compelled to go further than originally intended because of a 'ganging-up against him of a hard-line Blaney wing.' The challenge was serious, he said, and was based on an 'emotional appeal for physical intervention by the Republic in the event of any repetition of the disorders of last August.' Lynch felt that at the ard-fheis he had 'dampened down this enthusiasm (much of it premeditated) as best he could.'[85] Referring to the militant wing of the party, Lynch told Gilchrist that 'I had to get my way on these people at the end by rattling a lot of old bones—and some of them not even buried yet, by God!'[86]—a reference to his final words at the ard-fheis, in which he said that his policy was the same as that of de Valera and Lemass.

Lynch emphasised that his position required the British Government to ensure that Northern nationalists would not be victimised by the RUC, militant Protestants or the British army. With a candour rarely extended to his party colleagues, he told the British ambassador that in the event of a renewed conflict on the scale of the previous August the Blaneyites favoured the creation of an 'international incident'.

Because of the small scale envisaged, and because of lack of co-operation from within the North, it would be difficult for him to discover such a plot in advance. This was not connected with Sinn Féin or the IRA, which, Lynch implied, were under tight surveillance and whose threat did not alarm him. He then asked:

> Tell me, ought I to believe in a general good will towards the unity of Ireland on the part of this British Government and of succeeding British Governments? A great deal must depend on our understanding of this point.

Gilchrist replied that no Government decision had been taken on this, and he saw no sign of any in the future; but, 'speaking personally and off the cuff,' he said that many British statesmen would welcome a 'closer approach to the ideal of Irish unity' if unionist opinion could be brought along.

Lynch appeared content with the meeting and said that he had no need to meet the Prime Minister, Harold Wilson, in the near future.[87]

THE ARMS CRISIS

Meanwhile the quest for arms continued. Captain James Kelly and John Kelly made several trips to the Continent to set up an arms deal, accompanied by Albert Luykx, introduced to them by Blaney, who was to act as their interpreter. A deal concluded with the arms dealer Otto Schleuter in Hamburg secured £35,000 worth of mainly Czechoslovak weapons.[88] The deal was fraught with difficulties and setbacks. Eventually, after several mix-ups, the consignment was ready and was loaded onto the *City of Dublin*, the necessary customs clearance having been arranged by Haughey.

When the ship arrived at Alexandra Quay, Dublin, on 25 March 1970 there were no arms on board. Captain Kelly and John Kelly got the Customs and Excise officer at Dublin to telex Antwerp, from where the ship had sailed, and they received a message that the shipment had been stopped by the Belgian customs, as the shippers had not got an export licence. A few days later Captain Kelly reported to the Minister for Defence on what had taken place; and, after consulting the Director of Intelligence, he returned to the Continent to arrange for the arms to be transported by a chartered plane.

By this time, however, too many people not directly involved in the project had become aware of it. The attempt to charter a plane raised eyebrows in the Department of Transport and Power and in Aer Lingus, which in turn contacted the Department of Justice. As late as 18 April, Haughey asked Berry whether the arms would be let through if it could be guaranteed that they would go directly to the North. When Berry replied that this was not possible and that the arms would be seized on arrival, Haughey realised that the essential secrecy of the operation no longer existed, and he tersely replied: 'I had better have it called off.'

Berry contacted President de Valera, who directed him to Lynch, to whom he explained the details of the plan to import arms, expecting prompt action. However, when he met Lynch on 30 April the latter told him that he had seen Haughey and Blaney, that there would be no repetition of what had happened, and that the matter was closed. Berry was shocked, and he asked incredulously:

Does this mean that Mr. Haughey remains Minister for Finance? What will my position be, he knows I have told you of his conversation with me on 18 April and of the earlier police information.

Lynch, according to Berry, replied: 'I will protect you.'[89]

On the following day, 1 May, there was a meeting of the Government. Haughey was absent because of a riding accident,[90] but Blaney was in attendance. Lynch opened the meeting by stating that there had been allegations of an attempt to illegally import arms but that the matter was now closed.

However, the leader of the opposition, Liam Cosgrave, had now been informed of events by an anonymous message. This is referred to as the 'Garda note', though the source is more likely to have been British intelligence, which had been aware of the attempts from an early stage.[91] Cosgrave's first instinct was to leak the information to the press; but, doubting its veracity, the press declined to print it. At 8 p.m. on 5 May, Cosgrave went to see Lynch and informed him that it had come to his attention that Captain Kelly, Colonel Hefferon, Gibbons, Haughey and Blaney were involved in a plot to bring in $80,000 worth of arms for the North. Though the anonymous 'Garda note' specifically implicated Gibbons, Lynch denied, during his private meeting with Cosgrave, that Gibbons was involved.

Confronted with Cosgrave's information, which he presented in writing, Lynch's hand was forced, and he had to devise a strategy. He could have summoned Gibbons to have him tell Cosgrave that the operation was official, conducted by the Department of Defence with a view to providing Northern nationalists with weapons should the situation in the North deteriorate further. Instead he chose to take the line, which would be defended trenchantly in the coming months and years, that the arms importation had no authority, and that his subsequent Government purge was necessary because ministers must be above the 'slightest suspicion' of wrongdoing.[92]

Lynch sacked Blaney and Haughey, while Boland and Paudge Brennan (Parliamentary Secretary to the Minister for Local Government) resigned in protest. Mícheál Ó Móráin, known for his anti-Lynch views, had been forced to resign two days earlier, ostensibly on health grounds.

At 2 a.m. on 6 May 1970 Lynch made an announcement to the nation. The Arms Crisis broke on an entirely unsuspecting public. Through it Lynch's position was bolstered, as more than a quarter of the Government would be replaced within a week by Lynch loyalists.

Lynch's version of events hinged on Gibbons, as Minister for Defence, knowing nothing of the plan and certainly not authorising it, and both he and Cosgrave tailored their Dáil speeches accordingly. Lynch told the Dáil that, as far as his ministers were concerned, the 'Garda note' implicated only Blaney and Haughey.[93] Cosgrave dutifully played along, saying that 'those involved are a Captain Kelly, the former Minister for Finance [Haughey], the former Minister for Agriculture [Blaney] and two associates of the Ministers.'[94] Here we see the first sign that Gibbons was going to be plucked from the Government plan to import arms and instead be the chief advocate of the new Lynch line that there had been an illegal plot to import arms, with Captain Kelly at the centre.

Lynch had been aware of the central idea of the plan to provide arms, though the implementation was not of his devising. From August 1969 he had allowed the formulation of Northern policy to be dictated by those who were, in principle, his subordinates. However, the fact that he delegated his authority to formulate the principal aspects of Northern policy to others does not allow him to abdicate from his responsibilities as Taoiseach. His acquiescence was perceived as compliance, his knowledge as consent.

The central question is the extent to which the plan to import arms was in line with Government policy. To answer this, reference must be made to the Government directive issued to the army by the Minister for Defence, Jim Gibbons, on 6 February 1970. This directive, the fruit of previous Government deliberations, was dictated by Gibbons in the presence of the chief of staff, Lieutenant-General Seán Mac Eoin, and the Director of Intelligence, Colonel Michael Hefferon.

> The Government directs that the army (1) prepare to train the forces for incursions into Northern Ireland (2) make weapons and ammunition available and (3) make gas masks available.[95]

This directive demonstrates beyond doubt that the provision of arms for distribution in Northern Ireland when the Government felt the situation warranted it was official policy. The chief of staff's notes of his meeting of 6 February with Gibbons also confirm that preparations for incursion and for the provision of weapons was Government policy.

> a. At a meeting held this morning (Friday 6 Feb 70) I was instructed to direct you to prepare for Army incursions into Northern Ireland.
> b. The Taoiseach and other Ministers have met delegations from the North. At these meetings urgent demands were made for respirators [gas masks], weapons and ammunition the provision of which the Government agreed. Accordingly truck loads of these items were put at readiness so that they may be available in a matter of hours.[96]

Lynch and his Minister for Defence later denied that the provision of arms was ever contemplated. And yet a month after the crisis broke, by which time Lynch had already sacked the ministers and proclaimed that force was not an option, the implications of the February directive remained, as is clear from the secret minutes taken by the army of a meeting on 9 June between Lynch and Mac Eoin.

> a) In reference to the direction of 6 February, which was made known to An Ceann Foirne [the chief of staff] by the Minister of Defence (Mr. James Gibbons) and which required the Army to be trained and prepared to make incursions into Northern Ireland, the Chief of Staff assumed that these incursions would be made in circumstances in which there would be a complete breakdown in law and order in which the lives of the minority would be in grave danger and in which the Security Forces in Northern Ireland would be unable or unwilling to protect the minority.

b) The Taoiseach confirmed that the circumstances envisaged by the Government were those assumed by the Chief of Staff.[97]

What is clear now is that the Government had decided during the meetings of August 1969 to bring the army to a state of maximum preparedness. To this end, reserves were to be called up, an extensive recruitment campaign was launched and a serious commitment to a rearmament process was undertaken (eventually to be used against the IRA). After the initial conflict in the North had subsided, the emphasis shifted from the prospect of incursions into the Six Counties (though this always remained an option) to the procurement of arms for Northern nationalists. In line with this policy, the army moved five hundred rifles from Cathal Brugha Barracks in Dublin to a warehouse in Dundalk on 2 April 1970 during widespread rioting in the Ballymurphy district of Belfast. Gibbons was entirely at a loss at the subsequent trial of the two ministers to explain why these arms were moved to Dundalk if they were not for the use of Northern civilians.

There is also the question of the training of Derry republicans at Fort Dunree in Buncrana. On 8 May 1970 Gibbons told the Dáil that

there is an obligation on me to point out that this kind of talk is very destructive in the country at a time like this. There was some reference to the training of civilians in Donegal. I want to point out the position of the Defence Forces in this regard. The Defence Forces train only members of their own ranks, whether they be FCA or Army or Naval personnel. That is the extent of their training. This story first got currency in the *Protestant Telegraph* [edited by Ian Paisley]. It is time that stories of this kind ceased.[98]

What Gibbons's account deliberately concealed was the fact that the Derry civilians were temporarily provided with addresses in Co. Donegal and were enlisted in the FCA for the duration of their training. Lynch and Gibbons later explained this exercise by saying that it was common knowledge that unionists were better armed and trained than nationalists. It raises the question, however, of the point of training people in the use of arms if they are not going to have any. It must also be remembered that Captain Kelly kept his superiors informed on all aspects of the plan to import arms and that both Blaney and Haughey were intimately involved in its execution. Finally, the result of the Arms Trials endorsed the legality of the operation, for if it was not Government policy the accused would hardly have been acquitted of the charge of illegally importing arms.

John Kelly stated at the trial that he was 'in no doubt whatsoever but that what was being done was being done in the full knowledge and consent not only of Mr. Gibbons but of the Government as a whole.'[99] The court accepted this view. By refusing to reinstate Blaney and Haughey, and by promoting Gibbons, despite a trial verdict that vindicated the sacked ministers and rejected Gibbons's testimony, Lynch continued as if the Arms Trials had never taken place; and the establishment of a parliamentary committee to investigate the same events was part of a strategy to have a third attempt at the right verdict but this time by a jury less unpredictable than one drawn from the general public.

THE ARMS TRIALS

In May 1970 Kevin Boland drafted a circular describing the events leading to the Arms Crisis. It was, in essence, a detailed critique of Lynch's handling of the affair, and it was to be signed by Neil Blaney, Charles Haughey, Paudge Brennan and Mícheál Ó Móráin as well as Boland himself. Each Fianna Fáil cumann was to receive a copy, requesting that it meet as soon as possible to request a special ard-fheis. 'Whatever view your Cumann may hold as to the future leadership of Fianna Fáil in the light of recent happenings a special ard fheis to dispel confusion seems to be highly desirable if not essential.'[100]

To Boland's disappointment, his attempts to muster the support of the other four former ministers proved unsuccessful.[101] Blaney and Haughey had issues other than 'rescuing' Fianna Fáil to contend with, having found themselves before the High Court accused of serious criminal offences. Incredibly, the case against Blaney was dismissed in July because of insufficient evidence. Haughey, Captain Kelly, John Kelly and Albert Luykx were committed to trial, and the courtroom saga aroused great public interest throughout the autumn of 1970.

While preparing for the trial, Colonel Hefferon sought access to the files necessary to corroborate his own notes of meetings and personal recollections. Despite being called as a state witness, he was flatly refused permission, as was Mícheál Ó Móráin, the former Minister for Justice. From a document written in October 1970 by Hefferon's successor in Military Intelligence, Colonel P. J. Delany, we can understand why.

> Paragraphs 1a, 1b and 1e of Addendum [army incursions and provisions of arms] can NOT be released because NO Government can afford to publish openly what could be called its normal SECRET military plans especially if these plans are directed against a friendly State. Such a revelation in open Court would cause a diplomatic furore of the first order. This is just NOT done by any State, regarded as friendly.[102]

Colonel Delaney remarked that it was 'most unlikely' that Colonel Hefferon and Captain Kelly had possession of the ministerial directive of 6 February or related documents, as these were numbered copies and were in their rightful places after Hefferon left the army, and Captain Kelly had not been given an opportunity to look at them since Hefferon's departure. Finally, Delaney surmised that Hefferon would not have asked for access to the documents had he made photocopies of them. He concluded that 'the Directive should not be released because of the contents of paragraph 2.a, as this paragraph alone is open to misinterpretation.'[103] And yet the archives show that Jim Gibbons was allowed to consult Department of Defence files.[104] In particular, he sought and received permission from his successor, Gerry Cronin, to freely consult papers relating to the directive of 6 February.

What makes this selective distribution of classified files particularly perverse is that it was clearly conducted with a view to denying one side access to files crucial to the exoneration of those charged while allowing Gibbons to prepare his case with a view to misrepresenting their actions. During the Dáil debate in May, Gibbons defiantly disavowed any knowledge of the plan to import arms, and he tried hard to create an unsavoury picture of Captain Kelly.

> I want to intervene in this debate to clarify some points which have been raised . . . I have been informed that Mr Patrick Kennedy MP, in the course of a Radio Éireann interview, suggested that any participation by Captain James Kelly in an attempt to smuggle arms could only have been made with my knowledge and consent. I wish emphatically to deny any such knowledge or consent. I was aware, through the Director of Intelligence, that attempts to smuggle arms were a constant danger, and these attempts were kept under surveillance at all times. I wish to say I discharged my duty to the full extent of my knowledge of the situation. I want to say also that in recent times I formed the opinion that Captain Kelly was becoming unsuitable for the type of work that he was employed on. I want to say that certain suspicions were forming in my mind. I was kept informed by the Director of Intelligence, but nothing concrete emerged. I am satisfied that at all times I honoured the obligation that was placed on me by the Taoiseach when he made me Minister for Defence.[105]

Apart from that of Gibbons, the state case placed much importance on the testimony of Colonel Hefferon. The testimony Hefferon gave to the Gardaí was edited to chime with the Gibbons-Lynch line. Only in 2001 (with the release of state papers after the lapse of thirty years) did the full extent of the alterations become known. Hefferon made nineteen references to Gibbons in his testimony, but anything that stated that the minister had authorised the importing of arms and that he was fully cognisant of the progress of the plan was removed. A fifth of Hefferon's testimony was excised before being given to the barristers, including the following vital passages:

> Mr. Gibbons knew Capt. Kelly was involved in assisting the Defence Committees in the North to procure arms . . . I told Mr. Gibbons at this time about Captain Kelly's involvement with the Defence Committees in the North regarding the procuring of Arms and ammunition for their defence . . . Around this particular time Captain Kelly told him that he might have to go to Germany again in connection with the arms and ammunition for the North and that a lot of snags had developed with them . . . About this time I saw Mr. Gibbons again in his office, and I told him that Captain Kelly intended travelling to the Continent again in connection with the arms deal. This would be at the end of March or early April . . . Captain Kelly he would be required as Duty Officer at GHQ on the weekend he was going to the Continent. I told Mr. Gibbons that in the event of him not performing this duty I would have difficulty in explaining his absence, and if he was not relieved of this duty he would be subject to normal Army Disciplinary Action unless some authority was given to relieve of him of the duty. Mr. Gibbons was prepared to take the necessary steps to have him relieved of duty in order that he could travel to the Continent.[106]

Not only was Colonel Hefferon's testimony amended, it was tailored to give it the opposite meaning. Without such passages as those quoted above it seemed there was no Government authorisation, that Captain Kelly was somehow a loose cannon and that Gibbons knew nothing of his activities. Unaided by official files, Colonel Hefferon proceeded to recount what had actually taken place, so that after the first trial collapsed he was pointedly not called as a witness by the state in the second trial, having failed to corroborate Gibbons's story.

The second trial gave the state prosecution another bite of the cherry, but Gibbons's version of events was still very difficult to maintain. Just before he left for New York to address the United Nations, and while the trial was in progress, Lynch had confided in the British Ambassador, Sir John Peck, who recorded that

> he was furious with Mr. Gibbons for his performance as a witness, and that he seemed to be getting into an impossible situation. I thought it very likely that his resignation would be ready to put in the Taoiseach's hands when he returned. But it has not worked out that way. Mr. Lynch has retained Mr. Gibbons in his Government and has given his full backing.[107]

On the eve of the verdict, 22 October, Lynch addressed the twenty-fifth commemorative session of the United Nations General Assembly, speaking on the theme of 'peace, justice, and progress.' His speech criticised previous British and Northern governments, but it was clear that these criticisms referred exclusively to bygone days. When Northern society had 'broken down' the Government had 'charged Britain with her responsibility.' Britain, he said, had responded with the Downing Street Declaration, which contained a firm promise that human rights would be established and protected in Northern Ireland.

> We accepted that declaration as the true decision of a country which, despite many unhappy things in the past—and there comes a time to stop feeding on such things—we know herself to be a democratic and freedom-loving country with which Ireland has many ties of friendship and mutual interest. We accepted the concurrent guarantees of the Northern Ireland Government that justice would prevail, and I do not question the honesty of purpose of the Prime Minister, nor of his predecessor. I don't question their dedication in the face of the petty intrigues and manoeuvres of lesser men. We have inherited this historic problem. We are determined to solve it peacefully. We have asked those who have suffered to be patient . . . We have said to those who have suffered from deprivation of human rights in the North of Ireland that Britain will keep her word. My Government have guaranteed this. In this we have put our trust in the good faith between out countries.[108]

This remarkably moderate speech was believed to be an attempt to bolster Chichester-Clark's position as well as to restore confidence in the Fianna Fáil Government in the aftermath of the Arms Crisis and subsequent trials, two objectives that had become inter-dependent. Lynch's optimism about reforms 'created surprise,' the *Irish Times* wrote, and his references to Britain as a freedom-loving country 'caused many eyebrows to raise, for few Irishmen or women have ever thought of

Britain in these terms.' The paper also wondered whether the Fianna Fáil leader was 'running too far ahead of his grassroots.'[109]

In Dublin, the jury in the Arms Trial, after a mere two hours' deliberation, returned a verdict of 'not guilty' in the case against all four defendants.[110] The verdict raised serious questions about Lynch's support for Gibbons. Boland and Blaney both called on him to resign.[111] Buoyed up by his victory, Haughey imprudently broke his five-month silence and joined with Boland and Blaney in claiming that 'those who are responsible for this debacle have no alternative but to take the honourable course that is open to them.' When asked about his own political future he said that he had been mentioned in the past as a candidate for Taoiseach, and that 'I am not ruling anything out.'

Lynch made clear his intention of meeting any challenge head on when he returned from New York. All but two members of the Government were at the airport to greet him (and the Government Information Bureau had explanations for their absence).[112] Almost the entire Fianna Fáil parliamentary party, including senators, also turned out, making it known that this was no ordinary return from abroad. While no ultimatum was issued, Des O'Malley recalls that 'they were told that it would be appreciated if they did turn out, that to show support for Lynch was important at that particular time and circumstance.'[113] Significance was attached to the presence of 'the 1916–1923 Republican Old Guard' of Frank Aiken, Seán MacEntee, Paddy Smith and Michael Hilliard. The attendance of 'the solid hard-core of the foundation establishment' was interpreted as 'a demonstration of traditional Republican support' for Lynch.[114] To add to this impressive array was President de Valera's secretary, Máirtín Ó Flaitheartaigh, whose attendance many saw as 'the complete traditional Republican blessing.'

Haughey's challenge quickly crumbled in the face of this show of party strength. Indeed, within days he voted confidence in Jack Lynch and in Jim Gibbons, the minister whose word in court could have put him behind bars for twenty years. As one British Government report predicted, 'it is unlikely [that] the rebels would risk their political future by bringing down the Government . . . It has been observed that deputies sometimes make valiant declarations late at night which upon sober reflection fail to be translated into dramatic action.'[115]

Shortly before the crucial Dáil vote, Hillery met the British ambassador, Sir John Peck, and relayed Lynch's gratitude for checking whether his request for the Prime Minister, Edward Heath, to issue a public declaration of support still stood. In the circumstances, Lynch 'now feels that any overt support from Westminster or Stormont might be counterproductive, so the less said publicly the better.'[116] Hillery proceeded to give Peck

> a revealing account of the political battle inside Fianna Fáil since the acquittals in the arms conspiracy trial. Hillery himself was exhausted. He said he had been the hatchet man and had spent the last four days and nights twisting the arms of the dissidents. He seemed content with the results.[117]

Despite Kevin Boland's resignation from the Dáil, the Fianna Fáil parliamentary party closed ranks and narrowly survived the vote of confidence. Lynch now felt emboldened to embark on a new anti-republican drive.

THE 'RAPE OF THE FALLS'

The shadow of the Arms Crisis would loom over Jack Lynch and Fianna Fáil for a considerable time. Dissent remained within the parliamentary party, though this was camouflaged by Fianna Fáil's legendary discipline. On 12 June 1970 *Hibernia* estimated that up to twenty-five Fianna Fáil TDs opposed Lynch's line on the North, but this was an estimation of sentiment rather than of voting intentions.[118] The fact that *Hibernia* published the names of the deputies ensured that those considered as wavering would be subjected to additional pressure from Lynch loyalists.

Speculation about an early election, while a popular topic in the media, proved ill-founded, given Fianna Fáil's will to power and the belief entertained by almost all dissidents that the cause of Irish unity would be even more in jeopardy if it were placed in the hands of Fine Gael and the Labour Party, neither of which had sufficiently overcome their ideological antipathy to contemplate coalition. Determined to make as much political capital from the debacle as possible, the opposition parties harried the Government; but Lynch rejected their calls for an all-party committee on the North, reiterating instead his now-standard offer of *ad hoc* meetings with the party leaders.[119] When it was pointed out that both the Belfast and London Parliaments were discussing the crisis, and that the Dáil had an equal duty to respond, Lynch's reply that there was 'no reason why we should not be different from Stormont or Westminster'[120] was considered extremely unsatisfactory.

The biggest threat to Lynch's Northern policy came arguably from the results of the British general election of 18 June, which returned a Conservative majority. In the North the Ulster Unionist Party obtained 54 per cent of the vote and eight seats in the British House of Commons.[121] The new Secretary of State for the Home Department, Reginald Maudling, made his first visit to the North on 30 June. He had not been the shadow home secretary while in opposition, and his ignorance of the Northern situation staggered many of those he met.[122]

The election of a Conservative Government brought with it an intensified campaign to crush the IRA. On 3 July, Lieutenant-General Ian Freeland declared a curfew on the entire Falls Road area in Belfast, and a helicopter descended to announce that anyone who remained on the streets would be shot.[123] It was not an idle threat: in the following thirty-six hours the British army killed five people and injured dozens more. 1,600 canisters of CS gas were fired into the tightly knit streets, and the situation was exacerbated by the manner in which the British army conducted house-to-house searches.

> Troops broke down doors with pick-axes and rifle butts. They ransacked houses, ripping up floorboards, tearing out fireplaces and smashing holes in walls and ceilings. Religious statues were broken and crucifixes pulled down causing some residents to regard the British Army as no different from the sectarian gangs who threw rocks through church windows.[124]

The two-day curfew soon became known in the nationalist community as the 'Rape of the Falls'. While the number of arms discovered was considered significant at the time,[125] strategically the curfew was an unmitigated blunder. By attacking the entire Falls Road area the British army had given the impression that it considered the enemy to be not the IRA but the entire nationalist community. The curfew acted as a significant recruiting agent for the IRA,[126] and it is universally accepted as a watershed in relations between the British army and the Catholic community.[127] The army's presence was now seen as another oppressive arm of the Stormont regime,[128] an image reinforced when, after the curfew was lifted, two Unionist ministers travelled in a British armoured patrol on 'a triumphal tour of the subjugated area.'[129] In the House of Commons, Maudling told members that 'the rule of law, not the rule of the gun, would be maintained.'[130] For nationalists in Belfast, the two had become indistinguishable.

In Dublin the Government Information Bureau issued a statement on Saturday 4 July that expressed the Taoiseach's 'deep concern at the continuation of unhappy events in the North' and his sympathy to the bereaved. Lynch's terse statement made two requests of the British Government: the impartial disarmament of civilians and the prohibition of provocative parades for the remainder of the year.[131] The Government met for two hours on Sunday and issued another statement.

> The Government know full well that partition is basic to the whole problem. There can be no doubt whatsoever about our commitment to the reunification of our country and to the safety and wellbeing of all the Irish people.[132]

While it attempted to convey a trenchant and purposeful image, this statement, combined with an embargo on Northern Ireland debates in the Dáil, did little to quell confusion regarding Government policy. Once again it took a crisis to force the issue. The statement noted that

> last year very specific guarantees of safety and protection were given. There has now been the unilateral disarmament of one section of the Belfast people—the Catholic minority in the Falls area. This inevitably creates fears amongst the people which can only be allayed by the absolute guarantee of their protection and the equally effective disarmament of all others who hold arms illegally.[133]

This statement was noteworthy more for what it omitted than for what it said. There was no reference to the curfew, and while sympathy was expressed for the bereaved, the perpetrators were not explicitly mentioned. There was no reference to the use of CS gas, to the demolition of homes or to indiscriminate shooting and killing. The only issue relevant to the curfew was the desirability of a non-partisan approach to civilian disarmament, while the tone of the statement gave the impression that the British army had stumbled on an isolated arms dump rather than having conducted the systematic brutalisation of a community. Indeed Lynch's emphasis on the need for bicommunal disarmament suggested that the Government would have been entirely satisfied with the British army's actions if the people of the Shankill Road had received a similar visit. Finally, Lynch's faith in the fears of

Catholics being assuaged by the removal of all *illegal* weapons—a reference to loyalist arms—was evidence of his blinkered interpretation of events. In the aftermath of the curfew, nationalists were more afraid of the British army, whose arms, needless to say, were legally possessed.

Lynch's proclivity for understatement was bitterly resented by the nationalist community, which expected him to adopt a more pugnacious posture.[134] It was welcomed, however, by the darling of the unionist right, Brian Faulkner, who described Lynch's approach as 'statesmanlike.'[135] There was a time when Lynch's statement—which reaffirmed a belief that partition was central to the problem, and which committed the Government to the realisation of a united Ireland—would have been vehemently attacked by Faulkner. Considering the gravity of the situation, Faulkner must have skipped over the rhetoric and noted what the statement did not say. There was no explicit criticism of the British or Northern Governments, and the Irish Government did not threaten any action.

In Dublin the Government met in emergency session on 5 July, with the chief of staff, the Garda Commissioner and the Secretary of the Department of Justice, Peter Berry, also present. The meeting was called at the joint request of the new Ministers for Justice and Defence, Des O'Malley and Gerry Cronin, and its purpose was to discuss the possibility of a *coup d'état* in the Republic. Neither the chief of staff nor the head of the Garda Síochána had any new information on such a possibility, and Berry's impression was that 'the two inexperienced, newly appointed security Ministers had added two and two and come up with five.'[136] However, the fact that such a meeting was summoned at all illustrates the siege mentality afflicting the Government at that time.

Later that month the National Executive of Fianna Fáil again dealt with a request from the Six Counties to extend the party organisation there by recognising the Wolfe Tone Cumann, established in Belfast, as a branch of Fianna Fáil. As with all such requests made since the 1920s, it was turned down.[137]

THE INTERNMENT SCARE

Since the purge of the Government, Lynch and his new Minister for Justice, Des O'Malley, had considered various anti-republican initiatives, but they thought it imprudent to act before the conclusion of the Arms Trial. Now the gloves were off.

On 7 November 1970 eight IRA men were arrested in Coolock, Dublin, and on the following day fifteen were arrested outside Dundalk and charged with the illegal possession of arms. The arrests were interpreted as a serious change in policy, away from the 'blind eye' afforded to republicans active in the North and resident in the South. *Hibernia* argued that 'the reasonable assumption must surely be that the arrest of these men is much more than a local issue. One sees it as a hardening of attitude by the Gardaí, by the Minister for Justice, and by the Taoiseach.'[138]

On 4 December, Lynch announced that, following an identifiable threat to national security, the Government had notified the Council of Europe of its intention to derogate from the European Convention on Human Rights with a view to introducing internment should the threat persist. Lynch wished to quell speculation that the statement stemmed from talks with either the Belfast or London Governments, and he denied 'unequivocally' that the matter had been discussed with any other government either before or since the announcement. Despite insisting that the Government was working on 'the very best evidence available,' evidence that was 'absolutely reliable,' Lynch and O'Malley could not explain why the ordinary legal process could not be used to meet the purported threat to the state.[139]

When the opposition parties tried to have the matter discussed in the Dáil, Lynch put up a number of obstacles, the most novel being the argument that there was so much legislation the Dáil had to enact before Christmas that there would not be sufficient time to discuss any extraneous issue.[140] This excuse, if genuine, was totally counter-productive, as it proved impossible for the Dáil to discuss parliamentary business for the rest of the day.

Dáil business was suspended for twenty minutes when the Ceann Comhairle turned down requests by the Labour Party for a debate. The acrimonious exchanges continued when the Dáil reassembled. Eventually the leader of the Labour Party, Brendan Corish, was suspended from the Dáil, and he was followed by Noël Browne and Stephen Coughlan, both of whom were forcibly removed. Coughlan's contributions were particularly emotive. Accusing Lynch of 'moving in the direction of civil war because of his own cowardice,' he proclaimed that 'we will have no executions and no hunger strikes, such as we had before.'[141] After Coughlan was removed the Dáil adjourned until the following morning, only to be subjected to more interruptions, leading to the suspension of Conor Cruise O'Brien.

Des O'Malley has since claimed that the plot that prompted the Government to act was one involving the kidnapping of Government ministers. He has insisted that his information was reliable and the threat serious.[142] According to O'Malley the internment threat was aimed at Saor Éire, which was believed to be behind the conspiracy.

We made that statement publicly at the time in order to encourage the Provisional IRA particularly and the Official IRA also, who were very strong and active at that time, to come the heavy if you like on this very small group, Saor Éire, and to put a stop to their activities. I don't mean come the heavy in the sense of actually shooting them or anything but of threatening them, that they would desist from their activities.[143]

While this clarifies the motivation for the Government's public threat of internment, it was a bizarre way of getting its message across. Existing legislation was considered worthless by the Minister for Justice, as Saor Éire 'hadn't done what they were proposing to do,' and 'you can't convict someone for something that hasn't yet happened.'[144] As for O'Malley's contention that he didn't mean that the IRA would force Saor Éire to desist by 'shooting them or anything,' it is not clear how this was communicated to the IRA. Indeed Seán Mac Stiofáin recalled that he sent two IRA men 'to the two people in Saor Éire' and said, 'Look, if your people are responsible for internment down here you're all dead.'[145] Saor Éire got the message, and the internment threat subsided.

But there was a price. By openly embracing internment as a possible strategy Lynch played into the hands of those in the Ulster Unionist Party who favoured the introduction of internment to meet a much greater threat. Lynch said that the

Government had considered the ramifications, for the North and the South, and concluded that 'the warning should have no repercussions in terms of similar action in the north as it is directed against a specific plot here.'[146] Nationalists and civil rights leaders were appalled, believing that Lynch's unexpected announcement made internment north of the border almost a certainty. 'Dear God, have we gone back to this!' exclaimed the Nationalist Party leader, Eddie McAteer, who described internment on suspicion as 'a medieval panic measure [that] in modern times smacks of fascism.' He pleaded with the Government to 'think again in the name of justice.'[147]

The Grand Master of the Orange Order, Rev. Martin Smyth, commended Lynch on his 'statesmanship,' which he compared to the stance of the Canadian Prime Minister, Pierre Trudeau, in dealing with the Front de Libération du Québec.[148] Though the Northern Government had been reported as believing that Lynch's announcement did not mean that internment would be reactivated in the North,[149] Chichester-Clark was forced to admit that 'the argument for internment in Northern Ireland was now strengthened.'[150] For O'Malley the end clearly justified the means. While acknowledging that 'undoubtedly' his proposal could have been exploited by the Unionist Party, he also maintained that 'there are some times when it is necessary to do things which are going to give ammunition to your opponents or your critics, but you still have to do them; and it worked.'[151]

THE 1971 ARD-FHEIS

As the time for the Fianna Fáil ard-fheis approached, the British ambassador, Sir John Peck, wrote to the Foreign and Commonwealth Office to relate that Lynch had told him that Captain Kelly was working flat out to get his account of the Arms Crisis published. 'His aim,' Peck reported, 'is clearly to get it out just before the Ard Fheis in order to have the most damaging impact possible.' Peck ruminated that Collins, the publishing house with which Captain Kelly had negotiated a contract, should scrutinise the work well, 'as otherwise it might become very expensive.' He also recommended informing Collins that they would do well to wait until after the Public Accounts Committee had reported, as it was widely believed that Lynch's Government 'see the enquiry as tantamount to a re-run of the Arms Trial, getting the verdict right this time.'

The Foreign and Commonwealth Office responded with a litany of questions regarding the book. Peck asked, in the event of there being a publication date before the ard-fheis, 'Can you make these points to your friend?' The day after Peck's message arrived in London, A. C. Thorpe of the Foreign and Commonwealth Office met his contact at Collins, who promised a proof of the book. The British Government's influence may have proved decisive, for Collins withdrew from the contract two weeks later.

With Collins dropping the publication, and no doubt having insisted on acquiring the Irish rights, Thorpe commented that Kelly's search for a publisher would 'have to start again from scratch.'[152] Kelly pressed ahead but was forced to publish his book, *Orders for the Captain*, by himself. With its explosive content and its critique of the Lynch leadership, it missed the ard-fheis by some months.

In the weeks before the ard-fheis in February 1971 a small caucus met intermittently in a private house in Dublin to ensure, in Kevin Boland's words, 'that an effort would be made to retain the Republican character of the party.'[153] These endeavours, however, were minuscule compared with the preparations made by the leadership, which proved indefatigable in its attempts to stage-manage the gathering.[154] The letter to each delegate from the general secretary stated that 'no tickets are being issued for the Presidential Address because of lack of space.'[155] This break from normal procedure seems all the more curious in the light of the fact that for the first time the ard-fheis was being held in the Main Hall of the RDS, the biggest indoor venue in the country, capable of accommodating three thousand more people than the traditional venue, the Mansion House. The honorary secretaries' report stated cryptically that 'many cumainn because of their failure to register in time, found they were not entitled to representation at the current ard fheis.'[156]

Other anomalies were evident in the new procedures introduced for the election of honorary secretaries and treasurers. The normal procedure had been to notify nominees that they had been nominated and then to formally seek confirmation by a certain date of their consent to their names going forward. Boland, however, received no such notification but sent his acceptance by registered post, and his name duly appeared on the ballot paper. It was later discovered that a number of cumainn that had nominated Boland did not receive delegates' tickets.[157] On the eve of the ard-fheis a leak to the *Irish Press* made it clear that a change had been made to the voting system. This made it compulsory to vote for two candidates for these positions, otherwise the votes would be invalid. None of the delegates were officially notified of these changes, nor did an explanation for them appear in the agenda or in any of the reports distributed to delegates on their arrival.

The motive for the change, however, was plain enough to Boland and Blaney.[158] Boland was one of three candidates running for the two positions of honorary secretary, a position he had held for several years. The other two candidates were (unofficially) official candidates. The new system compelled those who wished to vote for Boland's re-election to vote both for and against him. As the change had been concealed until after nominations had closed, the obvious counter-action of putting forward a second candidate was unavailable.

The result was never really in doubt. Blaney, despite receiving more than 1,500 votes, also fell foul of the new system and was narrowly defeated. Next came the list of nominations for the Committee of Fifteen and the Officer Board. A list of 'approved' candidates was widely circulated by TDs and senators to delegates, and this was complemented by many informal conversations.[159] Not surprisingly, therefore, the Committee of Fifteen and the Officer Board all corresponded to the list of approved candidates that had been distributed to delegates.

The 1971 ard-fheis produced an important victory for the leadership, already bolstered within the Government by four new loyal ministers. It was clear to some, and is even clearer now, that the ard-fheis was a defining moment in the history of Fianna Fáil. It was to be the moment when the two wings of the party—divided over the most appropriate response to the Northern crisis—clashed swords and decided the party's future direction. The events leading to the Arms Crisis and the departure of five ministers provided the immediate background for the ard-fheis. It was clear also that the leadership was anxious to minimise anything that might ignite the ard-fheis on issues pertaining to the North or to the fall-out from the Arms Trials.

The honorary secretaries' report was a model of understatement. The resignations of Kevin and Gerry Boland were referred to as 'changes in the Officer Board', without further elaboration (save that their replacements were named, both of whom were staunch Lynch loyalists). Neither the honorary secretaries' report nor the agenda referred directly to the Arms Crisis. On the cover of the agenda there was a large photograph of Lynch, looking pensive but determined. Inside, the introduction laconically reported that

> the year which has passed since our last ard fheis has been an eventful one, a year in which Fianna Fáil had to face serious problems and difficulties. Because the heart of Fianna Fáil was sound, because the members of our great organisation remained true to our fundamental beliefs and ideals, because their loyalty to Fianna Fáil principles and their faith in the basic Fianna Fáil policies could not be shaken Fianna Fáil emerged triumphant.[160]

In seeking a full discussion on Northern Ireland the dissidents adopted a three-pronged strategy. The first action was to oppose the adoption of standing orders (procedural rules). For as long as anyone could remember, the adoption of standing orders was a formality, and the rules had not been altered in any way for some years. In 1971, however, several substantial changes had been made, all of which had the effect of diminishing rights formally available to delegates.[161] No explanation for the changes was offered, nor indeed was there any indication that the standing orders proposed were any different from before. Believing that the leadership was attempting to amend the standing orders surreptitiously, the dissidents demanded an explanation, and called for a vote should this be unsatisfactory. At this point they also intended to raise the question of the changes to voting procedures (mooted in the *Irish Press*) after nominations had closed but before they were ratified by the ard-fheis. The second part of the strategy was to initiate a discussion on the honorary secretaries' report, to call a vote on its contents, and, in view of the wide circulation of an inner-circle list of preferred National Executive candidates, to call for joint supervision of the election process. Kevin Boland would speak at this point in the agenda and explain his reasons for resigning as honorary secretary. Finally, the dissidents would try to ensure that, after the preliminaries had been dispensed with, the ard-fheis would be devoted, if necessary, to the debate on Northern policy.

None of these objectives was achieved, as the ard-fheis descended into a bitter and acrimonious fight among factions that often came to blows.

Most of what Lynch said that day went unheard by delegates, who shouted rival chants of 'We want Jack!' and 'Union Jack!' As the *Irish Times* commented, Lynch's address 'will go into the files as the most difficult three hours a Fianna Fáil president has ever had to endure in public.' The speech itself contained 'something for everyone from Major Chichester-Clark to the most rabid Kerry Republican'; but, as one reporter put it, no leader signals the changes in the basic articles of faith by underscoring the changes. You had the feeling, however, that for every two advancing steps towards Stormont, he took one reassuring step back—and the cheers were predictable when the familiar reassuring lines were used.[162]

The Minister for External Affairs, Patrick Hillery, was perhaps Lynch's most ardent defender, trading his normally placid demeanour for a more combative stance. He shouted that they now had to recognise that they were dealing with 'the enemies of Fianna Fáil.' Fianna Fáil's policy was Jack Lynch's policy, and it was the same as that of de Valera and Lemass. The party would survive 'in spite of any bully boys within or without the organisation.' Lynch would not be frightened out of office, he said, and added: 'You can have Boland but you can't have Fianna Fáil.'[163] Nell McCafferty described the scene in the hall:

> The leaders pointed at each other, Government Ministers of this country with swelling veins, curled lips, enraged, outraged, contorted faces, shouting into a battery of microphones. Paddy Hillery, Minister for External Affairs, shouted hysterically across the floor at Kevin Boland, his former companion in the Cabinet. Boland, with a curling index finger invited Hillery to 'come on, come on.' They stood apart, above the crowd below; Hillery, all urbanity gone, screaming now, Boland shaggily baiting him. The crowd came to blows, and a woman pushed past me, advising me to get out of the arena.[164]

Contradictions were apparent throughout the ard-fheis, as delegates found themselves cheering a variety of irreconcilable political stances.

> In the matter of Kevin Boland and his stand, there was more feeling for him than that represented in the 'walk-out' during the Taoiseach's speech: at times it seemed that 40 per cent of the audience was going along with some of his views (as articulated by the 'rebel' speakers). The name of John Kelly rated a 60 per cent ovation and this was rather symbolic of this 1971 ard fheis . . . It could cheer John Kelly's name and Neil Blaney's name: it did cheer Jack Lynch's Republicanism wildly even as he was *de facto* recognising Stormont . . . as wildly, indeed, as it cheered him when he said, in a departure from script, that nothing had changed—and nothing would fundamentally change.[165]

The tactic seems to have been to let Boland speak and to have him followed by a succession of party elders, who would parade their revolutionary credentials in defiance of the dissidents. After Boland was ushered off the rostrum, Seán MacEntee was on his feet, and he gave a detailed account of his upbringing in Belfast, his service in the Irish Volunteers and his part in the 1916 Rising.

> I fought against partition and like your chairman, Paddy Smith, I was sentenced to death for it. I was in the staff of the Belfast Brigade in 1920–21. During that Black and Tan period, there were three hundred casualties in Belfast, most of them

comrades of mine, but many of them ordinary civilians, slain because they were suspected of being supporters of Sinn Féin.[166]

Addressing hecklers, MacEntee said he was talking to a generation of Irish people who were free men—not slaves—because of what they had done for them. (There were shouts of 'Time up!' at this point.) When MacEntee said that Fianna Fáil had never forsaken its principles he was met with cries of 'Who are you fooling!' And as he embarked on a discussion of realism his words became inaudible, though he was heard to conclude that 'because in the long run they preferred partition to war, that is the basic situation.'

Nóirín Ní Scolláin, a member of the outgoing National Executive and a prominent Boland supporter, entered the debate, saying that

> mere sympathy for our brothers and sisters in the North is not enough. For fifty years we have ignored them and have done nothing. Have we lost our soul? Our people who came to us in need were refused and offered platitudes. The chief executive of the state is responsible for all the actions and obligations of the state. The chief executive is responsible for the arrest of John Kelly.[167]

Joe Groome pointed out that he had been honorary secretary of the party under de Valera, Lemass and Lynch (so, indeed, had Boland) and that the dissidents were 'a disgrace.' They thought they had 'a softy' when they elected Lynch, but they now realised that 'they had made the biggest mistake in their lives.' There were now cries of 'Put them out! They're not Fianna Fáil men! They're blackguards!'[168]

The physical violence that erupted was unprecedented. John Healy wrote:

> I have not, since my days as a youngster and the Bolshie and Blueshirt rallies of my childhood, seen such naked passion exhibited publicly, and while it makes great copy for a media man, there is something frightening when, in the middle of the R.D.S. Main Hall, you see men in their 40s rip off their glasses before making a lunge at a neighbour.[169]

The second day of the ard-fheis was little better, particularly during the speech of Jim Gibbons, now Minister for Agriculture, the vitriolic nature of the 'debate' heightened by the fact that Gibbons had received his portfolio at the expense of Neil Blaney. Throughout his speech Gibbons was continually heckled with shouts of 'Liar!', 'Perjurer!' and 'Out, out!' As he spoke on a motion recommending the extension of the beef cattle incentive scheme a Co. Donegal delegate asked how small farmers 'could look up to a man in high office who was a perjurer.' Gibbons responded:

> I was never a traitor. That man there [pointing to Lynch] is leader of the Fianna Fáil party, and I would not betray him, because if I betrayed him I would betray you.

Having merged leader and cause into one, Gibbons went on the offensive, describing his opponents in the audience as 'a rent-a-crowd . . . hired to interrupt,' who should 'go back to Trinity College.'[170] After a particularly bad bout of heckling Gibbons declared that

> I am one of you, and they [pointing to the hecklers] are not. Look at their beards. I am much too proud of the people who went before me to be associated with anything treacherous or anyone false. But these people over there would sell their country and sell their leader.

The ard-fheis ended suddenly in something of an anti-climax. The motions on justice, which it was feared would be the occasion for yet another fireworks display, were shelved, along with other remaining business, to be dealt with by the incoming National Executive. Lynch, who had seemed throughout to be in a state of denial, made a quick reappearance and closed the conference by complimenting the remaining delegates on 'the most successful ard-fheis that Fianna Fáil has ever had.' In a line that the *Irish Times* described as 'contemptuous of the intelligence of the people' he described the tumult as 'a little letting off of steam,' which 'did everybody good.'[171]

According to the British Government's report on the ard-fheis, this was always going to be the 'crucial battle', and Lynch's victory relied on the fact that 'the selection of delegates had clearly been weighted in favour of the party leadership.' Filling the eighty or so party leadership positions and demonstrating majority support for Lynch's Northern policy had been the twin aims of the conference, and both aims were

> triumphantly achieved, mainly because of the immense effort made by the party machine in the preparations for the conference, particularly during the Christmas recess. When Fianna Fáil determines to pursue a certain course, follow a certain leader, and crush internal opposition, it is efficient, ruthless and none too scrupulous.

The protests of the Boland faction, the British report concluded, were motivated more by helplessness than anything else.[172]

Dick Walsh of the *Irish Times* wrote that 'some went out to wake Fianna Fáil Republicanism, but most went home sensing rather than fully understanding that from here on in it was a whole new ballgame.'[173] The paper's editorial described the ard-fheis as 'not only a personal triumph for the Taoiseach, but the burial of some part of Fianna Fáil.'[174]

Chapter 13 ~

| DOOMSDAY, 1971–3

INTERNMENT

Despite Lynch's well-orchestrated triumph at the February 1971 ard-fheis, his position remained precarious so long as the Northern situation continued to deteriorate. His command of domestic politics was heavily influenced by British actions in the Six Counties.

On 28 April, Deputy Joe Lenehan was expelled from the parliamentary party for voting against the Government four days earlier. Lynch was able to sidestep a motion of no confidence in Jim Gibbons when it was ruled out of order by the Ceann Comhairle.[1] In the same month Neil Blaney made a blistering attack on the party leadership at a Fianna Fáil meeting in Arklow, in which he denounced the 'peaceful-means hypocrites', claiming that he knew the names of twenty-five Oireachtas members who had given their own guns in August 1969 for use in the North. He called on the rank and file to stop the party running away from its core principles.

> We want to get back to republican traditions and the removal of the Treaty, for which Fianna Fáil was founded. I said at Letterkenny and I say it again now, that if the minority in the Six Counties are under murderous attacks they are entitled to make up their own minds if they want to use arms to defend themselves, and we who claim responsibility for every one of the 32 counties are the last who should say Don't. If any of us feel we wanted to help them it was for us to decide what help to give and let them use it whatever way they liked.

He went on to claim that Lynch, since his commendable speech of 13 August, had made no comparable attack on British actions in the North. In contrast to the sentiments of that speech, Lynch now expressed regret at the deaths of British soldiers but ignored the dead of the Northern minority, and the more than a thousand people incarcerated for as little as shouting 'Up the IRA!' Blaney condemned the threatened introduction of internment in the South as Lynch's most scandalous action since the speech made on the night of Blaney's and Haughey's dismissal.[2]

In response to Blaney's speech the National Executive, now composed almost entirely of Lynch acolytes, began an inquisition of all cumainn, including Arklow, that had given a platform to prominent republican critics.[3] It was also recommended that dissidents expelled from the parliamentary party who retained party membership should be ineligible to attend or be invited to party meetings at any level, including social functions organised by cumainn other than their own. Such rights were to be the sole privilege of those holding high office.[4] This was to prevent fraternisation among those who subscribed to irregular opinions on party policy and to ensure a homogenisation of views, conforming to those of the party leadership.

Alive to Lynch's vulnerabilities, the British ambassador, Sir John Peck, reported in June that, for the first time since the Arms Crisis, Lynch and Hillery were seriously concerned about internal party unity on the North. Despite 'hair-raising moments,' Lynch's political skills, combined with party loyalty, had allowed him to retain the leadership as well as an endorsement of 'his policy of a peaceful approach to the problem of unification' and of 'working with the British.' Now there were signs that Lynch's position was crumbling.

> I have not so far over the last year rung alarm bells, but I am doing so now . . . I am bound to give warning that Mr. Lynch's position as Taoiseach is not now secure, and I urge most seriously that Ministers should consider the consequences of his being forced out of office.

No visible progress could be seen on the three issues considered to be crucial to Government policy—reunification, North-South co-operation, and justice for Northern Catholics—and Hillery had identified

> the beginning of a crisis of confidence among the Fianna Fáil stalwarts—the active party members and officers of the constituencies. They are still loyal to the Taoiseach but are beginning to ask themselves whether his policies concerning Northern Ireland are right.

Pre-empting suggestions that he might have been sold a line by the Fianna Fáil leaders, Peck cautioned that Hillery was speaking

> as Party Secretary (and as a friend) rather than as Foreign Secretary. I stress this because it was not a devious attempt to put pressure on us, and it would be a mistake to so regard it.

Peck pointed out that the alternatives to the status quo was 'a Fianna Fáil government under rougher, tougher, leadership who could cause us great trouble in Northern Ireland, the Common Market and the United Nations' or 'a weak and implausible Fine Gael-Labour coalition.' While the latter might superficially appear more pliant to British interests, it would result in 'increased political influence and physical strength of the IRA, to whom many hard hard-core Fianna Fáil supporters, freed from the inhibitions of the ruling party, would turn out of sheer frustration.' He concluded that

> on the sole grounds of internal security and law-and-order in the North there are strong reasons for giving what help we can to Mr. Lynch and the forces of moderation in the Republic. I need not enunciate the disadvantages of having an

embittered and possibly reckless government in Dublin at this stage, nor those of an accretion of active sympathy for the IRA in the South.[5]

In essence, Peck was telling his superiors in London that Lynch needed a tangible reform programme to convince party supporters that his policies were yielding results. Instead Lynch would get internment in the North, resulting in an explosion of violence and renewed pressure for a tougher line towards Britain.

The path to internment was paved during the leadership transition within the Ulster Unionist Party. In March, James Chichester-Clark relinquished office, ostensibly on the grounds that he was receiving insufficient military support from the British Government.[6] The election of Brian Faulkner as his replacement reflected the continuing drift to the right within Ulster unionism and a break with the ascendancy class. In contrast to the good old days when Unionist politicians, such as James Craig and Basil Brooke, could expect to serve two decades as Prime Minister, the political life-span of the incumbent was shrinking as the position became less a glittering prize than a poisoned chalice (though it was no less sought after for that). O'Neill had lasted six years, Chichester-Clark two; Faulkner would serve only one.

Faulkner immediately organised a reshuffle in an effort to establish what he called 'a broadly based government.'[7] What he meant in practice, however, was a government representative of the different shades of unionist opinion, not of Northern Ireland as a whole. His primary aim was to unite the Unionist Party and to heal the post-O'Neill rifts before an all-out assault on the republican community. To this end, one of the most hard-line opponents of reform, Harry West (sacked by O'Neill four years earlier), was brought back into the Government.[8] By now Faulkner's plans for internment were well advanced, and the British Government endorsed them on 5 August, promising to supply the necessary military resources (without being overburdened with the exact details).[9] Four days later, at 4 a.m. on Monday 9 August 1971, the British army descended on five hundred homes and managed to arrest 342 men listed in their outdated files as being worthy of internment.

It is generally accepted that internment was a political and military disaster, even by its own criteria. Within twenty-four hours fifteen people had been killed and hundreds injured; by the following day the number of deaths had risen to twenty-one. Ten thousand people in Belfast alone moved out of their homes.[10]

Up to the introduction of internment 34 people had been killed in 1971; in the remaining five months the figure rose to 174. Nearly five hundred people would be killed in 1972. This was despite the fact that the Dublin leadership of the Official IRA (whose activists were hardest hit) used internment to wind down its campaign, contrary to a desire among the rank and file to 'expand the struggle.'[11] Reports soon emerged of detainees being tortured at holding centres by 'deep interrogation' techniques.[12] (Dissatisfied with the conclusions of the subsequent British Government inquiry,[13] the Irish Government took the matter to the slow-moving European Court of Human Rights, which eventually, in January 1978, found the British Government to have been guilty of 'inhuman and degrading treatment.'[14])

Internment reactivated the civil rights movement, and produced a new generation of republicans educated in the 'university of revolution'—Long Kesh internment camp, outside Lisburn.[15] The fact that the extraordinary power of imprisonment without trial was directed exclusively against the Catholic population (the first loyalist was not interned until 1973) illustrated its partisan purpose and heightened inter-community tensions. Internment presented a particular problem for those Catholics who had joined the Ulster Defence Regiment—a part-time reserve attached to the British army as a replacement for the B Specials—and who now felt 'disillusioned and vulnerable.'[16]

Edward Heath had stressed at his meeting with Faulkner on 5 August that, in the interests of appearing impartial, 'those interned should include some Protestants,'[17] and this was the position up to the draft message prepared for Lynch, which stated that 'Protestant as well as Catholic and IRA extremists will be liable to internment.'[18] Significantly, this line was crossed out in the draft and did not appear in the final version that Lynch received. In fact at a secret meeting with the British ambassador at the end of July, Lynch had been told that interment was imminent, and he was asked to consider parallel internment in the South. After carefully reading the British proposal, Lynch, according to Peck, stated categorically

> that he could not contemplate internment at the present time . . . and if he tried to introduce it in consequence of our doing so, neither his nor any Irish Government could survive such a measure.[19]

Lynch repeatedly cautioned Peck against the introduction of internment, arguing prophetically that only a small minority of those interned would be 'bad', the others would be alienated by the experience, and the moderates would identify with the internees. Lynch's warnings had no effect on the British Government, which had already decided to give Faulkner this weapon; but it is worth noting that the British never publicised the fact that Lynch had been told almost two weeks earlier of the impending swoops. This suggests that they accepted Peck's observation that Lynch would come under intense pressure to say whether he had been consulted and that it was imperative that he be in a position to deny it.[20]

Within thirty-six hours of internment more than six thousand people had left their homes and moved to the South, where they were directed to five army camps.[21] Hillery was sent to London, but he failed to extract any concessions.[22] At one anti-internment meeting in Navan, Paddy Kennedy MP suggested that residents should put up barricades should internment be introduced in the South. Reports were coming in of a group of officers and NCOs in the FCA who had threatened to join the Provisional IRA 'unless the Government takes a more militant line on Northern Ireland.' They advocated a guerrilla campaign against the British army in border areas, the with-drawal of Irish peacekeeping forces from Cyprus, a boycott of British goods and the breaking off of diplomatic relations with Britain.[23]

Lynch's internment threat in December had encouraged some in Stormont to expect that, once internment was in operation in the North, Dublin would introduce a similar measure. Speaking in New York, the Northern Minister of Home Affairs, John Taylor, said that internment in the South 'must be accompanied by con-demnation of the IRA by Cardinal Conway.' He claimed that internment in the North and South in 1956, combined with the condemnation and excommunication of republicans by Cardinal D'Alton, had succeeded in defeating the IRA. He concluded, however, that the IRA would be defeated without the assistance of the Republic; it would just take longer.[24]

Faulkner questioned the Irish Government's critical stance, pointing out in a BBC interview that the Tánaiste, Erskine Childers, had said only a few months earlier that if internment was introduced in the Republic it would have the support of 'eighty per cent of the country.'[25] Des O'Malley, however, has rejected any connection between his planned internment and that implemented by the Unionist Party eight months later.

> To compare what I spoke about in December 1970 with what subsequently happened in the North in 1971 some time is just crazy. We had in mind the intern- ment of a small number—a *small* number—of very violent, clearly identifiable individuals. What they did in the North was mad.[26]

O'Malley's disavowal of any responsibility for the introduction of internment in the North raises two issues. Firstly, the use of an indiscriminate weapon for a discrim- inate purpose has traditionally proved difficult for governments, and the initial net inevitably widens if the primary aim of reducing the threat of violence is not quickly achieved. Indeed it should be remembered that the Northern Government intimated that internment would be used only against hardened terrorists, and for a relatively short period; in fact thousands were detained over four-and-a-half years. If O'Malley's sole intention was to put a few Saor Éire members behind bars, intern- ment would be like cracking a nut with a sledgehammer. Secondly, while O'Malley could not be blamed for how internment was *implemented* in the North, the Government can, arguably, be accused of having given respectability to the principle. Within a month of its introduction (and just before his meeting with Heath) Lynch undermined his own objections to internment by suggesting that a similar measure in the South was still possible and would 'depend completely on the security situation within the Republic': internment would be introduced only when Lynch's advisers were 'convinced that the security of the state was menaced.'[27] Faulkner could not have employed a better rationale for introducing internment in the North.

On the eve of its introduction Heath dissolved the British Parliament and, with maximum insensitivity, embarked on the Fastnet Race in his yacht. Despite the orgy of violence raging in the North as a result of his authorisation of internment, he would stay with the yacht race until the end, not returning to his desk until three days after the new conflagration had erupted. Heath could not be contacted until the day after the first internment swoop, when his officials communicated—employing an appropriate maritime metaphor—that the 'best news is the good "catch".'[28]

When Lynch eventually caught Heath on the phone he confessed his desperation. 'The press are in hordes around the place here, so I might just as well have a considered statement on the general position . . . I can't continue just saying nothing.' He delicately tried to tell Heath that there was a 'strong feeling' among the many people flooding over the border (he studiously avoided saying whether it was his own) that 'the army up there are not being completely impartial,' and 'again, without telling you your business, I think the army ought to be told of their true role.'

Heath was having none of it, and went so far as to blame the nationalist community for their own exodus. 'If it were not for a lot of the pressure which is being brought by the IRA in the Catholic communities, often deliberately to get them out of Northern Ireland, then your refugee camps would not be full.' In keeping with this separation from reality, he proceeded to defend Faulkner's policies towards the nationalist community. Faulkner's proposal to offer enhanced Catholic representation in parliamentary committees meant that 'it must be accepted that he has gone a very long way towards the Opposition . . . much further than we have in the British Parliament,' as if the differences between the Labour Party and the Conservative Party in Britain were comparable to those dividing people in Northern Ireland.

As the conversation drew to a close, Lynch confessed his worry that, having opted out of the system, moderate nationalists might be superseded by the IRA. He then raised the UN option, in his inimitable style.

> Lynch: . . . There is just one thing. Again it has been canvassed here—it was not mentioned yesterday in the talks between Maudling and Hillery—a United Nations presence. I take it that has not come into your reckoning at all. I know the answer to that and I know the difficulty about it, but I take it that you have not contemplated that at all in present circumstances.
> Heath: Not for a moment, no. This is part of the United Kingdom.
> Lynch: That is right, yes, and—well, anyway, I know all the arguments here. Very well, Mr Prime Minister . . . My boys [the Government] are meeting downstairs and I shall rejoin them . . . Thanks very much for calling back . . .
> Heath: Now what about this afternoon's telephone conversation . . . Do you want it not to have taken place?
> Lynch: No, I prefer it not to have taken place . . .
> Heath: Quite.
> Lynch: So this conversation need not have taken place either . . .
> Heath: We will do the same . . . Thank you.[29]

As Lynch had intimated to Heath, he now felt compelled to go on the offensive publicly, if only to counter accusations of inertia. Conveniently forgetting his own threat of internment eight months earlier, he described the reactivation of legislation for detention without trial as 'deplorable evidence of [the Northern Government's] political poverty.' While the Irish Government had acted with 'responsibility and restraint' during the previous two years, the new vista

> compels us to state our position with complete clarity. The administration of Northern Ireland is now, and has been since it was created, directed at the suppression of the civil and human rights of more than a third of the population . . . The Stormont regime, which has consistently repressed the non-Unionist population and bears responsibility for recurring violence in the Northern community, must be brought to an end.[30]

The speech marked a reversal of stated policy in a number of important ways.[31] The Unionist Government—not the IRA—was now considered to be responsible for the violence. Stormont, *from its creation,* had suppressed nationalists; but this was the first time that Lynch had explicitly called for its abolition, on the grounds that it was employing a repressive weapon (one that the Irish Government had introduced to deal with the same enemy in much less threatening circumstances).

Lynch had pinned his hopes on the Downing Street Declaration of August 1969, in which the British and Northern Governments had committed themselves to fair and equal treatment for all citizens in Northern Ireland. Now Lynch was forced to recognise that his favoured policy of functional co-operation was effectually at an end, and that the Downing Street Declaration was a dead letter, its implementation having been 'delayed and distorted.'[32]

In its editorial headed 'Mr. Lynch's new language' the *Irish Times* noted that his speech—'a big break from past attitudes . . . in language at any rate'—was 'not his normal style and, arguably, represents a concession to his more expressive followers and a hoped-for containment of them.'[33]

A telegram from Lynch to Heath, released simultaneously to the media by both sides, suggested that internment had already failed; that, should military solutions such as internment persist, he would support the passive resistance campaign being pursued by the non-unionist population; and that he remained willing to discuss possible political solutions with interested parties 'without prejudice to the aspiration of the great majority of the Irish people to the reunification of Ireland.'[34] Without waiting for Heath's reply, Lynch spoke in more forthright terms to the media, describing internment as 'a deliberate decision by the Stormont administration to attempt the outright repression of the minority' and again calling for the abolition of the Stormont regime, previously entrusted with implementing the desired reform programme.

Heath's response came quickly and, in retaliation for Lynch's discourtesy, was handed to Lynch just before being announced on the evening television news. It fell to the British ambassador, Sir John Peck, to travel to Lynch's home to deliver what he himself described as 'a fair stinker.'[35] He watched as Lynch carefully read Heath's note, which described Lynch's telegram as 'unjustifiable in its contents, unacceptable in its attempt to interfere in the affairs of the United Kingdom and can in no way contribute to the solution of the problems of Northern Ireland.'[36] Lynch could not be drawn on the contents of the note but instead turned to Peck and said, 'We better have a drink.' With that, Peck and his son, who acted as chauffeur, were invited to stay and, in Peck's words, enjoyed 'a charming and relaxed chat with the Taoiseach . . . He seemed quite reluctant to see us go.'[37] Peck reported that Lynch could be under no illusions about the folly of provoking public exchanges with the British, but he feared that 'he is no longer master in his own house'; and while he didn't expect an election in the near future 'we must be prepared for another leadership crisis in Fianna Fáil.' Lynch's 'apparently wild' actions since internment reflected Government decisions, Peck wrote; and party defections, resignations and dissidence, arising from the Northern issue, had 'shaken his position severely.'[38]

An Anglo-Irish summit meeting, which had been scheduled before internment, was due in the autumn. Though eager to bring the date forward so as to solicit Irish support, the British Government realised that it had compounded Lynch's problems by introducing internment and that Lynch was under sustained pressure for action from his party. In a report compiled within a month of the introduction of internment the British Government noted that Fianna Fáil had lost many members at the local level, disaffected by the leadership's performance on the North. Kevin Boland's putative party, soon to be named Aontacht Éireann, was 'a pressure group aimed at toppling Mr. Lynch and replacing him by the more militant Republicanism' of Blaney or Haughey.[39]

The British again speculated about what would happen within Fianna Fáil should Lynch lose power. While Dr Hillery was an obvious replacement, he lacked a political base and in attempting to build one would probably prove difficult to deal with, at least at the beginning. The other likely contenders—Blaney, Boland and Haughey—would be 'avowedly opposed' to British policies in Northern Ireland, and whatever the limitations of governmental action 'extremists and the IRA would draw comfort (and possibly also material comfort) from such an administration.'[40]

A Fine Gael government, or, more likely, a coalition with the Labour Party, was 'unlikely to amount to anything very effective.' Relieved of the responsibility of power, the 'extremist wing' within Fianna Fáil would increase in strength if in opposition, and Lynch's grip on the party would be correspondingly weakened. 'Therefore,' the report concluded, 'in practice the IRA would still be likely to enjoy greater material encouragement than they do now. Mr. Lynch therefore remains the best Irish Prime Minister in sight.'[41]

The British were wise enough to know that advertising their confidence in Lynch could, in the circumstances, only damage his reputation, not to mention his republican credentials within Fianna Fáil. As a result, when addressing Lynch's battles with republicans within and without Fianna Fáil the report claimed that 'in domestic political terms he stands to gain by being seen to be confronting a British Prime Minister.'[42] The British Government, therefore, should do its best to augment the impression that Lynch was heroically putting it up to them.

Before the summit meeting the British noted that if Lynch could not come away with tangible successes to confound his critics 'he will have to demonstrate to Irish opinion that he stood up for Ireland; i.e. he can more easily return bloody but unbowed than return empty handed.'[43] The British understood well Lynch's difficulties and, believing him to be the most malleable of the alternatives and to represent the best chance of complementing London's Irish policy, made gestures to help his position. The report—written before the meeting took place—concluded that 'it would do Mr. Lynch no harm were it to be reported that he had contended vigorously with the Prime Minister.'[44]

The British Government's aims were twofold: 'to persuade Mr. Lynch to take effective action against the IRA' and to get him 'to use his influence with the Roman Catholic minority in the North . . . so that they turn away from violence and look again to constitutional solutions at Stormont.'[45] As both issues were urgent, the British did what they could to persuade Lynch to bring forward the planned meeting by a month. It was also felt that, while Lynch shared some of his compatriots' reservations and concerns about Northern Ireland, he was 'too experienced and sensible a man to accept all the horror stories published in Dublin.'[46] The British realised that the hardening of Lynch's public statements was a response to public opinion and to demands within his party and that it did not necessarily spring from his own instincts and passions.

The Secretary of the Cabinet, Sir Burke Trend, was dismayed by 'the bareness of the landscape and the absence of any realistic prospect of making progress on the basis of our present assumptions.' In particular, 'we should be warned—by Vietnam and Rhodesia if we have forgotten our own earlier experience in dealing with recalcitrant colonies—against allowing ourselves to be drawn deeper in a situation from where there is no escape other than capitulation at the eleventh hour.'[47]

The high-level meeting took place on 6–7 September 1971. Not since 1921 had the heads of the Irish and British Governments met for the purpose of discussing the 'national question'.

Arrangements for the meeting were shrouded in secrecy. Early on Monday 6 September, Lynch arrived at the Prime Minister's official country residence, Chequers, in Buckinghamshire, accompanied by the Irish ambassador to Britain, Dr Dónal O'Sullivan. Heath was accompanied by the Secretary of the Cabinet, Sir Burke Trend. After lunch they were joined by Reginald Maudling and the Secretary of State for Foreign and Commonwealth Affairs, Sir Alec Douglas-Home. Lynch declined the invitation to stay overnight at Chequers, preferring to lodge at the Irish embassy. He returned for further talks on Tuesday morning, then travelled home to Dublin.

There was no discussion of the much-publicised telegrams of 19 August. When pushed on introducing internment in the Republic, Lynch, given his previous flirtation with this emergency measure, could not rule it out in principle, but he argued that it would 'only be considered if the internal situation in the Republic required it.'[48] Lynch and Heath also differed over the composition of possible future meetings. Heath suggested tripartite talks, to include Faulkner, which Lynch rejected: for him this was an issue between himself and Heath; and Faulkner was not the prime minister of a sovereign state. He countered with the suggestion of four-party talks, to include representatives of both the unionist and the nationalist community of Northern Ireland. Heath flatly refused, as this would suggest that Faulkner was just another political leader, rather than a prime minister.[49]

The British in their post-meeting pronouncements reiterated that 'the border is not an issue.' The meeting had resulted in 'a clearing of the air rather than any major agreement on future policy,'[50] though as this expression first emerged in drafts prepared before the meeting it is fair to assume that Heath had limited expectations and would judge its success purely according to how much co-operation Lynch was willing to afford the British security effort. They followed the advice of the Dublin embassy in their unattributable press briefings after the meeting, and they did their best to convey the image of a combative Fianna Fáil leader who fought Ireland's corner. By insisting on the Irish Government's participation in future talks the press briefings claimed that Lynch had sought to ignore Northern Ireland's constitutional status, and this had 'formed the main subject of the Chequers talks.' The reports also revealed that Lynch had turned down an offer of a tripartite meeting that would included the Prime Minister of Northern Ireland.[51]

Within a few days Lynch had backed down on his principled rejection of a tripartite meeting, and his own preferred option of a quadripartite meeting was pushed aside.

On 27 September, Heath, Lynch and Faulkner met at Chequers. Though heralded as the first meeting of its kind in almost five decades, it was something of a damp squib. Heath stood aside as if he was trying to adjudicate the rival positions, allowing Lynch and Faulkner to slug it out on internment, cross-border security, the causes of the problem and possible solutions.[52] Some of the disagreement related to the sequence of possible reforms: Lynch felt that reforms could bring an end to violence, whereas Faulkner was adamant that only an end to violence could facilitate reforms. Lynch said that he could not introduce internment, as conditions in the South did not warrant it, and in any case the trouble originated in the North. When he tried to divine how far Stormont would go to bring Northern nationalists into its institutions he met stiff resistance from Faulkner, who maintained that his government must govern and that it could not include people who sought ultimately to destroy the state. The best he could offer was enhanced representation on parliamentary committees (ignoring the fact that at this time Nationalist and SDLP members were refusing to take their seats).

When the meeting resumed the following day the tripartite format was abandoned and Heath met Lynch alone and then Faulkner.[53] Lynch left Heath with the prediction that if Faulkner prevaricated much longer he might find that by the time he was ready to talk constructively there would be no moderates to deal with, only the IRA.[54]

Despite British efforts to put a favourable spin on the meetings, it was clear that, at best, there had been a frank exchange of views—though these were already on the record. There were no concrete achievements to show. Lynch again left Chequers empty-handed, and he communicated to the British side that he could not countenance another trip to London 'in present circumstances,' for three reasons: the results of the Chequers meetings had been 'almost entirely negative'; even if he felt he should go his Government and party 'would not let him'; and he 'may have a political crisis on his hands in the near future.'[55]

TROUBLES WITHIN FIANNA FÁIL

With the bilateral and tripartite meetings producing no results, with violence spiralling out of control in the North and with Lynch facing internal dissent, the British Government again began mulling over the alternatives if Lynch should fall. A Fianna Fáil Government headed by any major party figure, including Hillery, Colley and Haughey, would

> take a more republican line on the North than does Lynch. We could expect such a government to refuse all cooperation with us over security matters, to have recourse to the UN and to attempt to stir trouble for us in third countries. They would be less explicit than Lynch in condemning violence and might give some more overt encouragement to the IRA.

The other possibility—a general election—was also unattractive from the British Government's viewpoint. It would be 'preceded by a period in which the Republic would have no real Government and in which hotheads in every party would be tempted to outdo one another in republicanism.' In the existing climate a presence in the Dáil of Aontacht Éireann or Official Sinn Féin was a possibility. Provisional Sinn Féin might also win seats, though they would not take them; it was pointed out that the last time there was an election during an IRA campaign the party had taken four seats (including one by Ruairí Ó Brádaigh, now the president of Provisional Sinn Féin). A repeat of the 1957 performance 'clearly cannot be ruled out,' while a coalition of Fine Gael and the Labour Party, the only alternative, 'would probably provide a weak and hesitant Government.' None of these alternatives would suit Britain's interests 'so well as the survival of Mr. Lynch.'[56]

The British also feared that Lynch and Hillery were diverging on Northern policy, which was prompting comment in Dublin, though not yet publicly.[57] Hillery's address to the Foreign Press Association in London on 22 September did little to assuage British unease. He said that a phased British withdrawal from the North 'would force the unionists to come to terms with a united Ireland,' a position 'dangerously close to the traditional republican line of Blaney and Boland.' The British noted that this was 'quite at variance with the Taoiseach's thinking' (though it might be added that it was not at variance with Fianna Fáil grass-roots understanding of policy), as was the idea of a UN peace-keeping force, which Hillery revived as a possibility at the same meeting.[58]

Lynch had more on his mind with a Dáil motion of no confidence in Jim Gibbons, the *bête noire* of Fianna Fáil's republican wing. The opposition motion was framed in such a way as to maximise the likelihood of Fianna Fáil dissidents voting in favour, emphasising the contradiction between Gibbons's statements in the Dáil in May 1970, in which he disavowed knowledge of the plan to import arms, and what had subsequently emerged. Seán Sherwin, the Fianna Fáil TD for Dublin South-West, had announced that he was almost certain to join the newly formed Aontacht Éireann; but his solitary stance among Fianna Fáil deputies was not enough to give the new party vital momentum.

Weeks passed in speculation about who would be next to defect—but none did. Instead, dissidents such as Neil Blaney, Paudge Brennan and Des Foley adopted a policy of 'external relationship' with Fianna Fáil, biding their time until better circumstances might see them return triumphantly to the fold under a new leadership. But lower-level resignations and defections continued throughout the autumn and winter of 1971. These included the chairman of Lynch's own cumann in Cork, who added his name to a letter announcing their intention of organising a new republican party. 'Fianna Fáil had abandoned the last vestige of Republicanism,' the letter maintained, as Lynch's position 'was virtually Cumann na nGael policy, to oppose which Fianna Fáil was founded.'[59]

On 29 October, Des Foley, Fianna Fáil TD for North County Dublin, launched a strong public attack on Lynch, who, he said, had 'deliberately betrayed the Northern Minority' and failed to deal more aggressively with British violence in the North. 'The Taoiseach should have roused the nation and waged diplomatic war against Britain. History would condemn the Taoiseach as a leader who parleyed with the enemy.'[60]

Foley pre-empted his expulsion and resigned before the motion of no confidence in Gibbons.[61]

Lynch went full steam ahead. Given that the opposition motion aimed to bring down the Government, he told the National Executive on 8 November that the issue was confidence in the Government as a whole, not in any individual minister. He warned that any TD voting for the no-confidence motion or abstaining 'would have voted against the Government and against Fianna Fáil,' which would result in expulsion from the party, and they would be deprived of official Fianna Fáil status if selected by the local party organisation in the forthcoming general election.[62] Pointing out that the time for debate on Fianna Fáil's policy on partition had passed, he stated that 'the Government's policy is Fianna Fáil's policy, as it has been from its foundation, and Fianna Fáil's policy is my policy.'[63]

The Government survived the challenge, by 72 votes to 69. Haughey and Foley voted with the Government, Blaney and Brennan abstained, and Sherwin voted against. The Government had survived, but only with the support or acquiescence of avowed dissidents. At the press conference afterwards Lynch said he would move for the withdrawal of the whip from Blaney and Brennan at the next party meeting, and neither would be confirmed as Fianna Fáil candidates in the next election.

With the resignation of Foley, Sherwin and Boland, with Blaney and Brennan on their way to expulsion and with Haughey domesticated, Lynch could look forward to having a party firmly under his control and one less likely to be divided on Northern policy. Other potential dissidents could be kept in line with the threat of expulsion or with an imminent election that might weaken the 'national position'. The Government would continue to depend for survival on the support of erstwhile colleagues; but these were unlikely to bring the house down, given that a coalition of Fine Gael and the Labour Party was the only alternative.

It seems that Lynch's inner circle were far more flexible about introducing internment in the South than their public utterances suggested. An illuminating meeting took place in late November between the former British ambassador to Ireland, Sir Anthony Gilchrist, and the Irish ambassador to Britain, Dónal O'Sullivan, over a 'quiet drink' at the Irish embassy to discuss a 'deal'. O'Sullivan contested with 'earnest emotion' the suggestion that, were Lynch dislodged, his successor would rapidly adopt something similar to the Lynch line. He presented a number of negative scenarios. For the party leadership a Hillery-Haughey partnership was likely, which in his view would be 'a reckless combination and infinite trouble.' An election victory for the opposition would be 'a disaster,' for 'they were incompetent and could not possibly cope with the IRA the way Lynch could.' Gilchrist surmised: 'One could translate this by saying that Fianna Fáil are closer to the IRA than Fine Gael and the Irish Labour Party; which is true.'

O'Sullivan repeatedly held out the lure of internment in the South as part of a political deal. In the existing climate it would be politically impossible and deeply unpopular to make a significant move against the IRA, but O'Sullivan's prospect was a package that, according to Gilchrist, made for:

(a) ... some (public) light at the end of the tunnel for the Republic. This would point not so much to a unified Ireland which they are scared to death of—but towards their entitlement to have some say in considering the future of the North; (*b*) a constitutional change in Northern Ireland by which the minority would have a fair share in the management of affairs; (*c*) the internment of the IRA by the Dublin Government.

O'Sullivan was 'quite emphatic' that the Government could deliver, saying that Lynch was 'on side.' Hillery, while 'in many ways an awkward customer,' had told O'Sullivan, 'We would certainly do it—I would be for it.'[64]

When Lynch summoned Peck for a meeting on 7 January 1972 he again worried about the lack of a political initiative; but he had new concerns about persistent unemployment in the North. 'The Devil found mischief for idle hands to do,' he complained, 'and there would be a lot of idle young men on the streets for the IRA to exploit.' He was also concerned about rumours circulating in the media that women, hitherto excluded, would also be subject to internment. 'There were some bad ones,' he mused, but he was 'afraid that Irish traditions and attitudes being what they were we should turn the whole island against us if we interned them.'[65]

Lynch elaborated on these points when he met Heath in Brussels two weeks later, on 23 January, where they signed the Treaty of Accession to the EEC.[66] Lynch told Heath that he had eighty thousand unemployed people to contend with, and there was

clearly a danger that these people would be tempted to drift into the IRA. There was passive support for the IRA all over the Republic, and this could easily become more active, if frustration with the rate of progress in Northern Ireland or with his own Government grew.

Lynch complained that after his last meeting at Chequers there had been another raft of internment orders as well as cratering by the British army of roads connecting the North and South. When the British had pushed for the extradition of suspected republicans he had promised 'to see if there was anything they could do,' but he pointed out that 'if a member of the IRA was extradited to the North in current conditions, it would increase public sympathy for the IRA who would immediately make a hero of the man concerned.' The fact that the number of internees continued to grow, and that another camp was being opened close to the Donegal border, was also a source of unease. Lynch equivocated when he told Heath that he

recognised that it would be difficult to bring internment to an end. While he thought that many of those interned were probably harmless, undoubtedly some would carry guns if released, and he could see that the security authorities would not wish to risk releasing them.[67]

Heath, for his part, was tired of hearing the SDLP hymn of 'no talks before internment is ended,' and he claimed that the party 'seemed less and less to represent anybody but themselves.' The SDLP, which had been founded in August 1970 as a reformist party with national unification as its declared aim, had yet to contest an election, and Lynch agreed with Heath that its support had declined. He felt that the Nationalist Party might now be more moderate, before concluding that it was unlikely to make concessions beyond those contemplated by the SDLP, lest it be accused of being 'soft'.

According to Lynch, the IRA had placed the prime ministers in a dilemma. If it was felt that the IRA's violence had precipitated a serious political initiative it would be possible for it to claim a victory. On the other hand, if it was crushed militarily before a new political dispensation had been negotiated it might encourage the unionists to 'freeze their position.' The situation was drifting, and people were saying that Faulkner was dictating events, leading to an increase in fear and frustration. If the British could not do something, Lynch said he would 'do something himself.' He proposed to 'talk to all the people of Ireland . . . in a major speech.' Heath thanked Lynch for coming and said if he was going to proceed in that manner it 'might be helpful if he [Lynch] were to let Sir John Peck see a draft of his speech, in case he were able to offer helpful suggestions.' They agreed to tell the press nothing beyond the fact that they had 'reviewed the situation in both parts of Ireland.'[68]

BLOODY SUNDAY

As it became clear that internment had not delivered its promised ending of violence, Faulkner came under unprecedented pressure from unionist extremists for 'decisive' action. On 30 January 1972 fourteen people were fatally wounded and dozens seriously injured when the British army's Parachute Regiment opened fire on a civil rights march in Derry. What happened is well known and well documented.[69] There appears to be little doubt that the massacre was premeditated. Indeed, even two decades later the abiding memory of one of the most senior British officers was his surprise on hearing of the number of deaths: he had been expecting at least fifty.[70] In an interview with Peter Taylor of the BBC, a company sergeant-major of the Parachute Regiment who was in Derry that day recalled that

> one thing that really surprised me when we first arrived and drove up the drive was [that] members of the RUC actually stood along the driveway and were clapping and cheering, waving their hats. The RUC were actually quite pleased that we'd done what we'd done.[71]

During the next few days no British passenger aircraft was allowed to land at any state airport in the Republic, and airport workers refused to handle British newspapers.[72] Tens of thousands marched in Cork, Waterford, Limerick, Galway and dozens of other towns.[73] In driving rain, more than 100,000 people made their way to Dublin city centre in what the *Irish Times* described as 'the biggest demonstration the Republic has seen in a generation.'[74] Placards were critical of the Irish as well as the British Government: one read, 'Jack Lynch can go to Copenhagen for a foreign king's funeral. He couldn't go to Derry.' The climax of these demonstrations occurred when the British embassy was burnt down by an angry crowd of more than 30,000 people.

Northern nationalists looked to Dublin to draw attention to their case, as British political opinion remained unmoved and was united in a vigorous defence of its soldiers. Lynch, however, fell far short of fulfilling this task. On the night of Bloody Sunday he rang Heath and began by apologising for phoning so late, 'but you will probably have heard the unfortunate news about Derry this afternoon.' This diffident opening set the tone for the conversation, with Lynch timidly trying to express his apprehensions while an irritated Heath blamed the marchers for the deaths and Lynch for not doing more to combat republicans. 'If you had dealt with them this would have been over long ago,' he charged.

During the conversation Lynch expressed concern for his own position in the wake of the deaths in Derry. He told Heath that

> from reactions received around the country at the moment it looks as if a very serious point has now been reached, and the situation could escalate beyond what any of us would anticipate at this stage ... If this kind of thing is going to have its repercussions south of the border ... I can assure you that my role is becoming more and more difficult, and I am very, very fearful of what is likely to happen. I just want to tell you how gravely apprehensive I am.

The following extract from the phone conversation gives some indication of its tenor.

> Lynch: I am told that, according to reports I received and checked on the spot, the British troops reacted rather beyond what a disciplined force might be expected to, and, as you know, there were thirteen killed and as many again injured ...
> Heath: Well, now, as far as any accusations are concerned I obviously cannot accept that.
> Lynch: I assure you I can understand your point of view.
> Heath: I will obviously consider anything which you say. But I must also point out that this arose out of a march which was against the law, which was banned. You have always asked me to ban marches . . . Now the people therefore who deliberately organised this march in circumstances which we all know in which the IRA were bound to intervene carry a very heavy responsibility for any damage which ensued—a very heavy responsibility—and I hope that you would at least condemn the whole of that unequivocally and publicly.
> Lynch: Well, I am waiting to get further clarification of the situation, but—
> Heath: So am I.
> Lynch: I accept at this stage anyway—
> Heath: There is absolutely no doubt. It was a march, it was against the law and should never have been held or countenanced by anybody.
> Lynch: Yes. On the other hand I am told now that ... I know it was against the law ... It was, I think—
> Heath: The reason it was against the law was that we have all known that if you have a march of this kind it will lead to a clash between the communities, and it will also lead to gunmen intervening, and everybody was warned yesterday quite specifically again that it was against the law, and the people who were organising it were going to carry a very heavy responsibility if the IRA intervened.

Lynch: Well, now, there is no indication at all that the IRA intervened before shots
　were fired from the British side. Now again you can disagree with that, but this
　is the information I have got, and—

Heath: I am not going to prejudge it . . . Well, you know it is very difficult to accept
　a condemnation of Stormont for doing something which you yourself have
　requested, you have constantly requested. You spoke to me last summer that
　marches should be banned.

Lynch: Because I think these marches are provocative.

Heath: Well, then, this was a provocative march today.

Lynch: But the fact is that—

Heath: And against the law.

Lynch: Well, it was a peaceful march up to the point when—

Heath: It was against the law.

Lynch: Yes.

Heath: And it was provocative.

Lynch: Yes. Well, I admit, but on the other hand—

Heath: Well, I cannot therefore take this as a criticism of Stormont.

Lynch: On the other hand—well, the fact is that the whole thing arises as a result
　of the Stormont regime. It arises as a result of the—

Heath: It arises as a result of the IRA trying to take over the country.

Lynch: Well, we have no intention of letting them do that.[75]

This dialogue amply demonstrates the British strategy of blaming the protesters
and the IRA for Bloody Sunday, a verdict later upheld by Heath's hand-picked tribunal
of inquiry, headed by Lord Widgery. Indeed, six months later the man in charge of the
Parachute Regiment in Derry that day, Lieutenant-Colonel Derek Wilford, was
awarded membership of the Order of the British Empire. Another consistent strategy
was to convince Lynch that the lesson to be learnt from Bloody Sunday was the danger
presented by the IRA, which both Governments had an interest in suppressing.

Just before Lynch went to the Dáil for an emergency debate on the political fall-
out from Bloody Sunday he was visited by Peck. It was noon, and, according to Peck,
Lynch 'looked grey and ghastly.' Lynch's mood was no doubt influenced by the fact
that he had sent Peck a message asking him not to visit him until after the emergency
debate. Now that Peck was here, Lynch felt, he would hear what he had to say; but he
asked for it to be quick so that he could prepare his speech.

Despite being the representative in Ireland of a government responsible for a
massacre in Derry, Peck went on the offensive, concentrating on the destruction of the
British embassy and seeking to draw political capital from it. While he acknowledged
that the Irish Government had promised to pay full compensation, reports of 'insane
hooliganism' in Dublin meant that Peck could 'only conclude that there was a total
breakdown in law and order.' He knew that a breakdown of such a description had
previously been described as the only circumstance in which the Government would
consider introducing interment. Plans were well advanced to evacuate all British
embassy staff from Dublin, but Peck was postponing a decision until it became clear
whether a planned march in Newry would go ahead. He repeatedly pointed out that,

while ostensibly peaceful, the march was illegal and would be exploited by republicans. Throughout the meeting Peck stuck to the position that the British army in Derry had merely responded to attacks, and he argued that the same could happen in Newry. He linked events in Derry and Dublin by saying that the IRA was the common link.

> If you study carefully what actually happened in Londonderry, and compare it with what happened in Dublin last night you will see that the IRA are making the running in these situations, North and South, and surely it can be understood that we have a common interest in preventing the breakdown of law and order.

This was perhaps the strongest card to play, emphasising that the British and Irish Governments had more in common than Fianna Fáil might have with protesters in Derry, Dublin or Newry. When Lynch complained that he was always the one sticking his neck out, Peck fell back on the familiar track of speaking vaguely of new British initiatives, which (it was usually implied) might be jeopardised by imprudent words or actions on Lynch's part. He said that Conservative Party backbenchers also had to be contended with, because of 'a belief that the Irish Government was incapable of standing up to the IRA.'

Lynch retorted that he had met Heath five times and 'each time had come away empty-handed.' But Peck got in two more shots before the meeting concluded. Firstly, he advised Lynch to desist from meeting Harold Wilson (leader of the opposition), as such meetings posed 'constitutional problems' for the British side, and in any case it was the Conservative Government that took the decisions. Secondly—referring, it seems, to Hillery's putative UN and European tour—Peck said that Hillery should control his public utterances, as 'while I understood Dr Hillery's desire to win friends and influence people, the terms in which he couched his public appeals were liable to have a result exactly opposite to that intended.'

Answering the first comment, Lynch said that he had consulted Wilson merely to see if his ideas were progressing with the British Government. There is no record of a retort to the latter.

Peck returned to the issue of the safety of British embassy property. He presumed that, should there be further disturbances, his own residence would be a target, and he wanted to know whether the Government intended to defend it. Lynch promised at once to contact the Minister for Justice; yet Peck reported to London that he remained worried, as there were only '2000 unarmed, unhelmeted police in the whole Dublin area,' and he bemoaned the fact that the Government 'would never use the Army against their own people.'

By the end of the meeting the atmosphere had 'thawed out considerably,' according to Peck, and, speaking personally, he urged Lynch to 'hold on as this might be the lowest point in Anglo-Irish relations.'[76]

Lynch made his way to the Dáil. Getting a debate had proved remarkably difficult, as he had attempted to prevent it for the previous two days. Blaney pointed out that every government that had any connection to the tragedy had already discussed the matter by way of emergency debate, including the slow-moving House of Lords and the American House of Representatives. He appealed for a two-day debate so that the views of the country might be expressed through the elected representatives (and not outside the Dáil in other ways). Lynch proposed a three-hour discussion, which Blaney said would be 'worse than useless.' Lynch explained that while it was one thing to extend a sitting day it was quite another to add an additional day, as ministers and deputies had other commitments. Blaney countered by arguing that, given the gravity of the situation, procedure and precedent were irrelevant; and eventually a two-day debate was agreed.

Lynch, who was 'still quite obviously pinning hopes on a reformed Stormont,'[77] concentrated on the IRA threat, describing the burning of the British embassy as 'the action of people who are dangerous and who are, above all, a danger to our freedom and democracy.'[78]

THE INTERNATIONAL INITIATIVE

After signing the EEC Treaty on 23 January 1972—a week before Bloody Sunday— Lynch had been asked if it was his intention to raise the issue of the North at the United Nations. Such action, he replied, was 'unlikely', as the UN precluded the government of one state calling for UN intervention in the territory of another. Unfortunately, he said, 'the Six Counties were, in the UN context, British territory.'[79]

This policy of inertia was dramatically reversed in the aftermath of Bloody Sunday. After the emergency Government meeting of 31 January it was announced that Hillery was again to be despatched to the UN.[80] What had been considered a futile exercise was once again the Government's great diplomatic hope. Hillery's brief was also to include a tour of European capitals. Lynch stated that British Government policy was 'might is right' and that the Government was prepared to accept aid from 'any nation in the world.'[81] This open-ended policy was reiterated the following day when Lynch declared that their mission was 'to seek support wherever we can find it.'[82] Remarks like these were widely interpreted as including the possibility of visits to Moscow, Warsaw and other communist and former colonial states.[83] However, the dominant impression was that the Government's international initiative was hastily prepared and formulated with little care or thought.[84]

On his arrival in New York, Hillery convened a press conference at which he accused Britain of provoking a war against a nation that, to a large extent, was unarmed. His Government was now confronted by a neighbour

> practising the arts of war on our people. They have had internment without trial and torture in these camps. And now we are faced with the death sentence for those that protest.

The Government had received 'brutal clarification of Britain's policies in our country,' and the Northern conflict was now an issue for the 'free world'. Relations with the British Government were 'never worse,' and his Government had taken the unprecedented step of withdrawing its ambassador from London. Hillery's objective, as Minister for External Affairs, in coming to New York was 'to end the reign of terror which Britain is perpetrating on our people.' He regarded recent events as constituting 'an act of war', and it was now his Government's policy 'to get British troops out of Ireland.' Questioned about growing support for the IRA, Hillery argued that it was a response to British policies.

> The locking up of adults, the harassing of children, the beating up of women have called the IRA into being. When I last spoke in New York there was no IRA. Britain calls her opponents IRA to justify attacks on what she called 'terrorists.'

According to Hillery, among the nationalist population in the Six Counties there was 'total support' for those viewed as 'resistance fighters.' However, despite the recent 'unwarranted savage attack' Hillery ruled out the possibility of Irish soldiers crossing the border. This was something the Government would never do, because, he declared paradoxically, the 'six north-eastern counties' were 'part of Ireland.'[85]

Hillery never addressed the UN General Assembly, as it was not in session, and the Security Council was meeting in Addis Ababa. As the Secretary-General, Kurt Waldheim, was otherwise engaged, Hillery spoke to the Under-Secretary-General, Chakravarthi Narasimhan. Narasimhan made no comment after the meeting but promised to report to Waldheim on his return from Ethiopia the following week.

Another press conference was summoned, this time in the UN's principal conference hall. Hillery again insisted that the IRA was 'a product of the repression in the North of Ireland' and 'a response to the institutional violence by the state.' He rejected, however, the suggestion that the Government should furnish nationalists with arms and ammunition, and he referred cryptically to the 'tragic division' that previous efforts in this direction had caused.

There were similar ambiguities in Hillery's attitudes towards the Northern unionists. He stressed that Ireland needed 'the Protestant Irish, with their particular background and their particular ethics.' It would be 'a disaster' if the new Ireland did not include the Northern Protestants, and he made vague allusions to possible constitutional changes to facilitate their inclusion. However, earlier in the press conference he described unionists as a 'privileged group,' their government an 'instrument of coercion.' But was their privilege not part of their 'particular background,' and their coercion an example of their 'particular ethics'? Hillery's emphasis depended primarily on the wording of the questions asked. Questions relating to Northern *Protestants* evoked a generous response. They were an integral part of the Irish nation, and their contribution to the 'new Ireland' would be a rich and rewarding one. Questions relating to Northern *unionists*, however, were met with an entirely different response. The sentiments were hostile, the language pugnacious. Thus, Hillery was able to express conflicting sentiments towards this community by calling them two different names. The intersection between Northern Protestantism and Northern unionism was never addressed in a substantive way.

Hillery's meeting with the US Secretary of State, William Rogers, was a fiasco. The British ambassador to the United States, Lord Cromer, had met Rogers the previous night to discuss the crisis.[86] Cromer delivered a message from Sir Alec Douglas-Home 'setting forth the views of his Government' on Ireland,[87] and he urged Rogers to dampen increasing congressional calls for a more active American role in the Irish situation. It was clear that Cromer had made a great impact on Rogers—if only in reinforcing his sentiments on the issue. Rogers's rebuff to Hillery was stinging.

> Personally, I have serious reservations about any useful role we could play. . . We feel [that] any intervention would be counter-productive and inappropriate . . . Suggestions that we can solve it in a diplomatic way are *outrageous*.

Considerable emphasis was placed on the last word. Hillery's suggestion, according to the *Irish Times*, had been rejected 'with rare vehemence.' Reuters reported Rogers as saying that when he told Hillery that the United States was not in a position to intervene, Hillery had said he understood this and was making no such request. Rogers said he would not even make private suggestions to the British Government on how to resolve the crisis. This was believed to have been a central aim of the Irish Government.

Obviously embarrassed by this rebuke, Hillery said afterwards that he did not expect Rogers 'to agree with any statement of mine in relation to a nation with which his Government has friendly relations.' This, of course, raises the question of the purpose of meeting Rogers in the first place. It creates the suspicion that the Government was more concerned with impressing domestic opinion than with achieving tangible results in the international arena. The only positive statement to emerge from the meeting was a reference by Rogers to President Nixon, who was apparently 'deeply concerned by the recent tragic events in Northern Ireland'—not a very helpful diplomatic gesture, considering that he had not been sufficiently perturbed to meet Hillery personally.[88]

Hillery's visits to Ottawa[89] and Paris[90] were equally fruitless. By 8 February the international campaign, only five days old, was already sagging, and enthusiasm among Government ministers had waned. On his arrival from Paris, Hillery submitted an interim report to the Government. Many believed that the Government's diplomatic offensive had backfired, eliciting only indifference in some quarters and ill-concealed contempt in others.[91]

Hillery travelled to Rome on 11 February to meet the Italian Foreign Minister, Aldo Moro. Few details were released, and the press conference was 'low-key,' as was coverage at home.[92] Hillery rejected suggestions that the tour would have a negative effect on British attitudes, as Britain 'could not be more rigid.'[93] He met the Belgian Foreign Minister, Pierre Harmel, on 16 February and the Dutch Foreign Minister, Norbert Schmeizer, the following day. Yet again nothing tangible was achieved, and domestic coverage was negligible.[94]

The Government never made a serious attempt to use the few options open to it at the United Nations. Before leaving for New York, Hillery was aware that the secretary-general was in Ethiopia and that the General Assembly was not in session. A number of factors contributed to the reluctance to approach the United Nations. Firstly, there was the reticence that had been a consistent feature of Government policy since Ireland became a member of the United Nations in 1955. Secondly, it was common knowledge that the UN initiative of 1969 after the Battle of the Bogside had not been a success. Finally, there were the limitations imposed by article 2.7 of the Charter of the United Nations, which prohibits intervention within the internal jurisdiction of a member-state. And the Government ruled out the possibility of taking the matter to the Security Council without Britain's prior consent.

The most the Government appeared to hope for was that the United Nations would use its 'good offices' to mediate in the crisis.[95] This the Secretary-General offered to do on 7 February, prompting Eddie McAteer to describe the move as 'something of a triumph for Irish diplomacy.' It was, of course, nothing of the sort. Waldheim stressed that Northern Ireland was a matter of 'the internal policy of a member-state,'[96] and this statement was seized on by the British Foreign Office.[97] More important was Waldheim's assertion that the United Nations would act only 'if both parties agree to it.' As Britain had made it clear that it would not consent to this—and had reiterated that stance the day after Waldheim's offer—the issue ended there. The Secretary-General did not specify what form UN assistance would or could take. In theory he could have made himself available for discussions, or sent an envoy to the North, and neither action would have constituted mediation.[98] He could have raised the matter in the Security Council on his own initiative; but, as Britain retained its veto, such moves were always highly unlikely.

The idea of raising the dispute in the Security Council was never actively considered. The anachronistic structure of the United Nations, which entrusts the British delegation with a permanent veto, provided the most compelling argument for this policy. This had not prevented Hillery from addressing the Security Council in 1969, but that dispensation had relied on the indulgence of the British representative, Lord Cromer, who understood the need of the Irish side to vent their feelings on the subject.[99] British attitudes had hardened considerably in the intervening years, and it was unlikely that Hillery would be similarly indulged on this occasion.

Article 2.7 was the insurmountable obstacle, but there are strong arguments that could have been used to counter it. If applied to the letter, article 2.7 would prevent the United Nations from addressing the great majority of international issues. Apartheid in South Africa, for example, could not have been discussed, as it would be considered an internal affair of the South African Government. In reality, common sense usually prevailed, and article 2.7 was often loosely interpreted (and sometimes flagrantly ignored), depending on the contingencies of the day.

Fianna Fáil had adopted a consistent policy of not raising the issue of the North in the Security Council, for fear of a negative vote. Such a vote, it was believed, would damage efforts to secure a united Ireland and would make the matter *res judicata* (a matter already judged and no longer subject to appeal) in international politics. It is not clear, however, that in 1972 this policy was the most appropriate for the circumstances. It is true that a motion in the Security Council would not have been passed, but it is not apparent that this would have resulted in anything other than a pyrrhic victory for the British.

Nine affirmative votes were required from the fifteen-member Security Council. However, of the five permanent members, Ireland was guaranteed the support of two, the Soviet Union and China,[100] with the United States and France most probably abstaining.[101] Of the temporary members it might have expected the support of Yugoslavia and the former colonies of India, Somalia, Sudan and Guinea. The other members—Belgium, Italy, Japan, Panama and Argentina—would probably have abstained.[102] There would thus have been seven affirmative votes, with seven abstentions, leaving Britain as the sole dissenter. Such a vote, while it would not have achieved its ostensible aim of securing a resolution censuring Britain (which it never could with the British veto), could hardly be considered a catastrophic defeat for the Irish Government. Indeed the fact that Britain would be the only member to explicitly reject the motion could only have created a sense of international isolation for Britain.

The presidency of the Security Council changed every month, and the incumbent could play a significant role in determining the agenda. In April the position would be held by the British representative, Sir Colin Crowe, and in May by the US representative, George Bush. From the Irish Government's point of view there were strong reasons for March being the most auspicious month, as the presidency would be held by the Soviet representative, Jakob Malik. Seán Cronin noted that Malik could 'on his own authority . . . allow the Irish Question to be brought up, but Dublin would have to make the request first, naturally.'[103] By March, however, the Government had lost interest in the campaign.

A second criticism that might be suggested in any evaluation of the Government's tactics relates to its refusal to enlist the support of communist and former colonial states and of the Soviet Union in particular. When Hillery arrived in New York he declared that 'my orders are to seek help wherever I can get it.'[104] As the week progressed, however, it became clear that he had no intention of seeking assistance from the only world power sympathetic to such a request.[105] The views expressed in the Soviet Union were mirrored in other communist states, particularly Poland[106]; yet the Government never considered visiting Warsaw or any eastern European capital.

Relations between the SDLP and the Fianna Fáil leadership continued to deteriorate in the aftermath of Bloody Sunday, and there was 'no meeting of minds' when the two sides met. A British Government report assessed the SDLP—which was already coming under criticism for its moderation within the Northern nationalist community—as substantially more radical in its demands than Lynch's Government, which believed the formula of 'no talks until internment ends' to be unrealistic.[107] However, as the Fianna Fáil leadership would be approaching the referendum on membership of the EEC with the argument that membership would help usher in a united Ireland, compliance with this reasoning by the SDLP (as the self-appointed spokespersons for the Northern nationalist community) was highly desirable. The SDLP, however, had not co-ordinated a consistent position on the EEC, and it certainly had not maintained that Irish and British membership would hasten reunification. Those SDLP leaders who engaged in the debate refused to follow the Fianna Fáil line and went so far as to complain of being used as a political football for winning the referendum. In a letter of 23 February 1972 to Lynch, later released publicly, Paddy Devlin wrote that,

having considered the devious way in which these specific matters were raised, and the party political advantage sought by you at all meetings of this nature, I have decided in future to attend only meetings where representatives of all the Irish Parliamentary Parties attend. Again, I am most unhappy at the way your Government has been manoeuvring our party to give the impression that we are subservient to your direction in the North. Furthermore, I intend to exercise my constitutional rights as an Irishman to speak publicly or privately here or in the Republic on any issue concerning the future of my country, and I will tolerate no interference with this right.[108]

Devlin illustrated the fragility of the relationship a few days later when he publicly recounted, both to the Common Market Defence Campaign and to the annual conference of the Labour Party, details of the meeting between the SDLP and Fianna Fáil. George Colley—'the most arrogant man I ever met'—told Devlin that he had 'no right to comment on the affairs of the Republic,' referring to Devlin's part in the anti-EEC campaign. 'I told him that I intended to speak at every anti-EEC meeting in this country, and moreover I promised the help of my colleagues in the same manner.' Colley's performance, according to Devlin, 'had shown how little they thought of the people in the North . . .They regarded them as election props.'[109]

In the immediate aftermath of Bloody Sunday the Government had decided to recall Dónal O'Sullivan, the Irish ambassador to Britain. This very public interruption in diplomatic relations proved to be entirely cosmetic, as the British ambassador in Dublin, Sir John Peck, though bereft of an embassy building, remained in regular contact with O'Sullivan and with the Fianna Fáil leadership. He began improvising an embassy at his home in Sandyford, Co. Dublin—though this fact was not publicly disclosed—and he went about his business as usual. Peck met O'Sullivan two weeks after Bloody Sunday, at O'Sullivan's instigation, at a lunch contrived for the purpose by the Canadian ambassador, and he learnt that O'Sullivan was already 'trying to return to London at the earliest possible moment.'

O'Sullivan remained worried about Lynch's position and said that alternatives to his leadership included a 'new Fianna Fáil probably led by Haughey,' or a *coup d'état*. When asked if it would be the Official or Provisional IRA that would engineer this coup, O'Sullivan surprised Peck by replying that it would be 'more probably police and young Army officers.' Despite the mayhem of the embassy burning, and the likelihood that there had been 'an upsurge of sympathy for the IRA, or rather against us, in the Army, FCA and police,' Peck concluded that he could not see a military or police regime in the Republic 'at the moment.' He acknowledged, however, that Lynch was 'likely to have a very rough time at the party conference . . . He will do his best to damp down the post-Derry fury and endeavour to be constructive.'[110]

THE 1972 ARD-FHEIS

Hillery's international initiative had effectually expired by the time Fianna Fáil met for its annual ard-fheis during the weekend of 18–20 February 1972. Despite some hard-hitting motions from branches (which were never discussed),[111] the honorary secretaries' report made no reference to the North—an omission that attracted the criticism of Blaney and others. It was also the last item in the printed agenda, in which it was stated by Lynch that

this year too will, I hope, mark a significant step forward towards the attainment of a united Ireland. No matter how great the frustrations and the difficulties, we will not be deflected in our task. As so often before, Fianna Fáil has a leading role in the shaping of the Ireland of the future and in achieving our country's true destiny.[112]

As the ard-fheis came only three weeks after Bloody Sunday, it was generally expected that Lynch would revert to a more traditional anti-British speech for his presidential address,[113] a perception accentuated by Hillery's vehement denunciations during his international tour. In the immediate aftermath of the Derry killings there had been a widespread feeling that the British army should withdraw from the North, something reflected in a more moderate way by Lynch when he called for British soldiers to be withdrawn from Catholic areas. In his ard-fheis address this demand was watered down further to a request that the British army 'cease their aggressive activities in densely populated Catholic areas.'[114]

If Lynch's address represented the approach of sweet reason, it was complemented by a more pugnacious outlining of harsh realities by Des O'Malley. O'Malley declared that they 'must deal effectively with the IRA,' and he floated the possibility of introducing special courts to deal with the menace. Perhaps the most ominous portent was his declaration that

> within the existing law it is necessary for us to take every possible step to see that the will of the people of the country and the law enacted by, on behalf of, and for the benefit of the people will not be thwarted by some strange or inexplicable decision of a district justice or other members of the judiciary.[115]

The assurance that this would be done within the existing law was meaningless, as the law as it stood covered almost every contingency.[116] Equally deceptive was O'Malley's assurance that he had already discussed the matter with the Attorney-General, who was 'independent of the Government and made up his own mind about these things.' The Attorney-General was in fact a party nominee, and it was clear from O'Malley's contribution that he had asked the Attorney-General to ascertain whether there was existing legislation that would allow the Government to pursue such a course. O'Malley informed the delegates that the Attorney-General had already decided to re-arrest 'certain people' who had been released by the courts, and that those individuals would be made to stand trial again.

Brian Faulkner welcomed O'Malley's announcement, describing it as 'certainly a step in the right direction.'[117] The *Irish Times* commented that, while no-one had quite said 'aren't we all right here,'

> one of the most negative aspects of Fianna Fáil solidarity is that it turns the members more and more into themselves, will more and more consolidate the party as a Twenty-six County unit, and possibly nurture the thought that all Northerners are spiky, difficult people and that this problem, while quite useful as an emotional outlet, does not call for planned effort from Government or party.[118]

In this regard it was noteworthy that the big loser of the ard-fheis was Neil Blaney, who represented the most northerly constituency in the country.[119]

But if Blaney's star was on the wane, the ard-fheis was also significant in marking the first step of Charles Haughey in his tortuous journey back to the top. Evidence of this rehabilitation could be seen in the result of the elections for party officers, in which Haughey obtained the coveted position of honorary vice-president. During the ard-fheis there had been bitter exchanges on Northern Ireland, with delegates divided along pro and anti-IRA lines; but most commentators reported that Lynch basked in a wave of overwhelming approval. 'The Taoiseach's triumph was complete,' Michael McInerney wrote in the *Irish Times*. 'There are no more rebels in Fianna Fáil.'[120] Indeed the ard-fheis was a model of unity when compared with the Labour Party conference the following weekend.[121]

Lynch's moderation may have been influenced by his contacts with the British Government. When the Government met two days after the ard-fheis the North again dominated the agenda, and it was reported that the British Government was planning a new package of initiatives, and that Lynch had been given a briefing on the main proposals. The British diplomatically passed on to Lynch a request to 'avoid specific proposals or comments on ideas that are being publicly canvassed,'[122] and after the ard-fheis Heath thanked Lynch for the 'moderate and steadying line that you took.'

But Heath immediately turned to an 'unexpected' and 'unwelcome' development. The case arising from the arrest in 1971 of John Hume, an SDLP leader, had demonstrated that the British army, in executing powers conferred by the Special Powers Act, had been acting since 1969 *ultra vires* (beyond its powers). Heath pointed out that the British army in the North was 'carrying out a wide range of essential duties connected with the maintenance of law and order, including search and arrest,' and that while appeals could be contemplated this would leave the army in the intolerable situation of being unsure about the legality of its actions. Therefore, Heath told Lynch, the British Government was going to introduce an emergency validating bill that would retrospectively legalise the actions of the British army so that the law would correspond to what they had always believed it to be.[123] The message was given orally to the Secretary of the Department of External Affairs, Hugh McCann, because, Peck wrote, 'any visible contact between the Taoiseach and myself today would at once be construed as arm-twisting over the IRA.'[124]

Three weeks after Bloody Sunday, Peck found the Irish people in 'a chastened and conciliatory mood.' Hillery's lack of success in rousing the indignation of foreign governments, disgust at IRA murders and the alleged breakdown of public order in Dublin (combined with 'the discovery that burning an embassy is not like setting fire to a barn') had all played their part. The cancellation of a Scotland v. Ireland football match had 'brought home to the Irish how many British [people] regard the Republic' and drew attention to the already calamitous damage done to the tourism industry. There was also 'a realisation of the folly of trying to use the economic weapon against us,' fears about Ireland's EEC prospects and regret at signs of diminishing Anglo-Irish relations. At the same time Peck felt that there was a 'mood of expectancy', based on an assumption that a significant political initiative was in the offing and that unionism was visibly crumbling.[125]

The British knew that Lynch felt that a Northern initiative was necessary to secure his position. 'Since frustration in the Republic is dangerous to his position and the

State,' Peck noted, 'I would therefore expect him to go along with any proposals [of the British Government],' so long as they provided some movement and did not exclude unification. Peck also felt that Lynch could dump the SDLP should it prove less enthusiastic about an offer. 'The susceptibilities of the SDLP would not carry much weight with Mr. Lynch who would regard them in the last resort as expendable.'[126]

But as the country continued to reel from internment and from Bloody Sunday, the British detected signs that divisions were emerging over how best to deal with the IRA. Erskine Childers had made a series of speeches welcoming tougher anti-IRA measures, but his view was not shared by some other members of the Government. During a discussion between Peck and Hillery in early March 1972 Hillery 'twice went out of his way to say that Childers was quite wrong in his approach, that the Government only looked ridiculous if they detained IRA members against whom no charges could stick and they were obliged to release them.' Hillery said that 'strong arm methods would only rally people behind the IRA and against the Government,' and that 'the only way to deal with the IRA was political,' by which he meant political initiatives that lay in the gift of the British Government. Peck records that Hillery

then propounded a theory that, while the Irish were very emotional, the people in the South, on the whole and with exceptions, were not given to violence and murder. It was the men from the North who were cruel and violent and it was noteworthy that many of the recent bank raids and other crimes of violence in the South have been committed by northerners.

Peck saw his opportunity to make political capital from Hillery's pseudo-psychological musings. 'I pointed out that plenty of them [Northerners] were skulking in the South and the problem in the Republic might be eased if they could be handed back.'[127]

When Peck met Lynch again on 3 March he received 'a warm and friendly welcome.' The tone of the conversation certainly suggested that although the Irish ambassador to Britain continued to be withdrawn this was merely decorative diplomacy, for public consumption. Peck began by commenting on the 'very welcome news' that the Gardaí had arrested eight Northerners in Co. Monaghan, as well as making a substantial arms haul, and reiterated the link between crushing the IRA and political initiatives, hoping that 'the Irish Government would maintain pressure on the IRA and produce visible results.' Lynch spoke of a general air of expectancy about a new initiative, and Peck emphasised that 'the minority in the North and their supporters in the Republic should not open their mouth too wide at this stage.'

Peck then questioned the wisdom of Ireland establishing diplomatic relations with the Soviet Union, as was widely rumoured. Lynch expressed surprise at the level and volume of British representations and pointed out that diplomatic relations would not only help redress a large trade imbalance but would rectify the anomaly whereby Ireland was the only Common Market country not to have a Soviet embassy. While conceding that, having a Soviet embassy themselves, the British could hardly press the Irish not to do likewise, Peck foresaw numerous possible drawbacks. 'Certainly a Soviet presence in Ireland would add to our problems in the UK and the

North but I wanted to stress the trouble that the Russians could stir up in the Republic through the Official IRA, the subversion of officials and students and so on.' He told Lynch that a Soviet embassy might engage in 'talent-spotting for future agents for influence and subversion, finding out how to use the IRA in order to prevent a peaceful settlement and friendly relations with Britain, damaging Irish standing in the Common Market.' Peck felt that Lynch was now 'in no doubt about our views and the reasons and I think I made some impression.'[128]

DIRECT RULE

With internment still an obvious failure and Bloody Sunday drawing negative international publicity, Heath summoned Faulkner to London and demanded that all security powers be transferred to London. When Faulkner refused, Heath claimed that he was left with 'no alternative to assuming full and direct responsibility for the administration of Northern Ireland.'[129] With the affable William Whitelaw as the first Secretary of State for Northern Ireland, the British Government was now responsible for the day-to-day running of part of Ireland for the first time since 1920. Unionists— not least those who had served in the Stormont Government—felt betrayed. Considering that the British Government had endorsed and authorised each new security measure, there was a feeling within the Unionist Government that they had been used as scapegoats for the failure of policies approved in London.[130]

The Irish political elite welcomed the suspension of the Northern Parliament, and it was announced that Dónal O'Sullivan, who had been itching to return to London, would resume his post within days.[131] This move, while understandable, was premature, as the issue that occasioned this unprecedented diplomatic gesture in the first place—Bloody Sunday—had yet to be resolved.

This became clear when Lord Widgery published the result of his inquiry into the Derry massacre a few weeks later. His verdict—in effect a whitewash that exonerated the British army—was greeted with disbelief in Ireland. Eddie McAteer claimed that the decision was a 'political judgement by a British officer and British judge upon his darling British Army,' and he added: 'I suppose we are lucky he didn't also find that the thirteen committed suicide.'[132] Despite its obvious disappointment at the result of the inquiry, the Irish Government remained firmly committed to the Anglo-Irish process, still very much in its embryonic stages.

The unity of purpose of the British and Irish Governments had been evident when both signed the Treaty of Accession to the EEC in January; both states were due to become full members on 1 January 1973. First, however, there was the matter of a referendum. In early March, Hillery had confided to Peck

that something was needed in the Republic, some cause that would divert public attention from the IRA. He thought that this could be the EEC, and he felt there was scope for a campaign that would show the Irish people the blessings of the Common Market. He expressed the opinion that, whereas membership would make reunification more probable and more rapid, the activities of the IRA were designed to prevent EEC membership and hence reunification.

Peck concluded: 'Presumably it is all to the good if Hillery stumps the country preaching this doctrine, and I do not suppose that Mr. Lynch will see any contradiction between this and a policy of being as tough against the IRA.'[133]

The referendum would be an important test of strength for Fianna Fáil and Jack Lynch. The Government's main tactic—much to the chagrin of its opponents—was to suggest that the Irish people had no real choice but to accept EEC membership. Michael O'Kennedy threatened 'economic collapse' if the referendum was rejected, and a 'grim struggle for survival' awaited an electorate that scorned this golden opportunity.[134] On the eve of the referendum Fianna Fáil took full-page advertisements in the national newspapers, in which Lynch told the electorate in almost Orwellian tones:

To put it simply: if you vote Yes tomorrow, the future, both for yourself and for your children now growing up, is bright with hope and prosperity. If you vote otherwise, I am convinced that the outlook is bleak in the extreme.[135]

The proposal was passed with an overwhelming majority (83 per cent). While ostensibly the issue was the merits of joining the Common Market, others attached a deeper significance to the result. In a front-page headline the *Irish Times* proclaimed that the decision ended the 'epoch of romantic nationalism.' In the article the chief political correspondent, Michael McInerney, wrote:

In the Irish political sense the million voters have resolved decisively all the problems of the Taoiseach, Mr. Lynch, swamping Aontacht Éireann, the Fianna Fáil dissidents, and other 'Republican' parties and groups, and they have also illustrated a nation's utter disapproval of the militant wings of 'Republicanism', strengthening the discipline of a people. Mr. Lynch—and the party—has won an election without the bother of declaring a general election; there is now no need for any other mandate.[136]

McInerney was not alone in believing that Lynch had won an important ideological debate. Lynch felt that the electorate had rejected both wings of Sinn Féin, which, he said, had used the campaign to further its own sinister ends. 'I think the people have emphatically rejected these groups and what they stand for.'[137] He was now subjected to renewed pressure from the British Government, which was reported as believing 'that an Irish vote for EEC entry was also a vote against the IRA and the Fianna Fáil dissidents.'[138] Heath, it was reported, had understood Lynch's internal party difficulties but believed he had received an enormous mandate and should now act decisively.[139] Des O'Malley's hints at the possibility of re-establishing special courts had provoked considerable interest, and there was a 'desire for a gesture from the Dublin Government.'[140]

What type of gesture Lynch would make as a result of his new-found 'mandate' was a matter of some speculation. However, the EEC vote, combined with strong British pressure, ensured that it was a question of when rather than if new anti-IRA measures would be introduced. Lynch was presented with a tailor-made opportunity on 18 May when republican prisoners rioted in Mountjoy Prison, held several prison officers captive for six hours and occupied and barricaded a wing of the prison against a large force of gardaí and soldiers. The prisoners were protesting against the fact that most of them had been on remand for several months without being committed for trial, which, they argued, amounted to *de facto* internment. After negotiations between the prisoners' representatives and senior Garda officers the prisoners returned voluntarily to their cells and released the hostages unharmed.[141]

Lynch reacted swiftly and 'spoke with greater confidence than ever of the Government's will to crush the IRA.'

> The disruptive forces in our midst, some of them fronting ideologies alien to and rejected by the Irish people, never more emphatically than in the recent referendum, are using the current situation in Northern Ireland, masquerading under the guise of patriotism, to pull down our democratic institutions.[142]

Private armies, he said, would not be permitted to use the territory of the Republic 'to impose their will on the people of Northern Ireland or indeed on the people of the 26 Counties.' He hinted at more repressive legislation and promised that if the law proved ineffectual he would ask the Government to strengthen those laws. In addition, he welcomed British initiatives in the North, describing them as

> an initial step in a genuine attempt to avoid these evils, to redress past grievances and to foster and promote reconciliation between the Northern communities. The British Secretary of State for Northern Ireland, Mr. Whitelaw has earnestly pursued this objective.[143]

Lynch's praise for Whitelaw's efforts and his implied support for more stringent anti-IRA legislation were not considered to be coincidental. Referring to the pressure on Lynch after the referendum to act decisively against republicans, Dick Walsh commented in the *Irish Times* that Heath was reported as having indicated that he would 'not agree to further discussions with the Taoiseach until Mr. Lynch kept his side of the "initiative bargain".'[144] This view was shared by both wings of Sinn Féin. Official Sinn Féin argued that Heath was pressuring Lynch to suppress all republican activity in the South to complement London's repressive measures in the North; Provisional Sinn Féin claimed that Lynch had tolerated an illegal army—the British army—on Irish territory for a long time.

> When members of this illegal army crossed into the 26 Counties today and were apprehended by the Gardaí, Mr. Lynch ordered their immediate release. Had they been Republican guerrillas who had strayed into Co. Monaghan they would now be in Mountjoy or the Curragh. Mr. Lynch always bows to his British masters.[145]

This statement referred to an incident in which a British armoured car containing ten soldiers was apprehended by gardaí and Irish soldiers outside Clones and was allowed to return unhindered to Co. Fermanagh.[146] Such events were occurring with increased frequency. A few days earlier Brian Lenihan had told the Dáil that there had been eighty-eight *recorded* incursions into the Republic during the two-year period ending 31 March 1972.[147]

The Prisons Bill—ostensibly Lynch's response to the Mountjoy riots but in reality the product of a legislative programme formulated over some time—was passed in all its stages within twenty-four hours.[148] It was then submitted to the Seanad, where it passed in record time without amendment. The Seanad also passed a resolution requesting that the President sign the bill that day, as provided for by the Constitution in relation to security matters, and it took immediate effect.[149] The act authorised the Minister for Justice to transfer prisoners to military custody. Such transfers, O'Malley claimed, could take place only in 'exceptional circumstances'; but as the bill provided for transfers when ordinary prison accommodation was considered by the minister to be inadequate or insufficient, it soon became obvious that such transfers would not be unusual. The severity of the bill, and the alacrity with which it was expected to pass, was defended by Lynch when he told the Dáil in sombre tones that 'there are occasions in any emergency when it is necessary to implement legislation quickly in the interest of public order and the maintenance of democracy and the national institutions.'[150]

The Labour Party was divided on the issue and voted accordingly. Dr David Thornley TD, the bill's most eloquent opponent, claimed that the measure was a 'back door to internment.' Fine Gael supported the Government but qualified this with suspicions regarding Lynch's future intentions. Fine Gael's spokesperson on justice, Paddy Cooney. wondered if, in view of Lynch's recent speech on illegal organisations, the Government was 'gearing itself for something drastic.' If such measures were on the horizon, Cooney warned that they would receive no support from his party.

On 26 May the Government reactivated part v of the Offences Against the State Act (1939), establishing the no-jury Special Criminal Court. This was not approved by the Dáil, as the act permits the section to be activated by Government proclamation. While this was a pertinent consideration in 1939, with a world war approaching, it was difficult to justify in 1972. There was little reason to believe that opposition would be vehement or that the bill would be rejected. Lynch may have been sensitive to the misgivings of some Fianna Fáil deputies and have wished to spare them and the party the inevitable conflict of conscience if it could be avoided. The opposition parties, not unnaturally, attributed the move to Government arrogance and a desire to evade the scrutiny of the Dáil.[151]

Part v of the act permits extraordinary measures when the Government is satisfied that the ordinary courts are 'inadequate to secure the effective administration of justice and the preservation of public peace and order.' Many people were unconvinced, however, that such conditions existed, or they believed that, if they did, they must have been in existence for a considerable time. As an editorial in *Hibernia* commented,

> there have been vague suggestions of intimidation of juries. But where are the facts? Had any justice of the courts or any single jury foreman complained of intimidation? And by what criteria are the ordinary courts deemed to be inadequate now compared to say six months or a year ago.[152]

O'Malley had claimed that jurors were being intimidated, but he refused to cite one example of this when challenged by Paddy Cooney. The reintroduction of such draconian legislation on so unsubstantiated a pretext disturbed many, including two journalists of the period, Derek Dunne and Gene Kerrigan, who wrote:

> Intimidating juries is a criminal offence, yet there was no attempt to solve the problem—if it existed—by using the gardaí to collar the alleged criminals. Instead, the whole structure of the judicial system was altered and what was in theory to be temporary use of emergency legislation was in practice the setting up of a permanent juryless court.[153]

The position of jury members was perhaps best described by the British ambassador, Sir John Peck, who wrote in his autobiography that 'whereas up till [Bloody Sunday] it had been hard enough to convict anyone charged with a crime that was even remotely anti-British, it would now be impossible.'[154] This account confirms the intense pressure applied on the Government by the British leading up to the anti-IRA initiatives. Peck relates how he was continually instructed to relay British concerns on the 'inadequacy' of the Irish judicial system.

> Known members of the IRA were appearing before District Justices in some border areas, charged with illegal possession of arms or some such offence, and the cases against them were being dismissed. More serious charges involving trial by jury invariably ended in acquittal. Requests for the extradition of the wanted men were consistently refused on the grounds that the offences were political. It was frustrating and also embarrassing, since I was under constant pressure to twist the arm of the Irish government on the subject and *we all knew that it was just as frustrated over much of this as we were* . . . At the end of some interminable conference of officials in London, I was asked rather aggressively when the Irish government was going to get *the right verdict* from an Irish court. [Emphasis added.][155]

Peck's reports of his meetings with Lynch were compulsory reading for the British. Many of his encounters were never publicised or acknowledged, and often he and Lynch met on the understanding that the meetings were to be secret and that, even if the fact of the meeting somehow reached the press, the substance of their discussions should never be divulged.[156] The British were also keen to build up a psychological profile of Lynch. 'It would be useful to know,' Kelvin White of the Foreign and Commonwealth Office wrote to Peck, 'the points on which he is sensitive, so that we can avoid rubbing him the wrong way in future, if we do get results from the Border [i.e. security co-operation], and continue to work on that sore patch if we do not.'[157]

The Government's security effort received an unexpected boost when the Official IRA called a permanent ceasefire on 29 May 1972. The revulsion arising from the bomb in Aldershot military camp in Hampshire (headquarters of the unit responsible for the killings on Bloody Sunday), which killed seven civilians and no soldiers, was reinforced by the killing of nineteen-year-old William Best, a member of the British army who was home on leave in Derry, which was deeply unpopular with local people.[158] However, it would be an oversimplification to attribute the suspension of activities to Best's death. For some time there had been a movement within the Officials that was 'concerned that the armed campaign would jeopardise their efforts to build a political machine.'[159] Bloody Sunday had propelled the organisation back into action, but the ending of its campaign was inevitable. Together with the botched assassination attempt on the Unionist hard-liner John Taylor, these killings strengthened the hand of those on the Army Council of the Official IRA who favoured an end to the campaign.

The withdrawal of the Official IRA from the conflict did not greatly affect Northern life, as about 90 per cent of republican operations were carried out by the Provisional IRA.[160] However, it simplified matters for the Provisionals. For them, all that remained was for the British to invite the IRA to take part in talks so that a phased withdrawal could be negotiated; and that is what they did.

TALKS, OPERATION MOTORMAN AND THE STRASBOURG CASE

While the Provisional IRA had initially been short of arms, by 1972 it had secured reliable channels for acquiring weapons, in particular from America and Libya.[161] British army casualties soared during 1972, becoming a serious cause of concern for the British Government. There were also pressures on the Provisional IRA leadership. War-weariness was setting in among the nationalist population, and many felt that the Official IRA ceasefire had set an example that the Provisionals should follow.

It was against this background that the first face-to-face meetings between the British Government and the IRA since 1921 took place. The difficulty of conducting such negotiations in the Ireland of 1972 was evident when it was arranged that the IRA representatives would travel to London. The only reason that the British Government had agreed to the idea was the high level of casualties the IRA had managed to inflict once it had embarked on an offensive military strategy. Almost four hundred people had been killed since the introduction of internment eleven months previously, and the 'acceptable level of violence' that Reginald Maudling had spoken of was proving elusive.

However, this was possibly the worst time to seek an accommodation with the IRA. Believing, understandably, that they had brought down the seemingly immovable Northern Government, republicans concluded that all that was required was one final push before the British would disengage, politically and militarily. The fact that talks were taking place only confirmed the view that the British were looking for a way out. To the IRA, the position was a return to that of 1921, and it was determined that the same mistakes would not be made again. During the meeting the Provisional IRA chief of staff, Seán Mac Stiofáin, read out the IRA demands, the most important of which was a declaration from the British Government that Britain would leave Northern Ireland by 1 January 1975.

One of the British negotiators, Frank Steele, recalled that Mac Stiofáin acted 'like the representative of an army which had fought the British to a standstill and as if we British wanted out,' comparing his manner to Field-Marshal Montgomery at Lüneburg Heath (site of the German surrender at the end of the Second World War) 'telling the German Generals what they should and shouldn't do if they wanted peace.'[162] The talks got nowhere; and an incident in the Lenadoon housing estate in Belfast, when the British army prevented dispossessed Catholic families moving into houses vacated by Protestants, was seen by both sides as a breach of faith and led to the resumption of hostilities. Even though negotiations had broken down, the British Government must have wondered about the prospects of a breakthrough, given the radical nature of Mac Stiofáin's demands.[163]

The news that the British Government had been holding talks with the IRA came as 'a shattering blow' to Lynch and his Government. The *Irish Times* reported that

> those negotiations have created quite an extraordinary new situation for the Government, as Mr. Whitelaw has, in effect, recognised the Provisionals and in one view he saw them as 'representing Ireland.' It will be held by many people that the British Government by-passed the Dublin Government by negotiating with the IRA.[164]

A serious military offensive was an obvious alternative to talks, and the British Government was given the opportunity when a series of bombs exploded in Belfast, killing nine civilians and two soldiers and leaving more than a hundred people injured, many with horrific injuries. Images of charred remains being scooped into plastic bags had a chilling effect on television viewers, and the day was quickly dubbed 'Bloody Friday' by the Northern Ireland Office.

Within days the British army launched 'Operation Motorman'. In the biggest British military offensive since the Anglo-French intervention in Egypt in 1956, 21,000 British soldiers advanced with armoured cars on the 'no-go' areas of Derry and Belfast.[165] The army had been expecting many casualties, but in the event only two civilians were killed. Those who escaped over the border to Co. Donegal were met by the Irish army and police, and in a 'mopping-up' operation following the offensive on 'Free Derry' many senior Provisionals were arrested.

After the suspension of Stormont, the British Government maintained pressure on the Fianna Fáil leadership to help suppress the IRA's campaigns against British military forces. 'The real issue surely,' one British report surmised, 'is how the two governments can best cooperate in isolating the leadership of both IRAs from their supporters, both North and South.'[166] Believing that 'internally, the Government's main headache [since Bloody Sunday] has been the threat posed by the IRAs,'[167] the British rarely missed an opportunity to tell Lynch that anti-republican action

> is as much in his interest as in ours. The IRA is as much, if not more, of a potential menace to Mr. Lynch than it is to HMG [Her Majesty's Government]. Unless the IRA can be kept too weak to be effective on either side of the Border, security in both Northern Ireland and the Republic is under threat.

Security co-operation could be publicly denied by both governments, Lynch was promised, and North-South co-operation could be a reward for good behaviour on the much-prized security front. 'Mr. Lynch might be reminded that there is a clear relationship between co-operation on security matters and co-operation on other matters.'[168] The British, however, realised that any Irish Government would have its work cut out for it.

> There is a latent virus of violent Republicanism in many people in the Republic, which can quickly spread to infect the country's whole personality. Moreover, although few are willing to give their active support to the IRA, many share its aims and resent or dislike too open interference with it.[169]

The burning of the British embassy, from the British point of view, was an example of an outbreak of this virus, and the British assiduously argued that the republican disease attacked all political entities it infected, be they in Belfast, London or Dublin. Though Hillery had put it to the British that the people of the 26 Counties had, compared with their Northern kin, developed a resistance over time to violent emotionalism, events had shown that they were still some way short of complete immunity.

In the same month that the British Government was secretly negotiating with the IRA, Lynch went on the offensive. On 14 July the Dáil adjourned until 25 October, and in his adjournment speech Lynch stated his view that IRA activities and support were motivated by a perverted romanticism rather than by a response to repressive conditions.

> They should speak out clearly and display no lingering romanticism or idealism which might surround the violence. Appeals to history or a roll call of patriots of the past did not legitimise the squalid acts of bloodshed. It was an insult to the Irish leaders of the past to link their names with these acts of violence. It was a travesty to equate the motives of those who prolonged the present agony. If violence was pursued to the point of provoking civil strife in the North, he would like to say to those who did so that they need expect no support, no resources, nor sympathy from here or from anybody in this part of the country.[170]

The British Government's report of this speech noted approvingly that Lynch had hit out at the IRA and its supporters 'more strongly than ever before.' There was no criticism of the British Government, 'nor much gratuitous advice.'[171] When Lynch took his message to the United States later that month, however, and told the Ancient Order of Hibernians that 'the actions of the current IRA . . . are anathema to the men of the old IRA who fought for freedom over fifty years ago,'[172] the response was less enthusiastic. Some, such as Judge James Comerford of New York, himself an Old IRA man, described the Provisionals as 'the legitimate inheritors of the IRA of the 1920s, and their violence alone had brought politicians to the conference table.' The order's national vice-president also disagreed, saying that 'most of us feel that British soldiers are enemies on Irish soil and to kill them is all right with us.' The order's president came to Lynch's aid and argued that Lynch 'knows the situation better than we do.'[173]

A month after Operation Motorman an opportunity arose for Lynch to meet Heath in Munich on 4 September.[174] It was their first encounter since January, and Lynch began by expressing good will towards William Whitelaw and appreciation for what the British Government had done for the Northern minority. The Irish Government had supported Operation Motorman, Lynch said, but warned that 'the Provisionals gained from the widely held view that the security forces were concentrating on the ghettos of the minority and leaving Protestant extremists alone.' Could Heath describe his Government's long-term policies, particularly in view of the conference of Northern parties to be convened by Whitelaw in September?

Heath neither acknowledged nor reciprocated Lynch's appreciation but congratulated his own Government, which, by suspending Stormont and introducing anti-discrimination legislation, had 'taken fully effective steps to safeguard the position of the minority,' while facing down considerable opposition, particularly from unionists, contradicting the argument that London could not stand up to Protestant pressure. Despite all these benign words there nevertheless existed a 'widespread feeling' in Britain and the North that 'the IRA could have been quickly suppressed if the Republic had taken action earlier.' While the greater assistance rendered along the border was to be welcomed, British opinion could not understand why the Irish Government would not go further, particularly when Lynch seemed to command a strong political position.

Lynch responded that additional courts had been established, border security had been tightened and more stringent controls over explosives had been introduced. 'The IRA could not operate freely south of the border and, short of internment, he believed that they had done all they could.' Heath then turned to individual IRA leaders. Could Lynch not make a special effort to arrest Seán Mac Stíofáin? Lynch replied that Mac Stíofáin had gone to ground, and that evidence against him was flimsy, but that IRA leaders would be charged whenever practicable.

Heath then raised the Irish Government's case against the British Government at the European Court of Human Rights in Strasbourg arising from the torture of prisoners by the British army. If it went ahead it would be defended vigorously. The relevant events had happened before the suspension of Stormont, so Heath 'hoped that lawyers on both sides could get together and arrange for the case to be dropped.'[175]

The case was to be a running sore in Anglo-Irish relations. For the rest of Fianna Fáil's time in office the British Government tried every method to induce the Irish Government to abandon it, threatening that if it had to fight the case it would do so in a manner aimed at maximising discomfort for the Irish Government.[176] It was pointed out that the British Government's derogation under article 15 of the European Convention on Human Rights was merely what the Lynch Government had done 'when threatened last December with a possible need to intern,' reinforcing the sheer folly of Lynch's flirtation with special powers months earlier.

In fact Britain was not being taken to task for introducing internment (Dublin had no high moral ground there) but for the mistreatment of those who were detained. On the question of inhuman and degrading treatment, as described in article 3 of the Convention, no derogation was permitted. Lynch instead would be asked whether he would be 'aligning his Government behind those who made such allegations until the facts are duly established' (i.e. by the British commission of inquiry).[177] Essentially, the British Government was advocating a procedure whereby politics should dictate the law—a logical extension of internment. The first line of argument was that the British understood that Lynch had been forced to take the case because of a popular clamour for justice in Ireland but could now abandon it, having made his point.

> We have impressed upon Mr. Lynch that although we understand the domestic political pressures to which his Government were subjected at the time of the original application (December 1971), to continue the application in present circumstances will only produce a sterile debate about past discontents.

The British continued to believe, perhaps influenced by previous post-crisis Irish Government initiatives, that the Irish case was not a legal one for upholding human rights but merely a device for pandering to domestic political opinion. The argument that these were 'past discontents' complemented the assertion that internees were not being ill-treated (though the British Government was not eager to seek international verification of this claim). The British contended that they had held their own investigations into the alleged wrongdoings, implying that to ask an international judicial body to assess the case was to question its good will. 'We are acutely aware of the necessity of safeguarding the human rights of the individual,' the brief prepared for Heath asserted, 'and it cannot be seriously contended that acrimonious discussion at Strasbourg is needed in order to heighten our awareness.' Again the British were stressing present attitudes, as if the law was a judgement of present intentions rather than of past actions. (The Irish side had recently had the appalling example of the Widgery Tribunal's investigation into Bloody Sunday to illustrate the absurdity of a government investigating its own crimes.) The Irish Government was also to be warned that public and parliamentary pressures in Britain might stymie co-operation between the two countries, as 'it will be impossible for Ministers in the UK to justify a policy of close consultation with Ministers in the Irish Republic, if on the very day (25 September) that talks involving the parties concerned in Northern Ireland begin, we have to defend ourselves at Strasbourg against the Irish Government's accusation.'[178]

Much to the consternation of the British Government, the European Court of Human Rights decided that the Irish case was admissible and that it should proceed. In response, the British continued to raise the stakes, as confirmed by a confidential briefing prepared for a later meeting of Lynch and Heath, in Paris on 21 October.

> Should [the] opportunity occur, Mr. Lynch should be corrected, and told that HMG will continue their search for a just and peaceful settlement, and that irrelevant sideshows at Strasbourg are a needless irritant which could arouse Parliamentary anger and make HMG less, not more, willing to listen to Dublin's views.

The report went on to state that 'it is not suggested that the Prime Minister should take the initiative; indeed protesting too much would risk confirming Irish ideas that HMG are badly scared.' While presenting Dublin's case at Strasbourg the Attorney-General, Colm Condon, was 'obviously angered by our criticisms of the Irish, and by our drawing attention to the measure of responsibility they bear for the present situation.' If the Irish side refused to drop the case similar tactics would be used, 'and this could mean publicising all the failures with which Mr. Lynch's Government could be taxed. The damage to Anglo-Irish relations will be considerable, but it will be of Dublin's choosing.'[179]

For a government that was pushing Dublin hard to get tough on law-breakers, the British adopted a markedly different approach to their own wrong-doings. Frequently explaining unpalatable acts with such phrases as 'the law must take its course,' they now used all manner of intimidation to prevent the case being heard. Lynch, whatever his personal feelings, could not drop the case without severe political repercussions; and once Strasbourg accepted the admissibility of the case there was no going back.

The British were dismayed also by the Irish media's reporting of events in the North since internment. The press, they believed, had maintained that internment was ill-conceived and arbitrarily implemented and that it represented London's decision to abandon reform and to support Faulkner's repression at all costs. In these circumstances the underlying message of the media, according to the British Government, was that 'civil disobedience is fully justified; and [that] there is much to be said for the IRA.'[180]

The British Government had its own sources within the Irish media. The political correspondent of the *Irish Times*, Michael McInerney, was reporting information—including private conversations with Jack Lynch—to the British embassy, in particular to the information officer. Peck reported to London that 'Irish ministers are aware of McInerney's close relations with my information officer,' though the same could hardly be said for readers of the *Irish Times*.[181]

THE GREEN PAPER

Having failed to secure an arrangement with the IRA, the British Government belatedly began to look at the possibility of a political accommodation. The SDLP made a formal submission for consideration by the British Government and the parties that would be attending the conference called by Whitelaw. The thrust of the document was the need to secure an immediate declaration from the British Government that 'it would be in the best interest of all sections of the communities in both islands if Ireland were to become united on terms acceptable to all the people of Ireland, and that the United Kingdom will positively encourage such a development.'[182] Pending this settlement, a condominium arrangement would exist, with the two governments exercising joint sovereignty over the Six Counties. An 84-member Assembly would be established, elected by proportional representation, and this in turn would elect a 15-member Executive. There would be no Northern Ireland representation in the British House of Commons or in the Dáil, but a new national Senate would be established, encompassing the whole of Ireland.[183] This would be composed of an equal number of representatives from the Dáil and the Assembly, and its function would be 'to plan the integration of North and South and agree on an acceptable constitution.' All this would be supervised by commissioners representing both Governments, to whom all legislation would be referred and by whom executive appointments would be approved.

Paul Bew and Henry Patterson have commented that, as the Irish Government concurred generally with Whitelaw's policies and was not seeking representation at the conference to be convened in September, the SDLP document 'put the party in a more stridently anti-partitionist position than Lynch's government.'[184] Dennis Kennedy made a similar observation in the Belfast current affairs magazine *Fortnight*, arguing that, despite the continual affirmations of solidarity, the Government was becoming increasingly disillusioned with the SDLP.

> Dublin policy—Government and non-Government—has long been based on the hope that the SDLP would provide the rigorous political leadership that would keep Catholic opinion in the North out of the hands of the IRA. But this does not mean, whatever the ambiguity of its own position, that the government wants the SDLP to do this by reverting to a revised Nationalist Party calling for a united Ireland or nothing. The SDLP is arguably 'greener' now than any party in Dublin.[185]

Unionists, meanwhile, had yet to reconcile themselves to the new reality of life without Stormont. Many of their leaders shunned compromise and made vitriolic attacks against direct rule, hinting at the possibility of a unilateral declaration of independence. On 19 October the most prominent of these critics, William Craig, a former Stormont minister and leader of the breakaway Ulster Vanguard, made a speech to a meeting of the right-wing Monday Club in London,[186] in which he informed his receptive Conservative audience that he could mobilise eighty thousand men to oppose the British Government should it attempt to impose an unwanted solution on the unionist people.

> We are prepared to come out and shoot and kill. I am prepared to come out and shoot and kill. Let us put bluff aside. I am prepared to kill, and those behind me have my full support.[187]

While Northern politicians tried to acclimatise themselves to the new political terrain, all looked to Britain to impose their preferred solution, for only Britain had the power to decide. As a stopgap created to remove the 'Irish question' from mainstream British politics, Stormont had exceeded expectations by surviving for half a century, and with its demise Britain again sought to extricate itself from day-to-day government in Ireland. It was obvious to the Conservative Government that Stormont could not realistically be resurrected in its original form, and the search began in earnest for a reformed administration that would quell nationalist dissent by offering moderates a vested interest in the state through direct participation in government.

The first attempt was the holding of a three-day conference at Darlington on 25–7 September 1972 at the behest of the Secretary of State for Northern Ireland, William Whitelaw. It was clear before the conference began that it would not achieve its ostensible aim of securing inter-party agreement on a new form of government in the Six Counties, for the simple reason that not all parties were in attendance. Only three of those invited—the 'Official' Unionist Party, the Alliance Party and the tiny Northern Ireland Labour Party—attended. Sinn Féin was not invited. Each party submitted a policy document, as did the SDLP, which refused to attend, as it continued to demand an end to internment before it would agree to enter formal talks with the British Government.[188] The Democratic Unionist Party—another Unionist breakaway, founded by Ian Paisley in 1971—refused to attend, as it demanded complete integration with Britain (a policy it was subsequently to reverse), while Craig's Ulster Vanguard was flirting with the idea of an independent Six-County state.

Shortly after the Darlington talks, and eleven days after Craig's outburst, the British Government published its Green Paper, *The Future of Northern Ireland*. While the basic ingredients of Britain's policy remained the same, there was evidence of a softening of attitude towards the Irish Government and towards the nationalist community in the North. The British Government's interest in the North was clearly expressed: it should be a stable and prosperous entity so as not to destabilise the United Kingdom or to detract from the prosperity of the British state. The British Government was also concerned that the North would not provide a base for any external threat to British security. Britain's sovereignty 'over all persons, matters and things' in Northern Ireland was reaffirmed; acceptance of this fact was described as a prerequisite for negotiations. In effect, the contested 'unionist veto' had to be recognised and accepted as a *sine qua non* for political progress.

It was the section headed 'The Irish dimension,' however, that most interested the Irish Government. This stated that any settlement 'must also recognise Northern Ireland's position within Ireland as a whole,' and that, while an agreement must meet the wishes of the United Kingdom, it should also 'be so far as possible acceptable to and accepted by the Republic of Ireland.'[189] The SDLP and the Irish Government were also heartened by the document's assertion that there were 'strong arguments' for giving 'minority interests a share in the exercise of executive power.'[190]

The Irish Government warmly welcomed the Green Paper[191]; but when Lynch and Heath met again in October on the margins of a meeting in Paris, Lynch again tried, without success, to get a sense of Heath's long-term thinking. Lynch said he could take difficult decisions if he knew that the British were ultimately well disposed towards a united Ireland. He later told Peck that a public declaration would not be necessary: it would perhaps be enough to know that 'in his heart of hearts' Heath thought reunification would be a blessing. But when Lynch pressed Heath, the latter confined his replies to the short term.[192]

Lynch told the British that he had sent Des O'Malley to the United States to try to prevent Irish-Americans sending money to republican organisations; but Government zeal for anti-IRA measures had been obstructed by constitutional niceties. Now wedded to co-operating with the British on security matters, Lynch was clearly frustrated with the Supreme Court, as the application of the Offences Against the State Act depended on the judiciary. When Peck said he had heard rumours that O'Malley was going to introduce new anti-IRA legislation during the current Dáil session Lynch replied:

> Well, I don't know about new legislation. Our quarrel is not with the law but with the lawyers. We have a standing group of seven barristers working with us to see how the safeguards in our constitution need not be used by Ó Dálaigh's boys [the Supreme Court] to block security measures—anyway you have seen that we have shunted Ó Dálaigh into Europe.

This was a reference to the Government's appointment of Mr Justice Cearbhall Ó Dálaigh, president of the Supreme Court, as Ireland's first judge in the European Court of Justice, ostensibly a promotion but, as Lynch makes clear, implemented with a view to removing an obstacle to pushing through legislation designed to combat the IRA. Peck reported to his superiors that this was the first indication he had had that Mr Justice Ó Dálaigh 'was regarded as an obstacle to internal security measures.'[193]

HUNGER STRIKE

In parallel with improving Anglo-Irish relations, the Government renewed its offensive on the IRA. On 6 October another section of the Offences Against the State Act was reactivated and was used to close down the head office of Provisional Sinn Féin in Kevin Street, Dublin, and its other Dublin office in Blessington Street. Máire Drumm, the vice-president, was arrested and imprisoned for a speech she had delivered,[194] and two weeks later the IRA chief of staff, Seán Mac Stiofáin, was arrested and charged before the Special Criminal Court. He immediately went on hunger strike and, with characteristic bravado, decided to go on a thirst strike as well. The prosecution's case was one that some prominent Fianna Fáil members had faced in the past. The state would

> try to prove that Mac Stiofáin's objectives were to fight the British in the North, to free prisoners in jails in both the North and the Twenty-Six Counties, and to fight for a free Ireland, North and South—these objectives to be achieved by force of arms.[195]

Barely audible during his trial, and accompanied by a doctor, Mac Stiofáin was convicted by the no-jury court and was sentenced to six months' imprisonment. Emotions ran high in the coming days, but, despite large demonstrations in Dublin, the Government refused to contemplate his release, believing it would be wrong in principle, would be politically counterproductive and would set an intolerable precedent.[196] During his incarceration Mac Stiofáin was visited by, among others, the Catholic Archbishop of Dublin, Dermot Ryan, and his predecessor, John Charles McQuaid, who gave him absolution. Both men were vociferously attacked by critics, including Noël Browne (who no doubt relished a clash with his old adversary McQuaid). A rescue attempt by armed men dressed as priests, who burst into the Mater Hospital in Dublin, was foiled, and Mac Stiofáin was flown by army helicopter to the Curragh Camp to prevent a recurrence.

On the tenth day of his hunger strike Mac Stiofáin was near death and was expected to survive only for another twenty-four hours. The intervention of the republican priest Father Seán McManus at this crucial point proved decisive.[197] McManus pleaded with Mac Stiofáin to come off the strike and to avoid the widespread bloodshed that would inevitably follow his death. Mac Stiofáin agreed, but his credibility in the republican movement suffered a fatal blow, and he was never again to hold a high-ranking position in the IRA.[198]

SECTION 31, THE EMASCULATION OF THE MEDIA AND THE ERASURE OF MEMORY

Mac Stiofáin's arrest and imprisonment stemmed from a series of events of much more enduring significance than his hunger strike. Within weeks of the introduction of internment in the North the Minister for Posts and Telegraphs, Gerry Collins, issued a Government directive under section 31 of the Broadcasting Authority Act (1960), requesting RTE to

> refrain from broadcasting any matter that could be calculated to promote the aims or activities of any organisation which engages in, promotes, encourages, or advocates the attaining of any political objective by violent means.[199]

The directive put RTE in an impossible position, and it obfuscated rather than clarified the official position. Somewhere there existed a line between reporting the IRA and promoting it, but nobody in RTE seemed to know where that line was, and, worse, would not know until, in the view of the Government, they had crossed it. The inevitable confrontation came in November 1972 after Heath paid a two-day visit to the North, during which he presented his new proposals.[200] As part of RTE's coverage of the visit, Kevin O'Kelly interviewed Mac Stiofáin to find out whether there was anything in Heath's proposals that would alter the IRA's position. In deference to the directive, RTE did not broadcast the interview, but a summary of its contents was read out by O'Kelly on 'This Week', a current affairs programme. Just after his interview Mac Stiofáin was arrested by members of the Special Detective Unit. O'Kelly's house was then raided, and the director-general of RTE was ordered to hand over the recording of the interview, which would be used in the Special Criminal Court against Mac Stiofáin.

Citing traditional journalistic ethics, O'Kelly refused to identify Mac Stiofáin in court as the person he interviewed, and he was sentenced to three months' imprisonment, later reduced on appeal to a fine of £250. No court of appeal was available, however, for the RTE Authority, which was unceremoniously sacked in its entirety.

Speaking at the airport in London on his way home from talks with Heath, Lynch described the sacking as an 'exercise in democracy', and he explained that the Government had acted because it saw the need for 'protecting our community.'[201] RTÉ closed down from Saturday evening to Tuesday morning in protest against the sacking and the sentence imposed on O'Kelly. For the same reasons, none of the three Dublin morning papers were published on 29 November 1972, nor were the evening papers of the previous day.

In any battle between RTE and the Government, the balance of power was always very much in the Government's favour.[202] The British Government's confidential report stated that Lynch had seized the opportunity to divert attention away from the Mac Stiofáin trial, which opened on the same day as the sacking, and to muzzle the RTE Authority, 'whom they resented for their criticisms of many aspects of Government policy.'[203] Critics of the sacking suggested that the Government's belief that the mere representation of the IRA's views would lead to an abundance of new recruits displayed a curious lack of faith in democracy. Others pointed out that the 'public interest' was a very broad expression, capable of wide interpretation, and that 'what the public interest requires should not be confused at any one moment with what the Government currently considers to be in its interest.'[204]

While controversial at the time, these events are not surprising when seen in the context of the historical relationship between Fianna Fáil and the media, one of authoritarianism and censorious paternalism. Because of its long periods in office, Fianna Fáil had used the press to cement its hegemonic control over the hearts and minds of the people and to articulate a state nationalism distinguishable in degree but never in substance from that of the party.[205] Just as Radio Éireann had done much to 'flatten out' regional accents and styles of music,[206] the centralisation of the dissemination of information led to the centralisation of ideas and the conformity of opinions. A kind of state language had developed, made familiar by repetition, with 'terrorists' the updated version of 'irregular', the slur that was cast on the founders of Fianna Fáil in their revolutionary days. Recourse to alternative modes of discourse provoked the question whether one was using the same state-approved vocabulary.[207]

The nature of the relationship between the Government and RTE was described by the former Taoiseach Seán Lemass, who informed the Dáil in 1966 that

> Radio Telefís Éireann was set up as an instrument of public policy, and as such is responsible to the Government. The Government has overall responsibility for its conduct, and especially the obligation to ensure that its programmes do not offend against the public interest or conflict with national policy as defined in legislation.[208]

For these reasons the Government rejected the view that RTE should be 'independent of Government supervision.' As a public institution, operating under statute and supported by public funds, its role was 'to sustain public support for the institutions of Government' and 'to assist public understanding of the policies enshrined in legislation enacted by the Oireachtas.' The Government, Lemass warned, 'will take such action by way of making representations or otherwise as may be necessary to ensure that Radio Telefís Éireann does not deviate from the due performance of this duty.'[209]

This proved to be no idle threat. Six months after Lemass's warning, when he had been succeeded as Taoiseach by Lynch, the RTE news division proposed sending a television team to Vietnam to cover the war, only to have its wrists very firmly and publicly slapped. After consulting the Minister for Posts and Telegraphs, Lynch spoke to the chairman of the RTE Authority and told him that the national interest would not be served by sending a television crew to Vietnam.[210] The Authority backed down and issued a statement declaring meekly that, following an examination of 'new circumstances brought to its notice,' it would not be proceeding with the project. In January another news team, this time reporting for the current affairs programme 'Seven Days', was in Lisbon *en route* to Africa to cover the breakaway province of Biafra in Nigeria when it was recalled. In the Dáil the Minister for External Affairs, Frank Aiken, declared that 'it would be wise for semi-state [state-sponsored] bodies, when they went outside their formal function across the line of international relations, to consult the Department of External Affairs.'[211]

The advent of the Northern conflict only accelerated this pattern of censorious intervention. One RTE producer, Peter Feeney, recalled after the eruption of armed conflict in 1969 that 'all other issues between RTE and [the] government were to pall into insignificance.'[212] Another current affairs producer, Betty Purcell, has written that

> the Government was sensitive enough about its image in the period of relative stability in the 1960s. When Northern Ireland erupted at the end of that decade the censorship allowed under the Broadcasting Act was seized like clifftop scutch in the slipping man's grip.[213]

The vagueness of the Government directive issued in October 1971 had been a continual source of confusion for RTE journalists,[214] but the sackings defined in the most forceful manner the exact relationship between the RTE Authority and the Government. The Authority had always been hand-picked; now it would be chosen with extreme care, with potential candidates screened for 'deviant' tendencies.[215] The psychological impact on broadcasters and journalists cannot be underestimated. As Niall Meehan has pointed out, 'no other law or internal regulation within RTE has functioned as a so-called "sacking offence"'—not even the stealing of records for use by the illegal pirate radio stations, or the breach of the rule of membership of political parties.[216] A culture of fear and paranoia developed within RTE. Betty Purcell has given a useful insight into the implications of section 31.

> People err on the cautious side where there is doubt. Whole neighbourhoods were silenced because they are too close to a possibility of breaking the ban. The question is not, 'Who is in Sinn Féin?' but 'Who is definitely *not* in Sinn Féin?'[217]

The pervasive censorship promoted by the Fianna Fáil Government during the wartime emergency period had been primarily (though by no means exclusively) directed at the press. That the ban in the 1970s on interviews with republicans was confined to television and radio was not surprising, for, as Russell Weaver and Geoffrey Bennet have suggested,

> Television and radio . . . probably have a far greater impact on public opinion than the print media because more people watch television and listen to the radio than read the newspaper. In addition, television and radio can have a far greater impact because they allow the viewer or listener actually to see or hear the speaker.[218]

Bans on seditious literature remained, however. In November 1972 employees of Drogheda Printers were prosecuted for printing a booklet entitled *Freedom Struggle of the Provisional IRA*. The court ordered all copies of the booklet to be confiscated and the type used for its production melted down.[219] Apart from the symbolic gesture of erasing the narrative, the message to printers was clear.

Depriving the IRA of the 'oxygen of publicity' meant that the life blood of independent debate was drained from RTE. Whatever independence existed among the station's journalists prior to the ban was replaced with a carefully monitored robotic reiteration of the Government line. The kernel of Fianna Fáil's case for introducing section 31 was that it would deprive republican insurgents of avenues for explaining or justifying their actions, as well as deny them an important source of new recruits. This assumption, popular among Government ministers and counter-insurgency theorists alike, has been trenchantly argued by, among others, Walter Laqueur, who claims that 'the media are of paramount importance in [terrorist] campaigns . . . The terrorist act by itself is next to nothing, whereas publicity is all.'[220]

There are some obvious flaws in this assessment. It assumes that all insurgent movements are composed of a small number of highly motivated (and necessarily evil) individuals who are divorced from the community. Cognisant of this absence of a popular base or even an awareness of their cause, the insurgent seeks to promote their particular ideology by recourse to 'terrorist' acts, which, by their horrific character, will receive widespread coverage by attentive media always hungry for sensational events. In essence, it is opting for the facile method of shock rather than the patient means of persuasion. For such a group, Lacqueur's analysis would hold particular weight: if they are denied access to the press and the air waves their actions cannot be explained to the public, who are left with a natural distaste for a brand of politics that demands the destruction of life and property to demonstrate its potency. (It is for this reason that such groups as the 'Red Army Faction' and the Baader-Meinhoff group never succeeded in spreading their particular gospel or achieving a modicum of popular support.)

This analysis, however, does not fit the particular circumstances of the IRA. Republican activity did not exist in a vacuum: it was symptomatic of a reality that affected hundreds of thousands of Northern nationalists. Moreover, the adverse position of this clearly identifiable group had been part of a collective historical experience that was centuries old, and its adverse position was institutionalised. It was from this group that the IRA emerged, just as similar organisations had sprung up over the centuries. In the North, republican insurgents did not need to convince: they were a direct response to events that directly affected their community. They enjoyed solid support within this community, ranging from active support to passive acquiescence (for example not informing the authorities).[221] Only those outside this community, and not exposed to these realities, could be affected by not hearing the articulation of the republican case—and this was precisely the constituency that the Fianna Fáil Government, by means of section 31, sought to influence.

Subsequently, coverage tended to concentrate on reporting violence at the expense of political background. The adopted role of RTE, dominated by official sources, was to delegitimise republican insurgents while promoting official views on the conflict. The themes considered worthy of coverage, and the pejorative terminology employed, reflected Government assumptions. The role of the media would be to facilitate the manufacturing of a consensus sympathetic to the ruling party and hostile to those seeking to overthrow the Northern state. A result of this process was the production of a cosy set of reassuring assumptions that could resist unpalatable realities. (In this respect, a consideration of earlier examples of moral censorship is relevant.) These assumptions would become deeply embedded in the political discourse permitted on the air waves and—it was hoped—in the public imagination. (It is ironic that the BBC—also a state service, and despite heavy restrictions—continued to interview republicans.)[222] In such an indoctrination model

> the power of the media is closely identified with the state . . . 'official sources' supply the themes and issues with which, in turn, the media work. In some cases the media are seen simply as instruments of the state.[223]

As Lemass had made clear, this was precisely the role that the Government had carved out for the state broadcasting organisation. This maxim was religiously adhered to by his successors.

It would not be long before attempts were made to erase all forms of republican or even nationalist discourse from popular culture. Paul McCartney's song 'Give Ireland Back to the Irish' (1972) was banned from being broadcast, possibly the first example in Ireland of overt censorship of politically inspired popular music.[224] A collection of avowedly pro-IRA songs by John Lennon suffered a similar fate and was unavailable for decades.[225] Also banned was 'The Helicopter Song', recorded by the Wolfe Tones in 1973 to celebrate the escape of three IRA prisoners from Mountjoy Prison.[226]

The presentation of history also proved to be a contentious subject. The practice of commissioning historical documentaries came to an abrupt halt. A new wave of historians emerged who redefined their role as one of finding historical reasons to support the constitutional status quo and to oppose political violence. At a time when the legitimacy of the Northern state (and, indeed, its Southern counterpart) was being contested and challenged in the eyes of many, the acclaimed historian F. S. L. Lyons declared in December 1971 that

> in the present situation, with the dire past still overhanging the dire present, the need to go back to fundamentals and consider once more the meaning of independence, asserts itself with almost intolerable urgency. The theories of revolution, the theories of nationality, the theories of history, *which have brought Ireland to its present pass,* cry out for reexamination and the time is ripe to try to break the great enchantment which for too long has made myth more congenial than reality. [Emphasis added.][227]

While what was perceived as a teleological nationalist view of Irish history was dismissed with paternal arrogance, a concerted effort was made to rehabilitate and resurrect neglected parliamentarians as models of virtue.[228] Many historians took up Lyons's call to produce the necessary polemics to bolster the existing order in the battle of conflicting ideas. The new school's objectives were to educate Southern opinion to accept the border (and the British presence it inevitably entailed). This would be done by adopting an approach that eschewed favourable references to the physical-force tradition in Irish history while rigorously questioning its motives, efficacy and ethics. Simultaneously, the parliamentary tradition would be elevated (but not subjected to vigorous interrogation). British colonialism, which constituted such a large part of Irish history, was de-emphasised, and new and exotic explanations were offered to rationalise it.[229] The new school of thought—or rather its more recent variant—would strive to modify nationalist opinion in the South. Accordingly, close links were established with those in the media and the political establishment who had similar designs.

Had revisionism remained within the confines of the university departments its influence would still have been significant; but perhaps its greatest importance was that it succeeded in giving an intellectual rationale to existing political policy. Echoing Yeats's fears after 1916, Conor Cruise O'Brien warned the Dáil that schoolchildren were in danger of being taught 'the philosophy of bombs,' and he asked rhetorically: 'Were the seeds of Aldershot sown in some Irish schoolroom?'[230] Cruise O'Brien's observations were intuitive rather than empirical and were certainly unverifiable. They did, however, exert a considerable influence in promoting a new wave of measures that not only sought to undermine the place of republicanism in Irish history but also questioned the origins of the state itself.

In 1971 Fianna Fáil's National Executive recommended that the firing of a volley at the 1916 Commemoration in Arbour Hill military cemetery should be stopped.[231] The following year the Government refused to commemorate the 1916 Rising at all, because of 'the Northern situation.'[232] From 1974 the ceremony was discontinued indefinitely, thus leaving the republican high ground to the Provisionals.[233] When Sinn Féin organised a ceremony outside the GPO in 1976 to commemorate the sixtieth anniversary of the rising it was promptly banned. The ten thousand people who defied the ban were met with a heavy Garda presence, and seventy people were prosecuted, including David Thornley TD (who was expelled from the Labour Party for his attendance), Fiona Plunkett (daughter of the executed 1916 leader Joseph Plunkett) and 83-year-old Máire Comerford (who had participated in the Rising). A daughter of James Connolly, Nora Connolly-O'Brien, managed to escape arrest.[234] Comerford was convicted and sentenced to a term of imprisonment. As Kenneth Griffith and Timothy O'Grady commented, Comerford, 'as much as anyone alive today in Ireland, personifies the Irish government's troubled relationship with its own founding fathers.'[235]

THE BOMB, THE BILL AND THE PROVOCATEURS

The zenith of the Fianna Fáil Government's anti-republican measures was the Offences Against the State (Amendment) Bill, introduced in the Dáil in November 1972, which would permit the sworn opinion of a Garda superintendent that an individual was a member of an unlawful organisation to be accepted as evidence. It would be up to the accused to prove otherwise, thus reversing the legal norm that the accused is presumed to be innocent until proved guilty.[236] When the head of the Special Detective Unit, Chief Superintendent John Fleming, had given evidence on oath the previous year to the Public Accounts Committee of the Oireachtas, which was investigating the £100,000 expenditure allocated for 'relief in the North,' Charles Haughey claimed that he 'gave false evidence against me' and that his evidence 'should be thrown in the wastepaper basket.' Still trying to rehabilitate himself in the party, Haughey would now vote to give a mere superintendent the power to make un-corroborated statements that could lead to the imprisonment of people on similar evidence.[237] Other controversial features of the bill included a provision that failure to deny published reports of a person's alleged membership of an unlawful organisation could be admitted as evidence of membership—though such a denial would not of itself be proof of innocence.[238] Section 4 would make unlawful any statement, procession or meeting considered to be 'interference with the course of justice'—a phrase so vague as to render its interpretation and application open to serious abuse.[239] An obvious result of this provision was the serious curtailment of public criticism of the Special Criminal Court and the act itself.

The introduction of special courts had already resulted in the end of trial by jury for certain offences, and the amendment bill appeared to signal the end of trial by the judiciary. For many parliamentarians the Government had crossed the line that divides defensive and dictatorial powers. The Labour Party was committed to voting against the bill, while some dissident Fianna Fáil deputies were expected to abstain. Liam Cosgrave, alone among his parliamentary party colleagues, was disinclined to vote against the Government on the issue. Fine Gael proposed amendments to lessen the impact of the bill's most draconian provisions; but, smelling blood, Fianna Fáil refused to entertain them and began to make plans for a snap election. Des O'Malley recalled the political elite's feeling of being under siege.

At one stage during the passage of the Offences Against the State (Amendment) Bill 1972 it was estimated [that] there were 7,000 or 8,000 people outside the gates, many of whom were in a fairly violent frame of mind. There were 300 troops here, at the back of Leinster House in the part that was then the Department of Agriculture. I remember being told that they were armed and that there was no question of them firing blanks, that their orders were to shoot to kill, if necessary.[240]

The Government had overcome its queasiness about using the army to fire on Irish citizens—a queasiness that had so distressed the British ambassador in February. Indeed O'Malley recalled that attitudes in this regard were 'very much coloured by the events in Merrion Square at the beginning of February . . . when the British Embassy . . . was burned down.'[241] The essential difference between February and December was that the target of the anger had shifted from London's political elite to Dublin's.

One of the most outspoken critics of the bill in the Dáil was the Fine Gael spokesperson on justice, Paddy Cooney (soon to undergo a radical transformation on taking the portfolio himself the following year). In opposition he presented himself as the leading spokesperson of liberal democratic values. He asked the minister how he could 'come into this parliament and ask it to support a bill the like of which can only be found on the statute book of South Africa.' Cooney's argument was that the Government was destroying democracy in order to preserve it: 'there is a limit to the measures a democracy is entitled to adopt in order to protect itself. I am suggesting that limit is exceeded in this bill.'[242] Bernadette Devlin proclaimed that 'if the bill is passed through the Dáil, may the hand of the President who signs it wither as he signs it, and may every one of his dead comrades who fought and died for this country appear before his dim eyes and curse his beating heart.'[243] But de Valera had signed many similar acts, and had appended his signature to death warrants for erstwhile brothers in arms. Indeed the purpose of the bill was merely to amend legislation that de Valera himself had introduced in 1939 and 1940 to meet an earlier crisis. It was unlikely that now, at the end of his political career, he would cause a constitutional upset by refusing to provide the necessary presidential seal of approval.

The bill was signed and became law, but not before a bizarre series of events had occurred—events that revealed the extent of British undercover activities in Ireland.

As the Dáil debated the 'IRA bill', as the media had dubbed it, two car bombs exploded in Dublin, one in Sackville Place, off O'Connell street, the other outside Liberty Hall in Beresford Place. A bus driver and a bus conductor were killed and seventy-three people were injured. During the first explosion, barely audible within the Dáil chamber, Tom O'Higgins was on his feet for Fine Gael, opposing the bill; he was still speaking when the second bomb went off, this one clearer to those assembled. Three minutes later Fianna Fáil was already making political capital out of Dublin's dead. Deputy Noel Davern entered the chamber and asked O'Higgins if, in opposing the bill, he supported those who had set off the two bombs. When O'Higgins told Davern 'not to be a bloody ass,' Davern taunted deputies to 'give us the means to deal with these people'; in the argument he called one Fine Gael TD 'a filthy pup.'[244] Des O'Malley declared that 'the situation in which the country finds itself had been amply demonstrated' by the bombs.[245]

Confused and demoralised, Fine Gael fell in behind Cosgrave. At 9:45 p.m. Paddy Cooney entered the chamber to make a statement. Fine Gael had 'decided to put nation before party' and was withdrawing its amendment, lest it have the effect of 'plunging the country into a political crisis.'[246] The Dáil adjourned for an hour as Fine Gael deputies reassessed the situation. Lynch travelled the short distance to the RTE studios in Donnybrook (now firmly under Fianna Fáil control) to make an address to the nation.[247]

As the bill passed, at 4 a.m., Mary Holland described the scene in the Dáil.

> The corridor outside the Members' Bar was like a Kilburn pub on a Friday night, Guinness bottles rolling on the floor and elderly deputies swaying up to young women to lurch unsteadily against their bosoms. One Fianna Fáil back bencher, who had dutifully voted for a law to make it easier for the courts to jail republicans, lay back on a leather couch shouting: 'Up the Republic!'[248]

Many people presumed that republicans were responsible for the bombs; but doubts soon emerged. Why would the IRA bomb Dublin—and why of all times during a debate in which the Government was going to be defeated on emergency legislation aimed primarily at republicans? Some began to suspect London's hidden hand,[249] and their suspicions were confirmed when it emerged that the bombing had been the work of two English brothers in the employment of British intelligence.[250]

Keith and Kenneth Littlejohn had carried out a number of crimes in the Republic during the previous year, including the sending of letter bombs and the petrol-bombing of Garda stations. They also embarked on a series of armed bank robberies, the most significant being at the Grafton Street branch of Allied Irish Banks in Dublin, from which they stole more than £67,000. All these activities were aimed at discrediting the IRA and strengthening the hand of the British Government and of those sections of Irish political opinion that sought more draconian anti-IRA measures.

When he was out of office, Jack Lynch gave an interview to ITN on 11 August 1973 in which he stated that he had suspicions that British agents might have been involved in the Dublin bombings in December 1972, as no organisation had claimed responsibility. Two days later he was forced to admit that in January he had been shown a report by the Secretary of the Department of Foreign Affairs (as the department was now called), Hugh McCann, that had confirmed the involvement of the Littlejohn brothers.[251] In what was considered an 'extraordinary admission,' Lynch claimed to have forgotten that the British had admitted that the Littlejohns were working for them.[252]

Such undercover activities had a significant effect on political events. They facilitated the introduction of a series of anti-republican laws in the South, and the bombs in Dublin gave the vital impetus necessary to get the Offences Against the State (Amendment) Act (1972) through the Dáil. Of equal political significance was the effect the bombs had on Fine Gael's electoral performance. Garret FitzGerald has stated his belief that Lynch had been 'deprived by a matter of minutes of the opportunity to call a snap election,' and that 'had we opposed the Bill we would, I believe, have been severely beaten in a post-Christmas law-and-order election.'[253] Lynch temporised, and by the time he called an election eight weeks later Fine Gael and the Labour Party had been adequately forewarned and had prepared a joint programme for government.

The British embassy in Dublin compiled a detailed report on the circumstances surrounding the Dáil vote, in which it reported that, since August, riots in the South, UDA reprisals in border towns and attacks on property had 'begun to terrify armchair Republicans with the spectre of disorder in the South,'[254] creating an opportunity to introduce tough anti-IRA legislation. The bill had been pushed through despite protests from the media, liberals, republicans and opposition and former Fianna Fáil TDs, who could not co-ordinate their efforts; but 'the two bombs on 1 December clinched the matter.'[255] According to this report, Lynch had come out very well, having held his nerve against Mac Stiofáin and against protests arising from the latter's hunger strike and succeeding in having his legislation passed while dividing the opposition. Lynch's achievement was all the more impressive considering that 'perhaps 20 of the Government back benchers who helped bring in the law designed to help jail the Provisionals are Provisional sympathisers.' The party remained united, at least superficially, and the affair had 'demonstrated again that Fianna Fáil have no ideological convictions; as the story goes in Dublin, if Fianna Fáil said that the moon was made of green cheese, 70 deputies would be on their feet asserting the fact.' The report also noted that the Dublin bombs came as

a considerable shock to the man in the street. Despite the preoccupation of the Dublin press with the North, many Irish have managed to get through the last

3 years as though the North was thousands of miles away. For the first time, bombs have killed people in Dublin . . . This, and the realisation that a breakdown of law and order is possible in Dublin, have done much to turn people's minds even further against violence and the IRA. There is widespread and open speculation that the Provisionals are finished.[256]

In mid-December further evidence of British espionage in the Republic surfaced with the arrest in Dublin of Detective-Sergeant Patrick Crinnion of the Special Detective Unit and John Wyman, an officer in the Secret Intelligence Service (commonly known by its former name, MI6). As private secretary to Chief Superintendent John Fleming, Crinnion had access to highly sensitive files not only on republicans but also on Government security strategies and processes. His being caught red-handed passing secret documents to a foreign intelligence agent made it potentially one of the most serious cases of espionage in Ireland since independence.[257] Yet within two days of the arrests the Irish ambassador to Britain, Dónal O'Sullivan, was able to assure Heath's private secretary, Robert Armstrong, that Wyman was unlikely to serve a prison sentence. In Armstrong's 'top secret and personal' note for the British Prime Minister he emphasised 'two points which are for your eyes only':

(1) For public relations reasons his [O'Sullivan's] government would have to oppose bail; but the strength with which they would do so was another matter.
(2) You had expressed concern about the effects of a long sentence. He had the impression that this was unlikely; indeed he said there might be no sentences at all.[258]

The note confirms the Government's obsequious sensitivity to Heath's concerns, despite the fact that it was the British who had been caught spying and paying an extremely well-placed member of the Special Detective Unit for state secrets. There is also something rather pathetic in the fact that O'Sullivan offered to communicate these assurances in person to Heath, only to be told not to bother and that it was sufficient for them to be communicated to his secretary. Equally noteworthy is the admission that the judicial process, such as it was, would be carried out with a view to public relations rather than to justice.

O'Sullivan's confidence about the token sentencing was no doubt bolstered by the fact that the new no-jury Special Criminal Court had effactually taken the judicial process under more direct Government control. By entering a *nolle prosequi* (a decision not to prosecute) the state decided to forgo an embarrassing trial and to simply make the whole affair disappear without any damaging admissions in court, which would have exposed the level of British penetration of the Irish police. On 27 February 1973 the court ordered that the British agent and the Garda collaborator be released, after which they were never seen again.[259]

It is worth contrasting Wyman's and Crinnion's treatment with that of the president of Sinn Féin, Ruairí Ó Brádaigh, who in the same month was charged with membership of the IRA under the new Offences Against the State (Amendment) Act. The only 'proof' accepted as evidence by the court was the word of the head of the

Special Detective Unit, Chief Superintendent Fleming. Though Fleming confessed that his opinion of Ó Brádaigh was not based on personal knowledge, and that he had been mistaken with his information in the past (and specifically about Ó Brádaigh), the court convicted Ó Brádaigh on Fleming's testimony alone. Despite Government protestations to the contrary during the Dáil debate on the act, the burden of proof had shifted to the accused, at least for republicans.[260]

THE GENERAL ELECTION

Superficially at least, the 1973 general election was similar to those of 1932 and 1948, in which parties in power for a long time had become bereft of ideas and whipped up a security scare that ultimately failed to rouse the electorate. In 1932 Cumann na nGaedheal claimed that it needed a strong mandate to prepare for the imminent Eucharistic Congress and the Commonwealth Conference in Ottawa and to combat the bands of communists and IRA men bent on the destruction of the state. In 1948 Fianna Fáil sought a renewed mandate to tackle post-emergency issues and to deal effectively with international and domestic communism and the non-existent IRA threat. The ostensible reason for the 1973 election was the imminent release of the British White Paper on the future of the North. As it turned out, Irish Governments— both incoming and outgoing—had no influence on the contents of the White Paper in the crucial months before its publication.

On the day of the announcement of the election Lynch said he would be meeting Heath within two weeks and that 'the General Election would not interfere with any plans.'[261] The next day the Government announced that there would be no such meeting after all, 'because of the General Election campaign.'[262] After that the White Paper quickly receded into the background, to be replaced by the issue of 'security', a theme the Government had planned to use since the introduction of the the the Offences Against the State (Amendment) Act two months earlier.

The Tánaiste, Erskine Childers, told a convention in Castleblayney, Co. Monaghan, that Fianna Fáil could not survive if its members listened to dissidents who had been expelled from the party. 'These were the people who would have brought the Border areas of the Republic, such as County Monaghan, into civil war.'[263] In Co. Donegal one Fianna Fáil candidate said that the proposed White Paper 'could cause a bloodbath that could overspill across the border' and that 'we will require a strong Government headed by Jack Lynch to deal with the situation.'[264] It was a measure of how far the party had recovered that it could taunt its opponents on their commitment to security and anti-IRA measures less than three years after a quarter of the Fianna Fáil Government had resigned as a result of disputes arising from a plan to import arms destined for Northern nationalists.

The impact of the North meant that, whereas only three parties contested the 1969 election, three new parties—all formed as a result of the Northern crisis—threw their hat into the ring: Aontacht Éireann, Official Sinn Féin, and 'Independent Fianna Fáil'.[265] There were now five parties in the Republic representing 'real' republicanism; in 1969 there were only two.

Aontacht Éireann put up thirteen candidates in twelve constituencies.[266] Though most of its candidates came from a Fianna Fáil background,[267] the party found itself closer to the Labour Party, which also opposed the raft of security legislation and membership of the EEC. The presence of Conor Cruise O'Brien on the Labour ticket, however, and his pivotal position as spokesperson on Northern Ireland made the Labour Party suspect on the national question for the Aontacht Éireann leadership. Official Sinn Féin put forward ten candidates committed to taking their Dáil seats if elected.[268] Neil Blaney and a few of his fellow-malcontents contested the election under the banner of Independent Fianna Fáil.[269]

The major parties all claimed that Northern Ireland was above electioneering and too tragic an issue to exploit for political gain. However, after a week of campaigning this undeclared consensus was broken by Fianna Fáil's director of elections, George Colley, who identified Cruise O'Brien as the Labour Party's Achilles heel.[270] Noël Browne's refusal to stand for the Labour Party had deprived Fianna Fáil of the Red card it had so adroitly played during the 1969 election, while the Labour Party itself jettisoned its 'seventies will be socialist' slogan for a more modest set of policies. Instead of challenging the 'doctrinaire socialism' of Browne and the Labour left, Fianna Fáil speakers contented themselves with attacking the Labour Party's Northern policy and in particular Cruise O'Brien. Colley claimed that the 'O'Brien line', as he called it, represented 'the height of folly,' and any Government foolish enough to adopt it would be yielding to 'Orange blackmail.'[271] Despite the White Paper and security being made significant issues by Lynch in the campaign, most of what he had to say on these subjects was woolly in the extreme. A typical example can be found in his explaining why his Northern policies merited support.

> In relation to the tragic situation in Northern Ireland I put it to you that we have pursued, and are pursuing, the only policy which makes sound common sense— the only sane policy which can bring about a true reconciliation of the communities and a lasting peace with justice to all.[272]

In this as in similarly vague statements Lynch never elaborated on what this sane, commonsense policy was, nor did he treat the electorate to a detailed exposition of the issues that this policy addressed. While the need for a strong Government to deal with the forthcoming British White Paper was continually stressed, no attempt was made, publicly at least, to consider its widely discussed contents, such as power-sharing, a Council of Ireland and cross-border institutions. No party in Ireland or Britain—with the possible exception of some of the unionist organisations— articulated a set of objectives explicitly precluding the aim of reconciliation and justice: it was the means of achieving those objectives that divided the parties. Similarly, when Lynch argued that Fianna Fáil was 'the only political organisation in the state capable of applying sound, long-term policies based on fundamental objectives,'[273] he again decided that it was unnecessary to burden the electorate with any explanation of what those fundamentals or policies actually were.

Fianna Fáil was never keen to reveal what exactly its mandate was for, or how it was to be used. The underlying message was 'Trust us.' Moreover, many of the arguments and rallying cries used during the election were reminiscent of the dominant slogan used for the 1944 snap election (also called ostensibly to meet a national emergency, i.e. Fianna Fáil without a majority): 'Don't change horses while crossing the stream.' The *Irish Times* claimed that 'no matter how it is dressed up, the issue which Fianna Fáil will put to the country in the current campaign will almost certainly be—Jack Lynch. Just that.'[274]

The Fianna Fáil advertising campaign imported much from the cruder American style of electioneering. An election broadcast was transmitted on RTE television in which scenes of bombing in Belfast were juxtaposed with scenes of serenity in the South. The broadcast reflected a renewed faith in security as an electoral trump card, pitting Fianna Fáil against an opposition that had failed to give full support to its anti-republican security legislation. In his campaign comment in the *Irish Times*, John Healy wrote:

Some people may object to Fianna Fáil hawking in the Northern troubles and using bomb blast scenes to market the politics of fear. Labour's Frank Cluskey said yesterday that the Alternative Government candidates would not seek to crawl into office over the corpses of the Northern dead and, of course, that's what makes Fianna Fáil such a great party: they have no such scruples, and whether they are the corpses of the Northern dead or of the dead busmen all are fair game for vote milking when your back is to the wall . . . That's professionalism and, frankly, it is hard to beat it.[275]

Neither Official Sinn Féin nor Aontacht Éireann was allocated any time on RTE television or radio during the election campaign.[276] RTE denied that the parties were banned, but the difference between being censored and not receiving any air time seemed a fine one.[277]

The theme of national security was repeated from Fianna Fáil platforms throughout the country. In Co. Monaghan, Childers claimed that the 'most important problem,' that of national security, provided the most convincing proof of 'coalition futility.' The alternative Government had no agreed policy on the issue, and he warned that 'people should think before they delivered desperately serious decision-making to a coalition, one of whose parties included extremist left-wingers who patted the IRA on the head.'[278] Seán Moore TD reiterated the point when he told an audience in Donnybrook, Dublin, that 'if you want peace and security, vote Fianna Fáil'; the alternative was 'a coalition including people who have been seen openly flirting with the IRA.'[279]

Liam Cosgrave responded by declaring that Fianna Fáil was reverting to its traditional strategy of attempting to frighten the electorate. 'Everybody knows where I stand on national security,' he said, 'and that any Government with which I am associated will in fact be firm but fair in dealing with any challenge to the authority of the state.'[280]

Fianna Fáil's elevation of security to the status of the most important problem facing the country divided the provincial press. The party's reliance on its record was supported by the *Westmeath-Offaly Independent*, which agreed with the contention that 'with so much trouble and uncertainty prevailing in the North,' Lynch was uniquely qualified 'to pull the nation through the difficulties that lie ahead.'[281] The paper urged electors to vote according to past performance on the issue and not on unproven promises. The *Western People*, on the other hand, claimed that the opposition was more consistent than Fianna Fáil on law and order and that Fianna Fáil was 'offering the Fine Gael policy of fifty years ago which it then rejected at the cost of civil war.'[282]

The election results demonstrated that Fianna Fáil remained as the premier constitutional nationalist party; its rivals for the mantle of 'the Republican Party' failed to make an impact. Aontacht Éireann's twelve candidates received an average of 1,027 votes each, while Official Sinn Féin received an average of 1,536, though the combined vote for the two parties was less than 30,000.[283] The former Fianna Fáil TDs Paudge Brennan and Des Foley stood as independents. Though they polled respectably, both failed to take a seat.[284] Neil Blaney, in contrast, demonstrated the importance of organisation by retaining his seat in Donegal North-East, topping the poll in the process. Outside Co. Donegal his colleagues did less well, and it is fair to say that Independent Fianna Fáil was more a small collection of local notables than a real national organisation.[285] Louis Maguire received a paltry vote in Dublin South-Central, while Des Foley did considerably better in the north of the city, though not enough to retain his seat.[286]

As far as the larger electoral picture is concerned, the results contrasted sharply with those of 1969, when Fianna Fáil had lost votes but gained seats. In 1973, on the other hand, its vote increased by more than 22,000 but it obtained six fewer seats than in 1969. The effect of the electoral pact paid handsome dividends for the opposition parties: although the combined vote of Fine Gael and the Labour Party fell by more than 14,000, they gained five seats. Fianna Fáil's second sixteen-year reign had come to an end.

Following the 1923 election, William Cosgrave headed the Irish Government and was ably assisted by his Minister for External Affairs, Desmond FitzGerald and Attorney General, John A. Costello. Cosgrave's government had to contend with a state under siege and the North in turmoil. As a result of the 1973 election, a new administration came to power led by Liam Cosgrave, son of William, and flanked by Foreign Minister Garret FitzGerald, son of Desmond, and Attorney General, Declan Costello, son of John A. Their political challenges remained much the same as those confronted by their fathers a half century earlier. The cycle of Irish history continued.

Chapter 14 ～

CONCLUSIONS: THE DESTINY OF THE SOLDIERS

DE VALERA AND REPUBLICAN POLITICS

The origins and development of Fianna Fáil are inextricably linked to the political personality of its founder, Éamon de Valera. There is little doubt that de Valera's decision to oppose the Treaty, for whatever motives, gave the anti-Treaty side a political—as opposed to a military—prestige that it would otherwise not have enjoyed to the same extent. It gave the republican movement a political focus and a credibility that disguised the imbalance in electoral support and military might.

That is not to say that the anti-Treatyites were bereft of notable political figures, simply that none were as well known as de Valera. This point was particularly significant with regard to international opinion, especially American opinion. While individuals such as Austin Stack, Cathal Brugha and Mary MacSwiney were known to those Irish-Americans who took an active interest in Irish affairs, de Valera was known by friend and foe alike as the man who had been President of the Republic during the War of Independence. De Valera fully appreciated the value of the Irish-American bloc and was indefatigable in securing its support, addressing rallies of fifty thousand people in several American cities. And while American support was a poor substitute for that of the majority of Irish people it was a useful base to fall back on. It allowed de Valera to maintain the image of international statesman in a way that was, arguably, more impressive than the attendance of William Cosgrave or Kevin O'Higgins at international forums such as the League of Nations and Imperial Conferences.

De Valera was something of a cuckoo in the nest of republican militants during the Civil War. Clearly he was not in control of events, and yet, despite his impotence, he continued to present himself as leader of the republican forces. He disagreed with most of the important actions taken by the IRA leadership, such as their repudiation of the Dáil and the continuation of hostilities, but in public he gave vocal support to every decision taken. He enjoyed responsibility without power, explaining republican actions retrospectively without being consulted about them. His response to this unenviable predicament was to form a republican government of which he was president. He showed considerable private ambivalence about this action; but there is much to suggest that these qualms were expressed to secure titular supremacy within the anti-Treaty movement.

De Valera's desire to bring hostilities to an end was frustrated by more bellicose elements in the movement; but the death of prominent militants—through active service or by execution—strengthened his position, and by the end of the Civil War his supporters held pivotal positions within the IRA, thus facilitating a ceasefire.

It is not unreasonable to suggest that de Valera was using the republican movement, and that it was using him. Many figures in Sinn Féin doubted de Valera's commitment to the Republic and were discomfited by his tendency to flirt with compromise, even if those flirtations were often purely intellectual. Yet they accepted him as leader. He had a poor opinion of some of his colleagues, but he may have felt more comfortable with them than with Collins or other pro-Treaty leaders. While in credibility de Valera was undoubtedly an asset to the republican movement, what he endowed he debilitated. He was, and continues to be, subjected to criticism from both pro-Treaty and anti-Treaty factions.[1] Those sympathetic to the Free State regime point to his actions during the crucial years 1921–3, during which his refusal to accept the Treaty made civil war inevitable. That he took the oath and appeared to accept, by his actions, the veracity of the 'stepping-stone' argument created additional bitterness. Republicans maintain that de Valera manipulated their movement, crippled it financially and politically, weakened its morale and betrayed the principles he had espoused. He succeeded in wrecking the Free State and the republican movement before settling for the curious hybrid of Fianna Fáil, whose ideology was similar to that espoused by Sinn Féin but whose actions differed little from those practised by Free-Staters (frustrating Sinn Féiners and Free-Staters alike).

During the Civil War de Valera accepted the position of President of the Republic, and he headed an underground republican government replete with council of state.[2] However, he began to feel a prisoner of the ideology that few others had so publicly espoused. He believed that Sinn Féin had entered a dead end, and he was anxious to get back on the main road to power with the minimum of embarrassing U-turns. He also feared that political impotence would lead to the gradual erosion of the electoral base on which his brand of republicanism depended. Despite the fact that the imposed Free State constitution contained seventeen articles that made reference to the British King, the oath of allegiance began to assume disproportionate importance in de Valera's mind. Private meetings took place between de Valera and a number of theologians, Daniel Mannix being the most prominent of them, in which the binding nature of the oath was discussed and examined in minute detail.

The split in Sinn Féin, which led to the birth of Fianna Fáil, was one manufactured by de Valera. Had he brought a majority of Sinn Féin with him he could have retained the name and enjoyed an immediate electoral and ideological advantage. As it turned out, he failed to conclusively convince Sinn Féin of the merits of his proposed new departure. With his most doctrinaire colleagues remaining in Sinn Féin, his defeat allowed him much greater flexibility, and it led directly to the establishment of Fianna Fáil.

THE EARLY DEVELOPMENT OF FIANNA FÁIL

After Sinn Féin split, the newly formed Fianna Fáil took with it many of the most radical elements of its parent party. An initial period of rapid expansion followed, culminating in the establishment of a cumann in almost every parish in the Free State.

Many of those who threw in their lot with de Valera's new venture were inspired by mixed motives and sentiments. Some party members, particularly those who were members of, or close to, the IRA, might have been content to remain outside Free State political institutions, so blurring the differences between the two parties, both of which advocated abstention from the Free State parliament. In this sense, the taking of the oath was a defining moment for Fianna Fáil. While it would be portrayed by the leadership and accepted by supporters as a great sacrifice, it was in reality an opportunist relinquishing of fundamental principle to the needs of organisation, a sacrifice made for love of party, despite being in violent conflict with the party's professed ethos and in opposition to the leadership's ideological convictions. These intellectual gymnastics, crowned by de Valera's 'empty formula' ritual when taking the oath, were inspired by the need to close the gap between stated ideological convictions and contemporary political realities.

Fianna Fáil's entry into the Dáil transformed that institution in regard to representation and legitimacy. Once inside the Free State political institution the party contested everything, going so far as to revise its previously held position on participation in the Seanad. Nothing compelled it to contest Seanad elections, and indeed there was considerable unease in the party about the move. However, a motion at the 1928 ard-fheis retrospectively disapproving of the leadership's decision to contest the election was defeated. The success of all six Fianna Fáil candidates in the Seanad election of December 1928 was considered vindication enough of the leadership's decision to contest. Rank-and-file supporters were assured that the party's attitude towards the Seanad remained unchanged and that 'their purpose in entering the Senate is the same as that of those who entered the Free State Parliament—to batter down the obstacles and clear the road to the Republic.'

Particular emphasis was placed on the discomfort that the elections had allegedly caused in pro-government circles and on the revolutionary credentials of the candidates, of whom Kathleen Clarke was the most famous. They had given 'loyal service in the days of danger,' and the party was confident that 'the task of meeting and defeating Imperialism in the Free State Senate will be safe in their hands.'[3]

Fianna Fáil's route to Leinster House may have been haphazard, but it was the logical next step for a mass party that had committed itself to altering the constitutional status quo within the existing political institutions (however flawed they were thought to be). Before August 1927 Fianna Fáil was in the anomalous position of being the second-largest party in the Free State but without a parliament to attend. Two competing institutions existed—both called Dáil Éireann—but, despite the embarrassment of choices, neither of them was attractive. The so-called 'second Dáil', which since the defections led by de Valera had become increasingly impotent, was ideologically pure but bereft of power. The Free State Dáil, on the other hand, had exclusive power but was repulsive as an institution. Faced with the choice between purity and power, the party had clearly opted for power.

The speed with which Fianna Fáil established an impressive network of cumainn demonstrated a singularity of purpose that had to have some focal point. Indeed the party appointed parliamentary whips some months before it formally entered the Dáil.[4] Despite its participation in the Free State institutions it was eager to stress that the pursuit of power was not an end in itself but was merely the most appropriate tactic available in the circumstances for achieving 'Republican Party' objectives.

Fianna Fáil's attention to organisation was in marked contrast to the relative neglect of the governing party's political machine. Cumann na nGaedheal's leadership had formed a government before it set about establishing a party, and throughout the 1920s duties of government predominated over attention to party— so much so that party and state were viewed as synonymous by both Cumann na nGaedheal and its opponents. The establishment of Fianna Fáil jolted Cumann na nGaedheal from its organisational lethargy, but not to a sufficient degree. The party found little with which to mobilise or inspire its supporters, save a call to defend the status quo. Fianna Fáil, on the other hand, as the opposition party, had little else to do but to build up an organisational machine that would propel it to power.

One issue on which the demands of ideology and organisation clashed was partition (and the question whether the party would actively organise in the Six Counties). It is not widely known that for three years Northern Ireland had a Fianna Fáil MP. Though the seat had been contested in 1921 and again in 1925 under the Sinn Féin banner, when de Valera left that party to establish Fianna Fáil he became *ipso facto* Fianna Fáil MP for Co. Down. A clear break was detectable, however, when Fianna Fáil did not contest the 1929 election for the Belfast parliament. In essence, the party leadership found it prudent, from an organisational point of view, not to establish Fianna Fáil in the Northern state, even if this was difficult to explain ideologically. It was strongly implied that such an initiative would have to wait until the primary task of attaining power in the Free State had been achieved. But with Fianna Fáil firmly ensconced in power from 1932, the leadership showed no inclination towards transforming it into a 32-County party. To do this it had to rebuff persistent overtures from Northern nationalists and initiatives from its own members. In essence, while the issue of the 'fourth green field' was exploited at election time and at ard-fheiseanna to mobilise the faithful, the North was viewed as a distraction from the main objective of maintaining its hold on power in the 26-County state. Nationalists alienated from the Northern state were offered sympathy—but little else.

During its campaign of 'slightly constitutional' opposition between 1926 and 1932 Fianna Fáil succeeded in presenting itself as the only credible political alternative to Cumann na nGaedheal for control of government. It consistently sought to polarise political debate and thus to squeeze out smaller parties. Much of its success in retaining its traditional support and in attracting new supporters can be attributed to its socio-economic polices, which offered a dynamic alternative to the governing party. While Cumann na nGaedheal's policies tended to favour the large farmer,[5] Fianna Fáil successfully charmed its potential support by emphasising the predicament of the small landholder, as its policies favoured 'the low paid at the expense of the rich, the small farmer rather than the rancher.'[6] But while the party's 1932 election manifesto emphasised economic, social and health policies it was clear that 'economic concerns and national ambitions were inextricably intertwined.'[7]

The land annuities campaign was explicitly anti-British, and it promised economic advantages to small farmers. The IRA leader Peadar O'Donnell had vociferously advocated a policy of withholding payment as part of a class struggle that would inspire a republican resurgence.[8] While O'Donnell and de Valera differed markedly in their approach to the issue, and in their objectives,[9] de Valera's modification of O'Donnell's strategy robbed the republican left of one of its most powerful rallying calls and handed it to Fianna Fáil.[10] It also accelerated the flight from Sinn Féin to Fianna Fáil, making de Valera undisputed leader of nationalist Ireland and condemning his republican opponents to the political margins.[11]

The establishment of Saor Éire, the brainchild of Peadar O'Donnell and the republican left, contributed to the Red Scare, in which church and state united to paint opponents of Cumann na nGaedheal's imperial politics and *laissez-faire* economics as part of a conspiracy manufactured in Moscow. The emphasis on the alleged spread of Bolshevism reflected the desperation of the Free State government amid mounting economic and political crises, but it proved a popular theme for the Catholic bishops, who issued a joint pastoral letter condemning the IRA. The Red Scare ultimately proved unsuccessful, and possibly counter-productive, when 'the horrible communists could not be found or turned out to be the Murphy lad down the lane.' In addition, 'the suppression of the IRA had created as many problems as it had solved, with Fianna Fáil going about the country howling to free the political prisoners.'[12] As Jeffrey Prager argues, 'neither Cumann na nGaedheal nor the Labour Party shared the same cultural universe as most Irish men and women,' and 'the government party's anti-republican policies produced a cultural unease that Fianna Fáil was able to exploit.'[13]

Fianna Fáil during its early years was highly critical of the police, particularly of the CID (later the Special Branch). Moreover, the party vehemently opposed all legislation aimed at combating the IRA. Such verbal bellicosity was partly motivated by the need to placate influential dissidents who were uncomfortable with the notion of mere political agitation. It also reflected a genuine ambivalence towards the institutions of the Free State. For the Fianna Fáil leadership the state was at the same time an object of repulsion and attraction. The party's political *culture,* and the circumstances and the tradition from which it sprang, repelled it from the Free State, which was portrayed as an inherently flawed institution, unworthy of popular support or party endorsement; Fianna Fáil's political *programme,* however, necessitated access by the party to the state machinery, without which its policies could not be implemented. Strident anti-state rhetoric was also useful in pandering to those republicans who had refused to join the party but who retained a certain usefulness in providing enhanced republican legitimacy and votes.

Ideologically pure but bereft of an organisation and finances, Sinn Féin entered a period of rapid decline in personnel and influence, and by 1929 it was moribund. Not until the 1950s would it re-emerge as a significant political force. By contrast, both Fianna Fáil and the IRA flourished and expanded between 1926 and 1932. In retrospect it is easy to see the alliance between Fianna Fáil and the IRA as a marriage of convenience (or perhaps a shotgun wedding). The IRA contained a considerable number of dedicated members, who, though ultimately expendable, could provide valuable assistance. This utility was amply demonstrated during the 1932 election, which brought Fianna Fáil to power.

CONSOLIDATION AND STAGNATION, 1932–48

After fighting a civil war to preserve the Treaty, Cumann na nGaedheal had found increasingly little to offer the electorate, and it fell back on presenting itself as a bulwark against anarchy. The Treaty became less a stepping-stone than a stick with which to beat its opponents. Similarly, Fianna Fáil had run out of ideas by 1938—a fact disguised only by the outbreak of the Second World War, during which the preservation of the state's neutrality and the attendant problems of feeding a people effectually blockaded by the outside world consumed the party leadership.

A comparison of the 1932 and 1948 elections demonstrates how close Fianna Fáil had come to the Cumann na nGaedheal party it had reviled. So great was the campaign in 1932 to portray Fianna Fáil as a Bolshevik party that de Valera was forced to declare that he was 'not a communist.' The Fianna Fáil manifesto stated that the party had 'no leanings towards communism and no belief in communistic doctrines.'[14] Even two years after taking office de Valera was being described by Fine Gael as the 'arch-Communist agent' and Fianna Fáil as 'the vanguard of the Communist policy here.'[15] By 1948 Seán MacEntee had become the chief red-baiter, who periodically erupted before his audiences, fulminating against the bogeymen who were out to undermine Fianna Fáil and destabilise the state. Seán MacBride, like de Valera before him, was forced to claim that his policies coincided with Papal encyclicals and that there were 'no Communists' in his party.[16]

As in the days of Cumann na nGaedheal, state and party were considered inter-changeable entities. Cumann na nGaedheal's 1932 election slogan of 'Safety first' differed little from that adopted by Fianna Fáil after sixteen years in power: 'Play safe.'

Similarly, Fianna Fáil's relationship with the Labour Party revealed the length of the ideological journey it had travelled. While in opposition, Fianna Fáil had derided the Labour Party for being insufficiently left-wing and mocked it for being 'the most respectable party' in the state. 'So long as they cannot be accused of being even pale pink in politics,' Seán Lemass told the Dáil in 1930, 'they seem to think they have fulfilled their function to the Irish people.'[17] By the 1940s, however, Fianna Fáil had moved to the right, and, though the Labour Party remained inoffensive, the 1943 election demonstrated that Fianna Fáil's transformation had left a vacuum that any party professing itself to be the voice of the left might exploit. The Labour Party's mild-mannered leader, William Norton, was therefore described by Fianna Fáil as 'the Kerensky of the Labour party ... preparing the way for the redshirts.'[18] So fearful was the Labour Party hierarchy of the Red Scare inspired by Fianna Fáil that it obligingly split in two in 1944. The results of this carefully orchestrated split are well en-capsulated by Kieran Allen.

> Just as McCarthyism gave the funeral rites to the radical sentiment that began in us labour in the mid-1930s, so the Red Scare in Ireland buried for decades most traces of left-wing ideas that had been in existence during the revolutionary years from 1916 to 1923.[19]

As it turned out, Clann na Poblachta was to be the party that moved into the vacated left wing of Irish politics. Just as the Cumann na nGaedheal campaign to link

Fianna Fáil with gunmen and communists began several months before a general election was called, so too did Fianna Fáil's efforts to discredit Clann na Poblachta begin in earnest well before the 1948 election. No effort was spared in presenting all opposition to Fianna Fáil as benefiting the agents of communism and presenting Clann na Poblachta as unreconstructed militarists bent on the destruction of Catholic Ireland.

During its sixteen-year reign between 1932 and 1948 Fianna Fáil proved unbeatable. The Labour Party's electoral performance fluctuated between mediocre and abysmal, while a plethora of small parties shone brightly and briefly before breaking up in the inhospitable political atmosphere. Fine Gael became a shadow of its former self and it watched with bitter-sweet satisfaction as Fianna Fáil continued and intensified its campaign against the 'gunmen'. Like rejected soothsayers, Fine Gael could only bemoan the fact that 'we performed the miracles, but they were unseen.'[20]

FIANNA FÁIL AND THE IRA

Fianna Fáil's evolving relationship with the IRA and Sinn Féin provides perhaps the best example of the process of institutionalisation at work within 'the Republican Party'. Much of Fianna Fáil's official response to the IRA was dictated by de Valera himself, and any assessment of evolving relations between Fianna Fáil and the IRA would be incomplete without a consideration of the personal journey he travelled.

In a letter to his friend Mick McDonnell shortly before he died, Joe McGarrity acknowledged that throughout his long friendship with de Valera they had been in fact pursuing different goals.

> Dev! His very name makes me sick. What has he not done in reverse of everything he taught? We made him a little god here [in America], and I now believe, and have for some time, that after Easter Week he was through with any physical contest with England.[21]

Whether it was Michael Collins during the War of Independence, Liam Lynch during the Civil War, Austin Stack in the period following the Civil War or Seán MacBride or Seán Russell during the late 1920s and 30s, de Valera had always been a restraining influence on militant republicanism. While always eager to secure the support of militants, and at times presenting himself as an ardent radical, he was at heart a constitutionalist.[22] It is worth noting that a year after the 1916 Rising de Valera was assuring the voters of Co. Clare that 'those who went out in Easter Week had achieved their ends, and another Easter Week would be a superfluity.'[23]

Attempts to give consistency to de Valera's views on the issue of physical force[24] do not reveal sufficiently the studied ambiguity of statements made in the course of a varied political career. Moreover, they tend to adopt an approach promoted by de Valera himself: that he was being 'as constant as the Northern Star,' never deviating from previously declared principles. But, as T. Desmond Williams has written, one of de Valera's notable political skills was 'his capacity to conceal the precise nature' of subsequent policy.

Few politicians have paid more attention to the significance of detail in the use of words. All phrases were to be considered in the light of the use they might serve under altering circumstances. Hence the constant recurrence in those years [1920–39] of firm statements followed by intricate qualifications.[25]

The greatest advantage derived from such an ambiguous style of discourse was that it allowed de Valera to extract those elements of a speech that sustained whatever policy was in vogue and to present them as consistent with long-standing principles. On the issue of republicanism in particular, de Valera did not welcome a diversity of views in the party. Burnt by his solitary delegation of powers during the 1921 Treaty negotiations, he did not allow any other spokesperson on foreign affairs (read: Anglo-Irish relations). During the early 1920s, when he had set himself up as President of the Republic in opposition to the Free State, he dominated (though never quite monopolised) party and government discussions on the republican cause. While in power from 1932 and 1948 he combined his role of prime minister with that of foreign minister, and he personally conducted all important negotiations.

The divergence between rhetoric and reality, between the promises of opposition and the policies of power, disillusioned some, such as Joseph Connolly, a member of the first Fianna Fáil Government, who recalled:

> In my later talks with de Valera I formed the opinion that he no longer welcomed discussion much less criticism, and that what he wanted beside him was a group of 'yes men' who agreed with everything that the party, with himself as leader, approved. I think he achieved this![26]

The origins of Fianna Fáil, according to the party itself, were to be found in the 1916 Rising. Fianna Fáil leaders referred to the party as the guardian of the 1916 tradition, and few opportunities were lost to stress the revolutionary credentials of its leaders. All but two of the party's first seven-member executive had fought in the Rising, and every member of the executive had fought in the War of Independence and on the republican side in the Civil War. A national record of this calibre was of inestimable value to Fianna Fáil's morale and self-image, and it enabled the leadership to dampen criticisms of its anti-republican legislation and of its lack of progress in attaining the objectives for which it was established. For the founders of Fianna Fáil, the IRA and Sinn Féin went from being comrades in a common struggle to competitors for the republican mantle.

The legacy of 1916, though largely beneficial for Fianna Fáil, proved to be a mixed blessing. On the one hand it provided a new party with a ready-made glorious history of armed resistance to imperial rule. However, the incomplete nature of the nationalist project, with partition institutionalised in the 1921 and 1925 agreements, also made the example of 1916 a problematic one for a party increasingly committed to constitutional politics.

When Fianna Fáil came to power in 1932 all republican prisoners were released. Anti-republican security legislation was allowed to fall into disuse—but, crucially, was not abolished. As in 1922, a concerted effort was made to integrate those republicans who had not subscribed to the Free State regime. During the 1930s de Valera induced a considerable number of IRA men to join a plethora of security organisations—the Gardaí, the Special Branch and the Volunteers (army reserve) among them—while still more were assimilated through pensions or positions in state-sponsored organisations.

Rather than abandon formal republicanism altogether, as Fine Gael had done, the party sought to monopolise it. Fianna Fáil continued to attend Bodenstown annually and to commemorate the 1916 Rising (in ever-decreasing numbers) while simultaneously prohibiting by law others from exercising the same right. It is probable that these bans were partly motivated by embarrassment at the fact that, after an initial attempt to out-commemorate the militants, Fianna Fáil found it could muster only a small fraction of the twenty thousand republicans who turned out. Less successful still were attempts to replicate republican institutions and symbols by giving them a distinctively—and, it was hoped, exclusively—Fianna Fáil quality. The launch of the Torch, intended to supplant the Easter Lily, was an early example of this policy. The new symbol never caught on, not least because many Fianna Fáil members continued to purchase and wear the Easter Lily (the proceeds from which still went to the republican movement). Rather than submit to the verdict of the republican market, the leadership banned the selling of Easter Lilies; but nonetheless the Torch was soon withdrawn from distribution.

More republicans were interned during the emergency years of the Second Worl War than at any time since the Civil War, during which most of what became the Fianna Fáil leadership had been incarcerated. Following the policies of the previous British and Free State governments, political status was denied to republican prisoners. In 1940 two men imprisoned for three months for refusing to give their name and address to Gardaí were allowed to die on hunger strike, only days before they were due for release. Equally noteworthy is the fact that the Fianna Fáil Government meted out harsher treatment to IRA prisoners than its Unionist counterpart in Belfast. For Fianna Fáil there appears to have been the added element of vindictiveness, as the IRA posed an ideological challenge to the Fianna Fáil leadership, a menace not comparable to any threat to the Unionist Party.

The Fianna Fáil leadership hoped that by denying the continuity of militant republicanism they would upset the continuous narrative and so destroy the IRA. In killing the IRA, as Gerry Boland boasted they had done, the leadership were, in their view, ridding themselves of an ideological burden that had outlived its value the moment Fianna Fáil assumed power. The IRA predated Fianna Fáil, and, like a dutiful heir, the party had first indulged the eccentricities of its parent organisation, but it quickly tired of toleration, until its existence became a blight. The killing of republicanism, like most acts of euthanasia, was portrayed as a merciful act, motivated by an altruistic desire to minimise the pain. What was not publicised was the strong vested interest involved in the silent and speedy extermination of the intended victim. For, with the IRA banished to history, Fianna Fáil stood to gain considerably as the sole beneficiary of the valuable republican ideology left behind, which it could now treasure and parade around as its own.

In the poetic retelling of Seán Ó Faoláin, Fianna Fáil was 'haunted like Richard III by the ghosts they had deposed,' and they treated militant republicans 'as they themselves had been treated in their own ghostly days. They imprisoned the ghost, starved it, executed and apparently crushed it.'[27] In opposition during the 1920s, Fianna Fáil had been the outsiders looking in, but after sixteen years in power they had become the insiders looking out. The siege mentality that had afflicted Cumann na nGaedheal by the end of its reign was evident within the Fianna Fáil hierarchy. There was a perception that the state it controlled was under relentless attack and in constant danger.

This affliction manifested itself in many ways. A sensitivity to criticism, bordering on paranoia, was evident. The Fianna Fáil hierarchy produced a monolithic set of definitions that was considered irrefutable. Those who challenged the imposed orthodoxies were condemned to political exile or classified in the vague constellation of 'enemies of the state.'

THE 1950s

De Valera proved adept at milking the sacred cow of republicanism at election time, but in the late 1940s Clann na Poblachta successfully challenged Fianna Fáil on its own ideological ground. The result was that de Valera and his Government found themselves out of office for the first time in sixteen years. A brief but intense period followed during which all political parties competed with each other to present themselves as the most vociferous anti-partitionists. De Valera hoped to revive his party's fortunes by embarking on a world anti-partition tour. Clann na Poblachta and its coalition partners raised the stakes by refusing to join NATO in protest against partition, and, more dramatically, by declaring the Irish state a republic. With the tenuous link to Britain severed, the pull towards the last remaining constitutional grievance—partition—became irresistible. Among the tangible, if transient, results of this anti-partition drive was the all-party Mansion House Committee and the nomination of Northern MPs to the Seanad and to various government bodies.

During this brief period all parties vied to give Northern anti-partitionists a blank cheque, though there was no political institution at which they could be cashed. More accurately, they were given a collection of IOUs, which were quickly forgotten about after the 1951 election. As with all other issues for Fianna Fáil, partition became the subject of auction politics, and the party simply sought to outbid its opponents. Influenced by the desire to secure tactical party advantage, the anti-partition campaign otherwise had little momentum of its own. Once Fianna Fáil was back in power the issue was discreetly shelved, much to the chagrin of many Northern nationalist leaders, who had believed that their Southern allies were in earnest. Nationalist attempts to gain admission to the Dáil during the 1950s were met with derision and sometimes outright hostility. De Valera's much-publicised 'world tour' proved to be international only in the geographical sense and was primarily aimed at keeping de Valera centre stage and keeping Fianna Fáil's electoral prospects alive. Indeed, on the subject of partition many of de Valera's speeches and actions demonstrated the features of what A. C. Elms has called 'superego-tripping'. Elms defines this as acting on the assumption that whatever behaviour best satisfies the demands of one's superego will be most effective in attaining one's realistic goals. In other words, if you judge the effectiveness of your overt acts in terms of whether they make you feel good morally, rather than whether they have changed external reality in the ways you had planned, you're superego-tripping.[28]

The Constitution of Ireland, in this regard, was a superego-trip on de Valera's part. In his definitive response to Chamberlain's unity proposals he wrote that the Constitution represented 'the limit to which we believe our people are prepared to go to meet the sentiments of the Northern Unionists.'[29] It is not clear whether there were any compromises that de Valera would have been willing to make to facilitate re-unification. A policy of absorption was promoted, and yet he sometimes acknowledged that Ulster unionists were indigestible, and in his more desperate moments he flirted with the idea of 'ethnic swaps' between Ireland and Britain.

When Con Lehane, a veteran of the IRA and Clann na Poblachta, was asked during the 1950s to speak on a university society motion relating to the Government's policy on partition he said that 'you cannot support a vacuum. You cannot support something which does not exist.' This suggested that the Fianna Fáil Government had not got a policy on partition; but it is more accurate to say it was Government policy to do nothing. Such a policy of inertia was not the same as having no policy at all, though its appearance and effect were much the same. It entailed a refusal to entertain a number of policy options that might have weakened partition but might also upset Fianna Fáil's absolute discretion over how power was exercised.

The frustration among Northern nationalists was reflected in the large vote received by Sinn Féin in the 1955 British elections, in which two abstentionist MPs were elected to the House of Commons. Heartened by what was perceived as a heightened interest in the national question, the IRA embarked on a five-year armed campaign in an effort to destabilise and ultimately destroy the Northern regime. In view of the anti-partition campaign of 1948–51 and the ritual denunciations of partition, the IRA naïvely hoped that, as the object of its campaign was to bring to fruition the stated objective of all parties in the Oireachtas, the Government would not interfere in its endeavours. In this belief it was supported by a number of Fianna Fáil TDs. They arranged a meeting between the IRA and de Valera, who firmly ruled out any accommodation.

Essentially, the IRA was attempting to reach an understanding similar to that reached with Michael Collins in 1922, when the head of the Provisional Government—then a hate figure for many de Valera supporters—gave assistance to IRA attacks in the North. Thirty-five years later not only did Fianna Fáil offer no support, moral or otherwise, but internment was introduced, suspected republicans were rounded up and a new wave of security laws was introduced. This exceptional power had been used by Cumann na nGaedheal during the Civil War and by Fianna Fáil during the wartime emergency period to meet a perceived threat to the internal security of the 26-County state. On this occasion, however, internment was used in response to a threat that was exclusively aimed at the destruction of the Six-County state.

FUNCTIONAL CO-OPERATION

As the sun set on de Valera's political destiny there were some indications that a new debate was taking place. An article by Dónal Barrington in *Studies* openly questioned the efficacy of the 1948–51 anti-partition campaign, which he viewed as an incomprehensible breach of de Valera's policy of saying little on partition—a strategy that Barrington contended had resulted in 'the liberalisation of Northern politics.'[30] Barrington argued for a policy of *rapprochement* with the Northern Government and with the unionist people, while leaving the political issue of partition on the back burner. The article was ostensibly a review of Frank Gallagher's book *The Indivisible Island*, a trenchant restatement of the traditional nationalist position that drew attention to the discriminatory practices of the Unionist regime. The influence of Gallagher, one of the few from the original Northern coterie that still surrounded de Valera, was, like that of his Chief, coming to end. Barrington, on the other hand, represented a new generation of aspiring stars only now beginning to make their mark. In 1962, the year before Gallagher died, Barrington was adopted by Fianna Fáil as a candidate for the Seanad, and he was later appointed by the party to the Supreme Court. Elements of his analysis were embraced by Seán Lemass, who embarked on a dual strategy of dismantling traditional Fianna Fáil policies of self-sufficiency and ostracising Stormont and replacing them with an 'open' economy based on foreign investment and functional co-operation with the Unionist Government.

The economic rationale of Lemass's repudiation of Fianna Fáil's traditional protectionist policies propelled him into an alliance with the country's nearest trading partner. This was reflected in the free trade agreement with Britain in 1965, but more particularly it necessitated a reappraisal of the Republic's relationship with the Northern regime. Economic pragmatism broke down many ideological barriers, and, as Pádraig O'Malley has noted, Lemass's meeting in 1965 with Terence O'Neill 'amounted to a *de facto* recognition of partition.'[31] The question of recognition, however, remained one of studied ambiguity. Unlike his predecessor, Brookeborough, O'Neill did not request a formal statement, realising, perhaps from his own experience, the difficulty in formally debunking previously articulated ideological certainties. Instead he contented himself with the belief that Lemass, in travelling through the gates of Stormont to visit the Prime Minister of Northern Ireland, had expressed through actions what words could not.

The meetings with O'Neill also complemented the new policy of 'reconciliation before unity'. Traditional Fianna Fáil ideology had assumed that the Unionist Party and the unionist population as a whole would never consider national reunification until the British Government severed the economic and political relationship with Northern Ireland that allowed unionists to enjoy a privileged position relative to their nationalist counterparts. The new thinking was that, however long a process was required, unification would have to be preceded by reconciliation between nationalists and unionists. The problem was essentially an Irish one, to be solved in Ireland among Irish people; all that was required from Britain was its blessing and a statement that it had no vested interest in maintaining partition or in preventing unification.

Functional co-operation occasioned surprisingly little soul-searching within

Fianna Fáil. By 1959, when Lemass came to power, Fianna Fáil, and perhaps the Republic in general, was ready for a new relationship with the North. De Valera had already made the leap, but he, like Lemass, found Brookeborough unreceptive to the idea of economic co-operation before a formal recognition of Northern Ireland. The advent of O'Neill made such a *rapprochement* possible.

Functional co-operation proved popular in the South, though the Fianna Fáil and Unionist Party leaderships were 'cautious if not leisurely' in implementing the new policy.[32] It was to be a mutually beneficial relationship (with no strings attached, its architects hastened to add). Yet the one issue that was to dominate politics in the coming years and that was to fundamentally change the political landscape in Northern Ireland—civil rights—was never discussed. Relations between the Fianna Fáil Government and representatives of the Northern nationalist community deteriorated, as functional co-operation reversed the traditional channels of communication to Northern Ireland. Whereas in the past Irish Government contact with the Six Counties was almost exclusively with representatives of the nationalist tradition (who were dutifully listened to but largely left to themselves), the new policy meant bypassing nationalists and reaching out to the Unionist Party. Nationalist leaders, such as Eddie McAteer, found themselves relegated to the role of political pawns in the much larger scheme of Anglo-Irish relations and North-South *détente*. As part of their dependence on Dublin, the Nationalist Party dutifully adhered to Lemass's request to enter Stormont as the official opposition—an act that, like Fianna Fáil's entry into the Dáil four decades earlier, conferred an unprecedented legitimacy on the state institutions. Of necessity, the injustices suffered by the nationalist community were de-emphasised in an effort to normalise relations between Dublin and Belfast. This proved to be the fatal flaw in the process of functional co-operation.

Functional co-operation never really amounted to much in practice—a fact acknowledged by O'Neill, who claimed that the main benefits would be in the non-economic sphere. The occasional bilateral meetings achieved little; the barrier between North and South remained.

O'Neill never succeeded in allaying the suspicions of the Unionist right wing. The complete secrecy surrounding Lemass's visit, motivated by a fear of a leak by Government hard-liners, only accentuated fears that O'Neill could not be trusted and that he was engaged in some underhand deal with the South. It gave ammunition to those already discomfited by O'Neill's ostentatious if shallow liberalism, which was unprecedented in the parochial and sectarian world of Unionist Party politics. O'Neill's manoeuvrability was further curtailed by the advent of the civil rights movement, which his Unionist opponents insisted on labelling an IRA front—not a legitimate, non-violent demand for fundamental civil liberties.

By the time of the much-delayed Lynch-O'Neill meetings the process of functional co-operation was already in reverse gear. The photo opportunities that the two meetings generated reflected a desire to keep up appearances as the political landscape changed rapidly; it would soon change irrevocably. Throughout 1968 O'Neill found himself under relentless attack from civil rights activists as well as from the right wing of his own party. The demands of these two groups—equality versus supremacy—were irreconcilable, and ultimately O'Neill could satisfy the demands of neither. Lynch, firmly wedded to the inherited principle of functional co-operation, could only watch helplessly as O'Neill's power crumbled and then collapsed, destroying all hopes of a successful *détente* between Dublin and Belfast. O'Neill's successor, Chichester-Clark, was of his cousin's mould: genial, aristocratic and utterly out of his depth. His victory over the darling of the right, Brian Faulkner, was too narrow (22 to 21) to permit a reactivation—let alone an intensification—of functional co-operation.

THE PASSING OF THE REVOLUTIONARY ELITE AND THE INSTITUTIONALISATION OF THE PARTY

Seán Lemass's departure from the Fianna Fáil leadership formalised a trend that had been developing in the previous decade towards the steady demise of the revolutionary generation's political ascendancy. Their dominance following independence was only to be expected, and yet the duration of their reign was remarkable. S. M. Lipset and Stein Rokkan observed in 1967 that the party-political alternatives confronting European citizens appeared to be frozen in the 1920s.[33] The Irish experience did little to challenge this claim, but what was unusual was the fact that not only did the party alternatives remain static but so too did the individual personnel who collectively personified the identities of political parties in the Republic. This apparent anomaly has been explained by demonstrating how Irish politics possessed the features of a post-colonial state.[34] Unique among its European neighbours in having conducted a successful guerrilla campaign against a colonial power, Ireland can be usefully compared to the developing revolutionary states of Africa, Asia and Latin America.

When set against this background, the tendency of Irish revolutionary leaders to linger at the centre of political power is not as extraordinary as it may at first appear. However, the reluctance of some Fianna Fáil ministers of the revolutionary generation to retire from active politics was, by the 1960s, a source of political ammunition for critics, as demonstrated by Liam Cosgrave's contribution to the debate on Lynch's nominations for Government: 'The remark Deputy Lemass made recently about not wishing to become an historical relic certainly was hard on some of his colleagues. Some of them had to be nearly carried out.'[35] One can detect in this reluctance to retire a fear that Fianna Fáil would not survive the departure of its founding fathers. This is an anxiety not uncommon among revolutionary elites. Al Cohan has made a useful comparison between the Irish and Chinese revolutionary generations, and he comments that Mao 'was most concerned with maintaining the revolutionary fervour among those who were too young to have participated in the revolution.'[36] His conclusion that the Irish experience demonstrates the impossibility of instilling the same vigorous radicalism in the post-revolutionary generation is accurate, but it does not dilute the fear of revolutionary generations that their ethos will not survive their political demise.

One of the most salient consequences of this prolonged hold on power was the creation of a 'missing generation' in Irish politics. The excessively long tenure of the revolutionary cadre precluded the possibility of ambitious young politicians gaining access to office during the 'middle period' of 1940–57. When the revolutionary generation eventually relinquished exclusive control they entrusted power to a younger elite who had bypassed the middle generation. This reality is starkly illustrated by the fact that when Neil Blaney and Charles Haughey entered the Government in 1957 they were forty and forty-three years younger, respectively, than their party leader, de Valera.

Jack Lynch was the first leader of Fianna Fáil who had not participated in the republican struggle of 1916–23, and his Government contained only one IRA veteran, Frank Aiken. The historic nature of Lynch's assumption of power was not lost on those who participated in the Dáil debate on the new appointments. The Labour Party deputy Michael O'Leary claimed that

> this administration represents a break, probably the first real break in Irish politics over the past forty years. Now, at last, we have turned the corner and the revolutionary legacy and that period is behind us.[37]

Indeed O'Leary went so far as to advocate the amalgamation of Fianna Fáil and Fine Gael in a single political entity in an effort to inaugurate a new era of left-right politics and to consign the Civil War to history. Needless to say, it was not a proposal that gained much support in either of the parties. While it has been suggested that by the 1960s the post-revolutionary generation in Fianna Fáil had more in common with their contemporaries in Fine Gael and the Labour Party than they had with their party predecessors,[38] the Irish party system, based largely on the partisan divisions of the early 1920s, remained intact. Seemingly anachronistic party alternatives persisted, despite the substantial degree of uniformity that had developed between the three parties.

What differences, if any, were there between the revolutionary and post-revolutionary elites, and what effect had this on Irish politics? In the life of a political party the transfer of power from the founding fathers to a new generation of politicians is a significant juncture. John Wilson has written that

> it is almost certainly true that the vast majority of social movements which survive to the second generation suffer a loss of zeal among their membership and fail to reproduce the sense of world rejection shown by the original members. The people of the second generation are much more concerned with accommodation to their social world and with relating harmoniously to one another than they are with disruption and ideological purity.[39]

The importance of this generational shift within Fianna Fáil was illustrated by Kevin Boland, who told a Fianna Fáil gathering in early 1969 that

> the process of transferring from the generation that founded it which has already taken place at the top of Fianna Fáil is gradually developing at Cumann level. At this stage it is important to be sure that the younger members fully appreciate the type of organisation Fianna Fáil is and above all the fundamental reason for its existence.[40]

After de Valera's departure from active party politics in 1959 there was, according to Boland, 'something of an influx into Fianna Fáil of people whose nature and tradition it was to be on the winning side.'[41] An antipathy towards de Valera personally had prevented some from aligning themselves with Fianna Fáil; but, as in the aftermath of the Treaty, pragmatism led many to join the party of power. Boland was one of those rare second-generation activists in a movement who 'are zealous in their attempts to preserve the old enthusiasm, even among those born into it.'[42] Boland's zeal can partly be explained by the fact that he did not have to go through the arduous path to the top that was forced on his contemporaries. He never served in local government, he was made a minister on his first day in the Dáil and he held that position until his voluntary resignation thirteen years later.

John Wilson notes that 'an extremely potent way of sustaining a strong orientation towards radical goals is to present the movement as being constantly under threat from those who oppose it.'[43] This was a clear Fianna Fáil strategy, but by the 1960s only the issue of Irish as an obligatory school subject could be cited as evidence of a significant policy difference influenced by ideological considerations. The view persisted, however, that on the issue of the North only Fianna Fáil could be trusted to safeguard the national (or nationalist) interest; and it is significant that Kevin Boland postponed his resignation in August 1969 when de Valera pointed out that the result of his action would be to usher Fine Gael into government to face the crisis of the Six Counties.

One important difference between the revolutionary and post-revolutionary generations is the marked contrast in the participation of Northerners in the political institutions of the Republic. The national independence movement of 1916–23 contained a large number of activists from what became Northern Ireland. Their contribution was reflected in the composition of government in the new 26-County state. In the Cosgrave government of 1922–32 there were three ministers of Northern extraction: Eoin MacNeill, Ernest Blythe and Patrick McGilligan. This trend continued under de Valera, whose first government in 1932 also contained three ministers from the North out of a total of nine. Two of these—Seán MacEntee and Frank Aiken—were to be central figures in Fianna Fáil in subsequent decades.[44]

Partition and the normalisation of politics in the Republic meant that the post-revolutionary elite was entirely Southern in its composition. One can only speculate about the impact this shift had on political life in the Republic and more specifically on government deliberations relevant to the North. At one level, the effects can be exaggerated. Those from the North in the governments of the revolutionary generation did not differ greatly from their Southern colleagues in their views on objectives or tactics. Blythe, though a Protestant, and a realist in matters pertaining to Northern policy, was a devout cultural nationalist, as was the Antrim Catholic MacNeill, and both were instrumental in the formulation of the government's language policy during the 1920s. As this policy has been criticised for accentuating the divide between unionist and nationalist, and is often cited as an example of Southern indifference to unionist sensitivities, it cannot be argued that the presence of Northerners in the government altered official policy in this significant area. (It should be remembered also that MacNeill participated in the ill-fated Boundary Commission in 1925 and was responsible for the botched partition settlement.)

The same applies to Seán MacEntee and Frank Aiken, who were strong traditionalists and who were among the chief advocates of creating an economic autarky and a conservative state that reflected the ethos and doctrines of the Catholic Church. These policies have also been presented as partitionist in nature, and it cannot be demonstrated that those government members from the North displayed any greater insight into the effects of these policies than their Southern counterparts. In addition, neither Aiken nor MacEntee deviated from the Government consensus on Northern policy; nor did they pursue the issue with a vigour that distinguished them from their peers. In fact it can be argued that, rather than the Northerners making a substantial impact on the ideological certainties and policy options of their government colleagues, their experience in Dublin governments moulded their personal and political outlooks.

Northern ministers represented constituencies in the 26 Counties, and the concerns of their constituents therefore were different from those of the nationalists who found themselves on the other side of the border. It can be argued that five decades at the centre of politics in the Republic had made MacEntee and Aiken 'Southern' in mentality.[45] While Al Cohan points out that no member of the post-revolutionary elite was born in the North, indicating 'growing localism and actual separation from the North,'[46] it cannot be demonstrated that the participation of those from the North in Dublin governments of the revolutionary generation impinged greatly on the formulation or implementation of policies relevant to North-South relations.

We must look for other possible differences between the generations. The experience of conducting a guerrilla campaign against a colonial power is one obvious demarcation influencing the emergence of new concerns and political values. Common experience in a revolution engendered a camaraderie among participants in post-independence governments that diminished the possibilities for friction and so made factionalism unlikely.[47] The post-revolutionary elite did not inherit this *esprit de corps*, having undergone an entirely different socialisation process. Cohan notes that

> the shift from revolutionary to post-revolutionary environment is thought to be the major factor in explaining differences between earlier and later elite groups. Those who participated in the revolutionary era were cultural as well as political nationalists and set goals that were based upon their perceptions of what an Irish Ireland should be. The members of the political elite today [1972] have not been through the revolutionary experience—most were not born at the time. In brief, although no doubt subject to graphic descriptions of the period as children, these younger members have not shared the same intense experience as actual participants.[48]

The emergence of the Men in the Mohair Suits was a logical development, arising from the ascendancy of a new generation accustomed to relative affluence and political stability and less content with aspirations of frugal comfort and constitutional change. While the revolutionary elite were unswervingly loyal to their erstwhile military commanders, who became their political leaders, the 1960s marked the advent of what Maurice Duverger describes as 'teams of leaders', which are a result of a 'spontaneous fellowship arising out of shared origins or training' and are 'are not united by any personal attachment to a dominant chief.' Such groups, according to Duverger, are not hierarchical in nature, and bonds develop horizontally rather than vertically, possibly because ambition and pride prevent deference to a recognised leader. They generally belong to a 'new generation, who unite in order "to shake the fruit tree," to win the positions of control from those in possession, and to monopolise them for their own advantage.'[49]

The evolution of such a phenomenon is also linked to increasing localism in Irish politics, which contrasted with the experience of the revolutionary elite, for whom a lack of local orientation was a strong feature of their period of political dominance. Almost a third of those deputies represented constituencies other than their home districts,[50] and, initially at least, the more prominent among them represented more than one constituency. Some were elected to both the Dublin and the Belfast legislature. De Valera exemplifies this trend. He was born in New York, grew up in rural Co. Limerick and lived in Dublin. He was elected for Co. Clare, not because of any local connections but because it presented the first suitable by-election that could be contested. He was also elected for East Mayo in 1919 before deciding to allow a colleague to take the seat. In addition he was MP for South Down, and he had contested West Belfast, only to be defeated by the sitting nationalist representative.

This feature of revolutionary politics freed representatives from dependence on a local bailiwick and permitted them to view issues from a national rather than a parochial viewpoint. Conversely, the localism that typified the post-revolutionary elite had the opposite effect, restricting the manoeuvrability of deputies and encouraging a provincial outlook. Whereas national prominence in the revolutionary era usually preceded local supremacy, for the new generation local dominance was the only means of achieving distinction at the national level. The contrasting routes to political eminence created different political creatures. Leaders of the revolutionary elite were politicians by accident, thrust into a political life few had envisaged when taking up arms against the established regime in 1916. Their successors were politicians by design, and they had to undergo a more gradual and less dramatic progression to high office. This development contributed to the intensification of the deradicalisation of the political elite and the institutionalisation of political ideologies and party organisation.

The inevitable normalisation of politics that follows a revolution (and the consequent localism that developed in the Republic) is illustrated by comparing the proportion of members of the revolutionary elite who had served on a local government council with that of the post-revolutionary elite. 29 per cent of politicians of the revolutionary elite had been a member of a local council, the majority beginning their tenure shortly before their election as MPs or TDs. By the 1960s the figure had risen to 51 per cent, as membership of a local council rapidly became a *sine qua non* for entry to politics at the national level.[51] In addition, the majority of the aspiring politicians of the post-revolutionary generation had to serve longer at the local level before achieving Dáil success. This gradual progression to high office in a political system whose legitimacy was uncontested inculcated a more gradualist and constitutional approach to political problems. While the revolutionary elite was typified by its 'lack of connection with any formal governing apparatus that came before,'[52] its successors grew up in a stable political environment that enjoyed the support of the majority of the population. This in turn made the concept of radical constitutional or political change more alien and unorthodox than it had appeared to many 'slightly constitutional' politicians of the earlier generation.

Participation in an insurgent movement was another factor that separated the elites of two generations. With the passing of the revolutionary elite, new issues emerged, and different criteria were required for determining the qualities necessary for political advancement. For the early Fianna Fáil governments, as with similar social movements, 'arrest and time in jail were often more important as job qualifications . . . than technical knowledge or expertise.'[53] This attitude coloured the distribution of all positions of authority, from ministerial appointments to the allotment of posts in the public service. The demise of the old guard meant that aspiring politicians had to find a new means to elicit support and justify their position in the national parliament. Writing during Jack Lynch's first period as Taoiseach, Marten Bax noted that during the early years of the state the importance of the Civil War was such that it was

possible for politicians to be elected on the basis of their attitudes towards the issue. Now that the issue is dying out and new ones are lacking, it is difficult for them to attract a following on a 'moral' basis. Under the present circumstances in Ireland the electoral system not only provides new opportunities for politicians, it also forces them to play another role to attract voters, namely the role of broker.[54]

In this way the Irish political system changed from one in which politicians secured votes through patriotic exhortations to one in which a political reputation was established by 'going about persecuting civil servants' on behalf of constituents.[55] As the realisation of the party's national aims became more aspirational, the emphasis shifted to objectives that could be achieved within the 26-County state, such as combating the problems of unemployment, poverty and emigration.

Lynch represented a new generation, the first leader drawn from the post-revolutionary cadre. There is little doubt that he was initially 'thought of as a stop-gap.'[56] Lynch also inherited a Government of prima donnas, and he was unable during the vital years of 1966–70 to impose his authority. A reshuffle was a theoretical option, being the 'well-worn standby of the beleaguered Prime Minister,'[57] but Lynch was constrained by powerful ministers who had no intention of being demoted by someone they viewed as a caretaker Taoiseach.[58] Instead, he delegated executive authority (most notably Northern policy) to others—a practice that always carries the risk that the agent may not faithfully execute the intentions of the principal. In 1969 Lynch lacked policy power on Northern Ireland (that is, the ability to get policies adopted and see them defended and implemented as desired). A vital part of the leadership equation is sufficient knowledge of those who are to be led—their strengths, weaknesses, institutional codes and customs; but Lynch never understood the emotional patriotism of Blaney, deeply rooted in the Civil War politics of his upbringing; nor did he comprehend the rigid, dogmatic adherence to principle that made Boland such a cantankerous colleague. Equally, the ambition for power of Haughey and Colley was alien to him, and he shared little of the flamboyant charisma that personified the Men in the Mohair Suits.

Lynch would eventually prove immensely popular with the electorate, but by the time his first official endorsement as Taoiseach came, in 1969, the damage to his confidence had already been done, and he continued, right up to May 1970, to exert little political mastery within the Government. The Arms Crisis enabled him to purge his most dangerous rivals, and his authority remained relatively undisputed until his resignation in November 1979.

The outbreak of renewed conflict in the North reignited long-submerged emotions. Whereas some viewed the crisis as opening up possibilities for radical change, Fianna Fáil could only see danger, and it sought to continue its policy of inertia. The Minister for External Affairs at this critical juncture, Dr Patrick Hillery, recalled:

> The ones I felt for were men in Clare who came to me [and said], 'What's happening?' Again, they thought this was the time to deal with this aspect [Irish unity], I suppose it was the main aspect . . . I suppose that's why they came into the democratic process, the potential and promise of the Republican Party. And I had to talk to a lot of them and tell them, 'I don't think this is the time for that.'[59]

As Sydney Smith observed in 1824:

> Procrastinator's Argument—'Wait a Little; This is Not the Time.'—This is the common argument of men who, being in reality hostile to a measure, are ashamed or afraid of appearing to be so.[60]

The struggle between the British army and a reinvigorated brand of militant Irish nationalism raised awkward questions that many in Fianna Fáil wished to leave unanswered. The intercommunal conflict of the mid-1970s had yet to take root, and it seemed to many that the 'unfinished business' of 1916–21 had re-emerged in the form of a straight fight between the IRA and the British-controlled state. What attitude would the Irish Government, which claimed jurisdiction over the whole of the national territory, take? What role did it see itself playing? What sacrifices was it willing to contemplate to facilitate reunification? There seems little doubt that the conflagration in Northern Ireland 'challenged the party's long-established but largely symbolic republicanism,'[61] and that Lynch chose to adopt a policy 'which put the stability of the Irish Republic before re-unification aspirations.'[62] Though Brendan O'Leary claims that such a policy 'continued the tacit revisionism which Lemass had initiated,' this reversal of priorities can clearly be traced back to de Valera.

THE INSTITUTIONALISATION OF POLITICAL PARTIES

It would be wrong, of course, to think that Fianna Fáil was the first or the only radical party to have embarked on a path that was to take it far from its ideological roots. Indeed, as a mass party bent on national electoral victories in a democratic polity, if its militant republicanism remained undiluted it would have deviated from similar types of parties that have emerged in Europe since the extension of the franchise in the early twentieth century. That is not to say that it was inevitable that Fianna Fáil would execute IRA members or allow republican hunger-strikers to die over principles that de Valera and his Fianna Fáil had struggled for in earlier times. However, as a party wedded to winning state power Fianna Fáil would have been a significant source of academic curiosity had it not abandoned revolutionism for reformism. Electorally successful radical parties, so the formula goes, generally become institutionalised and swap rigid principles for tangible power. Otherwise they die or remain on the margins.

The German political philosopher Robert Michels is the doyen of theorists adopting an institutionalisation model for the study of political parties. Michels was a conviction politician (*gesinnungsethiker*) who became progressively disenchanted with what he identified as the deradicalisation and institutionalisation of the German Social Democratic Party, in which he had originally vested much hope. He was interested in, among other things, determining the effect of intra-party structures on ideology, on role perceptions and on the motivation of party members and leaders at different levels of the hierarchy.

For Michels the fundamental question is whether the structural properties of political parties are conducive to the realisation of the final goal (*endzeil*). Power, according to Michels, is always conservative. As the organisation grows, the struggle for 'great principles' becomes impossible. Intellectual and ideological decline is reflected in the subject matter of internal party debate. Clashes occur, of course, but these are more likely to be grounded in differences of personality than of ideology. Considerations of a superficial nature, such as personal ambitions, increase, while conflicts over abstract ideals are ever diminished. Meanwhile the battle between the parties is no longer one based on principle but on competition. The once-revolutionary party no longer seeks to fight its opponents: it seeks simply to outbid them. The electorate and party supporters must content themselves with being merely the pedestal of an oligarchy. Michels's description of the SPD's evolution could quite easily be applied to Fianna Fáil.

> During the first years of its existence, the party did not fail to make a parade of its revolutionary character, not only in respect of its ultimate ends, but also in respect of the means employed for their attainment—although not always in love with these means. But as soon as it [reached] political maturity, the party did not hesitate to modify its original profession of faith to affirm itself revolutionary only 'in the best sense of the word,' that is to say, no longer on lines which interest the police, but only in theory and on paper.[63]

The capacity of the state, and what Gaetano Mosca calls the 'political class', to defend itself and to absorb new elements rarely fails 'to exercise an influence even upon the most embittered and uncompromising of its adversaries.'[64] The socialists might conquer, but never socialism; and Michels was tempted to see the whole process as a tragi-comedy in which the masses devote all their energies to effecting merely a change of masters.

With power and influence the radical movement acquires a stake in the political order in which that success has been achieved, and this vested interest is no less significant for the fact that it may go unacknowledged. Michels stressed this point in his study of socialist parties, but his analysis is equally valid for the republicans who ended up in Fianna Fáil. The revolutionary party, according to Michels, is 'a state within the state'—a description that neatly fits Sinn Féin during the 1920s—which organises with the avowed objective of replacing the existing order. The growth of the party organisation, however, weakens the movement's commitment to the revolutionary aim, as radical anti-state militancy only endangers the position attained through constitutional agitation within the framework permitted by the state (for example mass membership, party bureaucracy, financial interests). So it is, Michels concludes, that 'from a means, organisation becomes an end . . . The party grows increasingly inert as the strength of its organisation grows, it loses its revolutionary impetus, becomes sluggish, not in respect of action alone but also in the sphere of thought.'[65]

Frank Parkin has identified a similar feature in the early stages of the development of left-wing parties. As the party grows in size and influence, a gradual process of *embourgeoisement* occurs among the membership, accompanied by a shift to bureaucratisation.[66] Such a trend makes the party more attractive to moderate leaders of middle-class origins. The party provides avenues of vertical mobility for ambitious individuals and 'methods of acquiring power, wealth and prestige . . . to persons of energy and talent.'[67] The influx of these individuals slowly changes the character of the party, as leadership potential is decided more on meritocratic criteria and less on egalitarian principles. This new type of member uses the organisation as a mechanism for furthering their career and interests, while in return supplying the party with a particular area of expertise. The party becomes acceptable to the dominant class in society as it adopts an accommodating stance to vested interests in the state. The meritocratic ladder is embedded within the party framework, excluding all but a tiny minority of aspirants incapable of mouthing the required platitudes and participating in sentimental genuflections to the party's radical origins. In this way the party's radicalism suffocates as its members and leaders allow ideological vigour to be sacrificed for party organisation. Such ideological asphyxiation is inevitable when the party is committed to capturing the largest vote possible, demanding flexibility if the conflicting desires of sectional interest groups are to be satisfied.

In the 1940s Philip Selznick had already identified a process he termed 'goal displacement', whereby the original aims of a movement are replaced by organisational goals that have little in common with the avowed objectives, and indeed may be obstacles to their attainment.

Running an organisation, as a specialised and essential activity, generates problems which have no necessary (and often opposed) relationship to the professed or 'original' goals of the organisation. The day-to-day behaviour of the group becomes centred around specific problems and approximate goals which have primarily an internal relevance. Then, since these activities come to consume an increasing proportion of the time and thoughts of the participants, they are—from the point of view of actual behaviour—substituted for the professed goals.[68]

The most common form of goal displacement is the process whereby the organisation reverses its priorities—where the means becomes the goal and the goal becomes a means. As the organisation secures increased income, personnel, resources and status, many of its members become more concerned with preserving and building up the organisation than with assisting the attainment of its initial purpose. The goals of Fianna Fáil—foremost among them the reunification of the national territory as a republic—became the means to bind its members together, to gain votes and to legitimise its role in Irish society. It was impossible to stimulate the interest of members or to rationalise a desire for power unless it was articulated as a great 'cause' or mission. The value of the goal of a united Ireland was to conceal what became merely a basic desire to rule.

Writing in the 1960s of the mass people's parties (*volksparteien*), of which Fianna Fáil was a prime example, Otto Kircheimer argued that 'there is need for enough brand differentiation to make the article plainly recognisable, but the degree of differentiation must never be so great as to make the potential customer fear he will be out on a limb.'[69] Principles were revered but ultimately elastic, and Fianna Fáil's main threat when in government was competition from a more attractively packaged brand of a nearly identical product. Writing of Fianna Fáil in the 1980s, Michael Gallagher commented that

it has aims and aspirations rather than policies and thus can be entirely flexible in its attitude to specific questions as they arise. It has a powerful and positive image, of 'standing for' a thirty-two-county Irish Republic, which cements its members' loyalty to it. Whereas a party which claims to 'stand for,' say, the attainment of state control of the economy, must once in office either increase the state's control and alienate some floating voters or not increase it and annoy its own members, Fianna Fáil Governments are not committed to any specific policies as a result of the party's declared goal of a united Ireland, except the 'policy' of repeatedly declaring that goal. Mere verbal dedication to the goal is enough to keep the members satisfied, while floating voters, recognising that placating the faithful is its main purpose, ignore it and are not repelled.[70]

During the period 1926–73 Fianna Fáil was transformed from a movement with links to an anti-state army into one conforming to Maurice Duverger's definition of political parties as 'electoral machines . . . not ideological groups nor class communities . . . Teams of men expert in the winning of votes.'[71] The old *esprit de corps* was replaced with a formal and artificial camaraderie based on occupation and interests.

The post-Civil War Sinn Féin had conformed to what Gareth Morgan has termed an 'egocentric organisation'. Such groups have a rather fixed notion of who they are, or what they can be, and are deter-mined to impose or sustain that identity at all costs. This kind of egocentricism leads organisations to become preoccupied with and to overemphasise the importance of themselves, while underplaying the significance of the wider system of relations in which they exist.[72]

The differences within Sinn Féin over matters of principle and policy revealed a distinction between the issue-oriented and party-oriented members. Denis Sullivan detected similar divisions within American political parties, that is, between those who take pride in dogmatic purity and participate in politics to achieve a particular ideological objective and those who are professional party organisers and whose lives centre on the party rather than on any particular ideological goal.[73] In essence, the purists worry about issues, the professionals about organisation, and each views the other with suspicion. Professionals have learnt from bitter experience the value of mutual adjustment and party unity, and they view purists as political amateurs. Moreover, they see purists as lacking the skill necessary to accommodate differences, making them poor negotiators and inept strategists, innocent of the political bargaining required to achieve change incrementally.[74] Therefore, while the purist may at times be of use to the professional—in raising morale at meetings, at party conferences, during elections or in the media—they are considered at best simple-minded and at worst destructive and a threat to party cohesion. Purists, on the other hand, see professionals as ideologically unsound and as unable to resist the temptation to test success on the basis of organisational achievements and power rather than on the fulfilment of the movement's ideological mission.

The clash between purists and professionals within Sinn Féin eventually rested on the party's policy of refusing to recognise or participate in the Free State legislature and on its maintenance of an alternative republican government. As the Free State became firmly established as an internationally recognised institutional entity, the party split on this fundamental issue. The result was that, whereas the old Sinn Féin was an uneasy cocktail of differing outlooks and temperaments, Fianna Fáil was an election-focused professional party from the beginning. However, divisions between purists and professionals continued within the newly established Fianna Fáil in a diluted and much more containable fashion. The debate within Sinn Féin—and later between that party and Fianna Fáil—is one common to radical social movements, and it has occurred within most socialist parties on their road to becoming a constitutional 'peoples' party'.[75]

INSTITUTIONALISATION FORETOLD?

Classical theorists of social movements agree that the longer an organisation lasts the more structured and formalised it becomes. While not excluding the possibility that a movement may achieve its objectives quickly, John Wilson has argued that the longer the movement exists the more oriented it becomes towards the less lofty aim of self-maintenance. 'Social movements typically experience a transformation of mission in which the orientation of the majority of members switches from the extraneous goals for which the movement was set up to the solitary and immediate benefits accruing from participation in the movement itself.'[76] The movement begins when like-minded people unite to agitate for social and political change and are usually convinced that their goals can be achieved swiftly. This optimism, and the promise of rapid advances, causes the movement to swell. However, when these objectives are not attained within a comparatively short time, formalisation and routinisation set in. Consequently, it is fair to say that the formalisation process in Fianna Fáil was at the same time a symptom of failure and of success. The party failed to achieve its ideological objectives, but this was compensated for by the movement's political and electoral achievements.

After the 1918 landslide and the establishment of Dáil Éireann, Sinn Féin and republicans had every reason to hope for a speedy resolution to the struggle for independence. However, the Treaty and the Civil War shattered these expectations, and while the more doctrinaire continued to hold out for a united republic others did not enjoy life on the political periphery and the consequent repression that membership entailed. A desire for order, predictability, security and success grew among many in the Sinn Féin movement, and the division over tactics for achieving agreed political objectives was embodied in the widening chasm between de Valera and his opponents in Sinn Féin.

Two speeches were made during the Treaty debates that alluded to the effect that power might have on the ideological purity of the republican movement. The first was made by Liam Mellows, who asked:

Who will tell the British Government when the time has come to tell it, keep its hands off. Human nature, even the strongest human nature, is weak and the time will inevitably come, if this Free State comes into existence, when you will have a permanent government in the country; and permanent governments in any country have a dislike to being turned out and they will seek to fight their own corner before anything else. Men will get into positions, men will hold power and men who get into positions and hold power will desire to remain undisturbed and will not want to be removed—or will not take a step that will mean removal in case of failure.[77]

An almost identical view was expressed by his fellow-Republican deputy Seán Etchingham, who declared during the same debate:

Do not have the idea that in one year, or two years, or five years or ten years you are going to have your country free, for if the iron of the truce has entered your souls, after six months of it, and you are not prepared to fight, you will not do so after one year, two years or ten years, when you have Colonial or Free State fat in your bodies.[78]

Viewed from the standpoint of subsequent decades, these comments, directed at the pro-Treaty section of Sinn Féin, are equally relevant to Fianna Fáil. It is significant, perhaps, that both Mellows and Etchingham died during the Civil War, allowing for simple reverence of the men in Fianna Fáil folklore while their political warnings were quietly ignored. One of de Valera's first actions after the Civil War was to visit Etchingham's grave and pay homage to the dead leader; a portrait of Liam Mellows still hangs in the Fianna Fáil head office. Kevin Boland recalled that Fianna Fáil 'had its own special group of martyrs to guide it safely in all dangers, temptations and afflictions,' but the Civil War republican dead 'went to their graves without ever hearing of Fianna Fáil.'[79]

Dead martyrs are safe martyrs: they are inarticulate sources of inspiration, their words and actions frozen in history. The complexity of their characters and vision can be overlooked and their words selectively presented for approval, or even misrepresented. Fianna Fáil emphasised those remarks that were considered compatible with contemporary political realities while neglecting the most embarrassing or politically inconvenient statements. Differences of personality and policies between de Valera and the Treaty's most ardent opponents were ignored, while the mere mention of the 'Seventy-Seven' was guaranteed to secure a rapturous applause for the conclusion of a Fianna Fáil ard-fheis. The heroes were remembered, their message quietly forgotten.

NOTES

Chapter 1: Legion of the Rearguard: The revolutionary origins of Fianna Fáil, 1920–23 (p. 1–24)

1. Lee, *Ireland, 1912–1985*, p. 45.
2. Lee, *Ireland, 1912–1985*, p. 45. Michael McDonald makes a similar point in *Children of Wrath*, p. 55.
3. *Official Report, House of Commons* (Hansard), 127/1322 (31 March 1920), quoted by Frank Gallagher, *The Indivisible Island*, p. 138. In an effort to subdue any feelings of guilt that the imposition of partition might arouse, it was made clear by all contributors to the debate that the objective of the act was to facilitate the reunification of Ireland. A future signatory of the Anglo-Irish Treaty, Sir Laming Worthington-Evans, claimed that 'whenever they like, without any reference back to us, they can form one Parliament' (Hansard, 127/1031, 29 March 1920), while the Chancellor of the Exchequer, Austen Chamberlain, stated that the bill was the only one that could 'secure what we all desire: a United Ireland within the Empire who shall flourish in prosperity and peace as mistress of her own destiny' (Hansard, 127/944, 29 March 1920). The Chief Secretary for Ireland, Ian MacPherson, agreed with these sentiments and said: 'All of us hope that the division may be temporary only and our objective has, therefore, been to frame the Bill in such a manner as may lead to a union between the two parts of Ireland' (Hansard, 127/928, 29 March 1920). Indeed the Government of Ireland Act itself—the act that partitioned Ireland—states paradoxically, and implausibly, that it does so 'with a view to the eventual establishment of a Parliament for the whole of Ireland' (Government of Ireland Act (1920), section 2 (1); see also Summary of Main Provisions, p. 2).
4. See Fraser, *Partition in Ireland, India and Palestine*.
5. Eoin MacNeill (1867–1945); born in Co. Antrim and educated at Queen's University, Belfast; joint founder (with Douglas Hyde) of the Gaelic League 1893; appointed professor of early Irish history at University College, Dublin, 1908. A founder-member of the Irish Volunteers in 1913 and later its chief of staff, he controversially called off the planned rising in April 1916 but by 1917 had been rehabilitated in some republican circles, largely through the efforts of Éamon de Valera. Elected Sinn Féin MP for the National University of Ireland and also for Derry in the 1918 general election, he was briefly Minister for Finance in 1919 before becoming Minister for Industries 1919–21. He held the pivotal position of Ceann Comhairle during the debate on the Treaty, which he supported. Minister for Education 1922–5; the Boundary Commission fiasco forced his resignation in 1925 and he lost his Dáil seat in 1927.
6. British military casualties were 116 dead, 368 wounded and 9 missing. In addition, 16 policemen were killed and 29 wounded. 64 members of the republican forces died. Civilian deaths reached 254 by the end of the conflict.
7. A sixteenth leader, Roger Casement, was hanged for treason in Pentonville Prison, London, on 3 August.

8. The Irish Party is a generic name applied to the home-rule members of the British House of Commons (also called the Irish Parliamentary Party, Home Rule Party and Nationalist Party) and their various support and electoral organisations in Ireland (including the Home Rule League, Irish National League and United Irish League) from 1870 to 1918, when the party was displaced electorally by Sinn Féin.

9. Chief among the institutions promoting this cultural revival were the Gaelic Athletic Association and the Gaelic League (Conradh na Gaeilge). Many revolutionaries combined military activity with membership of such organisations, but they enjoyed a popularity far beyond republican circles. Between 1893 and 1916 there was also a flowering of Irish literature in English. See Mandle, *The Gaelic Athletic Association and Irish Nationalist Politics*, Mac Aonghusa, *Ar son na Gaeilge*, and Ó Tuama, *The Gaelic League Idea*.

10. Founded in 1791, the Society of United Irishmen would become a secret oath-bound movement dedicated to breaking the connection with England by uniting people of all religious denominations. A rebellion in 1798 was defeated with the loss of thirty thousand lives, including that of Theobald Wolfe Tone. See Elliott, *Wolfe Tone*, and Davis, *The Young Ireland Movement*.

11. During the early 1840s Young Ireland was connected with Daniel O'Connell's campaign for repeal of the Act of Union, but political failure and famine drove some of its leaders to rebellion in 1848. See Davis, *The Young Ireland Movement*.

12. One of the best accounts of the origins and development of the IRB is León Ó Broin, *Revolutionary Underground: The Story of the Irish Republican Brotherhood 1858–1924* (Dublin: Gill & Macmillan, 1976).

13. See F.S.L. Lyons, *The Irish Parliamentary Party, 1890–1910* (London: Faber and Faber, 1951).

14. George Noble Plunkett (1851–1948). Made a papal count by Pope Leo XIII 1877; director of the National Museum 1907–16. Father of Joseph Plunkett (1887–1916). Elected Sinn Féin MP for North Roscommon 1917 and again in 1918 general election. Member of first Dáil Éireann and Minister for Foreign Affairs 1919–21. Took the anti-Treaty side; elected Sinn Féin TD in the 1921, 1922 and 1923 elections before being defeated in June 1927.

15. Éamon de Valera (1882–1975). Born in New York of Irish mother and Spanish or Cuban father. Moved to Ireland in 1885. Commandant in Irish Volunteers, in command of Boland's Mill, Dublin, in 1916 Rising. President of Sinn Féin 1917–26. Won East Clare by-election in 1917 and re-elected in 1918 general election. Elected President of Irish Republic by Dáil Éireann 1919; elected TD for Clare at all elections between 1921 and 1957. Northern Ireland MP for Down 1921–9 and South Down 1933–7. Leader of Fianna Fáil 1926–59, President of Executive Council (head of government) of Irish Free State 1932–7; Taoiseach 1937–48, 1951–4, 1957–9; Minister for External Affairs 1932–48; President of Ireland 1959–73.

16. Quoted by Finnan, *John Redmond and Irish Unity*, p. 214–15.

17. See Kotsonouris, *Retreat from Revolution*.

18. See Ryan, *Seán Treacy and the Third Tipperary Brigade, IRA*, p. 50–51; also Kevin Haddick Flynn, 'Soloheadbeg: What really happened?,' *History Ireland*, 5/1 (spring 1997, p. 42–6.

19. Arthur Griffith (1871–1922). Published *The Resurrection of Hungary* (1904) and the following year founded Sinn Féin, with the objective of establishing a dual monarchy

for Britain and Ireland on the Austria-Hungarian model. Elected MP for Cavan East in 1918 by-election and held the seat in the general election a few months later as well as taking seat for Tyrone North-West. Minister for Home Affairs 1919–21; president of Sinn Féin 1908–17, vice-president 1917–22.

20. Davis, *Arthur Griffith and Non-Violent Sinn Féin*, p. 28.

21. Michael Collins (1890–1922). A member of the IRB from 1909. Fought under Pearse in the GPO during the 1916 Rising. Interned in Frongoch, 1916–17. Member of the Sinn Féin Executive and director of organisation of the Irish Volunteers 1917. Elected Sinn Féin MP (TD) for Cork 1918, 1921 and 1922 and for Armagh 1921. Minister for Home Affairs, January–April 1919, Minister for Defence 1919–22, chairman of the Provisional Government, January–August 1922. On hearing of the execution of twelve British spies on Collins's orders, Griffith exclaimed: 'How can we justify this? The killing of men on a Sunday morning in their homes in the presence of their wives.' Davis, *Arthur Griffith and Non-Violent Sinn Féin*, p. 30.

22. Richard Mulcahy (1886–1971). Member of Irish Volunteers and Gaelic League before participating in 1916 Rising. Elected Sinn Féin MP 1918 and member of first Dáil. IRA chief of staff, 1919–22. Minister for National Defence, January–April 1919, Minister for Defence 1922–4, Minister for Local Government and Public Health 1927–32; Leader of Fine Gael 1944–59. Minister for Education 1948–51, 1954–7, Minister for the Gaeltacht 1956.

23. Mitchell, *Revolutionary Government in Ireland*, p. 266.

24. *New York Times*, 10 November 1920, p. 1.

25. The land annuities stemmed from loans provided by the British exchequer in the late nineteenth and early twentieth centuries to Irish tenants to enable them to buy back land seized from them during the colonisation process. When the Irish Free State was established the British Government insisted that the loans should continue to be collected by the Irish state and paid to the British state.

26. Frank Gallagher, *The Anglo-Irish Treaty*, p. 174; Ryan, *Unique Dictator*, p. 146.

27. *Parliamentary Debates: Dáil Éireann: Official Report*, 3/129 (22 December 1921). Similar statements made earlier in the debate provoked a rhetorical question from Mary MacSwiney: 'If Mick Collins went to Hell in the morning would you follow him there?' *Parliamentary Debates: Dáil Éireann: Official Report*, 3/114 (21 December 1921).

28. Michael Collins. He continued: 'We had not beaten the enemy out of our country by force of arms . . . I say that rejection of the Treaty is a declaration of war until you have beaten the British Empire.' *Parliamentary Debates: Dáil Éireann: Official Report*, 3/32–3 (19 December 1921). Richard Mulcahy agreed: 'I personally see no alternative to the acceptance of the Treaty. I see no solid spot of ground upon which the Irish people can put its political feet but upon the Treaty. We are told that the alternative to the Treaty is war . . . We have not been able to drive the enemy from anything but a fairly good-sized barracks.' *Parliamentary Debates: Dáil Éireann: Official Report*, 3/142–3 (22 December 1921).

29. Barton disclosed that Lloyd George, 'with all the solemnity and the power of conviction that he alone, of all men I met, can impart by word and gesture . . . declared that the signature and recommendation of every member of our delegation was necessary, or war would follow immediately.' *Parliamentary Debates: Dáil Éireann: Official Report*, 3/49 (19 December 1921). Seán Moylan rejected the threat of war in the following terms: 'If there is a war of extermination waged on us, that war will also exterminate British interests in Ireland; because if they want a war of

extermination on us, I may not see it finished, but by God, no loyalist in North Cork will see it finish, and it is about time somebody told Lloyd George that.' *Parliamentary Debates: Dáil Éireann: Official Report*, 3/146 (22 December 1921).

30. *Parliamentary Debates: Dáil Éireann: Official Report*, 3/85–7 (21 December 1921).
31. *Parliamentary Debates: Dáil Éireann: Official Report*, 3/21 (19 December 1921).
32. *Parliamentary Debates: Dáil Éireann: Official Report*, 3/27 (19 December 1921).
33. *Parliamentary Debates: Dáil Éireann: Official Report*, 3/229 (4 January 1922).
34. Forester, *Michael Collins*, p. 267.
35. De Valera had not wanted the contents of the documents to become public and was angered (and embarrassed) when the compromises conceded became the subject of debate outside the Dáil. It was intolerable, he told the Dáil, that 'the workings of one's mind' was 'shown to those with whom we are dealing' (i.e. the British). *Dáil Éireann: Public Session*, 5 January 1922, p. 267.
36. When explaining why the text of the Treaty, according to the instructions given to the plenipotentiaries, was to be submitted to the Dublin government before signing, de Valera told the Dáil that 'in the case of a treaty, even verbal, the exact form of words is of tremendous importance.' *Parliamentary Debates: Dáil Éireann: Official Report*, 3/8 (14 December 1921). Lloyd George had described negotiating with de Valera as 'like trying to catch a man on a merry-go-round or picking up mercury with a fork,' but it remains a matter of conjecture whether he would have approached the mercurial de Valera with a spoon, as de Valera advocated. See McMahon, *Republicans and Imperialists*, p. 30.
37. *Parliamentary Debates: Dáil Éireann: Official Report*, 3/345 (7 January 1922).
38. *Parliamentary Debates: Dáil Éireann: Official Report*, 3/376 (9 January 1922).
39. *Parliamentary Debates: Dáil Éireann: Official Report*, 3/377–80 (9 January 1922).
40. Laffan, 'The unification of Sinn Féin,' p. 353–79.
41. Garvin, *Nationalist Revolutionaries in Ireland*, p. 154.
42. Brian P. Murphy, *Patrick Pearse and the Lost Republican Ideal*, p. 24.
43. This split manifested itself as early as 1907 when Bulmer Hobson, a Belfast Quaker, broke from Sinn Féin to establish a separate republican organisation, the Dungannon Clubs. See Hobson, *Ireland Yesterday and Tomorrow*, in particular p. 19–30. Michael Laffan notes that most of the Irish Volunteers 'resented being called "Sinn Féiners", partly because of Griffith's pacifist and monarchist views but also because his party was already regarded as a failure.' Laffan, 'The unification of Sinn Féin,' p. 356.
44. Quoted by Griffith and O'Grady, *Curious Journey*, p. 106.
45. Father D. Riordan, Abbeyfeale, 1 June 1917, quoted by Laffan, 'The unification of Sinn Féin,' p. 369, n. 56. The militant *Irish Nation* wrote that Sinn Féin's supporters 'are making headway in the country because they are supposed to stand for the principles of the men who died at Easter [1916], otherwise they would not win a solitary constituency. This is the real Sinn Féin, the Hungarian policy is merely a parody.'.
46. Morgan, *Labour and Partition*, p. 192.
47. Brian P. Murphy, *Patrick Pearse and the Lost Republican Ideal*, p. 96–7.
48. For a penetrating study of the evolution of the native intellectual see, for example, Franz Fanon, *The Wretched of the Earth* (London: Penguin, 1963).
49. *Sinn Féin*, 27 December 1913, p. 3.
50. Arthur Griffith, 'Pitt's policy,' in *The Resurrection of Hungary* (UCD Press reprint), p. 116. 'Pitt's policy' was a series of articles that originally appeared in *Sinn Féin* in 1911. 'Hodge' was a nickname for the typical English farm labourer.

51. Connolly had articulated the irritation of trade unionists who felt that Griffith had 'promised lots of Irish labour at low wages to any foreign capitalist who cares to establish in Ireland' (*Peasant*, 23 January 1909, p. 2). Griffith's outrage at the economic exploitation of Ireland was based on anti-British rather than pro-labour principles. In 1913 he was bitterly opposed to Larkin and extended little sympathy to the workers affected by the lock-out. Frederick Ryan encapsulated the objections and fears of those who rejected the evolving objectives of Griffith's Sinn Féin: 'We have Mr. Griffith telling the Irish landlords that their best chance of retaining their privileges against Irish democracy lies in Home Rule. In other words political freedom is not to be sought as a means of social liberation and the uplifting of a people but as a means of preserving the anti-social privileges of a class. A sort of clerical-Tory nationalism is to rise on the ruins of the old *United Irishman.*' Quoted by Davis, *Arthur Griffith and Non-Violent Sinn Féin,* p. 141.

52. See Griffith, *The Resurrection of Hungary,* chap. 11.

53. *United Irishman,* 4 March 1899, p. 2. Griffith did not believe that it was right that Africa should be 'civilised' in the name of British consumerism but agreed with the 'civilising' mission.

54. Indeed Friedrich List described the Act of Union (of Britain and Ireland) as 'a great and irrefutable example of the efficiency of free trade between united nations.' He was equally dismissive of Indian nationalism, predicting with equanimity that India was destined to remain underdeveloped and subjugated: 'all Asiatic countries of the torrid zone will pass gradually under the dominion of the manufacturing commercial nations of the temperate zone.' List, *The National System of Political Economy.* See vol. 2 (The Theory), chap. 11. 'Political and cosmopolitical economy.'

55. List, *The National System of Political Economy,* p. 175.

56. 'Grattan's Parliament' (1782–1800) was exclusively aristocratic in composition, the majority of members enjoying hereditary ownership of their seats. In addition, Catholics were not allowed to participate. The integrity of the majority of its members can be gauged from the fact that the parliament voted for its own abolition in return for bribes totalling a million pounds from the British Government.

57. Hobson, *Ireland Yesterday and Tomorrow,* p. 10, 19–20.

58. Michael O'Flanagan, *The Strength of Sinn Féin* (Dublin: Sinn Féin, 1934), p. 8.

59. Davis, *Arthur Griffith,* p. 23.

60. De Valera's request may have been motivated by a genuine desire to bolster the unity of the party, though there is little doubt that the shared public appearances were mutually beneficial. He was able to exploit MacNeill's extensive contacts with the Catholic clergy, while MacNeill was politically rehabilitated by his association with the only surviving 1916 commandant. Kevin J. Browne, *Éamon de Valera and the Banner County,* p. 44; David Fitzpatrick, 'De Valera in 1917: The undoing of the Easter Rising,' in O'Carroll and Murphy, *De Valera and His Times,* p. 101–12. For an examination of some aspects of the political atmosphere in Co. Clare during this period see Peadar McNamara, 'The Great War (1914–18) and some effects on Clare,' *The Other Clare,* March 1989, p. 53–7, and Kieran Sheedy, *The Clare Elections,* Dún Laoghaire: Bauroe Publications, 1993, p. 321–34.

61. Rumpf and Hepburn, *Nationalism and Socialism in Twentieth-Century Ireland,* p. 68.

62. Garvin, *Nationalist Revolutionaries in Ireland,* p. 141. Michael Hayes ('Michael Collins,' *Capuchin Annual,* 1969, p. 275) notes that 'the unity which had existed before

the Treaty had been moulded by aggression and pressure from British forces.'

63. Tom Garvin, 'Great hatred, little room: Social background and political sentiment among revolutionary activists in Ireland, 1890–1922,' in Boyce, *The Revolution in Ireland*, p. 106.

64. Garvin, *Nationalist Revolutionaries in Ireland*, p. 148–9.

65. See Griffith and O'Grady, *Curious Journey*, p. 168–9.

66. Rumpf and Hepburn, *Nationalism and Socialism in Twentieth-Century Ireland*, p. 34.

67. Garvin, *Nationalist Revolutionaries in Ireland*, p. 145.

68. Garvin, *Nationalist Revolutionaries in Ireland*, p. 148.

69. Rumpf and Hepburn, *Nationalism and Socialism in Twentieth-Century Ireland*, p. 35.

70. De Vere White, *Kevin O'Higgins*, p. 169.

71. Fanning, *Independent Ireland*, p. 13.

72. Letter from Annie MacSwiney (sister of Terence MacSwiney) to Richard Mulcahy, 4 December 1921 (UCD Archives, Mulcahy Papers, P7/D/1).

73. Quoted by Griffith and O'Grady, *Curious Journey*, p. 264.

74. Quoted by Garvin, 'Great hatred, little room: Social background and political sentiment among revolutionary activists in Ireland, 1890–1922,' in Boyce, *The Revolution in Ireland*, p. 106.

75. Quoted by Garvin, 'Great hatred, little room: Social background and political sentiment among revolutionary activists in Ireland, 1890–1922,' in Boyce, *The Revolution in Ireland*, p. 106. See also Garvin, *Nationalist Revolutionaries in Ireland*, p. 144.

76. Quoted by Fanning, *Independent Ireland*, p. 13.

77. For the text of the agreement see Neeson, *The Civil War*, p. 331–2.

78. Quoted by Lawlor, *Britain and Ireland*, p. 176.

79. Younger, *Ireland's Civil War*, p. 295.

80. Coogan, *Michael Collins*, p. 322.

81. Coogan, *Michael Collins*, p. 368.

82. Coogan, *Michael Collins*, p. 341.

83. Gilbert, *World in Torment*, p. 714–15.

84. Gilbert, *World in Torment*, p. 715.

85. Gilbert, *World in Torment*, p. 716; Younger, *Ireland's Civil War*, p. 294. Lloyd George concurred, stating that the British Government was drifting towards a position where they would have to 'abandon or reconquer.' He would not abandon, and so they 'might have to reconquer.' Quoted by Lawlor, *Britain and Ireland*, p. 178.

86. Gilbert, *World in Torment*, p. 716.

87. Neeson, *The Civil War*, p. 22; Younger, *Ireland's Civil War*, p. 293.

88. Gilbert, *World in Torment*, p. 716.

89. Gilbert, *World in Torment*, p. 716.

90. Younger, *Ireland's Civil War*, p. 301.

91. Collins had placed the British side in a delicate position by alluding to the conduct of three of the Privy Council judges: Mr Justice Summer, Sir George Cave and Sir Edward Carson. Lloyd George acknowledged to his Cabinet that these three judges had 'publicly taken up a very hostile attitude to the Irish Free State' and 'had placed His Majesty's Government in a very awkward and indefensible position.' Younger, *Ireland's Civil War*, p. 304.

92. Younger, *Ireland's Civil War*, p. 296.

93. Coogan, *Michael Collins*, p. 327.

94. Quoted by Neeson, *The Civil War*, p. 107–8.

95. Younger, *Ireland's Civil War*, p. 307.

96. Forester, *Michael Collins*, p. 311–12.

97. For a useful study of this election see Michael Gallagher, 'The Pact Election of 1922.'

98. Michael Hayes, 'Michael Collins,' *Capuchin Annual, 1972*, p. 276.

99. Neeson, *The Civil War*, p. 21. Neeson adds: 'Clearly what is meant here is "if he were unable to deal with the situation *to the satisfaction of the British Government . . .*"' (Emphasis in original.).

100. Coogan, *Michael Collins*, p. 374–5.

101. Gilbert, *World in Torment*, p. 738.

102. Coogan, *Michael Collins*, p. 330.

103. Gilbert, *World in Torment*, p. 741.

104. Coogan, *Michael Collins*, p. 332.

105. Sir Andrew 'Andy' Cope had been Assistant Under-Secretary for Ireland during the War of Independence. During 1922 he was the chief liaison for the British Government with the Provisional Government. His role in communicating with Collins and other prominent political figures, including the Catholic hierarchy, often understated, is extensively treated in Brian P. Murphy's ground-breaking *Patrick Pearse and the Lost Republican Ideal*, chap. 5.

106. Gilbert, *World in Torment*, p. 746.

107. Gilbert, *World in Torment*, p. 746.

108. William T. Cosgrave (1880–1965). Sinn Féin member of Dublin City Council, 1909–22, member of the Irish Volunteers and a participant in the 1916 Rising; elected MP for Kilkenny in the 1917 by-election and the 1918 general election. Minister for Local Government, 1919–22, President of Dáil Éireann and President of the Provisional Government, August–December 1922; President of the Executive Council (head of government), 1922–32, leader of Cumann na nGaedheal, 1923–33, and of Fine Gael, 1934–44.

109. Regan, *The Irish Counter-Revolution*, p. 82.

110. When Cosgrave met the Northern Prime Minister, Sir James Craig, for the first time he protested that 'I've been pushed into this. I'm not a "leader of men".' Quoted by Joseph M. Curran, *The Birth of the Irish Free State*, p. 251.

111. Gilbert, *World in Torment*, p. 746–7.

112. Winston S. Churchill, *The World Crisis, 1911–19* (New York and London: Free Press, 1959) p. 349.

113. Gilbert, *World in Torment*, p. 747.

114. Lawlor, *Britain and Ireland*, p. 174.

115. Dwyer, *De Valera*, p. 104.

116. Lawlor, *Britain and Ireland*, p. 173.

117. Dwyer, *De Valera*, p. 105.

118. *Parliamentary Debates: Dáil Éireann: Official Report*, 3/379 (9 January 1922).

119. Moynihan, *Speeches and Statements by Éamon de Valera*, p. 98.

120. Moynihan, *Speeches and Statements by Éamon de Valera*, p. 99.

121. 'Document No. 20,' Dáil Éireann, *Correspondence of Mr. Éamon de Valera*, p. 14–15. De Valera's letter, dated 13 September 1922, referred to 'Rory O'Connor's unfortunate repudiation of the Dáil, which I was so foolish to defend even to a straining of my own views in order to avoid a split.'

122. Dwyer, *De Valera*, p. 105.

123. Dwyer, *De Valera*, p. 106.

124. 'Document No. 13,' Dáil Éireann, *Correspondence of Mr. Éamon de Valera*, p. 8. The letter quoted above is a private letter to an unnamed person dated 7 September 1922.

125. I use the term 'Dublin Parliament' here because within a short space of time the same institution was referred to by different names. From 16 January to 6 December 1922 it was officially the Parliament of Southern Ireland; after that date it was called Dáil Éireann. The corresponding government was the Provisional Government of Southern Ireland (also called the Provisional Government of Ireland) and after December 1922 the Executive Council of the Irish Free State.

126. 'Document No. 13,' Dáil Éireann, *Correspondence of Mr. Éamon de Valera*, p. 8. De Valera concluded: '4. Hence, summing up, I am in favour of non-attendance. Let them keep guessing as to the reason for the present' (p. 9). It would appear that de Valera was attempting to deflect attention from his desire to retain a certain ideological flexibility by arguing that his favoured strategy of not outlining a policy would confuse their opponents.

127. 'Document No. 15,' Dáil Éireann, *Correspondence of Mr. Éamon de Valera*, p. 9–12. The document was signed 'on behalf of the Army' by Oscar Traynor, Barney Mellowes, Éamonn Corbett, Liam Pilkington, Tomás de Barra (Tom Barry) and Peadar Ó Domhnaill (Peadar O'Donnell) and 'on behalf of the Citizens of the Irish Republic' by Áine Ní Rathghaille and Nel Mhic Amhlaoibh.

128. 'Document No. 15,' Dáil Éireann, *Correspondence of Mr. Éamon de Valera*, p. 9. This was a brief note, dated 11 September, written to COM (Cathal Ó Murchadha), a former Republican TD, also known as Charles Murphy.

129. 'Document No. 11,' Dáil Éireann, *Correspondence of Mr. Éamon de Valera*, p. 7 (6 September 1922); 'Document No. 17,' p. 13 (12 September 1922). In the second letter de Valera said: 'If the army executive were at hand and would definitely give allegiance to that Govmt. I'd think it wise to try it.'

130. 'Document No. 8,' Dáil Éireann, *Correspondence of Mr. Éamon de Valera*, p. 5. Private letter from Lynch to de Valera, 30 August 1922; de Valera received the letter on 12 September.

131. Neeson, *The Civil War*, p. 269.

132. 'Document No. 18,' Dáil Éireann, *Correspondence of Mr. de Valera*, p. 13. Private letter to Cathal Ó Murchadha, 12 September 1922.

133. 'Document No. 20,' Dáil Éireann, *Correspondence of Mr. Éamon de Valera*, p. 14.

134. Gaughan, *Austin Stack*, p. 220.

135. Neeson, *The Civil War*, p. 271.

136. The composition of the Council of State is interesting in a number of respects. The selection of Austin Stack and Robert Barton reflected the continuity with the last pre-Treaty government, in which they were Minister for Home Affairs and for Economic Affairs, respectively. George Plunkett (father of the executed 1916 leader Joseph Plunkett) had been Minister for Foreign Affairs under the first Dáil and was the first Sinn Féin TD ever elected. J. J. O'Kelly and Laurence Ginnell had been elected vice-president and treasurer, respectively, of Sinn Féin at the unity conference in 1917. The inclusion of Seán O'Mahony is significant, in that he was elected for the first and second Dálaí for the constituency of Fermanagh, now excluded from the jurisdiction of the Dublin legislature. The fact that two women, Mary MacSwiney and Kate

O'Callaghan, were selected is also important when it is considered that the Cosgrave government (1922–32) did not contain a single woman. Fianna Fáil would continue this tradition, and it was not until 1979 that Máire Geoghegan-Quinn, appointed Minister for the Gaeltacht, became the first woman minister since Constance Markievicz. The remaining four members—Seán T. O'Kelly, Seán Moylan, P. J. Ruttledge and M. P. Colivet—would all become prominent members of Fianna Fáil, the first three holding ministerial portfolios.

137. For more on Joe McGarrity's role see Tarpey, *The Role of Joseph McGarrity in the Struggle for Irish Independence.*

138. Gaughan, *Austin Stack*, p. 220.

139. King, *The Orange and the Green*, p. 171–2; Neeson, *The Civil War*, p. 280–5; Gaughan, *Austin Stack*, p. 218.

140. 'Seventh year of the Republic,' *Poblacht na hÉireann War News*, no. 178, 26 October 1922.

141. Gaughan, *Austin Stack*, p. 221.

142. Dwyer, *De Valera*, p. 119.

143. See Burke Williamson, *The Zeal of the Convert: The Life of Erskine Childers* (Gerrards Cross, Bucks: Colin Smythe, 1978), p. 216–30.

144. Bell, *The Secret Army*, p. 37. The 'crimes' attributed to the executed men had been committed before the proclamation of 12 October establishing the Military Court. See Ward, *Unmanageable Revolutionaries*, p. 191.

145. Rory O'Connor had been best man at the wedding of Kevin O'Higgins the previous year. O'Higgins opposed his execution in the government but defended it in public. See de Vere White, *Kevin O'Higgins*, p. 131–5.

146. Dwyer, *De Valera*, p. 114; Longford and O'Neill, *Éamon de Valera*, p. 198.

147. On the death of Collins, de Valera declared: 'He is a big man and if things fall into the hands of lesser men anything might happen'; quoted by Neeson, *The Civil War*, p. 251.

148. Dwyer, *De Valera*, p. 123.

149. The most detailed study of the killings at Ballyseedy and Cahersiveen remains Dorothy Macardle's account, *Tragedies of Kerry*. Other accounts include Blake, *The Irish Civil War*, p. 54–5, Neeson, *The Civil War*, p. 254–5, and Younger, *Ireland's Civil War*, p. 501.

150. Dwyer, *De Valera's Darkest Hour*, p. 139.

151. On the role of Liam Lynch during the Civil War and the circumstances and implications of his death see O'Donoghue, *No Other Law.*

152. Dwyer, *De Valera*, p. 126.

153. See Neeson, *The Civil War*, p. 291–3.

154. *Irish Times*, 29 May 1923, p. 7.

155. *Irish Times*, 29 May 1923, p. 7.

156. Dwyer, *De Valera*, p. 105.

157. Dwyer, *De Valera*, p. 124; *Freeman's Journal*, 17 February 1923.

158. Letter dated 10 September 1922, quoted by Dwyer, *De Valera's Darkest Hour*, p. 126.

Chapter 2: Removing the straitjacket of the Republic, 1923–6 (p. 25–45)

1. Macardle, *The Irish Republic*, p. 788.

2. One Cumann na nGaedheal election poster in Ennis asked: 'Who looted your crops? Who robbed your banks? Who burned your bridges? Who murdered your sons?' before requesting a vote for de Valera's opponent, Eoin MacNeill. The poster appears

in a photograph included in Younger, *Ireland's Civil War*, p. 257.

3. Even when republicans had decided to emigrate they often found it impossible to procure a reference from the local Catholic clergy—an important document, which assisted in securing employment in the Irish communities of England and America. This information was imparted to me by Dr Seán Maguire, son of Tom Maguire (1892–1993), commanding officer of the 2nd Western Division and the last surviving member of the second Dáil. He recalled being told by Frank Butler, a prominent figure in the Clare IRA, that republicans in the county were refused references by the Catholic Church but were able to secure them from Church of Ireland ministers.

4. Bell, *The Secret Army*, p. 42.

5. Bell, *The Secret Army*, p. 42.

6. Regan, *The Irish Counter-Revolution*, p. 149.

7. Bell erroneously claims (*The Secret Army*, p. 42) that 'in Wexford Sinn Féin polled sixty per cent of the vote, in Kerry seventy six, and in Clare eighty per cent.' In fact the vote came nowhere near those figures. In Co. Wexford, Sinn Féin did indeed emerge as the largest party, with two seats out of five, but obtained only 26 per cent of the vote. In Co. Kerry the party secured four seats out of seven with 45 per cent of the vote, while in Co. Clare it took two seats out of five. Its vote in Co. Clare, 48 per cent, was the highest achieved by the party in any constituency. Other areas where it did particularly well were Mayo, Roscommon, Leitrim-Sligo, Longford-Westmeath and Laois-Offaly. Figures taken from Vincent Browne, *The Magill Book of Irish Politics*, p. 55, 216, 337, and Rumpf and Hepburn, *Nationalism and Socialism in Twentieth-Century Ireland*, p. 60.

8. Bell, *The Secret Army*, p. 42.

9. Brian P. Murphy, *Patrick Pearse and the Lost Republican Ideal*, p. 144.

10. Minutes of Comharile na dTeachtaí, 7 August 1924 (UCD Archives, De Valera Papers, P150/1946).

11. Austin Stack, Minister for Home Affairs and Finance; Art O'Connor, Economic Affairs and Local Government; Frank Aiken, Defence; Patrick Ruttledge and Robert Barton, ministers without portfolio; Seán T. O'Kelly, chairman. De Valera, in addition to his position of President of the Republic, held the External Affairs portfolio.

12. See minutes of Comhairle na dTeachtaí (UCD Archives, de Valera Papers, P150/1945). See also 'A Decree to establish the validity of certain acts done and omissions made by Comharile na dTeachtai during the period between the 7th day of August 1924 and the 18th day of December 1926' (UCD Archives, MacEntee Papers, P/67/91/1).

13. Dwyer, *De Valera*, p. 134.

14. Peter Pyne, 'The new Irish state and the decline of the republican Sinn Féin Party,' *Éire-Ireland*, 11/3 (1976), p. 42.

15. Dwyer, *De Valera*, p. 136.

16. Mortimer O'Kelly, private papers, SDM, 11 December 1924, p. 7, quoted by Brian P. Murphy, *Patrick Pearse and the Lost Republican Ideal*, p. 145.

17. Quoted in 'Gentlemen, the King,' a one-page pamphlet by Mortimer O'Kelly.

18. Mortimer O'Kelly, private papers, SDM, 18 March 1925, p. 3, quoted by Brian P. Murphy, *Patrick Pearse and the Lost Republican Ideal*, p. 146.

19. Quoted by Cronin, *The McGarrity Papers*, p. 141.

20. Brian P. Murphy, *Patrick Pearse and the Lost Republican Ideal*, p. 146. See also Fallon, *Soul of Fire*, p. 118–25, for an account of MacSwiney's American tour.

21. *Sinn Féin*, 25 April 1925, p. 3.

22. 'President refutes new rumour,' *An Phoblacht*, 17 July 1925, p. 3. This statement was made in the course of an interview given on 13 July 1925 at the request of the *Irish Times* that was not subsequently published by the paper. The rumours surfaced in an article in the *Sunday Independent*, 10 July 1925, that claimed that at the meeting on 28 June the entire position of the Sinn Féin organisation was discussed. Attempts to bridge the gap between the government and 'de Valera's followers' were allegedly discussed, as was the prospect of Sinn Féin TDS entering the Dáil. It was reported that this proposal met with strong opposition from a number of deputies. The report continued: 'It was strongly urged, states our informant, that an open letter should be addressed to the Free State Government restating the principles and the position of the Party, and urging the removal of the oath as the principal obstacle which prevented them from representing their constituents in An Dáil, and suggesting that they should be allowed to take their seats in the Dáil without taking the oath.' In his *Irish Times* interview de Valera admitted that the meeting had discussed national policy and that the position of the party had been reviewed. He denied, however, that a letter to the Free State government had been suggested or any similar proposal considered. In the absence of minutes for the relevant meeting, the veracity of the *Sunday Independent* report remains a matter for speculation.

23. Brian P. Murphy, *Patrick Pearse and the Lost Republican Ideal*, p. 147.

24. De Valera's connection with Mannix went back to 1912, when Mannix, then president of St Patrick's College, Maynooth, offered him a part-time post as professor of mathematics. At Maynooth de Valera extended his contacts among the clergy. Shortly after his appointment Mannix emigrated to Australia, where he became Catholic Primate. See Dwyer, *De Valera*, p. 11. Mannix played a prominent part in peace negotiations during the 1919–21 period and was the most important Catholic ecclesiastic to defend de Valera's position against the condemnations of the Irish hierarchy during the Civil War.

25. Rector of the Irish College in Rome, Hagan had defended the republican position at the Vatican after the Treaty.

26. Magennis was the head of the Carmelite Order. As president of the Friends of Irish Freedom he had welcomed and assisted de Valera during his American tour in 1919. He also supported de Valera after the Treaty.

27. The visit of Archbishop Mannix lasted several months and received extensive coverage in the republican press. See *An Phoblacht*, 10 July 1925, p. 1 (Mannix arrives), 24 July, p. 5 (Cork), 7 August, p. 6 (Limerick), 14 August, p. 5 (Limerick) and p. 6 (Waterford), 4 September, p. 3 (Wexford), 11 September, p. 3 (Wexford) and p. 6 (Drogheda), 16 October, p. 3 (Dublin), 30 October, p. 3 (Dublin), 6 November, p. 3, 6 (Rotunda, Dublin), 13 November, p. 1 (Liverpool).

28. Keogh, *The Vatican, the Bishops and Irish Politics*, p. 132.

29. Interview with Seán MacBride, quoted by Mac Eoin, *Survivors*, p. 121. See also interview in the *Irish Press*, 12 April 1986, quoted by Brian P. Murphy, *Patrick Pearse and the Lost Republican Ideal*, p. 148–9.

30. Tom Maguire, interviewed by Uinseann Mac Eoin, *Survivors*, p. 298.

31. Brian P. Murphy, *Patrick Pearse and the Lost Republican Ideal*, p. 149. Dr Patrick McCartan, a former IRB leader who had followed Collins on the issue of the Treaty, was the Free State representative, and it was he who informed McGarrity of his role as an intermediary.

32. Brian P. Murphy, *Patrick Pearse and the Lost Republican Ideal*, p. 149.

33. Brian P. Murphy, *Patrick Pearse and the Lost Republican Ideal*, p. 150.

34. Coogan, *The IRA* (second edition), p. 125–7. See also Michael McInerney, 'Gerry Boland's story,' *Irish Times*, 11 October 1968; Foley, *Legion of the Rearguard*, p. 40–41.
35. Brian P. Murphy, *Patrick Pearse and the Lost Republican Ideal*, p. 150. During the previous year more than £11,000 in American donations was used to support the IRA.
36. Quoted by Edmonds, *The Gun, the Law, and the Irish People*, p. 137.
37. Quoted by Brian P. Murphy, *Patrick Pearse and the Lost Republican Ideal*, p. 150–51.
38. *An Phoblacht*, 27 November 1925, p. 3. For a detailed report on the ard-fheis see *An Phoblacht*, 20 November 1925, p. 3, 8, and 27 November 1925, p. 3, 5–6.
39. Quoted by Brian P. Murphy, *Patrick Pearse and the Lost Republican Ideal*, p. 151.
40. See above and Coogan, *The IRA* (second edition), p. 76.
41. Coogan, *The IRA* (second edition), p. 75. See also Fallon, *Soul of Fire*, p. 125–6.
42. For the view of Sinn Féin on the Boundary Commission before the publication of the *Morning Post* report see *An Phoblacht*, 4 September 1925, p. 3.
43. As has been demonstrated, the Sinn Féin ard-fheis that took place weeks before the Boundary Commission report devoted the greater part of its time to the question of de Valera's position on the oath.
44. *An Phoblacht*, 13 November 1925, p. 3; 20 November 1925, p. 1, 3; 27 November 1925, p. 1, 3.
45. See Ronan Fanning, *The Irish Department of Finance, 1922–58* (Dublin: Institute of Public Information, 1978), p. 164–8.
46. *An Phoblacht*, 27 November 1925, p. 3.
47. *An Phoblacht*, 13 November 1925, p. 3.
48. See *An Phoblacht*, 4 December 1925, p. 1, 3–5; 11 December, p. 1–6; 18 December, p. 1–5, 7, 9; 25 December, p. 1–4.
49. *An Phoblacht*, 11 December 1925, p. 1.
50. *An Phoblacht*, 11 December 1925, p. 1.
51. Dwyer, *De Valera*, p. 136.
52. Transcript of public statement by de Valera, 15 January 1926, in response to queries by the press about the reasons behind his call for an extraordinary ard-fheis of Sinn Féin (Fianna Fáil Archives, FF/22).
53. 'Abridged report of ard-fheis,' *An Phoblacht*, 16 April 1926, p. 3.
54. 'Abridged report of ard-fheis,' *An Phoblacht*, 16 April 1926, p. 3.
55. Moynihan, *Speeches and Statements by Éamon de Valera*, p. 129–30.
56. Quoted by Michael McInerney, 'The name and the game,' *Irish Times* special supplement, 19 May 1979, p. 55.
57. Brian Farrell, *Seán Lemass*, p. 17.
58. Michael McInerney, 'Gerry Boland's story,' *Irish Times*, 11 October 1968.
59. Peter Pyne, 'The third Sinn Féin party, 1923–1926,' *Economic and Social Review*, 1/1 (1969), p. 46. The term 'galaxy of cranks' belongs to Lemass; quoted by Brian Farrell, *Seán Lemass*, p. 16.
60. Brian P. Murphy, *Patrick Pearse and the Lost Republican Ideal*, p. 153.
61. Brian P. Murphy, *Patrick Pearse and the Lost Republican Ideal*, p. 153.
62. Brian P. Murphy, *Patrick Pearse and the Lost Republican Ideal*, p. 155.
63. Minutes of Comhairle na dTeachtaí, 28 March 1926 (Fianna Fáil Archives, FF/22; UCD Archives, De Valera Papers, P150/1948).
64. Minutes of Comhairle na dTeachtaí, 28 March 1926 (Fianna Fáil Archives, FF/22; UCD Archives, De Valera Papers, P150/1948).

65. Minutes of Comhairle na dTeachtaí, 28 March 1926 (Fianna Fáil Archives, FF/22; UCD Archives, De Valera Papers, P150/1948).

66. Minutes of Comhairle na dTeachtaí, 28 March 1926 (Fianna Fáil Archives, FF/22; UCD Archives, De Valera Papers, P150/1948). The debate in 1922 on de Valera's position as President of the Republic resulted in a vote of 60 to 58 against, with several abstentions. As de Valera did not himself vote—ostensibly on the grounds that he was indifferent to his fate—he was in effect defeated by one vote.

67. Brian P. Murphy, *Patrick Pearse and the Lost Republican Ideal*, p. 160–6.

68. Ceannt had an impeccable republican pedigree, dating from the days of the Land League, when he was imprisoned. He was wounded in 1916, and his brother, Éamonn Ceannt, was one of the seven signatories of the Proclamation of the Irish Republic and one of the fifteen men executed for their part in the rising.

69. Minutes of Comhairle na dTeachtaí, 28–29 March 1926 (UCD Archives, De Valera Papers, P150/1948).

70. Minutes of Comhairle na dTeachtaí, 22–23 May 1926 (UCD Archives, De Valera Papers, P150/1948).

71. Minutes of Comhairle na dTeachtaí, 22–23 May 1926 (UCD Archives, De Valera Papers, P150/1948).

72. Minutes of Comhairle na dTeachtaí, 22–23 May 1926 (UCD Archives, De Valera Papers, P150/1948).

73. Minutes of Comhairle na dTeachtaí, 22–23 May 1926 (UCD Archives, De Valera Papers, P150/1948).

74. Brian P. Murphy, *Patrick Pearse and the Lost Republican Ideal*, p. 168.

75. Joe McGarrity, for example. See Cronin, *The McGarrity Papers*, p. 141–5.

76. See, for example, his speech at Melbourne on 19 May 1926. 'Archbishop Mannix on the Campaign Against the Oath,' 1926 (Fianna Fáil Archives, FF/22).

77. 'Archbishop Mannix on the Campaign Against the Oath,' speech on 26 June 1926 (Fianna Fáil Archives, FF/22, p. 1–2). .

78. 'Archbishop Mannix on the Campaign Against the Oath,' speech on 26 June 1926 (Fianna Fáil Archives, FF/22, p. 2–4). Speech delivered in New York, 11 July 1926, Philadelphia, 18 July, Boston, 21 July.

79. 'Archbishop Mannix on the Campaign Against the Oath,' speech on 26 June 1926 (Fianna Fáil Archives, FF/22, p. 4).

80. Art O'Connor to Mary MacSwiney, 2 August 1926. Brian P. Murphy, *Patrick Pearse and the Lost Republican Ideal*, p. 170.

81. The 1920 loan had raised £5,236,065, the second, in 1921, $622,720. See 'The Dáil bonds litigation: Serious blow to Free State prestige,' *Nation*, 21 May 1927, p. 2. The history of the Dáil bonds case since the Treaty is outlined in this article.

82. *Fianna Fáil Weekly News Bulletin*, no. 8, 22 February 1927, p. 1 (Fianna Fáil Archives, FF/25). $6.5 million was worth £1.3 million in 1927.

83. *Nation*, 21 May 1927, p. 2.

84. Quoted by Brian P. Murphy, *Patrick Pearse and the Lost Republican Ideal*, p. 173.

85. *Fianna Fáil Weekly News Bulletin*, no. 8, 22 February 1927, p. 1 (Fianna Fáil Archives, FF/25).

86. *Fianna Fáil Weekly News Bulletin*, no. 6, 8 February 1927, p. 1 .

87. *Fianna Fáil Weekly News Bulletin*, no. 9, 1 March 1927, p. 1.

88. *Fianna Fáil Weekly News Bulletin*, no. 12, 22 March 1927, p. 1.

89. See *Fianna Fáil Weekly News Bulletin*, no. 10, 8 March 1927, p. 1; no. 11, 15 March 1927, p. 1; no. 12, 22 March 1927, p. 1–3; no. 13, 29 March 1927, p. 1; no. 15, 12 April 1927, p. 1.

90. See the *Nation*, 9 April 1927, p. 1, 2; 16 April 1927, p. 6; 7 May 1927, p. 7.

91. *Fianna Fáil Weekly News Bulletin*, no. 12, 22 March 1927, p. 1.

92. *Fianna Fáil Weekly News Bulletin*, no. 12, 22 March 1927, p. 1.

93. *Fianna Fáil Weekly News Bulletin*, no. 15, 12 April 1927, p. 1.

94. *Nation*, 21 May 1927, p. 2.

95. *Fianna Fáil Weekly News Bulletin*, no. 8, 22 March 1927, p. 1.

96. Legal representation was provided by Martin Conboy of New York. In his letters to de Valera he greeted him as 'My Dear Mr. President,' which seems to indicate that, like many other Irish-Americans, he considered de Valera to be the head of the Republican government. He remained in contact long after the conclusion of the Dáil funds case. See Conboy to de Valera, 28 December 1928, and Asch to de Valera, 27 April 1927 (Fianna Fáil Archives, FF/26).

97. An edited copy of the Supreme Court judgement and appendix is reprinted in the *Nation*, 9 July 1927, p. 3.

98. *Nation*, 21 January 1928, p. 1.

99. See chap. 4.

100. On the issue of uniting Fianna Fáil and Sinn Féin see *An Phoblacht*, 16 April 1926, p. 3.

101. De Valera to Mary MacSwiney, 14 May 1927; quoted by Brian P. Murphy, *Patrick Pearse and the Lost Republican Ideal*, p. 175.

102. Brian P. Murphy, *Patrick Pearse and the Lost Republican Ideal*, p. 174.

103. Peter Pyne, 'The third Sinn Féin party, 1923–1926,' *Economic and Social Review*, 1/1 (1969), p. 29–50, and 1/2 (1970), p. 229–57.

104. Peter Pyne, 'The third Sinn Féin party, 1923–1926,' *Economic and Social Review*, 1/2 (1970), p. 229.

105. Peter Pyne, 'The third Sinn Féin party, 1923–1926,' *Economic and Social Review*, 1/1 (1969), p. 41.

106. Report of the Honorary Treasurers, 1927 Ard-Fheis, 24–25 November 1927 (Fianna Fáil Archives, FF/701).

107. This is clear from the Fianna Fáil cashbook for 1927. It documents a surge in foreign donations before the June 1927 election followed by a dramatic lull, only to be surpassed by another surge in the period immediately before the September election (Fianna Fáil Archives, FF/24).

108. Report of the Honorary Treasurers, 1928 Ard-Fheis, 25–26 October (Fianna Fáil Archives, FF/702). See also the *Nation*, 17 November 1928, p. 2.

109. Report of the Honorary Treasurers, 1929 and 1930 Ard-Fheisanna (Fianna Fáil Archives, FF/703 and FF/704).

110. Report of the Honorary Treasurers, 1931 and 1932 Ard-Fheiseanna (Fianna Fáil Archives, FF/705 and FF/706). These figures, with the exception of the financial year 1928/9, record the amount raised in national collections. However, the difference between the national collection figure and total income was never large, a fact indicated in the 1928/9 figures. America became less important as a source of party funds. A separate fund was established for setting up the *Irish Press*, and this venture did rely heavily on fund-raising in the United States. See the *Nation*, 3 March 1928, p. 8.

111. Peter Pyne, 'The third Sinn Féin party, 1923–1926,' *Economic and Social Review*, 1/1 (1969), p. 42.

112. Report of the Honorary Secretaries, 1927 Ard-Fheis, 24–25 November (Fianna Fáil Archives, FF/701).

113. Report of the Honorary Secretaries, 1928 Ard-Fheis (Fianna Fáil Archives, FF/702). See also the *Nation*, 3 November 1928, p. 2.

114. The honorary secretaries' report for 1929 lists only the number of registered cumainn.

115. There were 52 new cumainn, while 287 disappeared, a net decline of 235.

116. Report of the Honorary Secretaries, 1929 Ard-Fheis (Fianna Fáil Archives, FF/703). See also the *Nation*, 19 October 1928, p. 7.

117. Prager, *Building Democracy in Ireland*, p. 210.

118. Peter Pyne, 'The third Sinn Féin party, 1923–1926,' *Economic and Social Review*, 1/1 (1969), p. 42.

119. See Macardle, *The Irish Republic*, p. 802.

120. Macardle, *The Irish Republic*, p. 804.

121. O'Leary, *Irish Elections*, p. 23.

122. R. K. Carty (*Party and Parish Pump*, p. 101), for example, writes that Sinn Féin's 'early successes in establishing an organisation proved to be ephemeral, and by 1924 their party was disintegrating.' Carty's sole source for this judgement is Peter Pyne, 'The third Sinn Féin party, 1923–1926,' *Economic and Social Review*, 1/2 (1970), p. 252.

123. In fairness to Pyne it must be said that he makes a modest claim at the outset, stating that his study 'is offered only as an investigation of a preliminary nature, for synthesis must await the study of all relevant sources.' Peter Pyne, 'The third Sinn Féin party, 1923–1926,' *Economic and Social Review*, 1/1 (1969), p. 29.

124. Peter Pyne, 'The third Sinn Féin party, 1923–1926,' *Economic and Social Review*, 1/2 (1970), p. 252.

125. Letter reproduced by Cronin, *The McGarrity Papers*, p. 141.

126. Cronin, *The McGarrity Papers*, p. 141.

Chapter 3: Fianna Fáil—the Republican Party (p. 46–69)

1. Moynihan, *Speeches and Statements by Éamon de Valera*, p. 131–2. This statement treats the Irish Volunteers as a homogeneous entity and appears to forget that the Volunteers were themselves divided, the majority joining the British forces during the First World War, a small minority remaining at home. In addition, the minority were headed by Eoin MacNeill, who attempted to call off the Rising that declared the Irish Republic. The 'spirit of devotion' de Valera refers to can therefore be assumed to apply to that section that in 1916 was a minority of a minority within the Volunteers. 'Fianna Fáil' (literally 'warrior bands of Ireland') was an alternative name for the Irish Volunteers put forward in 1913 by Eoin MacNeill, reflected in the monogram FF in the Volunteers' badge. 'Soldiers of destiny' was a mischievous mistranslation popularised in the 1960s by the journalist John Healy.

2. Moynihan, *Speeches and Statements by Éamon de Valera*, p. 131.

3. This claim was reiterated on a number of occasions. See transcript of address to first Fianna Fáil ard-fheis (Fianna Fáil Archives, FF/22).

4. Moynihan, *Speeches and Statements by Éamon de Valera*, p. 134. An original copy of this speech is available in the Fianna Fáil Archives (FF/22).

5. Moynihan, *Speeches and Statements by Éamon de Valera*, p. 136.

6. Moynihan, *Speeches and Statements by Éamon de Valera*, p. 140.

7. Fallon, *Soul of Fire*, p. 128.

8. Letter to editor, *Irish Independent*, 6 June 1926, p. 7.

9. Fallon, *Soul of Fire*, p. 128.

10. Private letter from Frank Barrett to T.D., 7 June 1926 (Fianna Fáil Archives, FF/22). One can only hazard a guess about the identity of the recipient, though the presence of the letter in the Fianna Fáil Archives suggests it was a high-ranking member of the new party, perhaps Thomas Derrig.

11. Tom Maguire, a Sinn Féin TD, recalled that 'you had the virtual dissolution of this thriving organisation with its 44 seats in the South in order to create Fianna Fáil. That was almost inevitable, once de Valera had made his decision to take part, in view of the great personal magnetism of the man'; quoted by Mac Eoin, *Survivors*, p. 298–9.

12. Economics was always subservient to politics; as Horace Plunkett once remarked, in Ireland the term 'political economy' was invariably spelt with a capital 'P' and a lower-case 'e'; quoted by James Meenan, *The Irish Economy since 1922* (Liverpool: Liverpool University Press, 1970), p. xxvii.

13. Davis, *Arthur Griffith and Non-Violent Sinn Féin*, p. 127. The high priority given to this policy is demonstrated by the fact that the original Sinn Féin programme sought a 'protective system for Irish industries and commerce' as the first necessary step towards achieving its objective of 'the re-establishment of the independence of Ireland.' Considerably less attention was given to 'non-recognition of the British Parliament and the establishment of a National Assembly,' listed as the fourteenth proposal in pursuance of national independence. See de Blacam, *What Sinn Féin Stands For*, p. 46–7.

14. Gearóid Ó Crualaoich, 'The primacy of form: A "folk ideology" in de Valera's politics,' in O'Carroll and Murphy, *De Valera and His Times*.

15. Fianna Fáil, *A Brief Outline of the Aims and Programme of Fianna Fáil*, p. 2.

16. See Boland, *The Rise and Decline of Fianna Fáil*, p. 33; also 'The function of the cumainn' (editorial), *Nation*, 15 October 1927, p. 4.

17. Briscoe, *For the Life of Me*, p. 230.

18. Boland, *The Rise and Decline of Fianna Fáil*, p. 18.

19. Boland, *The Rise and Decline of Fianna Fáil*, p. 19.

20. The figures for 20 February are from *Fianna Fáil Weekly News Bulletin*, no. 8, 22 February 1927, p. 2, and for 10 April from no. 15, 12 April 1927, p. 2. The bulletin, which lasted for fifteen weeks before being superseded by the *Nation*, provided weekly updates on the number of cumainn from 3 January to 12 April 1927, after which similar figures were provided by the *Nation*.

21. Honorary Secretaries' Report, 1927 Ard-Fheis (Fianna Fáil Archives, FF/701).

22. See chap. 4 and 5.

23. *Nation*, 3 September 1927, p. 4.

24. Financial details are taken from Fianna Fáil cashbook for 1927 (Fianna Fáil Archives, FF/24). Entries for the dates cited above are: 28 April, £2,055; 3 May, £2,057 3s; 5 May, £4,110. These were all sent by Patrick Lyndon, secretary of the American Association for the Recognition of the Irish Republic, to the honorary treasurers of Fianna Fáil.

25. Fianna Fáil cashbook, 1927. See entries for 12 May and 27 May 1927.

26. Fianna Fáil cashbook, 1927. See entries for 5 September and 12 September 1927.

27. Report of the Honorary Treasurers, 1927 Ard-Fheis (Fianna Fáil Archives, FF/701). The party had received £30,402 2s 5d and spent £30,021 11s 8d, leaving a surplus of £380 10s 9d.

28. Report of the Honorary Secretaries, 1927 Ard-Fheis (Fianna Fáil Archives, FF/701).
29. This was recognised almost immediately after the September election. Writing in the *Nation* (12 November 1927, p. 2), Leo Murtagh stated: 'In every parish in the Free State there is a Fianna Fáil cumann, and now to all intents and purposes, this organisation is idle. Such machinery, to keep it in perfect order, must have work to do, and its periods of activity should not be limited to election times.'.
30. Report of the Honorary Secretaries, 1928 Ard-Fheis (Fianna Fáil Archives, FF/702). See also the *Nation,* 3 November 1928, p. 2. Attendance figures at ard-fheiseanna taken from the *Nation,* 26 October 1929, p. 7, and 8 November 1930, p. 7.
31. The party collected 96,000 signatures (the constitutional requirement was 75,000). This can be broken down as follows: Munster, 28,593; Leinster, 26,639; Connacht, 29,704; Ulster (three Free State counties), 11,143. See *Parliamentary Debates: Dáil Éireann: Official Report,* 28/1499–50 (16 May 1928).
32. *Nation,* 3 December 1927, p. 3.
33. See for example, Honorary Secretaries' Report, 1929 Ard-Fheis (Fianna Fáil Archives, FF/703).
34. See the *Nation,* 25 February 1928, p. 5.
35. Honorary Secretaries' Report, 1929 Ard-Fheis (Fianna Fáil Archives, FF/703).
36. Minutes of National Executive, 5 January 1928. See also the *Nation,* 14 January 1928, p. 8.
37. *Nation,* 14 January 1928, p. 8.
38. *Nation,* 31 January 1931, p. 8.
39. *Nation,* 26 May 1928, p. 8, and 2 June 1928, p. 8.
40. Statement of 18 April 1926 (Fianna Fáil Archives, FF/26); *Nation,* 25 June 1927, p. 1.
41. The National Group consisted of nine Cumann na nGaedheal TDs who left the party in 1924. The dissidents protested against the manner in which the demobilisation of the army was being implemented (favouring, they felt, ex-officers of the British Army over republican veterans) and what they perceived as a drift away from the republican position espoused by their former IRB chief, Michael Collins. Their resignations necessitated a by-election in November 1924, but only one of the group, Joe McGrath, put himself forward, while the others 'opted out of political life.' See John Coakley, 'Minor parties in Irish political life, 1922–1989,' *Economic and Social Review,* 21/3 (April 1990), p. 279. Clann Éireann was formed in the wake of the Boundary Commission fiasco in December 1925 when three Cumann na nGaedheal TDs and one senator resigned in protest against the Cosgrave government's Northern policy. The party put up seven candidates in the June 1927 election and received a negligible vote. Between the two groups of defectors Cumann na nGaedheal lost almost a fifth of its deputies elected in 1923.
42. The figure of £3 3s 3d is cited by J. Bowyer Bell (*The Secret Army,* p. 78), though he characteristically does not give any source.
43. His premature demise, the result of a long stint on hunger strike in the early 1920s, received generous coverage in the Fianna Fáil paper, but while his exploits of 1916–23 were mentioned in detail no reference was made to his parting with the Fianna Fáil leadership in 1926. Seán T. Ó Ceallaigh, 'The late Austin Stack,' *Nation,* 4 May 1929, p. 4–5.
44. *Fianna Fáil Weekly News Bulletin,* no. 15, 12 April 1927, p. 1.
45. Bell, *The Secret Army,* p. 78.

46. Coogan, *De Valera*, p. 398.
47. For examples of the ideological and policy debates between the Labour Party and Fianna Fáil during this period see the *Nation*, 16 April 1927, p. 2; 7 May 1927, p. 3; 28 May 1927, p. 6; 4 June 1927, p. 4; 11 June 1927, p. 6; and 16 July 1927, p. 7.
48. *Nation*, 19 October 1929, p. 4.
49. *Parliamentary Debates: Dáil Éireann: Official Report*, 34/318 (2 April 1930).
50. *Parliamentary Debates: Dáil Éireann: Official Report*, 21/1899 (24 November 1927). As was characteristic of Fianna Fáil deputies at the time, Lemass refrained from using the term 'Dáil', preferring instead 'this house.'
51. Cronin, *Frank Ryan*, p. 25.
52. John Horgan, *Irish Media: A Critical History since 1922* (London: Routledge, 2001), p. 6.
53. See chap. 5.
54. The existing daily papers were accused, for example, of 'bowdlerising' Fianna Fáil contributions in the Dáil. See the *Nation*, 2 November 1929, p. 1. In one article (*Nation*, 12 November 1927, p. 2) the dangers were stated in the following terms: 'On certain mentalities the written word exercises almost a hypnotic effect, and with reiteration, a half-truth becomes a truth.' The same article used the following descriptions of the daily press: 'the distorting mirrors of an anti-national press . . . so-called Irish newspapers . . . pro-British newspapers . . . our reptile Press.'
55. *Nation*, 12 November 1927, p. 2.
56. Full-page advertisement, *Nation*, 15 September 1928, p. 8.
57. Quotations from Father Richard Devane and Prof. T. F. O'Rahilly, respectively. Both authors were cited in detail from articles originally published in the philosophical quarterly *Studies*.
58. When Cosgrave visited New York in 1928 the *Daily Telegraph* noted that 'almost as many policeman as spectators lined the streets.' See the *Nation*, 28 January 1928, p. 4–5; *Irish Independent*, 21 January 1928.
59. 'Farewell to Mr. de Valera leaving New York: Mayor Walker cheered as he speaks in farewell to Republican leader,' *Nation*, 3 March 1928, p. 3.
60. *Irish World*, 26 May 1927, quoted by Bowman, *De Valera and the Ulster Question*, p. 103.
61. Quoted by Coogan, *De Valera*, p. 418.
62. Coogan, *De Valera*, p. 418.
63. Coogan, *De Valera*, p. 418.
64. *Nation*, 3 September 1928, p. 3. The article gives a lengthy account of O'Malley's exploits as a guerrilla leader from 1919 to 1924 but does not enlighten its readers about the details of his American tour, only that it had been undertaken 'at the special request' of de Valera.
65. *Nation*, 17 March 1928, p. 8.
66. Coogan, *De Valera*, p. 420.
67. The party's entry to Dáil Éireann is discussed in detail in the following chapter.
68. *Nation*, 23 june 1928, p.1.
69. Minutes of Parliamentary Party, 29 November 1928 (Fianna Fáil Archives, FF/438). The motion was proposed by T. O'Reilly, seconded by Domhnall Ó Buachalla.
70. Minutes of Parliamentary Party, 29 November 1928 (Fianna Fáil Archives, FF/438). The motion was seconded by Dr Ward.
71. Minutes of Parliamentary Party, 10 May 1929 (Fianna Fáil Archives, FF/438). The motion was proposed by Deputy Corry, seconded by Domhnall Ó Buachalla.

72. A motion passed three months earlier, sponsored by the whips' department of the party, compelled members to name deputies who were 'visibly under the influence of drink in the Dáil' at the following party meeting. Minutes of Parliamentary Party, 28 February 1929 (Fianna Fáil Archives, FF/438).

73. Minutes of Parliamentary Party, 10 May 1929. The motion was proposed by T. Ó Raghallaigh and seconded by D. Ó Buachalla.

74. Minutes of Parliamentary Party, 21 February 1928 (Fianna Fáil Archives, FF/438).

75. See Minutes of Parliamentary Party, 28 February 1929, 7 March 1929 and 14 November 1929. That some excuses enjoyed less credibility than others was underlined by a motion submitted by Deputy Corry on 21 March 1929, that 'the resolution requesting a Doctors Certificate for illness be rescinded, as same is useless.'

76. Minutes of Parliamentary Party, 23 February 1928.

77. Minutes of Parliamentary Party, 28 February 1929, 7 March 1929 and 14 November 1929.

78. Eight issues were considered to fall under this classification. They were, in order of importance: Treaty questions, language, land policy (including land annuities), development of industry (including tariffs, protection etc.), local government, army, education, and the manufacture and sale of alcohol. While Northern Ireland was not mentioned specifically, it can be assumed that this came under 'Treaty Questions'. Minutes of Parliamentary Party, 18 May 1928.

79. Minutes of Parliamentary Party, 19 July 1928 and 11 July 1929 (Fianna Fáil Archives, FF/438).

80. The statement of accounts from the whips' department for the period 1 November to 30 April 1929 revealed that subscriptions from TDs amounted to £581 14s—a large sum for the time. Senators contributed £40. Minutes of Parliamentary Party, 21 March 1929.

81. Minutes of Parliamentary Party, 11 November 1928.

82. Minutes of Parliamentary Party, 8 November 1928.

83. Constitution of Fianna Fáil (Fianna Fáil Archives, FF/26), p. 8.

84. Mr Nolan, delegate for North Dublin, called the attention of the ard-fheis to the fact that no mention had been made in the honorary secretaries' report of what had been done to put into effect the resolution that committed the party to fostering alliances with 'other oppressed nations.' In addition, Joe Groome (a future honorary secretary of the party) asked what action had been taken to put into effect the resolution pledging the support of Fianna Fáil to Fianna Éireann and 'kindred Republican organisations in their efforts to organise the youth of Ireland.' See Report of Ard-Fheis, Nation, 10 November 1928, p. 2.

85. Lenin, the advocate par excellence of democratic centralism, maintained that '"broad democracy" in party organisation . . . is nothing more than a useless and harmful toy.' Quoted by Keith Graham, The Battle of Democracy (Brighton: Wheatsheaf Books, 1982), p. 212.

86. Nation, 4 June 1927, p. 7. This was part of a one-page Fianna Fáil advertisement issued before the June election. It stated that 'Fianna Fáil can give you a NATIONAL GOVERNMENT because it is the only party whose members have not taken an oath to PARTITION.'

87. Nation, 2 July, p. 2.

88. Nation, 20 August 1927, p. 1.

89. Statement of Éamon de Valera outlining attitude to Clann Éireann, issued by Fianna Fáil HQ, 18 April 1926 (Fianna Fáil Archives, FF/22).

90. Transcript of first Constitution of Fianna Fáil, rule 2: Membership (Fianna Fáil Archives, FF/22).

91. This did not include members of the teaching profession, who—almost uniquely among public servants—were not required to make a political declaration. Fianna Fáil believed that this omission was the result of expediency, as such a directive would be very difficult to implement. The party also argued that the omission proved that the oath was not mandatory but selectively imposed for political reasons.

92. This pledge required the prospective candidate to declare that they would 'not take any position involving an oath of allegiance to a foreign power.' Fianna Fáil, *A Brief Outline of the Aims and Programme of Fianna Fáil*, p. 6.

93. *Nation*, 9 July 1927, p. 2; statement issued by Fianna Fáil headquarters, 29 June 1927.

94. *Nation*, 28 May 1927, p. 1. The Minister for External Affairs, Desmond FitzGerald, was taken to task for claiming that the Constitution of the Irish Free State meant that power was derived from the people and that there were no barriers to the nation's advance. The *Nation* argued that such statements were meaningless when compared with his statement that the removal of the oath would entail 'another round with England.'

95. *Nation*, 18 June 1926, p. 2.

96. *Nation*, 11 June 1927, p. 4, and 25 June 1927, p. 3.

97. *Nation*, 25 June 1927, p. 1, 3.

98. *Nation*, 11 June 1927, p. 4.

99. *Nation*, 23 April 1927, p. 2–3; 7 May, p. 5; 14 May, p. 4–5; 21 May, p. 5; 28 May, p. 6; 11 June, p. 2–3; 18 June, p. 2; 25 June, p. 2; 2 July, p. 6; 9 July, p.6; 16 July, p. 6; 30 July, p. 2; 6 August, p. 3; 13 August, p. 7; 20 August, p. 2; 3 September, p. 3; 17 September, p. 3; 24 September, p. 5; 8 October, p. 3.

100. *Nation*, 16 July 1927, p. 8.

101. *Nation*, 11 June 1927, p. 4.

102. *Nation*, 9 July 1927, p. 5.

103. De Valera statement, 18 April 1926 (Fianna Fáil Archives, FF/22).

104. Speech by Gerald Boland, *Fianna Fáil Weekly News Bulletin*, no. 4, 24 January 1927, supplement, p. 1.

105. Speech by de Valera at Navan and Kells, *Fianna Fáil Weekly News Bulletin*, no. 8, 22 February 1927, supplement, p. 2. See also his speech in Limerick reported in the 15 February issue (supplement, p. 1).

106. See *Fianna Fáil Weekly News Bulletin*, no. 5, 31 January 1927, p. 1.

107. Edmonds, *The Gun, the Law, and the Irish People*, p. 138.

108. *Fianna Fáil Weekly News Bulletin*, no. 7, 15 February 1927, supplement, p. 1–2.

109. Constitution (Amendment No. 6) Bill. *Parliamentary Debates: Dáil Éireann: Official Report*, 19/91–94 (6 April 1927).

110. *Nation*, 16 April 1927, p. 1.

111. *Nation*, 4 June 1927, p. 4.

112. *Nation*, 4 June 1927, p. 7.

113. Statement issued by Fianna Fáil HQ, 14 June 1927, reported in the *Nation*, 18 June 1927, p. 2.

114. Minutes of Parliamentary Party, 22 June 1927 (Fianna Fáil Archives, FF/437).

115. *Nation*, 9 July 1927, p. 4.

116. One option pursued was to argue through the courts that the Treaty did not make the

oath a condition for participation in the Dáil. See Minutes of Parliamentary Party, 22 June 1927 (Fianna Fáil Archives, FF/437), and the *Nation*, 25 June 1927, p. 2; 9 July, p. 7, 8; 16 July, p. 8; and 23 July, p. 8.

117. According to article 48, a petition signed by 75,000 voters obliged the government to hold a referendum on the relevant issue. On 14 June, de Valera declared that 'if a referendum were held . . . if the single issue of the oath were put before the people, this infamous penal legislation would be repudiated by an indignant nation' (*Nation*, 18 June 1927, p. 2). This claim was repeated during de Valera's radio broadcast of 20 June (*Nation*, 25 June 1927, p. 1). The suggested text of the referendum proposal issued by the Fianna Fáil Publicity Department on 1 July asked voters to delete article 17 of the Constitution of the Irish Free State and to substitute the following: 'Every member of the Oireachtas shall sign the Roll of Members of the House to which he shall have been elected and thereupon shall be entitled to sit and vote therein and to have and enjoy all the rights and privileges of members thereof' (*Nation*, 9 July 1927, p. 1, 2).

118. *Nation*, 16 July 1927, p. 8.

119. The ability of the government to propose amendments to the constitution at will rested on the fact that it was a flexible document that could be amended by the Dáil. This was so from the time of its introduction in 1922 until it was replaced by the Constitution of Ireland in 1937. See Chubb, *The Constitution and Constitutional Change*, p. 15.

120. Minutes of Parliamentary Party, 18 July 1927 (third meeting of the Fianna Fáil party) (Fianna Fáil Archives, FF/437).

121. *Nation*, 30 July 1927, p. 6.

122. *Nation*, 30 July 1927, p. 6. The resolution was signed by P. J. Brennan, honorary secretary.

123. Minutes of Parliamentary Party, 5 August 1927 (fifth meeting of the Fianna Fáil party) (Fianna Fáil Archives, FF/437). The motion for expulsion was proposed by Seán T. O'Kelly and seconded by P. J. Ruttledge.

124. Letter to editor, *Irish Independent*. When it was published a copy was pasted into the minutes of the Fianna Fáil Parliamentary Party for 5 August 1927 (Fianna Fáil Archives, FF/437).

125. Statement issued by Fianna Fáil Publicity Department, 25 July 1927, published in the *Nation*, 30 July 1927, p. 5.

126. Statement issued by Fianna Fáil Publicity Department, 25 July 1927, published in the *Nation*, 30 July 1927, p. 5.

127. The Labour Party and the National League were non-government parties that had taken their seats in the Dáil.

128. Minutes of Parliamentary Party, 26 July 1927 (Fianna Fáil Archives, FF/437). On the motion of Seán French, seconded by Seán Lemass, the party consented to the action taken by de Valera, who was authorised to sign the document on behalf of the party.

129. Minutes of Parliamentary Party, 26 July 1927 (Fianna Fáil Archives, FF/437).

130. Coogan, *De Valera*, p. 403.

131. Clarke, *Revolutionary Woman*, p. 211.

132. Minutes of Parliamentary Party, 5 August 1927 (Fianna Fáil Archives, FF/437).

133. Minutes of Parliamentary Party, 5 August 1927 (Fianna Fáil Archives, FF/437).

134. Clarke, *Revolutionary Woman*, p. 211.

135. Minutes of Parliamentary Party, 5 August 1927 (Fianna Fáil Archives, FF/437).

136. Minutes of Parliamentary Party, 5 August 1927 (Fianna Fáil Archives, FF/437).

137. Longford and O'Neill, *Éamon de Valera*, p. 254.

138. Official declaration, 10 August 1927, published in the *Nation*, 20 August 1927, p. 1.

139. The National League was established in 1926 by the veteran MPs William Redmond and Thomas O'Donnell as a pro-Treaty party and attracted the votes of many former Irish Party supporters. Eight members were elected in the June 1927 election, but as a result of defections and poor finances this number fell to two in the September election. The party dissolved in 1931, with most of its supporters, including Redmond, drifting into Cumann na nGaedheal, though O'Donnell joined Fianna Fáil. See J. Anthony Gaughan, *A Political Odyssey: Thomas O'Donnell MP* (Dublin: Kingdom Books, 1983).

140. Minutes of Parliamentary Party, 11 August 1927.

141. Longford and O'Neill, *Éamon de Valera*, p. 256.

142. As he left Leinster House de Valera declared that he would one day burn the book he had just signed. The account is taken from Longford and O'Neill, *Éamon de Valera*, p. 256, Coogan, *De Valera*, p. 405, and Dwyer, *De Valera*, p. 147. See also *Parliamentary Debates: Dáil Éireann: Official Report*, 41/1102 (20 April 1932), where de Valera gave a brief synopsis of his experience that day as he introduced a bill to abolish the oath.

143. Minutes of Parliamentary Party, 12 August 1927. Seventh Meeting of the Fianna Fáil Party (Fianna Fáil Archives, FF/437).

144. *Parliamentary Debates: Dáil Éireann: Official Report*, 20/1644–6 (12 August 1927).

145. Minutes of Parliamentary Party, 13 August 1927. Eighth Meeting of the Fianna Fáil Party (Fianna Fáil Archives, FF/437).

146. *Irish Independent*, 12 August 1927, p. 7.

147. For a detailed account of the Jinks episode, its context and consequences see Arthur Mitchell, 'The government that never was,' *Capuchin Annual, 1969*, p. 55–60. For a brief profile of Jinks see Vincent Browne, *The Magill Book of Irish Politics*, p. 309. Jinks later made it clear that he had stayed away because of his objections to de Valera, though rumours circulated at the time that he had been detained. See *Irish Independent*, 12 August 1927, p. 7, and *Irish Times*, 20 August 1927, p. 8.

148. *Parliamentary Debates: Dáil Éireann: Official Report*, 20/1747–50 (16 August 1927).

149. Constitution of Fianna Fáil, p. 8 (Fianna Fáil Archives, FF/26).

150. *Nation*, 13 August 1927, p. 3.

151. *Nation*, 13 August 1927, p. 3.

152. *Nation*, 20 August 1927, p. 4.

153. *Nation*, 10 September 1927, p. 6.

154. Quoted in the *Nation*, 3 September 1927, p. 2.

155. *Nation*, 3 September 1927, p. 2. It is of course possible that 'Sacerdos' was simply a pseudonym of Diarmuid Ó Cruadhlaoich.

156. *Nation*, 24 September 1927, p. 5.

157. Text of the cable issued by the party's publicity department on 21 August and published by the *Nation*, 27 August 1927, p. 8. On 4 September, Archbishop Mannix made his authoritative contribution to the oath controversy. See the *Nation*, 17 September 1927, p. 4–5. (This issue of the paper is incorrectly dated 10 September.) At a time when clerical support for Fianna Fáil was in short supply, Mannix's support was gratefully received and was given pride of place in much of the party's election literature. See one-page advertisement in the *Irish Independent*, 10 September 1927, p. 5.

158. *Nation,* 27 August 1927, p. 8.
159. Foremost among these was the American Association for the Recognition of the Irish Republic, whose national secretary, W. P. (Patrick) Lyndon, cabled de Valera stating that members of the organisation 'generally express their confidence in you and assure you of their support' (*Nation,* 27 August 1927, p. 8).
160. Letter dated 29 August 1927 (Fianna Fáil Archives, FF/26).
161. *Irish Independent,* 21 July 1927, p. 7.
162. Letter to de Valera, 16 August 1927, sent from France (Fianna Fáil Archives, FF/26).
163. Minutes of Parliamentary Party, 5 August 1927.
164. Resolution No. 2. Report of the Second Ard-Fheis of Fianna Fáil (Fianna Fáil Archives, FF/701).
165. Bowman, *De Valera and the Ulster Question,* p. 97.

Chapter 4: Fianna Fáil and the Irish Free State, 1927–31 (p. 70–102)

1. For a detailed account of the circumstances of his assassination see the *Irish Independent,* 11 July 1927, p. 7–8.
2. See de Vere White, *Kevin O'Higgins,* passim.
3. Contrary to common belief, O'Higgins had not initiated the policy of executing prisoners but in fact was the last, bar one, within the government to assent. As he was Minister for Justice, however, he was considered the chief architect of the policy, which he ardently defended in public.
4. Speech by W. T. Cosgrave, *Parliamentary Debates: Dáil Éireann: Official Report,* 20/757 (12 July 1927).
5. Speech by W. T. Cosgrave, *Parliamentary Debates: Dáil Éireann: Official Report,* 20/757 (12 July 1927).
6. Senator McLaughlin, *Parliamentary Debates: Seanad Éireann: Official Report,* (9 August 1927); quoted also in *Irish Independent,* 10 August 1927, p. 8.
7. *Irish Independent,* 21 July 1927, p. 5.
8. *Nation,* 23 July 1927, p. 1.
9. *Nation,* 16 July 1927, p. 1.
10. *Nation,* 16 July 1927, p. 5.
11. Coogan, *De Valera,* p. 401.
12. For a profile of Timothy Coughlan see *An Phoblacht,* 8 February 1930, p. 3. The other two assassins were Archie Doyle and Bill Gannon. The responsibility of the trio for O'Higgins's death was revealed only in 1985 by Harry White in *Harry,* p. 106, n. 1. At least one Fianna Fáil cumann (in Inchicore, Dublin) is named after Tim Coughlan— though a member of the cumann for forty years with whom the author spoke did not know who Coughlan was.
13. Briscoe, *For the Life of Me,* p. 234.
14. Briscoe, *For the Life of Me,* p. 234.
15. Part II, section 4.1.
16. Section 4.5.
17. Section 4.6.
18. Section 4.1 (*d*).
19. Sections 9–10.
20. Section 4.1 (*f*).
21. *Parliamentary Debates: Dáil Éireann: Official Report,* 20/825–6 (27 July 1927).

22. *Parliamentary Debates: Dáil Éireann: Official Report*, 20/826–37 (27 July 1927).

23. *Parliamentary Debates: Dáil Éireann: Official Report*, 20/839 (27 July 1927).

24. *Parliamentary Debates: Dáil Éireann: Official Report*, 20/1012 (27 July 1927).

25. Deputy Gorey (Cumann na nGaedheal), *Parliamentary Debates: Dáil Éireann: Official Report*, 20/1034 (28 July 1927).

26. *Irish Independent*, 10 August 1927, p. 8.

27. Michael Gallagher, *Irish Elections*, p. 113.

28. Conor Brady, *Guardians of the Peace*, p. 69.

29. Conor Brady, *Guardians of the Peace*, p. 82–3. This was to have important implications for the future development of the force, for, as Brady argues, 'if the Republicans had gunned down the first pioneers, unarmed and defenceless, in cold blood . . . the ideal of the unarmed Guard would not have survived very long.'

30. Conor Brady, *Guardians of the Peace*, p. 44–8.

31. Conor Brady, *Guardians of the Peace*, p. 44.

32. Regan, *The Irish Counter-Revolution*, p. 124.

33. 'The Free State's squint-eyed justice' (editorial), *Nation*, 27 April 1929, p. 4.

34. 'The Free State's squint-eyed justice' (editorial), *Nation*, 27 April 1929, p. 4.

35. Quoted in the *Nation*, 17 November 1928, p. 4.

36. 'The successors of the RIC' (editorial), *Nation*, 17 November 1928, p. 4.

37. 'The successor of Hamar Greenwood,' *Nation*, 7 July 1928, p. 1. Edward Shortt (1862–1935) was Chief Secretary for Ireland between 1918 and 1919; he failed to introduce conscription and to stem the rise of Sinn Féin. Sir Hamar Greenwood, first Viscount Greenwood of Holbourne (1870–1948), was the last Chief Secretary, occupying that position and a seat in the British Cabinet between 1920 and 1922. Greenwood attracted much of the blame for the excesses of British forces during the War of Independence.

38. Clár [agenda] of 1929 Ard-Fheis, motion no. 9 (Fianna Fáil Archives, FF/703).

39. *Nation*, 2 November 1929, p. 4.

40. *Nation*, 2 November 1929, p. 4.

41. Clár of 1929 Ard-Fheis, motion no. 25 (Fianna Fáil Archives, FF/703).

42. *Nation*, 8 November 1930, p. 6. Earlier in the day the ard-fheis considered two motions that condemned the alleged inactivity of Fianna Fáil regarding the plight of IRA prisoners and the party's refusal to countenance the wholesale dismissal of the Garda Síochána when Fianna Fáil would come to power. The party leadership questioned the authenticity of these motions.

43. Briscoe, *For the Life of Me*, p. 240.

44. *Parliamentary Debates: Dáil Éireann: Official Report*, 29/2225 (16 May 1929).

45. Briscoe, *For the Life of Me*, p. 240.

46. Report of the Commissioner, Garda Síochána, for period 1 January to 5 May 1931 (National Archives, D/T S5864B).

47. Briscoe, *For the Life of Me*, p. 228.

48. This decline in the public presence of the army can probably be attributed to a desire not to give belligerent status to the IRA. Entrusting the main anti-IRA measures to the police would complement attempts (ultimately unsuccessful) at implementing a criminalisation policy within the prisons.

49. 'The Free State army debate,' 3 November 1928, p. 1.

50. Speaking on second reading of the Defence Forces (Temporary Provisions) Bill.

Parliamentary Debates: Dáil Éireann: Official Report, 18/399 (8 February 1927).

51. *Fianna Fáil Weekly News Bulletin*, no. 7, 15 February 1927, p. 2. See also 'Britain the greatest danger' (editorial), *Nation*, 18 August 1928, p. 4.

52. Fianna Fáil refused to accept this and maintained that 'more is intended than merely to make "croppies lie down"' ('Ireland's place in the next war,' *Nation*, 3 November 1928, p. 1). The party therefore asked the government why the cost of the Free State army should not be considered an imperial charge. Deputy Kerlin, *Parliamentary Debates: Dáil Éireann: Official Report*, 26/977–8 (25 October 1928).

53. See contributions of Gerry Boland, *Parliamentary Debates: Dáil Éireann: Official Report*, 32/1035–7 (7 November 1929), and Seán Lemass, 33/1958–9 (14 March 1930).

54. *Parliamentary Debates: Dáil Éireann: Official Report*, 32/2193–4 (4 December 1929).

55. These details received extensive coverage in the *Nation* throughout 1929, coinciding with an attempt by Fianna Fáil in November to force the government to get the Comptroller and Auditor-General to examine the *bona fides* of all pension beneficiaries.

56. Carol Coulter, *Ireland: Beteen the First and Third World* (Dublin: Attic Press, 1990), p. 8.

57. Indeed the Dáil Supreme Court had declared the Treaty to be unconstitutional.

58. V. T. H. Delany, *The Administration of Justice in Ireland*, fourth edition (Dublin: Institute of Public Administration, 1975), p. 37.

59. See Kotsonouris, *Retreat from Revolution*, p. 131.

60. Gerard Hogan, 'Irish nationalism as a legal ideology,' *Studies*, 75/300, Winter 1986.

61. George Gavan Duffy and Hugh Kennedy being two significant, if lonely, examples.

62. Quoted by Gerard Hogan, 'Irish nationalism as a legal ideology,' *Studies*, 75/300, winter 1986, p. 530. The judgement was made in 1934.

63. Fanning, *Independent Ireland*, p. 67.

64. See *An Phoblacht*, 30 October 1925, p. 3.

65. In comparing the role of the British-controlled judiciary during the war of 1919–21 and that of the subsequent judiciaries in the Irish Free State and Northern Ireland, Colm Campbell (*Emergency Law in Ireland, 1918–1925*, Oxford: Clarendon Press, 1994, p. 350) notes that 'the attitude of the judiciary towards emergency powers were remarkably similar in all three.

66. A rare note of humour can be found in the case of a youth who declared defiantly that he refused to recognise the court. 'The court will recognise you,' Judge Gleeson angrily replied (*An Phoblacht*, 27 July 1929, p. 1).

67. Quoted in the *Nation*, 18 February 1929, p. 4.

68. *Nation*, 18 February 1928, p. 4–5. The article was written under the pseudonym Fear Dlighe ('Man of the Law').

69. *Saorstat Éireann High Court of Justice: Attorney-General v. Seán T. Ó Ceallaigh*. Sworn affidavit dated 19 March 1928 and submitted on behalf of Seán T. Ó Ceallaigh by Messers Ruttledge and Corr, Solicitors, para. 3.

70. *Saorstat Éireann High Court of Justice: Attorney-General v. Seán T. Ó Ceallaigh*. Sworn affidavit dated 19 March 1928 and submitted on behalf of Seán T. Ó Ceallaigh by Messers Ruttledge and Corr, Solicitors, para. 4.

71. *Saorstat Éireann High Court of Justice: Attorney-General v. Seán T. Ó Ceallaigh*. Sworn affidavit dated 19 March 1928 and submitted on behalf of Seán T. Ó Ceallaigh by Messers Ruttledge and Corr, Solicitors, para. 6–8.

72. *Saorstat Éireann High Court of Justice: Attorney-General v. Seán T. Ó Ceallaigh*. Sworn

affidavit dated 19 March 1928 and submitted on behalf of Seán T. Ó Ceallaigh by Messers Ruttledge and Corr, Solicitors, para. 11–12, 16.

73. *Nation*, 24 March 1928, p. 1, 4.

74. Quoted in the *Nation*, 28 April 1928, p. 2.

75. *Fianna Fáil Weekly News Bulletin*, no. 7, 15 February 1927, p. 2.

76. 'To Irish Citizens—Break the Connection with the British Empire.' Leaflet headed 'Ghosts,' n.d. [1929].

77. He was Albert Armstrong, who was shot by armed men at the rear of his home in Kilmainham, Dublin, on 20 February 1929. Department of Justice report, August 1931, p. 11 (National Archives, D/T S5864B).

78. The deputy was Robert Briscoe. He was not suspected of being involved in the killing but was questioned in relation to people with whom he was associated (National Archives, D/T S5862).

79. Quotations from 'The Jurors Bill,' *Nation*, 18 May 1929, p. 1, and the editorial on p. 4 of the same issue.

80. Thomas Ashe (1885–1917). A member of the influential Keating Branch of the Gaelic League, president of the IRB and a leader of the 1916 Rising. Ashe was the majority favourite to contest the East Clare by-election for Sinn Féin in 1917, but he was reluctant to accept the nomination, because, in his own words, 'a small but solid group is supporting de Valera with great persistence. If I accept I believe it may cause disunity in our ranks.' In August 1917 he was arrested with other republican leaders. He went on hunger strike in protest and on 25 September he died while being forcibly fed. His death had an enormous impact on public opinion and injected renewed momentum into the Sinn Féin movement. His body lay in state for four days in City Hall, Dublin, and Michael Collins delivered his famous one-line oration at his funeral, after Volunteers fired a volley over his grave: 'That volley which we have just heard is the only speech which it is proper to make above the grave of a dead Fenian.' See Brian P. Murphy, *Patrick Pearse and the Lost Republican Ideal*, p. 89–92. Terence MacSwiney (1879–1920) was a founder of the Celtic Literary Society and Cork Dramatic Society and wrote many plays for the latter. A founder-member of the Cork Brigade of the Irish Volunteers and president of Sinn Féin in Cork, he was elected unopposed for Mid-Cork in the 1918 election. Following the killing of Tomás Mac Curtáin by British forces on 20 March 1920 MacSwiney succeeded him as commander of the IRA in Cork and Lord Mayor of the city. After his arrest in August 1920 he was sentenced to two years' imprisonment but immediately went on hunger strike in Brixton Prison, London, and died on 25 October after seventy-four days without food. MacSwiney's famous dictum (taken from his posthumously published *Principles of Freedom*) that 'it is not those who can inflict the most but those who can endure the most that will conquer' is one of the most succinct descriptions of the IRA's philosophy. MacSwiney's sister, Mary MacSwiney (1872–1942), was elected to his Cork seat, voted against the Treaty, and subsequently became one of Fianna Fáil's most ardent republican critics. His brother, Seán MacSwiney, remained in the IRA and was imprisoned by the military tribunal re-established by Fianna Fáil in the 1930s. The actions of both Ashe and MacSwiney quickly became an essential part of the Irish nationalist narrative and have been cited to legitimise the actions of subsequent generations of hunger-strikers. In 1974 the coffin of the IRA hunger-striker Michael Gaughan was draped with the same Tricolour that had been placed on MacSwiney's coffin half a century earlier. See Costello, *Enduring the Most*.

81. 'Release the prisoners' (editorial), *Nation*, 17 December 1927, p. 4.

82. *Nation*, 28 April 1928, p. 1.

83. *Nation*, 14 July 1928, p. 1.

84. Quoted in the *Nation*, 7 July 1928, p. 3.

85. Minutes of Parliamentary Party, 28 February 1928 (Fianna Fáil Archives, FF/438). The four members of the sub-committee were P. J. Ruttledge, Frank Aiken, P. J. Little and Hugo Flinn.

86. Minutes of Parliamentary Party, 28 February 1928 (Fianna Fáil Archives, FF/438). The other three representatives were P. J. Ruttledge, Hugo Flinn and Deputy Kennedy.

87. Minutes of Parliamentary Party, 17 May 1928. The decision regarding representation on visiting committees was passed by thirty votes to three, while the second motion, proposed by Martin Corry and seconded by William Kent, was defeated by a similar margin.

88. Minutes of Parliamentary Party, 7 June 1928 (Fianna Fáil Archives, FF/438).

89. Quoted in the *Nation*, 23 June 1928, p. 6. The MacPherson cited is James Ian Macpherson, first Baron Strathcarron (1880–1937), who was Chief Secretary for Ireland, 1919–20. Edward Shortt was his predecessor; Sir Hamar Greenwood was the last Chief Secretary

90. *Nation*, 16 June 1928, p. 1.

91. *Nation*, 15 September 1929, p. 6.

92. *Nation*, 2 June 1928, p. 8.

93. *Nation*, 5 May 1928, p. 8.

94. A small notice appeared every week on p. 8 of the *Nation*.

95. *Nation*, 22 October 1927, p. 8.

96. Tuarascáil [report] of 1928 Ard-Fheis, resolution no. 7 (Fianna Fáil Archives, FF/702).

97. Clár of 1929 Ard-Fheis, resolution no. 18 (Fianna Fáil Archives, FF/703).

98. Clár of 1930 Ard-Fheis, Justice Section, resolution no. 13 (Fianna Fáil Archives, FF/704).

99. Edmonds, *The Gun, the Law, and the Irish People*, p. 141.

100. Nelligan's account of Harling and the events that led to Coughlan's death can be found in Griffith and O'Grady, *Curious Journey*, p. 338–9.

101. *Nation*, 17 March 1928, p. 8.

102. Quoted by White, *Harry*, p. 106n.

103. *Nation*, 4 February 1928, p. 6. For the record, no inquiry was opened during Fianna Fáil's time in office. Harling was despatched to America by the Free State government and stayed there for some months before returning to take up a position in the Revenue Commissioners. He retired in 1966.

104. Minutes of Parliamentary Party, 13 February 1928. See also minutes for 14 February meeting (Fianna Fáil Archives, FF/438).

105. *Nation*, 4 February 1928, p. 6.

106. *Irish Times*, 23 April 1928, p. 7.

107. *Nation*, 28 April 1928, p. 1.

108. *An Phoblacht*, 9 November 1929, p. 3.

109. *An Phoblacht*, 2 November 1929, p. 4.

110. '1916—How do we stand today?' *Nation*, 7 April 1928, p. 4.

111. These were De Valera (president), P. J. Ruttledge and Seán T. O'Kelly (vice-presidents), Dr James Ryan and Seán MacEntee (honorary treasurers), Seán Lemass and Gerry Boland (honorary secretaries).

112. *Nation*, 28 January 1928, p. 3.

113. 'We honour the Fenians,' *Nation*, 25 August 1928, p. 4.

114. Some individual Fenians did successfully contest elections, but in general the IRB treated constitutional politics with suspicion.

115. *Nation*, 9 June 1928, p. 7.

116. *Nation*, 28 January 1928, p. 6.

117. *Nation*, 14 April 1928, p. 4.

118. 'Wolfe Tone and ourselves,' *Nation*, 23 June 1928, p. 4.

119. 'Parliament and the people,' *An Phoblacht*, 27 July 1929, p. 4.

120. See *An Phoblacht*, 22 June 1929, p. 1, 3; 29 June, p. 1, 3; 13 July, p. 1, 3; 20 July, p. 1; 27 July, p. 1; also *Nation*, 4 May 1929, p. 3; 27 July, p. 4–5; 10 August, p. 4; 17 August, p. 5.

121. *An Phoblacht*, 10 August 1929, p. 3.

122. 'An Phoblacht's strange attitude,' *Nation*, 3 August 1929, p. 2. The word 'speedy' is of significance here, as is the use of the statistic of 75 per cent of the electorate: it implies that the remaining 25 per cent who voted for Fianna Fáil would countenance a swift resort to armed revolt.

123. 'Parliamentarians and physical force: Candid criticisms of policies,' *An Phoblacht*, 10 August 1929, p. 3–4; 'An Phoblacht's strange attitude: A Criticism and a reply,' *Nation*, 10 August 1929, p. 7.

124. Quoted in the *Nation*, 17 August 1929, p. 2.

125. Approved resolution no. 9, Fianna Fáil Ard-Fheis, 25–6 October 1928 (Fianna Fáil Archives, FF/702).

126. Sales of *An Phoblacht* reached a peak of forty thousand. The temporary suppression of the paper in 1929 interfered with production. However, in a letter to Joe McGarrity in 1929 Frank Ryan stated that it sold an average of eight thousand copies a week, compared with six thousand of the *Nation*; quoted by Cronin, *The McGarrity Papers*, p. 141. These figures need not be taken at face value, considering their source, but the one major academic study of Fianna Fáil (Dunphy, *The Making of Fianna Fáil Power*, p. 138) does not question them.

127. 'Force as a means towards Irish freedom,' *Nation*, 14 January 1928, p. 2.

128. 'Force as a means towards Irish freedom,' *Nation*, 14 January 1928, p. 2.

129. Minutes of Parliamentary Party, 7 October 1927 to 17 December 1931 (Fianna Fáil Archives, FF/438, passim).

130. See, for example, Minutes of Parliamentary Party, 14 February 1928, 27 March 1928, 18 May 1928, 15 November 1928, 20 February 1929, 28 November 1929.

131. 'First things first' (editorial), *Nation*, 13 July 1929, p. 4.

132. 'The Free State's squint-eyed justice' (editorial), *Nation*, 27 April 1929, p. 4.

133. *Nation*, 13 July 1929, p. 4.

134. 'Wrongs of Northern minority,' *Nation*, 20 October 1928, p. 7.

135. For a sample of these party resolutions and local government motions see the *Nation*, 23 February 1929, p. 7, 2 March 1929, p. 3, and 9 March 1929, p. 6. See also National Archives, D/T S2278.

136. Resolution passed unanimously on 20 February 1929. Copies of the resolution were sent to the Dublin and Belfast governments on 23 February (National Archives, D/T S2278).

137. Resolution passed unanimously on 13 February 1929. Copies of the resolution were sent to Cosgrave and Craigavon on 21 February (National Archives, D/T S2278).

138. Cable from Rev. M. D. Collins (in the United States) to de Valera (Belfast Jail), 1 February 1929 (Fianna Fáil Archives, FF/26).

139. De Valera to Rev. M. D. Collins, 9 March 1929 (Fianna Fáil Archives, FF/26).

140. *Irish World*, 22 March 1930, quoted by Bowman, *De Valera and the Ulster Question*, p. 104.

141. *Nation*, 16 February 1929, p. 4.

142. *Nation*, 23 February 1929, p. 2.

143. *Nation*, 2 March 1929, p. 1.

144. The meeting, which was addressed from two platforms, was presided over by P. T. MacGinley and the Fianna Fáil TD Robert Briscoe and addressed by several high-ranking party leaders. McGinley was announced by his well-known pseudonym Cú Uladh ('Hound of Ulster'), a name that echoed the mythic deeds of Cú Chulainn.

145. Seán Lemass described partition as 'the greatest wrong ever perpetrated by Britain against the Irish people' and stressed that it was up to Fianna Fáil to ensure that the question 'did not recede into the shadows' (*Nation*, 23 February 1929, p. 7).

146. *Nation*, 23 February 1929, p. 2.

147. *Nation*, 23 February 1929, p. 2.

148. Rule 2 (Fianna Fáil Archives, FF/22).

149. *Irish Independent*, 25 November 1926, p. 7.

150. *Irish Times*, 26 November 1926, p. 9.

151. Report of the Honorary Secretaries (1 October 1928), 1928 Ard-Fheis, 25–26 October (Fianna Fáil Archives, FF/702).

152. Report of 1928 Ard-Fheis. *Nation*, 3 November 1928, p. 2.

153. Report of the Honorary Secretaries, 1929 Ard-Fheis (Fianna Fáil Archives, FF/703).

154. Report of the Honorary Secretaries, 1929 Ard-Fheis (Fianna Fáil Archives, FF/703).

155. Michael Farrell, *Northern Ireland*, p. 113–16. Nationalists took three seats in Co. Tyrone, two each in Belfast, Derry and Down and one each in South Armagh and South Fermanagh. While the abolition of PR was disadvantageous from a nationalist viewpoint, and had wiped out nationalist control of local councils, the primary target in the 1929 Stormont elections was rival Unionist and Labour parties and individuals, which, Craig believed, blurred the lines between unionist and nationalist candidates.

156. Report of the Honorary Secretaries, 1929 Ard-Fheis (Fianna Fáil Archives, FF/703).

157. Report of the Honorary Secretaries, 1929 Ard-Fheis (Fianna Fáil Archives, FF/703).

158. Tuarascáil, 1928 Ard-Fheis. Motions referred to National Executive and approved, no. 50 (Fianna Fáil Archives, FF/702).

159. Report of Honorary Treasurers, 1929 Ard-Fheis (Fianna Fáil Archives, FF/703).

160. Report of Honorary Secretaries, 1929 Ard-Fheis (Fianna Fáil Archives, FF/703). See also the *Nation*, 10 October 1929, p. 7.

161. Report of Honorary Secretaries, 1929 Ard-Fheis (Fianna Fáil Archives, FF/703).

162. *Nation*, 7 September 1929, p. 7.

163. *Parliamentary Debates: Dáil Éireann: Official Report*, 22/1615–16 (21 March 1928).

164. Interview by Pat Kenny on 'Kenny Live', RTE 1, 1994. The programme was in part an appreciation of the life of Lemass and coincided with the publication by Michael O'Sullivan of *Seán Lemass: A Biography*.

165. *Parliamentary Debates: Dáil Éireann: Official Report*, 28/1400 (14 March 1929).

166. *Nation*, 23 March 1929, p. 4.

167. Clár of 1929 Ard-Fheis. Resolution no. 23 (Fianna Fáil Archives, FF/703).
168. *Nation,* 26 October 1929, p. 7.
169. Andrews, *Man of No Property,* p. 119.
170. 'Independence,' *Nation,* 24 March 1928, p. 1.
171. 'Purging Ireland of crime' (editorial), *Nation,* 23 March 1929, p. 4.
172. 'Politics and parliament' (editorial), *Nation,* 7 September 1929, p. 4.
173. Seán T. O'Kelly, quoted in the *Nation,* 25 February 1928, p. 4.
174. Fianna Fáil publicity handbill for June 1927 election (Fianna Fáil Archives, FF/787).
175. Fianna Fáil election handbill for Dr Con Lucey, September 1927 (Fianna Fáil Archives, FF/787).
176. Statement on the candidacy of Oscar Traynor for North Dublin by-election in March 1929 (*Nation,* 2 March 1929, p. 1).
177. These statements were made during the Kildare by-election campaign of June 1931; quoted in the *Nation,* 27 June 1931, p. 5.
178. *Nation,* 4 July 1931, p. 1.
179. 'Politics and parliament,' *Nation,* 7 September 1929, p. 4.

Chapter 5: Election time, 1931–2 (p. 103–29)

1. Carroll had been officer commanding C Company, 3rd Battalion, Dublin Brigade. An editorial in *An Phoblacht* (14 February 1931, p. 4) suggestively headed 'Executed by the IRA' noted the past fate of individuals guilty of 'the crime of Judas' but made no reference to Carroll. The killing is referred to in several security reports in the National Archives (D/T S5864B).
2. See *An Phoblacht,* 28 March 1928, p. 1, 8.
3. Quoted by Bell, *The Secret Army,* p. 82.
4. See appendix to Department of Justice Report (August 1931) (National Archives, D/T S5864B).
5. Bell, *The Secret Army,* p. 83.
6. *Nation,* 28 March 1931, p. 4. According to the paper, the *Irish Independent* refused to publish his accusations.
7. *Cork Examiner,* 23 March 1931, p. 7.
8. 'The Tipperary murder,' *Nation,* 28 March 1928, p. 4.
9. *Irish Independent,* 9 February 1931, p. 9.
10. *An Phoblacht,* 14 February 1931, p. 4.
11. *An Phoblacht,* 11 April 1931, p. 1. See also 'The Rising and today: What of its message,' *Nation,* 4 April 1931, p. 4.
12. A Dublin Protestant, educated at Trinity College, Theobald Wolfe Tone (1763–98) was one of the leaders of the Society of United Irishmen, founded in Belfast in 1791 with the object of breaking the connection with England. He solicited French support and helped to organise a rebellion, which was viciously put down during the summer of 1798 with more than thirty thousand deaths. Tone is considered to be the founding father of modern Irish republicanism and is commemorated every year at his grave in Bodenstown, Co. Kildare. See Marianne Elliot, *Wolfe Tone: Prophet of Irish Independence* (New Haven, Conn.: Yale Univeristy Press, 1990).
13. *Nation,* 30 May 1931, p. 8; 6 June 1931, p. 8; 13 June 1931, p. 8; 20 June 1931, p. 8.
14. *Nation,* 20 June 1931, p. 8.
15. *An Phoblacht,* 27 June 1931, p. 4.

16. *An Phoblacht,* 27 June 1931, p. 3. For an account of their trial see, p. 5.

17. *Nation,* 20 June 1931, p. 8.

18. Bell, *The Secret Army,* p. 85.

19. *An Phoblacht,* 27 June 1931, p. 3.

20. *Nation,* 27 June 1931, p. 1.

21. *Nation,* 27 June 1931, p. 1.

22. *Nation,* 27 June 1931, p. 4.

23. 'Mr. Blythe's bogies' (editorial), *Nation,* 13 June 1931, p. 4.

24. 'Kildare,' *Nation,* 13 June 1931, p. 1.

25. '"The Star" again,' *Nation,* 13 June 1931, p. 1.

26. 'As a man who fought under James Connolly, and was wounded in 1916, and who has since remained steadfast to the cause of nationality and independence, he can be depended on to uphold the national interest' (*Nation,* 27 June 1931, p. 1).

27. For Fianna Fáil support for Peadar O'Donnell's land annuities campaign see the *Nation,* 13 June 1931, p. 8, and 20 June 1931, p. 1.

28. *Nation,* 4 July 1931, p. 1.

29. James Meenan, *The Irish Economy since 1922* (Liverpool: Liverpool University Press, 1970), p. 208.

30. See Garvin, *The Evolution of Irish Nationalism,* p. 110.

31. See chap. 1, n. 24.

32. See, for example, Maurice Moore, *British Plunder and Irish Blunder* (Dublin: Gaelic Press, [c. 1929]).

33. McInerney, *Peadar O'Donnell,* p. 127–8.

34. Quoted by Mac Eoin, *Survivors,* p. 33.

35. Honorary Secretaries' Report, 1929 Ard-Fheis (Fianna Fáil Archives, FF/703). See also the *Nation,* 19 October 1929, p. 7.

36. M. A. G. Ó Tuathaigh, 'The land question, politics and Irish society, 1922–1960,' in J. Drudy, *Ireland: Land, Politics and People,* p. 175.

37. Rumpf and Hepburn, *Nationalism and Socialism in Twentieth-Century Ireland,* p. 107.

38. Bew et al., *The Dynamics of Irish Politics,* p. 46.

39. Ryan also represented the IRA with Peadar O'Donnell at the World Congress of the Anti-Imperialist League, held in Brussels in 1927. Two years later Seán MacBride and Dónal O'Donaghue attended the congress in Frankfurt. In 1930 Peadar O'Donnell formally opened the European Congress of Peasants and Working Farmers in Berlin. See Cronin, *Frank Ryan,* p. 24; Coogan, *The IRA* (second edition), p. 94; Jordan, *Seán MacBride,* p. 51; *An Phoblacht,* 5 April 1930, p. 1, and 12 April 1930, p. 5.

40. See memorandum by Patrick McCartan on mission to Russia and on draft Russo-Irish Treaty, May 1920, No. 33 (National Archives, D/FA ES, box 32, file 228), and Memorandum by Patrick McCartan on hopes of recognition of the Irish Republic by Soviet Russia, June 1921, No. 88 (National Archives, D/FA ES, box 32, file 228).

41. Bell, *The Secret Army,* p. 65.

42. Cronin, *Frank Ryan,* p. 28.

43. See Cosgrave's report to his private secretary, 6 September 1930, of his meeting with William O'Brien, a prominent figure in the labour movement, who put the proposal to the President of the Executive Council (National Archives, D/T S2430).

44. 'Department of Justice Report on the present position [August 1931] as regards the activities of unlawful and dangerous associations in the Saorstát with a summary of

similar activities in recent years' (National Archives, D/T S5864B).

45. Section 1, p. 1.

46. Section 1, p. 2.

47. Section 1, p. 2.

48. Section 1, p. 2.

49. Section 10, p. 9. This point is reiterated in section 9, p. 7, which states: 'The policy of the Government . . . has been, throughout, to be as lenient and patient as possible, to avoid provoking further violence, and to hope that public opinion, and religious influence would bring the offenders to a realisation of the criminal and futile nature of their campaign.'

50. Section 2, p. 3–4.

51. Section 7, p. 6.

52. Section 6, p. 6.

53. Section 5, p. 5.

54. See section 9, p. 9.

55. Section 7, p. 6–7.

56. The congress was advertised in *An Phoblacht* (26 September 1931, p. 1) and the *Irish Press* (24 September 1931, p. 6), both of which stated that the conference would begin in the Peacock Theatre on Saturday at 7:30 p.m. and continue the following day in the Abbey Theatre. According to the *Irish Times* (28 September 1931, p. 10), the organisers were informed by the theatres, hours before the congress was due to start, that they were revoking permission, as they 'did not wish to be involved in any political organisation.' The government had forced the proprietor of the Peacock, Lennox Robinson, to reverse his original decision, linking the act with government approval for continued subsidies and a renewed patent. See National Archives, D/T S6194.

57. The members of Saor Éire's National Executive were May Laverty (Belfast), Seán McGuinness (Mountjoy Prison; substitute: Fionan Walsh, Kerry), Seán Hayes (Clare), Helena Moloney, Peadar O'Donnell, Sheila Dowling, Seán MacBride, David Fitzgerald, Sheila Humphries, Michael Price, D. McGinley (Dublin), M. Hallisey (Kerry), M. O'Donnell (Offaly), P. McCormack (Antrim), T. Kenny (Galway), L. Brady (Laois), N. Boran (Kilkenny), J. Mulgrew (Mayo), and T. Maguire (Westmeath). See *An Phoblacht*, 3 October, p. 1.

58. *An Phoblacht*, 26 September 1931, p. 1.

59. See *An Phoblacht*, 3 October 1931, p. 5–7.

60. *Irish Independent*, 5 October 1931, p. 9. *An Phoblacht* reported that the deputies had been asked 'politely but firmly' by their constituents whether they intended voting for the proposed bill (*An Phoblacht*, 10 October 1931, p. 1). A similar attitude was taken by one Fianna Fáil representative, who said during a session of Galway County Council that 'those who visited deputies and senators were not trying to intimidate them, but merely to find out their opinion' (*Irish Independent*, 12 October 1931, p. 7). It is difficult to test the veracity of these conflicting claims. It is likely that some deputies were treated in an intimidatory manner. However, the example given by the Longford-Westmeath deputy M. P. Connolly of being 'accosted' by a man in the main street in Longford suggests that some deputies, at least, drew a thin line between irate constituents confronting their local representative and 'organised intimidation' by 'subversives.' See *Irish Independent*, 7 October 1931, p. 9.

61. *Irish Independent*, 7 October 1931, p. 9. One government source said that 'a challenge

has been thrown down to the people of the country. When Deputies and Senators are intimidated it means that the country is being intimidated, and that the writ of the constituted Government runs only so far as an unlawful organisation is willing to permit it to operate. The Government will not stand for that, and the attempt to intimidate members of the Legislature will guarantee the passage of the bill' (*Irish Independent*, 8 October 1931, p. 9).

62. This order was implemented regardless of the sentiments of individual TDs. When the independent Cavan deputy J. F. O'Hanlon found a body of gardaí at his home, sent to protect him, he asked them to leave, only to be told that this was not possible. After telegraphing Dublin requesting that the men be taken off at once he was informed that they 'could not be withdrawn at present' (*Irish Independent*, 10 October 1931, p. 9).

63. *Irish Independent*, 8 October 1931, p. 9, 10 October 1931, p. 9.

64. *An Phoblacht*, 17 October 1931, p. 1.

65. Among the public bodies that issued protests against the bill were Kerry County Council, Sligo Corporation [Town Council], Westmeath County Council, Limerick Corporation, Limerick Board of Health, Clare Board of Health, Galway County Council, Cavan County Council, Laois County Board of Health, Meath County Council, Youghal Urban District Council, Westmeath Board of Health, Kilkenny Corporation, Tuam Town Commissioners, Offaly County Council, Athy Urban District Council, Nenagh Urban District Council, Carlow Urban District Council, Mountmellick Town Commissioners, Leitrim County Council. See National Archives, D/T S2266; *Irish Times*, 12 October 1931, p. 8; *Cork Examiner*, 10 October 1931, p. 12.

66. *Irish Independent*, 7 October 1931, p. 9.

67. Speaking at Baltinglass, Co. Wicklow (*Irish Independent*, 14 October 1931, p. 10).

68. B. M. Egan TD (Cumann na nGaedheal), speaking at a party meeting at Ballincollig, Co. Cork (*Irish Independent*, 12 October 1931, p. 10).

69. Constitution (Amendment No. 17) Act (1931), part II, section 4.1. The five appointees were Col. Francis Bennett, Col. Daniel McKenna, Maj. John V. Joyce, Comdt Conor Whealan, Comdt Patrick Tuite. Cabinet Minutes, 20 October 1931, item 1 (National Archives, C.5/95).

70. Sections 4.2 and 5.1.

71. Section 7.1.

72. Section 6.5. It is curious that no-one at the time commented on the fact that technically this was untrue, as there existed a provision in the Constitution of the Irish Free State for appeals to the Privy Council. This may be due to hostility towards the judicial body from both sides. The government viewed the Privy Council as a superfluous irritant and had a vested interest in not drawing attention to this avenue of redress, as it could impede the work of the tribunal, while republicans may have omitted reference as it would have posed ideological dilemmas.

73. Section 7.5.

74. Section 8.1–8.3.

75. Report of Commissioner, Garda Síochána, for period 1 January to 5 May 1931 (National Archives, D/T S5864B).

76. Despite the fact that the list had been drawn up well in advance, the official authorisation for proscribing these organisations was decided by the government on 20 October. Cabinet Minutes, 20 October 1931, item 1 (National Archives, C.5/95). The

ubiquitous Peadar O'Donnell now had the distinction of being a member not merely of one illegal organisation but of more than half a dozen.

77. Department of Justice Report (National Archives, D/T S5864 B).

78. *Parliamentary Debates: Dáil Éireann: Official Report*, 40/32–3 (14 October 1931).

79. *Parliamentary Debates: Dáil Éireann: Official Report*, 40/232 (15 October 1931).

80. *Parliamentary Debates: Dáil Éireann: Official Report*, 40/37 (14 October 1931).

81. *Parliamentary Debates: Dáil Éireann: Official Report*, 40/37 (14 October 1931). Later, Cosgrave quoted a recently distributed pamphlet issued by the Publicity Department of Cumann na mBan that declared: 'Arming and drilling of Ireland's faithful soldiers of the Irish Republican Army is taking place all over Ireland. And in spite of the special Juries Acts passed recently by the Irish Free State Government no jury can be got to convict Irish patriots.' This pamphlet, entitled *To Foreigners Visiting Our Country*, was published in August 1931; there is a copy in the National Archives (D/T 5864A). The quotation used by Cosgrave is from p. 4. He responded by saying that 'no Government, and no self-respecting nation, can allow itself thus to become enslaved by the terrorist actions of a small minority' (cols. 42–3).

82. *Parliamentary Debates: Dáil Éireann: Official Report*, 40/41 (14 October 1931).

83. *Parliamentary Debates: Dáil Éireann: Official Report*, 40/37 (14 October 1931).

84. *Parliamentary Debates: Dáil Éireann: Official Report*, 40/57 (14 October 1931).

85. *Parliamentary Debates: Dáil Éireann: Official Report*, 40/39 (14 October 1931).

86. 'I do not believe that the IRA is a secret organisation,' de Valera declared, before claiming that the people had more to fear from the government than from the IRA. *Parliamentary Debates: Dáil Éireann: Official Report*, 40/57 (14 October 1931).

87. Deputy Tommy Mullins, *Parliamentary Debates: Dáil Éireann: Official Report*, 40/130–31 (14 October 1931).

88. *Parliamentary Debates: Dáil Éireann: Official Report*, 40/52–3, 56 (14 October 1931).

89. *Parliamentary Debates: Dáil Éireann: Official Report*, 40/54 (14 October 1931).

90. *Parliamentary Debates: Dáil Éireann: Official Report*, 40/55 (14 October 1931).

91. *Parliamentary Debates: Dáil Éireann: Official Report*, 40/55 (14 October 1931).

92. *Parliamentary Debates: Dáil Éireann: Official Report*, 40/56 (14 October 1931).

93. *Parliamentary Debates: Dáil Éireann: Official Report*, 40/98 (14 October 1931).

94. William Redmond, *Parliamentary Debates: Dáil Éireann: Official Report*, 40/123 (14 October 1931). See also Richard Mulcahy, 40/143 (14 October 1931).

95. *Parliamentary Debates: Dáil Éireann: Official Report*, 40/133(14 October 1931).

96. *Parliamentary Debates: Dáil Éireann: Official Report*, 40/125–6 (14 October 1931).

97. *Parliamentary Debates: Dáil Éireann: Official Report*, 40/130 (14 October 1931).

98. *Parliamentary Debates: Dáil Éireann: Official Report*, 40/138–9 (14 October 1931).

99. *Parliamentary Debates: Dáil Éireann: Official Report*, 40/298 (15 October 1931).

100. *Parliamentary Debates: Dáil Éireann: Official Report*, 40/289 (15 October 1931). Dark Rosaleen (from the Irish *Róisín Dubh*) was one of several common metaphors for Ireland used in nationalist prose and poetry. Its origins were in the time of the Penal Laws, when it was impossible to publish overtly patriotic verse, so this was often disguised as love songs or poems in which the hero struggled to save his 'Dark Rosaleen'.

101. *Parliamentary Debates: Dáil Éireann: Official Report*, 40/291–2 (15 October 1931).

102. *Parliamentary Debates: Dáil Éireann: Official Report*, 40/302 (15 October 1931).

103. *Parliamentary Debates: Dáil Éireann: Official Report*, 40/273 (15 October 1931).

104. Deputy Corry, *Parliamentary Debates: Dáil Éireann: Official Report*, 40/274 (15 October 1931).

105. *Parliamentary Debates: Dáil Éireann: Official Report*, 40/310–11 (15 October 1931).

106. *Parliamentary Debates: Dáil Éireann: Official Report*, 40/308 (15 October 1931).

107. *Parliamentary Debates: Dáil Éireann: Official Report*, 40/216 (15 October 1931).

108. *Parliamentary Debates: Dáil Éireann: Official Report*, 40/217 (15 October 1931).

109. *Parliamentary Debates: Dáil Éireann: Official Report*, 40/217 (15 October 1931).

110. *Parliamentary Debates: Dáil Éireann: Official Report*, 40/56 (14 October 1931).

111. *Parliamentary Debates: Dáil Éireann: Official Report*, 40/289 (15 October 1931).

112. Cabinet Minutes, 17 October 1931, item 1 (National Archives, C.5./94).

113. Cabinet Minutes, 17 October 1931, item 2 (National Archives, C.5./94).

114. Letter from Cosgrave to Cardinal MacRory, 10 September 1931 (National Archives, D/T S5864B). The discussion that took place on 18 August is referred to at the beginning of the letter, though there is no record of the substance of the conversation. It is likely that the conversation took place over the phone. The method and timing of the delivery of the material to Cardinal MacRory is revealed by the Secretary of the Department of External Affairs, J. P. Walshe, in a handwrriten note.

115. National Archives, D/T S5864B. Bishop Fogarty of the Diocese of Killaloe, probably the most vehement anti-republican member of the hierarchy, whose spiritual jurisdiction encompassed most of de Valera's constituency of Co. Clare, was sent a copy of the IRA interview by the *Daily Express* that Cosgrave was to quote in its entirety in the Dáil a month later. *Parliamentary Debates: Dáil Éireann: Official Report*, 40/34–6 (14 October 1931).

116. *Irish Independent*, 19 October 1931, p. 9.

117. Copy of a standard letter sent to all correspondents from the United States to be signed by the private secretary (National Archives, D/T S2267). See also file S4469/17. For the varying effects of the pastoral letter on correspondents it is worth comparing the letters to Cosgrave from P. J. Kilroy (dated 2 December 1931 and 25 January 1932) and Joseph Gallagher (dated 9 November 1931 and 25 January 1932) (National Archives, D/T S2267).

118. Cronin, *Frank Ryan*, p. 36.

119. 'The Coercion Act—our attitude and tasks.' Óglaigh na hÉireann [IRA], GHQ, to the commander of each independent unit (Roinn A/G, Uimhir BB 45), 27 October 1931, (National Archives, D/T S5864C). Subsequent quotations are from the same source unless otherwise stated.

120. The managing director of Fodhla was the War of Independence and Civil War veteran Oscar Traynor, then a senior Fianna Fáil TD and a future minister. Traynor's central role illustrates the connection between the slightly constitutional republican party and the physical-force republican movement.

121. It had also ceased publication in April 1929 for similar reasons.

122. See *Irish Independent*, 26 January 1932, p. 10; 27 January 1932, p. 6; 30 January 1932, p. 11; 5 February 1932, p. 11; 6 February 1932, p. 7; 10 February 1932, p. 11.

123. Óglaigh na hÉireann [IRA], Adjutant General to the commanding officers of each independent unit (Roinn A/C, Uimhir B.B. 47), 12 January 1932 (National Archives, D/T S5864C).

124. Quoted by Fanning, *Independent Ireland*, p. 105.

125. These included the state of the railways (*Irish Independent*, 27 January 1932, p. 6; 29 January, p. 11; 6 February, p. 10; 10 February, p. 7), pay cuts for the Gardaí (*Irish*

Independent, 30 January 1932, p. 11; 8 February, p. 9) and the hostility of the INTO to proposals to prohibit married women from entering the teaching profession (*Irish Independent,* 16 February 1932, p. 6).

126. In the case of Ottawa it was implied that experienced negotiators would be required to secure the best deal possible. This was a common theme in the editorials of the *Irish Independent* (see in particular that of 6 February 1932, p. 8). As regards the Eucharistic Congress, at the time of the Constitution Act it had been mooted that republican-inspired instability could necessitate the cancellation of the event.

127. See, for example, the speech of Fitzgerald-Kenney as reported in the *Irish Independent,* 9 February 1932, p. 7. The Statute of Westminster (1931), passed by the British Parliament in December 1931, established the principle of equality between Britain and other members of the British Commonwealth.

128. Prof. O'Sullivan in Killarney (*Irish Independent,* 1 February 1932, p. 8).

129. Speaking in Limerick (*Irish Independent,* 2 February 1932, p. 7).

130. Speaking in Kilkenny (*Irish Independent,* 8 February 1932, p. 9).

131. Lawrence O'Toole, speaking in Arklow (*Irish Independent,* 2 February 1932, p. 8).

132. Speaking at Westport, Co. Mayo (*Irish Independent,* 5 February 1932, p. 10).

133. James Fitzgerald-Kenney, speaking at Ballinrobe, Co. Mayo (*Irish Independent,* 10 February 1932, p. 7).

134. See pastoral letters reported by *Irish Independent,* 8 February 1932, p. 9–11. For 9 February alone the *Irish Independent* reported anti-Fianna Fáil speeches by Father M. Leahy, accompanying the Minister for Agriculture, Paddy Hogan, at Eyrecourt, Co. Galway; Father Egan, accompanying the Minister for Justice, James Fitzgerald-Kenney, in Ballinrobe, Co. Mayo; and Father C. Coyne, accompanying the President of the Executive Council, W. T. Cosgrave, in Portlaoise (*Irish Independent,* 9 February 1931, p. 7). Local clergymen involved themselves in the Fianna Fáil campaign also but were not afforded the same publicity.

135. It is interesting to compare Conservative Party election posters for the 1931 British general election, in which a Conservative-dominated coalition government (called the National Government) emerged victorious, with those of Fianna Fáil. The imagery of one poster showing unemployed men at a dock watching goods being imported is almost identical to a Fianna Fáil poster issued for the 1932 election. (The Fianna Fáil poster is reproduced by Lee and Ó Tuathaigh in *The Age of de Valera,* p. 65.) Another Conservative poster shows a poor farmer gazing over a hill where the word PROTECTION is emblazoned in the sky, and the slogan *The dawn of brighter days* is followed by the exhortation to *Vote Conservative and support the National Government.* See A. J. Davies, *We, the Nation: The Conservative Party and the Pursuit of Power* (London: Abacus, 1995), following p. 260.

136. Section 7 of the Fianna Fáil manifesto dealt with cuts in 'waste and extravagance.' A copy of the manifesto is available in the Fianna Fáil Archives (FF/789). It was also published in the national press during the election: see, for example, *Irish Independent,* 11 February 1932, p. 5.

137. See, for example, the *Nation,* 7 September 1929, p. 7.

138. Robert Briscoe TD, *Irish Independent,* 16 February 1932, p. 11.

139. From a brochure entitled *North Dublin Election News.* The copy in the National Library is reproduced by Arthur Mitchell and Pádraig Ó Snodaigh, *Irish Political Documents, 1916–1949* (Dublin: Irish Academic Press, 1985), p. 192–4.

140. The incident is also referred to by Margaret Mulvihill, *Charlotte Despard: A Biography* (London: Pandora, 1989), p. 178.

141. *Irish Independent*, 1 February 1932, p. 8.

142. *Republican File*, 13 February 1932, p. 1.

143. *Irish Independent*, 1 February 1932, p. 8.

144. Batt O'Connor, speaking in Shankill (*Irish Independent*, 1 February 1932, p. 8).

145. *Irish Independent*, 12 February 1932, p. 1.

146. Cumann na nGaedheal election advertisement for the County Dublin Constituency (*Irish Independent*, 13 February 1932, p. 6).

147. James Fitzgerald-Kenney, speaking at Ballinrobe, Co. Mayo (*Irish Independent*, 10 February 1932, p. 7).

148. Speaking at Ballinrobe, Co. Mayo (*Irish Independent*, 10 February 1932, p. 7).

149. *Irish Independent*, 10 February 1932, p. 7.

150. *Irish Independent*, 8 February 1932, p. 6.

151. *Irish Independent*, 5 February 1932, p. 10.

152. Election Manifesto, 9 February 1932 (Fianna Fáil Archives, FF/789). See also *Irish Independent*, 11 February 1932, p. 5.

153. The Ancient Order of Hibernians, a conservative Irish and Irish-American political organisation, was founded in New York in 1836 with the aim (among other things) of defending Irish Catholics against pervasive discrimination. Though the Irish Party disappeared in 1918, its supporters remained a force in Irish politics. The National League was one of many parties formed in the 1920s that was composed of former home-rule politicians and supporters.

154. *Irish Independent*, 13 February 1932, p. 11. William Archer Redmond (1886–1932) was the son of John Redmond, who led the Irish Party from 1900 until his death in 1918. William Redmond was a member of the British Parliament from 1910 to 1922 and, when Waterford ceased to be represented in the British House of Commons, was elected to the Free State Dáil in 1923 and at the three subsequent elections until his death in April 1932. In 1926 he was a joint founder of the National League, but after this party's dissolution in 1930 he joined Cumann na nGaedheal.

155. Redmond was reported to have spoken on government platforms in Cos. Clare, Galway, Dublin, Wexford and Waterford.

156. Speaking in Kilrush, Co. Clare (*Irish Independent*, 2 February 1932, p. 8).

157. Speaking in Waterford (*Irish Independent*, 10 February 1932, p. 7).

158. *Irish Independent*, 9 February 1932, p. 9.

159. Text of letter dated 20 January 1932, published in the *Irish Independent*, 9 February 1932, p. 10. Byrne's reply is also quoted.

160. 'To the people of Ireland from the Lord Mayor of Dublin: Why I am fighting this election' (*Irish Independent*, 16 February 1932, p. 6).

161. *Irish Press*, 26 November 1931, p. 1. The letter noted that potential subscribers, while aware of the threat that republicans posed to the state, might be reluctant to align themselves publicly with Cumann na nGaedheal. For this reason the letter promised that all contributions and communications would be 'treated as confidential.'

162. See, for example, the statement by Major Myles (Donegal) (*Irish Independent*, 4 February 1932, p. 11).

163. See *Irish Press*, 27 January and 6 February 1932.

164. *Irish Press*, 15 February 1932.

165. Speaking in favour of the candidacy of John Good at Dalkey Town Hall (*Irish Independent*, 8 February 1932, p. 6). Dr James Craig should not be confused with James Craig (Lord Craigavon) who was Prime Minister of Northern Ireland at this time.

166. The Royal Irish Constabulary was the armed police force in Ireland between 1822 and 1922.

167. *Irish Independent*, 15 February 1932, p. 9.

168. *Irish Independent*, 16 February 1932, p. 10.

169. *Irish Independent*, 16 February 1932, p. 10. The *Irish Independent* printed details of the deceased deputy's final speech, in which he condemned de Valera's policies as promoting disorder. It also noted that Detective-Garda McGeehan had been a witness at the inquest on John Vaugh in Drumshanbo, Co. Leitrim, the previous day, at which he denied allegations that he and other detectives had violently beaten Vaugh while he was in custody.

170. *Irish Independent*, 16 February 1932, p. 10.

171. *Irish Independent*, 16 February 1932, p. 9.

172. See Moss, *Political Parties in the Irish Free State*, p. 178.

173. 'Protect your state—Vote Government' was a typical slogan. In addition, advertisements regularly called for a 'vote for the Government Party' as opposed to a vote for Cumann na nGaedheal.

174. 'President on shameful attempt to deceive people,' *Irish Independent*, 15 February 1932, p. 10. The advertisement to which Cosgrave referred asked voters to 'give Fianna Fáil the chance to prove its sincerity' (*Irish Independent*, 3 February 1932, p. 10).

175. 'Carlow-Kilkenny thanks,' *Irish Independent*, 15 February 1932, p. 10.

176. *Cork Examiner*, 16 February 1932, p. 1. A similar advertisement appeared on the front page of the *Irish Independent* the previous day.

177. *Irish Independent*, 16 February 1932, p. 8.

178. See *Irish Independent*, 17 February 1932, p. 7–8.

179. Data taken from Vincent Browne, *The Magill Book of Irish Politics*, p. 216–17.

180. Vincent Browne, *The Magill Book of Irish Politics*, p. 57, 203, 260, 282, 292, 300, 317.

181. The relevant statistics are: Louth 34 per cent, Dublin County 29 per cent, Wicklow 26 per cent. Vincent Browne, *The Magill Book of Irish Politics*, p. 107–8, 270, 346–7.

182. MacMillan, *State, Society and Authority in Ireland*, p. 208.

183. See León Ó Broin, *Just Like Yesterday: An Autobiography* (Dublin: Gill & Macmillan, 1985), p. 91–2.

184. Maye, *Fine Gael*, p. 24. The Round Table also concluded that Cosgrave's defeat was due to the fact that 'his political organisation was far inferior to that of its opponents'; quoted by Carty, *Party and Parish Pump*, p. 106.

185. Óglaigh na hÉireann [IRA], Adjutant-General to the Commanding Officers of each Independent Unit (Roinn: A/G, Uimhir: B.B. 48), 12 January 1932 (National Archives, D/T S5864C).

186. White, *Harry*, p. 43.

187. A typical Fianna Fáil advertisement proclaimed: 'Now's your chance—PUT THEM OUT! Vote FIANNA FÁIL' (*Irish Independent*, 10 February 1932, p. 6). J. Bowyer Bell (*The Secret Army*, p. 92) claims that Peadar O'Donnell 'ran a banner headline in *An Phoblacht*' exhorting the electorate to 'Put Cosgrave out.' This is impossible, as *An Phoblacht* was not being published at the time.

188. Quoted by Ulick O'Connor, *Brendan Behan* (London: Granada, 1979), p. 84.

189. Bell, *The Secret Army*, p. 93. Bell also claims that 'some active Volunteers tripped from booth to booth judiciously casting fifty ballots,' but he is characteristically coy about sources.

190. Dermot Keogh, *Ireland and Europe, 1919–1989: A Diplomatic and Political History* (Cork and Dublin: Hibernian University Press, 1990), p. 34.

191. One of the more popular stories—probably apocryphal—illustrating the ambivalence felt by some army officers reports the new Minister for Defence, Frank Aiken, reviewing a section of the army. Looking at the man who had been chief of staff of the IRA from 1923 to 1925, one Free State officer reportedly said to another, 'Do we salute him or shoot him?'

192. See Conor Brady, *Guardians of the Peace*, p. 166–9.

Chapter 6: Fianna Fáil in power, 1932–8 (p. 130–51)

1. Quotations from Cronin, *The McGarrity Papers*. This book is a collection of letters and documents that were the possession of Joe McGarrity, a native of Co. Tyrone, the most important figure in republican Irish America between 1920 and 1940. The original documents are in the National Library in Dublin.

2. *An Phoblacht*, 19 March 1932, p. 1.

3. *An Phoblacht*, 25 June 1932, p. 8.

4. These statements were made in a letter to the *Evening Herald* and *Evening Mail*. The *Evening Herald* did not publish the letter, while the *Evening Mail* published a portion of it in its early edition but removed it from subsequent editions. The full text was published in *An Phoblacht*, 2 July 1932, p. 1.

5. Moynihan, *Speeches and Statements by Éamon de Valera*, p. 237.

6. *Irish Independent*, 15 February 1932, p. 11.

7. *Parliamentary Debates: Dáil Éireann: Official Report*, 41/573 (27 April 1932). The first stage of the bill was introduced on 20 April (*Official Report*, 41/171–5). De Valera did not put forward an explanation for the bill at this time, preferring, as was the custom, to wait until the second stage. Contrary to the norm, Frank MacDermott offered a detailed critique of the proposal. The second stage was taken on 27 April.

8. James MacNeill (1869–1938). Brother of Eoin MacNeill; High Commissioner of the Irish Free State in London.

9. Terence de Vere White, 'Social life in Ireland, 1927–1937,' *Studies*, 54/213 (spring 1965), p. 78.

10. The post of Governor-General was particular to the British Commonwealth and a relic of colonial times, when governors ruled territories on behalf of the Crown. Their role was downgraded considerably during the 1920s and 30s as a result of successive negotiations between Britain and the dominion states of the British Commonwealth. Certain duties remained, however, such as receiving ambassadors and signing legislation into law.

11. F. S. L. Lyons, *Ireland since the Famine* (London: Fontana, 1981), p. 518.

12. Domhnall Ó Buachalla (1866–1963) was a Gaelic League activist and a member of the Irish Volunteers. He was arrested after the 1916 Rising and in 1918 was elected to the first Dáil.

13. *An Phoblacht*, 30 April 1932, p. 4.

14. *An Phoblacht*, 14 January 1933, p. 3.

15. See *An Phoblacht*, 21 January 1933, p. 3.

16. The official name of the party was United Ireland Party—Fine Gael, but it soon became known exclusively as Fine Gael.

17. Col. Éamonn (Ned) Broy (1887–1972) was a valuable source of information for Michael Collins during the War of Independence, using his position in the Dublin Metropolitan Police to provide republicans with intelligence. In the film *Michael Collins*, directed by Neil Jordan, he is erroneously portrayed as being tortured and killed by British forces on the evening of Bloody Sunday (21 November 1920).

18. Conor Brady, *Guardians of the Peace*, p. 218.

19. *Parliamentary Debates: Dáil Éireann: Official Report*, 55/353 (6 March 1935).

20. *Parliamentary Debates: Dáil Éireann: Official Report*, 55/1 (27 February 1935).

21. The Republican Congress was established by several prominent IRA leaders, including Peadar O'Donnell, Frank Ryan, George Gilmore and Michael Price, and represented a more left-wing approach to Irish republicanism. It published a weekly paper, *Republican Congress*, during 1934 and 1935 but was suppressed by the Fianna Fáil government. Many members would later fight in defence of the Spanish Republic between 1936 and 1939, but their strength in Ireland had by that time diminished. See Gilmore, *The Republican Congress*, and Byrne, *The Irish Republican Congress Revisited*. Seán Cronin's biography, *Frank Ryan: The Search for the Republic*, also provides a detailed account of the Republican Congress.

22. See Patrick Kissane's question on hunger strike by Kerry prisoners, *Parliamentary Debates: Dáil Éireann: Official Report*, 55/183–4 (28 February 1935).

23. See Coogan, *De Valera*, p. 484.

24. *Republican Congress*, 20 April 1935, p. 4.

25. See *Republican Congress*, 1 June 1935, p. 1.

26. *Irish Press*, 15 April 1935.

27. *Fianna Fáil Bulletin*, March 1936, p. 2.

28. Minutes of Parliamentary Party, 28 March 1935 (Fianna Fáil Archives, FF/439).

29. *Fianna Fáil Bulletin*, March 1936, p. 4.

30. See *Parliamentary Debates: Dáil Éireann: Official Report*, 55/660–8 (7 March 1935).

31. There appears to be a consensus that the killing of More-O'Ferrall was an accident and that the initial decision to 'rough him up' had not been sanctioned by IRA headquarters. In the case of Egan, most agree that the killing resulted from an IRA court-martial and was sanctioned by headquarters. Opinions differ, however, on what level of sanction was given for the killing of Somerville. J. Bowyer Bell (*The Secret Army*, p. 119–20, 126–7) claims that the operation was ordered by the commanding officer of the Cork IRA, Tom Barry, and was approved by headquarters. He also suggests that the intention was to intimidate Somerville but not to kill him. Tim Pat Coogan, on the other hand (*The IRA* [second edition], p. 120–22), claims that the intention was indeed to murder Somerville but that the operation was not sanctioned: he attributes the action to the Cork IRA, which was 'strongly anti-British and anti-Protestant.' See also Foley, *Legion of the Rearguard*, p. 149–50, 158.

32. *Irish Independent*, 18 June 1936, p. 9. See also *Parliamentary Debates: Dáil Éireann: Official Report*, 63/2408–68 (16 June 1936), 63/2469 ff. (17 June 1936).

33. *Irish Independent*, 22 June 1936, p. 9.

34. *An Phoblacht*, 4 July 1936, p. 1.

35. *Irish Independent*, 22 June 1936, p. 10.

36. *Parliamentary Debates: Dáil Éireann: Official Report*, 63/2173–4 (29 July 1936).

37. Quoted by Coogan, *De Valera*, p. 484.

38. Maud Gonne MacBride, 'Ireland, 1936,' *Irish World* (New York). This paper was traditionally a strong supporter of de Valera and Fianna Fáil. The article was reprinted in *Irish Freedom*, September 1936, p. 1.

39. Michael Farrell, *Northern Ireland*, p. 67.

40. Bowman, *De Valera and the Ulster Question*, p. 132.

41. Michael Farrell, *Northern Ireland*, p. 99–100.

42. Bowman, *De Valera and the Ulster Question*, p. 132.

43. Buckland, *The Factory of Grievances*, p. 72–3.

44. Bowman, *De Valera and the Ulster Question*, p. 133.

45. Bowman, *De Valera and the Ulster Question*, p. 133.

46. Bowman, *De Valera and the Ulster Question*, p. 133. George Gilmore, a socialist republican who was to become a leader of the breakaway Republican Congress, advocated a more radical policy to Healy. His strategy was to boycott both the Belfast and Dublin parliaments and to convene an all-Ireland assembly, believing that 'Fianna Fáil could not refuse to cooperate.' Bowman, *De Valera and the Ulster Question*, p. 134.

47. Bowman, *De Valera and the Ulster Question*, p. 134–5.

48. *Irish Times*, 4 November 1936. The phrase was a clever adaptation of Parnell's famous speech, which declared that 'no man has the right to fix the boundary of the march of a nation.'

49. Minutes of National Executive, 21 December 1936 (Fianna Fáil Archives, FF/342).

50. The term 'interventionist wing' is used by John Bowman (*De Valera and the Ulster Question*) to describe those in Fianna Fáil more active on the partition issue.

51. Minutes of National Executive, 4 January 1937 (Fianna Fáil Archives, FF/342). The motion was seconded by P. Fogarty.

52. The National Executive had already met on 18 January. The date for this special meeting, therefore, was not the earliest available.

53. Minutes of National Executive, 1932–48 (Fianna Fáil Archives, FF/341–3), passim. This contrasts with de Valera's regular attendance at meetings while in opposition. Minutes of National Executive, 1927–31 (Fianna Fáil Archives, FF/340), passim.

54. Minutes of National Executive, 1 February 1937 (Fianna Fáil Archives, FF/342).

55. *Parliamentary Debates: Dáil Éireann: Official Report*, 67/110 (11 May 1937).

56. Minutes of National Executive, 1 February 1937 (Fianna Fáil Archives, FF/342). John Bowman (*De Valera and the Ulster Question*, p. 341) has noted de Valera's reluctance to commit anything to paper.

57. Bowman, *De Valera and the Ulster Question*, p. 156.

58. Bowman, *De Valera and the Ulster Question*, p. 149. See below for the text of articles 2 and 3.

59. Minutes of National Executive, 8 November 1937 (Fianna Fáil Archives, FF/342).

60. Bowman, *De Valera and the Ulster Question*, p. 172.

61. Minutes of National Executive, 22 November 1937 (Fianna Fáil Archives, FF/342).

62. Donnelly was excused attendance for the meetings of 6 and 20 December 1937. At the meeting of 3 January 1938 he was present, but there is no record of any discussion on the issue. He was again absent on 17 January 1938, returned on 31 January without discussion on the motion, was absent on 14 February and was present on 28 February, but again the motion was not considered. Minutes of National Executive (Fianna Fáil Archives, FF/342).

63. Fanning, *Independent Ireland*, p. 117–18.
64. Chubb, *The Constitution and Constitutional Change*, p.15.
65. Ronan Fanning, 'Mr. de Valera drafts a constitution' in Brian Farrell, *De Valera's Constitution and Ours*.
66. Moynihan, *Speeches and Statements by Éamon de Valera*, p. 364.
67. Quotations from the Constitution of Ireland unless otherwise stated.
68. As 'loyalty' and 'fidelity' are interchangeable words, one can only conclude that, rather than the article being needlessly repetitious, it was seeking to demonstrate again that the nation could not be equated with the state.
69. Article 1 declares that the Irish nation has an inalienable right to chose its own form of government. Article 6 declares that all powers of government, executive, legislative and judicial, derive from the people. Article 5 states that 'Ireland is a sovereign, independent, democratic state.'
70. For example, article 40.4.1 states that 'no citizen shall be deprived of his personal liberty save in accordance with law.' Article 40.5: 'The dwelling of every citizen is inviolable and shall not be forcibly entered save in accordance with law.' The right to freely express convictions and opinions is enshrined in article 40.6.1 'subject to public order and morality.' The publication of blasphemous, seditious or indecent matter is a punishable offence under article 40.6.1 (i). The right of citizens to assemble peaceably and without arms is guaranteed but may be negated if such an assembly is deemed 'to be calculated to cause a breach of the peace or to be a danger or nuisance to the general public' (article 40.6.1 (ii)). Citizens are granted the right 'to form associations and unions,' but this is followed by the qualification: 'Laws, however, may be enacted for the regulation and control in the public interest of the exercise of the foregoing right' (article 40.6.1 (iii)). Other rights are defended 'as far as practicable.' Furthermore, it is stated in article 40.4.6 that 'nothing in this section . . . shall be invoked to prohibit, control, or interfere with any act of the Defence Forces during the existence of a state of war or armed rebellion.'
71. The main effect of this article was to facilitate section 31 of the Broadcasting Authority Act (1960), which permitted the Government to prohibit certain individuals and opinions from gaining access to RTE. Failure to comply with such directives resulted in the sacking of journalists, the trial of broadcasters, and in 1972 the sacking of the entire RTE Authority when RTE television reported the substance of an interview with the then chief of staff of the IRA.
72. The leader of the Labour Party, William Norton, raised this matter during the Dáil debate on the issue and sought assurances that a state of emergency would not be declared in the eventuality of a war breaking out, for example, between China and Japan. Such assurances were given, but the threat of abuse remained just as real. See *Parliamentary Debates: Dáil Éireann: Official Report*, cols. 18–19 (2 September 1939).
73. See Chubb, *The Constitution and Constitutional Change*, p. 58.
74. *Parliamentary Debates: Dáil Éireann: Official Report*, 82/1209 (2 April 1941).
75. See the statements of Seán Lemass in Dáil Éireann, *Parliamentary Debates: Dáil Éireann: Official Report*, 185/615 (6 December 1960), 209/3 (21 April 1964). The emergency was rescinded only in 1995. See *Parliamentary Debates: Dáil Éireann: Official Report*, 448/1538–87 (7 February, 1995) and *Seanad Éireann: Official Report*, 141/2013–61 (16 February, 1995).
76. The state of emergency was eventually rescinded in response to the IRA ceasefire

declared on 31 August 1994. However, article 28.3.3 remains in the Constitution, and the state of emergency can be reactivated at any time. The fact that this was not done after the collapse of the IRA ceasefire in February 1996 demonstrates that the continuation of the 'emergency' was largely superfluous. In addition, the Offences Against the State Act remains on the statute book. In the aftermath of the IRA ceasefire it was retained on the grounds that it was needed to combat a new wave of drug-related crime. This changing rationale illustrates the reluctance of successive Governments to repeal any of their powers once they are established.

77. Article 15.6.1.

78. Articles 38.3.1 and 38.3.2.

79. From the 1960s journalists began using the term 'cabinet' to refer to the Government, and the practice was later taken up by politicians.

80. See Constitution of Ireland, article 28.6. This befits the meaning of the titles, as *taoiseach* literally means 'chief', while the *tánaiste* was the heir to the chief in ancient Ireland. During Fianna Fáil's periods in office between 1945 and 1959 Seán Lemass was Tánaiste before succeeding de Valera. In coalition Governments the position of Tánaiste has traditionally been reserved for the leader of the second-largest party.

81. For the power of the President see Constitution of Ireland, articles 12–14; for the powers of the Taoiseach see article 28.

82. See Constitution of Ireland, articles 18–19.

83. Minutes of Parliamentary Party, 7 June 1928 (Fianna Fáil Archives, FF/438).

84. *Irish Independent*, 10 February 1932, p. 9.

85. Moynihan, *Speeches and Statements by Éamon de Valera*, p. 333, quoted by Lee, *Ireland, 1912–1985*, p. 211.

86. Bowman, *De Valera and the Ulster Question*, p. 116–17.

87. McMahon, *Republicans and Imperialists*, p. 247.

88. Clare O'Halloran, *Partition and the Limits of Irish Nationalism: An Ideology under Stress* (Dublin: Gill & Macmillan, 1987), p. 182. See also Bowman, *De Valera and the Ulster Question*, p. 164.

89. Bowman, *De Valera and the Ulster Question*, p. 181. See also Foster, *Modern Ireland*, p. 561.

90. *Parliamentary Debates: Dáil Éireann: Official Report*, 71/41–2 (27 April 1938).

91. See *Parliamentary Debates: Dáil Éireann: Official Report*, 71/32–60 (27 April 1938) and 71/164–304 (28 April 1938).

92. Quoted by Bowman, *De Valera and the Ulster Question*, p. 183.

93. Jack Lynch repeated this achievement when he led Fianna Fáil to victory in the 1977 election.

94. In a speech made in the presence of the returning officer, Seán MacEntee declared: 'I should like to thank also those who supported our party for the first time. I know that many of them in some quarters might be described as ex-unionists. To me they are "unionists" in the true and happy sense of that word. They have given it a new connotation, because they are helping to accomplish the true union of hearts in Ireland, north and south.' (MacEntee Papers, UCD Archives, P67/361/2).

95. *Irish Times*, 21 June 1938, quoted by Lee, *Ireland, 1912–1985*, p. 215.

96. Fianna Fáil suggested that the opposition parties would discard PR at the first opportunity. In fact, frustrated by its inability to regularly get an absolute majority, Fianna Fáil introduced constitutional referendums in 1959 and 1968 to abolish PR with

a view to replacing it with the British 'first past the post' system. Both were unsuccessful, despite an attempt to link the 1959 vote with de Valera's candidature for the presidency by holding the referendum and the presidential election at the same time.

97. Letter to all voters, 10 June 1938, from William Black (Dalkey). (UCD Archives, MacEntee Papers, P67/359/10).

98. Double-sided election leaflet, which is a reproduction in full of a letter dated 6 June 1938 from a Mr R. G. L. Leonard SC to Mr William Black SC (Fianna Fáil candidate with MacEntee) (UCD Archives, MacEntee Papers, P67/359/7).

99. 'Fianna Fáil spent £1,210. Dublin townships election. Striking figures,' *Irish Independent*, 12 August 1937 (UCD Archives, MacEntee Papers, P67/358/1). This was considered extravagant by the economising honorary secretary, Gerry Boland, who raised the matter with Seán MacEntee. In a letter to Boland, 22 September 1937, MacEntee defended the spending. 'The expenditure in the Constituency was undoubtedly heavy, but the Constituency is an overwhelmingly middle-class, residential district, the residents of which do not come to public meetings. I feel certain, therefore, that we could not have won the election upon any other plan than that which I adopted, of newspaper advertisement and written individually-addressed personal appeals' (UCD Archives, MacEntee Papers, P67/358/6).

100. Carty, *Party and Parish Pump*, p. 107–8.

101. Boland (*The Rise and Decline of Fianna Fáil*, p. 63) was not sure whether it was a meeting of the National Executive or of the Officer Board.

102. Boland, *The Rise and Decline of Fianna Fáil*, p. 63–4.

103. Personalised letters sent out to voters in MacEntee's constituency, dated 10 June 1938 (UCD Archives, MacEntee Papers, P67/359/5).

104. Speaking at Ballygarret during the 1936 Wexford by-election (UCD Archives, MacEntee Papers, P67/356/5).

105. Russell commanded the 2nd Battalion of the Dublin Brigade, and his unit had been responsible for the killing of thirteen British agents on Bloody Sunday, 1920. He was appointed to GHQ by Michael Collins, as Director of Munitions, and had remained on the IRA Executive despite the plethora of splits, deaths and defections, until his (temporary) dismissal in 1936. See Foley, *Legion of the Rearguard*, p. 174.

106. See Fearghal McGarry, *Irish Politics and the Spanish Civil War* (Cork: Cork University Press, 1999), and R. A. Stradling, *The Irish and the Spanish Civil War, 1936–9* (Manchester: Manchester University Press, 1999). Ironically, Ryan was to die a guest of Nazi Germany in 1944. Russell died in his arms aboard a German submarine headed towards Ireland in 1940. See Stephan, *Spies in Ireland*, p. 139–52, 259–63. For a relatively marginal figure in Irish politics Ryan has managed to capture the attention of several authors, his left-wing internationalism making him something of a Che Guevara figure. Among the works devoted to his life are Michael O'Loughlin, *Frank Ryan: Journey to the Centre* (Dublin: Raven Arts Press, 1987), Fearghal McGarry, *Frank Ryan* (Dundalk: Dundalgan Press, for Historical Association of Ireland, 2002), and Adrian Hoar, *In Green and Red: The Lives of Frank Ryan* (Dingle: Brandon Books, 2004), though arguably none have surpassed the ground-breaking biography by Seán Cronin, *Frank Ryan: The Search for the Republic*.

107. Bell, *The Secret Army*, p. 152.

Chapter 7: Revolutionary crocodile, 1939–40 (p. 152–73)

1. Speaking on the Offences Against the State Bill. *Parliamentary Debates: Dáil Éireann: Official Report*, 74/1394–5 (2 March 1939).
2. *Parliamentary Debates: Dáil Éireann: Official Report*, 74/1575 (7 March 1939).
3. Cabinet Minutes, 17 May 1938, item 3 (National Archives, G.C. 1/27).
4. *Wolfe Tone Weekly*, 4 February 1939, p. 1.
5. For the circumstances of this botched operation see Bell, *The Secret Army*, p. 161–2. For an account of Behan's trial see the *Irish Independent*, 8 February 1940, p. 7.
6. Cabinet Minutes, 10 February 1939, item 1 (G.C. 2/47).
7. See Coogan, *The IRA* (first edition), p. 131.
8. This had some amusing side effects. The *Irish Times* journalist John Healy recalled that under the act 'it was forbidden to call the organisation "the Irish Republican Army" or use the designation "IRA." Even if you were quoting an eye witness, we had to change the actual phrase "IRA" into "a member of an illegal organisation." Thus if an armed man said: "Hands up—this is the IRA" you had to render it: "Hands up— we are members of an illegal organisation".' John Healy, *Healy, Reporter: The Early Years* (Achill: House of Healy, 1991), p. 161. (In the book Healy inadvertently refers to the Offences Against the State Act as the Special Powers Act.)
9. Part IV, section 30 (1).
10. Part IV, section 30 (5).
11. *Parliamentary Debates: Dáil Éireann: Official Report*, 74/1437 (3 March 1939).
12. *Parliamentary Debates: Dáil Éireann: Official Report*, 74/1309–10 (2 March 1939).
13. *Parliamentary Debates: Dáil Éireann: Official Report*, 74/1455–6 (3 March 1939).
14. *Parliamentary Debates: Dáil Éireann: Official Report*, 74/1460 (3 March 1939).
15. William Davin, *Parliamentary Debates: Dáil Éireann: Official Report*, 74/1474 (3 March 1939).
16. *Parliamentary Debates: Dáil Éireann: Official Report*, 74/1395–6 (2 March 1939).
17. *Parliamentary Debates: Dáil Éireann: Official Report*, 74/1408–9 (2 March 1939).
18. See contributions of Deputy Davin, *Parliamentary Debates: Dáil Éireann: Official Report*, 74/1565 (7 March 1939), and Seán Mac Eoin (col. 1567). Patrick McGilligan asked: 'Is this the sort of legislation that we, having certain feelings for certain people in the Six Counties, would like to see operated by the present Government there in peaceful ordinary times?' (col. 1398, 2 March 1939).
19. *Parliamentary Debates: Dáil Éireann: Official Report*, 74/1323 (2 March 1939).
20. *Parliamentary Debates: Dáil Éireann: Official Report*, 74/1567–8 (7 March 1939).
21. *Parliamentary Debates: Dáil Éireann: Official Report*, 74/1331 (2 March 1939).
22. *Parliamentary Debates: Dáil Éireann: Official Report*, 74/1395 (2 March 1939).
23. *Parliamentary Debates: Dáil Éireann: Official Report*, 74/1438 (3 March 1939).
24. *Parliamentary Debates: Dáil Éireann: Official Report*, 74/1574 (7 March 1939).
25. *Parliamentary Debates: Dáil Éireann: Official Report*, 74/1390 (2 March 1939). De Valera introduced the issue, unprovoked, when opening his speech in defence of the proposed legislation. He chose as evidence of misrepresentation the speech he made on 17 March 1922, known as the 'wading through blood' speech. Incredibly, he sought to use it to demonstrate that he had never deviated from previously held political beliefs. 'If there is to be force used in future, that force can only be used effectively by the Government which is responsible to this Parliament. No other body can use force effectively, or can be allowed to use it, in the name of the Government, so long as the

Government here exists. The two things are incompatible, impossible and cannot remain together. This is not a new doctrine for me to enunciate.' It was at this point that de Valera alluded to his speech of March 1922, but he demurred when requested by opposition deputies to quote from it directly.

26. *Parliamentary Debates: Dáil Éireann: Official Report*, 74/1434 (3 March 1939).

27. *Republican Review*, June 1939, p. 1.

28. See above. The Emergency Powers Bill had been drafted as early as January 1939.

29. The power to intern without trial was specifically excluded by section 2 (*k*); but this exemption proved short-lived and disappeared altogether with the enactment of the Emergency Powers (Amendment) (No. 2) Act in January 1940. Like its predecessor, this amendment was not approved by referendum, because of the flexible period provided for by the Constitution of the Irish Free State.

30. *Parliamentary Debates: Dáil Éireann: Official Report*, 78/1430 (3 January 1940). After MacEntee had said, 'The fact that I am here tonight making a speech on behalf of this bill—' the Labour TD for Wicklow, James Everett, interjected: 'Which you may consider unjust in another few years' time.'

31. *Parliamentary Debates: Dáil Éireann: Official Report*, 78/1531–2 (4 January 1940).

32. See Labour Party, 10th Annual Report (incorporating Report of the Administrative Council for 1940 and Report of the Proceedings of the 10th Annual Conference held from 21 to 23 April 1941), p. 7–8.

33. The other members were Seán T. O'Kelly (Tánaiste and Minster for Finance), Frank Aiken (Minister for Co-ordination of Defensive Measures), Gerry Boland (Minister for Justice), Oscar Traynor (Minister for Defence) and Paddy Ruttledge (Minister for Local Government and Public Health). The Attorney-General (Kevin Haugh) and the Secretary of the Government (Maurice Moynihan) also attended on occasions. (National Archives, D/T S14433B).

34. Certainly many in the republican movement looked at the world through this prism. In December 1938 Joe McGarrity declared: 'We are not fighting de Valera and de Valera's government. De Valera is a past patriot; he is today what John Redmond was in 1916. We shall simply ignore him as we ignored Redmond. We are after the real enemy, and the only enemy, and that enemy is England. The fighting, therefore, will be wholly in the occupied Six Counties of Northern Ireland and in England.' Quoted by Cronin, *The McGarrity Papers*, p. 168.

35. Cronin, *Washington's Irish Policy*, p. 105.

36. See Ó Drisceoil, *Censorship in Ireland*, p. 269.

37. Lee, *Ireland, 1912–1985*, p. 237.

38. Fisk, *In Time of War*, p. 161.

39. Fisk, *In Time of War*, p. 161.

40. Foster, *Modern Ireland*, p. 560–61.

41. See Fisk, *In Time of War*, p. 190–206.

42. Fisk, *In Time of War*, p. 215.

43. Fisk, *In Time of War*, p. 77–8.

44. Fisk, *In Time of War*, p. 323.

45. Fisk, *In Time of War*, p. 324–5.

46. Though labouring under the delusion that Churchill was reviving the Chamberlain offer of 'neutrality for unity,' de Valera firmly rejected the idea and refused to entertain the notion of travelling to London, which, he argued, would be

misunderstood. See Bowman, *De Valera and the Ulster Question*, p. 247.

47. Fanning, *Independent Ireland*, p. 141.

48. These veiled threats continued throughout the war, and Churchill appears to have derived a mischievous pleasure from them at times. As late as 1944 he told President Roosevelt that, following Gray's lead, they had decided that it was still too soon to begin reassuring de Valera and that he thought it much better 'to keep them guessing for a while.' He concluded that, 'far from allaying alarm in de Valera's circles we should let fear work its healthy process.' Telegram from Churchill to Roosevelt, 19 March 1944, quoted by Churchill, *The Second World War, Volume 5: Closing the Ring* (London: Penguin, 1985), p. 614–15.

49. Quoted by Dwyer, *De Valera*, p. 250.

50. Private conversations between de Valera and the editor of the *Irish Press* were not recorded by either side. However, the fact that the Fianna Fáil leadership intervened in the administration of the paper is indicated in the minutes of the parliamentary party. In early 1934, for example, the issue of the 'unsatisfactory reporting of speeches in the *Irish Press*' was raised, and de Valera promised to take up the matter with the paper and asked deputies to keep an eye out for similar examples. Minutes of Parliamentary Party, 15 February 1934 (Fianna Fáil Archives, FF/439). The close connection between Fianna Fáil and the *Irish Press* was also demonstrated during the 1948 election and was an integral part of the party's reorganisation drive while in opposition. Shortly after Fianna Fáil's departure from office, Seán Lemass, who had taken over as managing director of the paper, asked the Fianna Fáil National Executive whether it would be interested in financing an illustrated record of de Valera's anti-partition tour of the United States, a suggestion that was supported by the Executive. Minutes of National Executive, 12 April 1948 (Fianna Fáil Archives, FF/343).

51. Rex Cathcart, 'Broadcasting: The early decades,' in Brian Farrell, *Communications and Community in Ireland*, p. 44.

52. The text of the cancelled broadcast was printed in full in the *Irish Independent*, 6 January 1934.

53. Quoted by John A. Murphy, 'Censorship and the moral community,' in Brian Farrell, *Communications and Community in Ireland*, p. 53–4.

54. Robert Greaves, *Irish Times*, 22 June 1950; John A. Murphy, 'Censorship and the Moral Community,' p. 54.

55. *Parliamentary Debates: Dáil Éireann: Official Report*, 67/1634–5 (2 June 1937).

56. Gaughan, *Memoirs of Senator Joseph Connolly*, p. 400. Connolly was Controller of Censorship until 1941, when he was replaced by his deputy, T. J. Coyne.

57. Ó Drisceoil, *Censorship in Ireland*, p. 61.

58. Ó Drisceoil, *Censorship in Ireland*, p. 62; also National Archives, D/J 'Postal Censorship: Organisation and Administration.'

59. Gaughan, *Memoirs of Senator Joseph Connolly*, p. 400. Sometimes individual letters were passed to the Department of Justice. Peter Berry, the man who, as secretary of the department, would play a pivotal role in the Arms Crisis a quarter of a century later, worked at a junior level in the Department of Justice at that time.

60. Ó Drisceoil, *Censorship in Ireland*, p. 63; also National Archives, D/J 'Postal Censorship: Organisation and Administration.'

61. Ó Drisceoil, *Censorship in Ireland*, p. 74.

62. Coyne to Curry, 19 June 1940 (National Archives, D/J, No. 19); quoted by Ó Drisceoil, *Censorship in Ireland*, p. 234–5.

63. A secret report by the Department of Justice in August 1931 stated that the IRA was 'the direct descendant of the armed forces which opposed the Free State Army in 1922/3: the succession of Headquarters Officers has never been broken.' Department of Justice report on the present situation as regards the activities of unlawful and dangerous associations in the Saorstát with a summary of similar activities in recent years (National Archives, D/T S5864B, section 1, p. 1).

64. National Archives, D/J, Press Censorship Monthly Reports, September 1942.

65. Ó Drisceoil, *Censorship in Ireland*, p. 235.

66. Joseph Clarke had played a prominent role in 1916. With eleven others he held out in Mount Street. In what was the most significant action of the Rising the group inflicted 216 casualties on the British forces while losing only three men. He continued his military endeavours during the War of Independence and Civil War and was arrested several times throughout the twenties and thirties. The editor of the *Wolfe Tone Weekly*, Brian O'Higgins, had been an active republican before the 1916 Rising and was elected with de Valera as Sinn Féin TD for Clare in the second Dáil. See Mac Eoin, *The IRA in the Twilight Years*, p. 719, 736.

67. Another publication, *Republican Review*, had ceased publication in June because of the Offences Against the State Act.

68. *Republican News*, no. 5, December 1942, p. 4. The only copies of this publication that seem to be publicly available are those in the Government files in the National Archives (D/T S11564A). According to Uinseann Mac Eoin (*The IRA in the Twilight Years*, p. 412), *War News* was produced at 17 Percy Place, Dublin. Seven people, including McNeela and Mac Eoin, were involved. See also *The IRA in the Twilight Years*, p. 692–3, 791. Mac Eoin's interviewees suggested that the publication was issued weekly from late 1939 to mid-1940. Unless there was another publication of the same name, existing copies do not suggest that it was published so frequently.

69. Quoted by Stephan, *Spies in Ireland*, p. 91.

70. Görtz had been disappointed with the IRA and wrote after the war that, 'in spite of the fine qualities of individual IRA men, as a body I considered them worthless.' When one IRA leader boasted of five thousand sworn members in one district Görtz was unimpressed. 'I answered him that I personally would be completely satisfied with 500 men who knew how to obey an order. I would march with them to Belfast and destroy the Harland and Wolff shipyards, and these men would have done more for Ireland than 5,000 talking about the Second Dáil and Third Dáil and their legality.' However, the IRA felt that Görtz's motivation in seeking the destruction of the Belfast shipyards had more to do with serving Germany's interests than Ireland's. The republican leaders who met Görtz disliked his abrasive manner and his propensity to give orders, and it is not surprising that he found co-operation with the IRA difficult at the best of times. See Hermann Görtz, 'Mission to Ireland,' *Irish Times*, 25 August to 10 September 1947.

71. Coogan, *The IRA* (second edition), p. 222. In 1949 Veesenmayer was sentenced to twenty years' imprisonment for his involvement with the Nazi regime, though he was released in 1951.

72. Nigel West, *MI5* (London: Triad-Panther, 1983), p. 420.

73. Bell, *The Secret Army*, p. 178–9.

74. Barney Casey was commanding officer of the Longford IRA before his internment. See McGuffin, *Internment,* chap. 4, and White, *Ruairí Ó Brádaigh,* p. 29–30.
75. See County Longford Branch, National Graves Association, *Longford Remembers,* p. 12; Bell, *The Secret Army,* p. 180.
76. 'I expect to be British amateur golf champion in 1944,' one internee wrote facetiously to his father; quoted by Dwyer, *Guests of the State,* p. 39.
77. Dwyer, *Guests of the State,* p. 39.
78. Bell, *The Secret Army,* p. 171.
79. Cabinet Minutes, 31 October 1939, item 5 (National Archives, G.C. 2/111). The following day the prisoners were informed of the decision. Letter from Secretary of Department of Defence to Secretary of Department of the Taoiseach, 1 November 1939 (National Archives, D/T S11515).
80. Department of the Taoiseach memo, 7 November 1939, signed by Leas-Runaí (National Archives, D/T S11515).
81. Letter from Margaret Pearse to Éamon de Valera, 15 November 1939. Addressing him as 'My dear Chief,' she said that she understood de Valera's position, but 'for Ireland's sake I don't hesitate to say that more tragedy will ensue if Paddy dies now. I am asking Mother, Pat and Willie to pray for you and your Ministers and for Paddy' (National Archives, D/T S11515). Separate but equally poignant letters were sent to de Valera by McGrath's sister, Josephine, and his brother, James, writing from Crooksling Sanatorium, November 1939 (National Archives, D/T S11515).
82. Letter from Liam Tobin to de Valera, 8 November 1939. The department secretary's note dated 13 November indicates that a meeting took place (National Archives, D/T S11515). An apostle of Michael Collins, Liam Tobin took the pro-Treaty side and was rewarded with a senior position in the Free State Army; by 1924, however, he had become disillusioned with the manner in which demobilisation was being carried out and with what he felt was the betrayal of Collins's ideals. The result was a showdown between two factions within the Free State camp, which ended in the defeat of Tobin and his supporters. See *Parliamentary Debates: Dáil Éireann: Official Report,* 6/2204–38 (19 March 1924).
83. Letter to de Valera, 8 November 1939 (National Archives, D/T S11515).
84. *Parliamentary Debates: Dáil Éireann: Official Report,* 77/1208–11 (9 November 1939).
85. Burke became known subsequently in republican circles as Séamus 'Habeas Corpus' Burke.
86. Hogan and Walker, *Political Violence and the Law in Ireland,* p. 178.
87. *Parliamentary Debates: Seanad Éireann: Official Report,* 24/510 (4 January 1940).
88. Hogan and Walker, *Political Violence and the Law in Ireland,* p. 188, n. 26.
89. Her brother, Edward Daly, had also been executed in 1916.
90. Maud Gonne MacBride had sent a detailed letter personally to de Valera on 19 March (National Archives, D/T S11515).
91. These were Máire Nic Shuibhne, Honora Murphy, May Delaney, Brigit Fitzgerald and Gregory Ashe. Máire Nic Shuibhne (better known as Mary MacSwiney) was the sister of Terence MacSwiney, who had died on hunger strike in 1920. The other four were related to Joseph Murphy, Michael Fitzgerald and Thomas Ashe, respectively.
92. National Archives, D/T S11515.
93. *Connacht Tribune,* 20 April 1940, p. 7. See also *Irish Press,* 17 April 1940, and *Irish Independent,* 17 April 1940, p. 8.

94. Among the witnesses called was Dr Andrew Cooney, who stated that he had been approached by relatives of the hunger-strikers in an effort to secure a resolution. As a result he had made contact with de Valera and sought permission to visit the prisoners to bring about a settlement, but the necessary authorisation had been denied. Rev. John J. O'Hare also testified that he had applied to the Minister for Justice three times for permission to meet the prisoners with a view to settling the dispute but was refused on each occasion. 'I have every reason to believe that the hunger strike would have been settled a fortnight ago if I had been allowed to enter Mountjoy.' When asked by MacBride whether he had made this clear to de Valera and Boland he replied that he did and that 'they had no explanation for their refusal.'

95. *Connacht Tribune,* 20 April 1940, p. 7.

96. *Connacht Tribune,* 27 April 1940, p. 9.

97. *Connacht Tribune,* 20 April 1940, p. 7.

98. The department was aware that it could be argued that the making of such an order would 'be used as evidence to accuse the Government of being afraid to face a public investigation.' The memo warned, however, that at any such inquest Government officials and medical officers 'would be exposed to attacks by Counsel [for the families of the deceased] who would be brought for that purpose.' Even more alarming was the possibility that ministers might be subpoenaed, and that 'the occasion would be availed of to cause the maximum amount of trouble and expense.' The provisions of the draft order were also extended to include cases of people who were interned. There had been two cases of internees going on hunger strike, and even though they had since abandoned their strike the department feared that similar cases might occur, and that 'it is probably better to make provision for them.' This would have created a rather unusual situation whereby men or women who had not been charged with or convicted of any crime would be denied an inquest into their deaths or their release for burial. Department of Justice memo, 15 April 1940 (National Archives, D/T S11828).

99. Memo, para. 6. See also Draft Order 2 *c* (ii).

100. A statement describing the prisoners' demands was sent by Rita E. Byrne to de Valera on 10 March. 'We do not demand release, though we do not recognise the Free State or their authority to hold us.' She added: 'Since there appears to be some confusion as to the issue on which the Republican prisoners have gone on hunger strike, I would like to draw your attention to the above since I understand that you yourself fought on a similar issue in 1917' (National Archives, D/T S11515). See also the statement issued by Cumann na mBan, 11 April 1940 (National Archives, D/T S11533).

101. The document, headed 'Political Prisoners: Treatment of,' is unsigned and undated, but a letter submitted the following day indicates that it was composed by Stephen Roche and Michael Byrne on 18 April 1940 (National Archives, D/T S11515).

102. *Connacht Tribune,* 27 April 1940, p. 7. A coachbuilder by profession, Kilroy had been active in the Irish Volunteers and the IRA, becoming officer commanding the 1st Battalion (Castlebar), West Mayo Brigade 1920–21, and leader of a flying column. He was promoted to commanding officer of the 1st Western Division from 1921 to 1922. He opposed the Treaty, was on the Executive of the anti-Treaty IRA, and was officer commanding the Western Command of the anti-Treaty forces during the Civil War. Captured by the Free State army in November 1922, the following June he was elected Sinn Féin TD for Mayo South with Tom Maguire. Elected to Mayo County Council in 1925, he followed de Valera into Fianna Fáil and was elected for that party at every

election between June 1927 and 1933. He stood unsuccessfully for Mayo North in 1937 and for Mayo South in 1944 and 1954. See also Vincent Browne, *The Magill Book of Irish Politics*, p. 282. The *Irish Press* (22 April 1940) referred to Kilroy as an uncle of McNeela and former TD but did not mention his party affiliation or occupational status.

103. In a manifesto issued on 17 October 1923 Kilroy had announced that a number of IRA men were embarking on a hunger strike until they had, in the words of Terence MacSwiney, achieved freedom or the grave. Hunger Strike Manifesto issued by prisoners on hunger strike in Mountjoy Prison for unconditional release. Signed by Michael Kilroy and Mícheál Mac Giollaruaidh (officer commanding prisoners) and published by the Sinn Féin Publicity Department, 17 October 1923 (National Library of Ireland, LO P117, no. 70).

104. Skinner, *Politicians by Accident,* p. 206.

105. 'You are in the dock as far as the Irish nation is concerned, Mr Boland,' declared MacBride, to which the minister replied that the Irish people would soon have an opportunity to express a verdict. On another occasion MacBride declared: 'I put it to you, Mr Boland, that out of your intolerance you allowed these two men to die. I put it to you that you refused to make any concession to Father O'Hare until D'Arcy had died and until you saw that the Irish nation would not stand for this.' Boland replied, 'I was going to say, "Is that a speech or a question?"' Transcript of Inquest, p. 83 (National Archives, D/T S11515).

106. *Connacht Tribune,* 27 April 1940, p. 7.

107. The sporadically produced republican journal *War News* (no. 2, July 1940, p. 2) commented sardonically that 'it is felt that this important seizure will greatly affect the future course of the European War.'

108. Fine Gael had stepped aside, an act that the Government had described as patriotic and that demonstrated to the satisfaction of Fianna Fáil that 'Mr. Cosgrave's party are behind the Government four-square.' Éamon de Valera and Tom Derrig, speaking in Oughterard, Co. Galway (*Connacht Tribune,* 25 May 1940, p. 7). Fine Gael's support in the area was little more than 20 per cent.

109. Tom Derrig, speaking in Oughterard, Co. Galway (*Connacht Tribune,* 25 May 1940, p. 7).

110. Biographical information from the *Irish Times,* 22 January 1948, p. 1. The paper was covering the death of 48-year-old Gantly, who was shot and accidentally killed by one of his own men during a raid in pursuit of a wanted man. His funeral was attended by Gerry Boland (Minister for Justice), Frank Aiken (Minister for Finance) and Oscar Traynor (Minister for Defence) (*Irish Times,* 24 January 1948, p. 5).

111. Bell, *The Secret Army,* p.187.

112. Bell, *The Secret Army,* p. 191.

113. Bell, *The Secret Army,* p. 216.

114. White, *Harry,* p. 105.

115. Foley, *Legion of the Rearguard,* p. 207.

116. Coogan, *The IRA* (second edition), p. 248.

117. See White, *Harry,* p. 104–6.

118. Conor Brady, *Guardians of the Peace,* p. 237.

119. Archie Doyle recounted that 'it was a case of who got whom first.' White, *Harry,* p. 105.

120. Demonstrating the ambivalence that permeated many levels of the state, the soldier brought White first to an isolated farmhouse, where he fed him and nursed his

wounds over a number of days before bringing him to his family home. He then made contact with the IRA and brought him to Dublin. See Mac Eoin, *The IRA in the Twilight Years*, p. 450, 523–8.

121. Mac Eoin, *The IRA in the Twilight Years*, p. 501, 533, 698. Griffiths' father, a compositor at the *Irish Press*, took up the telex message about his son's death and fainted over his machine. Bell, *The Secret Army*, p. 233.

122. These included Seán Gaffney and Joe McGinley, who died in November 1940 and August 1943, respectively, on the prison ship *Al-Rawdah*, brought into Strangford Lough to accommodate additional IRA prisoners. Others reported to have died as a result of ill-treatment while in prison are Bob Clancy (12 June 1941, Curragh Internment Camp), Joe Malone (21 January 1942, Parkhurst Prison, Isle of Wight), Terence Perry (7 July 1942, Parkhurst Prison), John Hinchy (October 1942, Mountjoy Prison) and Charlie O'Hare (2 June 1944, Isle of Man). Seán Dolan and James Keenan died within weeks of being released from *Al-Rawdah* and Belfast Prison (Crumlin Road), respectively.

123. Mac Eoin, *The IRA in the Twilight Years*, p. 450.

Chapter 8: The showdown, 1940–46 (p. 174–99)

1. Peter Barnes was a 32-year-old native of Banagher, Co. Offaly, who gave up his job with Offaly County Council to go to England in 1939. James McCormack, who was sentenced under the alias Frank Richards, was a 29-year-old native of Mullingar.

2. Barnes, for example, was sentenced to death for possession of a receipt for a flour bag and suitcases that were used in the incident. He was not in Coventry when the bomb was prepared or when it exploded.

3. See the *Irish Independent*, 1 February 1940, p. 10; 2 February, p. 8; 5 February, p. 11; 6 February, p. 7–8; 7 February, p. 7–8.

4. Letter from de Valera to Eden, 29 January 1940 (National Archives, CJ 1/62).

5. Letter from de Valera to Chamberlain, 2 February 1940 (National Archives, CJ 1/62).

6. Telephone message from de Valera to Chamberlain, 5 February 1940 (National Archives, CJ 1/62).

7. If anything, the position of the Catholic hierarchy fell some way short of that of its counterparts in the Protestant and Jewish communities. In addition to the usual warnings against drinking, dancing, evil literature and immodest dress, the Lenten pastorals contained strong condemnations of the IRA, combined with the threat of excommunication. No reference was made to the imminent execution of Barnes and McCormack. The alleged communistic nature of the IRA was stressed, and the Bishop of Waterford stated that 'members of the IRA are unworthy of the sacraments of Penance and the Blessed Eucharist and confessors should refuse them absolution unless they have left the society ... Other societies, whether of men or women, which are allied to the IRA, or have similar objects, come under the same condemnation, and their members are to be dealt with in the same way by confessors' (*Irish Independent*, 5 February 1940, p. 6–7).

8. *Irish Independent*, 7 February 1940, p. 7.

9. Message from Chamberlain to de Valera, 6 February 1940; quoted by Longford and O'Neill, *Éamon de Valera*, p. 360.

10. Thomas Pierrepoint (1870–1954), principal executioner in Britain from 1908 to 1945. Believed to have killed approximately three hundred people, including a number in

Ireland under the British, Free State and Fianna Fáil regimes. His brother, Henry Pierrepoint (1878–1922), was also a hangman, 1903–14. Henry's son, Albert Pierrepoint (1905–1992), one of the last people to carry out this work for the British Government, executed an estimated 435 men and women. His autobiography, *Executioner: Pierrepoint* (London: Harrap, 1974), deals extensively with his work in Ireland during de Valera's period in office (Coronet edition, 1998, p. 99–110, 158–60). He also recounts a visit to his pub in Lancashire by members of the IRA who were interested to know the route he took when travelling to Ireland (p. 160–6).

11. Such public indignation was not captured in the newspaper editorials; the *Irish Independent,* for example, editorialised on 'Birds in war-time' the day after the executions and offered no editorial comment throughout the entire episode (*Irish Independent,* 8 February 1940, p. 6).

12. *Irish Independent,* 10 February 1940, p. 9, 11.

13. *Irish Independent,* 2 February 1940, p. 9. The question whether the assailants identified themselves is central in assessing the case against Mac Curtáin. At the same time as Mac Curtáin's trial a similar case, that of William Mulligan, was being adjudicated by the Special Criminal Court. Mulligan was charged with resisting arrest and obstructing gardaí in the execution of their duty, though the sequence of events that led to his arrest was almost identical to those in the Mac Curtáin case. Mulligan refused to plead (which suggests IRA membership) but defended himself. As the gardaí admitted that they had not produced identification, the president of the court concluded that 'there may have been some doubt in the prisoner's mind with regard to the identity of the police, and the Court is inclined to give him the benefit of the doubt' (*Irish Independent,* 3 February 1940, p. 9).

14. Born in Mallow, Co. Cork, Hickey was a trade union official, elected Labour Party TD for Cork City in 1938. Defeated in 1943, he did not contest the 1944 election but was elected for the National Labour Party in 1948 and for the reunited Labour Party in 1951 before being defeated again in 1954. He was Lord Mayor of Cork, 1939–40.

15. National Archives, D/T S11974, annex A. The number of signatures, according to an estimate carried out by the author, is 13,692 (± 150).

16. At the bottom of some petition forms is the statement 'Owing to the shortness of time at our disposal to seek vast numbers of signatures it is intended rather to confine our efforts to securing the signatures of a number of people representative of the national life of the country. Please ask anyone in your neighbourhood whose name would be of value to sign the Petition' (National Archives, D/T S11974, annex B). This point is borne out in a letter from Aodh Mac Giolla Pheadair of Ballyshannon, Co. Donegal, dated 30 June 1940. Submitting four petition pages containing ninety-two signatures from the town, he informed the Reprieve Committee that 'had time and space permitted I could have obtained ten times the number of signatures enclosed herewith; as it is I have endeavoured to obtain the most representative list possible' (National Archives, D/T S11974, annex B).

17. The petition from these groups was acknowledged by the secretary after consultation with de Valera, who said he did not want the communication sent by post. A telegram was sent to the Lord Mayor, James Hickey, at 6:30 p.m., which stated that the petition had been 'carefully considered' but that the Government had 'decided law must take its course' (National Archives, D/T S11974).

18. Telegram, 29 June 1940 (National Archives, S11974.

19. Telegram 1 July 1940 (National Archives, D/T S11974.

20. During one evening, 9 July 1940, an estimated 1,800 signatures were collected at the Mansion House by Clarke (National Archives, D/T S11974, annex B).

21. These included Mrs O'Mahony, whose son was executed in Cork Barracks on 28 February 1921 after the Dripsey ambush; Mrs Mullane, whose son was one of five people killed by the Black and Tans at Ballycannon on 23 March 1921; Mrs Murphy, whose son, Joe, died on hunger strike in Cork Jail after seventy-six days on 25 October 1920; Mrs Trahey, whose husband was murdered in Cork on 20 November 1920; and Miss Delaney, whose two brothers and uncle were killed by the Black and Tans on 12 December 1920.

22. The father and brother of James M. Quain, killed in action on 10 May 1921; mother, sister, aunt and cousin of Michael Fitzgerald, executed by Free State forces on 20 January 1923; brother, two sisters and two nieces of John Ahern, who died on 19 September 1922 from ill-treatment received in British prisons; mother, three sisters, uncle and cousin of Vice-Comdt Patrick O'Reilly, 10th Battalion, Cork No. 1 Brigade, killed in action on 25 October 1922; three sisters and cousin of Capt. Liam Hoare, officer commanding 4th (Gartroe) Battalion, Cork No. 1 Brigade, killed in action on 10 April 1921.

23. Cabinet Minutes, 4 July 1940 (National Archives, G.2/167). The order stated that the Government could 'at absolute discretion' defer such cases. See schedule A to the minutes for the text of the order.

24. Cabinet Minutes, 4 July 1940, item 3 (National Archives, G.2/167).

25. Cabinet Minutes, 10 July 1940 (National Archives, G.2/170).

26. Interview with Lt-Col. Seán Clancy by the author. Clancy, who had previously worked with Michael Collins, became friendly later in life with Peadar O'Donnell. It is likely that O'Donnell did indeed meet Boland to make a personal appeal, but it is impossible to establish whether this was decisive. In the aftermath of Mac Curtáin's reprieve there were probably many individuals and organisations who felt that their protest had exerted a decisive influence. Tim Pat Coogan offers a different explanation, stating that it is 'authoritatively supposed' that a sister of Cathal Brugha's widow, the head of a convent in Co. Armagh, interceded with Cardinal MacRory, who persuaded de Valera to commute the sentence to penal servitude for life. Coogan, *The IRA* (first edition), p. 150.

27. Quoted by Fisk, *In Time of War*, p. 347–8.

28. Quoted by Fisk, *In Time of War*, p. 347–8.

29. Quoted by Fisk, *In Time of War*, p. 347–8.

30. Such a belief is not as fanciful as it may at first appear. The head of the Special Branch, Chief Supt Seán Gantly, was accidentally killed by one of his own men in 1948 while participating in a raid that sought to capture an unarmed wanted man. See *Irish Times*, 22 January 1948, p. 1. According to one commentator, the incident clearly demonstrated that 'the American system of calling out squads of heavily armed and irresponsible policemen, while not over effective in accomplishing its purpose—one of the men is still at large—is highly dangerous to the members of the force, to say nothing of the general public, whom the police are ostensibly trying to protect' (*Irish Times*, 23 January 1948, p. 4).

31. Seán O'Mahony, *Frongoch*, p. 222–5.

32. Cabinet Minutes, 21 August 1940 (National Archives, G.2/183).

33. Cabinet Minutes, 23 August 1940, item 2 (National Archives, G.2/185). See the schedule to the minutes for the text of Emergency Powers (No. 45) Order (1940).

34. Cabinet Minutes, 23 August 1940, item 3 (National Archives, G.2/185).

35. Anonymous, *Tom Harte and His Comrades of the Forties* (Dublin: Irish Freedom Press [1990]), p. 17.

36. Cabinet Minutes, 4 September 1940 (National Archives, G.2/190).

37. Clarke, *Revolutionary Woman*, p. 224.

38. *Irish Independent*, 6 September 1940, p. 4.

39. *Irish Independent*, 18 December 1940, p. 6.

40. The censorship of the time is reflected in standard works on the IRA. The execution of Goss merits only one line in Bell's *The Secret Army* and two in Coogan's *The IRA* and is not mentioned in Foley's *Legion of the Rearguard*. Biographical information is mainly taken from County Longford Branch, National Graves Association, *Longford Remembers*, p. 12, 15–24.

41. Walsh is erroneously described as Mayor of Dundalk in the report of the Secretary of the Government. I am grateful to Mrs Monica McGuill of Dundalk for being able to recollect the political affiliation of Joseph O'Hagan.

42. See National Archives, D/T S12127.

43. Telegram from Lawrence Clifford, Philip Daly Cumann (60th), 2 August 1941 (National Archives, D/T S12127).

44. Telegram received on 7 August 1941 (National Archives, D/T S12127).

45. Telegram received on 7 August 1941 and signed by 'Carroll', district secretary of Old IRA, Louth Brigade (National Archives, D/T S12127).

46. Letter not dated but written on the first Sunday in August 1941. In return she received a standard reply, dated 5 August: 'A Chara, I am directed by the Taoiseach to acknowledge receipt of your recent letter. Mise le meas, P. Ó Cinnéide, Leas-Runaí.' The deputy secretary's signature is a rubber stamp (National Archives, D/T S12127).

47. It was stipulated by emergency legislation that the death sentences be carried out 'not later than 72 hours' after the sentence was confirmed by the Executive. The very short interlude between announcement and execution was probably aimed at limiting the amount of public opposition that could be mustered.

48. Brian Farrell, *Chairman or Chief?*

49. Lindsay, *Memories*, p. 154.

50. Mac Eoin, *The IRA in the Twilight Years*, p. 540–41.

51. Bell, *The Secret Army*, p. 168.

52. See Department of the Taoiseach file, National Archives, S12249.

53. Quoted by Coogan, *De Valera*, p. 625.

54. The most important effect of the Emergency Powers Order on the Plant case was that it empowered the prosecution—but not the defence—to read at any stage in a trial a statement taken down in writing and signed by any person, even if such a person was not called as a witness or refused to give evidence. The order further empowered the Military Court to 'act on such a statement as evidence.' See *Irish Independent*, 5 January 1942.

55. The case was transferred from the military tribunal to the Military Court (often called the 'Death Court' by its opponents). That this was done bolsters the belief that the Government wished to rid itself of Plant as expeditiously as possible, for the court was empowered only to hand down a death sentence; there was no right of appeal;

and the judgement had to be executed within seventy-two hours of being confirmed by the Government.

56. *Irish Times*, 26 February 1942; quoted in Sinn Féin, *George Plant*, p. 14.

57. Commenting on the Emergency Powers Order, Tony Gray (*The Lost Years*, p. 174) wrote that 'with legislation like this ranged against them how could the IRA possibly have survived?'

58. Walsh and Daveran were also sentenced to death, but these sentences were commuted to life imprisonment by the Government.

59. Fisk, *In Time of War*, p. 182.

60. Fisk, *In Time of War*, p. 378.

61. Fisk, *In Time of War*, p. 379.

62. C. J. McDonnell, on behalf of United Press Associations of America, draft to censor in 31 August 1942, passed in full save for minor grammatical corrections (National Archives, D/J R35).

63. Coogan, *The IRA* (second edition), p. 249. The man in question was Harry White, who was on the run at the time.

64. The Manchester Martyrs—William Allen, Michael Larkin and Michael O'Brien—were hanged in England in 1867. An early and, as a result, vivid account of their trial and execution can be found in Anonymous, *The Dock and the Scaffold: The Manchester Tragedy and the Cruise of the Jacknell* (Dublin: A. M. Sullivan, 1868). A succinct account can be found in John Newsinger, *Fenianism in Mid-Victorian Britain* (London: Pluto Press, 1994), p. 60–64.

65. Draft of articles from the *Tipperary Star*, 2 September 1942 (National Archives, D/J R35).

66. Extract from 'A Londoner's Diary' in the *Evening Standard*, reprinted by the *Irish Independent*, draft of article dated 26 August submitted to censor. Bevan was on a visit to Ireland (National Archives, D/J R35).

67. Deleted from issues of the *Irish Times* and *Irish Press* dated 27 August 1942 (National Archives, D/J R35).

68. Deleted from issue of the *Irish Press* dated 30 August 1942 (National Archives, D/J R35).

69. Descriptions in National Archives, D/J R35. Williams was buried in an unmarked and unconsecrated grave in the grounds of Belfast Prison, where he had been hanged. The closure of the prison in 1996 and the efforts of the National Graves Association led to the release of the remains and their reburial on 19 January 2000. The event was attended by several thousand people, including Joe Cahill (1920–2004), who had been condemned to death with Williams but reprieved. Cahill went on to become a prominent figure in the Provisional IRA and was its representative sent to the United States in 1994 to secure agreement for a ceasefire. See Brendan Anderson, *Joe Cahill: A Life* (Dublin: O'Brien Press, 2002).

70. Deleted from issue of the *Irish Times* dated 2 September 1942 (National Archives, D/J R35).

71. C. J. McDonnell, United Press Correspondent in Dublin, draft to censor, 2 September 1942, passed in full except for one line (National Archives, D/J R35). However, Eason's bookshop was stormed and compelled to close during the designated hour of mourning.

72. J. Kenny, *Daily Express* correspondent, draft for censor, 2 September 1942, partially deleted (National Archives, D/J R35).

73. Tim Pat Coogan (*The IRA* [second edition], p. 247) states incorrectly that the incident occurred in November.

74. A native of Courtown, Co. Wexford, George Mordaunt served in the Free State army from 1922 until 1935, when he joined the Special Branch.

75. See Coogan, *The IRA* (second edition), p. 250.

76. *Irish Press*, proof for censor, 8 November. The Government statement was printed, but the heading 'Maurice O'Neill: Death sentence to stand' was changed to 'Government decision: Donnycarney death sentence' (National Archives, D/J R47).

77. Minutes of Parliamentary Party, 29 October 1942, item 3 (Fianna Fáil Archives, FF/440).

78. Minutes of Parliamentary Party, 29 October 1942, item 2 (Fianna Fáil Archives, FF/440).

79. *Irish Independent,* proof for censor, 8 November 1942, stopped in entirety (National Archives, D/J R47).

80. Bell (*The Secret Army,* p. 228) states incorrectly that he was hanged by the British hangman, Pierrepoint.

81. *Irish Press*, proof for censor, 12 November 1942 (National Archives, D/J R47).

82. *Irish Independent*, handwritten report to censor, 12 November 1942 (National Archives, D/J R 47).

83. *Irish Independent,* handwritten note, 13 November 1942; *Irish Press,* proof for censor, 13 November 1942 (National Archives, D/J R47).

84. *Irish Independent*, 8 July 1943.

85. Memorandum on the policy of the Government with regard to Offences Against the State, p. 14 (National Archives, D/T S11564A).

86. Clarke, *Revolutionary Woman*, p. 225–6. De Valera did not reply personally; instead a note was sent by his secretary that stated that her letter had been received by the President and that her resignation would be considered at the subsequent meeting of the National Executive. On 17 May she received a letter informing her that her resignation had been accepted. There is an interesting epilogue. When Clarke died, in September 1972, aged ninety-four, she was given a state funeral from the Pro-Cathedral, Dublin, which was attended by President de Valera. Also in attendance were the Taoiseach, Jack Lynch, and several other Fianna Fáil ministers (fresh from the ard-fheis that had expelled Neil Blaney for his over-zealous attachment to traditional republicanism). In death, Kathleen Clarke had been reclaimed for state and party.

87. For a selection of suppressed items relating to McCool see letter to the national papers from the Political Prisoners Committee, which included Maud Gonne MacBride, Úna de Staic and Dr Kathleen Lynn (*Irish Independent,* proof for censor, 17 June 1943, stopped, and *Irish Press* and *Cork Examiner* advised); letter from Brian O'Higgins (*Sunday Independent,* proof for censor, 19 June 1943); reports of Fianna Fáil meetings in Cos. Donegal and Cork (*Irish Press,* proof for censor, 11 June 1943; *Irish Times* proof for censor, 6 June 1943, p. 3). All cited documents are in National Archives, D/J R37.

88. See, for example, the speeches of Seán MacEntee in Rathmines and Dr James Ryan in Wexford. *Irish Independent* and *Irish Times,* proofs to censor, 6 June 1943, and *Free Press* (Wexford), typed report to censor, 26 May 1943 (National Archives, D/J R37). All three papers were forced by the censorship to remove the remarks of the hecklers from their reports.

89. Allen, *Fianna Fáil and Irish Labour*, p. 77.

90. Labour Party election poster for Dublin Townships Constituency, Joseph Browne and James Cawley (UCD Archives, MacEntee Papers, P67/362/9).

91. Notes for Speakers and Canvassers, No. 1 (UCD Archives, MacEntee Papers, P67/362/1).

92. Dónal Ó Drisceoil, 'Keeping the temperature down: Domestic politics in emergency Ireland,' in Keogh and O'Driscoll, *Ireland in World War Two*, p. 180.

93. Dónal Ó Drisceoil, 'Keeping the temperature down: Domestic politics in emergency Ireland,' in Keogh and O'Driscoll, *Ireland in World War Two*, p. 179.

94. Speech in Ranalagh, Dublin, 8 June 1943 (UCD Archives, MacEntee Papers, P67/364/9).

95. Speech in Ranelagh, Dublin, 8 June 1943 (UCD Archives, MacEntee Papers, P67/364/9). In another speech, at Harold's Cross Bridge (Emmet Bridge) on 4 June 1943, MacEntee declared: 'The Comintern has been abolished in Russia but the Muscovites are active in Dublin. I might say they are triumphant in Dublin. They have captured Mr. Norton and are holding him as a hostage while the Dublin Communist organisation is infiltrating its advance elements into the Irish Labour Party' (UCD Archives, MacEntee Papers, P67/364/16).

96. Dónal Ó Drisceoil, 'Keeping the temperature down: Domestic politics in emergency Ireland,' in Keogh and O'Driscoll, *Ireland in World War Two*, p. 181.

97. Election letter to constituents, Dublin Townships Constituency (UCD Archives, MacEntee Papers, P67/362/5).

98. Election letter to constituents, Dublin Townships Constituency (UCD Archives, MacEntee Papers, P67/362/5).

99. Notable among these was that of the future Fine Gael leader and Taoiseach J. A. Costello, who told the Dáil on 28 February 1934: 'The minister gave extracts from various laws on the Continent, but he carefully refrained from drawing attention to the fact that the Blackshirts were victorious in Italy and that the Hitler Shirts were victorious in Germany, as, assuredly, in spite of this bill and in spite of the Public Safety Act, the Blueshirts will be victorious in the Irish Free State.' Quoted on Fianna Fáil 1943 election handbill entitled 'Fine Gael and Labour SAID this' (UCD Archives, MacEntee Papers, P67/362/3).

100. Election letter to constituents, Dublin Townships Constituency (UCD Archives, MacEntee Papers, P67/362/5.

101. Córas na Poblachta has not been given serious academic treatment. Its presence on the electoral scene was fleeting, and all five candidates in the 1943 election lost their deposit. The party did not contest any subsequent elections. Ailtirí na hAiseirghe put up a small number of candidates in both the 1943 and 1944 elections. An excellent assessment of the organisation can be found in Aoife Ní Lochlainn, 'Ailtirí na hAiseirghe: A party of its time?' in Keogh and O'Driscoll, *Ireland in World War Two*, p. 187–210; see also the more recent R. M. Douglas, *Architects of the Resurrection: Ailtirí na hAiseirghe and the fascist 'New Order' in Ireland* (Manchester: Manchester University Press, 2009).

102. Letter from Lemass to MacEntee, 10 June 1943 (UCD Archives, MacEntee Papers, P67/363/6).

103. O'Leary, *Irish Elections*, p. 102.

104. See Eunan O'Halpin, 'Irish-Allied security relations and the "American note" crisis: New evidence from British records,' *Irish Studies in International Affairs*, 11 (2000), p. 71–83.

105. Speech by Seán MacEntee (UCD Archives, MacEntee Papers, P67/364).

106. Joseph Lee (*Ireland, 1912–1985*, p. 240–41) emphasises the personal animosity between O'Brien and Larkin, while Kieran Allen (*Fianna Fáil and Irish Labour*, p. 78–82) stresses the political and ideological forces at play.
107. Quoted by Allen, *Fianna Fáil and Irish Labour*, p. 80.
108. Michael Gallagher, quoted by Maye, *Fine Gael*, p. 66.
109. Hogan, *Election and Representation*, p. 77.
110. Hogan, *Election and Representation*, p. 77–8.
111. Bowman, *De Valera and the Ulster Question*, p. 251.
112. Cronin, *Washington's Irish Policy*, p. 156.
113. Cronin, *Washington's Irish Policy*, p. 159.
114. Dwyer, *De Valera*, p. 276.
115. Dwyer, *Strained Relations*.
116. Lee, *Ireland, 1912–1985*, p. 241.
117. Hogan, *Election and Representation*, p. 70–71.
118. See letter to editor from Eithne Nic Shuibhne, *Irish Independent*, 25 May 1944 (National Archives, D/J R38).
119. See speech by Michael Donnellan at Headford, Co. Galway (*Connacht Tribune*, 25 May 1940), and his election address for the West Galway by-election (*Connacht Tribune*, 25 May 1940, p. 10).
120. *Connacht Tribune*, 25 May 1940, p. 7.
121. Election address of Michael Donnellan for West Galway by-election (*Connacht Tribune*, 25 May 1940, p. 10).
122. In the constituency of Cork South-West the party vote rose from 17 to 27 per cent, and it narrowly missed taking a second seat.
123. Brian Inglis, *West Briton* (London: Faber and Faber, 1962), p. 175.
124. Hugh McAteer was a brother of Eddie McAteer, leader of the Nationalist Party in Northern Ireland.
125. See chap. 8.
126. *Irish Press*, 3 October 1944.
127. Bell, *The Secret Army*, p. 234.
128. *Parliamentary Debates: Dáil Éireann: Official Report*, 95/1408–9 (30 November 1944). Ó Drisceoil, *Censorship in Ireland*, p. 87.
129. *Irish Press*, proof for censor, 23 November 1944; *Irish Independent*, copy of telegram sent by Kerry County Council, 23 November 1944; *Irish Independent*, handwritten submission, 24 November 1944; stopped in full.
130. *Cork Examiner*, written record of phone message from paper, 23 November 1944.
131. For example, the *Nationalist* (Clonmel) had to stop publication of a paid advertisement announcing a public meeting to be held on 26 November to appeal to the Government to reconsider Kerins's sentence and that the bishop and local clergy had been invited to attend. Handwritten account of phone message received by Peter Berry at 1:20 p.m. on 22 November 1944.
132. Department of Justice, 'Instructions to Press Censors,' 21 November 1942 (National Archives, D/J R48).
133. National Archives, D/J R48.
134. See *Irish Independent*, typed and handwritten submissions, 24 November 1944; *Irish Times*, 24 November 1944; *Irish Press*, 24 November 1944; *Cork Examiner*, 24 November 1944; *Irish Independent*, 26 November; all stopped.

135. At the Manchester Martyrs Commemoration Concert in the Mansion House, Dublin, Peadar Cowen, made an appeal for people to attend the forthcoming meeting for Charlie Kerins, as notices of the meeting had been prohibited and even telegrams sent to public representatives had been stopped. *Irish Independent,* proof dated 24 November 1944, stopped.

136. *Irish Independent,* proof for censor, 27 November 1944, stopped.

137. See *Irish Independent,* typed submission, 24 November 1944; *Evening Herald,* typed submission, 1 December 1944; both articles were stopped.

138. 'Many arrests follow move for reprieve,' *Irish Times,* proof for censor. See also *Irish Independent,* proof for censor, 26 November 1944, stopped in entirety.

139. *Evening Herald,* 28 November 1944, stopped. Statement by Con Lehane, solicitor for Kerins (National Archives, D/J R48). The number of signatures—77,000—was also considered symbolic by some, as seventy-seven IRA men had been executed by the Cosgrave government during the Civil War.

140. Covering letter to petition, 28 November 1944 (National Archives, D/T S13567/1).

141. 'Petition for reprieve,' *Evening Herald,* proof for censor, 28 November 1944, and *Evening Mail,* 28 November 1944; stopped totally.

142. Cabinet Minutes, 28 November 1944, item 1 (National Archives, G.4/31).

143. Attempts to raise the issue of Kerins's impending execution were ruled out of order the previous day. The Kerry deputy Pat Finucane (Clann na Talmhan) declared that 'if he is executed, his memory will live when Fianna Fáil is blasted into oblivion.'

144. During one bitter exchange Dan Spring (Labour Party) warned that Tom Derrig would not want to visit Co. Kerry in the near future. When Derrig asked whether he was making a threat, Spring replied that he could 'take it any way you like.'

145. 'Your citizenship of the American Republic was invoked in 1916 to save your life. Why now give the British rope to a soldier of the Irish Republic?' Telegram from Bridget Dudley Edwards to de Valera, 30 November 1944 (National Archives, D/T S13567/1).

146. Letter to de Valera, 28 November 1944 (National Archives, D/T S13567/1).

147. Kevin Barry (1902–20) was an eighteen-year-old medical student when he was captured by the British army. His IRA unit had ambushed a lorry transporting British soldiers on 20 September and killed three, and Barry was hanged for his part on 1 November. His youth and manner of execution (he had requested that he be shot as a soldier) outraged nationalist Ireland and resulted in a swelling of IRA ranks. See Cronin, *The Story of Kevin Barry,* and John Ainsworth, 'Kevin Barry, the incident at Monks' Bakery and the making of an Irish Republican legend,' *History,* 87/287 (2002), p. 372-87. On 14 October 2001 the Government (headed by Fianna Fáil) authorised the removal of Barry's remains from Mountjoy Prison along with those of nine other IRA volunteers. All ten men were given a state funeral, which was attended by thousands, and Barry is now buried in Glasnevin Cemetery.

148. Telegram from May Barry to de Valera, 30 November 1944 (D/T S13567/1). When May Barry died, in 1953, de Valera, as Taoiseach, attended the funeral. According to a nephew of Kevin Barry, the family ignored him. See O'Donovan, *Kevin Barry and His Time,* p. 186–9.

149. Letter to Ceann Comhairle, Frank Fahy TD, 6 January 1945 (National Archives, D/T S13567/1).

150. Note in margin of covering letter from Rory McHugh (National Archives, D/T S13567/1).

151. Submission from *Irish Press,* 5 January 1945. Advice sent to the *Irish Independent* and *Cork Examiner* (National Archives, D/J R48).

152. Submission from the *Irish Independent* and proof from the *Irish Press,* 1 December 1944. A directive was also sent to the *Cork Examiner.* The *Month's Mind* (31 December) suffered a similar fate. There was a curious sequel to this act. On Saturday morning, 2 December, two young clerical officers were discussing the censoring of the report of the mass for Kerins. The first declared that that the Chief Press Censor had done 'a terrible thing,' a statement with which the second concurred, saying that 'he will get into a hell of a row over that.' The conversation was overheard by a sister-in-law of the censor, who reported the matter to the Controller of Censorship. Handwritten note from Michael Knightly to Controller, n.d. (National Archives, D/J R48).

153. National Archives, D/J R48.

154. Handwritten note by Chief Press Censor, Michael Knightly, to Controller of Censorship, 4 December 1944 (National Archives, D/J R48).

155. Foley, *Legion of the Rearguard,* p. 208.

156. Bell, *The Secret Army,* p. 235, 239. John A. Murphy provides a similar assessment when he states that 'by the end of the war it seemed that the IRA was finished as an organisation commanding anything like substantial support.' John A. Murphy, *Ireland in the Twentieth Century,* p. 160.

157. National Archives, D/T S11574.

158. Hayes was well known in Co. Wexford, where he was a former county footballer. He became chief of staff of the IRA after the death of Seán Russell in 1940. For reasons that are still unclear, the majority of the IRA leadership became convinced, after a series of fiascos, that Hayes was an informer and in league with the Government. He was subjected to a prolonged period of incarceration and torture in a house in Rathmines, Dublin, where, under the eye of McCaughey, he wrote a detailed confession, the veracity of which is still contested. He managed to escape and contacted the Gardaí, who promptly arrested McCaughey. The majority of those interviewed by Mac Eoin in his magnum opus, *The IRA in the Twilight Years,* were certainly convinced of Hayes's guilt. See, for example, interviews with Liam Burke (present at the 'trial'), p. 445–7, Tomo Costello, p. 475–6, Paddy Murphy, p. 534, and Christy Quearney, p. 781. Moss Twomey, however, favoured the Scottish verdict of 'not proven' (p. 856).

159. The *Cork Examiner,* for example, reported three public demonstrations (10 May 1946, p. 5), while the *Connacht Tribune* reported an after-Mass meeting in Inch, Co. Clare (11 May 1946, p. 3). Clan na Gael in New York sent a telegram to the Prisoner Release Committee reporting a meeting of 'thousands of Gaels, assembled to protest at the inhuman treatment of Seán McCaughey and David Fleming' (*Irish Independent,* 7 May 1946, p. 6).

160. *Irish Independent,* 10 May 1946, p. 7.

161. *Parliamentary Debates: Dáil Éireann: Official Report,* 100/1239 (3 April 1946).

162. Quoted by Cronin, *Washington's Irish Policy,* p. 183.

163. Memorandum [dated 21 May 1946] of interview with Mr. de Valera on Saturday, 18 May 1946 (National Archives [London], DO 35/2094).

164. See report in the *Irish Independent,* 13 May 1946, p. 2.

165. *Cork Examiner,* 31 May 1946, p. 4.

166. *Parliamentary Debates: Dáil Éireann: Official Report,* 101/1128 (29 May 1946).

167. Quoted by Mac Eoin, *The IRA in the Twilight Years,* p. 541. A copy of the letter was also sent to de Valera.

168. *Connacht Tribune,* 25 May 1946, p. 2.
169. *Irish Independent,* 25 May 1946, p. 4; *Cork Examiner,* 4 June 1948, p. 7. At the meeting Boland was described as 'His Majesty's Chief Butcher in Ireland,' and it was claimed that the IRA 'would live as long as they had men like Charlie Kerins, Seán McCaughey and David Fleming.' The three men—J. J. Sheehy, Richie Eager and Seán Ryan, all prominent former Kerry footballers—were sentenced to six months' imprisonment.
170. It was contended that White had been handed over to the Dublin authorities on the assumption that the 'Death Court' in the South would mete out harsher punishment than what would be received had he been tried in the North. The head of the Special Branch, Chief Supt Seán Gantly, did little to allay this suspicion when he allegedly walked over to White after he was charged in Dublin and said: 'Don't worry, we'll get this over quick and you'll hang, you bastard.' White, *Harry,* p. 155.
171. See White, *Harry,* p. 158–63.
172. Even this seemingly innocuous programme fell foul of the censorship. When it was transmitted from Belfast in October 1942 the presenter, Joe Linnane, asked a competitor, 'Who is the world's best-known teller of fairytales?' Instead of the answer 'Hans Christian Andersen' he received the reply 'Winston Churchill,' upon which the mainly nationalist audience burst into laughter and cheers. As the programme was broadcast live, there was nothing Radio Éireann could do to prevent its transmission. All reports of the incident were stopped by the censorship, however, and it was 'a long time before a team from Radio Éireann crossed the border again.' See Maurice Gorham, *Forty Years of Irish Broadcasting* (Dublin: Talbot Press, 1967), p. 130–33; Ó Drisceoil, *Censorship in Ireland,* p. 101.
173. Mac Eoin, *The IRA in the Twilight Years,* p. 540. Noel Hartnett also appears to have believed that Little was not acting on his own initiative: in his letter to the *Cork Examiner* (31 May 1946, p. 4) he referred to 'the reason assigned by Mr. de Valera's Mr. Little for purging me.'
174. Some clues may be provided in a file that existed in the Department of Justice entitled 'Noel Hartnett and Seán McCaughey' (National Archives, D/J S10/46). I was informed by the National Archives, however, that this file is now missing.
175. *Irish Independent,* 31 May 1946, p. 2.
176. *Cork Examiner,* 31 May 1946, p. 4.
177. Quoted by Mac Eoin, *The IRA in the Twilight Years,* p. 540.

Chapter 9: A new republican rival, 1946–8 (p. 200–16)
1. *Cork Examiner,* 4 June 1946, p. 5.
2. *Cork Examiner,* 4 June 1946, p. 5. McGrath expressed the belief that Fianna Fáil was 'the only national party in the country at the present time and was the only party that could effectively end partition,' a position that must have seriously diluted the appeal of Barry, who (though this was not widely known) had advocated an armed offensive against the North when on the IRA Army Council in the late 1930s.
3. *Cork Examiner,* 17 June 1946, p. 5.
4. See Patrick Quinlivan and Paul Rose, *The Fenians in England, 1865–1872* (London: John Calder, 1982), p. 144–59.
5. See Bell, *The Secret Army,* p. 243–4.
6. Quoted by Rafter, *The Clann,* p. 39.

7. Michael Farrell, 'The extraordinary life and times of Seán MacBride: Part 2,' *Magill*, January 1983, p. 26.

8. P. D. O'Keeffe, 'The origins and development of Clann na Poblachta,' MA thesis, UCC, 1981; cited by Rafter, *The Clann*, p. 23.

9. *Irish Times*, 8 July 1946, p. 1.

10. The strike had cost the INTO £191,553 in strike pay alone. See *Irish Times*, 2 April 1947, p. 7.

11. Resolution passed by over one hundred Fianna Fáil supporters at INTO conference, 24 April 1946 (Fianna Fáil Archives, FF/72).

12. Quoted by Fanning, *Independent Ireland*, p. 156.

13. Jordan, *Seán MacBride*, p. 9.

14. Noël Browne, *Against the Tide*, p. 96.

15. John A. Murphy, *Ireland in the Twentieth Century*, p. 118.

16. See Fianna Fáil advertisement in the *Howth Review*, 18 October 1947, p. 4, and 25 October 1947 (Special Election Bulletin), p. 1.

17. *Parliamentary Debates: Dáil Éireann: Official Report*, 40/133 (15 October 1931). See chap. 5.

18. *Irish Times*, 30 October 1947.

19. *Irish Times*, 16 October 1947, p. 6. See also *Irish Press*, 17 October 1947.

20. See letter to editor by MacBride, *Irish Times*, 18 October 1947, p. 8.

21. *Irish Times*, 29 October 1947, p. 1.

22. Free-marketers such as James Dillon were increasingly critical of Fianna Fáil's rigid adherence to protection and import substitution. See report of Dáil debate on the Finance Bill (1947) in the *Irish Times*, 12 June 1947, p. 3.

23. *Irish Times*, 1 November 1947, p. 1.

24. *Irish Times*, 1 November 1947, p. 7.

25. *Irish Times*, 1 November 1947, p. 1.

26. *Irish Times*, 12 January 1948, p. 7.

27. Patrick Beegan TD speaking in Gort with de Valera (*Connacht Tribune*, 10 January 1948 (first edition), p. 5).

28. The logic of de Valera's decision was apparent to Seán MacBride, who, speaking in Cork (*Irish Times*, 8 January 1948, p. 6), accused the Government of putting the country through the unnecessary expense of a general election to further the interests of Fianna Fáil. While making good political capital, MacBride was naïve if he thought the timing of elections was influenced by any factor other than the need to secure the re-election of the governing party.

29. Four-page Clann na Poblachta recruiting leaflet, n.d. [1947] (Fianna Fáil Archives, FF/891).

30. Four-page Clann na Poblachta recruiting leaflet, n.d. [1947] (Fianna Fáil Archives, FF/891).

31. Lee, *Ireland, 1912–1985*, p. 295–6.

32. Speaking in Monaghan (*Irish Times*, 12 January 1948, p. 7).

33. Speaking in New Ross (*Irish Times*, 15 January 1948, p. 3). This point was made throughout the campaign. See, for example, the speeches by de Valera in Monaghan (*Irish Times*, 12 January 1948, p. 7), Clonmel (*Irish Times*, 17 January 1948, p. 5), Mallow (*Irish Times*, 19 January 1948, p. 1), Birr (*Irish Times*, 23 January 1948, p. 3) and Boyle (*Irish Times*, 31 January, p. 3). See also the speech of Oscar Traynor in Phibsborough, Dublin (*Irish Times*, 17 January 1948, p. 5), and that of Lemass in Navan (*Irish Times*, 7 January 1948, p. 7).

34. Donncadh Ó Briain, speaking in Ballingarry, Co. Limerick (*Irish Times*, 8 January 1948, p. 6).

35. Erskine Childers, speaking in Tyrrellspass, Co. Westmeath (*Irish Times*, 30 January 1948, p. 1).

36. Matt Feehan, speaking at final rally in Dublin (*Irish Press*, 4 February 1948), quoted by Bowman, *De Valera and the Ulster Question*, p. 265.

37. *Irish Times*, 31 January 1948, p. 3.

38. Speaking in Cork (*Irish Times*, 8 January 1948, p. 6).

39. *Irish Times*, 19 January 1948, p. 5.

40. *Irish Times*, 19 January 1948, p. 5.

41. Speaking in Letterkenny (*Irish Times*, 28 January 1948, p. 1).

42. Speaking in Donegal (*Irish Times*, 28 January 1948, p. 1). He made similar points during his speeches in Clonmel (*Irish Times*, 12 January 1948, p. 6), Templemore (*Irish Times*, 22 January 1948, p. 3) and Tullamore (*Irish Times*, 30 January 1948, p. 1). T. F. O'Higgins described de Valera's conception of strong government as 'a regimented army of dummies,' and he accused him of having made 'a god out of party and a farce out of parliament' (*Irish Times*, 12 January 1948, p. 6).

43. *Irish Times*, 14 January 1948, p. 5. Another editorial (17 January 1948, p. 7) claimed that 'single-party rule, particularly under a leader of Mr. de Valera's stamp, sooner or later would degenerate into dictatorship.' See also editorials of 2 January 1948, p. 5; 24 January 1948, p. 7; and 31 January 1948, p. 7.

44. See, for example, speech in Clonmel (*Irish Times*, 17 January 1948, p. 5).

45. For the views of Fine Gael see *Irish Times*, 7 January 1948, p. 7, and 12 January 1948, p. 6. For the views of the leader of the Labour Party, William Norton, see *Irish Times*, 31 January 1948, p. 4.

46. See, for example, the *Irish Times* editorial on 2 January 1948, p. 5.

47. From a pamphlet issued by John J. Humphreys; quoted in a letter by J. Douglas to the editor, *Irish Times*, 16 January 1948, p. 4. It might be noted that de Valera's views on coalition government had also evolved over the years. In 1922 he had promoted a pact between pro-Treaty and anti-Treaty members of the Dáil, with government positions divided in proportion to parliamentary strength. This was the first time that coalition government was advocated in Ireland.

48. The *Star*, 10 May 1930. The Cumann na nGaedheal paper had urged the government to abolish PR 'while there was still time,' which presumably meant before Fianna Fáil came to power or the expected proliferation of parties materialised. Despite a flexible constitution, such a bold initiative was impossible, as throughout its period in office Cumann na nGaedheal was dependent on an array of small political groupings and independents, who would not have committed political suicide by agreeing to the abolition of the only electoral system that facilitated their election.

49. Cumann na nGaedheal had also cited the advantages of stability but couched its arguments in nationalist tones by charging that PR was a system 'thrust upon this country by the British.' This was despite the fact that one of its initial attractions was that, in a constitution that followed the British model in so many respects, a distinctive electoral system satisfied a desire to emphasise differences with the British model. In addition, Arthur Griffith and most of the original Sinn Féin leadership considered PR to be an important concession to the unionist minority, which would be obliterated politically should the 'first past the post' system prevail.

50. Editorial, *Cork Examiner*, 1 June 1946, p. 4.

51. See coverage of a Fianna Fáil meeting at Rathmines Town Hall addressed by Seán MacEntee, *Irish Times*, 26 January 1948, p. 1. An hour before a Clann na Poblachta meeting in Dún Laoghaire Town Hall, persons unknown entered the hall and stole the party's banner from the platform and poured kerosene over the leather chairs on which the speakers were to sit (*Irish Times*, 15 January 1948, p. 3). Fianna Fáil denied that it was involved. Letter to editor, *Irish Times*, 23 January 1948, p. 4.

52. MacBride claimed that special forms were provided and completed by officials and then transferred to recruiting agents in Britain, and through the Department of Social Welfare the Government aided foreign agents in recruiting emigrants at £1 a head (*Irish Times*, 30 January 1948, p. 1, and 2 February 1948, p. 1). What MacBride was not aware of was that, throughout the war, one of de Valera's greatest concerns was that the hundreds of thousands who left to work in Britain or to join the British forces would return to Ireland following the end of the war—a fear that proved to be groundless.

53. Speaking in Callan, Co. Kilkenny (*Irish Times*, 22 January 1948, p. 3).

54. Dr J. P. Brennan, speaking in Dún Laoghaire (*Irish Times*, 15 January 1948, p. 3).

55. May Laverty, for example, speaking in Harold's Cross, Dublin, as a candidate for Dublin South-West, sought to remind 'those women who claim to leave politics to men that this attitude would date them' (*Irish Times*, 13 January 1948, p. 4).

56. Con Lehane, speaking in New Street, Dublin (*Irish Times*, 16 January 1948, p. 3).

57. Frank Aiken described Clann na Poblachta as the 'Compulsory English Party' (*Cork Examiner*, 26 January 1948, p. 5), while de Valera said that the saving of Irish was more important than the election (*Connacht Tribune*, 31 January 1948, city edition, p. 10). Conradh na Gaeilge intervened by placing advertisements in the papers that attacked those who questioned the policy of obligatory Irish (*Connacht Tribune*, 31 January 1948, city edition, p. 7). It is worth noting that a prominent member of Clann na Poblachta publicly resigned from the party on the grounds that it was 'prepared to sacrifice the language to get votes' (*Connacht Tribune*, 31 January 1948, city edition, p. 10).

58. Ruairí Brugha was later to join Fianna Fáil, becoming a member of the Seanad, 1969–73 and 1973–81. He was elected to the Dáil for a single term, 1973–7, becoming TD for Dublin South County in a contest notable for the attempt of Kevin Boland to reclaim his old seat as leader of the new republican party, Aontacht Éireann. Between 1973 and 1977 Brugha was opposition spokesperson on Northern Ireland. His father, Cathal Brugha, was Minister for Defence during the War of Independence and was killed when fighting on the Republican side in the Civil War. Terence MacSwiney, IRA leader and Lord Mayor of Cork, died on hunger strike in Brixton Prison, London, in 1920 after seventy-four days on hunger strike. See Costello, *Enduring the Most*. A brief profile of Ruairí Brugha was published in the *Irish Times*, 23 January 1948, p. 3. For information on Michael Barry see O'Donovan, *Kevin Barry and His Time*, p. 155–6.

59. Michael Hilliard (1903–83) was Minister for Posts and Telegraphs, 1959–65, and Minister for Defence, 1965–9. He successfully contested eight general elections and was a Fianna Fáil TD from 1943 to 1973.

60. Information on backgrounds from Vincent Browne, *The Magill Book of Irish Politics*, p. 293, and Rafter, *The Clann*, p. 75–6.

61. *Irish Times*, 17 January 1948, p. 5.

62. Speaking in Bray (*Irish Times*, 3 February 1948, p. 1).

63. *Irish Times*, 27 January 1948, p. 1.

64. *Irish Times*, 2 February 1948, p. 1.

65. Speaking in New Ross (*Irish Times*, 15 January 1948, p. 3).

66. See letter to editor by MacBride, *Irish Times*, 27 January 1948, p. 2, and editorial response, same issue, p. 5. See also editorial of 31 January 1948, p. 7.

67. E. Ginnell, candidate for Meath, speaking in Trim (*Irish Times*, 7 January 1948, p. 7).

68. Speaking in Portumna (*Irish Times*, 16 January 1948, p. 3).

69. Letter from MacEntee to Mullins, 5 January 1948 (Fianna Fáil Archives). The Security File documented the activities of the CPI from 12 January 1942 to 7 November 1943.

70. Letter from Jim Larkin Junior to *Irish Workers' Voice*, 10 April 1930.

71. Editorial, *Irish Times*, 17 January 1948, p. 7.

72. Editorial, *Irish Times*, 31 January 1948, p. 7.

73. Cited by MacBride when speaking in Kilrush (*Irish Times*, 16 January 1948, p. 3). MacBride was quoting from a series of articles written by Dr O'Rahilly in the *Cork Examiner*.

74. Speaking in Patrick Street, Cork (*Cork Examiner*, 26 January 1948, p. 5, 7).

75. See letter to editor from L. G. Carr Lett, honorary secretary of Irish Film Society (*Irish Times*, 30 January 1948, p. 3). The society had shown six Russian films during the previous years. MacEntee also accused the society of making the Clann na Poblachta films (which were in fact made at Ealing Studios in London). The *Irish Times* (editorial, 31 January 1948, p. 7) described the charges of disseminating communist propaganda as 'almost pathetically funny.'

76. *Connacht Tribune*, 24 January 1948, p. 8.

77. *Connacht Tribune*, 24 January 1948, p. 8.

78. Senator L. E. O'Dea, speaking with de Valera in Eyre Square, Galway (*Connacht Tribune*, 31 January 1948, city edition, p. 10). O'Dea does not seem to have considered the analogy between the Portuguese dictator and the Fianna Fáil leader to be inappropriate. See also the speeches of Lemass in Navan (*Irish Times*, 7 January 1948, p. 7) and Kissane in Ballybunnion (*Irish Times*, 12 January 1948, p. 7).

79. Speaking in Coolboy, Co. Wicklow. 'Will he deny that one of the leaders was secretary of the Communist Party in Ireland?' Everett taunted. 'Will he deny that one of them stood as a communist candidate in Dublin?' (*Irish Times*, 21 January 1948, p. 5).

80. *Irish Times*, 23 January 1948, p. 3. See also the speech of the Labour Party candidate William Davin in Enniscorthy (*Irish Times*, 22 January 1948, p. 3).

81. Speaking in Kilrush (*Irish Times*, 15 January 1948, p. 3).

82. Michael Mannion, candidate for North Galway, speaking in Ballymoe, Co. Roscommon (*Connacht Tribune*, 17 January 1948 (first edition), p. 3); Alderman Margaret Ashe, speaking in Clonbur, Co. Galway (*Connacht Tribune*, 31 January 1948, p. 5).

83. 'Divided Ireland,' *Irish Times*, 28 January 1948, p. 5. The paper reached similar conclusions in an editorial a week earlier: 'Through the medium,' *Irish Times*, 21 January 1948, p. 5.

84. The Labour Party's emphasis in improved economic standards as a means of ending partition was supported by the British Labour Party MP Geoffrey Bing, who, as a member of the anti-partitionist parliamentary group Friends of Ireland, visited Ireland during the election to support Labour Party candidates. Describing the Stormont regime as 'evil', he argued that 'to defeat it you must bring the economic

NOTES TO PAGES 210–13

standards here up to the level of those in the North' (*Irish Times*, 15 January 1948, p. 1). Lemass accused Bing of interfering in the affairs of an 'independent republic' (*Irish Times*, 15 January 1948, p. 3). For further information on the Friends of Ireland see Bob Purdie, 'The Friends of Ireland, British Labour and Irish nationalism, 1945–49,' in Tom Gallagher and James O'Connell (eds.), *Contemporary Irish Studies* (Manchester: Manchester University Press, 1983), p. 81–94.

85. *Irish Times*, 13 January 1948, p. 4.

86. See Tom Hales, speaking in Kinsale (*Cork Examiner*, 24 January 1948, p. 8).

87. For speeches other than those of MacBride on the subject see *Connacht Tribune*, 10 January 1948 (city edition), p. 5, and 17 January 1948 (first edition), p. 3, *Irish Times*, 7 January 1948, p. 7, and *Cork Examiner*, 24 January 1948, p. 8.

88. Speaking in Skibbereen (*Irish Times*, 30 January 1948, p. 1).

89. Speaking in Ballybay, Co. Monaghan (*Irish Times*, 31 January 1948, p. 3).

90. Cahir Healy had criticised those politicians in the South who offered no constructive policies but uttered 'some foolish comparison about the social services on both sides of the border' (*Irish Times*, 26 January 1948, p. 1).

91. *Parliamentary Debates: Dáil Éireann: Official Report*, 46/192 (1 March 1933).

92. *Irish Times*, 27 January 1948, p. 1.

93. For Fine Gael's response see the speech by Mulcahy in Letterkenny (*Irish Times*, 28 January 1948, p. 1).

94. *Irish Times*, 29 January 1948, p. 1.

95. *Irish Times*, 29 January 1948, p. 1.

96. *Irish Press*, 19 January 1948. See also *Irish Times*, 16 January 1948, p. 3.

97. Owen Smyth, speaking as director of organisation for the County Galway Executive of Clann na Poblachta in Ballygarron (*Connacht Tribune*, 17 January 1948 (first edition), p. 10). He concluded: 'While one sod of Irish soil is held in bondage, how dare any man say that Ireland is free!'

98. Speaking in Cavan (*Irish Times*, 22 January 1948, p. 3).

99. Speeches in Cavan and in Christ Church Place, Dublin (*Irish Times*, 22 January 1948, p. 3, and 31 January 1948, p. 3).

100. *Irish Times*, 22 January 1948, p. 3, and 31 January 1948, p. 3.

101. Dr B. Grace, speaking in Claremorris (*Irish Times*, 16 January 1948, p. 3).

102. *Connacht Tribune*, 31 January 1948 (first edition), p. 5; *Irish Times*, 16 January 1948, p. 3.

103. Speaking in Ranelagh, Dublin (*Irish Times*, 29 January 1948, p. 4).

104. Dr B. Grace, speaking in Claremorris (*Irish Times*, 16 January 1948, p. 3).

105. De Valera spoke of the unique capacity of the Fianna Fáil Government, while his supporters—from Government ministers to the humblest candidate—tended to stress the unique abilities of de Valera personally. See, for example, speech by P. J. Little in Tramore (*Cork Examiner*, 26 January 1948, p. 7).

106. Speaking in Monaghan (*Irish Times*, 12 January 1948, p. 7). See also speech at Parnell Monument, Dublin (*Irish Times*, 22 January 1948, p. 3), and speech of Cllr Michael Kitt at Fohanagh, Co. Galway (*Connacht Tribune*, 24 January 1948 (first edition), p. 5).

107. *Irish Times*, 29 January 1948, p. 4.

108. *Connacht Tribune*, 7 February 1948 (first edition), p. 4.

109. *Irish Times*, 23 October 1947, p. 6. See also *Irish Times*, 19 June 1947, p. 1.

110. Ailtirí na hAiséirghe ('Architects of the Resurrection') was a right-wing party that unsuccessfully contested a small number of seats during the 1940s. Led by Gearóid

Ó Cuinnegáin, it advocated a Christian, Irish-speaking, corporatist one-party state and a wide range of radical socio-economic policies. See Aoife Ní Lochlainn, 'Ailtirí na hAiséirghe: A party of its time?' in Keogh and O'Driscoll, *Ireland in World War Two*, p. 187–210.

111. *Irish Times*, 4 February 1948, p. 1.

112. These figures include the results from the constituency of Carlow-Kilkenny, where, because of the death of the Fine Gael incumbent, Éamonn Cogan, polling had been postponed until 10 February. Some works cite figures that do not include this constituency.

113. Cornelius O'Leary (*Irish Elections*, p. 40) puts forward the traditional claim that an examination of the results demonstrates that the number of candidates and poor intra-party transfers were the reason for Clann na Poblachta's poor showing. However, the results do not indicate this at all. At 70 per cent, the rate of Clann na Poblachta's transfers was high for a new party and compared favourably with those of Fianna Fáil, which was the model party as regards intra-party solidarity. A far more important factor was the relatively low number of transfers that Clann na Poblachta received from other parties, a problem common among new parties and accentuated by Clann na Poblachta's overt radicalism. While transfers from Clann na Poblachta candidates—which benefited Fine Gael against Fianna Fáil, and the Labour Party against all others—were instrumental in securing vital marginal seats for opposition parties, the flow was mostly one way, and none of Clann na Poblachta's seats were gained with the aid of inter-party transfers. See Michael Gallagher, 'Party solidarity, exclusivity and inter-party relationships in Ireland, 1922–1977: The evidence of transfers,' *Economic and Social Review*, 10 (1978), and 'The impact of lower preference votes on Irish parliamentary elections, 1922–1977,' *Economic and Social Review*, 11 (1979).

114. *Irish Times*, 28 January 1948, p. 5.

115. See David E. Schmitt, *The Irony of Irish Democracy: The Impact of Political Culture on Administrative and Democratic Political Development in Ireland* (Lanham (Md): Lexington Books, 1973), chap. 4.

116. The fact that traditional emigration routes were blocked during the First World War and during the Great Depression of 1929–31 was a factor contributing to the general radicalisation of politics that led to the 1916 Rising and Fianna Fáil's victory in 1932.

117. Cllr Peter Cooke, speaking in West Galway (*Connacht Tribune*, 10 January 1948 (city edition), p. 5).

118. Noel Hartnett, speaking in New Street, Dublin (*Irish Times*, 16 January 1948, p. 3).

119. In response to a query from the *Irish Times* to the director of elections of Fianna Fáil, Fine Gael and Clann na Poblachta (*Irish Times*, 4 February 1948, p. 1).

120. The nearest any party has come to the Clann na Poblachta performance was in 1987, when the Progressive Democrats obtained 12 per cent of the vote.

121. Quoted by O'Sullivan, *Seán Lemass*, p. 112–13.

122. This figure includes the four farmers' deputies who were not members of Clann na Talmhan.

123. A similar belief had sustained Cumann na nGaedheal in 1927 when there were suggestions that the National League and Fianna Fáil might unite in an effort to facilitate a change in government.

124. Michael Farrell, 'The extraordinary life and times of Seán MacBride: Part 2,' *Magill*, January 1983, p. 28. Noël Browne suggested (*Against the Tide*, p. 107) that Esmonde

was rejected because of his knighthood, though he does not specify whether he was rejected by Fine Gael or Clann na Poblachta.

125. Jordan, *Seán MacBride*, p. 95.
126. As chief of staff of the Free State army Mulcahy had personally authorised the seventy-seven official state executions and trenchantly defended the unofficial ones.
127. Michael Farrell, 'The extraordinary life and times of Seán MacBride: Part 2,' *Magill*, January 1983, p. 28.

Chapter 10: Drift, 1948–59 (p. 217–48)

1. Joseph Lee (*Ireland, 1912–1985*, p. 306) remarks that Costello had 'no commanding presence.'
2. For a sympathetic appraisal of Costello's tenure as Taoiseach see Brian Farrell, *Chairman or Chief?*, p. 42–54.
3. See Chubb, *The Government and Politics of Ireland*, p. 194.
4. Cronin, *Washington's Irish Policy*, p. 226.
5. Diarmuid Brennan, 'Dáil Diary,' *Waterford Standard*, 2 October 1948.
6. See, for example, the coverage of Plant's reburial, *Tipperary Star*, 25 September 1948. Three Clann na Poblachta TDs—Con Lehane, Patrick Kinane and J. J. Timoney—were in attendance.
7. Since the Government had taken office there had been nine instances of shots being fired over graves. The first five were during the reburial of the five men executed during the Emergency years (Tom Harte was buried in the North); the latter four funerals were of republican veterans. See National Archives, D/T S11564A.
8. Costello told the Dáil that he wanted 'to do all in my power to bring peace to this country and to put an end to that bitterness that was born of the Civil War and bring about a position where there shall be no necessity for guns or gunning and where we shall get some symbol around which our people can rally.' *Parliamentary Debates: Dáil Éireann: Official Report*, 113/378 (24 November 1948).
9. 1948 ard-fheis, Clár, section A, resolution 5. See also the agenda of the 1944 ard-fheis and reports of 1945 ard-fheis in the *Irish Press*, 7 November 1945.
10. *Parliamentary Debates: Dáil Éireann: Official Report*, 97/2570–72 (17 July 1945).
11. *Parliamentary Debates: Dáil Éireann: Official Report*, 107/94 (24 June 1947).
12. Ian McCabe, 'John Costello "announces" the repeal of the External Relations Act,' *Irish Studies in International Affairs*, 3/4 (1992), p. 71–2.
13. Shortly after assuming the leadership of Fine Gael, Richard Mulcahy declared that they 'stand unequivocally for membership of the British Commonwealth' (*Irish Times*, 27 January 1944). During the 1948 election he promised that 'we are not going to interfere with any constitutional affairs' (*Irish Times*, 26 January 1948). It could be argued that these speeches were made by a man who, though leader of Fine Gael, was not the man who became Taoiseach. However, in his election address as Fine Gael candidate for Dublin South-East in 1948 he stated that if Fine Gael was returned to power 'it will not propose any alteration in the present Constitution in relation to external affairs' (quoted in *Irish Times*, 12 November 1948).
14. Garret FitzGerald, who was twenty-two at the time of the 1948 election, recalls (*All in a Life*, p. 45) that 'my understanding . . . was that Fine Gael supported Commonwealth membership, and Joan and I canvassed accordingly; we particularly remember reassuring the inhabitants of Waterloo Road on this point.'

15. *Irish Times,* 25 November 1948, p. 9.

16. *Irish Times,* 12 November 1948, p. 9.

17. Michael Farrell, *Northern Ireland,* p. 184.

18. Lee, *Ireland, 1912–1985,* p. 300.

19. The issue of how best the party should respond to the Republic of Ireland Act was discussed at meetings of the National Executive on 21 March, 11 April and 25 April 1949.The retaliatory British act was discussed on 9 May.

20. See National Archives, D/T S14387B.

21. See the contribution of Seán Lemass to the second reading of the bill, as reported in the *Irish Times,* 25 November 1948.

22. *Parliamentary Debates: Dáil Éireann: Official Report,* 112/2441 (6 August 1948).

23. Longford and O'Neill, *Éamon de Valera,* p. 433–4.

24. As has been documented, Fianna Fáil made extensive reference to its constitutional achievements at every election from 1933 to 1948. In particular, the successful enactment of the Constitution of Ireland (1937) was accorded a prominent part in Fianna Fáil literature, and in December 1937 and December 1938 the electorate were urged to celebrate 'Constitution Day' (*FF Bulletin*). On the other hand, there was no parallel to the coalition Government's elaborate celebrations during 1949, which may have been a case of Fine Gael overcompensating for the perception that it was less 'solid' on the national question.

25. Quoted by O Connor, *In Search of a State,* p. 230.

26. Thomas E. Hackey, *One People or Two?: The Origins of Partition and the Prospects for Unification in Ireland* (London, 1975), p. 238. In his memoirs the former Prime Minister of Northern Ireland Brian Faulkner describes the move as 'an action which drove even further wedges between Irishmen, North and South' (*Memoirs of a Statesman,* London: Weidenfeld and Nicholson, 1978, p. 17).

27. Lee, *Ireland, 1912–1985,* p. 301.

28. Noël Browne (*Against the Tide,* p. 129–33) put forward the frequently quoted assertion that the declaration was occasioned by a precipitous reaction by Costello to an alleged slur while on an official visit to Canada in 1948. This view was contested by Seán MacBride in a detailed rebuttal in *Magill* (April 1989, p. 40–45). See also Fanning, *Independent Ireland,* p. 172–4, and Cronin, *Washington's Irish Policy.*

29. Section 1 (2).

30. *Parliamentary Debates: Dáil Éireann: Official Report,* 115/807 (10 May 1949).

31. *Irish Press,* 2 May 1949.

32. In 1970 a Dáil motion was proposed by Liam Cosgrave on behalf of Fine Gael that ruled out the use of force to achieve reunification. The motion was supported by the Fianna Fáil members present, though many expressed the opinion that they considered the motion unnecessary. The 1949 resolution is unique in that it was jointly proposed by the leaders of Fine Gael and Fianna Fáil.

33. *Parliamentary Debates: Dáil Éireann: Official Report,* 112/1520 (23 July 1948).

34. Bowman, *De Valera and the Ulster Question,* p. 273.

35. Moynihan, *Speeches and Statements by Éamon de Valera,* p. 522.

36. Rawle Knox, 'Six and twenty six,' *Spectator,* 30 April 1948. 'He has returned with his sense of indignation unimpaired and has now gone off to repeat his rampage in Australia.'

37. Lee and Ó Tuathaigh, *The Age of de Valera,* p. 109.

38. Garrett to Secretary of State, 5 March 1948; quoted by Cronin, *Washington's Irish Policy,* p. 190.

39. Cronin, *Washington's Irish Policy*, p. 193.
40. *Irish Press* supplement (copy in Gallagher Papers, National Library of Ireland).
41. Dwyer, *De Valera*, p. 304.
42. Speaking in Dún Laoghaire (*Irish Times*, 15 January 1948, p. 3).
43. See Eamon McKee, 'Church-state relations and the development of Irish health policy: the mother and child scheme, 1944–53,' *Irish Historical Studies*, vol. 25, no. 98 (November 1986), p. 159–94.
44. Advertisement. See, for example, *Dungarvan Observer*, 19 and 26 May 1951, p. 1; *Democrat and People's Journal* (Dundalk), 19 May 1951, p. 7; *Drogheda Argus*, 19 May 1951, p. 7; *Donegal Democrat*, 18 and 25 May 1951, p. 8; *Clare Champion*, 19 May 1951, p. 10; *Connacht Telegraph*, 19 May 1951, p. 3; *Nationalist* (Clonmel), 19 May 1951, p. 3; and *Ballina Herald*, 19 and 26 May 1951, p. 4.
45. See, for example, litir um thoghchán (election letter) for Dún Laoghaire-Rathdown constituency (Fianna Fáil Archives, FF/795). The three candidates were Seán Brady, Matthew Cullen and Matt Smith. Cullen's membership of Fianna Éireann from 1920 to 1922 is mentioned, as is his membership of the ARP service. Smith is described as a member of the 1st Battalion, Dublin Brigade, from 1919 to 1921. The participation of Brady—the only successful candidate—in the 1916 Rising and in the ARP service was given prominence, while his role on the Republican side in the Civil War was not referred to. (Brady was with Cathal Brugha in the Hammam Hotel in O'Connell Street, Dublin, when it became the headquarters of the IRA after the evacuation of the Four Courts.)
46. Quoted in *Ballina Herald*, 19 May 1951, p. 3. See also four-page pamphlet entitled 'To the Electors of Co. Louth' from Frank Aiken and Laurence Walsh, which also concentrated on achievements in the period 1932–8 (Fianna Fáil Archives, FF/795).
47. *Ballina Herald*, 19 May 1951, p. 3. The style adopted is quintessential in that it doesn't name the opposition parties, thus avoiding giving them publicity.
48. Litir um thoghchán (election letter), Dún Laoghaire-Rathdown constituency (Fianna Fáil Archives, FF/795).
49. One is reminded of Nikita Khrushchev's definition of politicians as people who promise to build bridges even where there are no rivers.
50. Liam de Paor, *Unfinished Business: Ireland Today and Tomorrow* (London: Hutchinson Radius, 1990), p. 93.
51. Quotations and information from Cruise O'Brien, *Memoir*, p. 161–5.
52. Cruise O'Brien, *Memoir*, p. 162. See also Donald Harman Akenson, *Conor: A Biography of Conor Cruise O'Brien*, Volume 1, Montréal and Kingston: McGill-Queen's University Press, 1994, p. 144–7.
53. Quoted by Bowman, *De Valera and the Ulster Question*, p. 281. F. H. Boland was made Secretary of the Department of External Affairs in 1946 after the move of J. J. Walshe to the Vatican and in 1950 became ambassador to Britain. For a biographical profile of Boland during this period see *Irish Times*, 1 November 1955, p. 1.
54. Bowman, *De Valera and the Ulster Question*, p. 282.
55. *Parliamentary Debates: Dáil Éireann: Official Report*, 126/2024 (19 July 1951).
56. *Parliamentary Debates: Dáil Éireann: Official Report*, 126/2279–85. See also question put by Noël Browne (126/951, 5 July 1951). Perhaps sensing the imminent demise of the coalition Government, four Anti-Partition League MPs, representing South Armagh, South Down, Fermanagh and South Tyrone and Mid-Tyrone, and two Northern

senators sought admission to the Dáil in March 1951 'as elected representatives of part of the national territory' but were refused. See *Parliamentary Debates: Dáil Éireann: Official Report*, 124 (1 March 1951).

57. This point was made by Seán MacBride. *Parliamentary Debates: Dáil Éireann: Official Report*, 126/2158 (19 July 1951).

58. Seán Mac Eoin, *Parliamentary Debates: Dáil Éireann: Official Report*, 126/2250 (19 July 1951).

59. *Parliamentary Debates: Dáil Éireann: Official Report*, 126/2279 (19 July 1951).

60. *Parliamentary Debates: Dáil Éireann: Official Report*, 126/2283–5 (19 July 1951).

61. *Parliamentary Debates: Dáil Éireann: Official Report*, 126/2281 (19 July 1951).

62. *Parliamentary Debates: Dáil Éireann: Official Report*, 126/2282 (19 July 1951).

63. Of the 82 deputies who voted against the motion, 67 were Fianna Fáil (who voted *en bloc*), 11 were Fine Gael and 4 were independents (2 of whom subsequently joined Fianna Fáil). Of the 43 who voted in favour of the motion there were 19 Fine Gael deputies, 8 Labour Party, 4 Clann na Talmhan, 2 Clann na Poblachta and 9 independents (two of whom subsequently joined Fianna Fáil and 2 of whom joined Fine Gael).

64. *Parliamentary Debates: Dáil Éireann: Official Report*, 126/2294 (19 July 1951).

65. *Parliamentary Debates: Dáil Éireann: Official Report*, 126/2294 (19 July 1951).

66. 'Deputation from Irish Anti-Partition League,' 3 August 1951, point 5 (National Archives, D/T S6390C).

67. Deputation from Fermanagh-Tyrone, 9 January 1952 (National Archives, D/T S6390C).

68. The full delegation consisted of Eddie McAteer MP, James Stewart MP, R. M. O'Connor MP and Senator P. F. McGill.

69. 'Deputation from Anti-Partition League' (27 August 1953, 11.30 a.m to 12.30 p.m.), notes taken by Mr. Mac Úgó, Department of the Taoiseach (National Archives, D/T S6390). See also details of the meeting of de Valera and Aiken with the Tyrone MP Joseph Stewart and the Dungannon priest Father Devlin on 21 May 1953 in Leinster House (National Archives, D/T S6390B).

70. In this regard it might be considered that when Aiken was not available on such occasions, de Valera was accompanied by Seán MacEntee, who was from Belfast.

71. See *Parliamentary Debates: Dáil Éireann: Official Report*, 135/987 (9 December 1952); 143/1181 (1 December 1953), 142/1465–6 (5 November 1953), 143/2542–3 (16 December 1953) and 143/2603–4 (17 December 1953).

72. In 1881 Dublin City Council had made a case before the British House of Commons on the issue of the electoral franchise. In 1913 it put forward Catholic demands and in 1916 it sought an inquiry into the North King Street shootings.

73. *Parliamentary Debates: Dáil Éireann: Official Report*, 143/2542–3 (16 December 1953).

74. Minutes of monthly meeting of Clare County Council, 10 November 1952. The motion read: 'That as Mr. Charles McGlennon was selected as an abstentionist candidate and was elected in South Armagh Constituency on a 2 to 1 majority on that mandate and as Mr. McGlennon was an officer of the Irish Republican Army and is still true to his oath to the Republic of Ireland in not entering Stormont or Whitehall, it is our opinion [that] he is entitled to admission to Dáil Éireann and we call on our TDs for the County for support for his admission.' For similar resolutions see National Archives, D/T S6390C.

75. The motion, which was submitted by the Clann na Poblachta deputies Seán MacBride, John Tully and Johnny Connor, read: 'Believing that, in order to achieve the unity of Ireland, a greater degree of contact and co-operation between the elected representatives of the people of the six occupied counties and members of the Oireachtas is required, Dáil Éireann requests the Government to initiate proposals for legislation in the Dáil or in the Seanad whereby all the elected representatives of the people of the six occupied counties of Ireland will be given a right of audience in the Dáil or Seanad, as may be determined.' A similar motion was put before the Seanad during the same month by Senators J. McHugh and Frank Hugh O'Donnell.

76. Quoted in *Evening Herald*, 13 November 1954 and *Irish Times*, 15 November 1954. The Taoiseach's decision to refuse McAteers's request was also raised in the Dáil by Deputy McQuillan. See *Parliamentary Debates: Dáil Éireann: Official Report*, 147/601–2 (17 November 1954).

77. *Parliamentary Debates: Dáil Éireann: Official Report*, 147/201–2 (28 October 1954).

78. Minutes, Committee of Ten, 19 May 1922 (UCD Archives, Mulcahy Papers, P7/A/145).

79. Minutes, Comhairle na dTeachtaí, 7 August 1924 (UCD Archives, MacSwiney Papers, P48/C/8).

80. See letter from Mary MacSwiney to J. J. O'Kelly, 8 June 1926 (UCD Archives, MacSwiney Papers, P48/D/25).

81. See *Irish Independent*, 25 November 1926, p. 7; *Irish Times*, 26 November 1926, p. 9; Honorary Secretaries' Report, 1928 Ard-Fheis (Fianna Fáil Archives, FF/702) and 1929 Ard-Fheis (Fianna Fáil Archives, FF/703); *Nation*, 3 November 1929, p. 3.

82. Cláracha (agendas), 1936 and 1937 Ard-Fheiseanna. Minutes of National Executive, 21 December 1936, 4 January 1937, 1 February 1937, 8 November 1937 and 14 February 1938 (Fianna Fáil Archives, FF/342).

83. Clár (agenda), section A, resolution 4 (Fianna Fáil Archives, FF/709).

84. Minutes, National Executive, 8 November 1937, 14 February 1938 and 12 July 1938 (Fianna Fáil Archives, FF/342).

85. See speeches by Seán MacBride in Cavan and in Christ Church Place, Dublin (*Irish Times*, 22 January 1948, p. 3, and 31 January 1948, p. 3) and Dr B. Grace, speaking in Claremorris, Co. Mayo (*Irish Times*, 16 January 1948, p. 3, and *Connacht Tribune*, 31 January 1948 (first edition), p. 5). For Fianna Fáil's response see speech of Seán MacEntee in Ranalagh, Dublin (*Irish Times*, 29 January 1948, p. 4). MacEntee contended that if Northern MPs acquired full voting rights in the Dáil 'it would follow logically that the Government, which was responsible to the Dáil, should undertake the task of extending the authority of the Oireachtas over all Ireland, even by force of arms.'

86. Memorandum for the Government, 'Six County Parliamentary Representatives: Question of attending Dáil and Seanad,' 10 March 1949. There are copies in the National Archives (D/T S6390) and in UCD Archives (McGilligan Papers, P35B/146).

87. MacBride had adopted such an attitude towards the issue of the repeal of the External Relations Act, arguing that his party had not received a mandate for radical constitutional change.

88. Coogan, *De Valera*, p. 644.

89. Bowman, *De Valera and the Ulster Question*, p. 284.

90. See report of the first ard-fheis in the *Irish Independent*, 25 November 1926, p. 7 and *Irish Times*, 26 November 1926, p. 9.

91. Report of the Honorary Secretaries (1 October 1928) to the Fianna Fáil ard-fheis, 25–26 October 1928 (Fianna Fáil Archives, FF/702).

92. Report of the Honorary Secretaries (1 October 1928) to the Fianna Fáil ard-fheis, 25–26 October 1928 (Fianna Fáil Archives, FF/702). See also the *Nation*, 3 November 1928, p. 2, and Report of the Honorary Secretaries, 1929 ard-fheis (Fianna Fáil Archives, FF/703).

93. See, for example, minutes of National Executive, 8 and 22 November 1937 (Fianna Fáil Archives, FF/342).

94. Quoted in the *Irish Independent*, 16 June 1949. In referring to a related motion de Valera added that 'the same was true in regard to Six Counties representatives sitting in Dáil Éireann.'

95. 'Deputation from South Armagh Constituency Committee of the Irish Anti-Partition League,' 19 May 1955. The question of 'what effect admission to the Dáil would have on the activities of those who sought force' was one in which Costello displayed an interest (p. 3) (National Archives, D/T S6390C).

96. *Irish Times*, 7 November 1951, p. 1.

97. *Irish Times*, 6 November 1952, p. 8.

98. Joe Dowling, Dublin South-West. Dowling was Fianna Fáil spokesperson on labour between 1973 and 1977.

99. Quotations from *Irish Times*, 7 November 1951, p. 7.

100. *Irish Times*, 5 November 1952, p. 7.

101. When MacEntee evaded the question of whether the British Government had requested that the Gardaí co-operate in preventing the importing of arms into the Six Counties he was asked whether he would give a reply in two months' time. MacEntee responded frankly by saying, 'It may be somebody else's job then. I will let them answer it.' Quoted in the *Irish Independent*, 10 March 1954, p. 7.

102. Quoted in the *Irish Independent*, 15 March 1954, p. 8.

103. Speaking in Limerick (*Irish Independent*, 11 May 1954, p. 10).

104. See speeches by Seán MacBride in Longford and Mullingar (*Irish Independent*, 17 May 1954, p. 10).

105. Speaking in Monaghan (*Irish Independent*, 6 May 1954, p. 12).

106. See, for example, speeches by de Valera in Ennis and Sixmilebridge, Co. Clare (*Irish Independent*, 22 March 1954, p. 8, and 8 May 1954, p. 12), and Lemass in Dún Laoghaire (*Irish Independent*, 6 May 1954, p. 12). See also 'Fianna Fáil and Coalition Government,' undated paper prepared by MOC (Fianna Fáil Archives, FF/796).

107. Report from Sir Walter Hankison to Lord Swinton; quoted in the *Irish Times*, 1–2 January 1985, p. 14.

108. See the contribution of Senator J. Walsh, sponsor of the anti-partition motion, *Irish Times*, 13 October 1954, p. 7.

109. *Irish Times*, 13 October 1954, p. 5.

110. The official title of the committee was the Permanent Committee on Partition Matters. It was not to be permanent. Details of to the deliberations of the committee can be found in the Fianna Fáil Archives (FF/42).

111. See letter sent to all members of the Anti-Partition Committee, 25 January 1955 (Fianna Fáil Archives, FF/42).

112. 'Partition', memorandum by Lt-Col. Matthew Feehan, 20 January 1955 (Fianna Fáil Archives, FF/42), para. 3, 4.

113. 'Partition', memorandum by Lt-Col. Matthew Feehan, 20 January 1955, para. 5, 6 (Fianna Fáil Archives, FF/42).

114. 'Partition', memorandum by Lt-Col. Matthew Feehan, 20 January 1955, para. 9, 10, 11, 13 (Fianna Fáil Archives, FF/42).

115. 'Partition', memorandum for the National Executive of Fianna Fáil, submitted by Tomás Ó Cléirigh Cumann, Dublin North-East, n.d. (February–March 1955), p. 3, point (d) (Fianna Fáil Archives, FF/42).

116. 'Partition', memorandum for the National Executive of Fianna Fáil, submitted by Tomás Ó Cléirigh Cumann, Dublin North-East, n.d. (February–March 1955), p. 2 (Fianna Fáil Archives, FF/42).

117. 'Partition', memorandum for the National Executive of Fianna Fáil, submitted by Tomás Ó Cléirigh Cumann, Dublin North-East, n.d. (February–March 1955), p. 5 (Fianna Fáil Archives, FF/42).

118. 'Partition', memorandum for the National Executive of Fianna Fáil, submitted by Tomás Ó Cléirigh Cumann, Dublin North-East, n.d. (February–March 1955), p. 6 (Fianna Fáil Archives, FF/42).

119. There was a more public articulation of divergent approaches to the national question three years later between Frank Gallagher and Dónal Barrington. While neither was a member of the Fianna Fáil leadership, both reflected the increasing tensions between the old and the new. Gallagher, a Northerner, a journalist and long-time associate of de Valera, published *The Indivisible Island,* a classic restatement of the traditional republican position on partition, largely based on the pamphlets he researched for the Mansion House Committee. In what was ostensibly a review article ('Uniting Ireland,' *Studies,* 46/184, winter 1957, p. 379–402) Dónal Barrington wrote a remarkably lucid counter-argument that questioned the basis of traditional attitudes to partition. Barrington was not at that time a member of Fianna Fáil but joined the party in 1961 and was later made a senator and a judge.

120. Reid, *Ireland,* p. 102.

121. See Bell, *The Secret Army,* p. 269.

122. See Michael Farrell, *Northern Ireland,* p. 209–11.

123. Saor Uladh was the military wing of Fianna Uladh. One of the best outlines of its policies and philosophy is contained in a short pamphlet published in April 1955 to coincide with the British general election (which the party did not contest). It viewed the Nationalist Party as 'a somewhat discredited and futile' entity and was a strong advocate of abstention from the British and Northern Parliaments. It thought that Sinn Féin's claim that the second Dáil was the only legitimate government in Ireland to be 'fantastic and unrealistic.' It declared itself also to be opposed to Sinn Féin's policy of refusing to recognise the Constitution of Ireland and felt that such a stance involved 'implies the overthrow of the Parliament and Government of the Republic.'

124. Quoted by Michael Farrell, *Northern Ireland,* p. 205.

125. The raids took place at Eglinton naval air base, Co. Derry, on 24 April and at Arborfield depot, Berkshire, on 13 August (Coogan, *The IRA* (second edition), p. 335–60). The dead Laochra Uladh member was Brendan O'Boyle.

126. Bell, *The Secret Army,* p. 270.

127. *Irish Times,* 2 November 1955, p. 1.

128. The ard-fheis is reported in the *Irish Times,* 23 November 1955, p. 1, 4, and 24 November, p. 7. Quotations from the ard-fheis are from this source unless otherwise stated.

129. See Government meeting of 20 January 1955 and notes of a meeting between the Secretary of State for Commonwealth Relations and the Irish ambassador, F. H.

Boland, 24 January 1954. The Commonwealth secretary said that IRA support was growing and that, whereas in November he had good reason to believe the Irish Government would take firm action, it now seemed that 'they are disposed to let matters drift' (National Archives [London], PREM 11/923).

130. *Irish Times,* 28 November 1955, p. 1.

131. There was a bizarre sequel to the assault. During the attack Connie Green, a former British soldier, was fatally injured. Through Seán MacBride, Kelly managed to have the inquest held clandestinely south of the border. The matter did not remain secret for long and was cited as evidence of Government connivance with militant republicanism in the North. See the *Irish Times,* 28 November 1955, p. 1, 9, and 29 November, p. 1, 3; Coogan, *The IRA* (second edition), p. 362–6; Michael Farrell, *Northern Ireland,* p. 212.

132. Quoted in the *Irish Independent,* 1–2 January 1990.

133. *Parliamentary Debates: Dáil Éireann: Official Report,* 153/1336–50 (30 November 1955).

134. *Parliamentary Debates: Dáil Éireann: Official Report,* 153/1336–45 (30 November 1955).

135. *Irish Times,* 28 November 1955, p. 1.

136. Memorandum [dated 21 May 1946] of interview with Mr. de Valera on Saturday 18 May 1946 (National Archives [London], DO 35/2094).

137. An interesting example of this is a motion of protest submitted to the National Executive in September 1951 by Charles Haughey on behalf of the Tomás Ó Clérigh Cumann in the Dublin North-East constituency. The cumann took issue with the fact that a member of the National Executive had proposed at a meeting of Dublin City Council that the council should attend the unveiling of a memorial to IRA men executed during the 1940s. The cumann argued that these men had been killed 'to protect the Nation during the Emergency,' and it deplored the failure of Fianna Fáil members of the city council 'to realise the implications of their action in this matter.' The National Executive was also informed that a letter had been sent to the chairman of the party group in the council instructing the party to meet and discuss the agenda before future council meetings so as to prevent future embarrassment. Minutes of National Executive, 10 September 1951 (Fianna Fáil Archives, FF/344).

138. Longford and O'Neill, *Éamon de Valera,* p. 444. The information regarding the identity of the intermediaries is given by Bowman, *De Valera and the Ulster Question,* p. 289, and was provided by one of de Valera's official biographers, Thomas P. O'Neill. There is no reference to the meeting in any of the standard works on the IRA.

139. *Irish Times,* 19 January 1956. See also J. H. Whyte, *Church and State in Modern Ireland, 1923–1979* (Dublin: Gill & Macmillan, 1980), p. 321.

140. The position was elaborated on by a Limerick priest, Monsignor Moloney, in the aftermath of the deaths of Sabhat and O'Hanlon. In a strongly worded attack he condemned the 'irresponsible conduct of certain public representatives faced with these tragic circumstances. "Silence in regard to responsibility" was one of the evils denounced by the Holy Father last Christmastime. What are we to make of the political playboys who dodged the terrible issues and sought to fish in the troubled waters of the moment? The existence of such sorry personages may be largely responsible for retarding political progress in the country. They were out of place in public life, and young and old might well unite to take the earliest opportunity of packing them back to the obscurity from which they should never have emerged.' Quoted in the *Limerick Leader,* 12 January 1957.

141. *Irish Times*, 1 January 1957, p. 1, 7, and 4 January 1957, p. 7.

142. *Irish Times*, 5 January 1957, p. 5.

143. *Cork Examiner*, 5 January 1957, p. 7, and 7 January 1957, p. 7. See also the *Limerick Leader*, 12 January 1957.

144. See the *Cork Examiner*, 12 January 1957, p. 7, and 15 January 1957, p. 7.

145. This mood was reflected somewhat by Ireland's permanent representative at the United Nations, F. H. Boland, who told the General Assembly that the experience of Ireland showed that partition was 'a facile and fatal expedient' (*Irish Times*, 22 February 1957, p. 1).

146. *Cork Examiner*, 12 January 1957, p. 7.

147. During his contribution to a debate organised by UCD Literary and Historical Society on 19 January 1957, Con Lehane of Clann na Poblachta asked: 'Why is it that our political leaders can salute the courage and sincerity of freedom fighters in Hungary and Cyprus, while reserving for freedom fighters in the Six Counties the draconian legislation of the Offences Against the State Act?' (National Archives, DT, S11564E).

148. *Cork Examiner*, 8 January 1957, p. 7; *Irish Times*, 8 January 1957, p. 7.

149. *Cork Examiner*, 7 January 1957, p. 7.

150. An exception was Kildare County Council, which decided not to discuss a Labour Party motion expressing sympathy with 'the relatives and comrades' of Fergal O'Hanlon and Seán Sabhat. Both Fianna Fáil and Fine Gael members explained their decision by citing the Taoiseach's broadcast in which he appealed to 'people of influence' not to encourage the recent activities across the border (*Irish Times*, 18 January 1957, p. 6). Similarly, when a member of Athy Urban District Council sought to criticise the Government for sending the army to patrol the border he was ruled out of order by the chairperson, who said that 'we were elected to look after the affairs of the town and not to discuss politics' (*Leinster Leader*, 12 January 1957).

151. *Western People*, 12 January 1957. See also *Cork Examiner*, 9 January 1957, p. 7, and *Irish Times*, 9 February 1957, p. 1.

152. Quotations from the meeting are taken from 'Members sympathise with relatives of men who lost their lives,' *Nationalist* (Clonmel), 12 January 1957, and 'Give republicans support of army,' *Tipperary Star*, 12 January 1957. See also *Cork Examiner*, 8 January 1957, p. 7, and *Irish Times*, 8 January 1957, p. 8. Even Fianna Fáil members who opposed the motion, such as Cllr William O'Dwyer, declared that 'they must admire O'Hanlon and South for their courage. They were prepared to lay down their lives for the freedom of their country and there was nothing more a man could do for Ireland.' Like the other members of the council, O'Dwyer voted in favour of the sympathy motion.

153. See Vincent Browne, *The Magill Book of Irish Politics*, p. 328; Michael Gallagher, *The Irish Labour Party in Transition*, p. 128. His views on the IRA had not changed by the 1970s; see Michael Gallagher, *The Irish Labour Party in Transition*, p. 140–153 passim.

154. *Irish Times*, 4 January 1957, p. 1. A similar motion was put before Dublin City Council by Frank Sherwin, requesting that the Government 'not . . . co-operate, or give any information to the occupying forces in the Six Counties on matters of a political nature affecting Irish nationalists in their efforts to end or protest against partition.' Sherwin, an independent and a Republican veteran of the Civil War, was to enjoy a surprise by-election victory in Dublin North-Central in November. Though receiving only a third of the first-preference vote, he gained heavily from Sinn Féin and Fine Gael transfers. He was re-elected in the 1961 general election but defeated in 1965.

155. *Irish Times,* 5 January 1957, p. 1.

156. *Cork Examiner,* 7 January 1957, p. 1, 7; a supportive editorial was published on p. 4. *Irish Times,* 7 January 1957, p. 1; an editorial supporting the Taoiseach, entitled 'Enemies of the people,' was published on p. 5.

157. *Cork Examiner,* 7 January 1957, p. 1; *Irish Times,* 7 January 1957, p. 1.

158. *Cork Examiner,* 7 January 1957, p. 1; *Irish Times,* 7 January 1957, p. 1.

159. Nor indeed did it do much to humour some people who wrote to Costello personally. The National Archives (D/T S11564E and 11564D) contain a number of letters, some of which are very threatening, protesting against the Government's policy on partition and the IRA. 'God Damn you Costello . . .' is the typical beginning of one letter, written by Mr. A. Gallagher, 14 January 1957.

160. *Cork Examiner,* 11 January 1957, p. 7.

161. *Cork Examiner,* 5 January 1957, p. 7; *Irish Times,* 5 January 1957, p. 5, and 7 January 1957, p. 8.

162. *Irish Times,* 7 October 1991.

163. Jordan, *Seán MacBride,* p. 150.

164. Tomás Ó Dubhghaill, speaking in Dublin (*Irish Times,* 23 February 1957, p. 9).

165. Mícheál Ó Tréinfhir, secretary of Sinn Féin, speaking in Dublin (*Irish Times,* 25 February 1957, p. 5), and Seán O'Sullivan, speaking in Donnycarney, Dublin (*Irish Times,* 26 February 1957, p. 4).

166. Synopsis of manifesto published in *Irish Times,* 15 February 1957, p. 4.

167. Advertisement for Pádraig Ó Dubhthaigh, candidate for the constituency of Cavan (*Anglo-Celt,* 2 March 1957, p. 8).

168. Sinn Féin advertisement, *Anglo-Celt* (Cavan), 2 March 1957, p. 8.

169. Speaking in Bandon (*Irish Times,* 4 March 1957, p. 1). See also *Irish Press,* 4 March 1957, p. 1. De Valera reiterated the point during speeches in Listowel and Limerick. The issue of whether or not Fianna Fáil had taken an oath was fought out in a series of letters in the *Irish Press* between de Valera and Senator T. J. O'Connell. See *Irish Press,* 15 March 1957, 16 March 1957, 18 March 1957 and 21 March 1957.

170. Speaking in Bandon (*Irish Times,* 4 March 1957, p. 1).

171. Handbill in Fianna Fáil Archives (FF/797). The rally was addressed by de Valera, Lemass and MacEntee. 'Medals to be worn' was the instruction for veterans.

172. Fianna Fáil advertisement, *Anglo-Celt* (Cavan), 2 March 1957, p. 16.

173. Half-page advertisement, *Anglo-Celt* (Cavan), 23 February 1957, p. 12.

174. See poster collection in Fianna Fáil Archives (FF/1188 and FF/1190).

175. Edmonds, *The Gun, the Law, and the Irish People,* p. 198.

176. O'Leary, *Irish Elections,* p. 44. See also Basil Chubb, 'Ireland, 1957,' in D. E. Butler (ed.), *Elections Abroad* (London: Macmillan, 1959), p. 183–222.

177. K. T. Hoppen, *Ireland since 1800: Conflict and Conformity* (London: Longman, 1989), p. 180.

178. Though Fine Gael was formed in 1933, most people, including Fine Gael itself, consider the establishment of Cumann na nGaedheal in 1923 to be the origins of the party.

179. Figure for nineteen constituencies, calculated from election results.

180. *Irish Press,* 8 March 1957.

181. The statistics are calculated from a list compiled by one of the prisoners, Éamonn Tomoney, a 29-year-old railway clerk from Derry. The list contains the name, address,

age, occupation and the year imprisoned of every prisoner held between 1956 and 1960 in Belfast Prison; the sample number is ninety-five. The list is reproduced by Cronin, *Irish Nationalism*, p. 332–5. The figure for prisoners from the 26 Counties decreases significantly when one assesses those imprisoned after January 1957 only. This decrease can largely be attributed to the introduction of internment in the South.

182. Bell, *The Secret Army*, p. 310. For his troubles, Mac Curtáin was arrested with three others the following day.

183. One typically abusive letter sent to Costello condemning the imprisoning of republicans said that 'you were never a soldier and so far as I can gather none of your family thus your ignorance of the proud principles of our brave boys and I can assure you that no body will believe that Mr. De Valera is behind you. As a soldier he could not back up a thick head prepared to fight for England's ideals (divide and conquer).' Letter from Mrs Brigid Griffin to John A. Costello, 7 January 1957 (National Archives, D/T S11564D).

184. Cabinet Minutes, 28 March 1957, item 5 (National Archives, G.C.3/3). The term 'local authorities' was defined as including employees of vocational education committees, committees of agriculture and harbour authorities.

185. Cabinet Minutes, 28 March 1957, item 6 (National Archives, G.C.3/3). At the time of its introduction seven people were liable for suspension under the ruling: two vocational teachers, two CIE employees, one employee at Shannon Airport, one rate collector and one engineer in the Department of Posts and Telegraphs. Some of the violations of the Offences Against the State Act were of relatively minor consequence. One teacher, Domhnall Ó Lubhlaí, was suspended because he had received fourteen days' imprisonment for possession of an 'incriminating document' (as defined by the Offences Against the State Act) and refusal to answer Garda questions. See Department of Education, 'Memorandum for the Government: The Offences Against the State Act, 1939: Removal of Domhnall Ó Lubhlaí, vocational teacher from office' (National Archives, D/T S11564F).

186. Cabinet Minutes, 9 April 1957, item 4, sections 2–3 (National Archives, G.C.8/5). See also Cabinet Minutes, 18 April 1957, item 5 (G.C.8/7).

187. See British reports on Fianna Fáil in the National Archives [London] (DO 35/7940), particularly those of 29 November 1955, 12–15 October 1956, Irish Republic Summary, 28 March 1957.

188. See *Parliamentary Debates: Dáil Éireann: Official Report*, 161/92–102 (26 March 1957). The minister was responding to questions from Deputies Finucane and McQuillan relating to the release of prisoners.

189. The power to intern was conferred by part II of the Offences Against the State (Amendment) Act (1940). A copy of the proclamation reactivating the special powers was published in *Iris Oifigiúil*, 8 July 1957. The internee figures to not include republican prisoners sentenced to imprisonment by due process. See aide-mémoire, 'Offences Against the State Activities' (National Archives, D/T S11564G).

190. *Parliamentary Debates: Dáil Éireann: Official Report*, 170/1025 (17 July 1958).

191. *Parliamentary Debates: Dáil Éireann: Official Report*, 170/1073 (17 July 1958).

192. *Irish Times*, 29 October 1958, p. 1.

Chapter 11: Approach to crisis, 1960–69 (p. 249–82)

1. Michael Gallagher, *The Irish Labour Party in Transition*, p. 46.
2. *Irish Times*, 27 September 1961, p. 7.
3. See Michael Gallagher, *The Irish Labour Party in Transition*, chap. 8.
4. Four-page leaflet issued by candidates in Co. Tipperary (Fianna Fáil Archives, FF/798). Despite being signed by, among others, Dan Breen, the leaflet's ten declared 'points to note' did not include any reference to partition, though piped water, forestry and land division were included.
5. There is a copy of the booklet in the Fianna Fáil Archives (FF/798). The quotation is taken from para. 14, p. 6.
6. Manning, *Irish Political Parties*, p. 90.
7. This served only to confuse the electorate and certainly did not aid voters' recognition of candidates. Such recognition was crucial, as ballot papers at the time did not give the name of the party a candidate was representing.
8. Sinn Féin's performance in Clare (9½ per cent) was surpassed only by that in South Kerry, where its TD retained 13 per cent of the vote. Moreover, the party secured 17 per cent of the vote during the 1959 by-election in Clare, despite the fact that it had failed to put up a candidate there in 1957. Similarly, in Donegal South-West the Sinn Féin secured 8 per cent of the vote, and yet the party did not contest either of the Donegal constituencies in 1957.
9. For example, Sinn Féin had received 11½ per cent and 9½ per cent in Galway North and Galway South, respectively. In the 1958 by-election in Galway South it obtained 17½ per cent of the vote. The boundaries of the Galway constituencies were revised for the 1961 election, creating the new constituencies of Galway East and Galway West; yet Sinn Féin put up only one candidate—in Galway East—securing 8½ per cent of the vote, its third-best performance of the twenty constituencies. Similarly, in Meath and Limerick East the party had gained 9 per cent and 8½ per cent, respectively, in 1957 but failed to put up any candidate in 1961. On the other hand, candidates were put up in such areas as Tipperary South, Waterford and Wexford, where the party had failed to contest in 1957, obtaining insignificant results (2¼ per cent, 2¼ per cent and 3¾ per cent, respectively).
10. Figures relevant to twenty constituencies calculated from results.
11. O'Leary, *Irish Elections*, p. 104.
12. Clann na Talmhan obtained 1½ per cent of the first-preference vote, the National Progressive Democrats 1 per cent. The NPD was established in 1958 by two former members of Clann na Poblachta, Noël Browne and Jack McQuillan, both of whom won a Dáil seat in 1961.
13. *Parliamentary Debates: Dáil Éireann: Official Report*, 192/1213 (6 December 1961).
14. *Parliamentary Debates: Dáil Éireann: Official Report*, 192/839–40 (23 November 1961). Lemass was responding to a private notice question from James Dillon requesting 'a statement to Dáil Éireann in the light of the Government's decision to provide Military Courts.'
15. *Parliamentary Debates: Dáil Éireann: Official Report*, 192/840–41 (23 November 1961).
16. This shift was reflected in the personnel of the candidates who contested the 1961 election, with many of the new standard-bearers, including Seán Garland, Tomás Mac Giolla and Seán Rogers, becoming prominent in the wing that was to become Official (as opposed to Provisional) Sinn Féin. John Joe Rice was expelled in 1966 as part of this process.

17. *Northern Ireland Progress* (Journal of the Belfast and Northern Ireland Chambers of Commerce), 15/8 (August 1965), p. 6. These figures are a little misleading, as they include goods transshipped (in both directions) through Northern Ireland.

18. *Parliamentary Debates: Dáil Éireann: Official Report*, 176/140 (23 June 1959).

19. *Irish Times*, 17 January 1962, p. 1.

20. Speaking in Leeds (*Irish Times*, 24 February 1962, p. 1).

21. *Parliamentary Debates: Dáil Éireann: Official Report*, 201/113 (2 April 1963).

22. *Parliamentary Debates: Dáil Éireann: Official Report*, 201/736 (4 April 1963).

23. *Irish Times*, 30 July 1963, p. 1. This speech is also quoted in part by O'Neill, *Ulster at the Crossroads*, p. 158.

24. *Irish Times*, 19 October 1963, p. 1.

25. *Irish Times*, 15 February 1964, p. 1.

26. *Irish Times*, 18 October 1963, p. 1.

27. See in particular Lemass's speech in Arklow, in which he described the North as a place 'where time never seems to move, where old animosities are carefully fostered and whose bigotry and intolerance seem to be preserved as a way of life,' before expressing his belief that there was a growing mood there to move 'in closer conformity to the spirit of the age' (*Irish Times*, 13 April 1964, p. 1). In a bitter reply, O'Neill attributed Lemass's speech to his failure in London 'to get the same economic advantages that Ulster has long enjoyed within the United Kingdom.' He concluded by saying that Lemass 'should not try and cover up his failures by making unsubstantiated and specious statements about us' (*Irish Times*, 14 April 1964, p. 1).

28. *Irish Times*, 1 January 1965, p. 1, 13. Faulkner revealed in an interview that he 'would be willing to meet Mr Lynch at any time,' to which Lynch replied: 'I hope it will be possible for Mr Faulkner and me to meet early in the new year.'

29. Lemass was the only Southerner at the meeting. He was accompanied by T. K. Whitaker (a native of Co. Down), while O'Neill was assisted C. J. Bateman (Secretary of the Stormont Cabinet), Ken Bloomfield (Assistant Secretary of the Stormont Cabinet) and Jim Malley (private secretary to the Prime Minister).

30. Undated memorandum, 'Meeting with the Prime Minister of the Irish Republic' (Public Record Office, Northern Ireland, CAB/9U/5/1).

31. *Irish Times*, 15 January 1965, p. 1.

32. Quoted by O'Neill, *The Autobiography of Terence O'Neill*, p. 72.

33. *Irish Times*, 15 January 1965, p. 1.

34. *Irish Times*, 16 January 1965, p. 15.

35. *Irish Independent*, 27 January 1965, p. 1, 7; *Irish Times*, 27 January 1965, p. 1, 11.

36. Interview by Wesley Boyd, *Irish Times*, 25 January 1965, p. 12.

37. See Ed Moloney, 'Stormont turned down united transport body,' *Irish Times*, 4 January 1982, p. 7; 'Rebuff for Bord Fáilte,' *Irish Times*, 1–2 January 1991, p. 6.

38. 'North-South free trade plan opposed strongly,' *Irish Times*, 1–2 January 1990, p. 9.

39. See interview given to British journalists in London (*Irish Times*, 19 March 1958, p. 1, 3).

40. Speech on 3 February 1965 (O'Neill, *Ulster at the Crossroads*, p. 158).

41. O'Neill, *Ulster at the Crossroads*, p. 159.

42. Interview with Kevin Boland by the author.

43. Speech by Tomás Mac Giolla, president of Sinn Féin, *Irish Times*, 10 February 1965, p. 1; Seán Ó Brádaigh, *Irish Independent*, 26 January 1965, p. 11. Éamonn Mac Thomáis, speech at AGM of Seán Russell Cumann of Sinn Féin, *Irish Times*, 28 January 1965, p. 14.

44. *Irish Independent,* 4 February 1965, p. 3; *Irish Times,* 4 February, p. 7. McAteer received a standing ovation for his contribution, though the motion was lost by 31 votes to 21.

45. *Irish Times,* 15 January 1965, p. 4.

46. Such a shift in vocabulary was not a direct result of the visit but derived from a slow evolution on the subject. See, for example, National Archives, D/T S1957C.

47. *Irish Times,* 22 January 1965, p. 1, 7; O'Neill, *The Autobiography of Terence O'Neill,* p. 73.

48. *Irish Independent,* 15 January 1965, p. 15.

49. Quoted by Frank Curran, *Derry,* p. 37–8.

50. Interview with Brian Feeney by the author.

51. Interview with Brian Feeney by the author. Regarding the de Valera quotation, Feeney was alluding to an extract from a recent work by Eamon Phoenix (*Northern Nationalism,* p. 389). When approached by a nationalist deputation in early 1940 de Valera had impressed upon Cahir Healy that (in the words of the notes taken at the meeting) 'the retention of the 26 County status was considered of such value that the loss of it could not be risked in any effort to reintegrate the country.'

52. Quoted by O Connor, *In Search of a State,* p. 231–2. Paddy McCrory became a prominent solicitor in Northern Ireland and was identified with many important human rights and civil rights cases.

53. Frank Curran, *Derry,* p. 37.

54. *Irish Independent,* 5 February 1965, p. 1, 10.

55. *Irish Times,* 12 February 1965, p. 1.

56. *Irish Times,* 10 February 1965, p. 1.

57. Election slogans and literature from Fianna Fáil Archives (FF/799).

58. Clár (agenda) and turascáil (report) of 1965 ard-fheis, 16–17 November, section A, resolution no. 1 (Fianna Fáil Archives, FF/732).

59. Copy of text in Fianna Fáil Archives (FF/732).

60. In interview by Michael Mills; quoted by O'Sullivan, *Seán Lemass,* p. 187–8.

61. Jack Lynch, 'My life and times,' *Magill,* 3/2 (November 1979), p. 43.

62. Lynch, 'My life and times,' *Magill,* 3/2 (November 1979), p. 42.

63. O'Sullivan, *Seán Lemass,* p. 186.

64. Walsh, *The Party,* p. 89.

65. Interview with Kevin Boland by the author.

66. Dwyer, *Charlie,* p. 54; O'Sullivan, *Seán Lemass,* p. 187.

67. Lynch, 'My life and times,' *Magill,* 3/2 (November 1979), p. 42.

68. Lynch, 'My life and times,' *Magill,* 3/2 (November 1979), p. 42.

69. Walsh, *The Party,* p. 90.

70. Vincent Browne, 'The Arms Crisis, 1970: The inside story,' *Magill,* May 1980, p. 38.

71. Brian Farrell, *Chairman or Chief?,* p. 75.

72. Olivia O'Leary, 'Neil Blaney—past and future' (interview), *Magill,* May 1985, p. 19.

73. Chubb, *Cabinet Government in Ireland,* p. 37.

74. Michael Gallagher, *Political Parties in the Republic of Ireland,* p. 19.

75. *Irish Times,* 23 November 1966, p. 1, 6. Subsequent quotations are from the same source unless otherwise stated.

76. *Irish Times,* 23 November 1966, p. 9.

77. *Irish Times,* 18 November 1966, p. 1.

78. Interview with Kevin Boland by the author.

79. *Irish Times*, 18 November 1966, p. 1, 11.

80. *Irish Times*, 19 November 1966, p. 1.

81. See O'Neill, *The Autobiography of Terence O'Neill*, p. 73–4, for an account of the meeting. Curiously, and erroneously, O'Neill claims that it was 'nearly two years since the previous meeting.'

82. It would be of interest to know whether Paisley received the news from the media or from one of O'Neill's Cabinet colleagues.

83. *Irish Times*, 12 December 1967, p. 9. Subsequent quotations are taken from this issue (p. 1, 7, 9, 14) unless otherwise stated.

84. *Parliamentary Debates: Dáil Éireann: Official Report*, 225/1946 (13 December 1966).

85. *Parliamentary Debates: Dáil Éireann: Official Report*, 225/2037–8 (13 December 1966). See also 225/1082–4 (16 November 1966).

86. *Irish Times*, 2 November 1967. Henry Patterson, 'Seán Lemass and the Ulster question, 1959–1965,' *Journal of Contemporary History*, 34/1 (January 1999), p. 149.

87. Mary Holland, 'How Wilson faltered before Stormont 30 years ago,' *Observer*, 4 January 1998, p. 2.

88. See Tom Bell, 'The struggle of the unemployed in Belfast, October 1932: The Falls and Shankill Unite,' *Communist International*, 1932, reprinted Cork: Cork Workers' Club, 1976; Leo Wilson, *Growing Up in the Hungry, Violent Thirties* (Belfast: Glendore Publishing, 1998); Michael Farrell, *Northern Ireland*, p. 120–49. Related issues can be found in Brendan O'Leary and John McGarry, *The Politics of Antagonism: Understanding Northern Ireland* (London: Athlone Press, 1993), p. 107–52, and Buckland, *The Factory of Grievances*.

89. Memorandum by Nicholas Nolan, 3 November 1967 (National Archives, D/T 99/1/76). See also John Bowman, 'Aiken warned Lemass about applying federal formula to Northern policy,' *Irish Times*, 2 January 1998.

90. The elaborate nature of this subterfuge is indicated by the fact that none of the committee's recommendations were implemented save the section relating to the electoral system, which was not a recommendation. As agreement could not be secured, the advantages and disadvantages of altering the system were outlined, but the committee did not come down on one side or the other. Some members of the opposition complained bitterly that they had devoted much valuable time (eighteen months) to producing a report when it was never intended that any of its recommendations would be implemented. It is true that the recommendation relating to article 44 was put to the people in 1972, but this was an *ad hoc* response to the Northern conflagration. It is almost certain that had it not been for the 'Troubles' the proposal would have gathered dust along with the others.

91. *Report of the Committee on the Constitution*, December 1967 (Dublin: Stationary Office), p. 5–6.

92. Interview with Kevin Boland by the author, 22 June 1993. Boland also pointed out that among the Fianna Fáil representatives there was a faction that was subsequently to leave the party.

93. Boland, *We Won't Stand (Idly) By*, p. 29.

94. The original, unexpurgated version of the five-page script, which Boland gave to Lynch at the Government meeting of 2 January, has never been published and is not in the National Archives. The original copy was provided to the author by Kevin Boland.

95. Boland, *We Won't Stand (Idly) By*, p. 36.

96. Speech at the annual dinner of Mallow Comhairle Ceantair of Fianna Fáil, 5 January 1969, p. 2; copy of speech in author's possession.

97. *Irish Times,* 16 December 1966, p. 1, 4.

98. See secret memorandum on North-South discussions (Public Record Office, Northern Ireland, cab/9U/5/2, and National Archives, dfa 98/3/33).

99. *Irish Times,* 9 January 1968, p. 1, 7, 9.

100. See *Violence and Disturbances in Northern Ireland in 1969* (Scarman Report), Belfast: hmso, 1972.

101. Vincent E. Feeney, 'The civil rights movement,' *Éire-Ireland,* vol. 9, no. 2 (summer 1974), p. 37.

102. *Disturbances in Northern Ireland: Report of the Commission Appointed by the Governor of Northern Ireland (Cameron Report),* London: hmso, 1969, para. 23.

103. O'Neill, *The Autobiography of Terence O'Neill,* p. 99.

104. *Disturbances in Northern Ireland: Report of the Commission Appointed by the Governor of Northern Ireland (Cameron Report),* London: hmso, 1969, chap. 4, para. 51.

105. *Disturbances in Northern Ireland: Report of the Commission Appointed by the Governor of Northern Ireland (Cameron Report),* London: hmso, 1969, chap. 4, para. 49.

106. Edmonds, *The Gun, the Law, and the Irish People,* p. 225.

107. It was an argument to which members of the Government were remarkably sensitive: see, for example, speeches by George Colley (*Irish Times,* 11 October 1968, p. 14) and Jack Lynch (*Irish Independent,* 15 October 1968, p. 14).

108. *Irish Times,* 7 October 1968, p. 1.

109. *Irish Times,* 9 October 1968, p. 1.

110. *Irish Times,* 12 October 1968, p. 9.

111. *Parliamentary Debates: Dáil Éireann: Official Report,* 236/2015 (5 November 1968).

112. *Irish Times,* 31 October 1968, p. 1.

113. *Irish Times,* 31 October 1968, p. 9.

114. *Irish Times,* 1 November 1968, p. 9.

115. *Irish Times,* 1 November 1968, p. 9.

116. Meeting at 10 Downing Street on 4 November 1968 (Public Record Office, Northern Ireland, cab/4/1413). O'Neill and Wilson met secretly before the main conference, which lasted for several hours. The official meeting also included the British Minister of State for Education and Science, Alice Bacon.

117. *Irish Times,* 5 November 1968, p. 1.

118. *Irish Times,* 1 November 1968, p. 1.

119. *Irish Times,* 31 October 1968, p. 1.

120. *Parliamentary Debates: Dáil Éireann: Official Report,* 236/2015 (5 November 1968).

121. *Irish Times,* 31 October 1968, p. 1.

122. *Irish Times,* 31 October 1968, p. 1.

123. *Parliamentary Debates: Dáil Éireann: Official Report,* 236/2487 (7 November 1968).

124. *Parliamentary Debates: Dáil Éireann: Official Report,* 236/2487–8 (7 November 1968).

125. *Irish Times,* 9 November 1968, p. 13.

126. *Irish Times,* 9 November 1968, p. 13.

127. Séamus Brady, *Arms and the Men,* p. 29.

128. *Irish Times,* 12 November 1968, p. 1.

129. *Irish Times,* 12 November 1968, p. 1.

130. *Parliamentary Debates: Dáil Éireann: Official Report,* 236/1088 (23 October 1968).

131. *Irish Times,* 12 November 1968, p. 1.

132. *Irish Times,* 13 November 1968, p. 1.

133. *Parliamentary Debates: Dáil Éireann: Official Report,* 237/162–3 (13 November 1968).

134. *Irish Times,* 13 November 1968, p. 1.

135. *Parliamentary Debates: Dáil Éireann: Official Report,* 237/162 (13 November 1968).

136. Meeting at 10 Downing Street on 4 November 1968 (Public Record Office, Northern Ireland, CAB/4/1413).

137. *Irish Independent,* 10 December 1968, p. 1, 12.

138. *Irish Independent,* 12 December 1968, p. 1; 13 December 1968, p. 1, 15. O'Neill's victory of 28 to 4, while significant, was not as comprehensive as might first appear. There were four abstentions, and two members walked out. Ten MPs, therefore—more than a quarter of the party—could not bring themselves to support O'Neill.

139. The definitive account is that of Bowes Egan and Vincent McCormack, *Burntollet* (London: LRS Publishers, 1969). Michael Farrell (*Northern Ireland,* p. 249–52) gives a fascinating and succinct recollection from the viewpoint of the organisers. See also Paul Arthur, *The People's Democracy, 1968–1973* (Belfast: Blackstaff Press, 1974), and Liam de Paor, *Divided Ulster* (Harmondsworth: Penguin, 1971), p. 186–95. A useful retrospective is provided in a special feature published in the *Irish Times,* 2–3 January 1989, p. 19, in which a number of the participants were interviewed twenty years later. Another PD member present at Burntollet, Tom McGurk, provided another interesting retrospective assessment in the *Sunday Business Post,* 3 January 1999.

140. *Disturbances in Northern Ireland: Report of the Commission Appointed by the Governor of Northern Ireland (Cameron Report),* London: HMSO, 1969, p. 73, para. 177.

141. Quoted by Bowes Egan and Vincent McCormack, *Burntollet* (London: LRS Publishers, 1969), p. 64.

142. *Irish Independent,* 29 April 1969, p. 1,12.

143. *Parliamentary Debates: Dáil Éireann: Official Report,* 238/1933 (27 February 1968).

144. *Irish Times,* 28 February 1969, p. 1.

145. Séamus Brady, *Arms and the Men,* p. 31.

146. *Parliamentary Debates: Dáil Éireann: Official Report,* 238/1933 (27 February 1968).

147. *Parliamentary Debates: Dáil Éireann: Official Report,* 238/1935 (27 February 1968).

148. Draft note by Frank Aiken, 21 April 1969 (National Archives, 2000/9/1 G.C.12/175; 2000/6/557). See also *Irish Times,* 22 April 1969, p. 9.

149. Interview with Kevin Boland by the author.

150. The delay in joining was due to the Soviet Union, which blocked Ireland's application on four occasions, in retaliation for the western powers blocking the admission of China. See Edwin Tetlow, *The United Nations: The First 25 Years* (London: Peter Owen, 1970), p. 89. The policy of not raising partition at the United Nations was contested in the Dáil on many occasions. When the IRA Border Campaign began in earnest during 1957, several county councils and other local bodies passed resolutions calling on the Government to demand the introduction of a UN peacekeeping force in the North. When this strategy was not adopted it gave rise to bitter responses from some deputies. As the Border Campaign was nearing its end, Deputy McQuillan, for example, claimed that 'we can be a sore thumb at UNO [the United Nations] on every other subject except Partition, and is it any wonder that these tragic events take place?' *Parliamentary Debates: Dáil Éireann: Official Report,* 192/841 (23 November 1961).

151. 'Aiken for President?,' *Hibernia,* June 1968, p. 3.

152. *Parliamentary Debates: Dáil Éireann: Official Report*, 240/6 (29 April 1969). De Valera had expressed a similar view when the question of membership of the United Nations first arose. He told the Dáil: 'I do not think myself, looking through the Charter, that one could reasonably hope that through the organisation itself we would be able to bring about the unity of our nation,' though he also speculated that 'circumstances might develop in the future which would lead in that direction.' *Parliamentary Debates: Dáil Éireann: Official Report*, 102/1323 (24 July 1946).

153. Interview with Kevin Boland by the author. Boland attributed some of this reluctance to the influence of Conor Cruise O'Brien, who had been a significant figure in the Department of External Affairs during Aiken's tenure as minister.

154. *Parliamentary Debates: Dáil Éireann: Official Report*, 240/7 (29 April 1969). The words are those of Brendan Corish. When Aiken explained that he had made no request of the Secretary-General, Corish said: 'The minister just told him about the situation. Is that not so?' to which Aiken replied simply, 'Yes.'

155. This account was similar to that given to the UN Correspondents' Club in New York. There the minister explained that he had met U Thant solely 'for the one purpose, and that [was to] advise the Secretary-General of the situation . . . I made no request of the Secretary-General.' See *Irish Times*, 4 April 1969, p. 1.

156. *Parliamentary Debates: Dáil Éireann: Official Report*, 240/8 (29 April 1969). Deputy Seán Dunne made a similar point and claimed that 'the minister could have had a chat with U Thant in London without going to the expense of travelling to the United Nations.'

157. *Irish Times*, 23 April 1969, p. 19.

158. *Irish Times*, 24 April 1969, p. 9.

159. *Irish Times*, 24 April 1969, p. 9.

160. *Parliamentary Debates: Dáil Éireann: Official Report*, 240/6. Aiken responded to the question of raising partition at the UN by stating that U Thant was 'well aware of the reasons why, in the 1920 act, the British partitioned Ireland,' but that he (Aiken) had 'concentrated upon advising him of the extreme gravity of the present situation in the Six Counties and the possibility of further deterioration.'

161. *Parliamentary Debates: Dáil Éireann: Official Report*, 240/1 (29 April 1969).

162. *Parliamentary Debates: Dáil Éireann: Official Report*, 240/1284 (20 May 1969).

163. *Parliamentary Debates: Dáil Éireann: Official Report*, 241/486 (15 July 1969).

164. *Parliamentary Debates: Dáil Éireann: Official Report*, 241/1301 (22 October 1969).

165. *Irish Times*, 22 January 1969, p. 1. Mac Gabhann had previously been a correspondent for the *Irish Press* and travelled with de Valera during his world anti-partition tour of 1948. As for his depiction of de Valera's attitude of 'carry on as if unhearing,' it should be noted that de Valera, now in his eighty-seventh year, may not have been able to hear the interruption. Other survivors, including Máire Comerford and Sheila Donoghue, simply stayed away. See 'Lessons of Remembrance,' a supplement to the *Irish Times*, 21 January 1969, p. 12. Máire Comerford published her own book, *The First Dáil*, to mark the anniversary. She was in her eighty-seventh year when, in 1976, she was arrested and sentenced to imprisonment for participating in a 1916 commemoration that had been banned by the Government.

166. See Fianna Fáil Archives, FF/735, for details of the 1969 ard-fheis.

167. *Irish Times*, 4 June 1969, p. 1.

168. See John A. Murphy, '"Put them out!": Parties and elections, 1948–1969,' in Lee, *Ireland, 1945–1970*, p. 1–17.

169. John A. Murphy, "'Put them out!'": Parties and elections, 1948–1969,' in Lee, *Ireland, 1945–1970*, p. 12.

170. *Irish Times*, 4 June 1969, p. 9.

171. *Irish Times*, 4 June 1969, p. 1.

172. *Irish Times*, 9 June 1969, p. 8.

173. *Irish Times*, 6 June 1969, p. 1. See also speech by Brendan Corish (*Irish Times*, 17 June 1969, p. 8).

174. *Evening Herald*, 17 June 1969, p. 3.

175. See Bruce Arnold, *Haughey: His Life and Unlucky Deeds* (London: Harper Collins, 1994), p. 69–70.

176. *Irish Times*, 5 June 1969, p. 1, 4. See also *Irish Times*, 9 June 1969, p. 1, 4.

177. *Irish Times*, 3 June 1969, p. 8. The comparison was made by Dónal O'Sullivan, Labour Party candidate for South County Dublin.

178. See chap. 3, p. 000.

179. *Irish Times*, 9 June 1969, p. 1,4.

180. *Irish Times*, 4 June 1969, p. 1, 13; *Irish Times*, 18 June 1969, p. 1, 8.

181. *Irish Times*, 10 June 1969, p. 1.

182. *Irish Times*, 18 June 1969, p. 1.

183. Quoted by Bew et al., *The Dynamics of Irish Politics*, p. 93.

184. *Irish Times*, 6 June 1969, p. 9.

185. *Irish Times*, 6 June 1969, p. 9.

186. *Irish Times*, 6 June 1969, p. 9.

187. *Irish Times*, 6 June 1969, p. 9.

188. *Irish Times*, 9 June 1969, p. 1.

189. *Irish Times*, 3 June 1969, p. 8.

190. *Irish Times*, 3 June 1969, p. 11. The two republican elders quickly came to regret their endorsement of the Labour Party candidate. Cruise O'Brien recalled a subsequent meeting with Peadar O'Donnell at which O'Donnell described the new stance of Gilmore and himself as akin to that of 'bishops': Cruise O'Brien had been 'excommunicated' by Gilmore, while O'Donnell was praying for the errant deputy. (Interview with Vincent Browne, RTE Radio 1, December 1998).

191. *Irish Times*, 6 June 1969, p. 1.

192. *Irish Times*, 7 June 1969, p. 10.

193. *Irish Times*, 4 June 1969, p. 17.

194. *Irish Times*, 14 June 1969, p. 9.

195. *Irish Times*, 17 June 1969, p. 3.

196. Speaking in Drumgohill, Co. Donegal (*Irish Times*, 17 June 1969, p. 8).

197. *Irish Times*, 17 June 1969, p. 8.

198. *Irish Times*, 7 June 1969, p. 5.

199. Joe Dowling, Fianna Fáil candidate for Dublin South-West, speaking in Inchicore (*Irish Times*, 4 June 1969, p. 6). Dowling, who topped the poll on this occasion, was to become a front-bench spokesperson for Fianna Fáil between 1973 and 1977.

200. *Irish Times*, 10 June 1969, p. 1.

201. See, for example, *Irish Times*, 9 June 1969, p. 1, 8.

202. *Irish Times*, 18 June 1969, p. 11.

203. Boland, *We Won't Stand (Idly) By*, p. 44.

Chapter 12: 'The moment of truth,' 1969–71 (p. 283–316)

1. Hillery travelled with the Secretary of the Department of External Affairs, Hugh McCann, and met John G. Molloy and Kevin Rush of the Irish embassy in London. Stewart was assisted by Sir Edward Peck, Deputy Under-Secretary at the Foreign Office, and officials from both the Home Office and Foreign Office.
2. Notes of discussion at the Foreign Office at 12.00 noon on Friday 1 August 1969 (National Archives, DFA 2000/6/557).
3. *Irish Times*, 6 August 1969, p. 13.
4. Public Record Office, Northern Ireland, CAB/4/1455, 3 August 1969, and CAB/4/1456, 4 August 1969.
5. *Irish Times*, 4 August 1969, p. 1.
6. *Irish Times*, 5 August 1969, p. 1.
7. These calls came mainly from members of the Campaign for Democracy in Ulster, a group of members of the British Parliament.
8. *Irish Times*, 8 August 1969, p. 1.
9. *Irish Times*, 4 August 1969, p. 11.
10. Bishop and Mallie, *The Provisional IRA*, p. 98.
11. Séamus Brady, *Arms and the Men*, p. 26.
12. For an account of Blaney's actions that night see the interview with Neil Blaney by Joe Jackson in 'Lawyers, guns and money', *Hot Press*, 14/11 (14 June 1990).
13. Séamus Brady, *Arms and the Men*, p. 34–5.
14. Séamus Brady, *Arms and the Men*, p. 36.
15. Boland, *The Rise and Decline of Fianna Fáil*, p. 67.
16. Interview with Neil Blaney by Peter Taylor, 'Timewatch,' BBC2, 27 January 1993.
17. Interview with Kevin Boland by the author.
18. Boland, *Up Dev!*, p. 11.
19. Ronan Fanning, 'Hillery acted as lightning rod on the North,' *Irish Independent*, 20 April 2008.
20. Interview with Kevin Boland by the author.
21. In an interview with the author, Des O'Malley, who was present at the Government meeting as chief whip, said that he didn't 'recall the detail' of what happened that day. He did state, however, that Boland and Blaney (in that order) were the most vociferous critics of Lynch's document. Haughey was the 'least strident', though O'Malley, like many others, claimed to have been surprised by Haughey's stance.
22. Interview with Des O'Malley by the author.
23. Indeed, two months earlier a detailed profile in the *Irish Times* over three days had failed to make any reference to Haughey's views on the North or republicanism generally. *Irish Times*, 9 June 1969, p. 6; 10 June 1969, p. 12; 11 June 1969, p. 12.
24. Hugh McCann (1916–81) had previously served as Irish ambassador to London, 1958–62, before taking up the position of Secretary of the Department of External Affairs, 1963–74.
25. According to Basil Chubb (*Cabinet Government in Ireland*, p. 37), this new statement was put to a vote and 'approved . . . by a narrow majority.' Chubb does not give a source for this important piece of information, and it contradicts the recollections of one of the Government members who participated. Interview with Kevin Boland by the author.
26. Interview with Kevin Boland by the author.
27. As is well known, the word 'idly' was not used by Lynch in this speech but was widely

reported afterwards. Numerous hypotheses have emerged to explain the discrepancy, but a convincing explanation was provided by Kevin Boland, who claimed that the word was in the original statement drafted by Haughey but was deleted after a discussion in the Government. Interview with Kevin Boland by the author.

28. Jack Lynch, 'Speeches and Statements on Irish Unity, Northern Ireland, Anglo-Irish Relations, August 1969 to October 1971' (Government Information Bureau, Dublin, 1971), p. 2.

29. Jack Lynch, 'Speeches and Statements on Irish Unity, Northern Ireland, Anglo-Irish Relations, August 1969 to October 1971' (Government Information Bureau, Dublin, 1971), p. 2.

30. Interview with Neil Blaney by Joe Jackson, in 'Lawyers, guns and money,' *Hot Press*, 14/11, 14 June 1990. This view was reiterated in an interview by Gay Byrne, RTE Radio 1, 1 February 1993.

31. *Evening Press*, 14 August 1969, p. 1. The article, headed 'Irish troops are on the border,' declared that 'Army spokesman admits large forces of Irish troops are at the moment on manoeuvres in Co. Donegal and in the Cavan area . . . Very large forces and convoys are moving near Border areas.' In the more tranquil atmosphere of Leinster House in October the *Evening Press* was criticised for the language employed. See *Parliamentary Debates: Dáil Éireann: Official Report*, cols. 1468–70 (22 October 1969).

32. Peter Taylor, *States of Terror: Democracy and Political Violence* (London: BBC Books, 1993), p. 213.

33. 'A State of Crisis,' RTÉ1 documentary on the Arms Crisis, 1999.

34. One is reminded of Seán Ó Faoláin's reference in 1951 to what he called 'a joke army, a joke navy, and a joke air force'; quoted by Bernard Share, 'Other Toms, Other Moores,' in John F. McCarthy, *Planning Ireland's Future: The Legacy of T. K. Whitaker* (Dublin: Glendale Press, 1990), p. 159.

35. James Dooney, *Them and Us: Britain, Ireland and the Northern Question, 1969–1982* (Dublin: Blackwater Press, 1983), p.36.

36. Boland, *Up Dev!*, p. 42.

37. James Downey, *Them and Us: Britain, Ireland and the Northern Question, 1969–1982* (Dublin: Blackwater Press, 1983), p. 36.

38. Tim Pat Coogan, *The IRA* (second edition), p. 465–6.

39. Interview with Neil Blaney by Peter Taylor, 'Timewatch,' BBC2, 27 January 1993.

40. *Irish Times*, 13 August 1969, p. 7.

41. Confidential report of discussion at Foreign Office, London, 15 August 1969 (National Archives [London], 2000/6/558).

42. 'Paddy Hillery Remembers', RTE1, 1992.

43. 'Discussion at Foreign and Commonwealth Office, London, on 15 August 1969 concerning Northern Ireland,' minutes circulated to Government at meeting of 18 August 1969 (National Archives [London], 2001/6/658).

44. 'Discussion at Foreign and Commonwealth Office, London, on 15 August 1969 concerning Northern Ireland,' minutes circulated to Government at meeting of 18 August 1969 (National Archives [London], 2001/6/658).

45. 'Discussion at Foreign and Commonwealth Office, London, on 15 August 1969 concerning Northern Ireland,' minutes circulated to Government at meeting of 18 August 1969 (National Archives [London], 2001/6/658).

46. Jack Lynch, 'Speeches and Statements on Irish Unity, Northern Ireland, Anglo-Irish

Relations, August 1969 to October 1971' (Government Information Bureau, Dublin, 1971), p. 2.

47. Information for this section is derived from interviews with Kevin Boland and from his books *Up Dev!*, p. 12–14, and *We Won't Stand (Idly) By*, passim.

48. Information for this section is derived from interviews with Kevin Boland and from his books *Up Dev!*, p. 12–14, and *We Won't Stand (Idly) By*, passim.

49. Letter from Quartermaster-General, Colonel Mac Donnchadha, to Secretary of Department of Defence, Seán Ó Cearnaigh, 19 August 1969 (National Archives, S650).

50. National Archives, S650 P&O file 1, para. 2.

51. Letter from Colonel Mac Donnchadha, Quartermaster-General, 21 August 1969 (National Archives, S650).

52. Memo from Secretary, Ó Cearnaigh, to Minister for Defence, 3 September 1969 (National Archives, S650).

53. Memo from Secretary, Ó Cearnaigh, to Minister for Defence, 3 September 1969 (National Archives, S650).

54. Memo from Secretary, Ó Cearnaigh, to Minister for Defence, 3 September 1969 (National Archives, S650).

55. 'Meeting of the Council of Defence held on 13 October 1969, in the Minister's Room, Parkgate' (National Archives 3-58367). When taken with what is known of men from Derry being trained by the army at Fort Dunree, Co. Donegal, the expression 'elements of the FCA' may refer to the training of Northern residents who joined the FCA during this period to be trained in the use of firearms.

56. Secret memorandum by Seán Ronan, 18 August 1969 (National Archives, 2000/9/2).

57. See evidence of Colonel Hefferon to the Committee of Public Accounts, para. 4102.

58. See James J. Kelly, *Orders for the Captain?*, p. 15–17.

59. The Belfast republican John Kelly commented: 'We were disappointed—well, maybe "disappointed" wasn't the word. As against that, training was already taking place inside in nationalist areas by the IRA on an ongoing basis, so people were getting weapons training. The disappointment might have been that official training had ceased. They gave the reason for that as being Intelligence, that they didn't want to get the Brits involved.' Interview with the author, 1993.

60. *Magill*, May 1980, p. 34.

61. *Magill*, May 1980, p. 34.

62. 'Peter Berry diaries,' entry for 17 October 1969, *Magill*, June 1980, p. 54.

63. Evidence of Colonel Hefferon to Committee of Public Accounts, para. 11167. From January 1971 the committee attempted to ascertain the destination of the money allocated for the 'relief of distress,' a fund that had been established in August 1969 for the benefit of those immediately affected by the conflict.

64. Interview with John Kelly by the author, July 1993.

65. Interview with the author.

66. Interview with the author.

67. Interview with John Kelly by the author, July 1993.

68. Interview with John Kelly by the author, July 1993.

69. Interview with John Kelly by the author, July 1993.

70. Telegram from British ambassador, Sir Anthony Gilchrist, to Foreign and Commonwealth Office (National Archives [London], FCO 33 759). The speakers included the Stormont MPs Austin Currie, Paddy Kennedy and Paddy O'Hanlon and

the Derry activists Eamonn McCann and Fionbarra Ó Dochartaigh.

71. *Irish Times,* 12 January 1970, p. 1, 12.

72. Bishop and Mallie, *The Provisional* IRA, p. 134.

73. See Taylor, *Provos,* p. 64–7.

74. Interview with Neil Blaney by Peter Taylor, 'Timewatch,' BBC2, 27 January 1993. Blaney mentioned Ballymurphy in particular, as he was referring to violent clashes between the British army and local civilians in March 1970, which had injected renewed urgency into the quest for arms.

75. Report of the Honorary Secretaries (Fianna Fáil Archives, FF/737).

76. Report of the Honorary Treasurers (Fianna Fáil Archives, FF/737).

77. Seán Sherwin, then aged twenty-six, became the youngest member of the nineteenth Dáil when he successfully stood in the Dublin South-West by-election for Fianna Fáil, but he failed to retain his seat at the subsequent general election, when he stood for Aontacht Éireann. He rejoined Fianna Fáil when Haughey became Taoiseach but failed to win a seat in Dublin West in the general election of November 1982. In 1985 he was appointed director of organisation for Fianna Fáil and is now the party's general secretary.

78. Noirín Ní Scolláin, who was twenty-eight at the time of the 1970 ard-fheis, later joined Aontacht Éireann. A member of Fianna Fáil from 1962 to 1971, she served on the party's National Executive.

79. All quotations are from the discussion on the honorary secretaries' report, taken from the *Irish Times,* 19 January 1970, p. 4.

80. Boland, *Up Dev!,* p. 35–6.

81. There is a copy of the Taoiseach's presidential address in the Fianna Fáil Archives (FF/737). The full text was also published in the *Irish Times,* 19 January 1970, p. 4.

82. Telegram from Sir Anthony Gilchrist to Foreign and Commonwealth Office, 18 January 1970 (National Archives [London], FCO 33/1201).

83. Telegrams between Sir Anthony Gilchrist, George Thomson and Michael Stewart, 19 and 20 January (National Archives [London], FCO 33/1201).

84. Telegram from Sir Anthony Gilchrist to Foreign and Commonwealth Office, 18 January 1970 (National Archives [London], FCO 33/1201). Lynch had already communicated to Gilchrist the desirability of a statement from Chichester-Clark and was disappointed when nothing emerged from Stormont in the immediate aftermath of the ard-fheis. According to Gilchrist's recollection, the speech did not need to be substantive: 'nothing very definite . . . just something to keep the situation sweet.' Notes of meeting between Sir Anthony Gilchrist and Jack Lynch and Patrick Hillery communicated in telegram to Foreign and Commonwealth Office, 20 January 1970 (National Archives [London], FCO 33/1201).

85. Notes of meeting between Sir Anthony Gilchrist and Jack Lynch and Patrick Hillery communicated in telegram to Foreign and Commonwealth Office, 20 January 1970 (National Archives [London], FCO 33/1201).

86. Confidential letter from Sir Anthony Gilchrist to the Minister for Foreign and Commonwealth Affairs, George Thomson, 20 January 1970 (National Archives [London], FCO 33/1201).

87. Notes of meeting between Sir Anthony Gilchrist and Jack Lynch and Patrick Hillery communicated in telegram to Foreign and Commonwealth Office, 20 January 1970 (National Archives [London], FCO 33/1201).

88. This was to consist of 200 submachine guns, 84 light machine guns, 50 general-purpose machine guns, 150 automatic rifles, 200 percussion grenades, 70 flak jackets, 200 pistols and 250,000 rounds of ammunition.

89. 'Peter Berry diaries,' entries for 18 and 30 April 1970, *Magill*, June 1980, p. 61, 63. See also *Magill*, May 1980, p. 54.

90. Speculation developed that the riding accident was feigned to avoid the confrontation; but according to Kevin Boland, Haughey's injuries were serious. Des O'Malley confirmed this, saying 'Haughey's injuries were too serious to be contrived.' Interviews with Kevin Boland and Des O'Malley by the author. June 1993 and January 1996, respectively.

91. The first attempt at securing arms had been in England, when John Kelly and Pádraig (Jock) Haughey (brother of Charles) entered negotiations with a Captain Randall, who later turned out to be a British agent. Kelly's initial suspicions were confirmed when Randall requested that he be taken on a tour of IRA training camps in the Republic. Kelly agreed to the suggestion while privately making plans for Randall's assassination in Dublin. Only the intervention of Captain James Kelly saved Randall from certain death. Proof, if any was needed, of surveillance by British Intelligence was provided when the Garda Special Branch received photographs of Haughey and Kelly in London. Herr Schleuter also seems to have been in contact with British Intelligence. Interview with John Kelly by the author, 19 July 1993.

92. *Parliamentary Debates: Dáil Éireann: Official Report*, 246/720 (7 May 1970).

93. *Parliamentary Debates: Dáil Éireann: Official Report*, 246/643 (7 May 1970).

94. *Parliamentary Debates: Dáil Éireann: Official Report*, 246/644 (7 May 1970).

95. National Archives, 2000/6/513.

96. Addendum to Memo of 10/2/70, Ministerial Directive to CF [chief of staff] (National Archives, MDA, copy no. 5, Rn P&O, CCA, 11 February 1970).

97. Secret: Meeting with An Taoiseach, Tuesday 9 June 1970 (National Archives, MI 5, p. 2–8).

98. *Parliamentary Debates: Dáil Éireann: Official Report*, 246/841 (8 May 1970).

99. John Kelly's speech in the dock can be found in Tom McIntyre, *Through the Bridewell Gate, A Diary of the Dublin Arms Trial.* p. 123–32.

100. The original copy of this previously unpublished circular was made available to the author by Kevin Boland.

101. Boland, *We Won't Stand (Idly) By*, p. 86–7.

102. Colonel Delaney, Comments on Government Directive and Addendum, 5 October 1970 (National Archives, MI 5/3).

103. Colonel Delaney, Comments on Government Directive and Addendum, 5 October 1970 (National Archives, MI 5/3).

104. On Friday 2 October 1970 Cronin instructed Hefferon's successor, Colonel P. J. Delaney, to have the files given to Gibbons, and this was done the following Monday, 5 October. Undated note of Col. Delaney (National Archives, MI 5/3). See Clifford, *Military Aspects of Ireland's Arms Crisis of 1969–70*, p. 124.

105. *Parliamentary Debates: Dáil Éireann: Official Report*, 246/838–9 (8 May 1970).

106. Prime Time Special, 'The Arms Trial Revisited,' RTE1, April 2001.

107. Peck to Sir Alec Douglas Home [Secretary of State for Foreign and Commonwealth Affairs], 10 November 1970 (National Archives [London], FCO 33/1207).

108. *Irish Times*, 23 October 1970, p. 1, 9.

109. *Irish Times*, 23 October 1970, p. 1, 9.

110. Without producing any proof, Garret FitzGerald has said of the jury decision: 'It was a totally perverse verdict. They were intimidated . . . they totally disregarded the evidence.' Justin O'Brien, *The Arms Trials* (Dublin: Gill & Macmillan, 2000), p. 220. When RTE contacted the four surviving jurors in 2001 they dismissed claims of intimidation. Prime Time Special, 'The Arms Trial Revisited,' April 2001.

111. Haughey also said: 'The verdict was not just "not guilty" for these men but one of guilty against one of his Ministers who he has officially endorsed in the Dáil. He is on record in the Dáil as endorsing this Minister who has now been repudiated by the Courts of Justice. I think the implications will be obvious for the Taoiseach.' *Irish Times*, 24 October 1970, p. 1.

112. The Minister for Lands was in London at a conference for World Conservation Year, while the Minister for External Affairs, Dr Hillery, was said (mysteriously) to be returning from New York by sea!

113. Interview with the author.

114. *Irish Times*, 27 October 1970, p. 1.

115. Telegram 351 of 28 October 1970, entitled 'Government Crisis' (National Archives [London], FC 33/120). See also telegram 354 of 29 October 1970.

116. Telegram 351 of 28 October 1970, entitled 'Government Crisis' (National Archives [London], FC 33/120).

117. Telegram 360 of 31 October 1970 (National Archives [London], FC 33/1201).

118. *Hibernia*, 12 June 1970. Certainly this is what happened when, in 1982, Bruce Arnold published the names of those considered anti-Haughey in the *Irish Independent*, 24 February 1982, p.1. As recollected by Charles McCreevey and Pádraig Flynn in 'Haughey,' RTE 1, 2005.

119. *Parliamentary Debates: Dáil Éireann: Official Report*, 248/53–4 (30 June 1970). This suggestion had been made during the previous debate on the North. See *Parliamentary Debates: Dáil Éireann: Official Report*, 241/1442 to 3 (22 October 1969). Then the Taoiseach had promised to consider the proposal (241/1598, 23 October 1969); he now considered it inappropriate 'in the present circumstances.' He had not, he said, considered Cosgrave's suggestion of a tripartite meeting between the British, Irish and Northern Governments (248/55, 30 June 1970). Cosgrave was to consistently advocate this action throughout this period. See, for example, *Irish Times*, 11 July 1970, p. 9.

120. *Parliamentary Debates: Dáil Éireann: Official Report*, 248/57 (30 June 1970).

121. The election returned 331 Conservatives and Unionists, 287 Labour, 6 Liberals and 6 others. Exclusive of the speaker (chairperson) and the Ulster Unionists, who were an integral part of the Conservative Party, the Government's majority was only 22. Harold Wilson had lost 33 of his 1966 majority of 96 seats during the previous four years through normal anti-Government swings at by-elections. The slim Conservative majority obviously enhanced the leverage of the UUP.

122. Hamill, *Pig in the Middle*, p. 36. 'Nothing is known of Mr. Maudling's views,' the *Irish Times* reported. 'He is not known to have any profound views on Northern Ireland or any exact knowledge of the situation.' Maudling had met Terence O'Neill on several occasions when he was Chancellor of the Exchequer (minister for finance) and was reported to be a social acquaintance of Chichester-Clark (*Irish Times*, 22 June 1970, p. 1, 7, 9). For these reasons his appointment was welcomed by Unionists, while the Irish

Government's preference for Quintin Hogg, who held the shadow portfolio in opposition, was well known. For a profile see *Irish Times*, 24 June 1970, p. 11, and W. D. Flackes and Sydney Elliot, *Northern Ireland: A Political Directory, 1968–1993* (Belfast: Blackstaff Press, 1994), p. 231.

123. Interview with Paddy Devlin by the author, 29 April 1994. Devlin, then a Stormont MP, provides a personalised account of the curfew, during which he was arrested, in *Straight Left: An Autobiography* (Belfast: Blackstaff Press, 1993), p. 128–31. See also the *Irish Times*, 4 July 1970, p. 1, 5, 8, 9, 11. The curfew was briefly broken when a thousand women from the Andersonstown area marched to the Falls Road with food supplies.

124. Kelley, *The Longest War*, p. 147. Tim Pat Coogan attributes the sectarian nature of the searches to the fact that the soldiers were primarily Scottish Protestants. 'It was like letting the Rangers supporters loose on the Celtic supporters.' Quoted from Martin Dillon, 'The Last Colony,' Channel 4, July 1994.

125. *Irish Times*, 6 July 1970, p. 9.

126. Bell, *The Secret Army*, p. 377; Reid, *Ireland*, p. 154.

127. Henry Kelly, *How Stormont Fell*, p. 9–10, Hamill, *Pig in the Middle*, p. 39, Dewar, *The British Army in Northern Ireland*, p. 47; Coogan, *Disillusioned Decades*, p. 208–9. The main beneficiaries were the Provisional IRA. The Lower Falls area had been an Official IRA stronghold, but the organisation's relative inaction during the curfew brought about a shift in republican allegiance in the area. As the Official IRA was a more moderate version of the Provisional wing, this shift was to have long-term implications for the British army, further emphasising the counter-productive nature of the curfew.

128. John A. Murphy, for example (*Ireland in the Twentieth Century*, p. 166), states that the curfew 'marked the final alienation of the Catholic population from the British Army which was now regarded as bolstering up the discredited Stormont regime.'

129. Michael Farrell, *Northern Ireland*, p. 274. One of the ministers, John Brooke (son of the former Prime Minister Lord Brookeborough), declared: 'It's a grand day for us' (Sunday Times Insight Team, *Ulster* (London: Deutsch, 1972), p. 221). The *Irish Times* (6 July 1970, p. 7) described the scene thus: 'Captain John Brooke . . . riding at the front . . . like a combat officer surveying a captured town, as did Captain Walter Long, who confided to journalists that it was always painful to lance a boil. He himself was not noticeably pained.'

130. *Irish Times*, 4 July, 1970, p. 1.

131. *Irish Times*, 6 July, 1970, p. 7.

132. Jack Lynch, 'Speeches and Statements on Irish Unity, Northern Ireland, Anglo-Irish Relations, August 1969 to October 1971' (Government Information Bureau, Dublin, 1971), p. 20–21.

133. Jack Lynch, 'Speeches and Statements on Irish Unity, Northern Ireland, Anglo-Irish Relations, August 1969 to October 1971' (Government Information Bureau, Dublin, 1971), p. 20–21.

134. See interview with Paddy Devlin by Kevin O'Kelly of RTE, in which Devlin implied that nationalists needed arms and not words from the Taoiseach (*Irish Times*, 6 July 1970, p. 1, 7). See also the account by Conor Cruise O'Brien (*States of Ireland*, p. 218), who visited the Falls Road the day after the curfew was lifted.

135. *Irish Times*, 6 July 1970, p. 7.

136. Extract from Berry's diary, 5 July 1970, as published in *Magill*, June 1980, p. 70. O'Malley remained adamant that his suspicions were not unjustified and pointed to

the Saor Éire threat five months later as proof that these apprehensions were not unwarranted. He had less than fond memories of Peter Berry. Interview with Des O'Malley by the author.

137. Fianna Fáil, Minutes of National Executive, 27 July 1970 (UCD Archives, P176/350). The petitioners appealed to the National Executive to reconsider, but the request was turned down again at the meeting of 14 September 1970.

138. *Hibernia*, 22 November 1970.

139. See *Parliamentary Debates: Dáil Éireann: Official Report*, 250/485–94 (9 December 1970).

140. *Parliamentary Debates: Dáil Éireann: Official Report*, 250/489 (9 December 1970).

141. *Parliamentary Debates: Dáil Éireann: Official Report*, 250/512–13 (9 December 1970).

142. Interview with Des O'Malley by the author, 11 January 1996.

143. Interview with Des O'Malley by Paul McGuill (copy in possession of author).

144. Interview with the author.

145. Interview with Seán Mac Stiofáin by Paul McGuill (copy in possession of author).

146. *Parliamentary Debates: Dáil Éireann: Official Report*, 250/486 (9 December 1970).

147. *Irish Times*, 5 December 1970, p. 1.

148. *Irish Times*, 7 December 1970, p. 1.

149. *Irish Times*, 7 December 1970, p. 1.

150. *Irish Times*, 8 December 1970, p. 1.

151. Interview with the author.

152. Letter from Sir John Peck to W. K. K. White, Western European Department, Foreign and Commonwealth Office, 11 January 1971; letter from A. C. Thorpe to P. J. Evans of Dublin embassy, 19 January 1971; P. J. Evans to A. C. Thorpe, 22 January 1971; A. C. Thorpe to P. J. Evans, 3 February 1971 (National Archives [London], FCO 33/1596).

153. Boland, *We Won't Stand (Idly) By*, p. 109.

154. The perception that the ard-fheis was to be stage-managed was widespread. One cartoon by 'Drake' depicted a group of older delegates approaching a bouncer at the door of the Main Hall and asking, 'D'ye think he'll let us in without an Oath?' (*Irish Times*, 20 February 1971, p. 12).

155. Letter to each delegate from Ard-Rúnaí (Fianna Fáil Archives, FF/737).

156. Report of the Honorary Secretaries (Fianna Fáil Archives, FF/737).

157. Boland, *We Won't Stand (Idly) By*, p. 109–10.

158. Interview with Kevin Boland by the author.

159. Letter from Tom Lally (Chairman of Fianna Fáil, Galway West) to secretary of Galway West Comhairle Ceantair, quoted in *Irish Times*, 19 February 1972, p. 7. Lally resigned from Fianna Fáil and joined Aontacht Éireann.

160. Clár (agenda) of 1971 ard-fheis (Fianna Fáil Archives, FF/737).

161. A cut in the time allocated to delegates' speeches was the most significant proposed change. The time made available to proposers of motions was to be reduced by almost 40 per cent and that allocated to other contributors by 25 per cent.

162. 'Rowdy ard-fheis backs Lynch against disruptive groups,' *Irish Times*, 22 February 1971, p. 8.

163. 'Uproar at opening of Fianna Fáil ard-fheis,' *Irish Times*, 22 February 1971, p. 7.

164. Nell McCafferty, 'Fianna Fáil's Weekend of the Long Knives,' *Irish Times*, 22 February 1971, p. 8.

165. 'Rowdy ard-fheis backs Lynch against disruptive groups,' *Irish Times*, 22 February 1971, p. 8.

166. 'Boland supporters in angry scenes,' *Irish Times*, 22 February 1971, p. 9.
167. 'Boland supporters in angry scenes,' *Irish Times*, 22 February 1971, p. 9.
168. 'Uproar at opening of Fianna Fáil ard-fheis,' *Irish Times*, 22 February 1971, p. 7.
169. John Healy, 'Political fervour stopped just short of mass hysteria,' *Irish Times*, 22 February 1971, p. 1.
170. Had Gibbons told his opponents to 'go back to college' one might have put it down to traditional anti-intellectualism. Trinity College, however, was considered a bastion of Protestantism and, to a lesser extent, West-Britishness. (Orthodox unionism was now something confined to Ulster.) Until 1971 Catholics had to receive permission from their local bishop to attend Trinity College; it was therefore considered an institution favoured by lapsed (or 'bad') Catholics and Protestants (Brian Faulkner had been educated at Trinity). Those members of the Fianna Fáil Government who had received a university education had attended NUI colleges, particularly UCD.
171. 'Gibbons asserts he stands by every word said in past,' *Irish Times*, 22 February 1971, p. 9.
172. 'Fianna Fáil Party Conference,' Diplomatic Report, 9 March 1971, p. 1–2 (National Archives [London], FCO/33/1596).
173. *Irish Times*, 22 February 1971, p. 8.
174. 'Letting off steam!,' *Irish Times*, 22 February 1971, p. 11.

Chapter 13: Doomsday, 1971–3 (p. 317–70)
1. British embassy in Dublin, telegram 136 of 29 April 1971 (National Archives [London], FCO33/1596). See also telegram 133 of 23 April 1971.
2. British embassy in Dublin, telegram 124 of 19 April 1971 (National Archives [London], FCO 33/1596).
3. Fianna Fáil, Minutes of National Executive, 26 April 1971 (UCD Archives, P176/350).
4. Fianna Fáil, Minutes of National Executive, 22 November 1971 (UCD Archives, P176/350).
5. Peck to Foreign and Commonwealth Office, 1 June 1971 (National Archives [London], FCO 33/1596).
6. See *Irish Times*, 22 March 1971, p. 1, 8, 9, 11. A full transcript of the phone conversation between Heath and Chichester-Clark, during which the latter announced his resignation, can be found in 'Note for the Record,' 25 March 1971 (National Archives [London] (PRO PREM 15/476).
7. See *Irish Times*, 26 March 1971, p. 1, 13.
8. *Irish Times*, 26 March 1971. One Unionist MP, Anne Dickson, resigned from the party in protest against the inclusion of West in the new Cabinet (*Irish Times*, 27 March 1971). She later joined the Alliance Party.
9. 'Note of a Meeting held at 10 Downing Street on Thursday, 5 August 1971 at 6.00 p.m.' (National Archives [London], PREM 15/478). Those representing the British Government included Heath, Maudling, Douglas-Home (Foreign and Commonwealth Affairs), Carrington (Defence) and Sir Philip Allen (Permanent Under-Secretary of State, Home Office), while only Faulkner and the Deputy Secretary of his Cabinet, Kenneth Bloomfield, were in attendance from Northern Ireland.
10. *Irish Times*, 24 September 1971, p. 1,7.
11. Holland and McDonald, *INLA*, p. 19.
12. *Irish Times*, 13 August 1971, p. 8; 19 August 1971, p. 1; 20 August 1971, p. 9. A study of the psychological effects of interrogation during internment can be found in Fields, *A*

Society on the Run, p. 67–98. Her analysis is based on psychological test and clinical interview data collected on a sample of 125 men. She concluded that the experience of internment and interrogation 'effects changes in a man's cognitive processes and in his concept of self which render him anomic and alienated—conditions characterised by feeling alone in a normless society and without a consistent positive identity.' For British media coverage of internment see Curtis, *Ireland: The Propaganda War*, p. 30–40.

13. The British Home Secretary, Reginald Maudling, wrote gleefully that the committee had 'found no evidence of physical brutality, still less of torture or brain-washing.' *Report of the Enquiry into Allegations against the Security Forces of Physical Brutality in Northern Ireland Arising out of Events on the 9th August, 1971* (Compton Report), London: HMSO, 1971, para 14.

14. By this stage the British Government was able to argue that the ECHR's conclusions were of historical value only and of no contemporary relevance. This was despite the fact that a new phase of 'deep interrogation' of detainees had begun at Castlereagh. See Peter Taylor, *Beating the Terrorists?: Interrogation at Omagh, Gough and Castlereagh* (Harmondsworth: Penguin, 1980).

15. See Bobby Devlin, *An Interlude with Seagulls: Memories of a Long Kesh Internee* (second edition) (London: Information on Ireland, 1985); Gerry Adams, *Cage Eleven* (Dingle: Brandon Books, 1990).

16. Chris Ryder, *The Ulster Defence Regiment: An Instrument of Peace?* (second edition) (London: Mandarin 1992), p. 45.

17. 'Note of a Meeting held at 10 Downing Street on Thursday, 5 August 1971 at 6.00 p.m.' (National Archives [London], PREM 15/478).

18. 'Draft Message to the Taoiseach,' p. 3 (National Archives [London], PREM 15/478).

19. Dublin telegram no. 290 of 30 July 1971 (National Archives [London], PREM 15/478).

20. Dublin telegram no. 298, 8 August 1971 (National Archives [London], PRO 33/1465).

21. *Irish Times*, 12 August 1971, p. 8.

22. Maudling had pressed Hillery to do all he could to combat the IRA, but Hillery replied that it would be politically impossible if viewed as helping the Stormont authorities. 'Northern Ireland: Dr. Hillery's discussion with the Home Secretary. Note of a meeting at the Home Office on Wednesday, 11 August' (National Archives [London], PRO PREM 15/478). See also *Irish Times*, 12 August 1971, p. 1.

23. *Irish Times*, 17 August 1971, p. 5.

24. *Irish Times*, 17 August 1971, p. 5; 18 August 1971, p. 4. Taylor made his contribution during a television discussion that included representatives of both wings of the IRA. Michael Flannery, an Old IRA man from Co. Tipperary who was to become prominent in Noraid, was also a member of the panel, as was Cormac O'Malley, son of Ernie O'Malley.

25. *Irish Times*, 12 August 1971, p. 8.

26. Interview with the author, January 1996.

27. *Irish Times*, 4 September 1971, p. 1.

28. Gregson to Prime Minister, 10 August 1971 (National Archives [London], PRO PREM 15/478).

29. Text of a Conversation between Mr. Lynch and the Prime Minister at 4.11 p.m. on Thursday, 10 August 1971 (National Archives [London], PRO PREM 15/478).

30. *Irish Times*, 13 August 1971, p. 1, 9.

31. *Irish Times*, 13 August 1971, p. 11.

32. *Irish Times,* 13 August 1971, p.9.

33. *Irish Times,* 13 August 1971, p.9.

34. Dublin telegram no. 335 of 19 August 1971 (National Archives [London], PREM 15/479).

35. Peck, *Dublin from Downing Street,* p. 130.

36. National Archives [London] PREM 15/479/T1296/71, 19 August 1971.

37. Peck, *Dublin from Downing Street,* p. 132. Dublin telegram no. 337 of 20 August 1971 (National Archives [London], FCO 33/1596).

38. Dublin telegram no. 337 of 20 August 1971 (National Archives [London], FCO 33/1596).

39. Undated confidential report in advance of Lynch visit of 6–7 September 1971 (National Archives [London], FCO 33/1613).

40. Undated confidential report in advance of Lynch visit of 6–7 September 1971, p. 2–3 (National Archives [London], FCO 33/1613).

41. Undated confidential report in advance of Lynch visit of 6–7 September 1971, p. 4–5 (National Archives [London], FCO 33/1613).

42. Undated confidential report in advance of Lynch visit of 6–7 September 1971, p. 1 (National Archives [London], FCO 33/1613).

43. Undated confidential report in advance of Lynch visit of 6–7 September 1971, p. 8 (National Archives [London], FCO 33/1613).

44. Undated confidential report in advance of Lynch visit of 6–7 September 1971, p. 23 (National Archives [London], FCO 33/1613).

45. Undated confidential report in advance of Lynch visit of 6–7 September 1971, p. 13 (National Archives [London], FCO 33/1613).

46. Undated confidential report in advance of Lynch visit of 6–7 September 1971, p. 8 (National Archives [London], FCO 33/1613).

47. Trend Note to Prime Minister, 3 September 1971 (National Archives [London], PRO PREM 15/486).

48. 'Report of discussions on 6th and 7th September 1971 at Chequers between the Taoiseach and the British Prime Minister' (National Archives, DFA 2003/13/6).

49. 'Report of discussions on 6th and 7th September 1971 at Chequers between the Taoiseach and the British Prime Minister' (National Archives, DFA 2003/13/6).

50. Unattributable Press Briefing, 7 September 1971, for immediate transmission to certain missions (National Archives [London], FCO 33/1613, FCO 271925Z).

51. Unattributable Press Briefing, 7 September 1971 for immediate transmission to certain missions (National Archives [London], FCO 33/1613, FCO 271925Z).

52. 'Record of a discussion with the Prime Ministers of the Irish Republic and Northern Ireland held at Chequers on Monday, 27 September, 1971 at 12 noon' and 'Record of a discussion with the Prime Ministers of the Irish Republic and Northern Ireland held at Chequers on Monday, 27 September, 1971 at 3.15 p.m.' (National Archives [London], PRO CAB 133/406).

53. 'Record of a discussion with the Prime Ministers of the Irish Republic and Northern Ireland held at Chequers on Tuesday, 28 September, 1971 at 3 p.m.' and 'Record of a discussion with the Prime Ministers of the Irish Republic and Northern Ireland held at Chequers on Tuesday, 28 September, 1971 at 3.45 p.m.' (National Archives [London], PRO CAB 133/406).

54. 'Record of a discussion with the Prime Ministers of the Irish Republic and Northern Ireland held at Chequers on Tuesday, 28 September, 1971 at 3.45 p.m.' (National Archives [London], PRO CAB 133/406).

55. Telegram no. 545 of 1 November 1971 (National Archives [London], PRO CAB 133/406). Lynch's views were communnicated to Peck in conversation with Hugh McCann.

56. Telegram no. 552 of 2 November 1971 (National Archives [London], FCO 33/1596). In telegram no. 342, 28 August, Hillery is considered the most likely successor, closely followed by Haughey. If Hillery was successful in succeeding Lynch the report concludes that he would most probably have to include Haughey and Blaney in his Government, while if Haughey was elected he would probably bring in Blaney and Boland. 'Both Hillery and Haughey would probably make more statements [like] Lynch's telegram of 19 August, go to the UN, bring back troops from Cyprus, police the border, declare emergencies and so on. They would probably also reassert strongly the republican position. All this would be mere hot air, but it would inflame the situation in the North even further and, perhaps, reduce feelings of frustration here [Dublin].' The report considered a 'national government' (coalition of all parties) to be 'a very remote possibility.'

57. A remark of the Irish ambassador in London, Dónal O'Sullivan, to the effect that Hillery would be 'quite happy to see the Lynch/Heath meeting fail,' was added to the fact that Hillery had failed to publicly see off or welcome back the Taoiseach from his vital meeting of 6–7 September with Heath. Instead, Peck's report stated, he had returned to Co. Clare, where he would be INCOMMUNICADO (double-underlined in the report) for more than a week, making no comments, receiving no phone calls and not even travelling to Dublin to sign the Sterling Area Agreement. All this would have been more comprehensible, the report speculated, 'if he had observed the common civilities when his master returned from Chequers. Instead, he has left the impression of an out-of-step minister having a fit of political sulks and taking considerable pains publicly to disassociate himself from the manner in which the Taoiseach conducts relations with ourselves.' Peck Telegram no. 408, 15 September 1971 (National Archives [London], FCO 33/1596).

58. Peck Telegram no. 437, 23 September 1971 (National Archives [London], FCO 33/1596).

59. David Blatherwick to A. C. Thorpe, 19 August and 27 August 1971 (National Archives [London], FCO 33/1596).

60. Peck Telegram no. 543, 1 November 1971 (National Archives [London], FCO 33/1596).

61. Fianna Fáil, Minutes of National Executive, 8 November 1971 (UCD Archives, P176/350).

62. Fianna Fáil, Minutes of National Executive, 8 November 1971 (UCD Archives, P176/350).

63. Peck Telegram no. 577, 11 November 1971 (National Archives [London], FCO 33/1596). The British ambassador's report of the meeting of the National Executive on 8 November provides more detail than the official Fianna Fáil minutes available in the party archives.

64. Gilchrist to Trend, 24 November 1971 (National Archives [London], PRO PREM 15/1000). Trend passed on the letter to Heath. See Trend to Heath, 10 December 1971 (National Archives [London], PRO PREM 15/1000).

65. Peck to UKREP [United Kingdom Representation to the European Union, Brussels], 7 January 1972 (National Archives [London], PRO PREM 15/1000).

66. Only McCann and Armstrong accompanied Lynch and Heath during the meeting, which began at 11 a.m.

67. The British side recognised the significance of what was conceded here and emphasised this statement in their report of the meeting.

68. 'Notes for the Record,' Meeting between Heath and Lynch, 23 January 1972 (National Archives [London], FCO 87/27).

69. See McCann et al., *Bloody Sunday in Derry*; Mullan and Scally, *The 'Bloody Sunday' Massacre in Northern Ireland*; Mullan and Scally, *Eyewitness Bloody Sunday*; Pringle and Jacobson, *Those Are Real Bullets, Aren't They?*; Joanne O'Brien, *A Matter of Minutes*; Hayes and Campbell, *Bloody Sunday*.

70. Interview with General Michael Carver by Martin Dillon, 'The Last Colony,' Channel 4, July 1994.

71. See transcript of Peter Taylor's submission to the Bloody Sunday tribunal at www.bloody-sunday-inquiry.org/reports/kstatements/Archive/M76.pdf.

72. *Irish Times*, 1 February 1972, p. 1.

73. *Irish Times*, 1 February 1972, p. 6. See also Eamonn McCann, *War and an Irish Town* (Harmondsworth: Penguin, 1973), p. 166.

74. *Irish Times*, 3 February 1972, p. 1.

75. As reprinted in the *Irish Times*, 2 January 2003. The transcript was also made available and publicised by the Bloody Sunday tribunal at www.bloody-sunday-inquiry.org.

76. Confidential record of meeting between Sir John Peck and Jack Lynch, 3 February 1972 (National Archives [London], FCO 87/26).

77. *Irish Times*, 4 February 1972, p. 1.

78. John Healy commented that Lynch 'was getting tough with the IRA in all its manifestations but I cannot honestly report that his brave sentiments were "hear-heared" by any one of the 30 Deputies then sitting alongside or behind him' (*Irish Times*, 4 February 1972, p. 1).

79. *Irish Times*, 23 January 1972, p. 1.

80. *Irish Times*, 1 February 1972, p. 1, 9.

81. *Irish Times*, 1 February 1972, p. 1.

82. *Parliamentary Debates: Dáil Éireann: Official Report*, 258/826 (1 February 1972).

83. *Irish Times*, 1 February 1972, p. 1; 2 February 1972, p. 6.

84. *Irish Times*, 1 February 1972, p. 11.

85. *Irish Times*, 2 February 1972, p. 6.

86. Cronin, *Washington's Irish Policy*, p. 305; *Irish Times*, 3 February 1972, p. 7.

87. *Irish Times*, 4 February 1972, p. 1.

88. Any support that did manifest itself in the United States came mainly from Irish-Americans. The British consulate in New York was taken over, and rallies were held in several cities. An example of such support was a strike called by the Long Island (New York) dockers' union, which refused to handle goods from British-registered ships (*Irish Times*, 7 February 1972, p. 1). Hillery briefly met Senators Ted Kennedy and Abraham Ribicoff, who had jointly sponsored a Senate motion urging British withdrawal and Irish reunification (*Irish Times*, 4 February 1972, p. 7).

89. While considerable sympathy had been aroused for nationalist Ireland in Québec, Canadian Government policy was markedly pro-British. Hillery's meeting with the Canadian Secretary of State for External Affairs, Mitchell Sharp, was his only official engagement in Ottawa. At the press conference afterwards Sharp said that Canada would be happy to pass on Dublin's views to London but stressed that the Canadian Government would not urge any particular point of view on Britain. He said he 'could not accept any suggestion' that the Canadian Government would use its 'good offices' to put pressure on the British Government and added that his Government had not

been asked to mediate in the dispute, and therefore the question of a mediation role for Canada did not arise. Hillery, for his part, described the meeting as 'very satisfactory' (*Irish Times*, 8 February 1972, p. 1).

90. For an account of French official attitudes see Fergus Pyle, *Irish Times*, 4 February 1972, p. 6. An article in *La Nation* possibly inspired by the Ministry of Foreign Affairs argued that Ireland and Britain should resolve their differences before being permitted to join the EEC. See *Irish Times*, 5 February 1972, p. 16.

91. See *Irish Times*, 8 February 1972, p. 1, for a preliminary assessment of Hillery's tour.

92. The meeting merited less than a single column on p. 11 of the *Irish Times*. It was 'very satisfactory,' the discussions 'very warm and friendly.'

93. *Irish Times*, 12 February 1972, p. 11.

94. The Dutch visit received three sentences in the *Irish Times*, the Belgian visit only one. *Irish Times*, 15 February 1972, p. 11; 16 February, p. 1.

95. *Irish Times*, 2 February 1972, p. 6.

96. *Irish Times*, 8 February 1972, p. 7.

97. *Irish Times*, 8 February 1972, p. 1.

98. Waldheim had discussed the issue of Northern Ireland with the Pope on 5 February. This was before Hillery's visit to the Vatican.

99. See chap. 12.

100. In 1971 the People's Republic of China took the seat previously occupied by the pro-Western 'Republic of China' (Taiwan).

101. Voting patterns based on analysis by Seán Cronin (*Irish Times*, 3 February 1972, p. 7).

102. While an abstention has the same effect as a negative vote, it can also be interpreted (or portrayed) as representing a desire not to take sides.

103. *Irish Times*, 3 February 1972, p. 7.

104. *Irish Times*, 2 February 1972, p. 6.

105. The Soviet press was highly critical of British policies in the North. *Komsomolskaya Pravda* spoke of 'the victims of the policy of terror and brute force in Ulster,' while *Sovetskaya Rossiya* and *Izvestia* compared Britain's role in Ireland to that of the Americans in Vietnam. *Pravda,* the official organ of the Communist Party of the Soviet Union, demanded 'an end to the bloody crimes of the English colonisers in Ulster.' See Séamus Ó Coigligh, 'The Soviet press on Derry,' *Irish Times*, 10 February 1972, p. 14.

106. 'Polish press urges U.K. to relent now' (Polish Interpress Agency). *Irish Times*, 5 February 1972, p. 9.

107. Peck political report to W. K. K. White of Foreign and Commonwealth Office, 14 February 1972 (National Archives [London], FCO 87/11).

108. Peck letter to Roger B. Bone, Foreign and Commonwealth Office, 28 February 1972 (National Archives [London], FCO 87/11).

109. Peck letter to Roger B Bone, Foreign and Commonwealth Office, 28 February 1972, and David Bletherwick to R. B. Bone, Republic of Ireland Department, Foreign and Commonwealth Office, 10 March 1972 (National Archives [London], FCO 87/11).

110. Peck political report to W. K. K. White, Foreign and Commonwealth Office, 14 February 1972 (National Archives [London], FCO 87/11). See also follow-up messages of Michael Alexander (Foreign and Commonwealth Office) to Peter Gregson (Office of the Prime Minister), 16 February, and Gregson's reply the following day.

111. The entire Taoiseach section was taken up with five motions on the North, which were, according to the agenda, 'representative of hundreds on the subject received

from all the constituencies.' The five motions were: (1) 'The Ard-Fheis affirms its support for the declared policy of the Taoiseach with regard to the unification of Ireland as a Republic'; (2) 'The Ard-Fheis calls on the Government to suspend diplomatic relations with Great Britain until the British Forces are withdrawn from the Six Counties of North East Ulster'; (3) 'The Ard-Fheis urges more vigorous action by the Government to expose the cruelties and injustices committed by the British Army in the occupied Six Counties'; (4) 'The Ard-Fheis asks the Government to outline the stages in its plan for national unity'; (5) 'The Ard-Fheis recommends that no move should be made to amend the Constitution pending the opening of negotiations for a United Ireland' (Fianna Fáil Archives, FF/738). Motion 5, though of relevance to the Northern situation, was deemed to be separate from the other four and so was debated, and defeated. There is no record of any discussion on motions 2, 3 or 4. The first motion was the official one sponsored by the leadership and the only one of these discussed. Motion 4 was a response to traditional resolutions (such as motion 1), which in the context of the turmoil of 1972 did little to clarify Fianna Fáil policy. Lynch was in favour of reconciliation, a political solution, and against violence. The detail of policy was not put to the ard-fheis for formal endorsement.

112. Clár of 1972 Fianna Fáil Ard-Fheis (Fianna Fáil Archives, FF/738).

113. Backbencher (John Healy), 'The ard-fheis and the green frenzy,' *Irish Times*, 19 February 1972, p. 12.

114. *Irish Times*, 21 February 1972, p. 8.

115. *Irish Times*, 21 February 1972, p. 1.

116. Section 62 of the Courts of Justice Act (1936) provided the Minister for Justice with the powers necessary to implement the substance of his proposals.

117. *Irish Times*, 21 February 1972, p. 1.

118. *Irish Times*, 22 February 1972, p. 11.

119. Blaney's formal expulsion from the party came some months later at a meeting of the National Executive on 26 June 1972, convened specifically for that purpose. In a letter to the Executive, Blaney asked, firstly, that the motion be dismissed and failing that that he be supplied with a 'full statement of the evidence to justify the motion so that he could defend himself whatever charges might be made against him.' If the Executive agreed to this he asked for a meeting at a later date at which he could defend himself against the charges. Seán MacEntee thought this a reasonable request and tabled an amendment to this effect, but only 6 of the 74 members agreed, after which Blaney was expelled on a vote of 71 to 2. Minutes of National Executive, 26 June 1972 (UCD Archives, P176/350).

120. *Irish Times*, 22 February 1972, p. 1.

121. See Michael Gallagher, *The Irish Labour Party in Transition*, p. 143–8.

122. Telegram from Douglas-Home to Peck, Telegram no. 41, 18 February 1972 (National Archives [London], FCO 87/11).

123. Foreign and Commonwealth Office to Dublin, telegram no. 45, 22 February 1972; letter from Peter Gregson, Prime Minister's Office, to John A. N. Graham, Foreign and Commonwealth Office, 22 February 1972 (National Archives [London], FCO 87/11).

124. Peck to Foreign and Commonwealth Office, telegram no. 92, 23 February 1972 (National Archives [London], FCO 87/11).

125. Peck to Foreign and Commonwealth Office, telegram no. 79, 20 February 1972 (National Archives [London], FCO 87/11).

126. Peck to Foreign and Commonwealth Office, telegram no. 80, 20 February 1972 (National Archives [London], FCO 87/11).

127. Peck to Kelvin White, Foreign and Commonwealth Office (and copied to Howard Smith), 2 March 1972 (National Archives [London], FCO 87/11).

128. Peck report of meeting with Lynch on 3 March 1972 (National Archives [London], FCO 87/26).

129. *Irish Times*, 25 March 1972, p. 1.

130. Interview with Roy Bradford by the author.

131. *Irish Independent*, 25 March 1972, p. 1, 8.

132. *Irish Times*, 20 April 1972.

133. Peck to Kelvin White, Foreign and Commonwealth Office (and copied to Howard Smith), 2 March 1972 (National Archives [London], FCO 87/11).

134. *Irish Times*, 6 May 1972, p. 9.

135. *Irish Times*, 9 May 1972, p. 3. Lynch was also to state that to vote No would constitute 'a wanton abuse of freedom' and would be symptomatic of a 'slavish attitude.' *Irish Times*, 8 May 1972, p. 1, 9, and 6 May 1972, p. 8.

136. *Irish Times*, 12 May 1972, p. 1. The article was headed DECISION JOINS REPUBLIC, N.I., AND BRITAIN IN ONE ECONOMIC UNIT—ENDS EPOCH OF ROMANTIC NATIONALISM. According to McInerney, the referendum had demonstrated 'the electors' insight in appreciating that Ireland in isolation from Britain and its market made no economic or political sense.' See also Tom Garvin and Anthony Parker, 'Party loyalty and Irish voters: The EEC referendum as a case study,' *Economic and Social Review*, IV (1972), p. 35–9.

137. *Irish Times*, 12 May 1972, p. 8.

138. *Irish Times*, 12 May 1972, p. 8.

139. *Irish Times*, 16 May 1972, p. 1.

140. *Irish Times*, 16 May 1972, p. 7.

141. *Irish Times*, 19 May 1972, p. 1, 17.

142. *Irish Times*, 19 May 1972, p. 1, 17.

143. *Irish Times*, 23 May 1972, p. 1.

144. *Irish Times*, 23 May 1972, p. 1.

145. *Irish Times*, 23 May 1972, p. 1, 9.

146. *Irish Times*, 23 May 1972, p. 9.

147. *Irish Times*, 16 May 1972, p. 9. Lenihan was replying to a question from Dr John O'Connell TD (Labour Party).

148. The second stage was passed on 23 May, by 97 votes to 6. It passed all remaining stages on 24 May by a margin of 114 to 8 after a twelve-hour discussion.

149. The usual procedure was for the President to allow five days' grace before signing a bill.

150. *Irish Times*, 24 May 1972, p. 10.

151. *Parliamentary Debates: Dáil Éireann: Official Report*, 24 May 1972.

152. Quoted by Dunne and Kerrigan, *Round Up the Usual Suspects*.

153. Dunne and Kerrigan, *Round Up the Usual Suspects*.

154. Peck, *Dublin from Downing Street*, p. 4.

155. Peck, *Dublin from Downing Street*, p. 125–6.

156. Peck to White, 13 April 1972 (National Archives [London], FCO 87/26).

157. White to Peck, 29 March 1972 (National Archives [London], FCO 87/26).

158. Best had never served in Northern Ireland but was stationed in Germany. It was

believed that he intended to leave the army after his leave was over. Mac Stiofáin, *Revolutionary in Ireland*, p. 242.

159. Holland and MacDonald, *INLA*, p. 16.

160. Reid, *Ireland*, p. 154.

161. Speaking at a rally in Tripoli, Colonel al-Gaddafi declared that 'we support the Irish revolutionaries who are fighting Britain' and that Libya had 'strong ties with the Irish revolutionaries to whom we have supplied arms' (*Irish Times*, 12 June 1972).

162. Quoted by Taylor, *Provos*, p. 142.

163. Whitelaw has outlined his impression of the talks in his autobiography and confirmed the euphoric mood of the IRA in the wake of the fall of Stormont. 'The meeting was a non-event. The IRA leaders simply made impossible demands which I told them the British government would never concede. They were still in fact in a mood of defiance and determination to carry on until their absurd ultimatums were met'. William Whitelaw, *The Whitelaw Memoirs*, p. 28 (London: Aurum Press, 1989).

164. *Irish Times*, 11 July 1972, p. 1. The British Government had indirectly maintained contact with the IRA since 1971. The leader of the British Labour Party, Harold Wilson, and his spokesperson on Northern Ireland, Merlyn Rees, had travelled to Dublin to meet the IRA leadership. An interesting account of how these contacts were maintained is provided by Dr John O'Connell TD, who acted as the conduit between the IRA and the British Government. See John O'Connell, *Dr John: Crusading Doctor and Poltician* (Dublin: Poolbeg, 1989), p. 124–44. The view of the British side is colourfully portrayed by Harold Wilson's adviser Joe Haines, who—unlike O'Connell—was present during the discussions. See Joe Haines, *The Politics of Power* (London: Coronet, 1977), p. 122–39. First-hand accounts from the IRA side are difficult to procure, with Mac Stiofáin's autobiography (*Revolutionary in Ireland*) being the sole published exception. In an interview with the author one of the IRA participants, John Kelly, recalled that Wilson stressed that he had not got the power to negotiate but that he would convey the views of the IRA to the British Government. Kelly felt that the meetings were a futile exercise, aimed merely at assessing the calibre of the IRA leadership and whether there was a possibility of a ceasefire.

165. *Irish Times*, 1 August 1972, p. 1, 6 7, 8, 11.

166. Letter from Peck to W. K. K. White, Republic of Ireland Department, Foreign and Commonwealth Office, 13 April 1972 (National Archives [London], FCO 87/26).

167. 'The Irish Political Scene since the Burning of the Dublin Embassy,' Diplomatic Report No. 340/72, 27 June 1972 (National Archives [London], FCO 87/11).

168. Brief by Northern Ireland Office and Foreign and Commonwealth Office prepared for Heath-Lynch [meeting], 4 September 1972 at 10.00 (National Archives [London], FCO 87/27).

169. 'The Irish Political Scene since the Burning of the Dublin Embassy,' Diplomatic Report No. 340/72, 27 June 1972 (National Archives [London], FCO 87/11).

170. *Parliamentary Debates: Dáil Éireann: Official Report*, 262/1992 (14 July 1972).

171. Telegram no. 490, 14 July, and telegram no. 497, 15 July 1972 (National Archives [London], FCO 87/11).

172. Foreign and Commonwealth Office, telegram no. 521, 28 July 1972 (National Archives [London], FCO 87/11).

173. Foreign and Commonwealth Office, telegram no. 522, 28 July 1972 (National Archives [London], FCO 87/11).

174. Lynch was accompanied by the Irish ambassador to West Germany, Seán Ronan, for the ninety-minute talk.

175. Report of Heath-Lynch meeting, 4 September 1972 (National Archives [London], FCO 87/27).

176. Record of meeting between Peck and Lynch on 23 October, 25 October and sent to W. K. K. White (National Archives [London], FCO 87/26.).

177. Undated confidential report in advance of Lynch visit of 6–7 September 1971, p. 17 (National Archives [London], FCO 33/1613).

178. Brief by Northern Ireland Office and Foreign and Commonwealth Office prepared for Heath-Lynch meeting of 4 September 1972 (National Archives [London], FCO 87/27.

179. Confidential Brief, 16 October 1972, prepared by Foreign and Commonwealth Office prepared for Heath-Lynch Paris meeting, 21 October 1972 (National Archives [London], FCO 87/27).

180. Undated confidential report in advance of Lynch visit of 6–7 September 1971, p. 6 (National Archives [London], FCO 33/1613).

181. Peck to Foreign and Commonwealth Office, telegram no. 82, 21 February 1972 (National Archives [London], FCO 87/11). Originally from Limerick, McInerney emigrated to England in the 1930s and worked as a railway clerk in London and later in Belfast. He joined the Communist Party of Great Britain and wrote for the *Daily Worker,* and in Belfast he edited the Communist Party of Ireland newspaper, *Unity.* He became a reporter for the *Irish Times* in 1946 and political correspondent in 1951, remaining in that position until the 1970s.

182. Northern Ireland Office, *The Future of Northern Ireland: A Paper.*

183. The word 'Senate' was substituted for 'Council' in an effort to minimise the impact on Unionist sensitivities. However, the SDLP reverted to the word 'Council' in its submission to the Darlington talks. See SDLP, *Towards a New Ireland* (Belfast: SDLP, 1975). This document was included as an annex to the British Green Paper along with other party submissions.

184. Bew and Patterson, *The British State and the Ulster Crisis,* p. 53.

185. Quoted by Bew and Patterson, *The British State and the Ulster Crisis,* p. 53.

186. The Monday Club frequently invited Unionist speakers to its its gatherings at the Conservative Party conference. An Ulster branch of the organisation was established in 1975.

187. Or (more likely) those in front of him. *Irish Times,* 20 October 1972. Craig never fired a shot in anger during the coming years; many others, inspired by his rhetoric, did.

188. This proved to be merely an opening gambit to match the increased radicalism within the nationalist community, as the SDLP within sixteen months would be participating in an assembly while internment continued. It was pointed out to the author during an informal conversation with Bernadette McAliskey (née Devlin) that the fact that the IRA had participated in talks with the British Government while internment continued eased the way for the SDLP to change its stance on this fundamental issue.

189. Para. 78.

190. Para. 79f.

191. Bew and Patterson, *The British State and the Ulster Crisis.* The *Irish Times* (31 October 1972) reflected the mood predominant in the South, that the Green Paper was 'a big victory for the North's minority and a big step towards cooperation and ultimate unity.'

192. Record of meeting between Peck and Lynch on 23 October and sent to W. K. K. White, 25 October (National Archives [London], FCO 87/26). It appears that Peck's account is the only record of the meeting.

193. Record of meeting between Peck and Lynch on 23 October and sent to W. K .K. White, 25 October (National Archives [London], FCO 87/26).

194. *Irish Times,* 6 November 1972, p. 1. She had been released by the Northern authorities the previous year after serving two six-month sentences in Armagh Prison, one of them for a speech at Free Derry Corner.

195. *Irish Times,* 25 November 1972, p. 1.

196. As Mac Stiofáin's condition worsened, the atmosphere in the Republic became tense. Tim Pat Coogan claims, perhaps with some exaggeration, that 'for a time it appeared that if he were to die the result would be civil war in the South of Ireland.' Coogan, *The IRA* (second edition), p. 518.

197. *Irish Times,* 29–30 November 1972, p. 1.

198. *Irish Times,* 29–30 November 1972, p. 1; Bishop and Mallie, *The Provisional IRA,* p. 243–5; Coogan, *The IRA* (second edition), p. 516–17; Bell, *The Secret Army,* p. 395–6.

199. *Irish Times,* 2 October 1971, p. 1.

200. *Irish Times,* 17 November 1972, p. 1, 4, 11; 18 November 1972, p. 1, 8, 13.

201. *Irish Times,* 25 November 1972, p. 1.

202. Neither of the Dublin evening papers of 28 November 1972 and none of the three morning papers of 29 November were published, in protest against the sentence of imprisonment imposed on Kevin O'Kelly.

203. 'Republic of Ireland—A Crowded Fortnight,' British embassy report for Sir Alec Douglas-Home and others, 12 December 1972 (National Archives [London], FCO 87/11).

204. Paul O'Higgins, 'The Irish TV sackings,' *Index on Censorship,* 3/1 (1973), p. 24.

205. See Desmond Bell, 'Proclaiming the Republic: Broadcasting policy and the corporate state in Ireland,' *West European Politics,* 8/2 (April 1985), p. 44.

206. See Gibbons, 'From megalith to megastore: Broadcasting and Irish Culture,' in *Transformations in Irish Culture,* p. 73.

207. For an insightful analysis of the importance that Governments and television stations attach to language see David Miller, 'Understanding "terrorism": US and British audience interpretations of the televised conflict in Ireland,' in Meryl Aldridge and Nicholas Hewitt (eds.), *Controlling Broadcasting: Access, Policy and Practice in North America and Europe* (Manchester: Manchester University Press, 1993). See also David Miller, 'Official sources and "primary definition": The case of Northern Ireland,' *Media, Culture and Society,* 15 (1993), p. 385–406, and David Miller, *Don't Mention the War* (London: Pluto Press, 1994). More general works on this subject include Noam Chomsky's *Pirates and Emperors, Old and New: International Terrorism in the Real World* (Cambridge, Mass.: South End Press, 1986) and George Orwell's celebrated essay 'Politics and the English language,' *Horizon,* April 1946.

208. *Parliamentary Debates: Dáil Éireann: Official Report,* 224/1045 (12 October 1966).

209. *Parliamentary Debates: Dáil Éireann: Official Report,* 224/1046 (12 October 1966).

210. Lynch's principal argument—that it would be assumed that the RTE crew was going with Government approval—was lacking in cogency, for the Government could, if it so wished, have informed the necessary authorities through its diplomatic agencies that though the television crew was going this was not to imply that their mission was

either sponsored or supported by the Government. After all, several crews from the United States had travelled to Vietnam.

211. *Parliamentary Debates: Dáil Éireann: Official Report,* 227/1664 (13 April 1967).

212. Feeney, 'Censorship and RTÉ,' *Crane Bag,* 8/2 (1984), p. 63.

213. Betty Purcell, 'The silence in Irish broadcasting,' in Rolston, *The Media and Northern Ireland,* p. 54.

214. Kevin Boyle, 'The legal context,' in British-Irish Rights Watch, *Conflicting Reports,* p. 5; Desmond Bell, 'Proclaiming the Republic: Broadcasting policy and the corporate state in Ireland,' *West European Politics,* 8/2 (April 1985), p. 45–6.

215. That is not to say that the RTE Authority had been a nest of subversives before the sackings. Its members were: Dónall Ó Móráin (chairman) (chairman of Gael-Linn), Stephen Barrett (barrister, former Fine Gael TD), Liam Hyland (prominent member of Muintir na Tíre, Fianna Fáil member of Laois County Council, later Fianna Fáil MEP for Leinster), James Fanning (editor, *Midland Tribune,* Birr), Noel Mulcahy (head of Business Management Division, Irish Management Institute), Seán Ó Murchú (secretary of Cork National Industrial Group, ITGWU), T. W. Moody (professor of modern history, Trinity College, Dublin) and Phyllis O'Kelly (widow of Seán T. O'Kelly, former President of Ireland). Appropriately, the new chairman appointed by the Government was a former Secretary of the Department of Posts and Telegraphs.

216. Niall Meehan, 'Ireland's censorship culture,' *Film Ireland* (1991), p. 31.   Betty Purcell concurs: 'The shock waves in RTE were enormous and are still felt. In the atmosphere of daily controversy in RTE, managers learn that most conflicts blow over. Only on the sensitive subject of Northern Ireland have heads rolled. And they were the most important heads in the organisation, those of the RTE Authority itself' (Betty Purcell, 'The silence in Irish broadcasting,' in Rolston, *The Media and Northern Ireland,* p. 61.) An interesting insight into the fate of those who served on the RTE Authority in the post-1971 environment is to be found in Marianne Heron's biography of Sheila Conroy, who served as chairperson of the authority from 1976 to 1979. The sacking of the authority 'tended to act as a powerful deterrent against flouting the ban . . . News and current affairs staff accused station executives of going further than the government intended and claimed that they were being intimidated in their work by needless extension of the law. Sheila's view of Section 31 was pragmatic. "As Chairman I had to uphold [the] ruling and the Authority is committed to upholding the Act which set it up. I felt that if I didn't support the Act then I shouldn't be working under it. But as Chairman it meant that I had to be more alert to any attempt to break the ban."' Marianne Heron, *Sheila Conroy: Fighting Spirit* (Dublin: Attic Press, 1993), p. 91–2. Conroy's account suggests that only those who felt they could conscientiously support section 31 could consider themselves as candidates for membership of the RTE Authority. This in itself is quite separate from the fact that their opinions on the act would have been established before they were considered as likely appointees by the Government of the day.

217. Bernedette McAliskey noted similar techniques from the viewpoint of the potential interviewee: 'The first question any journalist asks you in Northern Ireland is not, "Did you see what happened, have you any information, do you know anything?" The first question a journalist asks you is, "Are you in Sinn Féin?" In Coalisland they tell jokes about it, you know. They draw wee cartoons of journalists standing over corpses saying, "Are you in Sinn Féin?" before they can verify whether or not you are dead.'

Bernedette McAliskey, 'The ban in Northern Ireland' in British-Irish Rights Watch, *Conflicting Reports*, p. 13. (This is a verbatim report of a conference organised by British-Irish Rights Watch in London on 20 November 1993.)

218. Russell L. Weaver and Geoffrey Bennet, 'The Northern Ireland broadcasting ban: Some reflections on judicial review,' *Vanderbilt Journal of Transnational Law*, 22/5 (1989), p. 1148.

219. *Index on Censorship*, 2/4 (winter 1972/3), p. iii.

220. Walter Lacqueur, *Terrorism* (London: Abacus, 1978), p. 269.

221. See Frank Burton, *The Politics of Legitimacy: Struggles in a Belfast Community* (London: Routledge and Kegan Paul, 1978).

222. This does not imply that the British were more sympathetic: see Curtis, *Ireland: The Propaganda War*. Conor Cruise O'Brien complained of IRA terrorists 'wafting' into Irish sitting-rooms by courtesy of the BBC. Cruise O'Brien's views on the connection between broadcasting and terrorism were perhaps best characterised in his speech to the Seanad introducing the Broadcasting Authority (Amendment) Bill on 27 March 1975, reprinted in Cruise O'Brien, *Herod*, p. 110–27.

223. David Miller, 'Understanding "terrorism": US and British audience interpretations of the televised conflict in Ireland,' in Meryl Aldridge and Nicholas Hewitt (eds.), *Controlling Broadcasting: Access, Policy and Practice in North America and Europe* (Manchester: Manchester University Press, 1993), p. 2.

224. In one of those perverse examples of Anglo-Irish co-operation the British Government issued a similar dictate. As one English solicitor recalled, '"Give Ireland back to the Irish" was considered by the lawyers at the BBC to be so offensive that it not only had to be banned from the airwaves, but it had to be removed from the BBC library, and not only from the BBC library: it was removed from the EMI library. Not only that, you could not get the record anywhere. I went to enormous lengths to get that record, and it is only on the B-side of a single back in the 1970s, but no-one has singles any more, and nobody knows how to play them. It took us about six months to locate this song, because it had been removed from everywhere, while it is normal for the BBC to catalogue every record that they have ever played.' Mark Stephens, 'The ban in England,' in British-Irish Rights Watch, *Conflicting Reports*, p. 18.

225. John Lennon, 'Some Time in New York City' (1971).

226. Public taste triumphed, as both Paul McCartney and the Wolfe Tones went to number 1 in the Irish pop charts. McCartney's song also went to number 1 in Spain.

227. F. S. L. Lyons, 'The meaning of independence,' in Brian Farrell, *The Irish Parliamentary Tradition*, p. 223. See Fanning, 'The great enchantment', p. 131–147.

228. Since the establishment of the Irish state, figures such as John Redmond had been largely neglected and relegated from the premier league of heroes to the bottom division, along with a host of political undesirables from Diarmaid Mac Murchú to Sadlier and Keogh.

229. Fennell, *The Revision of Irish Nationalism*.

230. *Irish Times*, 24 February 1972, p. 1.

231. Fianna Fáil, Minutes of National Executive, 12 July 1971 (UCD Archives, P176/350).

232. *Hibernia*, 12 January 1973.

233. *Hibernia*, 26 April 1974.

234. *Irish Times*, 26 April 1976.

235. Griffith and O'Grady, *Curious Journey*, p. 316.

236. Section 3.2 (*b*).

237. In May 1973 Chief Supt Patrick Murphy swore on oath that he believed that a Noel Hanrahan of Poulovanogue had been a member of the IRA on 25 April. Under cross-examination he admitted that he had never seen the accused before and had merely been told by other gardaí that Hanrahan was a member. Asked how many Noel Hanrahans there were in Poulovanogue, Murphy admitted that he was not from the area and didn't know. Dunne and Kerrigan, *Round Up the Usual Suspects*, p. 73–4.

238. Section 3.6. This meant that one would have to read every paper every day lest one be described as an IRA member and fail to contest such a description. This power was employed to convict the editor of *An Phoblacht*, Éamonn Mac Thomáis. A photograph had appeared in a newspaper of Mac Thomáis and others attending what was described as 'an IRA press conference.' This and the evidence of Chief Supt John Fleming, who swore on oath that he believed him to be a member of the IRA, led to Mac Thomáis being sentenced to fifteen months' imprisonment. See *Hibernia*, 8 June 1973.

239. See *Hibernia*, 1 December 1972, p. 3. Under this provision a public statement, meeting or demonstration (including a token picket) intended to influence the decision of a court was declared unlawful and entailed a prison sentence of up to five years and a substantial fine. An insight into how this section was used can be derived from the case of a small group of prisoners' rights activists who were sentenced in July 1975 to twelve months' imprisonment for placing a picket outside the Circuit Criminal Court in protest against the incarceration of a mentally retarded man. See *Hibernia*, 26 July 1975.

240. Speaking to the Joint Committee on Justice, Equality, Defence and Women's Rights, vol. 80 (1 February 2005), Sub-Committee on the Barron Report.

241. Speaking to the Joint Committee on Justice, Equality, Defence and Women's Rights, vol. 80 (1 February 2005), Sub-Committee on the Barron Report.

242. *Parliamentary Debates: Dáil Éireann: Official Report*, 264/276, 280 (29 November 1972).

243. Quoted by: Conn McCluskey, *Up Off Their Knees: A Commentary on the Civil Rights Movement in Northern Ireland* (Dungannon: Conn McCluskey and Associates, 1989), p. 145. Devlin, for her part, was admonished as the bill began its passage through the Dáil by the Labour Party deputy Barry Desmond during a speech in the same Liberty Hall that had been bombed with the assistance of British Intelligence.

244. *Parliamentary Debates: Dáil Éireann: Official Report*, 264/830 (1 December 1972).

245. *Parliamentary Debates: Dáil Éireann: Official Report*, 264/858 (1 December 1972).

246. *Parliamentary Debates: Dáil Éireann: Official Report*, 264/858 (1 December 1972).

247. *Irish Times*, 2 December 1972, p. 1, 8, 9, 11, 13.

248. Quoted by Dunne and Kerrigan, *Round Up the Usual Suspects*, p. 50.

249. See statement of Seán MacBride, quoted by Faligot, *Britain's Military Strategy in Ireland*, p. 101.

250. See, for example, Murray, *The SAS in Ireland*, p. 75–90, 'The Littlejohn Affair,' *Time Out*, 181, 10–16 August 1973, and Bloch and Fitzgerald, *British Intelligence and Covert Action*, p. 102–8. The affair received extensive coverage in Ireland and Britain during August 1973, when it first became public knowledge. For an extensive bibliography on the media coverage surrounding the revelations see Father Murray's book, cited above, p. 465. Despite these well-established facts, some commentators have embarked on a process of revising events. Garret FitzGerald, for example, explains in his

autobiography (*All in a Life*, p. 108) that 'it transpired that they [the bombs] had been undertaken by loyalist paramilitaries from the North.' Interestingly, in 1983 a former British intelligence officer, Captain Colin Holroyd, wrote to Noel Dorr, then Irish ambassador in London, and to Garret FitzGerald, then Taoiseach, offering to help the authorities to investigate crimes committed by British agents in the Republic and by British agents within the Gardaí. He received no replies. See the *Phoenix*, 26 September 1986. Holroyd's claims were also made to Brendan O'Brien on the RTE1 programme 'Friendly Forces?' transmitted in 1996. See also the *Phoenix*, 9 May 1986, p. 13.

251. It also emerged that two days after the Government had been informed of the British Government's involvement in the affair the matter had been discussed at a meeting of the Minister for Justice, Des O'Malley, and the Attorney-General, Colm Condon, with the British Director of Public Prosecutions, Sir Norman Skelhorn.

252. *Irish Times*, 14 August 1973, p. 1, 13; 15 August 1973, p. 1, 8, 11; 16 August 1973, p. 1; 18 August 1973, p. 12. The fact that this information became public was not considered coincidental. Lynch's admission shifted the spotlight completely away from the British Prime Minister and to himself. There was no evidence that the coalition Government had confronted Heath on the issue, and its disclosure meant that it was Lynch rather than Heath who offered to resign in response to the revelations. According to the *Irish Times*, the effect of the statement was to embarrass Fianna Fáil and to neutralise criticism of the coalition's handling of the Littlejohn affair. The paper's editorial (14 August 1973, p. 1) claimed that 'the Government is still most anxious not to embarrass the British Government, whatever about Fianna Fáil, and reluctant to take advantage of the opportunities that have been presented by the clear exposure of London's involvement in acts of provocation in the Republic. Ministers seem satisfied that they have silenced a major source of criticism while remaining silent themselves on related issues; nothing has yet been said of the circumstances surrounding the Dublin explosions or the investigations of them and there has been no reaction to calls for disclosure of British agents' activities in the Republic.' Neither the Dáil nor the House of Commons was recalled; and despite the revelations the Minister for Justice, Paddy Cooney, reiterated that 'the Gardaí have no evidence linking any person, organisation or group with these explosions.' He denied a report in the *Evening Herald* that a file had been prepared by the Special Detective Unit that contained evidence of involvement by the SAS in the Dublin bombings (*Irish Times*, 22 August 1973, p. 1, 9; *Evening Herald*, 21 August 1973, p. 1). The British, for their part, claimed that the SAS had not been used either in the North or in the South, claims that can now be dismissed as false. (See Murray, *The SAS in Ireland*, p. 29–30.)

253. FitzGerald, *All in a Life*, p. 109. FitzGerald also claims that 'our emotional opposition to this Act was not subsequently justified by the use actually made of it.' The views of another Fine Gael elder on the divisions within the party at that time have more recently received the autobiographical treatment: see T. F. O'Higgins, *A Double Life* (Dublin: Town House, 1996) p. 238–57.

254. 'Republic of Ireland—A Crowded Fortnight,' British embassy report for Sir Alec Douglas-Home et al., 12 December 1972, p. 14 (National Archives [London], FCO 87/11).

255. 'Republic of Ireland—A Crowded Fortnight,' British embassy report for Sir Alec Douglas-Home et al., 12 December 1972, p. 15 (National Archives [London], FCO 87/11).

256. 'Republic of Ireland—A Crowded Fortnight,' British embassy report for Sir Alec Douglas-Home et al., 12 December 1972, p. 16–17 (National Archives [London], FCO 87/11).

257. Another British intelligence officer, Andrew James Johnstone, was sought but never found, and another garda was believed to have been recruited by the British at this time, suggesting that Wyman and Crinnion were probably part of a much larger conspiracy.

258. Éamonn McCann, 'Lynch sanctioned espionage cover-up: Secret files show Jack Lynch told Heath spying need not damage relations with UK,' *Sunday Tribune,* 16 March 2003.

259. Bloch and Fitzgerald, *British Intelligence and Covert Action,* p. 219–22.

260. White, *Ruairí Ó Brádaigh,* p. 198–201.

261. *Irish Times,* 6 February 1973, p. 1.

262. *Irish Times,* 7 February 1973, p. 1.

263. *Irish Times,* 12 February 1973, p. 8.

264. Dr Delap, speaking in Donegal (*Irish Times,* 12 February 1973, p. 8).

265. Whereas Aontacht Éireann was organised with the objective of replacing Fianna Fáil as the major constitutional republican party, 'Independent Fianna Fáil' was a loose collection of personalities sharing Neil Blaney's views on Northern Ireland. It never sought to create a national organisation and seemed to hope for a leadership change within Fianna Fáil that would produce a more militant Northern policy and then open up the possibility of a merger.

266. Fifteen candidates had been selected, but Éamonn Kane in Dublin South-East and Seán Harris in Kildare dropped out before polling day.

267. The party's candidate in Cork City South-East, Gerald Carroll, had been elected to Cork City Council in 1967 before defecting to Aontacht Éireann in August 1971. In order to contest the election he had to obtain an adjournment of his case before the Special Criminal Court, where he was charged with the illegal possession of firearms. Another former Fianna Fáil supporter, Joe Keohane, stood for Aontacht Éireann in North Kerry. A former Kerry football star and retired army officer, Keohane had been court-martialled in 1972 on charges relating to ammunition. The party's candidate in Galway West came from an established Fianna Fáil family, while in Laois-Offaly its candidate had run the Fianna Fáil TD Ber Cowan's election campaign in 1969. In Dublin the party had a former Fianna Fáil minister (Kevin Boland), a former Fianna Fáil TD (Seán Sherwin) and a former member of the National Executive (Nóirín Butler) all running under the Aontacht Éireann banner. In Louth the party ran two candidates, one of whom was a former secretary of the Cooley Comhairle Ceantair of Fianna Fáil; the other had campaigned for the Labour Party in the 1969 election, the only candidate with such a background. The other four candidates who contested for Aontacht Éireann had no previously declared political background.

268. *Irish Times,* 12 February 1973, p. 1, 8.

269. *Irish Times,* 12 February 1973, p. 9.

270. Colley had previously described Cruise O'Brien as 'the Tories' favourite Irishman' (*Irish Times,* 5 November 1971, p. 9). John Peck, British ambassador to Ireland, 1970–73, claimed (*Dublin from Downing Street,* p. 144) that Cruise O'Brien was 'regarded more as an analyst of the Irish than as a typical representative of them.'

271. Speaking in Dublin North-Central (*Irish Times,* 12 February 1973, p. 8).

272. *Irish Times,* 16 February 1972, p. 10.
273. *Irish Times,* 15 February 1972, p. 9.
274. *Irish Times,* 7 February 1973, p. 11.
275. *Irish Times,* 19 February 1973, p. 8.
276. *Irish Times,* 10 February 1973, p. 1.
277. RTE described the allegation that Sinn Féin was being excluded from political broadcasts as 'incorrect' (*Irish Times,* 12 February 1973, p. 8).
278. *Irish Times,* 20 February 1973, p. 9.
279. *Irish Times,* 20 February 1973, p. 9.
280. Speaking in Enniscorthy (*Irish Times,* 23 February 1973, p. 12).
281. Quoted in the *Irish Times,* 20 February 1973, p. 6.
282. Quoted in the *Irish Times,* 20 February 1973, p. 6.
283. Des Ferguson is erroneously described as a candidate for Aontacht Éireann in Vincent Browne, *The Magill Book of Irish Politics.*
284. In Wicklow, Paudge Brennan polled only 2,500 votes, a shadow of his performance during previous elections, while Des Foley's first-preference vote was 3,387.
285. A TD since 1954, Brennan had topped the poll at every election since 1957. His vote may have been adversely affected by the candidature of Séamus Costello (Official Sinn Féin), who obtained almost 2,000 votes, though they were on opposite ends of theconstituency.
286. Des Foley had entered the Dáil in 1965 as representative for Dublin County and retained his seat in the new constituency of Dublin North County in 1969. His seat was taken by Seán Walsh, who had unsuccessfully contested the 1965 and 1969 elections for Fianna Fáil.

Chapter 14: Conclusions: The destiny of the Soldiers (p. 371–96)
1. See, for example, Garvin, 1922, and Brian P. Murphy, *Patrick Pearse and the Lost Republican Ideal.*
2. His unwillingness to entrust others with major constitutional matters led de Valera to retain the External Affairs portfolio for himself, a stance maintained when he became President of the Executive Council and later Taoiseach.
3. 'The Senate elections' (editorial), *Nation,* 15 December 1928, p. 4.
4. Minutes of Parliamentary Party, 22 June 1927 (Fianna Fáil Archives, FF/437).
5. Daly, *Industrial Development and Irish National Identity,* p. 17.
6. Daly, *Industrial Development and Irish National Identity,* p. 60.
7. English, *Radicals and the Republic,* p. 164. English skilfully employs the minutes of various Fianna Fáil cumainn to demonstrate the important link between economic policy and the party's nationalist project.
8. English, *Radicals and the Republic,* p. 90–95.
9. Henry Patterson, 'Fianna Fáil and the working class: The Origins of the enigmatic relationship,' *Saothar,* 13 (1988), p. 85.
10. Daly, *Industrial Development and Irish National Identity,* p. 61; English, *Radicals and the Republic,* p. 93.
11. Sheila Humphreys, a prominent member of Sinn Féin during the wilderness years, reflected later: 'There were a lot of people that thought [de Valera] was going slowly but he was going somewhere—and they were happy with that.' English, *Radicals and the Republic,* p. 162.

12. Bell, *The Secret Army*, p. 93.

13. Prager, *Building Democracy in Ireland*, p. 192.

14. Fianna Fáil Manifesto, 9 February 1932 (Fianna Fáil Archives, FF/789).

15. *Irish Times*, 10 February 1934; quoted by Regan, *The Irish Counter-Revolution*, p. 349.

16. *Irish Times*, 15 January 1948, p. 3.

17. Seán Lemass, *Parliamentary Debates: Dáil Éireann: Official Report*, 34/318 (2 April 1930).

18. Speech by Seán MacEntee during the 1943 general election (UCD Archives, MacEntee Papers, P67/364).

19. Allen, *Fianna Fáil and Irish Labour*, p. 79.

20. 'Let Erin remember,' Fine Gael election handbill (one page) for 1948 election, outlining 'the Fine Gael tradition' (Fianna Fáil Archives, FF/891).

21. Quoted by Coogan, *De Valera*, p. 485.

22. Tim Pat Coogan (*De Valera*, p. 485) commented that de Valera was finished with the use of force to further independence after the 1916 Rising and that his support for the IRA after the Treaty 'came about through the injury to his pride inflicted by Collins and Griffith. Had it not been for that fateful rush of blood to the head on hearing of the Treaty's signing he would have parted from him and his associates far earlier. His goal had been "extremist support," not the extremists' objectives.'

23. *Freeman's Journal*, 9 July 1917, quoted by Lee, *The Modernisation of Irish Society*, p. 162.

24. See, for example, Ronan Fanning, '"The rule of order": De Valera and the IRA,' in Brian Farrell, *De Valera's Constitution and Ours*.

25. T. Desmond Williams, 'De Valera in Power' in MacManus, *The Years of the Great Test*, p. 33.

26. Gaughan, *Memoirs of Senator Joseph Connolly*, p. 416.

27. Seán Ó Faoláin, *The Irish* (revised edition) (Harmondsworth: Penguin, 1972), p. 156.

28. A. C. Elms, *Personality in Politics* (New York: Harcourt, Brace Jovanovich, 1976), p. 50.

29. Quoted by Fisk, *In Time of War*, p. 212.

30. Dónal Barrington, 'Uniting Ireland,' *Studies*, winter 1957, p. 386.

31. Pádraig O'Malley, *The Uncivil Wars: Ireland Today* (Belfast: Blackstaff Press, 1983), p. 73.

32. Patrick Keatinge, *A Place Among the Nations: Issues of Irish Foreign Policy* (Dublin: Institute of Public Administration, 1978), p. 115.

33. S. M. Lipset and Stein Rokkan, 'Cleavage structures, party systems and voter alignments: An introduction,' in *Party Systems and Voter Alignments* (New York: Free Press, p. 50).

34. Tom Garvin, 'Nationalist elites, Irish voters and Irish political development: A comparative perspective,' *Economic and Social Review*, 8 (1977), p. 161–86.

35. *Parliamentary Debates: Dáil Éireann: Official Report*, 225/726 (10 November 1966).

36. Cohan, *The Irish Political Elite*, p. 73.

37. *Parliamentary Debates: Dáil Éireann: Official Report*, 225/1084 (16 November 1966).

38. Coogan, *Ireland since the Rising*.

39. John Wilson, *Introduction to Social Movements* (New York: Basic Books, 1973), p. 356.

40. Speech at the annual dinner of Mallow Comhairle Ceantair, 5 January 1969, p. 1. Copy of speech in author's possession.

41. Boland, *Up Dev!*, p. 8.

42. John Wilson, *Introduction to Social Movements* (New York: Basic Books, 1973), p. 356.

43. John Wilson, *Introduction to Social Movements* (New York: Basic Books, 1973), p. 356.

44. MacEntee served under both de Valera and Lemass and held the Finance portfolio for thirteen years before his retirement in 1965. Frank Aiken was unique in having served under all three Fianna Fáil leaders and was Tánaiste and Minister for External Affairs in the Lynch Government of 1966–9.

45. This was certainly a perception held by Northern nationalists, as Conor Cruise O'Brien recounts from his visits to the North in the early 1950s. 'A typical comment I heard from Eddie McAteer was that, although Frank Aiken had been born in Armagh, he had been away from it a long time.' Cruise O'Brien, *Memoir*, quoted in *Sunday Independent*, 1 November 1998.

46. Cohan, *The Irish Political Elite*, p. 48.

47. Cohan (*The Irish Political Elite*, p. 72) cites the analysis by Charles Mokos of the revolutionary elite in Albania and concludes that the common experience of revolution encourages the elimination of dissension once independence is achieved.

48. Cohan, *The Irish Political Elite*, p. 43.

49. Duverger, *Political Parties*, p. 152–3.

50. Cohan, *The Irish Political Elite*, p. 61.

51. Cohan, *The Irish Political Elite*, p. 61.

52. Cohan, *The Irish Political Elite*, p. 59.

53. Elliott Rudwick and August Meier, 'Organizational structure and goal succession: A comparative analysis of the NAACP and CORE,' *Social Science Quarterly*, no. 52, p. 15. The fact that the authors refer to a phenomenon prevalent in civil rights organisations in the United States emphasises the similarity between Fianna Fáil and other radical social movements.

54. Marten Bax, 'Patronage, Irish style: Irish politicians as brokers,' unpublished paper, p. 8, quoted by Cohan, *The Irish Political Elite*, p. 65.

55. Basil Chubb, 'Going about persecuting civil servants: The role of the Irish parliamentary representative,' *Political Studies*, 10/3 (1963), p. 272–86.

56. Michael Marsh, 'Selecting party leaders in the Republic of Ireland: Taking the lid off party politics,' *European Journal of Political Research*, 24 (1993), p.300.

57. David Marquand, *Ramsey MacDonald* (London: Jonathan Cape, 1977), p. 541.

58. The reluctance of ministers to be moved sideways or out of the government altogether is a common restraining factor for prime ministers. See R. K. Alderman and J. A. Cross, 'The timing of Cabinet reshuffles,' *Parliamentary Affairs*, 40/1 (January 1987), p. 1–19; in particular p. 13. In the period just before the Arms Crisis, Lynch made a feeble effort to move Blaney to a new department, but once blaney refused the offer, Lynch let the matter drop.

59. Speaking on 'Seven Ages', RTE1, 27 March 2000.

60. W. H. Auden (ed.), *The Selected Writings of Sydney Smith* (New York: Farrar, Straus and Cudahy, New York, 1956).

61. Michael Marsh, 'Selecting party leaders in the Republic of Ireland: Taking the lid off party politics,' *European Journal of Political Research*, 24 (1993), p. 311.

62. Brendan O'Leary, 'An Taoiseach: The Irish prime minister,' *West European Politics*, 14/2 (April 1991), p. 148.

63. Michels, *Political Parties*, p. 220–21.

64. Michels, *Political Parties*, p. 234–5.

65. Michels, *Political Parties*, p. 221.

66. Frank Parkin, *Class Inequality and Political Order* (London: Paladin, 1972), p. 128–36.

67. Leiserson, *Parties and Politics*, p. 178.

68. Philip Selznick, 'An approach to a theory of bureaucracy,' *American Sociological Review,* vol. 8 (1943), p. 49.

69. Otto Kircheimer, 'The transformation of the western European party systems,' in Joseph La Palombara and Myron Weiner (eds.), *Political Parties and Political Development* (Princeton University Press, 1966), p. 192.

70. Michael Gallagher, 'Societal change and party adaptation in the Republic of Ireland,' *European Journal of Political Research,* 9 (1981), p. 282.

71. Duverger, *Political Parties,* p. 21–2.

72. Gareth Morgan, *Images of Organization,* Beverly Hills (Calif.): Sage Publications, 1986), p. 243.

73. Denis G. Sullivan, Jeffrey L. Pressman, Benjamin I. Page and John J. Lyons, 'Purists and professionals in party politics,' in David W. Abbot and Edward T. Ragowsky (eds.), *Political Parties* (second edition) (Chicago: Rand McNally, 1978), p. 44–50.

74. De Valera's decision not to send Mary MacSwiney to London as part of the negotiating team was an implicit recognition that she would be unable to negotiate a compromise that stopped short of full recognition of the Republic. Collins and Griffith also refused to accept her as a negotiating partner, though de Valera's account suggests that they had additional problems with accepting a woman in the delegation. Cathal Brugha and Austin Stack were also considered unsuitable companions for Griffith and Collins. De Valera claimed that if he had been negotiating he would have brought Brugha with him but that if he had gone with Griffith and Collins they would have sought to outmanoeuvre rather than to convince him. In a telling comment that illustrates the differences between professionals and purists, de Valera claimed that 'Cathal is the finest soul in the world, but he is a bit slow at seeing fine differences and rather stubborn' (letter from de Valera to Joe McGarrity, 21 December 1921, quoted by Cronin, *The McGarrity Papers,* p. 106–11). For additional information on the position of Mary MacSwiney see Fallon, *Soul of Fire,* p. 78.

75. In Germany the polemics of the 'Young Ones' (*Die Jungen*) against reformism were succinctly rebutted by Karl Kautsky, who claimed that 'we are too big to go on being a mere protest party.' Others, such as August Bebel, warned the Social-Democratic Party against 'the danger of dissipating its energies in detailed work and losing sight of its higher objective.' If one substitutes 'the Free State' for 'bourgeois society,' Paul Kampffmayer's analysis in 1899 of the German Social-Democratic Party's leading theoreticians and party leaders might equally be applied to the early years of Fianna Fáil: 'On the one hand they heap anathema after anathema upon bourgeois society; on the other hand they labour with burning zeal to patch up and improve it.' Quoted by Susanne Miller and Heinrich Potthoff, *A History of German Social Democracy* (Leamington Spa, Warks.: Berg, 1986), p. 45–6.

76. John Wilson, *Introduction to Social Movements* (New York: Basic Books, 1973), p. 332.

77. *Parliamentary Debates: Dáil Éireann: Official Report,* 3/231 (4 January 1922).

78. *Parliamentary Debates: Dáil Éireann: Official Report,* 3/55 (20 December 1921).

79. Boland, *The Rise and Decline of Fianna Fáil,* p. 14.

BIBLIOGRAPHY

PRIMARY SOURCES

Interviews
— Tony Benn (British Government minister, 1964–70; chairperson of British Labour Party, 1971–2)
— Kevin Boland (Government minister, 1957–70; founder of Aontacht Éireann, 1971)
— Roy Bradford (Stormont MP, 1965–73; Northern Ireland Government minister, 1969–72)
— Seán Clancy (East Clare Brigade, IRA, 1918–19; Dublin Brigade, 1919–21; Defence Forces officer, 1922–59, reaching position of commanding officer, 5th Infantry Battalion)
— Paddy Devlin (Stormont MP, 1969–72; joint founder of SDLP, 1970)
— John Kelly (Belfast IRA; chairman, Central Citizens' Defence Committee; Arms Trial defendant)
— Oliver Napier (leader, Alliance Party, 1972–84)
— Desmond O'Malley (Government minister, 1970–73)
— Rev. Martin Smyth (grand master, Grand Orange Lodge of Ireland, 1971–96)

Fianna Fáil Archives
These have been organised professionally by Philip Hannon and are now part of UCD Archives. They contain parliamentary party minutes, national executive minutes, party conference programmes, honorary secretaries' reports, honorary treasurers' reports from most ard-fheiseanna and sometimes presidential speeches. They also contain an array of fascinating memorabilia, including leaflets, posters, letters, and a wealth of internal documents.

UCD Archives (University College, Dublin)
— Frank Aiken Papers
— Ernest Blythe Papers
— Colonel Dan Bryan Papers
— Clann na Poblachta Papers
— Éamon de Valera Papers
— Seán MacEntee Papers
— Patrick McGilligan Papers
— Mary MacSwiney Papers
— Richard Mulcahy Papers
— George Noble, Count Plunkett, Papers
— Ernie O'Malley Papers

National Archives
— Department of the Taoiseach (D/T)
— Department of Justice (D/J)
— Department of Foreign Affairs (D/FA)

National Archives [London]
— Foreign and Commonwealth Office (FCO)
— Cabinet Papers (CAB)
— Home Office (HO)
— Prime Minister's Office (PREM)

National Library of Ireland
— Frank Gallagher Papers
— Joseph McGarrity Papers

Stationery Office (Government Publications)
— Dáil Éireann, *Correspondence of Mr. Éamon de Valera* (Dublin: Dáil Éireann, 1922)
— Acts of the Oireachtas

PARLIAMENTARY SOURCES
— *Parliamentary Debates: Dáil Éireann: Official Report*
— *Parliamentary Debates: Seanad Éireann: Official Report*

Periodicals
— *An Phoblacht* (1925–37)
— *Anglo-Celt* (Cavan)
— *Blueshirt*
— *Clann* (1947–8)
— *Connacht Tribune* (Galway)
— *Cork Examiner*
— *Fianna Fáil Bulletin* (1934–9)
— *Fianna Fáil Weekly Bulletin* (1926–7)
— *Fortnight* (Belfast) (1970–)
— *Hibernia*
— *Honesty*
— *Howth Review*
— *Iris*
— *Irish Freedom*
— *Irish Independent*
— *Irish Press*
— *Irish Republican Bulletin* (New York) (1946)
— *Irish Times*
— *Irish Worker*
— *Magill* (1977–89)
— *Nation* (1924–5)
— *Nation* (1927–31)

— *National Democrat* (1923)
— *Prison Bars* (1937–8)
— *Red Hand*
— *Republican Congress* (1934–5)
— *Republican File* (1931–2)
— *Republican News* (1940s)
— *Republican News* (Belfast) (1970–76)
— *Republican Review* (1939)
— *Resurgence* (1946)
— *Sinn Féin*
— *Sunday Business Post*
— *Sunday Independent*
— *Unionist* (1920)
— *United Irishman*
— *War News* (1922–3)
— *War News* (early 1940s)
— *Wolfe Tone Weekly* (1937–9)
— *Workers' Voice*

Journals
— *Administration*
— *Capuchin Annual*
— *Crane Bag*
— *Éire-Ireland*
— *History Ireland*
— *Ireland: A Journal of History and Society*
— *Irish Historical Studies*
— *Irish Political Studies*
— *Irish Reporter*
— *Irish Review*
— *Irish Studies in International Affairs*
— *Political Studies*
— *Social Studies*

Pamphlets and booklets
— Byrne, Patrick, *The Irish Republican Congress Revisited,* London: Connolly Association, 1994.
— Clann na Talmhan, *The Book of Clann na Talmhan,* Drogheda: Drogheda Argus, 1944.
— Clifford, Angela, *August 1969: Ireland's Only Appeal to the United Nations,* Belfast: Athol Books, 2006.
— Clifford, Angela, *Military Aspects of Ireland's Arms Crisis of 1969–70,* Belfast: Athol Books, 2006.
— County Longford Branch, National Graves Association, *Longford Remembers,* Aughnacliffe: Seán Lynch, on behalf of County Longford Branch, National Graves Association, n.d. [1990].
— de Valera, Éamon, *National Discipline and Majority Rule,* Dublin: Irish Press, 1936.

— Fianna Fáil, *A Brief Outline of the Aims and Programme of Fianna Fáil*, Dublin: Fianna Fáil, n.d. [1927].
— Fianna Fáil, *Archbishop Mannix on the Oath*, Dublin: Fianna Fáil, n.d. [1927].
— Fianna Fáil, *Fianna Fáil, 1926–1951: The Story of Twenty Five Years of National Endeavour and Historic Achievement*, Dublin: Fianna Fáil, n.d. [1951].
— Fianna Fáil, *Fianna Fáil's Work for the Nation*, Fianna Fáil, Dublin, n.d. [1948].
— Fianna Fáil, *Frank Aiken, T.D., On Fianna Fáil: A Call to Unity*, Dublin: Fodhla Printing Works, n.d. [1926].
— Fianna Fáil, *Some Opinions on Partition and the Oath*, Dublin: Fianna Fáil, n.d. [1927].
— Fianna Fáil, *'The Independent' versus the Truth*, Dublin: Fianna Fáil, n.d. [1927].
— Fianna Fáil, *What Fianna Fáil Stands For*, Dublin: Fianna Fáil, n.d. [1927].
— Fianna Fáil, *Who Caused the Civil War?*, Dublin: Fianna Fáil, n.d. [1927].
— Fields, Rona M., *A Society on the Run: A Psychology of Northern Ireland*, Harmondsworth (Middx): Penguin, 1973.
— Gilmore, George, *The Republican Congress*, Cork: Cork Workers' Club (Historical Reprints), 1978.
— Irish Press, *The New Ireland: Five Years of Progress* (supplement issued with *Irish Press*, 11 June 1937).
— Labour Party, *Prisons and Prisoners in Ireland: Report on Certain Aspects of Prison Conditions in Portlaoighse Convict Prison*, Dublin: Labour Party, 1946.
— Macardle, Dorothy, *Tragedies of Kerry*, Dublin, 1924.
— O'Flanagan, Michael, *The Strength of Sinn Féin*, Dublin: Sinn Féin, 1934.
— O'Neill, David, *The Partition of Ireland*, Dublin: M. H. Gill and Son, 1947.
— O'Reilly, Gerald, *They Are Innocent: The Story of Irish Republican Prisoners*, New York: Connolly Commemoration Committee, n.d. [c. 1946].
— Rice, George, *Charlie Kerins* (fiftieth anniversary commemorative booklet), Tralee, 1994.
— Sinn Féin, *George Plant* (50th anniversary commemorative booklet), Dublin: An Phoblacht / Republican News, 1992.

SELECT BIBLIOGRAPHY OF BOOKS AND ARTICLES

— Allen, Kieran, *Fianna Fáil and Irish Labour*, London: Pluto Press, 1997.
— Andrews, C. S., *Dublin Made Me*, Cork and Dublin: Mercier Press, 1979.
— Andrews, C. S., *Man of No Property*, Dublin: Mercier Press, 1982.
— Barrett, J. J., *The Name of the Game*, Dublin: Dub Press, 1997.
— Barry, Tom, *Guerrilla Days in Ireland*, Tralee: Anvil Books, 1949.
— Behan, Dominic, *My Brother Brendan*, London: Four Square Books, 1966.
— Bell, Geoffrey, *The Protestants of Ulster*, London: Pluto Press, 1976.
— Bell, J. Bowyer, *The Secret Army: The IRA, 1916–1979*, Dublin: Poolbeg, 1989.
— Bence-Jones, Mark, *Twilight of the Ascendancy*, London: Constable, 1987.
— Bennett, Richard, *The Black and Tans*, London: Four Square Books, 1961.
— Benton, Sarah, 'Women disarmed: The militarization of politics in Ireland, 1913–23,' *Feminist Review*, 50 (summer 1995), p. 148–72.
— Bew, Paul, and Patterson, Henry, *The British State and the Ulster Crisis: From Wilson to Thatcher*, London: Verso, 1985.
— Bew, Paul, et al., *The Dynamics of Irish Politics*, London: Lawrence and Wishart, 1989.
— Bew, Paul, et al., *The State in Northern Ireland, 1921–72: Political Forces and Social Classes*, Manchester: Manchester University Press, 1979.

— Bishop, Patrick, and Mallie, Eamonn, *The Provisional IRA*, London: Hamish Hamilton, 1987.
— Blake, Frances M., *The Irish Civil War, 1922–1923, and What It Still Means for the Irish People*, London: Information on Ireland, 1986.
— Bloch, Jonathan, and Fitzgerald, Patrick, *British Intelligence and Covert Action: Africa, Middle East, and Europe since 1945* (Irish edition), Dingle: Brandon Books, 1983.
— Boland, Kevin, *The Rise and Decline of Fianna Fáil*, Cork and Dublin: Mercier Press, 1982.
— Boland, Kevin, *Up Dev!*, Rathcoole (Co. Dublin): K. Boland, [1976].
— Boland, Kevin, *We Won't Stand (Idly) By*, Dublin: Kelly Kane, [1971].
— Bowman, John, *De Valera and the Ulster Question, 1917–1973*, Oxford: Clarendon Press, 1989.
— Boyce, D. G., *Nationalism in Ireland* (second edition), London and New York: Routledge, 1991.
— Boyce, D. G., *The Irish Question in British Politics, 1868–1986*, Basingstoke (Hants): Macmillan, 1988.
— Boyce, D. G., *The Revolution in Ireland, 1879–1923*, Dublin: Gill & Macmillan, 1988.
— Boyd, Andrew, 'Belfast riots, 1935: The reason why,' *Aquarius*, 5 (1972), p. 107–9.
— Boyd, Andrew, *Holy War in Ulster*, Tralee: Anvil Books, 1969.
— Brady, Conor, *Guardians of the Peace*, London: Prendeville Publishing, 2000.
— Brady, Séamus, *Arms and the Men: Ireland in Turmoil*, Bray: S. Brady, 1971.
— Breen, Dan, *My Fight for Irish Freedom*, Tralee: Anvil Books, 1964.
— Briscoe, Robert (with Alden Hatch), *For the Life of Me*, Boston and Toronto: Little, Brown, 1958.
— British-Irish Rights Watch, *Conflicting Reports: Reporting the Conflict in Northern Ireland*, London: British-Irish Rights Watch, 1993.
— Bromage, Mary C., *De Valera and the March of a Nation*, London: Hutchinson, 1956.
— Browne, Kevin J., *Éamon de Valera and the Banner County*, Dublin: Glendale Press, 1982.
— Browne, Noël C., *Against the Tide*, Dublin: Gill & Macmillan, 1986.
— Browne, Vincent, with Farrell, Michael, *The Magill Book of Irish Politics*, Dublin: Magill Publications, 1981.
— Buckland, Patrick, *The Factory of Grievances: Devolved Government in Northern Ireland, 1921–1939*, Dublin: Gill & Macmillan, 1979.
— Buckland, Patrick, *A History of Northern Ireland*, Dublin: Gill & Macmillan, 1981.
— Buckland, Patrick, *James Craig*, Dublin: Gill & Macmillan, 1980.
— Butler, Ewan, *Barry's Flying Column: The Story of the IRA's Cork No. 3 Brigade, 1919–21*, London: Tandem, 1972.
— Carty, R. K., *Party and Parish Pump: Electoral Politics in Ireland*, Waterloo (Ont.): Wilfred Laurier University Press, 1981.
— Chubb, Basil, *Cabinet Government in Ireland*, Dublin: Institute of Public Administration, 1974.
— Chubb, Basil, *The Constitution and Constitutional Change*, Dublin: Institute of Public Administration, 1978.
— Chubb, Basil, *The Government and Politics of Ireland*, London: Longman, 1982.
— Clarke, Kathleen, *Revolutionary Woman: An Autobiography*, Dublin: O'Brien Press, 1991.

— Clifford, Angela, *The Arms Conspiracy Trial*, Belfast: Athol Books, 2009.
— Cohan, Al S., *The Irish Political Elite*, Dublin: Gill & Macmillan, 1972.
— Collins, Michael, *The Path to Freedom*, London: Talbot Press, 1922.
— Collins, Stephen, *The Cosgrave Legacy*, Dublin: Blackwater Press, 1996.
— Coogan, Tim Pat, *De Valera: Long Fellow, Long Shadow*, London: Hutchinson, 1993.
— Coogan, Tim Pat, *Disillusioned Decades: Ireland, 1966–87*, Dublin: Gill & Macmillan, 1987.
— Coogan, Tim Pat, *Michael Collins: A Biography*, London: Hutchinson, 1990.
— Coogan, Tim Pat, *The IRA* (second edition), London: Fontana, 1980.
— Coogan, Tim Pat, *Ireland since the Rising*, London: Pall Mall, 1966.
— Costello, Francis J., *Enduring the Most: The Life and Death of Terence MacSwiney*, Dingle: Brandon Books, 1995.
— Cronin, Seán, *Frank Ryan: The Search for the Republic*, Dublin: Repsol, 1980.
— Cronin, Seán, *Irish Nationalism: A History of Its Roots and Ideology*, Dublin: Academy Press, 1980.
— Cronin, Seán, *The McGarrity Papers*, Tralee: Anvil Books, 1972.
— Cronin, Seán, *The Story of Kevin Barry*, Cork: National Publications Committee, 1965.
— Cronin, Seán, *Washington's Irish Policy, 1916–1986: Independence, Partition, Neutrality*, Dublin: Anvil Books, 1987.
— Cruise O'Brien, Conor, *Herod: Reflections on Political Violence*, London: Hutchinson, 1978.
— Cruise O'Brien, Conor, *Memoir: My Life and Themes*, Dublin: Poolbeg Press, 1998.
— Curran, Frank, *Derry: Countdown to Disaster*, Dublin: Gill & Macmillan, 1986.
— Curran, Joseph M., *The Birth of the Irish Free State, 1919–23*, Tuscaloosa: University of Alabama Press, 1980.
— Curtis, Liz, *Ireland: The Propaganda War*, London: Pluto Press, 1984.
— Curtis, Liz, *The Cause of Ireland*, London: Beyond the Pale, 1994.
— Daly, Mary E., *Industrial Development and National Identity, 1922–1939*, Syracuse (NY): Syracuse University Press, 1992.
— Davis, Richard, *Arthur Griffith* (Irish History Series, no. 10), Dundalk: Dundalgan Press, for Dublin Historical Association, 1976.
— Davis, Richard, *Arthur Griffith and Non-Violent Sinn Féin*, Dublin: Anvil Books, 1974.
— Davis, Richard, *The Young Ireland Movement*, Dublin: Gill & Macmillan, 1987.
— de Blacam, Aodh, *What Sinn Féin Stands For: The Irish Republican Movement, Its History, Aims and Ideals Examined as to Their Significance to Their World*, Dublin: Mellifont Press, 1921.
— de Vere White, Terence, *Kevin O'Higgins*, Tralee: Anvil Books, 1966.
— Dewar, Michael, *The British Army in Northern Ireland*, London: Arms and Armour, 1996.
— Drudy, P. J., *Ireland: Land, Politics and People*, Cambridge: Cambridge University Press, 1982.
— Dunne, Derek, and Kerrigan, Gene, *Round Up the Usual Suspects: Nicky Kelly and the Cosgrave Coalition*, Dublin: Gill & Macmillan, 1984.
— Dunphy, Richard, *The Making of Fianna Fáil Power, 1923–1948*, Oxford: Clarendon Press, 1995.
— Duverger, Maurice, *Political Parties: Their Organization and Activity in the Modern State*, London: Methuen, 1964.

— Dwyer, T. Ryle, *Charlie: The Political Biography of Charles J. Haughey,* Dublin: Gill & Macmillan, 1987.
— Dwyer, T. Ryle, *De Valera: The Man and the Myths,* Dublin: Poolbeg Press, 1992.
— Dwyer, T. Ryle, *De Valera's Darkest Hour, 1919–1932,* Dublin: Mercier Press, 1982.
— Dwyer, T. Ryle, *Guests of the State: The Story of Allied and Axis Servicemen Interned in Ireland During World War II,* Dingle: Brandon Books, 1994.
— Dwyer, T. Ryle, *Strained Relations: Ireland at Peace and the USA at War,* Dublin: Gill & Macmillan, 1988.
— Edmonds, Seán, *The Gun, the Law, and the Irish People,* Tralee: Anvil Books, 1971.
— Elliott, Marianne, *Wolfe Tone: Prophet of Irish Independence,* New Haven (Conn.): Yale University Press, 1989.
— English, Richard, *Radicals and the Republic: Socialist Republicanism in the Irish Free State, 1925–1937,* Oxford: Clarendon Press, 1994.
— Faligot, Roger, *Britain's Military Strategy in Ireland: The Kitson Experiment* (revised English-language edition), Dingle: Brandon Books, 1983.
— Fallon, Charlotte, *Soul of Fire: A Biography of Mary MacSwiney,* Cork: Mercier Press, 1986.
— Fanning, Ronan, 'Anglo-Irish relations: Partition and the British dimension in historical perspective,' *Irish Studies in International Affairs,* 2/1 (1985), p. 1–20.
— Fanning, Ronan, *Independent Ireland,* Dublin: Helicon, 1983.
— Fanning, Ronan, 'Neutrality, security and identity: The example of Ireland,' in Werner Bauwens et al. (eds.), *Small States and the Security Challenge in the New Europe,* London: Brassey's, 1996, p. 137–49.
— Fanning, Ronan, 'The great enchantment': Uses and abuses of modern Irish history,' in James Dooge (ed.), *Ireland in the Contemporary World: Essays in Honour of Garret FitzGerald,* Dublin: Gill & Macmillan, 1986, p. 131–47.
— Fanning, Ronan, 'The UCD debate: The meaning of revisionism,' *Irish Review,* no. 4 (spring 1988), p. 15–19.
— Farrell, Brian, *Chairman or Chief?: The Role of Taoiseach in Irish Government,* Dublin: Gill & Macmillan, 1971.
— Farrell, Brian, *Seán Lemass,* Dublin: Gill & Macmillan, 1991.
— Farrell, Brian, *The Founding of Dáil Éireann: Parliament and Nation Building,* Dublin: Gill & Macmillan, 1971.
— Farrell, Brian (ed.), *The Irish Parliamentary Tradition,* Dublin: Gill & Macmillan, 1973.
— Farrell, Brian (ed.), *Communications and Community in Ireland,* Cork and Dublin: Mercier Press, 1984.
— Farrell, Brian (ed.), *De Valera's Constitution and Ours,* Dublin: Gill & Macmillan, 1988.
— Farrell, Michael, *Northern Ireland: The Orange State,* London: Pluto Press, 1980.
— Farrell, Michael, 'The extraordinary life and times of Seán MacBride: Part 2,' *Magill,* January 1983, p. 24–37.
— Feeney, Peter, 'Censorship and RTE,' *Crane Bag,* 8/2 (1984), p. 61–4.
— Fennell, Desmond, *The Revision of Irish Nationalism,* Dublin: Open Air, 1991.
— Finnan, Joseph P., *John Redmond and Irish Unity, 1912–1918,* Syracuse (NY): Syracuse University Press, 2004.
— Fisk, Robert, *In Time of War: Ireland, Ulster and the Price of Neutrality, 1939–45,* London: Paladin, 1987.
— Foley, Conor, *Legion of the Rearguard: The IRA and the Modern Irish State,* London: Pluto Press, 1992.

— Forester, Margery, *Michael Collins: The Lost Leader*, London: Sphere, 1972.
— Foster, Roy, *Modern Ireland, 1600–1972*, London: Penguin, 1989.
— Fraser, T. G., *Partition in Ireland, India and Palestine: Theory and Practice*, London: Macmillan, 1986.
— Gallagher, Frank, *The Anglo-Irish Treaty*, London: Hutchinson, 1965.
— Gallagher, Frank, *The Indivisible Island: The Story of the Partition of Ireland*, London: Victor Gollancz, 1957.
— Gallagher, Michael, *Political Parties in the Republic of Ireland*, Dublin: Gill & Macmillan, 1985.
— Gallagher, Michael, *The Irish Labour Party in Transition, 1957–82*, Manchester: Manchester University Press; Dublin: Gill & Macmillan, 1982.
— Gallagher, Michael, 'The Pact Election of 1922,' *Irish Historical Studies*, 21/84 (1979), p. 404–21.
— Gallagher, Michael (ed.), *Irish Elections, 1922–44: Results and Analysis*, Limerick: PSAI Press, 1993.
— Garvin, Tom, *1922: The Birth of Irish Democracy*, Dublin: Gill & Macmillan, 1998.
— Garvin, Tom, *Nationalist Revolutionaries in Ireland, 1858–1928*, Oxford: Clarendon Press, 1987.
— Garvin, Tom, *The Evolution of Irish Nationalism*, Dublin: Gill & Macmillan, 1981.
— Gaughan, J. Anthony, *Austin Stack: Portrait of a Separatist*, Dublin and Tralee: Kingdom Books 1977.
— Gaughan, J. Anthony (ed.), *Memoirs of Senator Joseph Connolly (1885–1961): A Founder of Modern Ireland*, Dublin: Irish Academic Press, 1996.
— Gibbons, Luke, *Transformations in Irish Culture*, Cork: Cork University Press, in association with Field Day, 1996.
— Gilbert, Martin, *World in Torment: Winston S. Churchill, 1917–1922*, London: Minerva, 1990.
— Gorham, Maurice, *Forty Years of Irish Broadcasting*, Dublin: Talbot Press, 1967.
— Gray, Tony, *Mr Smyllie, Sir*, Dublin: Gill & Macmillan, 1994.
— Gray, Tony, *The Lost Years: The Emergency in Ireland, 1939–45*, London: Little, Brown, 1997.
— Griffith, Arthur, *The Resurrection of Hungary*, Dublin: Talbot Press, 1915.
— Griffith, Kenneth, and O'Grady, Timothy E., *Curious Journey: An Oral History of Ireland's Unfinished Revolution*, London: Hutchinson, 1982.
— Hamill, Desmond, *Pig in the Middle: The Army in Northern Ireland, 1969–1984*, London: Methuen, 1985.
— Hannon, Philip, and Gallagher, Jackie (eds.), *Taking the Long View: 70 Years of Fianna Fáil*, Dublin: Blackwater Press, 1996.
— Hayes, Patrick Joseph, and Campbell, Jim, *Bloody Sunday: Trauma, Pain and Politics*, London: Pluto Press, 2005.
— Healy, John, *Healy, Reporter: The Early Years*, Achill: House of Healy, 1991.
— Hobson, Bulmer, *Ireland Yesterday and Tomorrow*, Tralee: Anvil Books, 1968.
— Hogan, Gerard, and Walker, Clive, *Political Violence and the Law in Ireland*, Manchester: Manchester University Press, 1989.
— Hogan, James, *Election and Representation*, Cork: Cork University Press, 1945.
— Holland, Jack, and McDonald, Henry, *INLA: Deadly Divisions*, Dublin: Torc, 1994.
— Hopkinson, Michael, *Green Against Green: The Irish Civil War*, Dublin: Gill & Macmillan, Dublin, 1988.

— Hopkinson, Michael, 'The Craig-Collins pacts of 1922: Two attempted reforms of Northern Ireland government,' *Irish Historical Studies*, vol. xxvii, no. 106 (November 1990), p. 145–58.
— Horgan, John, *Seán Lemass: The Enigmatic Patriot*, Dublin: Gill & Macmillan, Dublin, 1997.
— Horgan, John, 'State policy and the press,' *Crane Bag*, 8/2 (1984), p. 51–8.
— Jordan, Anthony J., *Seán MacBride: A Biography*, Dublin: Blackwater Press, 1993.
— Keatinge, Patrick, *The Formulation of Irish Foreign Policy*, Dublin: Institute of Public Administration, 1973.
— Kelley, Kevin, *The Longest War: Northern Ireland and the IRA*, Dingle: Brandon Books, 1982.
— Kelly, Henry, *How Stormont Fell*, Dublin: Gill & Macmillan 1972.
— Kelly, James J., *Orders for the Captain?*, Dublin: Kelly, 1971.
— Keogh, Dermot, 'Ireland and Emergency culture: Between Civil War and normalcy, 1922–1961,' *Ireland: A Journal of History and Society*, 1/1 (1995), p. 4–43.
— Keogh, Dermot, *Ireland and Europe, 1919–1989: A Diplomatic and Political History*, Cork and Dublin: Hibernian University Press, 1990.
— Keogh, Dermot, *Jack Lynch: A Biography*, Dublin: Gill & Macmillan, 2008.
— Keogh, Dermot, *The Vatican, the Bishops and Irish Politics, 1919–1939*, Cambridge: Cambridge University Press, 1986.
— Keogh, Dermot, and O'Driscoll, Mervyn (eds.), *Ireland in World War Two: Neutrality and Survival*, Cork: Mercier Press, 2004.
— Kiely, Benedict, *Counties of Contention: A Study of the Origins and Implications of the Partition of Ireland*, Cork: Mercier, 1945.
— King, Clifford, *The Orange and the Green*, London: Four Square, 1967.
— Kotsonouris, Mary, *Retreat from Revolution: The Dáil Courts, 1920–1924*, Dublin: Irish Academic Press, 1997.
— Laffan, Michael, *The Partition of Ireland, 1912–1925*, Dublin: Dublin Historical Studies, 1983.
— Laffan, Michael, 'The unification of Sinn Féin,' *Irish Historical Studies*, vol. xvii (1970–71), p. 353–79.
— Lawlor, Sheila, *Britain and Ireland, 1914–23*, Dublin: Gill & Macmillan, 1983.
— Lee, J. J., *Ireland, 1912–1985: Politics and Society*, Cambridge: Cambridge University Press, 1989.
— Lee, J. J. (ed.), *Ireland, 1945–1970*, Dublin: Gill & Macmillan, 1979.
— Lee, Joseph, *The Modernisation of Irish Society, 1848–1918*, Dublin: Gill & Macmillan 1973.
— Lee, Joseph, and Ó Tuathaigh, Gearóid, *The Age of de Valera*, Dublin: Ward River Press in association with RTE, 1982.
— Leiserson, Avery, *Parties and Politics: An Institutional and Behavioural Approach*, New York: Alfred A. Knopf, 1958.
— Levenson, Leah, and Natterstad, Jerry H., *Hanna Sheehy-Skeffington: Irish Feminist*, Syracuse (NY): Syracuse University Press, 1986.
— Lindsay, Patrick J., *Memories*, Dublin: Blackwater Press, 1993.
— Lipset, S. M., and Rokkan, Stein (eds.), *Party Systems and Voter Alignments*, New York: Free Press, 1967.
— List, Friedrich, *The National System of Political Economy* [1841], London: Longmans, Green, and Company, 1909.

— Longford, Earl of, *Peace by Ordeal: The Negotiation of the Anglo-Irish Treaty, 1921,* London: Mentor, 1967.
— Longford, Earl of, and O'Neill, Thomas P., *De Valera,* Boston: Houghton Mifflin, 1971.
— Mac Aonghusa, Proinsias, *Ar son na Gaeilge: Conradh na Gaeilge, 1893–1993, Stair Sheanchais,* Dublin: Conradh na Gaeilge, 1993.
— McCann, Eamonn, et al., *Bloody Sunday in Derry: What Really Happened,* Dingle: Brandon Books, 1992.
— Macardle, Dorothy, *The Irish Republic: A Documented Chronicle of the Anglo-Irish Conflict and the Partitioning of Ireland, with a Detailed Account of the Period 1916–1923,* Dublin: Irish Press, 1951.
— McConville, Michael, *Ascendancy to Oblivion: The Story of the Anglo-Irish,* London: Quartet Books, 1986.
— MacDermott, Eithne, Clann na Poblachta, Cork Cork University Press, Cork, 1998.
— McDonald, Michael, *Children of Wrath: Political Violence in Northern Ireland,* Cambridge: Polity Press, 1986.
— Mac Eoin, Uinseann, *Survivors: The Story of Ireland's Struggle as Told through Some of Her Outstanding Living People . . .* Dublin: Argenta Publications, [1983].
— Mac Eoin, Uinseann, *The IRA in the Twilight Years,* Dublin: Argenta Publications, 1997.
— McGlynn, Pat (ed.), *Éirí Amach na Cásca: The Easter Rising, 1916,* Dublin: Republican Publications, 1986.
— McGuffin, John, *Internment,* Dublin: Anvil Books, 1973.
— McGuill, Paul, 'Political Violence in the Republic of Ireland, 1969–1997,' MA thesis, University College, Dublin, 1997.
— McInerney, Michael, *Peadar O'Donnell: Irish Social Rebel,* Dublin: O'Brien Press, 1974.
— McMahon, Deirdre, *Republicans and Imperialists: Anglo-Irish Relations in the 1930s,* New Haven (Conn.): Yale University Press, 1984.
— MacManus, Francis (ed.), *The Years of the Great Test, 1926–1939,* Cork: Mercier Press, 1967.
— MacMillan, Gretchen, *State, Society and Authority in Ireland: The Foundation of the Modern State,* Dublin: Gill & Macmillan, 1993, p. 208.
— Mac Stiofáin, Seán, *Revolutionary in Ireland,* Farnborough (Hants): Saxon House, 1974.
— Mac Suain, Séamus, *County Wexford's Civil War,* Wexford: Mac Suain, 1995.
— Mair, Peter, *The Changing Irish Party System: Organisation, Ideology and Electoral Competition,* London: Pinter, 1987.
— Mandle, W. F., *The Gaelic Athletic Association and Irish Nationalist Politics, 1884–1924,* Dublin: Gill & Macmillan, 1987.
— Manning, Maurice, *Irish Political Parties: An Introduction,* Dublin: Gill & Macmillan, 1972.
— Manning, Maurice, *The Blueshirts,* Dublin: Gill & Macmillan, 1971.
— Maor, Moshe, *Political Parties and Party Systems: Comparative Approaches and the British Experience,* London: Routledge, 1997.
— Maye, Brian, *Fine Gael, 1923–1987,* Dublin: Blackwater Press, 1993.
— Meehan, James, *The Irish Economy since 1922,* Liverpool: Liverpool University Press, 1970.
— Memmi, Albert, *The Colonizer and the Colonized,* London: Earthscan, 1990.
— Michels, Robert, *Political Parties: A Sociological Study of the Oligarchical Tendencies of*

Modern Democracy, Kitchener (Ont.): Batoche, 2001 (first published 1911, first English-language edition 1915).

— Miller, Susanne, and Potthoff, Heinrich, *A History of German Social Democracy* (translated by J. A. Underwood), Leamington Spa (Warks.): Berg, 1986.

— Mitchell, Arthur, *Revolutionary Government in Ireland: Dáil Éireann, 1919–22*, Dublin: Gill & Macmillan, 1993.

— Morgan, Austen, *Labour and Partition: The Belfast Working Class, 1905–1923*, London: Pluto Press, 1991.

— Moss, William Warner, *Political Parties in the Irish Free State*, New York: Columbia University Press, 1933.

— Moynihan, Maurice, *Speeches and Statements by Éamon de Valera, 1917–73*, Dublin: Gill & Macmillan, 1980.

— Mullan, Don, and Scally, John, *Eyewitness Bloody Sunday: The Truth* (second edition), Dublin: Merlin Publishing, 1998.

— Mullan, Don, and Scally, John, *The 'Bloody Sunday' Massacre in Northern Ireland: The Eyewitness Accounts*, Boulder (Colo.): Roberts Rinehart, 1997.

— Mulvihill, Margaret, *Charlotte Despard: A Biography*, London: Pandora, 1989.

— Murphy, Brian P., *Patrick Pearse and the Lost Republican Ideal*, Dublin: James Duffy, 1991.

— Murphy, Donie, *The Men of the South in the War of Independence*, Newmarket (Co. Cork): Inch Publications, 1991.

— Murphy, John A., *Ireland in the Twentieth Century*, Dublin: Gill & Macmillan, 1973.

— Murray, Raymond, *The SAS in Ireland*, Cork and Dublin: Mercier Press, 1990.

— Neeson, Eoin, *The Civil War, 1922–23*, Dublin: Poolbeg, 1989.

— Ní Dhonnchadha, Máirín, and Dorgan, Theo, *Revising the Rising*, Derry: Field Day Publications, 1991.

— Ní Lochlainn, Aoife, 'Ailtirí na hAiseirghe: A party of its time?' in Keogh and O'Driscoll, *Ireland in World War Two*, p. 187–210.

— O'Brien, Joanne, *A Matter of Minutes: Legacy of Bloody Sunday*, Dublin: Merlin Publishing, 2002.

— Ó Broin, León, *Just Like Yesterday: An Autobiography*, Dublin: Gill & Macmillan, 1985.

— O'Carroll, J. P., and Murphy, John A. (eds.), *De Valera and His Times*, Cork: Cork University Press, 1983.

— Ó Ceallaigh, Daltún (ed.), *Reconsiderations of Irish History and Culture: Selected Papers from the Desmond Greaves Summer School, 1989–93*, Dublin: Léirmheas, 1994.

— O Connor, Fionnuala, *In Search of a State: Catholics in Northern Ireland*, Belfast: Blackstaff Press, 1993.

— O'Connor, Séamus, *Tomorrow Was Another Day*, Tralee: Anvil Books, 1970.

— O'Connor, Ulick, *Brendan Behan*, London: Granada, 1979.

— O'Donoghue, Florence: *No Other Law: The Story of Liam Lynch and the Irish Republican Army, 1916–1923*, Dublin: Irish Press, 1954.

— O'Donovan, Dónal, *Kevin Barry and His Time*, Dublin: Glendale Press, 1989.

— Ó Drisceoil, Dónal, *Censorship in Ireland, 1939–1945: Neutrality, Politics and Society*, Cork: Cork University Press, 1996.

— Ó Duibhir, Ciarán, *Sinn Féin: The First Election, 1908* (North Leitrim History Series, no. 4), Nure (Co. Leitrim): Drumlin Publications, 1993.

— Ó Glaisne, Risteard, 'De Valera and the press: A case study in the history of politics,' *Crane Bag*, 8/2 (1984), p. 34–9.

— Ó hEithir, Breandán, *The Begrudger's Guide to Irish Politics*, Dublin: Poolbeg 1986.
— O'Farrell, Padraic, *The Ernie O'Malley Story*, Cork and Dublin: Mercier Press, 1983.
— O'Leary, Cornelius, *Irish Elections, 1918–77: Parties, Voters, and Proportional Representation*, Dublin: Gill and Macmillan, 1979.
— O'Mahony, Seán, *Frongoch: University of Revolution*, Dublin: FDR, 1987.
— O'Malley, Ernie, *Army Without Banners*, London: Four Square, 1967 (first published in 1936 as *On Another Man's Wound*).
— O'Malley, Ernie, *The Singing Flame*, Dublin: Anvil Books, 1979.
— O'Neill, Terence, *The Autobiography of Terence O'Neill*, London: Rupert Hart-Davis, 1972.
— O'Neill, Terence, *Ulster at the Crossroads*, London: Faber, 1969.
— O'Sullivan, Michael, *Seán Lemass: A Biography*, Dublin: Blackwater Press, 1994.
— Ó Tuama, Seán Óg (ed.), *The Gaelic League Idea*, Cork: Mercier Press, 1972.
— Parkin, Frank, *Class Inequality and Political Order*, London: Paladin, 1972.
— Peck, John, *Dublin from Downing Street*, Dublin: Gill & Macmillan, 1978.
— Patterson, Henry, *The Politics of Illusion: Republicanism and Socialism in Modern Ireland*, London: Hutchinson Radius, 1989.
— Phoenix, Eamon, Northern Nationalism: Nationalist Politics, Partition and the Catholic Minority in Northern Ireland, 1890–1940, Belfast: Ulster Historical Foundation, 1994.
— Prager, Jeffrey, *Building Democracy in Ireland: Political Order and Cultural Integration in a Newly Independent Nation*, Cambridge: Cambridge University Press, 1986.
— Pringle, D. G., 'Electoral systems and political manipulation: A case study of Northern Ireland in the 1920s,' *Economic and Social Review*, 11/3 (April 1980), p. 187–205.
— Pringle, Peter, and Jacobson, Philip, *Those Are Real Bullets, Aren't They?: Bloody Sunday, Derry, 30 January 1972*, London: Fourth Estate, 2000.
— Pyne, Peter, 'The new Irish state and the decline of the republican Sinn Féin party,' *Éire-Ireland*, XI, 3 (1976).
— Pyne, Peter, 'The third Sinn Féin party, 1923–1926,' *Economic and Social Review*, 1/1 (1969), p. 29–50, and 1/2 (1970), p. 229–57.
— Rafter, Kevin, *The Clann: The Story of Clann na Poblachta*, Cork and Dublin: Mercier Press, 1996.
— Regan, John M., *The Irish Counter-Revolution, 1921–36: Treatyite Politics and Settlement in Independent Ireland*, Dublin: Gill & Macmillan, 1999.
— Reid, David, *Ireland*, London: Larkin Publications, 1984.
— Rolston, Bill (ed.), *The Media and Northern Ireland: Covering the Troubles*, London: Macmillan, 1991.
— Rumpf, Erhard, and Hepburn, A. C., *Nationalism and Socialism in Twentieth-Century Ireland*, Liverpool: Liverpool University Press, 1977.
— Ryan, Desmond, *Seán Treacy and the Third Tipperary Brigade, IRA*, Tralee: Anvil Books, 1945.
— Ryan, Desmond, *Unique Dictator: A Study of Éamon de Valera*, London: A. Barker, 1936.
— Schmitt, David E., *The Irony of Irish Democracy: The Impact of Political Culture on Administrative and Democratic Political Development in Ireland*, Lanham (Md): Lexington Books, 1973.
— Sheedy, Kieran, *The Clare Elections*, Dún Laoghaire: Bauroe Publishing, 1993.

— Short, Con, *The Ulster GAA Story, 1884–1984,* Monaghan: Comhairle Uladh, CLG, 1984.
— Skinner, Liam C., *Politicians by Accident,* Dublin: Metropolitan Press, 1946.
— Smelser, Neil, *Theory of Collective Behaviour,* Glencoe (NY): Free Press, New York, 1962.
— Stephan, Enno, *Spies in Ireland,* London: Four Square, 1965.
— Tarpey, Marie Veronica, *The Role of Joseph McGarrity in the Struggle for Irish Independence,* New York: Arno Press, 1976.
— Taylor, Peter, *Provos: The IRA and Sinn Féin,* London: Bloomsbury, 1997.
— Valiulis, Maryann Gialanella, *Portrait of a Revolutionary: General Richard Mulcahy and the Founding of the Irish State,* Dublin: Irish Academic Press, 1992.
— Walsh, Dick, *The Party: Inside Fianna Fáil,* Dublin: Gill & Macmillan, 1986
— Ward, Margaret, *Hanna Sheehy Skeffington: A Life,* Cork: Cork University Press, 1989.
— Ward, Margaret, *In Their Own Voice: Women and Irish Nationalism,* Dublin: Attic Press, 1995.
— Ward, Margaret, *Unmanageable Revolutionaries: Women and Irish Nationalism* (second edition), London: Pluto Press, 1989.
— West, N. C., *The Truth about Ireland,* Dublin: Mahon's Printing Works, 1921.
— White, Harry (as related to Uinseann Mac Eoin), *Harry: The Story of Harry White,* Dublin: Argenta Publications, 1985.
— White, Robert William, *Ruairí Ó Brádaigh: The Life and Politics of an Irish Revolutionary,* Bloomington: Indiana University Press, 2006.
— Williamson, Burke, *The Zeal of the Convert: The Life of Erskine Childers,* Gerrards Cross (Bucks): Colin Smythe, 1978.
— Wilson, John, *Introduction to Social Movements,* New York: Basic Books, 1973.
— Woodman, Kieran, *Media Control in Ireland, 1923–1983,* Carbondale (Ill.): Southern Illinois University Press, 1986.
— Younger, Calton, *A State of Disunion,* London: Fontana, London, 1972.
— Younger, Calton, *Ireland's Civil War,* London: Fontana, 1970.

INDEX